100
Great
Nineteenth-Century Lives

100
Great
Nineteenth-Century
Lives

EDITED BY
JOHN CANNING

METHUEN

First published in Great Britain 1983 by
Methuen London Ltd
11 New Fetter Lane, London EC4P 4EE

Copyright © 1983 Century Books Ltd

Reprinted 1984

ISBN 0 413 51520 6

Printed in Great Britain by Butler & Tanner Ltd, Frome and
London

Contents

List of Illustrations   8
Introduction   9

Statesmen and Soldiers
Thomas Jefferson   *Stuart Andrews*   11
Talleyrand   *Lawrence Wilson*   17
James Monroe   *Esmond Wright*   23
Andrew Jackson   *Esmond Wright*   30
Napoleon Bonaparte   *Esmond Wright*   37
George Canning   *E. Royston Pike*   43
Metternich   *Lawrence Wilson*   49
Viscount Melbourne   *Reginald Pound*   55
Viscount Palmerston   *E. Royston Pike*   61
Sir Robert Peel   *David McIlwain*   67
Benjamin Disraeli   *Mollie Hardwick*   73
Robert E. Lee   *Charles Chilton*   79
Napoleon III   *Douglas Johnson*   86
Abraham Lincoln   *Esmond Wright*   92
William Ewart Gladstone   *E. Royston Pike*   98
Otto von Bismarck   *Esmond Wright*   105
Prince Albert   *Michael Hardwick* 111
Lord Roberts   *David McIlwain*   117
Joseph Chamberlain   *David McIlwain*   123
Charles Stewart Parnell   *Reginald Pound*   129
Sergei Witte   *Eileen Bigland*   135
James Keir Hardie   *Lawrence Wilson*   141

Scientists, Inventors and Engineers
Michael Faraday   *Lawrence Wilson*   147
Isambard Kingdom Brunel   *Geoffrey Hindley* 153
Charles Darwin   *Lawrence Wilson*   159
Louis Pasteur   *Anthony Burton*   165
Johann Mendel   *Anthony Burton*   171
Thomas Huxley   *E. Royston Pike*   177
James Clerk Maxwell   *Geoffrey Hindley* 183
Robert Koch   *Lawrence Wilson*   189
Alexander Graham Bell   *Ian Fellowes Gordon*   194

Writers and Poets

Georg W. F. Hegel	*Esmond Wright*	200
Stendhal	*Edward Ashcroft*	205
Percy Bysshe Shelley	*Michael Hardwick*	210
Thomas Carlyle	*Anthony Burton*	216
John Keats	*Peter Dale*	222
Heinrich Heine	*Lawrence Wilson*	228
Honoré de Balzac	*Edward Ashcroft*	234
Lord Macaulay	*E. Royston Pike*	240
John Stuart Mill	*E. Royston Pike*	246
Alfred Tennyson	*Lawrence Wilson*	252
William Makepeace Thackeray	*Michael Hardwick*	258
Charles Dickens	*Mollie Hardwick*	263
Samuel Smiles	*Asa Briggs*	268
The Brontë Sisters	*Mollie Hardwick*	274
Karl Marx	*Esmond Wright*	281
Ivan Sergeyevich Turgenev	*Eileen Bigland*	287
Leo Tolstoy	*Lawrence Wilson*	292
Jules Verne	*Michael Hardwick*	297
Henrik Ibsen	*Anthony Burton*	302
William James	*Lawrence Wilson*	308
Oscar Wilde	*Lawrence Wilson*	314

Religious Leaders and Thinkers

Hugh Bourne	*Lord Soper*	320
Pius IX	*Francis Edwards*	325
John Henry Newman	*Francis Edwards*	331
Joseph Smith	*E. Royston Pike*	338
Soren Kierkegaard	*E. Royston Pike*	344
William Booth	*David McIlwain*	350
Charles Haddon Spurgeon	*Gordon Baverstock*	356
St Bernadette	*Mollie Hardwick*	361

Reformers and Innovators

Francis Place	*E. Royston Pike*	367
Robert Owen	*David McIlwain*	373
Thomas Arnold	*Jean Liddiard*	379
Edwin Chadwick	*E. Royston Pike*	385
John Bright	*Asa Briggs*	391
Benjamin Jowett	*C. J. Carter*	397
Julius de Reuter	*Lawrence Wilson*	404

Florence Nightingale   *Mollie Hardwick*   410
Elizabeth Blackwell   *E. Royston Pike*   416
Josephine Butler   *E. Royston Pike*   422
Richard Norman Shaw   *Judy Moore*   428
Robert Applegarth   *John Burnett*   434
Octavia Hill   *David McIlwain*   440
W. T. Stead   *Michael Hardwick*   446

Discoverers and Explorers
Sir John Franklin   *Charles Chilton*   452
David Livingstone   *Charles Chilton*   459
Sir Richard Burton   *Lawrence Wilson*   465
Heinrich Schliemann   *C. J. Carter*   471
Henry Walter Bates   *Charles Chilton*   477

Legends and *Causes Célèbres*
John Brown   *Charles Chilton*   483
Charles Bradlaugh   *E. Royston Pike*   489
William Cody   *Charles Chilton*   495

Captains of Industry and Commerce
Thomas Cook   *Charles Chilton*   501
Alfred Krupp   *Lawrence Wilson*   508
William Whiteley   *Anthony Burton*   513
Iwasaki Yataro   *Richard Storry*   518
Andrew Carnegie   *Charles Chilton*   523

Composers, Artists and Artistes
Ludwig van Beethoven   *Michael Hardwick*   529
Franz Schubert   *Sarah Thomas*   535
Hector Berlioz   *Nadia Lasserson*   540
Frédéric Chopin   *Sarah Thomas*   546
Richard Wagner   *Mervyn Levy*   552
Jenny Lind   *Mollie Hardwick*   557
Sir John Everett Millais   *Michael Hardwick*   562
Sir Henry Irving   *David McIlwain*   567
Paul Cézanne   *Mervyn Levy*   572
Claude Monet   *Mervyn Levy*   578
Sarah Bernhardt   *Mollie Hardwick*   583
Index   589

List of Illustrations

Between pp 128-9; 160-1; 256-7; 288-9; 384-5; 416-17; 512-13; 544-5

1a	Thomas Jefferson	11d	Robert Owen
1b	Andrew Jackson	12a	Francis Place
1c	Napoleon Bonaparte	12b	Benjamin Jowett
1d	Talleyrand	12c	Florence Nightingale
2a	Prince Metternich	12d	Octavia Hill
2b	Otto von Bismarck	13a	W. T. Stead
2c	Albert, the Prince Consort	13b	Josephine Butler
		13c	Karl Marx
3a	Napoleon III	13d	James Keir Hardie
3b	Viscount Melbourne	14a	Sir John Franklin
3c	Sir Robert Peel	14b	Sir Richard Burton
3d	Benjamin Disraeli	14c	Sophie Schliemann
4a	William Gladstone	14d	David Livingstone
4b	Charles Parnell	15a	William Cody ('Buffalo Bill')
4c	Abraham Lincoln		
5a	Charles Darwin	15b	A poster for Thomas Cook's first conducted excursion
5b	Thomas Huxley		
5c	Louis Pasteur		
6a	I. K. Brunel		
6b	Michael Faraday	15c	Andrew Carnegie
6c	Alexander Graham Bell	16a	Ludwig van Beethoven
7a	Thomas Carlyle	16b	Richard Wagner
7b	John Keats	16c	Paul Cézanne
7c	Keats' grave	16d	Sarah Bernhardt
8a	Honoré de Balzac		
8b	W. M. Thackeray		
8c	Henrik Ibsen		
9a	Alfred, Lord Tennyson		
9b	Charles Dickens		
9c	Anne, Emily and Charlotte Brontë		
10a	Leo Tolstoy		
10b	Tolstoy's study		
10c	Oscar Wilde		
11a	Sören Kierkegaard		
11b	Cardinal Newman		
11c	William Booth		

Pictures 1a-d, 2a, 2b, 3b-d, 4c, 5a, 5c, 6b, 7a, 7c, 8a, 10a-c, 11a, 11b, 11d, 12a, 12b, 13a, 13c, 14c, 15a, 15b, 16a-d are from the Mansell Collection; 3a, 4a, 4b, 5b, 6a, 6c, 7b, 8b, 9a, 9b, 11c, 12d, 13b, 13d, 14b, 14d, 15c are from the BBC Hulton Picture Library; 2c, 9c, 12c and 14a are from the National Portrait Gallery; and 8c is from the Nasjonalgalleries, Oslo.

Introduction

It has for long been fashionable – indeed too fashionable – to see nineteenth-century history as shaped by great impersonal and near-anonymous social and economic forces, greater than the men and women caught up in them and sweeping them along as the tide sweeps flotsam. The nineteenth century was the century of socialism and dialectical materialism, of nationalism and imperialism, and of secularism and evangelicalism. History is usually written as if it was predetermined, and as if it was a matter of causes like these and of their consequences rather than of people. The individual, in Mary McCarthy's phrase, is deposited in a trend. Or as James Baldwin more aptly puts it: 'People are trapped in history, and history is trapped in them.'

Of course, nothing is given, nothing is written until we make it so. Important as these movements were, and profound as were their consequences, they were the work of men's and women's wills and ideas, of their impulses and inspirations. Marx might see it all as preordained, but who ordained Marx? And what were the forces that produced him? Personality and chance play decisive roles. It would almost be possible to say with Carlyle that 'History is the essence of innumerable biographies'.

Certainly the biographies assembled here demonstrate not only the part played by chance, but the diversity and the total unpredictability of genius. Ability of course can be nurtured by a favourable environment but, as most of these examples will demonstrate, it will rise despite poverty and adversity. It may even need adversity to nourish it. Most of these studies are the stories of an individual of humble origin and of his or her triumph against the environment not because of it. And for some, especially the musicians, the secret of their greatness remains a mystery. This is true of Beethoven – but then so it is with the Brontës and – in a different dimension – with Bernadette Soubirous.

Indeed after reading this book one is left asking: are there any patterns, any conclusions? Mothers would seem to be much more important than fathers in the training of the young;

many great men lived their public lives in permanent awe – like Napoleon – of Madame Mère. Yet in the last century anyway it is men rather than women who emerge to greatness, or at least that form of it that merits public notice and acclaim. Only ten of these hundred portraits are those of women. Yet, certainly where the poets are concerned, women seem required as inspiration – and sometimes also as protectresses? But clearly success has no single cause. For some it came late: as with Canning, with Melbourne and even with Gladstone; as it did (and in another country than his own) with Ibsen. And with most of the people described here their success owed most to themselves, to their own talents and their own capacity to develop and exploit them.

But two specific conclusions seem to arise from this book. The first is social/economic and the second political/ideological. There was in the nineteenth century an immense creative spirit at work, triggered largely by the application of a steam power to the operations of industry and by the coming of railways and electricity. It was an exciting and a challenging world to live in, notably but not only for inventors and engineers, with a sense of new worlds to explore and master; witness in their totally different ways the careers of Livingstone and Schliemann, of Andrew Carnegie, Charles Darwin and Thomas Cook. Even in the new field of consumerism there was – as to William Whiteley – immense opportunity. And the inventions and discoveries that made Europe then the dynamic centre of the world and bred the imperialism and the industrial power that led it to master the globe in turn bred their own problems, the problems that led Disraeli one way and Dickens in another to fame of their own.

The other conclusion is simpler. One of these figures bestrides the book like a Colossus. It is striking how many of the figures in this book were the legatees of the stirring and restless years of the first Napoleonic Empire and how they expressed, for at least the next two generations, in music, poetry and politics, either their devotion to or their revulsion from the ideas personalized by that Emperor of the French who was at heart always a Corsican soldier of fortune. The career open to talent, liberty in the guise of nationalism, equality, fraternity and a sense of adventure are at the heart of the dreams and the strivings of many of the fascinating individuals whose stories are so vividly recorded here.

Esmond Wright

Thomas Jefferson

(1743–1826)

Although Thomas Jefferson did not die until 1826, he was born in 1743 and thus belongs rather more to the eighteenth century than to the nineteenth. But his inclusion in this volume is justified on at least three counts: he was President of the United States from 1801 to 1809, he continued to defend liberal ideals even during the period of reaction that followed the French Revolution, and he founded the University of Virginia.

His father was a wealthy tobacco planter and his mother came from a distinguished Virginian family with a long Scottish and English pedigree. 'To which,' Jefferson was later to remark, 'let everyone ascribe the faith and merit he chooses.' Even today Virginia preserves many of the customs and attitudes of the English country gentry. In the mid-eighteenth century the best Virginian families rode in a coach, ate off crested silver, collected books befitting a gentleman's library, and imported their furniture and porcelain from Europe. They imported their political and philosophical ideas from Europe too – though at least one American historian, Daniel Boorstin, has claimed that Jefferson's ideas were of what he calls 'local lineage' and were evolved amid the harsh practical necessities of managing a large plantation.

At all events, when Thomas Jefferson arrived at William and Mary College in 1760 to study law, his tutor was a Scotsman, Dr William Small. Jefferson described him as 'a man profound in most branches of science, with a happy talent of communication, correct and gentlemanly manners, and an enlarged and liberal mind'. After Small's return to England in 1762, Jefferson studied law under George Wythe, later to become the first professor of law at William and Mary College. Jefferson was called to the bar in 1767 and entered politics in 1769, when he became a member of the Virginian House of Burgesses. He tried to introduce a measure permitting the emancipation of slaves, but this was rejected. 'Indeed,' he adds in the account given in his autobiography, 'during the regal government, nothing liberal could expect success.' He was later to play a leading part in the overthrow of regal government, but for the present he was more preoccupied with domestic matters: in

1769 he had begun building Monticello and in 1772 he married.

Monticello, which stands on a wooded hillside above the town of Charlottesville, was built and rebuilt over a period of half a century before Jefferson was satisfied with it – if indeed he ever was. Its dome and classical portico, though designed by Jefferson, owe much to the inspiration of the sixteenth-century Italian architect, Palladio. But Jefferson's interest in classical architecture took him back beyond the Palladian style to ancient Roman models. In 1787, during his diplomatic mission to France, he wrote from Nîmes to Madame de Tessé, Lafayette's cousin: 'Here I am, Madam, gazing whole hours at the Maison Quarrée, like a lover at his mistress... From Lyons to Nîmes I have been nourished with the remains of Roman grandeur.' When asked to suggest a design for the new Capitol at Richmond, Virginia, he had a model of the Maison Quarrée made in stucco and produced his own drawings for the interior arrangement. Apart from the Richmond Capitol and the Lawn of his new university, Jefferson designed a number of public and private buildings in Virginia, while the neo-classical style was also followed – though in more monumental manner – for the public buildings of the new city of Washington.

As a lucid draftsman of legal documents he was much in demand in his own day. He had, as John Adams remarked, 'a reputation for literature, science, and a happy talent of composition'. When he arrived at Philadelphia in 1774 to attend the First Continental Congress, he had already published *A Summary View of the Rights of British America*. Many of its arguments were incorporated in the Declaration of Independence, drafted by Jefferson and approved by Congress with only minor amendments on 4 July 1776. And Jefferson was still only thirty-three.

When he returned to the Virginian legislature in October 1776, he set about a reform of the laws of his home state. He completed the task in three years, but most of his new legislation was not enacted until after the end of the war – including the famous Act for Establishing Religious Freedom. The preamble began with the words, 'Well aware that Almighty God hath created the mind free', and ended with the brave assertion that 'truth is great and will prevail if left to herself, that she is the proper and sufficient antagonist to error, and has nothing to fear from the conflict . . .'

In 1779 he was elected Governor of Virginia at a time when the state was threatened by bankruptcy, by Indian incursions in the west and by the British fleet in the east. In 1781 the state legislature was forced to flee its capital, Richmond, in the face

of Cornwallis's advance. Jefferson was blamed for the ineffec-
tiveness of the Virginian defences. This was almost certainly
unfair, but at the end of his second year of office he resigned in
favour of a military governor and retired to Monticello. Barely
a year later the death of his wife persuaded him to return to
public life, and in the autumn of 1783 he was again appointed
to represent Virginia in the Congress at Philadelphia.

In the year between his retirement from the governorship
and his wife's death, Jefferson devoted himself to his books.
He shared the encyclopedic impulse of the age in which he
lived – the age that saw the publication of the French *Ency-
clopédie* and the *Encyclopaedia Britannica* – and he collected a
mass of observations about the country surrounding Monticello. These he published in 1784 as *Notes on the State of
Virginia*. The pamphlet had originated as a long and careful
reply to a series of questions about Virginia put to him by the
Secretary of the French Legation at Philadelphia, and it was
first published (without Jefferson's permission) in Paris and in
French. It contained, among much miscellaneous information,
an attack on the theories of the French naturalist, Buffon, who
had been incautious enough to argue that nature was less active
and vigorous in America than on the European continent, and
that the American versions of animal species common to both
continents were smaller than their European counterparts.
Jefferson had no difficulty in refuting this contention, as Buffon
later had the grace to admit.

Jefferson evidently felt a sense of kinship with the French
Encyclopédistes that went far beyond mere gratitude for the fact
that the intervention of the French fleet had led to the defeat
of Cornwallis. In 1784 his appointment as Minister Plenipotentiary to assist Benjamin Franklin and John Adams in arranging some commercial agreements enabled him to get to
know France at first hand. He was at once a welcome figure in
the Paris *salons*, which were still very much the centre of French
intellectual life; and in 1785, on Franklin's return to America,
Jefferson succeeded him as Minister Plenipotentiary to the
Court of France. When the French Revolution broke out he
was thus in a doubly privileged if embarrassing position: he was
an accredited minister at the French court and yet at the same
time the friend and confidant of Lafayette, who led the opposition to the privileged orders. Jefferson not only wrote to Lafayette urging him to side with the Third Estate, but drew up
a draft of a 'Charter of Rights' containing ten articles, the first
of which began: 'The States General shall assemble, uncalled,
on the first day of November, annually, and shall remain

together as long as they shall see cause . . .' When, after the Tennis Court Oath, Jefferson was invited to attend meetings of the committee that was to draft a new constitution, he was careful to decline. But a month later Lafayette brought eight 'Patriots' to dinner at Jefferson's house where they discussed constitutional issues until 10 p.m. The discussions, Jefferson considered, were 'truly worthy of being placed in a parallel with the finest dialogues of antiquity, as handed to us by Xenophon, by Plato and Cicero'.

Jefferson returned home before the end of 1789 and so did not witness the more violent phases of the Revolution – not even the march of the women to Versailles. In the following spring he wrote to Lafayette, 'I hope you will never see another 5th or 6th of October.' But he adds the reminder that 'we are not to expect to be translated from despotism to liberty in a feather-bed'. Jefferson continued to follow the course of the Revolution with interest, though news did not reach him very rapidly. He regarded the abolition of the French monarchy as 'of absolute necessity', and he continued to defend the Jacobins even after the September Massacres. It was Bonaparte rather than Robespierre whom he regarded as the true betrayer of the French Revolution.

After serving as Secretary of State under George Washington and as Vice-President under John Adams, Jefferson became President in 1801, not much more than a year after Napoleon had seized power in France. Some years later, in a letter written to the Papal Nuncio in 1818, Jefferson compared his rule with that of Napoleon. He had not, like Napoleon, caused five or ten million deaths, nor the devastation of other countries, nor the depopulation of his own:

> On the contrary, I have the consolation to reflect that during the period of my administration not a drop of the blood of a single fellow citizen was shed by the sword of war or of the law, and that after cherishing for eight years their peace and prosperity I laid down their trust of my own accord and in the midst of their blessings and importunities to continue in it.

Undoubtedly the greatest achievement of Jefferson's first term as President was the purchase (at a figure of $15,000,000) of the whole of Louisiana, which had recently been ceded to France by Spain. In authorizing this transaction Jefferson was painfully aware that he was acting out of character. As Washington's Secretary of State, he had argued fiercely against Alexander Hamilton's view that all powers not specifically reserved to the states by the constitution must reside with the federal government. Jefferson had contended that the federal government could exercise only those powers specifically allocated to it: all other matters were the prerogative of the state legislatures. Now he was called upon to demonstrate the most spectacular exercise of presidential power in the whole history of the presidency – before or since. No wonder he hesitated. But in the end he bought the territory – an area of one million square miles – and the Hamiltonian doctrine of 'implied powers' was finally vindicated by its most vehement opponent.

Jefferson's first term as President ended in a chorus of congratulation, and he was elected for a further term. His purchase of Louisiana had been largely prompted by the fear that France and Britain might combine to throttle the infant American republic. 'The day that France takes possession of New Orleans,' he wrote, 'seals the union of two nations who in conjunction can maintain exclusive possession of the ocean.' But his second term began in the year of Trafalgar, and it was Anglo-French hostility that posed the greater immediate threat, particularly when in 1806 Britain and France began their policies of mutual blockade. American shipping suffered, and Jefferson's chosen remedy was the Embargo Act of 1807 forbidding Americans to export to any European port. Jefferson described this extraordinary piece of self-denial as 'the last card we have to play short of war'. But as the scale of the consequent disruption of American trade became clear, it began to look as if war would be economically less damaging.

The Embargo Act was repealed on the day Jefferson retired from the presidency, and in 1812 the Anglo-American war that he had foreseen broke out. The famous boast of his first inaugural speech – that America was 'kindly separated by nature and a wide ocean from the exterminating havoc of one quarter of the globe' – now seemed a little hollow.

Nevertheless some of the other promises of his first inaugural had been fulfilled. He had looked forward to 'a wise and frugal government', and he was at some pains to play down the dignity of the presidential office. He professed to see himself as merely the executor of the decisions of Congress (though he proved very dextrous at getting it to decide as he wanted) and deliberately discarded the ceremoniousness so carefully cultivated by Washington and Adams. When he declined nomination for a third term and retired from the presidency in 1809, the spokesman of the Virginian state legislature congratulated him for, among other things, 'pomp and state laid aside'. He nevertheless continued to advise his successors Madison and

Monroe, both Virginians whom he knew well and whom he had advised in their youth.

He obviously enjoyed his retirement. In 1819, at the age of seventy-six, he could boast: 'Whether I retire to bed early or late, I rise with the sun. I use spectacles at night, but not necessarily in the day, unless in reading small print . . .' 1819 was the year of the foundation of the University of Virginia, the buildings of which were designed, down to the last window-pane, by Jefferson himself. His vigilance extended even to the diet of the students: 'their drink at all times water, a young stomach needing no stimulating drinks, and the habit of using them being dangerous'.

For his new university at Charlottesville, he provided for eight professorships: ancient languages, modern languages, mathematics, natural philosophy (physics and astronomy), natural history, anatomy and medicine, moral philosophy and law. Five of his professors were recruited in Europe – men whom Jefferson described as 'characters of the first order of science'. And the purpose of the university he defined thus in 1820: 'This institution will be based on the illimitable freedom of the human mind. For here we are not afraid to follow truth wherever it may lead, nor to tolerate any error so long as reason is left free to combat it.'

Probably the greatest of Jefferson's many claims to fame is that he ensured that the spirit of Voltaire and the ideals of the best of the French revolutionaries were carried on into the nineteenth century. In designing his own tombstone, Jefferson had made clear what he himself regarded as his contribution to civilization:

Here was buried
Thomas Jefferson
Author of the Declaration of American Independence
of the Statute of Virginia for religious freedom
and Father of the University of Virginia.

He did not think it important to record that he had also been President of the United States.

Talleyrand

(1754-1838)

Those most able to enjoy the pleasures of peace are least likely to favour war. Conversely it is the isolated, the bored, the dissatisfied, the potential megalomanics, who most often make trouble. It is one of the ironies of history that Napoleon's Foreign Minister Talleyrand belonged to the first category while Napoleon belonged to the second.

But the irony goes deeper. Talleyrand came from an aristocratic French family which traced their genealogy as far back as the Bourbons themselves. Napoleon, the upstart from Corsica, was quite unknown till as General Bonaparte he raised the siege of Toulon by the British. He was irascible, impetuous, ruthless, could be vulgar. Talleyrand, born in mid-eighteenth century, had the fastidious manners of one who had bandied witticisms in the drawing-rooms of Madame Du Barry, was an epicure in women, food and luxury, languid, impenetrable, lazy. Compared with Napoleon's tiger, one might have called him a harmless butterfly, but for his high intelligence and a determination carefully concealed beneath layers of reserve.

Charles Maurice de Talleyrand-Périgord, born at Paris in February 1754, was the son of a lieutenant general in the royal army. He had been destined as a youth to enter the Church, studied at the seminary of Saint-Sulpice and in due course was ordained, rising to the dignity of Bishop of Autun in the time of Louis XVI. But the priesthood was never his vocation and, after voting during the Revolution for the Civil Constitution of the Clergy, which in effect nationalized the Church, and consecrating bishops in defiance of the Pope, he was excommunicated and later, though still officially a priest, secularized, which meant he was allowed to wear lay garments. To the scandal of all believers he then married, and married a woman of low birth hardly better than a trollop.

All this made him deeply suspect to people of stern morals. But over the years worse was to come. As Foreign Minister he demanded as a matter of course large sums of money from foreign governments in return for favours conferred, so amassing a colossal fortune which he spent in luxurious living. Finally there was his 'seraglio', as contemporaries called it, a bevy of mistresses, mostly from high society, whom he captured, concurrently or in succession, by the undoubted charm of his wit and personality.

Not much here, one might think, to warrant his inclusion in a book of great lives. But the paradox of Talleyrand is that his amorality was combined with the coolest, the most brilliant, the most far-seeing insights in politics both at home and internationally. From these, in a career lasting forty-five years, he never wavered and they provide the thread by which we can follow his shifts of allegiance and his intrigues.

We first see him in March 1789, hastening to his diocese to help the clergy draw up a *cahier*, or book of requests, to be submitted to the States General, consisting of nobles, clergy and the Third Estate, recently summoned by Louis XVI to discuss the economic and social plight of France. Talleyrand entertained his Burgundians lavishly, persuading them to elect him as their representative and include certain points in the *cahier*. Coming from an eighteenth-century French bishop it is an astonishing list: no taxation, no legislation without the people's consent, trial by jury, *habeas corpus*, freedom of speech and of the press, educational and financial reform, regular meetings of the States General, which had not been summoned since 1614. It was a programme in fact to do credit to the most liberal-minded.

But within two months these wise suggestions were largely swept aside when the Third Estate (magistrates, squires, small landowners) voted itself into a National Assembly with power to make decisions without the nobles and clergy. Talleyrand, ever sensitive to the wind, saw here the beginnings of revolution and in a secret midnight meeting with the King's youngest brother, the Count of Artois, urged force to disperse the Assembly, but in vain. Years later, when anxious to establish his *bona fides* as the constitutional monarchist he had always been, he reminded the Count of that meeting.

The Count, ultimately to become King Charles X, was one of the first to emigrate. But despite the danger to himself as an aristocrat Talleyrand stayed, was elected President of the National Assembly and committed himself to one aspect of the Revolution by proposing the bill to make the Catholic Church a pensioner of the state and sequester its lands. His intention at this time was also to secure urgently-needed democratic reforms, including a two-tier monarchical system of government after the English model. But here again his hopes were swamped by the revolutionary impetus, the fall of the Bastille in July 1789, followed later by the invasion of the Tuileries and the imprisonment of Louis XVI and his Queen in the Temple.

Meanwhile, the French revolutionary armies were preparing
for war with Austria and Talleyrand, though opposed to such
plans, was sent to London as a semi-official emissary to secure
English neutrality, a policy which in fact Prime Minister Pitt
had already decided upon and needed no securing. But at the
back of Talleyrand's mind was a wider aim which throughout
his long career he never abandoned, an alliance with England.
Already he had written to the French Foreign Minister: 'Two
neighbouring nations, one of which founds its prosperity principally upon commerce and the other upon agriculture, are
called upon by the eternal nature of things to have good
understanding and mutually to enrich one another.' But here
too, and for the next twenty years, the prospects were nullified
by events.

In 1792 he returned to France for some months, then, foreseeing the coming bloodshed, obtained a passport from Dan-
ton and escaped to England, allegedly on private business,
only twenty-four hours before the September Massacres
began. From there in November he sent a memorandum to the
war mongering Convention now in power with an eloquent
plea for peace:

> We have learnt, a little late no doubt, that for states as for
> individuals real wealth consists not in acquiring or invading
> the domains of others, but in developing one's own. We
> have learnt that all extensions of territory, all usurpations,
> by force or by fraud ... are only the cruel jests of political
> lunacy, false estimates of power, and that their real effect is
> to increase the difficulty of administration and to diminish
> the happiness and security of the governed.

This plea, which if acted upon would have changed the course
of history, fell on deaf ears.

Meanwhile in England he was provoking mixed reactions,
as he did throughout his career. Thinking perhaps of his *re-
troussé* nose, which gave him a supercilious air, Lady Stafford
wrote to a friend: 'He is a disagreeable looking man, has a
baddish, tricking character, and supposed not very upright in
disposition of heart.' But after initial doubts Fanny Burney,
the famous diarist, was enchanted and wrote: 'I think him now
one of the finest members and one of the most charming of
this exquisite set [the French *emigrés*]. His powers of entertainment are astonishing.'

Suddenly in early 1794, probably on suspicion of being a
spy, Talleyrand was told he must leave England immediately.
He spent the next two and a half years in Philadelphia where

there was already a group of French *emigrés* awaiting their chance to return home. This for him came in late 1796, when France was being misgoverned by five corrupt and incompetent nonentities who styled themselves the Directory. To strengthen their team they made him Foreign Minister, whereupon, sizing up his colleagues, he turned his eyes elsewhere, to Bonaparte at that time conquering all before him in Italy.

They first met in December 1797 and liked one another, but it was not until November 1799 that the *coup d'état* took place which abolished the Directory and installed Napoleon as First Consul, a bloodless event for which Talleyrand worked with great secrecy and cunning. During the five years of the Consulate he worked loyally with Napoleon, even to the extent of tacitly agreeing to the murder (it was called an execution) of the Bourbon Duke of Enghien who, in March 1804, was abducted at night from the neighbouring state of Baden and shot in the dry moat of Vincennes castle. The deed was intended as a warning to royalist dissidents but aroused only universal horror, and Talleyrand had to admit it was a serious blunder, in his own words 'worse than a crime'.

In 1801 he negotiated two treaties, Luneville with Austria after Napoleon's victory at Marengo, and Amiens with England which he hoped would form a basis for peace. But after his early enthusiasm for Napoleon it was becoming clearer every year that there could be no peace, no stability, no prosperity for the French people, so long as he was in command.

Napoleon's military genius allied to limitless ambition made peace impossible. His assumption of the imperial crown in 1804 was followed in 1805 by his crushing defeats of the Austrians at Ulm and the Austrians and Russians combined at Austerlitz. In two memoranda written at this time Talleyrand implored Napoleon to treat Austria generously, to encourage her to become an ally as a bulwark against Russian expansion. But at the Peace of Pressburg, which Talleyrand was obliged to impose, the Habsburg Empire was stripped of nearly three million inhabitants, lost a sixth of its revenue and was saddled with a huge indemnity. Ironically, for these services Napoleon then made Talleyrand Prince of Benevento, a small enclave in the kingdom of Naples.

It was in 1807, after further French victories over the Prussians and Russians, that Talleyrand secretly decided to work for the downfall of the tyrant. In that year he was replaced as Foreign Minister and promoted to the post of Vice-Grand Elector, a highly paid sinecure which still gave him direct access to Napoleon, so that his situation remained virtually unchanged. Even so, he was obliged to watch helplessly for over a year while Napoleon carved up Prussia and Poland with Tsar Alexander at Tilsit and made insidious moves to get his grips on Spain. Then, in September 1808, Talleyrand was ordered to accompany his master to Erfurt for further talks with the Tsar and it was at this point that his independent actions (or, in the language of Bonapartists, his blatant treachery) began.

By day, Napoleon alone with Alexander urged him to hold Austria in check while he dealt with Spain. At night the Tsar reported the whole conversation to Talleyrand who then briefed him on what to say at the next day's meeting, so persuading him to stall and eventually draw nearer to Austria, already thirsting for revenge against Napoleon.

The Emperor never learnt of these secret meetings but later, while in Spain, got wind of Talleyrand's intrigues against him in Paris and in a terrible scene never forgotten by the bystanders, in January of the following year, screamed at him for a solid half hour before the whole privy council. Leaning against a mantelpiece to take the weight off his right foot, which had been crippled in childhood, Talleyrand never moved a muscle and afterwards merely drawled to a friend, 'What a pity so great a man should be so ill bred!'

Strangely, he was not dismissed, merely out of favour, and it suited him well to withdraw from the limelight. Already he foresaw the end of Napoleon and determined to hasten it, warning the Tsar as early as December 1810 that the tyrant was planning a war against him and once more in March 1811, this time giving a date for the start of the campaign: April 1812. For this invaluable news Alexander paid a vast sum of money which Talleyrand coolly pocketed according to his long-held maxim: 'Il ne faut jamais être un pauvre diable.'

As the disastrous Russian campaign unfolded, followed by Napoleon's heavy defeat at Leipzig, Talleyrand watched with clinical detachment. When the allies finally entered Paris in 1814 he alone was ready with a plan to form a provisional government, which he headed, and to install Louis XVIII under a constitution which he had worked out in two days. Justly thereafter he could claim that it was he who had restored the Bourbons in the face of allied dissension.

Appointed Foreign Minister by Louis, he was able, with the help of his Austrian counterpart Prince Metternich, to obtain a remarkably lenient peace treaty for France which left her with more territory than she had possessed at the start of the wars and no indemnity imposed. Both men were determined to ensure the pacification of Europe on the basis of legitimacy. At the Congress of Vienna, which Talleyrand attended as the French delegate, they worked to restrain excessive Russian and Prussian ambitions, Talleyrand with great finesse defeating an initial attempt by the Big Four (Russia, Austria, Prussia and Britain) to exclude France from their discussions and reach decisions without her. The final result in January 1815 was a secret defensive treaty between Britain, Austria and France which finally broke French isolation in Europe.

But Napoleon's escape from Elba put everthing in the melting pot. After his defeat at Waterloo Talleyrand, by no means confident that the restored monarchy could last, addressed a series of outspoken memoranda to Louis pleading for more liberalism, but Louis disregarded them. Faced with lack of royal support and the prospect of painful negotiations with the victorious allies over a second peace treaty, Talleyrand then resigned as Foreign Minister.

He was not in disgrace, he was still Grand Chamberlain, an honorary post which brought in 100,000 francs a year, and he still had his magnificent chateau of Valençay on the banks of the Loire, where he entertained his friends and kept in touch with political events, in the hope of returning to power as head of a new government. Though disagreeing with their politics, he even courted the ultra-conservatives who dominated events right through to the end of Charles X's reign in 1830.

But it was not until 1830, after the King's flight to England and the accession of Louis Philippe, that a new post was offered him, that of ambassador to Britain. 'That fabulous old man', as Lord Palmerston called him, had many friends in London and worked harmoniously with Tory and Whig governments to establish France yet again, after the July revolution, as a reliable partner in Europe.

Then at last, nearing eighty, he retired to Valençay, to enchant a throng of visitors with stories culled from his fabulous memory, stories that only he could tell, of the court of Louis XV, or Napoleon as a young man, of that turbulent era in history when he had been at the centre of affairs. Sometimes he would visit Paris with a young girl to whom he was devoted, Pauline, said to be his natural daughter by his constant companion for many years, the Duchess of Dino. Often he worked at his memoirs, not published till 1891, wherein he sought to explain his policies, and on his last day, 27 May 1838, not a moment too soon, he became reconciled with the Church and received extreme unction, with Pauline, his 'guardian angel' as he called her, by his side.

James Monroe

(1758–1831)

The fifth President of the United States – the last and the least
impressive of the 'Virginia dynasty' – has become immortal
because of the Doctrine given his name, but major parts of
which he did not write. Both as Secretary of State and President
he was seen as a foreign-policy specialist – yet all his own
diplomatic missions were failures. But of no other president
can it be said that his age is known as the 'era of good feelings',
as the *Columbian Sentinel* of Boston described it in 1817. And
that only one elector in the Electoral College voted against his
re-election in 1820 puts him almost on a par with the first
Virginian himself.

James Monroe was born of Scottish stock in 1758 in West-
moreland County, Virginia, in what Virginians know as the
'Northern Neck', and he came from the farmer rather than the
planter class. He left William and Mary College to join Washington's army and was wounded at Trenton. He saw action
also at Brandywine and Monmouth, and was a lieutenant-
colonel at twenty-one. On returning to Virginia he became a
close associate of Thomas Jefferson, in whose long shadow his
life was spent. He made his home at Ash Lawn, within sight of
Monticello; his politics were to be throughout his life those of
the Jeffersonian school.

He served in 1782 in the Virginia legislature and from 1783
to 1786 in the Congress of the Confederation. By instinct he
was a states' rights Republican. He accepted that the Articles
of Confederation needed strengthening and that the Congress
should have the power to regulate commerce, but he was no
friend of centralized government.

Monroe served as Senator from 1790 to 1794, when he was
sent as minister to the government of republican France, a
testing assignment. Robespierre was dead, the future uncertain. He got off to a good start and a stirring reception before
the whole Convention. But the French knew of the similar Jay
mission to Britain and were justifiably suspicious that Monroe
was there merely to placate them. To try to offset these fears,
Monroe went too far the other way; he was savagely critical
of the Jay Treaty and enthusiastically pro-French. Edmund

Randolph, who in 1795 replaced Jefferson as Secretary of State, had to rebuke him for his 'extreme glow'. He was recalled in 1796 by Randolph's successor Timothy Pickering.

He served from 1799 to 1802 as Governor of Virginia, but was again dispatched in 1803 on a mission to France. While not responsible for the Louisiana Purchase, since Napoleon offered the ex-Spanish west to American minister Robert Livingston before Monroe arrived, he showed himself prompt in accepting the obvious bargain and precise in working out the details. In 1803 he replaced Rufus King as American minister in London, an assignment he did not enjoy. In 1804 he went on to Madrid to assist Charles Pinckney in his unsuccessful attempt to secure the surrender of East Florida from Spain. And in 1805 he was back in London seeking to end the British practice of impressing American seamen into the British navy, and to obtain commercial concessions. He had as little success as John Jay eleven years earlier. Monroe had by this time, in one role or another, spent nearly six years abroad on diplomatic missions; his actions in Paris had been repudiated by Washington, his treaty in London was repudiated by Jefferson. It had been a strikingly unprofitable series of sojourns.

In the presidential election of 1808, Monroe allowed his name to go forward against Madison's, but he did not get a single vote in the Electoral College. He stayed loyal to the cause, however; in January 1811 he became once again Governor of the state, but only for two months. In March, Madison invited him to become Secretary of State, a post he held until his own election to the White House in 1816.

His term as secretary was as unfortunate as had been his own missions. Although he sought to avert the War of 1812, he knew enough of British opinion, as he thought, to judge its obduracy over impressment and its unwillingness, as he believed, to repeal the Orders-in-Council. The declaration of war of 18 June 1812 largely owed its form to a draft of Monroe's, yet the Orders had been in fact repealed two days before the war was declared; and the war need never have been fought. It was bitterly unpopular in New England, which saw it as 'Mr Madison's War'. In its Convention at Hartford in 1814, New England threatened to secede from the Union.

In 1814 the British army advanced on Washington unopposed, and Madison and his cabinet left the city in a hurry – the 'Blaydonsburg Races'. The American government was both in hiding and bankrupt, Washington was burnt, New England talked ominously of rebellion. American trade was practically at a standstill. Monroe took the lead in redeploying the troops and for ten days was hardly out of the saddle. He was for a time Secretary of War as well as Secretary of State. But the news of British reverses at Plattsburg and Baltimore led Britain to be willing to negotiate; after twenty years of war and a heavy burden of debt and taxes she was tired, too. With Napoleon safely, it seemed, on Elba, the case for ignoring the rights of neutrals and this side-show struggle lapsed. The American War, as Castlereagh rightly called it, had been a millstone.

The terms of the treaty made at Ghent in Belgium were very simple. British demands were dropped. Not a word was said on maritime rights, impressment and the rights of search or seizure. Nor were there any references to territory. Neither side gained or lost; it was peace without victory. The ending of the war was only in part Monroe's achievement, but it was his greatest good fortune. It initiated the era of good feelings of which he was the principal beneficiary. Though a sectional war in its origins it had a nationalizing effect. It taught the United States the impracticability of Republican distrust of centralization, the need for an army and navy, for a national bank, for protection against British competition and for the encouragement of domestic industry.

The election of 1816 was thus held in a mood of pride and relief. Monroe was the Republican choice, though there were signs of opposition in the caucus to the Virginia dynasty and some support for William Crawford of Georgia. Monroe was elected with 183 votes in the Electoral College to thirty-four cast for Rufus King of New York by three New England states. The country had never been so united.

In 1820 Monroe's second election was unchallenged. The Federalist Party offered no candidate and Monroe got all the electoral votes but one, which was cast for John Quincy Adams. It seemed that Washington's warning against political parties had been heeded, and that real unanimity could exist. It was not to last – sectional issues and personal rivalries began to show themselves the day after Monroe's second inaugural. But the results of this were not visible on the national stage until 1824.

Politically, Monroe's was then an important administration. Old John Adams once called it an 'administration without a fault'. But even in the midst of the era of good feeling, problems arose. Two of these were important, the Panic of 1819 and the Missouri Compromise.

The Panic of 1819 was due to two factors: first, the opening up of new lands in the west on the easy credit of the wild-cat banks of 1811; and second, the consequences of tariff protection in 1816.

The policy of over-expansion resulted in inevitable collapse in 1819, when the second Bank of the United States, in a sudden panic for its own safety, demanded that the state banks redeem their obligations to it in specie. Immediately arose the cry, so often heard before and since, of the western debtor against the eastern creditor. 'All the flourishing cities of the west,' cried Benton of Missouri, 'are mortgaged to this money power. They may be devoured at any minute. They are in the jaws of the Monster.' The panic resulted in an investigation and reorganization of the Bank. It led to the Land Act of 1820 which abolished the system of purchasing public lands on credit, liberalized the land policy by reducing the amount of land that must be purchased from 160 to eighty acres, and lowered the price from $2 an acre to $1.25. All these changes were improvements on the Harrison Act of 1800; the typical frontiersman was too poor to afford as much as 160 acres at the earlier price, and the credit system had promoted speculation and over-expansion. The advocates of protection attempted to pass a higher tariff in 1820, but consideration in the Senate was postponed. The votes, however, showed the north-west, where manufacturing was now well started, solid for protection, the south and south-west almost solid against it, and the north-east divided.

The Panic of 1819 had shown that there was a double basis for economic sectionalism in the conflict between the western debtor and the eastern creditor, and in the controversy over the tariff. The second conflict was destined to be more serious, the problem of slavery as against free labour. The territory of Missouri had applied for admission to the Union in 1818, and when the debate opened in the following year James Tallmadge of New York proposed an amendment that any further introduction of slavery in Missouri be prohibited, and that slave children be freed there when they reached the age of twenty-five. The House passed and the Senate rejected his amendment. There were several reasons why the South fought his proposal so bitterly: since the invention of Eli Whitney's cotton gin in 1793, cotton production had become very profitable and was becoming the economic mainstay of the South; there were eleven free and eleven slave states in the Union, hence the Tallmadge amendment would have given the North control of Congress; and Missouri was the first state wholly west of the Mississippi and anything done there would set a precedent for the rest of Louisiana Territory. Now aware that there existed a determined anti-slavery faction in the North, the South grimly resolved to defend its cherished institution.

The deadlock was broken by admitting Maine (since 1677 part of Massachusetts) as a free state and Missouri as slave. But slavery was excluded from all the Louisiana Territory north of 36° 30' except Missouri itself. This settled the question for twenty years. But, in Jefferson's phrase, the country had heard the sound of the firebell in the night. It would be heard more loudly, and with shattering effect, in the next generation.

The foreign policy of the administration reflected the prevailing mood of nationalism and of optimism. Shortly after the conclusion of the War of 1812 the United States negotiated two treaties with Great Britain. By the Rush–Bagot agreement of 1817, Britain and the United States pledged themselves to keep the Canadian–American border unfortified and to keep no armed war vessels on the Great Lakes. The next year the United States rectified the northern boundary of Louisiana Territory. The boundary was to extend along the forty-ninth parallel from the Lake of the Woods to the Rocky Mountains; Oregon was to be held by joint occupation for ten years.

Since the occupation of West Florida in 1810 the United States had been trying to obtain the rest of Florida. American desires were whetted by the fact that the British used East Florida as a base of operations in the War of 1812, and that after the war British officers incited Indians and runaway slaves to make attacks on American border settlements. In 1817 General Jackson received orders to end the disturbances and pursue the Indians into Spanish territory but to respect Spanish forts. Jackson invaded Florida and seized every Spanish fort except St Augustine, and he also executed two British subjects for inciting Indians. Spain protested, demanding the punishment of Jackson and the restitution of the forts. Monroe agreed on the latter, but J. Q. Adams insisted that Jackson be upheld. By the Treaty of 1819 the United States obtained all of Florida and agreed to assume Spanish obligations of five million dollars to American citizens. The western boundary of Louisiana was also agreed upon and the United States abandoned claim to Texas.

Spain did not ratify this treaty until 1821 because she hoped to prevent the United States from according recognition to the new republics of Latin America. There had grown up in the US a movement, led by Clay, for the recognition of the Latin American republics. This sentiment was based largely upon American sympathy for nations struggling for freedom. Eco-

nomic interests played little part in this sympathy, for trade
with South America was not very great and the US had more
to lose than gain. The Monroe administration was very
cautious in its Latin American policy, for it was unwise to
antagonize Spain until the Florida Treaty was signed. By 1821
the treaty had been ratified and the defeat of the Spaniards in
South America was completed. In 1822 Monroe recommended
to Congress that the new states be recognized as independent.

The first step in the actual formulation of the Monroe Doctrine was taken in August 1823 when Canning, the British
Foreign Secretary, speaking to the American minister, Richard
Rush, suggested a joint announcement by Britain and the
United States on the future of the new republics. Monroe was
in sympathy with his view but Adams was not, believing that
the United States ought to express its opinion, and to act
independently of Great Britain. He realized that Britain's navy
could stop French intervention at any time, making such a
joint declaration unnecessary; he feared that a disavowal of
intentions to acquire any portions of Latin America would
restrain the United States from any possible future acquisition
of Cuba or Mexico; and in any case the declaration did not
extend to Russia which, by 1821, had occupied portions of the
Pacific coast as far south as Fort Ross (1816) near San Francisco. If the US acted with Britain they might offend Russia,
and would surely lose prestige in South America and Europe.
Monroe announced his policy in his message to Congress in
December 1823.

The Monroe Doctrine consists of three broad principles.
The first, written by Adams and directed to Russia, states, 'the
American continents ... are henceforth not to be considered
as subjects for future colonization by any European powers'.
The second, written by Monroe, was a direct warning to the
Holy Alliance:

> The political system of the allied powers is essentially differ-
> ent ... from that of America ... we should consider any
> attempt on their part to extend their system to any portion
> of this hemisphere as dangerous to our peace and safety.
> With the existing colonies or dependencies of any European
> power, we have not interfered, and shall not interfere. But
> with the governments who have declared their indepen-
> dence, and maintained it, and whose independence we have
> ... acknowledged, we could not view any interposition for
> the purpose of oppressing them, or controlling, in any other
> manner, their destiny, by any European power, in any other

light than as the manifestation of an unfriendly disposition toward the United States.

The third principle was the proposition that the US did not intend to interfere in European affairs and they did not want the European powers to extend their political systems to the New World.

In 1824 a treaty was concluded whereby the Tsar of Russia accepted 54° 40' as the southern boundary of Alaska. Though the doctrine had little influence on Europe, increasingly it came to be seen as the Bible of American foreign policy.

Monroe was not the most gifted nor the most subtle of the Virginians, but he was clearly impelled by a strong sense of public service. He did not seek power for any reason of personal or party aggrandizement, and came to the presidency almost by inheritance. He brought to it transparent integrity, the memory and the record of service in the Revolution in what now seemed a distant and historic age; indeed the dress and style, the knee-length pantaloons and white-topped boots, of an earlier day. If he was not striking or flamboyant, he could rise above sectional conflicts and could choose excellent lieutenants – which could not be said of all who preceded him – and he could show administrative ability of a high order. On his work as statesman the Doctrine put the seal. In it he gave expression, in a form he chose himself, to a nation-wide popular sentiment. Here as elsewhere he could tap a national mood and sense the will of the people. It is by no means a common gift.

Public service was demanding and it was unrewarding. Like some of his predecessors, he left the White House in debt. Congress voted him $30,000 in 1826, but it was not enough to meet the claims. He was forced, on his wife's death in 1830, to sell his home and to leave Virginia to live with his daughter in New York. There he died on 4 July 1831. It was a hallowed day. On it five years before both Jefferson and John Adams had died. And fifty-five years earlier the Declaration of Independence had been signed. Monroe's death was indeed the end of the revolutionary era.

Andrew Jackson

(1767-1845)

It has become essential to the office of the presidency of the United States that around its occupant myths and legends should gather. It is not, of course, so written in the constitution. But the capacity to arouse popular emotion and to generate political excitements has come to be one of the tests of greatness in the man.

He is indeed a successful president to whom most easily legendry adheres: however remote from truth it be. He must be more than life-size and touched, if not by divinity, at least by the exotic. Thus Washington never told a lie, Lincoln was always quick with the apt anecdote and the tall tale, the story of John F. Kennedy will be permanently linked to 'the curse on the Kennedys' and the unfulfilled promise of a Camelot that never was. Of Washington, of Lincoln, of Theodore and Franklin Roosevelt, of J. F. Kennedy, this is true. And it is particularly so of Andrew Jackson.

He was the first of the really strong presidents, opinionated, explosive, forceful. He was the first president to be chosen by processes recognizably democratic. He was the first president to voice, and to be ready to defend by force, the idea of American national unity. And, though a wealthy cotton planter with a real scorn for the mob, he can claim with justice to be the first truly popular president.

The seventh President of the United States was born in 1767 at Waxhaws in the South Carolina backwoods. He came of poor Scotch-Irish stock, his father having left Carrickfergus just two years before; but the father died before the son was born. Two of his brothers were killed in the frontier war with Britain and he himself, though a mere boy, took part in the battle of Hanging Rock. He trained as a lawyer, but his schooling was inadequate and his spelling always idiosyncratic. He was a tall, hatchet-faced, high-tempered young man, and age never dulled the spirit; he was always prompter with his fists than with words.

He moved west with the frontier and settled in Nashville, then a village of log cabins. He lodged in the home of the widow Donelson. The daughter of the house, Rachel, had made an unhappy marriage with Lewis Robards; her friendship with Jackson led to her divorce, but their own marriage took place before the divorce decree was granted. Jackson was devoted to his wife and he was always sensitive about the marriage and its scandal; there was thereafter always in him a Wellingtonian promptness to defend women about whom gossip played.

The lawyer turned cotton planter and farmer; he bought and sold land; and he built his own home on the Hermitage tract. In 1796 he was a member of the Tennessee convention which framed the first constitution, and he served for a spell in the House and the Senate in Philadelphia. But neither legislating nor debating were to his taste. In 1802, however, he was elected major general of the Tennessee state militia. This was a decisive turning point. The job was no sinecure, for, in the west, the militia were often on call. Jackson made his reputation as a frontier soldier, like Washington before him.

In the War of 1812, when the Creeks rose in support of Britain, the Tennessee militia were called out. Jackson defeated the Indians at the battle of Horseshoe Bend on the Tallapoosa River (March 1814): not in itself a great victory but an achievement of logistics, of hard slogging along difficult untamed trails, and of the holding together of reluctant volunteers by the effort of a superior will-power. Jackson became a major general in the Army of the United States.

He was called on in 1814 to defend New Orleans against the veterans of the Peninsular War. He chose his ground well, and the British forces hemmed between marsh and river were forced to attack on a narrow untenable front. Over 2,000 British lives were lost: American casualties were eight dead and thirteen wounded. Again Jackson's skill lay in holding together a motley crowd of volunteers, prominent among them Jean Lafitte and his Bay pirates. The victory (January 1815) made Jackson's name a legend back east as well as on his native ground. Aged forty-eight, he was now a figure of national importance. The road to the White House became a clearer trail than the Natchez and New Orleans traces.

Nor was it checked by the clash with the Seminoles. In 1818 Jackson chased the Seminoles back across the line into Spanish Florida, and in an excess of zeal hanged two British traders, Ambrister and Arbuthnot, whom he allegedly mistook for spies. He was to be for a short time Governor of the new territory of Florida when it was acquired in 1821.

There gathered around this powerful image – soldier, Indian fighter, western expansionist, with a western programme of a

protective tariff and internal improvements – a group of friends
who saw in Jackson the west's first serious candidate for the
White House. They included his former fellow lodger at the
Donelson house, John Overton, and William Lewis and John
Eaton: later the nucleus of his Kitchen Cabinet. They began
the hard work of politics, feeding the press with stories, persuading, cajoling, making contacts in other states. Jackson
became the presidential choice for the Tennessee legislature in
1822, and in 1823 once again a Senator for Tennessee.

In 1824 the United States had in fact a one-party system.
Under the successive Virginian presidents – Jefferson, Madison, Monroe – and aided by the long years of isolation from
Europe and by the War of 1812, partisan politics had all but
disappeared. Against Monroe's election in 1820 only one Electoral College vote had been cast. Jefferson's party, the Republicans, had become the party of almost all the people.

In 1824 William H. Crawford of Georgia, the Secretary of
the Treasury, was named as a candidate by the Democratic
Republican caucus, but Crawford himself had suffered a paralytic stroke. Other Republicans, Calhoun, Clay and John Q.
Adams, as well as Jackson, aspired to the White House. Clay,
champion of the American system and of the South American
republics, was the 'favourite son of Kentucky'. Adams was
Secretary of State and was the only candidate known to oppose
slavery. Calhoun withdrew from the race to run for vice-president, unopposed. If the issues were far from clear there was
no shortage of colourful candidates.

When the Electoral College ballots were counted in 1824,
Jackson had ninety-nine, Adams eighty-four, Crawford
forty-one, Clay thirty-seven. Since no candidate had an overall
majority the election went to the House, voting by states as the
constitution prescribed, and choosing only from the three highest. Clay, now ineligible, threw his support to Adams, who was
elected by the House, and Adams promptly announced that
Clay was to be Secretary of State. John Randolph described
this as a union of the 'Puritan and the blackleg'; and an
inconclusive duel followed. The Jackson party had at first
counted upon Clay's favour, but when they learned of his
partiality for Adams, they decided to discredit him or compel
him to support Jackson. The resulting rivalry led to the division
of the Republican Party into the Adams–Clay and Jackson–
Calhoun wings. The former became known as National Republicans, the latter as Democratic Republicans or gradually
as Democrats.

The split wrecked the Adams presidency and left a legacy of

bitterness on which the Jackson campaign for 1828 fed. The
hero of the west had, it seemed, been denied his rightful place
by a corrupt bargain. Jackson was renominated for president
by the Tennessee legislature in 1825 and a savage three-year
campaign began. It was seen now as a nationwide and popular
vindication, an effort to rouse not caucuses but people to
ensure that the wrongs of 1824 were righted. There was no
need for a programme or a policy: personality was all.

But by 1828 the situation had changed. Clay withdrew from
the race, though not with benevolence. He hoped Jackson
would kill someone during the capaign. 'How hard it is to keep
the cowhide from these villains,' stormed Jackson, and was
with difficulty dissuaded from challenging Clay to a duel. By
1828 also, Crawford a sick man, was not a serious candidate.
So the struggle became a straight clash between Jackson and
Adams, between 'the man who can fight and the man who can
write'. Crawford's major ally of 1824, Martin Van Buren, of
New York, turned to Jackson, and carried with him the Crawford groups of Virginia and Georgia. The result was impressive: Jackson's popular vote was quadrupled over that of 1824.
He carried every state west of the Alleghenies and south of the
Potomac, plus half of New York and all Pennsylvania. In the
Electoral College, it was 178 to eighty-three.

Jackson's victory over Adams in the election of 1828 is
usually regarded as a great popular triumph. The fact is that
Jackson's success was made possible by the over-representa-
tion of the south in the Electoral College. And by 1828 the
Jackson machine (Lewis, Van Buren of New York and James
Buchanan of Pennsylvania) had won over the Crawford and
Calhoun groups in the south. The south had no love of the
hero of the west, but it hated the tariff and feared Adams's
nationalism. The north-west deserted Clay because of his advocacy of the Bank and swung to Jackson, because he wanted
to eliminate the Indian menace.

Two other major developments contributed to Jackson's
victory and to the success of his party through the next decade.
The first of these was the rapid growth of the west and the
influence of the western communities in promoting democracy.
The political codes of the western communities called for manhood suffrage, frequent elections, rotation in office and popular control of the judiciary. The seaboard states were in turn
compelled to abolish political and economic privilege. The
other major development which strengthened democracy was
the introduction of the factory system in the north-west. The
new labouring masses, suffering from political and social

discrimination, began to organize in the 1820s, forming labour unions and labour parties. The extension of the franchise made it possible for the wage-earners of the east to throw their support to the Democratic Party of Jackson, to make of it essentially a farmer-labour party.

Many factors explain then the Jackson victory. But if Jackson was the product of this new democratic spirit, he also knew how to capitalize on it and use the new masses of voters to political advantage. In his first two messages to Congress Jackson kept returning to the theme – 'To the people belongs the right of electing their chief magistrate'. His alliance with the bosses and machines, his use of the spoils system, his campaign against the Bank, all illustrate the popular nature of his administration.

One of Jackson's first acts as President was to dismiss many office-holders and replace them with his loyal followers. The 'spoils system' had already appeared in several states, especially New York and Pennsylvania. What Jackson did was to extend it to the federal administration. This of course was thoroughly in accord with the democratic principle, so cherished in the west, of rotation in office. In practice it meant that postmasters and customs collectors now used patronage as a weapon for creating a well-organized Jackson machine.

The man who expected to succeed Jackson was John Calhoun. Running again for the vice-presidency in 1828, Calhoun had given his support to Jackson and expected to have the deciding voice in the administration. Jackson's friendship for Calhoun dated back to the time of his invasion of Florida, for he always believed that Calhoun, then Secretary of War, had upheld him. In 1830, however, Jackson learned that Calhoun had in fact proposed to discipline him in 1818 and, when Calhoun tried to explain away his attitude, Jackson became embittered.

Van Buren was the one to reap the advantages from the feud between Jackson and Calhoun. In 1831 the cabinet was reorganized and the friends of Calhoun were replaced by men in sympathy with Jackson and his policies. Van Buren was nominated to be ambassador to England, and when the Senate rejected him Jackson avenged the affront by making him his running mate in 1832. Van Buren, a slick politician from New York, had cleverly identified his own cause with that of Jackson, the leader of the Democratic Party. The nucleus was formed of the federal alliance of New York with the south and west, or urban and rural, that was to be the characteristic feature of the Democratic Party over a century.

The quarrel between Jackson and Calhoun was far more than a personal feud. Calhoun's disgrace signified that the south had lost political influence, that the western farmers and eastern labouring masses were becoming the dominant elements in the Democratic Party. On no issue did this fact become more obvious than on the nullification question.

After the War of 1812 Calhoun had advocated the nationalist programme: internal improvements and the Bank of the United States. But industry was developing slowly in the South; she lacked skilled labour, fuel and water power; and she was increasingly hurt by protective tariffs imposed, it seemed, for northern benefit. Higher duties raised the planters' costs for clothing and tools. Calhoun, and his South with him, became savage critics of the tariff and in 1828 he drew up his Exposition and Protest, a statement of the states' rights case. Till then Jackson himself had shared this point of view: but when states' rights items were pushed to the extravagant lengths of the claim of Calhoun that a state could nullify the will of the federal government, Jackson drew a firm line. On 13 April 1830, at the annual Jefferson birthday banquet, angered by no fewer than twenty-four toasts to nullification, Jackson's was, 'Our federal union. It must and shall be preserved.'

The strong federalist where secession was concerned, however, was a states' rights man where the Bank was concerned. He had the westerner's fear of big monopoly which kept interest rates high and milked the poor and debtor classes. On this issue he was ignorant and prejudiced, but so were most westerners. The Bank Charter did not expire until 1836 but his opponents, especially Clay, his presidential rival again in 1832, demanded its re-charter before the election so that the Jackson veto would become an issue in the campaign. Indeed it did; and the more open political processes indicated that Jackson had a popular following on this issue. The President, with Van Buren as his running mate, was re-elected by a larger popular vote than in 1828 and made incursions into the alien territory of New England. The Bank duly went out of existence – but its disappearance, and the distribution of its funds among the states, which promptly dissipated them, was eventually a disaster, though hidden for a while by the boom of the Jackson years.

Jackson was a strong, vigorous and contradictory being, rich in prejudice and passion. On nullification he was a Unionist, and on the strength of it he got an honorary degree from Harvard – to John Quincy Adams's horror. When the Harvard students shouted, 'Give us a speech in Latin, Doctor,' he replied, 'E pluribus unum.' On the Bank he was a westerner. On internal improvements he was a states' rights man. On Indians he was all of these. He made ninety-four treaties with the Indians and opened up for white settlement millions of acres. When the Indians were slow to move, he was not: he harried the Seminoles in 1819, and when they repudiated a treaty he wiped out those who stayed behind in Florida. Creek, Choctaw and Cherokee were pushed across the Mississippi; when the Sac and Fox Indians under Black Hawk were slow to move they were ruthlessly massacred. Jackson was by nature an authoritarian, aware – as with many westerners – that the people have a taste less for democracy than for leadership, and a straightforward affection for character. Jackson was a natural leader who can best be described as a demagogic aristocrat. He owned slaves, and slavery seemed not to worry him at all.

He came up the hard way and never paused to reflect on theory or justification. He was the first westerner to become President, the first genuinely popular incumbent of the White House, and the most colourful and masterful politician between Jefferson and Lincoln.

He retired in 1837 to The Hermitage in Nashville, where he died in 1845. He was buried in his own garden alongside his wife Rachel. He had, he said on his deathbed, only two regrets: that he had not hanged John Calhoun and that he had not shot Henry Clay.

Napoleon Bonaparte

(1769-1821)

Napoleon Bonaparte was born in 1769 in Ajaccio, Corsica, a year after Genoa had sold its stormy island to France. Only a few months before his birth, French troops had crushed the Corsican rebellion led by Pasquale de Paoli. Bonaparte was the second son in a large family of the lesser nobility, and there were four brothers and three sisters, all dominated by their mother, *née* Letizia Ramolino, Madame Mère. His father saw him from the outset as a man of genius: he was lean and pinched in appearance, but with a piercing hawk-like gaze, great will-power and intensity. He went with a scholarship to the military school at Brienne and the École Militaire in Paris, and he went with a purpose – to free Corsica. He studied hard with this intent, and was utterly out of tune with the rich sons of the nobility around him who had come there by easy roads and with no such design. He was commissioned a second lieutenant of artillery in 1785; and he read assiduously, not least Rousseau and the *philosophes*.

Like Caesar before him and like Hitler after, the army was his ladder, his tool and his passion. He wrote a tract or two, but his weapon was the sword, not the pen. He exploited the Revolution and saw it as his cause, and made it at once Corsican and French. In 1792 and 1793 he tried to seize Ajaccio for the Revolution, only to be defeated by Paoli, fighting for Corsican independence and prepared to call on monarchists and Anglophiles as allies. In 1793 the Bonaparte family was expelled from Corsica, and the France of the Revolution now became his own cause – other, that is, than himself.

His batteries helped to expel the British from Toulon in 1793, and his commander, Du Teil, gave him most of the credit. By the age of twenty-four he was a brigadier. With Robespierre's death he lost his mentor, so he attached himself to Barras, the least reputable of the Directory. By 1795 France was in a state of civil war, divided between royalists dominating the south and west, and practising a counter-terror of their own; constitutionalists – the Clichiens, notably Carnot – hoping for a 'mixed order'; and the 'perpetuals' – mainly Girondins and notably Barras and Rewbell – who wanted to carry on the

Revolution and the war against the old order, against royalism, the clergy and the *émigrés*. France was threatened by foreign enemies, by the hunger riots of 1795, by a rising of the *sans-culottes* – of which the only result was the abortive Babeuf conspiracy (May 1796) – and by the royalist conspiracy of the Abbé Brottier (January 1797). There was rampant inflation, administrative chaos and business corruption. The situation called for leadership, and leadership came from this Corsican outsider, trained as an artilleryman caught up in revolutionary ideas but in no man's party except his own.

Vendémiaire and the 'whiff of grapeshot', 5 October 1795, brought him the command of the Army of the Interior, the rank of major-general and the hand of Josephine de Beauharnais, one of Barras's discarded mistresses. He may well have loved her for a while, if he had room for any other passions than war. She may have grown in her fashion to love him, for there was an incandescent quality in him and immense physical magnetism. However, four days after the marriage, Napoleon was on his way to Italy. The victories of 1796 (Lodi, Castiglione and Arcole) and of 1797 (Rivoli – to name only the most important of the twenty-six battles won in twelve months) made him a revolutionary hero at a time of economic discontent and political frustration, and, in a military sense, they were his greatest achievements. He dominated northern Italy as far as Rimini, occupied Florence and Leghorn, compelled the British to evacuate Corsica, and merged Milan, Modena and Bologna into the Cisalpine Republic. At Campo Formio the Machiavellian emerged: he gave much of the Venetian Republic to Austria, in return for the Ionian Islands, an advance base for a campaign in the east. To the Corsican, the Venetians, like everyone else, were expendable. And there followed the Egyptian campaign.

At the age of twenty-nine (1799) Napoleon was given command of the Army of England, but the Directory decided to strike at Britain through Egypt. Aware now that complete power in France was possible but that 'the pear is not ripe', and fascinated by the east – he had once thought of service with the Sultan – he was away for sixteen months, in the course of which he took Malta and routed the Mameluke forces at the battle of the Pyramids. But Nelson destroyed his fleet at Aboukir Bay, and he was checked at Acre; the army he abandoned had later to capitulate, and to evacuate Egypt – but his own reputation stayed unsullied.

He returned in September 1799, to help Sieyès, who, like a Madison, sought a Washington and found a Caesar. After

Brumaire (1799), he was First Consul. Only he could appoint and dismiss officials and promulgate laws. In 1802 he became First Consul for life, with the right to nominate his successor. He himself then crowned Josephine. He was thirty-four.

The roots of his success lay on the battlefield. Napoleon had a remarkable eye for the broad perspective of a campaign, and equally remarkable tactical insight on the day; he could see the weak spot of an enemy, as at Waterloo – and he was usually opposing uneasy coalitions; he was a master of timing, as Austerlitz showed; even when exhausted, he had striking powers of recuperation, as witness the manoeuvres against Blücher and Schwarzenberg in 1814. He was a great planner of campaigns, but he never in fact relied on plans when it came to action. The art of war, he said, was 'all in the execution'. And he was able to establish a *rapport* with his men of a rare kind. 'It is by speaking to the soul that men are electrified.' He had exceptional physical strength – in 1808 he rode from Valladolid to Paris in six days, and in the four days of the Waterloo campaign he was on horseback for thirty-seven hours and had less than twenty hours' sleep.

Bonaparte's success, however, was more than military. He was not only a successful soldier, but a natural authoritarian. He worked with the concentration, and the command of detail, of a Louis XIV; like the young Louis also he chose well, and his success and efficiency bred loyalty. He was superbly served – by Talleyrand as Foreign Minister (1799–1807); by Berthier, War Minister (1800–1807); by Fouché, Police and Interior (1799–1802, 1804–1810); and by a parade of brilliant marshals: Masséna, Soult, Ney, Davout, Murat, Augereau, Bernadotte. Some of these were noble indeed and paid the supreme price – for Ney, the 'bravest of the brave' who joined him after Elba, was executed by the Bourbons, and Berthier was pulled in both directions and died in 1815 – a possible suicide. Napoleon had no such emotions, nor such loyalties.

His revolutionary ardour soon cooled, and efficiency and merit became the watchwords. 'The more I read Voltaire,' he said, 'the better I like him ... Up to the age of sixteen I could have fought for Rousseau against all the friends of Voltaire. Today it is the opposite. Since I have seen the east, Rousseau is repugnant to me. The wild man without morals is a dog.' After 1799 the First Consul was in fact a supremo. The senators were nominated for life by the consuls, and they themselves selected both the tribunate, and a legislative assembly. After 1804 the Emperor himself nominated the senators. Local government in any event was controlled by a prefect, chosen

by Paris. Mayors of major cities were named by the Emperor.
Judicial posts became life appointments.

Gradually the trappings and ritual of authority were introduced also: the Legion of Honour, modelled on the Order of
St Louis, in 1802; at his coronation in 1804, princely titles for
the Bonapartes, with kingdoms to follow for all his brothers
except Lucien; in 1808, an imperial nobility with hereditary
titles and hereditary estates also – thirty-one dukes, 388 counts,
1,090 barons, 1,500 knights; sixteen generals became marshals
of France, and Murat, the ally of Vendémiaire, became Grand
Admiral; and in 1810, came marriage to the most august dynasty in Europe and an eighteen-year-old bride for himself, the
Archduchess Marie Louise of Austria, whom he found eminently satisfactory. In 1811 with the birth of a son, the King of
Rome, his own dynasty seemed assured. The basis of the
Napoleonic system however, was not honour but fear. If he
was the child of the Revolution, he was also its destroyer.

In the legal codes the emphasis was also authoritarian. The
authority of the father in the family was made clear – he could
imprison his children, withhold consent to their marriage and
control his wife's property. Family cohesion was seen as basic
to cohesion in the state. In criminal trials, there was no *habeas
corpus*.

Education too bore the marks of the despot. A new style of
grammar school appeared, the *lycée*, in which military training
was as important as the classics – it was to be one of Napoleon's
great contributions to France. In 1808 the Imperial University
was established, a degree from which was a prerequisite for
teaching. Écoles, set up by the Convention, notably the École
Polytechnique, to train engineers, and the École Normale Su-
perieure, to train teachers, were encouraged and supported.
But they too gradually reflected the authoritarianism of the
regime – by 1810 the École Polytechnique was no more than a
training school for the army, and primary education was sadly
neglected. French education, even after a century of shocks
and revolution, still bears the notably centralized and 'hot-
house' character that Napoleon gave it.

He saw religion as a necessity not for the sake of the Church
but for the stability and contentment of the state; it was a
useful buttress to patriotism. 'In religion,' he said, 'I do not see
the mystery of the Incarnation but the mystery of the social
order.' In 1802 a Concordat was signed with the Pope. Bishops
were required to resign their sees, and the bishoprics were
reduced to fifty in number, with ten archbishoprics; they were
nominated by Napoleon and consecrated by the Pope. In

exchange for a fixed salary, the clergy took an oath of obedience to the state. Roman Catholicism was recognized as the
'religion of the great majority', but equal rights were granted
to other faiths – a basic principle of the secular state which was
unknown anywhere before the Revolution.

Napoleon produced, then, a cohesive, highly centralized,
tightly disciplined state. His reforms were in the spirit of the
Revolution, a revolution made tidy and orderly. But it was as
if he knew the revolutionary words but had forgotten the tune.
His empire at once enshrined the ideas of the Revolution and
in the process undermined them. He had been prepared to
eradicate the mob with grapeshot; for him they were *canaille*.
His reforms in education sought and trained an elite; in his
codes and in his Concordat the emphasis was not on liberty
and equality, and certainly not on fraternity, but on discipline
and obedience – and on talent.

The reforms were largely the work of Napoleon as consul.
By 1804 he was an emperor, and he planned an all-out war
with Britain, with invasion for a time his dream. In the Rhineland, Italy and Poland he was seen as liberator rather than as
conqueror. Many Rhinelanders fought in his armies. And certainly 1806 was a year of total victory. After Austerlitz Austria
made peace; Russia withdrew into its own territory; and the
Holy Roman Empire was declared abolished. When Prussia
moved, she was defeated at Jena (October 1806), and the
Continental System – a vast blockade of Britain by Europe –
was announced in a series of decrees made in Berlin. And in
1807 the Russians were overwhelmed at Friedland. In July
1807, the two Emperors, of France and of Russia, met in high
ceremony on a richly decorated raft in the River Niemen and
signed the Treaty of Tilsit. Tilsit is the climax of his reign, and
it witnessed the carving up of Europe between the two men.

The last eight years were years of total absolutism and all
but total carnage. To enforce the Continental System, the
extremities of Europe as well as the French heartland had to
be controlled. Spain was torn by civil war, and in the struggle
against Napoleon the nationalist cause there gradually became
the cause of high conservatism; in the end, as he said himself,
the Spanish ulcer was to destroy him, but it was also to halt all
notions of progressive political change at the Pyrenees. By
1810 the uneasy alliance with the Tsar was over. The march on
Moscow in 1812, on which 600,000 set off but only 30,000
returned, was the beginning of the end, as decisive a turning
point as Hitler's invasion in 1941. The nationalism of the
peoples, the secret ally of the Revolution and of the early

Napoleon, was now turned against him. The arbitrary carving up of territories, the Corsican-style nepotism of the 'kingdoms', the reappearance in the satellite states not of liberators but of men of property, usually from the major families of the old regime, all these were anathema to the rising spirit of national resurgence and bourgeois assertion. And at the centre of the dream was less a new vision of Europe than an enlarged France.

In the end the spirit of nationalism, itself a product of 1789, was Napoleon's undoing, plus his failure by 1813 to be capable of any measure of moderation. Even after Leipzig (October 1813), by bargaining and blandishment he could still have retained his throne, even perhaps an imperial title. It was by that time not in him to compromise; the major cause of his final tragedy, first at Elba, and in the hundred days to Waterloo, was thus less the Spanish war or the Moscow campaign, Wellington's armies or nationalism, but the man's own megalomania. At the end, as at the beginning, the nature of the usurper and the *condottiere* was all too transparent. He had done it all. Why should it end?

Napoleon was passionately admired, in his own day and later, and not only by Frenchmen – by Hegel and Goethe, by Beethoven and Hazlitt, by Carlyle and Rosebery. Along with Byron, he became for nineteenth-century Europe the great embodiment of romantic individualism. Yet this was not an admirable man. Even if history is not a court of morals, Napoleon condemns himself by his own frank admissions – his comment on the 29,000 dead at Eylau was 'small change!' and on Borodino, where 80,000 lay dead, was that it was the most beautiful battlefield he had ever seen. In 1813 he told Metternich that a man like him did not care for the lives of a million men. As women conspicuously were but the instruments of his lust, so, most of the time, were men but the instruments of his quest for power. It is impossible to quarrel with the verdict and indictment of A. J. P. Taylor: 'He was a monster. He found France great; he left her small ... It would have been better for everyone if he had never been born; and there was nothing for it but to eliminate him.' Or, as Alexis de Tocqueville put it – and he was brought up as a boy in Napoleon's France: 'He was as great as a man can be without virtue.'

George Canning

(1770–1827)

Brilliant, erratic, dashingly self-confident, George Canning was Prime Minister of Britain for a mere one hundred days if one counts from when he completed his Cabinet – the shortest term of any prime minister. It is on his achievement as an outstanding Foreign Secretary that his reputation chiefly rests.

George Canning was born in London on 11 April 1770 of Irish, or Anglo-Irish, parents. The Cannings settled in Ulster in Queen Elizabeth's reign. In the middle of the eighteenth century the head of the family was one Stratford Canning, who had three sons. The eldest was George, the future statesman's father, who, having fallen in love with a beautiful but penniless girl of whom his father disapproved, was turned out into the world to make his own way. He went to London, where before long he was head over heels in debt. Then in 1768 he committed the further imprudence of marrying an eighteen-year-old girl from Connaught, Mary Anne Costello by name, who like his earlier love was beautiful but without a penny to her name. Soon his debts accumulated afresh and in 1771 he died, worn out with worries and disappointments. This was just a year after the birth of his son George.

The young widow was left practically destitute, but she was a woman of fine character and resource, and she formed the notion of going on the stage to keep herself and her boy. She appeared in productions at Drury Lane and Covent Garden, where at first her beauty and sad story aroused the interest of playgoers. But she was nothing much of an actress, and before long she could get engagements only in the provincial theatres. Then she took up with an actor-manager named Reddish, by whom she had several children.

Poverty and sometimes actual want, harsh treatment, disreputable companions – these must have been George's lot, and an actor friend of Mrs Canning's named Moody, when he first met the boy, concluded that he was 'on the way to the gallows'. He might indeed have ended up there but for this kind-hearted fellow. Moody learnt from Mrs Canning that George had an uncle, Stratford Canning, who was a successful merchant in the City. He presented the boy's case to such good effect that the old grandfather in Ireland agreed to make the boy an allowance of £200 a year, while Stratford Canning took him into his own home at Putney.

George's mother, it would seem, was left to carry on as best she could, with an ever-growing number of children to look after. In 1801 George Canning arranged to have transferred to her a pension of £500 a year to which he had become entitled in consequence of his official employment. He visited her when-ever he could, and wrote to her regularly every week. His affection for his mother is, in fact, one of the most engaging traits in Canning's character.

Canning was about eight years old when he was transferred to his uncle's care. Stratford Canning was a staunch Whig, and under his roof George made the acquaintance of other impor-tant figures in Whig society. Fox himself is supposed to have urged that the boy should be sent to Eton, where Canning stayed for six years from 1782, and did well there, winning a number of prizes and becoming top of the school. He also helped to launch and was the chief contributor to a school magazine called *The Microcosm*, and distinguished himself in the debating society.

Leaving Eton in 1788, when he was eighteen, Canning went on to Christ Church, Oxford, where he showed superiority in Greek and Latin. In 1791 he got his degrees and took the coach for London. On arrival there he started reading for the bar at Lincoln's Inn, but he was very soon deserting his law studies for the drawing-rooms queened over by the great ladies of Whig society, to which he was admitted on the strength of his Oxford reputation as a smart-tongued young man of promise and his uncle's connections in political circles.

At Oxford he had been a 'horrible Whig', and had inveighed against the policies of William Pitt. When the French Revolu-tion broke out, he hailed it as the dawn of an infinitely brighter and happier age, and at the radical clubs that met in such popular hostelries as the Hardwicke and the Crown and An-chor his spirited denunciations of tyranny were received with rapturous shouts. But before long he began to have doubts. As he explained in a letter to his friend, Lord Boringdon, while the French

were struggling for their own liberty ... my opinion, my hopes, and my prayers went with them, and I exulted in the defeat of their enemies; but now I find them a very different people, victorious everywhere ... not oppressed, attacked, and insulted but insolent beyond all bounds, professing universal oppression.

This was written in 1792, when he had already broken with his Whig friends and patrons. He had written to Pitt, offering his services, and in August the Prime Minister had received him at Downing Street in the most friendly fashion. From that moment Canning was Pitt's most devoted supporter. A seat in Parliament was the next step, and in July 1793 Canning was returned unopposed as MP for the borough of Newtown in the Isle of Wight.

Of course he was bitterly assailed by the Whigs for this 'desertion'. He in turn proceeded to attack in the columns of a satirical weekly called the *Anti-Jacobin* those Whigs who still adhered to Fox instead of hurrying to jump on to Pitt's bandwagon.

Early in the next year he made his maiden speech, and although it was not quite so good as his reputation had led people to expect, it made a favourable impression. Later on he developed into one of the greatest of parliamentary orators; Lord Aberdeen, who had an extensive knowledge of the subject, declared that he preferred Canning's oratory to that of such splendid performers as Fox and Pitt. But what most was to his advantage was the Prime Minister's obvious partiality, and the relationship between them developed into one of sincere affection. Pitt, it was remarked, seemed to look upon Canning almost as a son.

Canning's first experience of office was in 1796, when Pitt appointed him under-secretary at the Foreign Office. After three years of what he described as 'such slavery as never was slaved' he was given the much better paid post of joint Paymaster-General.

Shortly afterwards he made a highly advantageous marriage. His bride was Miss Joan Scott. Not only was she politically very well connected, but she was exceedingly well off. He met her for the first time at Walmer Castle, when he was staying there as Pitt's guest – the Prime Minister was then Lord Warden of the Cinque Ports – and whether or not Pitt actually arranged the meeting, he certainly encouraged Canning's suit. They had three sons and a daughter. The third son was the Lord Canning who was Governor-General of India at the time of the Mutiny in 1857 and earned the noble nickname of 'Clemency Canning'.

When Canning was appointed to the Pay Office he seemed well on the way to a successful political career, but within a

few months Pitt took it into his head to retire and Canning felt
obliged to follow his patron's lead. He opposed the Addington
government, sneering at its leader as 'The Doctor', and did his
best to further Pitt's return to office.

On Pitt's return to the premiership in 1804 Canning was
appointed Treasurer of the Navy. He was with Pitt the night
before he died, and he was deeply grieved. Immediately after
the funeral he wrote to his wife, 'It is all over, dearest Love. I
have seen poor Pitt laid in his grave, and I feel somehow a
feeling of loneliness and dismay which I have never felt so
strongly before.' And six years later, in a speech at Liverpool
to those who had recently become his constituents, he declared,
'To one man, while he lived, I was devoted with all my heart
and all my soul. Since the death of Mr Pitt I acknowledge no
leader.' This statement provides the key to an understanding
of his political career, so chequered in its various stages. He
was not cut out to be a sound party man. He proved an uneasy
and unreliable colleague. He was too clever for the ordinary run
of politicians, whichever side of the party fence they were on.

When Lord Portland became Prime Minister in 1807 he
made Canning his Foreign Secretary, in which capacity he
showed plenty of energy and enterprise. It was Canning who
decided on Spain as the battlefield on which Napoleon's power
might be undermined, and he gave his full support to the
selection of Wellesley as the commander of the British armies
in the Peninsula. His most remarkable stroke was the dispatch
of an expeditionary force to Denmark – a country with which
Britain was not then at war – which bombarded Copenhagen
and seized the Danish fleet, thereby preventing its falling into
Napoleon's hands. But his relations with Lord Castlereagh,
the War Minister, were always strained, and in 1809 the two
men fought a duel on Putney Heath. Canning was wounded in
the thigh, but shot a button off Castlereagh's coat.

Before the year was out Portland resigned, and Canning was
in great hopes of succeeding him as Prime Minister. It was a
deep disappointment when Spencer Perceval was chosen instead. For a number of years Canning was out of high office.
His greatest blunder was in 1812 when Lord Liverpool, who
had become Prime Minister on Spencer Perceval's assassination, offered him the Foreign Office, on the understanding that
Castlereagh should lead the House of Commons. In these
circumstances Canning refused the offer – and it was not long
before he realized what a fool he had been. He was quite glad
to receive in 1816 the comparatively minor appointment of
president of the Board of Control (the predecessor of the India

Office), and as a member of Liverpool's government he supported to the full all the repressive measures that characterized it. For although inclined to a liberal policy in foreign affairs, he was a hardened reactionary on most domestic issues. Thus he was strongly opposed to any measure of parliamentary reform. The exception to this attitude was his advocacy of Roman Catholic emancipation – and this did him no good with the Tories.

In 1822 his old rival Castlereagh cut his throat in a fit of insanity and Canning was offered the vacant post of Foreign Secretary. Such a wonderful second chance comes to few men, and Canning made the most of it. He ticked off His Majesty's Minister at Lisbon for his slovenly penmanship, and also for including packets of tea with his official correspondence. He sent a breath of fresh air blowing down the dusty corridors, and occasionally his old gay humour asserted itself. The most celebrated instance of this is the dispatch which he sent to the British Minister at The Hague to advise him that because the Dutch had been difficult in some commercial matters a levy of twenty per cent was about to be imposed on Dutch shipping. When deciphered, the message read:

> Sir, – In matters of commerce the fault of the Dutch
> Is giving too little and asking too much.
> With equal protection the French are content,
> So we'll clap on Dutch bottoms just twenty per cent.
> *Chorus.* Twenty per cent, twenty per cent.
> *Chorus of English Customs House Officers.* We'll lay
> on Dutch bottoms just twenty per cent.

As Foreign Secretary, Canning was brilliantly successful. He asserted Britain's independent attitude towards the Holy Alliance of the despotic emperors of the Continent. He supported the Greeks in their struggle to throw off the Turkish yoke. When Spain seemed likely to fall under French control, he furthered the efforts of the Spanish colonies in South America to achieve their independence as democratic republics; as he expressed it in the most memorable of his phrases, 'I called the New World into existence to redress the balance of the Old.'

When Lord Liverpool had a stroke early in 1827, Canning was laid up with a severe chill that he had caught at the Duke of York's funeral, when he had been obliged to stand for hours in the middle of the night on the cold flagstones of St George's Chapel at Windsor. But he recovered himself sufficiently to make a determined bid for the succession.

No one had a better claim to the premiership, and yet strong

influences were brought to bear against his appointment. The
King did not like him, and Wellington and the ultra-Tories
distrusted him. For weeks there was much wrangling behind
the scenes, and it was only on 10 April that Canning at last
kissed the King's hand as Prime Minister, First Lord of the
Treasury, and Chancellor of the Exchequer. But he had yet to
form a government; most of Liverpool's cabinet agreed to
serve under him, but Wellington and Peel were among those
who declined.

Canning's administration was given a rough passage in both
Houses. As the official opposition, the Whigs under Lord Grey
were very naturally opposed to everything he did, but far worse
were the Tories who sided with Wellington. On 1 June, as
Chancellor of the Exchequer, he introduced his budget. Three
weeks later, on the Corn Amendment Bill, he made what
proved to be his last speech in the House of Commons. The
young Benjamin Disraeli heard it from a seat in the gallery,
and many years afterwards he said that he could recall 'the
lightning flash of that eye and the tumult of that ethereal brow.
Still lingers in my ear the melody of that voice.'

Parliament rose at the beginning of July, but Canning had
to continue at high pressure. Among his last actions were the
signing of the treaty which gave freedom to Greece, and the
opening of negotiations with Brazil for the abolition of the
slave trade. Mentally he was as alert as ever, but he had never
properly recovered from the chill he caught some months
earlier. He went to see the King at Windsor on 30 July, and
George remarked how ill he looked.

When he got back to Chiswick he took to his bed and for a
week lingered in the most dreadful agony. The King sent his
own doctor to see him, and his diagnosis was inflammation of
the liver. Towards the end he lost consciousness. Early on the
morning of 8 August 1827 Canning died.

Grief and consternation were the mingled emotions when
the news became known. A grave in Westminster Abbey was
made ready; and though the funeral was private in accordance
with Canning's own expressed wish, and the rain descended in
torrents, immense crowds assembled to watch the simple
procession go past. The coffin was placed in a vault opposite
that containing the remains of William Pitt, the man whose
friend and disciple Canning had been most proud to be.

Metternich

(1773-1859)

It is impossible for us today to share the depth of horror experienced by the rulers and aristocracy of Europe over the events of the French Revolution of 1789. But what we can do is gauge its effects in the extreme conservatism which prevailed in Europe in the years following Napoleon's fall, and nowhere more clearly than in the words and actions of its chief protagonist, the Austrian Foreign Minister from 1809 to 1848, Prince Metternich.

Clement Wenzel Lothar von Metternich-Winneburg-Beilstein, a Rhinelander, was born in 1773 in Coblenz, son of a wealthy diplomat and Count of the Holy Roman Empire and of Beatrice née Countess Kagenegg. At sixteen Clement was sent to study at Strasbourg University where he acquired an interest in medicine, science and music. But his parents had other plans for him, and in 1795 after their Rhineland estates had been confiscated by Napoleon and they had moved to Vienna, they arranged the marriage of their handsome and brilliant son to the grand-daughter of Maria Theresa's famous Chancellor, Kaunitz, thus giving him a lift-up into high society. He had already made his mark in a minor diplomatic post. Now he was sent by the Emperor Francis as ambassador to the court of Saxony, then to Berlin and finally to Paris where he learnt to know Napoleon well.

By 1809 he had formed a close relationship with his master and they were agreed on the ultra-cautious policy to be followed at a time of Austria's lowest fortunes. She had twice been heavily defeated by Napoleon, at Austerlitz in 1805 and recently at Wagram with consequent massive loss of territory. At home there was runaway inflation, in 1806 Francis had been forced to declare the Holy Roman Empire dissolved and Napoleon's unstoppable armies were carrying the virus of revolution to the mutually hostile nationalities in Austria–Hungary, of which there were no less than eleven.

To cope with this situation Metternich aimed to achieve peace, stability and a balance of power in Europe, backed by regular discussion between the countries concerned. In this way progress and the growth of freedom would be secured by

49

'measured steps', both internally and externally, not by revolutionary 'leaps' which were self-defeating. Meanwhile it was clear that for the time being Austria could not risk another military encounter with Napoleon. 'Our system,' wrote Metternich, 'must be exclusively one of tacking, of obliterating ourselves, of accommodating ourselves to the victor. In this way alone we shall perhaps extend our existence to the day of general deliverance.'

But Metternich also realized that Napoleon was dependent for his throne on continuing military success and could ultimately be brought to heel only by military defeat. This entailed drawing his continental enemies, Russia and Prussia, into a fresh coalition without prematurely severing contact with him. Metternich also meant to ensure that after the hoped-for victory, if it came, the allies would not themselves be lured by expansionist dreams, thus upsetting the European balance yet again.

All this was to be triumphantly achieved. Contact with Napoleon was maintained by his marriage to Francis's daughter Marie Louise, a project eagerly furthered by Metternich who saw in it a useful smoke-screen behind which to develop his plans, and the coalition was more easily brought about by Napoleon's catastrophic defeat in Russia in 1812. The result was the first notable allied victory at Leipzig in the following year. Thereafter, at Metternich's insistence an Austrian general was given command of the allied armies as they advanced towards Paris in 1814, and after the occupation of the city in March he took a leading part in ensuring fair terms for France, including the restoration of the Bourbons, under the First Treaty of Paris, as part of his long-term aim of pacification.

At the Congress of Vienna which followed Napoleon's fall and banishment to Elba it remained to negotiate the allies' territorial claims and here again Metternich played a decisive role, bringing in France as a fifth member of the Big Four (Russia, Austria, Prussia and Britain) to outvote the Tsar Alexander's excessive demands on Poland and a project to allow Prussia to annex the whole of Saxony. Instead, Prussia became a member of a wider German Confederation under Austrian presidency, Austria was restored to suzerainty in northern Italy and, at British instigation, the Netherlands were set up as an independent kingdom. Napoleon's escape from Elba and subsequent defeat at the battle of Waterloo did not upset these arrangements except in so far as France, under the Second Treaty of Paris, was saddled with an indemnity and an army of occupation.

Thus in the space of six years Metternich had raised Austria from a state of near-disintegration to a position of unprecedented power and prestige. But this achievement was not to last. He was a product of the Enlightenment, the offspring of the Age of Reason, believing in a 'science' of politics and in time-tested orderly government. Not for him concessions extorted by popular unrest, whether liberal or nationalistic in tone. If there was to be progress it should be granted from above in times of stability, never demanded from below. Unfortunately for Metternich this typically aristocratic attitude was contrary to the spirit of the new century. In the thirty-three years that remained of his career times never were stable and his repressive policies probably made the explosion more violent when it came. This was tragic as his concept of a concert of European powers was truly prophetic, anticipating by more than a century the movement towards unity of our own time.

Meanwhile, after more than twenty years of war, the exhausted former allies were not inclined to squabble. They saw clearly that if they did not hang together they might hang separately, or, in the words of the British Foreign Secretary Castlereagh, with which Metternich would have heartily agreed:

> The immediate object is to inspire the States of Europe with a sense ... of the hazards they will incur by a relaxation of vigilance, to make them feel that the existing concert is their only perfect security against the revolutionary embers more or less existing in every State of Europe.

It was in this spirit, indeed, that in the previous month Castlereagh and Metternich had brought about a quadruple alliance between the big powers, guaranteeing the territorial *status quo* and providing for periodic consultations to ensure 'the repose and prosperity of nations'.

So was born the congress system, destined to last in its original form for seven years until Castlereagh's mental breakdown and suicide in 1822. There were four congresses: at Aix-la-Chapelle (1818), Troppau (1820), Laibach (1821) and Verona (1822). At the first it was agreed to bring France back within the comity of nations by cancelling what remained of the indemnity and withdrawing the occupation troops, at the same time secretly reaffirming a provision of the quadruple alliance to take joint action in case of future French aggression. The discussions went so smoothly that Metternich wrote he had never seen 'a prettier little congress'.

But trouble was looming. Metternich knew that for all his

sound principles Castlereagh would never act unless the European balance of power was seriously threatened, and the mer-
curial Tsar Alexander, whose mind swung perpetually between
airy mysticism and grasping opportunism, might easily be
tempted to upset that balance (already distorted by vast westward increases of Russian territory in the last fifty years) if the
chance arose. The chance came in 1820 with uprisings in Spain
and Naples. Under the influence of his liberal-minded minister
Capo d'Istria, Alexander wanted to intervene on the side of the
insurgents. Here was a serious crisis and at the congresses of
Laibach and Troppau Metternich strove, with ultimate success, to woo the Tsar away from his dangerous ideas. 'Sire,' he
wrote feelingly, 'let us be conservative; let us walk steadily and
firmly on well-known paths; let us not deviate from these lines
in word or deed ...'

But it was becoming increasingly difficult to follow the
well-known paths, those, that is, of peaceful balance and harmony. A Greek revolt against Turkish rule in 1821 developed
into a full-scale bid for independence and again brought a
Russian threat of intervention, on the side of the Greeks. This
was temporarily averted at Verona but already the congress
system was collapsing: Britain under Castlereagh's successor,
George Canning, France with reviving military ambitions,
Alexander lured by the chance to spread his influence into the
Mediterranean, no longer believed wholeheartedly in its principles. In the event Russia went to war against Turkey and
peace was not restored until 1829 when a new independent
kingdom of Greece was set up.

Throughout, Metternich's policy had been to support Turkey's 'legitimate' rule against the insurrectionists. Now, in
defeat, he felt the law of the jungle returning and wrote sadly to
the Emperor that the only hope for the future lay in Austria's
renewed military strength. Collective security was no longer
effective. Nevertheless for a few more years the Big Four
retained faith in conservatism and the *status quo*, and paradoxically this was strengthened by the revolutions of 1830,
which brought Louis Philippe to the throne of France and split
off Belgium from the United Netherlands as a separate kingdom. Only in Italy were there signs of chronic unrest pointing
to a different future. There the Vienna settlement had left
Austria in almost complete control of the northern states,
directly in Lombardy-Venetia and through junior members of
the Habsburg family in Parma, Modena and Tuscany. In these
areas there were many secret societies, divided in their aims but
all obscurely searching for greater freedom – and the only

Austrian response, instigated by Metternich and Francis, was repression, with eventual recourse to military action.

At the dawn of the 1840s Italy was not to be the only trouble-spot. Throughout Europe there was a rising tide of liberal and nationalistic fervour, in France, in Germany and throughout the provinces of the sprawling Austrian Empire: Bohemia, Hungary, Galicia, Dalmatia and Istria (on the Adriatic coast). Metternich was not directly responsible for internal administration in these areas, though for many years he had preached a modest form of devolution and reform of the central bureaucracy in Vienna. Such plans had been blocked by the ultra-conservative Francis, however, and since his death in 1835 they had become increasingly irrelevant as an answer to growing unrest. Now, despite mounting danger signals, Metternich made no great effort to put them into effect, perhaps because he knew it was too late, or because opposition from the bureaucracy was too strong, or simply that he was old and tired.

For over thirty years the Austrian Empire, always an artificial and unstable creation, had lost no territory and been engaged in no major war. This had been Metternich's achievement. Now his glittering career was about to end in humiliation. Early in 1848 the flame of revolution spread from Paris, where Louis Philippe was forced to abdicate and a republic declared, to Italy, Bohemia, Hungary, the German states and Vienna itself, where discontent was already rife among the professional classes fearful for the stability of the currency, university students seeking relaxation of oppressive laws and a throng of desperate, semi-starving peasants who had come to the city to find work.

Amid mounting scenes of violence the mentally retarded Emperor Ferdinand and the government dithered. Troops were sent in, then replaced by the civic guard, a force under the control of the burgomaster. At nine o'clock on the evening of 13 March the guard issued an ultimatum, threatening to join the rioters if Metternich, now the scapegoat for all dissatisfactions, was not dismissed. Metternich was summoned to an audience at the Hofburg and there, after some discussion, Ferdinand dismissed the man who had been created Prince by his father Francis in 1813 and Chancellor in 1821, saying simply: 'Tell the people I agree to everything.' Metternich was approaching seventy-five.

Next day, Metternich, his wife and children, with only the equivalent of £50 between them, were taken by friends to Feldsberg on the Moravian border to be out of harm's way.

From there they were persuaded to set out for the Dutch coast with the intention of settling in England, which they reached after a perilous journey through strife-torn Europe on 20 April. In London, with finance from the Rothschilds, they rented a house at 44 Eaton Square and soon the brave old man was appearing in public, imperturbable, impeccably dressed as ever, and winning a wide circle of friends. For some months they then moved to Brighton where Disraeli succumbed to his charms ('I've never heard such divine talk') and the Duke of Wellington became an attentive friend, devising endless schemes to keep Metternich amused. But this was hardly necessary. With amazing resilience the aged Prince was already eagerly interested in everything around him, devouring the English and French newspapers and keeping up a cautious but lengthy correspondence with his numerous friends at home.

Eventually exile in England began to pall and the Metternichs would have liked to return to Vienna. But this depended on an invitation from the young Emperor Francis Joseph, nephew of Ferdinand, and that was not forthcoming until two years later when an official investigation cleared Metternich of charges that during his term of office he had accepted bribes from Tsar Alexander and his successor Nicholas. On 24 September 1851, the Metternichs returned to their house on the Rennweg, to their delight finding it undamaged. Even more pleasing to the Prince was the discovery that, though free now from day-to-day responsibilities, he was not cold-shouldered by those in power and his advice was sought after.

It was not often followed, though, and increasingly he came to realize that he was speaking into the wind and that an old man's shadow was not welcomed by a younger generation at the helm. He could do nothing to avert the outbreak of the Crimean War, and in 1859 could not prevent Francis Joseph invading Piedmont. When on 5 June news reached him of a heavy defeat at Magenta he fell to the floor in a faint. Six days later he was dead. Already he had been almost forgotten and it was his son Richard, ambassador in Paris, whom people usually referred to when they spoke the name that had been a byword in Europe for forty years.

Viscount Melbourne

(1779–1848)

If the second Viscount Melbourne, Queen Victoria's first prime minister, had died before he was fifty, he would not have been deemed worthy of record here. For twenty years he was an undistinguished back-bencher in Parliament, sitting successively in the Whig interest for Leominster, Portarlington, Northampton and Hertfordshire.

He spoke rarely and made little mark when he did, though he commanded a far richer vocabulary than most MPs. His reading was prodigious and unusually well ordered. A pundit of the feared Edinburgh school of reviewers believed that Melbourne had it in him to rival Charles Lamb as an essayist, Rochefoucauld as a maker of aphorisms, Saint-Beuve as a critic. Exerting himself to such lofty endeavours, however, was no temptation to his indolent, reflective and somewhat cynical nature.

Melbourne, born William Lamb, was the son of Sir Peniston Lamb (1745–1828), the first Viscount Melbourne. The latter was not a particularly estimable character, of whom it was said that the only good taste he ever displayed was in choosing his wife. She was the daughter of Sir Ralph Milbanke, a Yorkshire baronet, and her good intelligence was combined with social graces that attracted men as notable and various as the Prince of Wales, Sheridan, the dramatist, Brougham and Canning, the statesmen, and Brummell, the man of fashion. William, her second son, was born on 15 March 1779.

After Eton and Cambridge, he went to Glasgow University as a substitute for the 'grand tour' denied to young Englishmen by the Napoleonic wars. He read law, was called to the bar and was making good progress in his chosen profession when his elder brother died, leaving him heir to the family title and estates.

Meanwhile, he had been captivated by the boyish figure and 'large hazel eyes' of Lady Caroline Ponsonby, only daughter of the third Earl of Bessborough. By her own account, she fell in love with William Lamb some time before she first saw him, enthralled by what she had heard of his good looks, cleverness and fine prospects. They became friends when she was thirteen and he twenty, were married in 1805 and took up residence on a top floor of Melbourne House, Piccadilly. In 1806 he was elected MP for Leominster in the Whig interest.

In the Commons, he supported reforming measures that included the betterment of prison conditions; otherwise, his attitude to burning issues was lukewarm. When he lost his seat he showed a certain dismay but did not care, he said, to ask his father for financial help in securing another. He was apparently indifferent to the prizes of life and set on an aimless course. That would certainly have been the judgement on his public performance thus far. Privately, he was preoccupied with the subject of the Peninsular War, the Greek and Latin classics and, curiously, with theological studies. There was also the conduct of his wife, whose energies were largely devoted to profligate activities.

His essential good nature tolerated much that would have impelled other husbands to drastic action. His mother wrote a forcible reminder to her daughter-in-law of 'the Decencies imposed by Society'. The last restraints gave way when Lady Caroline met Lord Byron. That occasion, and its disastrous sequel, led to William Lamb's temporary avoidance of social life in London. His marriage finally came to grief in 1825, by which time his wife's mental breakdown, as well as her desperate affair with Byron, was common knowledge.

That unpleasantness behind him, some of his friends in high places, including the Prince Regent, Castlereagh and Canning, were professing confidence in his political future. He still behaved as if disinclined to bestir himself in the public interest. In 1827 the prime minister of the day, Lord Liverpool, was stricken with paralysis. A government crisis followed, involving a split in which the warring factions were led by the Duke of Wellington and Canning. From the ensuing complications, William Lamb surprisingly emerged as chief secretary to the Lord Lieutenant of Ireland. He was forty-eight.

Lamb had been in favour of Catholic emancipation, one of the few causes on which he had spoken out in the House of Commons. It opened doors for him in Dublin, where he relaxed the formalities of official life, conducting himself as no chief secretary had before. He actually sat at his desk with the door of his room wide open to admit all and sundry. 'Come in,' he would shout as a visitor diffidently approached. 'Now, don't go too fast, don't ask for impossibilities, and don't do anything damned silly.' As a formula it worked wonders. Even the most obstreperous Irish fell under the spell of an Englishman who confounded their notions of race and class.

Popular as anyone holding his post could hope to be, he may not have deeply regretted his recall in a few months as the consequence of yet another political upheaval at home. George IV asked Wellington to form a government. During the negotiations, Lamb succeeded to the Melbourne title on the death of his father in 1829. The great issue before the public was the Reform Bill. Speaking against, Wellington alienated many of his supporters. The national unease was reflected in threats of labour agitation in the north. In the south, the temper of land workers flared up in ugly demonstrations.

It was a climate insupportable to the Tories, who gave way to a Whig administration with Lord Grey at its head. Melbourne was made Home Secretary, to the surprise of many. Greville, as clerk of the council, thought him 'far too inconsiderable' for the post. In fact, Melbourne's appointment to high office was not so astonishing as his efficiency in carrying out its duties. His casual air was soon seen to be deceptive. It glossed a far more penetrating mind than was realized.

His major task was to maintain order while the Reform Bill was going through Parliament. It meant enforcing the law at a time of great constitutional readjustments, involving much disturbance in the body politic. The situation was complicated by the forces of an even more profound change, that of the Industrial Revolution. Melbourne had to act with decision if the reforming measures were to cause a minimum of trouble in the country. Several southern counties were in a state of revolt, riots spreading from Kent into Sussex and Hampshire, and thence into a dozen other counties. Special constables were enrolled in most of them; in some, local sympathies were such that few volunteers for those duties came forward. Meanwhile, haystacks blazed, farmers' families were intimidated, pitched battles occurred between rioting labourers and the local yeomanry.

By the time the Labourers' Revolt was over, there were three hangings, between four and five hundred sentences to transportation, and a similar number of imprisonments for riotous assembly, damage to farm buildings and machinery, demanding money with menaces, and anonymous letter writing.

Events assumed a fresh momentum with the resignation of Grey from the premiership, his administration engulfed by the rising tide of Irish nationalism. Having, after a scene in the House of Commons announced his intention to retire, Grey handed Melbourne a sealed letter from the King. He desired 'Lord Melbourne's immediate attendance and advice on the existing state of affairs'. The date was 8 July 1834.

Melbourne's satisfaction in being called to the highest office was not profound. He seems to have considered himself in charge of an emergency cabinet that might at any time be dissolved. He watched the destruction of the Houses of Parliament by fire on the night of 16 October 1834 with a jauntiness that betrayed nothing of his fears for the future of the country. They were real enough. To him, the fire at Westminster symbolized the passing of old verities and assurances, even old glories, that could never be replaced. Readers of *The Times* of 15 November that year were astonished by its report that the Melbourne government was no more.

In a few months, the Whigs were back in office again, their parliamentary strength augmented by radicals and Irish. Melbourne took soundings for a coalition with the Tories. Once again Irish matters, this time mainly centred in the Church, stood in the way. Failing also to persuade Grey to resume the leadership, Melbourne reluctantly became prime minister for the second time.

Three years later William IV died, an unforeseen event that produced more political agitation and opened a new and glamorous chapter in Melbourne's career. At 9 a.m. on 20 June 1837, he presented himself at Kensington Palace in the full dress of a Privy Councillor. He was there to bow the head to the new monarch, the young Queen Victoria. 'I had a very important and very *comfortable* conversation with him,' she wrote in her diary at the end of the day. After a miserably strict upbringing, at last she had someone to turn to whose role was not suppressive, who helped her to realize herself and her place in the scheme of things, who in her eyes had heroic attributes and who yet treated her with gentle respect. It was not long before she was thinking of him in terms of fascinated regard.

That 'fine soft voice of his', as he read dispatches and speeches to her, made music in her ear, the more so when he spoke, at her prompting, about his boyhood and youth. 'He wore his hair long,' she was pleased to note, 'as all boys did then, till he was seventeen; (*how* handsome he must have looked!).' She thought it 'quite extraordinary' that he never carried a watch. He explained that he 'always asks a servant what o'clock it is'. Puzzling over that conceit, she also noted that he could not understand her dislike of rooks. 'They are my delight,' he told her. 'I could sit looking at them for an hour.'

Through the young Queen he attained a public eminence that he had never consciously aspired to. Now, as the confidant of the sovereign, he was at the peak of his political fortunes, admired and respected to a degree previously denied him.

It was idyllic while it lasted, for the ageing statesman a benison of the gods. Then came gathering clouds. Almost inevitably the relentless emphasis on the young woman's importance in the world produced imperious reactions. They worried Melbourne. He was more than once heard appealing to her: 'For God's sake, don't do that, Ma'am!'

Crisis intervened in 1839, this time arising from the recent abolition of slavery in Jamaica. Agreed apprenticeship schemes were being abused by the planters; prison reforms were being obstructed. The Whig government under Melbourne decided to suspend the Jamaican constitution. Radical opposition in Parliament reduced the government's majority to an unworkable level. Melbourne felt obliged to resign and recommended the Queen to turn to the Tories for his successor. That meant sending for Sir Robert Peel, 'the greatest member of parliament that ever lived'.

Peel desired the Queen's consent to the replacement of some of her ladies-in-waiting. She declined to give it, arguing that if she did so she might be 'surrounded by spies'. Soon, Peel was out and Melbourne in again. But his star was beginning to wane. Albert of Coburg – 'who is *beautiful*', Victoria wrote in her diary – arrived at Windsor. When she told Melbourne that she had resolved to marry the handsome young prince, he replied: 'Oh, you have? Well, I'm very glad of it. You'll be much more comfortable,' a prognosis that could not be applied to himself.

The Queen remarked on his tiredness at their private interview at Buckingham Palace immediately after the wedding ceremony in February 1840. 'It's this constant care,' he told her. A near-east crisis involving France and England intensified Melbourne's cares. The possibility of a new collision between the two countries loomed. Palmerston, the Foreign Secretary, was sure the French were bluffing. Melbourne was anything but confident. He was a deeply troubled man. The tensions collapsed in a few weeks. Melbourne's relief was extraordinary, as if he experienced a reprieve not from war but from the menace of old age.

It was a delusive remission. 'Lord Melbourne is looking as old as the hills,' remarked someone at court shortly afterwards. His government, too, was threatened by the nation's economic ills, with the Corn Laws a source of inflammation. At cabinet meetings he lapsed into absent-mindedness and showed a want of grip on state business. After one meeting had broken up,

departing ministers heard him call out after them: 'Stop a bit
– what did we decide?' Hearing that Palmerston was said to be
scheming with the Tories, he showed pleasure, as if at the
prospect of retiring.

When he did so with the fall of his government in 1841, the
Queen was 'dreadfully affected'. She wrote to her uncle Leopold, King of the Belgians: '*Eleven days* was the *longest* that I
ever was without seeing him, and this time will be elapsed on
Saturday, so you may imagine what the change must be.' That
she insisted on corresponding with him and continued to invite
him to Windsor produced complications that he foresaw but
could not easily obviate.

In October 1842 he suffered a slight paralytic stroke, and
was thereafter seen 'dragging one foot after the other and with
no speculation in his eye.' He would sit for hours gazing at the
portrait of his mother at Brocket Hall. Mention of the Queen
was apt to bring tears to his eyes.

He died on 24 November 1848, that year of unexampled
social and political upheaval in England and on the Continent.
The Queen wrote her own epitaph on him: 'Though not a *firm*
minister, he was a noble, kind-hearted, generous being.'

Viscount Palmerston

(1784-1865)

Henry John Temple, Viscount Palmerston, became British prime minister for the first time when he was seventy, and for the second time when he was seventy-five. He was called the 'Evergreen Premier' among other things, complimentary and otherwise, in the course of his almost unequalled career of long public service. Perhaps the most popular name given him was 'Old Pam' - a term of affection, for the people loved him with all his faults, and perhaps the more because of them.

He sprang from an old family which had been originally English but had been established for some generations in Ireland. His father, the second Viscount, made his home at Broadlands, near Romsey in Hampshire, and with his wife - born Mary Mee, daughter of a wealthy citizen of Bath and both good-looking and well-dowered - cut a fine figure in society. As a child the future prime minister accompanied his parents on their trips abroad, and in 1795 was sent to Harrow where he was not very good at his books but showed himself a jolly little fellow with lots of pluck.

At sixteen he went to Edinburgh University to attend the classes of the celebrated Scottish philosopher Dugald Stewart, and in the three years he spent there, he wrote later, 'laid the foundation of whatever useful knowledge and habits of mind I possess'. In 1802 his father died, and at the age of seventeen he became Viscount Palmerston. This was a title in the peerage of Ireland. If it had been an English title he could have been precluded from sitting in the House of Commons, but as it was there was no such bar.

The following year Palmerston proceeded to St John's College, Cambridge, and he was a student there when his mother died, to his bitter grief. At the university he paid much more attention to politics than to classical studies, and in January 1806, when he had only recently come of age and had not yet taken his degree, he decided to stand for Parliament as Tory candidate for the university. He canvassed energetically - and came last in the poll. He stood again for the same seat in 1807 and was again beaten, but this time by only four votes.

At the age of twenty-two he was appointed a junior lord of

the Admiralty through the influence of Lord Malmesbury, who had been one of his guardians during his minority, and shortly afterwards he was found a seat in the House of Commons as member for Newtown, in the Isle of Wight – the same seat that had been occupied by Canning at the outset of his career.

Early in 1808 he delivered his maiden speech. Canning was now Foreign Secretary, and he was being hauled over the coals for his action in ordering the seizure of the Danish fleet to prevent its falling into the hands of Napoleon. This was just the sort of spirited action that was to appeal to Palmerston in later years when he stood in Canning's place, and he spoke strongly in his defence. Having broken the ice, he spoke occasionally, when he had something useful to say, but he was never a fine speaker. Even when he had been years in the House, his style was slipshod and untidy, with innumerable hums and haws, noisy throat-clearings and much flourishing of his pocket-handkerchief, and he might be guilty of sucking an orange. But his dogged, determined manner, his bulldog tenacity and obvious love of a scrap – what the memoirist Greville was to call his 'bow-wows' – made men sit up and listen. Furthermore, he always managed to convey the impression that here was a man who was able to do things, and see that others did them.

This was the case even when he was a very young man, quite new to the game, as is evidenced by the letter that he received at Broadlands one morning from Spencer Perceval, the Prime Minister. Would he come up to town immediately, as he had a proposal he wished to make which Lord Palmerston might find agreeable?

'I went up to him, and he offered me the Chancellorship of the Exchequer.' Palmerston says he was a good deal surprised at so unexpected an offer, as well he might be. Most young men in politics would have jumped at it, but not Palmerston. He asked Perceval if he might have a little time to think it over and consult his friends; whereupon the Prime Minister told him that if he did not fancy the Treasury he might be able to offer him the War Office instead. This is what he chose. 'It is throwing a great stake,' he wrote later, 'and where much is to be gained, very much may also be lost. I have always thought it unfortunate for anyone, and particularly a young man, to be put above his proper level, as he only rises to fall lower.'

So in 1809, at the age of twenty-five, Palmerston became Secretary at War. At War, be it noted, not for War. The latter was a quite separate post, the holder of which was responsible for policy and field operations; the Secretary at War was in charge of the office, the business side of the department. Palmerston dealt with the business so successfully that he was at the War Office for not far short of nineteen years without a break. Prime ministers came and went – Spencer Perceval, Liverpool, Canning, Goderich, Wellington. While every other post in the government changed hands time after time, Palmerston stayed put. He was clearly the right man in the right job. In the earlier years of his tenure it was his responsibility to keep Wellington in the Peninsula supplied with everything – guns and ammunition, food and uniforms, stores, equipment of all kinds – necessary to maintain his army as a fighting force in the field of war.

He was content to continue with his duties at the War Office, making an occasional speech in the Commons, and enjoying his position in society. He was never without plenty of invitations to dinner and parties, for he had the knack of making himself agreeable, and he was quite a favourite with the ladies, who playfully dubbed him 'Cupid'. He also had his estate at Broadlands to look after, his racing stables, his Irish estate and his country pursuits.

Palmerston was still at the War Office when the Duke of Wellington became Prime Minister in 1828. But after a few months the Canningites in the government decided to break loose because of the Duke's ultra-Toryism, and Palmerston, who was one of the principal members of the group, decided to quit with them. He was really no longer a Tory. He had supported Roman Catholic emancipation when Wellington and Peel held out against it, and now he was feeling his way towards the necessity for some measure of parliamentary reform. He was not quite ready to join the Whigs, but, he told his brother, 'I like the Whigs much better than the Tories, and agree with them much more'.

After twenty-one years as a minister, Palmerston was out of office. But not for long. When in November 1830 Lord Grey set about forming his Whig government, he at once made an approach to Palmerston and offered him the post of Foreign Secretary. It was just the job for him. He had always taken a very keen interest in foreign affairs and his experience at the War Office had made him a master of international business. For most of the eleven years from 1830 to 1841 he remained at the Foreign Office, and he was immensely successful. He took a leading part in securing the independence of Belgium, supported constitutional government in Spain and in Portugal, worked harmoniously with Louis Philippe's France, and strove to protect Turkey from being absorbed by Russia. With truth it has been said of him that in those eleven years he 'raised the prestige of England to a height which she had not occupied since Waterloo'.

A few days before Christmas in 1839 Palmerston took the plunge into matrimony. He had left it rather late: he was fifty-five, an age when he had reached the status of a gay old bachelor. The woman he chose was the dowager Lady Cowper, only three years younger than he was. She had been Emily Lamb, Lord Melbourne's sister. It proved a wonderfully happy and successful match.

Throughout Peel's administration, Palmerston remained in opposition, but he supported wholeheartedly Peel's free trade measures and the abolition of the Corn Laws. When the dreadful famine struck Ireland he went to see how his tenants were faring, and he exerted himself in enabling as many of them as he could to emigrate to the United States and Canada.

When Lord Russell was forming his ministry in 1846 he invited Palmerston to return to the Foreign Office, although he was rather nervous of what he might do there. Palmerston gladly accepted, and proceeded to carry out his duties with his customary energy and aplomb. In 1848, the year of revolutions on the Continent, Palmerston did not disguise his sympathies with the peoples, in Italy and elsewhere, who were struggling to be free. A few months later, in the summer of 1850, occurred what became known throughout the world as the 'Don Pacifico case'.

Don Pacifico was a Jew, a native of Gibraltar, whose house in Athens had been sacked in broad daylight by a mob headed by the sons of the Greek minister of war. Don Pacifico was a dubious character, but he was a British subject, and that in Palmerston's eyes was enough. Palmerston demanded redress of the wrong that had been done him, and to others in similar cases; when the representations had been treated with contempt he ordered the British fleet into Piraeus where certain vessels were seized and held. His actions and his defence of them in the House made him a popular idol. Probably it was now that, for the first time, Palmerston must have realized that the premiership was not beyond his reach.

But in the cabinet he was distrusted, and at Windsor the Queen and Prince Albert were often shocked and indignant. The Queen disagreed strongly with his liberal policies, his encouragement of a new order in foreign arrangements. *She* was interested in dynasties, in royal and princely houses, nearly all of which were intimately connected with her by ties of blood or marriage; *he* was concerned with peoples and nations striving to liberate themselves from age-old thraldoms. The Queen remonstrated again and again with Lord John Russell, and implored him to keep his subordinate in order.

When Prince Louis Napoleon, whom he had known well for many years, executed his *coup d'état* in Paris in December 1851, Palmerston expressed something like approbation to the French ambassador, without thinking it necessary to consult the Queen or the Prime Minister beforehand. Whereupon Lord John, as kindly as he could, told Palmerston that he must relieve him of his office.

He did not have to wait long for his revenge. In February 1852 he moved an amendment to the Militia Bill which was carried, and Lord John Russell forthwith resigned. 'I have had my tit-for-tat with Johnny Russell!' remarked Palmerston in high good humour.

Lord Stanley – or Lord Derby as he was now – was called upon to form an administration, and he made one last effort to persuade Palmerston to return to the Tory fold. He offered him the Chancellorship of the Exchequer, although the Queen was strongly against it. Palmerston, thinking, no doubt, of the number of times he had been offered that same post before, declined. In less than a year, Derby had to make way for Lord Aberdeen, and Palmerston received an invitation to join the coalition. Not as Foreign Secretary, however; that went to Lord John Russell. It was the Home Office for Palmerston, and he accepted it with pleasure.

When the Crimean War was being fought Palmerston was still at the Home Office, and so his public image remained untarnished, his popularity unaffected. Early in 1855 Lord Aberdeen's well-meaning but bungling ministry petered out, and the Queen had to look for a new premier. At length, very much against her will – and Prince Albert's – she sent for Palmerston. He came, bursting with vitality and good humour, and on 4 February he was writing to inform Her Majesty that he thought 'he could undertake with a fair prospect of success to form an Administration which will command the confidence of Parliament and effectually conduct public affairs in the present momentous crisis'. On 10 February the ministry was complete.

Palmerston's first ministry lasted for just over three years, during which time he brought the Crimean War to a successful conclusion and weathered the storm of the Indian Mutiny. He did so well that the general election of 1857 gave the Liberals, as his following was now generally styled, a great majority.

(Palmerston himself, however, had been a Tory and had become a Whig, and was hardly to be called anything else.) Things seemed to be going so well with him that he remarked once that, like the Roman consuls in a triumph, he ought to have somebody to remind him that as a minister he was not immortal. In fact the reminder soon came, for on 19 February 1858 a combination of parties procured his defeat on a matter of no great importance and he resigned.

For a year Lord Derby was Prime Minister, but early in 1859 he suffered a defeat on a franchise bill and appealed to the country. The Liberals won the election, and on 18 June 1859 Palmerston was installed as Prime Minister for the second time. His government contained representatives, for the first time, of all the liberal elements in Parliament – Whigs, Radicals, Liberals, Peelites, and plain Palmerstonians. Gladstone was Chancellor of the Exchequer, and thus definitely joined the Liberal Party.

In the spring of 1865 he had a specially nasty attack of the gout, but he was well enough to go down to his constituency at Tiverton for his last election. The country people welcomed him with their usual warmth and again he was returned unopposed. And the country, invited again to vote 'Pam for Premier', did just that. After leaving Tiverton he went to Brocket Hall, his wife's country house which had belonged to her brother, Lord Melbourne. But on Thursday, 12 October, he woke feeling poorly, although he and 'Em' went out for a drive in the carriage later. He came home with a cold, was put to bed and lingered on for a few days. He died on the morning of 18 October 1865. In his will he had stated that he wished to be buried at Romsey Abbey, beside his ancestors, and arrangements had been made to that effect when Gladstone insisted on a public funeral and a grave in Westminster Abbey. Lady Palmerston's consent was obtained on the understanding that a place should be preserved for her by his side.

So on 29 October Lord Palmerston's body was buried in Westminster Abbey. 'The crowds were immense,' wrote Lord Shaftesbury afterwards,

> but in wonderful order; silent, deeply reverential ... Such a scene has seldom been seen ... The people loved the man, his open simplicity, his imperturbable good humour, his incapability of resentment, his readiness to stand up, at all times, for what he thought to be right ...

Sir Robert Peel

(1788–1850)

When Sir Robert Peel was thrown from his horse on Constitution Hill and three days later died from the effects of the fall,
there were the most widespread expressions of grief. Few
statesmen, indeed, have been so deeply and sincerely mourned.
And yet his long parliamentary career was, to say the least, a
chequered one. Even when he triumphed, as he always did,
there was – again almost always – poison in the cup of victory.

The future statesman was born at Chamber Hall, near Bury,
which was then the family home. Already the father of two
girls, the wealthy Robert Peel senior was so gratified at the gift
of a boy that (so it is said) he fell on his knees and vowed that
'he would give his child to his country'.

Young Robert was provided with a tutor at Bury, and after
the move to Tamworth he attended a school kept by the local
clergyman, until in 1801 he went to Harrow. Here he had
among his school-fellows no fewer than three future Prime
Ministers – Palmerston, Aberdeen and Goderich – and also
Byron. 'Peel was my form-fellow, and we were both at the top
of our remove,' wrote Byron. 'There were always great hopes
of Peel amongst us all, masters and scholars, and he has not
disappointed them.' From Harrow Peel proceeded in 1806,
when he was just on eighteen, to Christ Church, Oxford, where
he performed most brilliantly, winning a double first in classics
and mathematics, being the first man to do so under the new
and more stringent regulations recently introduced, but he was
no solitary student. He dressed in the fashion of the day, rode,
played cricket and boated; and in the vacations he went shooting. He rode to hounds, but he never became much of a
horseman, a fact which is not without significance in the matter
of his end.

Blessed with brains, personality, influential friends and a
father with an almost bottomless purse, young Peel had no
difficulty in obtaining a seat in the House of Commons. The
Irish borough of Cashel was on the market; Sir Robert bought
it and in April 1809 the young man took his seat among the
Tories next to his father who was the MP for Tamworth. His
maiden speech in the following January was hailed as 'the best

first speech since Mr Pitt's', and a few months later the Prime
Minister, the ill-fated Spencer Perceval, appointed Peel to an
under-secretaryship at the Colonial Office. Here his chief was
Lord Liverpool, and when in 1812 Liverpool succeeded Perceval in the premiership, he made Peel Secretary for Ireland.

At Dublin Peel acquitted himself in a way that commended
him to the Anglo-Irish governing class. So closely was he
identified with the Orangemen – the association of extreme
Protestants named after William of Orange (William III) –
that he was given the nickname of 'Orange Peel'. In 1817 he
became one of the two MPs chosen to represent Oxford University, and he owed this distinction in large measure to the
strong fight he had sustained against any proposals for the
emancipation of the Roman Catholics from their legal disabilities. After six years Peel had had enough of Irish administration and went back to London.

At Westminster Peel resumed his assiduous attendance as a
Tory Member, and in 1819 he was chairman of a select committee appointed to inquire into the expediency of the resump-
tion of cash payments by the Bank of England after the many
war years when paper money had been the rule. This had been
proposed some years before by Francis Horner, a Whig member, on which occasion Peel, prompted by his father, had acted
like a good Tory and had joined in defeating it. But now he
looked at the proposal with fresh eyes. To the disgruntlement
of many of his political associates he resolved at length to
support it. Cash payments were resumed, and Peel was as
much responsible as anybody. This was Peel's first 'conversion': there were more conversions to come.

While he was out of office, Peel found time to look for a
wife. He found her in the charming person of Miss Julia Floyd,
the twenty-five-year-old daughter of Sir John Floyd, a general
with a distinguished record. The marriage was an exceedingly
happy one. She bore him five sons and two daughters, and Peel
proved a fondly devoted father.

For eighteen months Peel was enwrapped in domestic bliss,
but in 1822 he accepted Lord Liverpool's invitation to become
Home Secretary. As such he was a decided success, revealing
a liberal streak in his composition that had not been hitherto
suspected. When he took office there were some two hundred
felonies that might entail the death penalty, and within a year
or so he had introduced five bills which reduced the number by
half. Nearly three hundred acts of parliament relating to the
criminal law which were antiquated and useless were swept
away. One of Peel's first reforms was to end the employment

of spies and *agents-provocateurs* in the investigation of cases arising out of social distress and industrial unemployment, and in 1829 he created the Metropolitan Police, the first of the country's forces of organized police. It was a tribute to his achievement that the first police constables were nicknamed 'Peelers' and 'Bobbies', and the latter perpetuates his fame to this day.

But apart from the Home Office his record was far from commending him to Tory rank-and-file. The winds of change were beginning to blow. Reform was in the air, and there was even talk of revolution. In theory Peel was against reform – until he had become convinced that it was more than necessary, it was inevitable. Then, as in the case of the penal laws, he moved quickly and decisively. In 1828 he voted against the repeal of the Test and Corporation Acts which had for centuries hampered and humiliated the Nonconformists, but as soon as the House of Commons agreed to it he used his influence with the House of Lords to effect a workable compromise. Then in 1829 it was proposed to repeal the laws against the Roman Catholics. As Secretary for Ireland Peel had resolutely opposed any such measure and he had won his seat at Oxford as the champion of the privileged position of the Church of England in Ireland as in England. With something like amazement, then, Tory MPs heard in the King's Speech that 'His Majesty recommends ... that you should take into your deliberate consideration the whole condition of Ireland, and that you should review the laws which impose civil disabilities on His Majesty's Roman Catholic subjects'. Of course they understood that His Majesty King George IV had had very little to do with it: it was Peel again. They were right; Peel had had another of his changes of mind, his 'conversions', and as on the previous occasions he got away with it.

But he had to pay the price of what was widely denounced as his apostasy. As an honourable man he felt obliged to resign his seat as MP for Oxford University, and although his friends renominated him immediately he was defeated at the election. Whereupon a vacancy was created for him at Westbury, and in 1830 he exchanged this for Tamworth, rendered vacant by his father's death.

Backed by the Duke of Wellington's immense prestige, the Roman Catholic Emancipation Bill became law, and thereby civil war in Ireland was prevented. Peel and the Duke were now hand-in-glove, and they employed very much the same tactics in the even more dangerous situation of 1830, when at the general election following upon George IV's death a large majority of pledged Reformers was returned. Peel, as leader of the Opposition in the House of Commons, resisted the Reform Bill as long as the struggle was kept within the four walls of Parliament; but when the riots began and there was bloodshed in towns and cities, he once again accepted the inevitable. Better reform than revolution, he argued, and the Duke of Wellington agreed. The bill went through. Once again Peel's 'conversion' had achieved a great result.

Thanks to him the Tories – now becoming known as Conservatives – were able to stage something of a 'come-back' much earlier than might have been anticipated. In 1834 Peel was Prime Minister for a few months, and the 'Tamworth Manifesto' that he drew up was a capable exposition of the new Conservatism that had taken the place of the ancient Toryism. At the general election in the spring of 1835 the Conservatives failed to get the majority they had hoped for, and Peel once more led the Opposition. But at the general election of 1841 they triumphed with a majority of ninety, and Peel became Prime Minister for the second time.

The cabinet he proceeded to form was one of the ablest and most distinguished of the century; his only mistake was in not finding a place for Benjamin Disraeli. At home and abroad he was confronted with a host of difficulties, but he tackled them not as a doctrinaire economist, not as a hidebound party politician, but as the consummate opportunist that he was. The budget of 1842 was epoch-making, with its income tax (seven pence in the pound) and the lowering of duties on a large number of articles in general consumption that were imported from abroad. The old protectionist policy that had endured for so long was doomed, and already he was a free trader without, perhaps, realizing it. Then the Anti-Corn Law League under Cobden and Bright went on the rampage, and Peel was moving slowly but surely in the same direction when the great famine in Ireland forced his hand. At first he had hoped that a gradual reduction in the duties that restricted corn imports would do the trick, but by October 1845, he had reached the conclusion that 'The remedy is the removal of all impediments to the import of all kinds of human food – that is, the total and absolute repeal for ever of all duties on all articles of subsistence.' The hour of his latest and last 'conversion' had struck.

When he submitted his proposals to his cabinet, only two – Gladstone and Lord Aberdeen – were prepared to follow him. He handed his resignation to the Queen, but when Lord John Russell, the leader of the Whig (or Liberal) opposition failed to form an alternative government, Queen Victoria sent again for Peel and begged him to resume the premiership, reconstruct his ministry and secure the abolition of the Corn Laws. 'I believe I can collect a ministry which will last long enough to carry Free Trade,' he told the Queen, 'and I am ready to make the attempt.' One of the first to join him was the Duke of Wellington. In the event all the previous ministers except one agreed to serve again under Peel.

The session of 1846 was one of the most memorable in the history of Parliament. Led by Disraeli, who had not forgotten or forgiven the slight of a few years before, the Tory protectionists representing the landed interest raged against the man whom they denounced as the arch-betrayer. For the most part Peel put up a strenuous defence, but there were times when he winced and was bludgeoned into silence. He stuck it out, however, and the bill passed all its stages in the House of Commons and was sent upstairs to the House of Lords. There it was passed on 25 June. On that same night the malcontents defeated an Irish measure put forward by the government, and Peel forthwith resigned.

The speech in which he announced his resignation was noble:

> I shall leave a name censured, I fear, by many who, on public grounds, deeply regret the severance of party ties; I shall surrender power severely censured by others who adhere to the principle of Protection ... I shall leave a name execrated by every monopolist who clamours for Protection because it conduces to his own individual benefit. But it may be that I shall leave a name sometimes remembered with expressions of goodwill in the abodes of those whose lot it is to labour and earn their daily bread with the sweat of their brow, when they shall recruit their exhausted strength with abundant and untaxed food, the sweeter because it is no longer leavened with injustice.

As he left the House on the day of his fall, crowds of people gathered to see him go by. The Queen offered him the Garter and any other honour he might care to name. He respectfully refused them all, and begged that he might never be invited to take office again.

Peel's last appearance in the House of Commons was on 28 June 1850, when he spoke against Lord Palmerston's rumbustious foreign policy. The next day he attended a meeting of the commissioners for the proposed Great Exhibition in Hyde Park, and then in the afternoon set out on his customary ride. Going along Constitution Hill his horse suddenly became restive, and Peel was flung violently to the ground. He was picked up and conveyed to his town house in Whitehall Gardens, and there, after three days of agony, he expired on 2 July 1850. A tomb in Westminster Abbey was offered, but by Peel's own wish, expressed in his will, he was interred in the family vault at Drayton Bassett church.

'The sorrow and grief at his death,' wrote Queen Victoria, 'are most touching, and the country mourns over him as over a father. Everyone seems to have lost a personal friend.' And Prince Albert: 'The feeling in the country is absolutely not to be described. We have lost our truest friend and trustiest counsellor, the throne its most valued defender, the country its most open-minded and greatest statesman.'

Benjamin Disraeli

(1804–81)

He liked people to think that he came from a distinguished Jewish family of Spanish origin, who had become rich merchants in Venice around the 1490s, dropped their old name and assumed that of Disraeli, 'a name never borne before or since by any other family in order that their race might be for ever recognized.' After the failure of the Jacobite rebellion of 1745 Benjamin's grandfather had come to England, in full confidence that the Hanoverian dynasty would be tolerant towards Jews – particularly rich ones.

Not a word of this was true. Benjamin the elder had indeed settled in England in 1748, but solely because he thought it a likely spot in which to ply the straw-bonnet trade. Neither Spain nor Venice figured in the paternal background. But that was Disraeli all over: romantic, bizarre, adding a touch of colour when life failed to do so.

He was born in London, near Gray's Inn, in 1804 and christened at St Andrew's, Holborn, in 1817. This statement is not as wild as it sounds, for his father, Isaac Disraeli, an intelligent dilettante much respected in the literary circles of his time, had broken away from Judaism when his eldest son was nine. Benjamin was brought up, very fortunately, as events proved, as a member of the Anglican Church. The family circumstances were comfortable, even luxurious by the standards of the day. Benjamin had a reasonably happy childhood in the company of his brothers and sister Sarah or 'Sa', who was always his most admiring and devoted audience.

He missed the torments of public school, being sent to private ones, possibly because his mother thought that Eton and its like were places 'where boys were roasted alive'. Benjamin profited by the fairly permissive atmosphere of his rearing, though his black curls, hooked nose and dark eyes caused much outspoken comment among his Anglo-Saxon schoolfellows; but his extraordinary wit, apparent at a very early age, arrested jeers and commanded admiration.

Of a lively intelligence, he learned quickly and by seventeen considered himself (whatever his teachers might think) a master of history, literature and the classics. He might with amusement have recognized himself in Oscar Wilde's character who observed that though others might play the piano with accuracy, *he* played with great feeling. Indeed, Wildeian parallels crop up throughout his literary career.

Leaving school, he flirted briefly with the law, being articled to a firm of solicitors. His father's £400 premium was wasted, for by 1824 he had transferred his energies to playing the stock market, with unfortunate financial results. Then he bulldozed the great John Murray, doyen of publishers, into issuing a new daily paper, which failed. Undaunted, he wrote his first novel, *Vivian Grey*. It was autobiographical, a 'society novel', full of portraits from life, presented with dash and verve. It had immediate success – *de scandale*, but that was all the better for Disraeli's publicity. It is unconsciously as well as consciously funny, overdrawn, and highly significant of the way its re-markable young author was going. He followed it by two more romantic effusions. At this time he was much helped by a solicitor's wife, Sara Austen, who seems to have had more than a literary interest in the decorative young dandy, so romanti-cally exotic, who, on a 'Grand Tour' of the east with Sara and her husband, revelled in the chance to revert to oriental cos-tume: 'red cap, red slippers, broad blue jacket and trousers', and a belt full of pistols and daggers. He worshipped the just-dead Byron, copied his style, even annexed as servant Byron's personal gondolier.

In the 1830s he arrived in society, with the help of his friend Bulwer, soon to be Bulwer Lytton. He acquired a mistress, a Clara Bolton, a doctor's wife, perhaps on his own epigram-matic principle: 'Every woman should marry – and no man.' But love was not enough for his ambitious soul. He decided to enter politics, like Bulwer. The Disraelis were moderate Tories, but he leaned towards reform and radicalism, and in 1832 offered himself as a candidate for the High Wycombe seat, his father being now established close by at Bradenham. Standing above the porch of the Red Lion Inn, he gestured towards the heraldic animal: 'When the poll is declared I shall be *there* [at the head] and my opponent will be *there* [the tail end].' He was wrong, being defeated by twenty votes to twelve; but at his country house, Hughenden, the red lion is still preserved, a memorial of his entry into politics and a solid proof that his boast was prophetic.

Again defeated in Buckinghamshire in 1835 he boldly con-tested the London seat of Marylebone, this time as a sort of off-pink Tory, his exact political outlook stated in a pamphlet entitled *What is He? by the Author of Vivian Gray*. He did not win Marylebone. Retiring from the political scene in disappointment, he turned again to love as a consolation. His new flame was Lady Henrietta Sykes, a lady of remarkable beauty and a temperament equalling his own in passion. His love-story *Henrietta Temple* commemorates her name and their passionate affair.

In these years, the mid-1830s, he wrote a volume of satires and two novels. Then, in 1837, the year of Victoria's accession, he at last entered Parliament as Conservative member for Maidstone, though greeted on nominating day with cries of 'Old Clothes!' and 'Shylock!' A certain Mrs Wyndham Lewis forecast that 'Mr Disraeli will in a very few years be one of the greatest men of his day'. He lost no time in justifying her opinion. The House would not listen to his maiden speech on the Irish topic: he warned them, 'The time will come when you *will* hear me.' They soon learned respect for his grasp of facts and their implications, his quick brain, the (as it were) electro magnetic quality of the man.

As well as brilliance, Disraeli had the advantage of sincerity, a fact which impressed his fellow-members when he spoke up in the debates on the Chartist petition and disturbances of 1839 and 1840. Though a species of foreigner in love with the English aristocratic ideal, Disraeli felt deeply for the condition of the oppressed workers, a feeling he demonstrated in practical terms in his novel *Sybil*. This, and the immense ability concealed by a histrionic manner and the verbal fireworks of his speeches, ensured his rise to power.

He needed money in order to rise. Also, he may have felt, in Mrs Pat Campbell's immortal phrase, that it was time to forsake the hurly-burly of the divan for the peace and quiet of the double bed. His choice was Mrs Mary Anne Wyndham Lewis, the very lady who had seen greatness in his stars. Now a widow, she was forty-four, twelve years older than himself, of middle-class origins, with a rudimentary education; 'a flirt and a rattle', in Disraeli's words. Against these disadvantages she was rich, pretty, uncommonly youthful for her age, witty in a down-to-earth way, kind-hearted and affectionate. Disraeli, to his own surprise, fell in love.

Mary Anne was not particularly anxious to give up the freedom of widowhood, but Disraeli forced her hand by a dramatic letter. They were married in 1839 and were for the rest of their wedded lives as happy as any couple could hope to be. Childless, Mary Anne gave her 'dear Dizzy' all the coddling, admiration, full-hearted devotion that he needed. He adored her, ignoring her occasional social gaffes and sternly suppressing any outside criticisms of them.

Squire and dame of their little Buckinghamshire kingdom (to purchase which Disraeli had, with characteristic *élan*, borrowed £25,000), they were well established for Disraeli's ascent to power. From 1841 to 1848 he was MP for Shrewsbury. His idealism and romanticism, contrasting with Peel's prudence and materialism, made him the natural leader of the 'Young England' movement, a group of young Tories who were strongly opposed to Peel's policy of wooing the wealthy manufacturing middle class. Disraeli supported their campaign with a novel, *Coningsby*, followed it up with *Sybil* and completed the trilogy with *Tancred*, thus expressing in terms of popular fiction his strong views on the condition of the parties, the condition of the people (the Two Nations of *Sybil*'s subtitle are the rich and the poor) and the fulfilment of Judaism through Christianity.

'A Conservative Government is an organized hypocrisy.' This he said in 1845, the year when a terrible harvest and the destruction of the Irish potato crop by disease forced Peel first into a recommendation to the government that the Corn Laws, bitterly attacked by the landed interest, should be repealed, and second into resignation. Next year Peel returned to office with a brilliant rebel in his ranks, Lord Stanley, who assumed supremacy in the Lords while Disraeli did so in the Commons. For the first time Disraeli sat on the front bench, with Peel and Lord George Bentinck. Bentinck died in 1848, Peel in 1850: it was as though the gods were giving a helping hand to ambitious genius. Now that the Tory party was split on the question of protective duties on foreign corn, Disraeli moved in and began to rebuild it, with some opposition, in his own image. Ever a champion of his own race, he managed to abolish the law that kept Jews out of Parliament: but for his father's adoption of Christianity he too would have been excluded. Now all that was changed. By 1852 he was Chancellor of the Exchequer and Leader of the House of Commons, the first man since Pitt to enjoy both honours without ever having held office.

His great Liberal rival Gladstone was already on the warpath against him on the vexed question of a revolutionary budget. It was, indeed, war for the rest of his long career. In February 1867 he was preparing a Reform Bill to replace that brought forward in the previous year by Gladstone, which had been heavily defeated. It was to offer household suffrage to personal ratepayers, provide a second vote for those who paid 20s. in direct taxation, and various franchises. But, led by Lord

Cranborne, the House rejected it. Undeterred, Disraeli produced a cunning modification of it, not entirely in accordance with his own principles: despite Gladstone's fierce opposition, it was passed.

In 1869, on Derby's retirement, he became Prime Minister, resigned in the face of a hostile majority, but resumed office in 1874.

Queen Victoria had once viewed him with grave doubts. When Stanley had put him forward as a secretary of state, the Queen had remarked that she did not approve of Mr D. and accepted him only on Stanley's guarantee. In maturity he became her beloved favourite, Leicester to her Elizabeth. Though he had remarked callously to Matthew Arnold: 'Everyone likes flattery; and when you come to royalty you should lay it on with a trowel,' he genuinely reverenced the Crown and had no difficulty in being more than agreeable to the early-widowed Queen. She basked in the sense of personal power Disraeli gave her. 'The Faery Queen waved her wand over him,' it was said, but it was he, Oberon, who waved his over her.

Very few ministers have been offered the Order of the Garter by their sovereign and given more pleasure by a 'beautiful' rejection than by acceptance; or have received a personal valentine from that sovereign. This was the courtier with the calm effrontery to use in literary chat with Her Majesty (who had produced one 'book', *Leaves from the Journal of our Life in the Highlands*) the phrase 'We authors, Ma'am'.

Without her on the throne, his later career might have been very different. A spirited foreign policy was his delight and hers. When trouble loomed eastwards, and it seemed that Britain and Russia would soon be fighting each other, it was suggested to the Queen that if she assumed her imperial title – Empress of India – Britain's position in the east might be strengthened. The bill to make her so was violently opposed in Parliament; but Disraeli carried it through, with consummate tact persuading the Queen that her imperial status applied to India alone. On 1 May 1876, she became Queen-Empress.

When Turkey, the 'sick man of Europe', became the victim of Bulgarian atrocities in 1875, it was Disraeli who cashed in on the situation by buying 177,000 Suez Canal shares at the right moment, thus making Britain half-owner of the canal. When in 1877, the Russians threatened to occupy Egypt, an hysterical Victoria infected her people with the new disease of jingoism and relied on Disraeli to give the word for battle. Instead, he brought about the Congress of Berlin, which took place in June 1878, gave Britain what Disraeli described as 'Peace with honour', and caused Bismarck to exclaim: 'Der alte Jude, das ist der Mann!'

By now 'der alte Jude' was alone. In 1872 Mary Anne had died. Four years previously he had entreated the Queen to create her a viscountess in her own right, that she might enjoy the honour while he remained a commoner and leader of his party. Victoria, embarrassed but unable to refuse Dizzy any-thing, elevated Mary Anne to the peerage as Viscountess Bea-consfield (Disraeli was created Earl of Beaconsfield in 1876).

His last years were personally lonely, though full of activity as ever. In the election of 1880 the Conservative Party suffered a shattering defeat, the result of revulsion against imperialism caused by the Afghan and Zulu wars, economic depression and the perennial Irish troubles. On 21 April of that year Disraeli held his last cabinet meeting and a bitterly disap-pointed Victoria found herself advised to ask the detested Gladstone if he were ready to form a government. Disraeli, out of power at last, tired and ailing, turned again to literature and produced the charming *Endymion*, a society romance with, curiously enough, a Whig hero. Then he began another novel, *Falconet*.

He did not live to finish it. Bronchitis, his old enemy, claimed him in the cold April of 1881. He died bravely and calmly, jesting as long as he could speak. When they asked him if he would like the Queen to visit him, he replied, 'No, it is better not. She would only ask me to take a message to Albert.'

'What wondrous times are these!' he had said of his age. Life to him had been a sort of perpetual Arabian Night and adven-ture; politics 'the great game'.

The most colourful figure ever to animate the drab world of Parliament, he had puzzled, irritated, antagonized many, charmed as many more. Charlatan or genius, eastern wizard of Jewish pedlar of the *Punch* cartoons, greater than Gladstone or less – the arguments continue still. Yet, virtual creator of popular Conservatism, advocate of social reform before a socialist party existed, loyalist and lover of Empire, his virtues have been remembered longer than his failures. His oratory still echoes in the House to which he was a Garrick and an Irving in one, his wit still scintillates in quotes, and he himself will be remembered above all politicians while the light burns in Westminster's tower.

Robert E. Lee

(1807-70)

Henry 'Light Horse Harry' Lee, father of Robert E. Lee, was the scion of a wealthy and illustrious Virginian family. He had been a distinguished cavalry commander during the Revolution, and for three years (1792-95) was Governor of Virginia. His second wife, Ann Carter, came from a wealthy plantation-owning family. Despite these achievements and advantages he managed to get into deep debt and involved in a number of scandals, so that by 1813, when Robert was only six years old, he was forced to flee into exile to Barbados. It was against such an impecunious and scandalous background that Robert's mother tried to raise him to be a Southern gentleman.

Robert E. Lee, born in 1807, was the youngest of three children of his father's second marriage. He grew up to be a tall, good-looking young man with many friends. He did not smoke, swear or drink, except an occasional glass of wine. He was never known to lose his temper. He was highly respected by all. In fact he did grow up to be a perfect Southern gentleman – the only thing he lacked was wealth.

He decided on a military career, entered West Point in 1825 and became an engineer. He was a hard worker and devoted to his profession. In 1831 Lee married Mary Anne Randolph Custis, daughter of George Washington's adopted son. Although the Washingtons (and the Custises) were known to possess considerable wealth, very little of it was transferred to Mary Anne until after her father's death. Consequently the Lees had to rear their seven children on army officer's pay.

Lee's first battle experience came in 1846 when the United States declared war on Mexico. Captain Robert E. Lee crossed the Rio Grande as an army engineer in 1847. At the request of General Winfield Scott, commander-in-chief and fellow Virginian, he was transferred to the general staff of the main task force preparing to march on Mexico City. Lee made a reputation as a reconnaissance officer and became something of a hero. This was the only war experience he underwent prior to 1861. The Mexican War ended in victory for the United States and the acquisition of the vast area of former Mexican territory from which were carved the states of California, Utah, Nevada, New Mexico, Arizona and part of Colorado.

By February 1861 seven states, all in the deep South, had dissolved their ties with the Union. They had formed the Confederate States of America and elected Jefferson Davis, a cotton planter from Mississippi as their president. The American Civil War began with the bombardment and capture by the Conferedate forces of Fort Sumter in Charleston harbour.

Before the fighting started Colonel Robert E. Lee was called to Washington to be offered a high command in the Federal Army. Lee did not uphold slavery and did not believe in secession, but he was totally and immovably loyal to his native 'country', the state of Virginia. Lincoln, the Northern president, declared the states to be at war and called upon all those remaining in the Union, including Virginia, to supply 75,000 volunteers to form a fighting force. He offered the command of this new army to Colonel Lee. Lee replied: 'If Virginia stands by the Union so will I. But if she secedes then I will follow my native state with my sword and, if need be, with my life.'

Soon after this Virginia voted to join the war on the side of the Confederacy. Lee returned home to Arlington, wrote out his resignation from the US Army and sent it to Lincoln's secretary of state in Washington, just across the river. Then he set out for Richmond, the Confederate capital. There the Governor offered him command of all the naval and military forces of his native state and the post of military adviser to President Davis. Lee accepted.

Statistics indicated that the North would win the war. Twenty-three Northern states were lined up against eleven in the Confederacy. Twenty-two million people inhabited the North. Nine million, of which 3,500,000 were slaves, inhabited the South. The North greatly exceeded the South in industrial output. It became a vast arsenal while the South remained a huge plantation. The South's bad economic position was aggravated by the tight blockade which the North maintained on all Southern ports.

The Appalachian Mountain range, which runs north to south between the Atlantic seaboard and the Mississippi River, neatly divided the theatre of war into two parts: eastern (from the Atlantic to the Appalachians) and western (from the mountains to the river).

A major campaign to take the Southern capital was launched in 1862. With a force of 100,000 men General George McClellan, the Union commander of the Army of the Potomac, began his advance on Richmond. The field commander of the Virginia forces was General Joseph E. Johnston. Lee figured that McClellan would advance from the south-east, and try to link up with Union troops led by General McDowell who would invade Virginia across the Potomac from the north-west. He set himself to defend Virginia. General 'Stonewall' Jackson was already patrolling the Shenandoah Valley. Lee instructed various scattered Confederate patrols in that area to link up with Jackson. By a series of brilliant moves through the mountains and valleys Stonewall Jackson, outnumbered by more than three to one, was able to pin down four Federal generals. Lincoln was so alarmed he ordered McDowell's army to remain on the north bank of the Potomac in order to protect Washington. Meanwhile McClellan's army was slowly making its way to Richmond up the peninsula.

By the end of May McClellan was within eight miles of the capital, General Johnston attacked the Federals while they were trying to cross the river at Seven Pines. General Lee and President Davis rode out to watch the battle. Johnston was seriously wounded and carried from the field, whereupon Davis offered command of the army of Virginia to Lee. Lee accepted gladly, and immediately his superiority as a general coupled with his intensive training as an engineer came to the fore. He ordered a line of entrenchments to be dug between Richmond and the enemy. This order almost caused mutiny in the ranks for, in the South, such menial tasks were performed by slaves. But Lee was firm, the trenches were dug and another reserve line prepared behind the main ones.

Lee's idea was to hold off McClellan's mighty army before Richmond with a small entrenched contingent while the rest of the Southern troops attacked his flank with overpowering force. Rapid fire, lots of noise and large tree trunks disguised as big guns convinced McClellan that he was totally outnumbered and outgunned. Lee sent word to Stonewall to leave the valley and help attack the enemy flank. Heavy fighting ensued. It lasted for the next seven days (25 June–1 July 1862); seven big battles were fought all within a few miles of Richmond.

McClellan now found himself isolated and surrounded in enemy country. He pulled out his troops from before Richmond and headed back to the James River. In his haste to retreat he left behind most of his supplies and 2,500 wounded men at Savage station hospital. Richmond had been saved. McClellan got safely back to Washington where he was relieved of his command.

Lee now became the South's hero. 'So great is my confidence

in General Lee,' said Stonewall Jackson, 'that I am willing to follow him blind-folded.' Lee's troops addressed him as 'Marser' Robert. They would go anywhere and do anything he asked them. His kindly bearded face, his smart grey uniform and his lively grey horse, Traveller, were known and respected by every Southern soldier and civilian.

A succession of Northern generals now took the field against Lee. John Pope invaded Virginia and advanced towards Manassas. There in August 1862 he was soundly defeated at the second battle of Bull Run.

Lee now took the initiative and, to the great alarm of the North, invaded Maryland, a border slave-state which had remained in the Union. Lee thought that his invasion would convince the Marylanders that the South would win the war and bring the state into the Confederate fold. Unfortunately as a result of the blockade many of the soldiers' uniforms were in rags – hundreds were barefoot. Could this bunch of scarecrows be the same that had defeated McClellan and Pope? All the enthusiasm Marylanders may have had for the Confederacy quickly faded away.

Lincoln, thinking Washington was about to be attacked, reinstated 'Slowcoach' McClellan as commander of the Army of the Potomac and ordered him to find Lee and destroy him. Even though he was in the depths of enemy territory Lee divided his army into four parts. He sent three of them to attack the Union arsenal at Harper's Ferry from three different directions. The fourth was to attack Haggerston on the border of Pennsylvania. Unfortunately when McClellan's advance scouts reached Frederick where Lee had camped, they found papers describing Lee's plan had been left behind (wrapped round three cigars). McClellan began a forced march to overtake the small part of Lee's army that was not engaged in attacking Harper's Ferry.

Lee decided to stand and fight near a little creek called Antietam. Eighteen thousand Confederates prepared to meet 90,000 Federals. The battle was intense. Even when reinforcements arrived (Harper's Ferry having fallen) Lee was still outnumbered by more than two to one. Lee, no doubt greatly puzzled as to how McClellan knew his intentions, had to accept that the South's attempted invasion had failed: 23,000 casualties, about 12,000 on each side, had rendered Antietam the bloodiest single day of the whole war. Lee had no choice but to lead his decimated army southward into Virginia. McClellan did not pursue him.

Once more Lincoln removed McClellan from his command

and replaced him by General Ambrose E. Burnside. Burnside invaded Virginia in November 1862 and met Lee's army at Fredericksburg on the River Rappahannock. Burnside's army crossed the river by pontoon bridge to find Lee's army lined up and waiting for him: 75,000 Southern veterans ready to fight the kind of defensive engagement in which they were virtually unbeatable. The Federals attacked with great vigour and valour. But the position was hopeless. By the end of the day they had lost 12,000 men. The Confederate losses were less than half that, and at no time had there been any danger of their being dislodged from their hill positions.

With the spring (1863) came 'Fighting' Joe Hooker, the latest Union commander, to make *his* attempt to invade Virginia and take Richmond. Lee met him at Chancellorsville. With help from an attack on Hooker's flank by Stonewall Jackson, Lee gave Hooker a terrible beating. The Northern general was compelled to retreat, leaving 17,000 casualties behind him. This great victory, however, was won at heavy cost; during the battle Jackson, Lee's ablest general, was mistaken for the enemy when riding back to his lines, shot by his own pickets and mortally wounded.

Lee headed north. He was hunted by the Union forces now under the command of Major-General Gordon Meade. Meade was at Frederick when Lee learned of his whereabouts. Knowing a battle must soon ensue, he tried to regroup his entire army at the little town of Gettysburg. Meade, informed of Lee's move, headed north and, quite by accident, collided with Lee just outside the town. And so began the greatest single battle of the war. It lasted for three days, during which time reinforcements on both sides came pouring into the area.

The Federals, only a part of their army having reached the field, were soundly beaten on the first day. During the next two days Lee did his utmost to crush the Army of the Potomac for all time. The climax came on the afternoon of the third day when 15,000 Virginians, led by General Pickett, assaulted the Federal position on Cemetery Ridge. The attack almost succeeded, but when it seemed the Southern troops were about to take the Union position the Federals rallied and drove them back. The repulse turned into a retreat. Five thousand of Pickett's original 15,000 were left lying on the field. Lee's great gamble had failed. He had lost a third of his army. He could do nothing but retreat. During the march back to Virginia he rode up and down the line comforting his men and placing responsibility for defeat solely on his own shoulders. This was the major turning point in the eastern theatre of war. Next day

Lee received news from the western theatre that the whole of the Mississippi was in Union hands and that the Confederacy had been cut in two.

Because of his successful 'blood-and-guts' method of fighting, General U. S. Grant was summoned to Washington by Lincoln and given supreme command of all Union armies. He was also ordered to do what McDowell, McClellan, Pope and Hooker had failed to do: take Richmond. Meanwhile General Sherman, Grant's second-in-command in the west, was given charge of Grant's old army and told to cut his way from Chattanooga in Tennessee, through Georgia to Atlanta and to Savannah on the Atlantic coast, thus dividing what was left of the Confederacy in two.

In 1864 Grant placed himself at the head of the Army of the Potomac and made his battle plans, the main object of which was to march on Richmond, destroying the Confederate army as he went. He crossed the Rapidan on 4 May 1864 and entered a scrubby jungle-like area of timber known as the Wilderness. Here he was attacked by Lee whose fighting men numbered about half of Grant's. In two days Grant lost more than 17,000 men. It was expected that, as he had been utterly defeated, he would return to Washington, re-equip, and start another campaign a month or so later – but he didn't. He withdrew certainly, but after reorganizing his forces he slipped sideways and headed south. It was Grant's intention to keep the Confederates fighting until they were completely worn out.

He made for Spotsylvania on the road to Richmond, hoping to reach it before Lee. Thus he would force the Southern general to attack and sustain heavy losses. But Lee divined Grant's intention, and by forced marching got to Spotsylvania first. The hard fight to gain the crossroads was the first incident in a battle that lasted twelve days. Lee was not defeated, but he was falling back closer and closer to Richmond. At a crossroads known as Cold Harbour he turned to defend his capital city. Grant hit him with everything he had, but failed to break the Southern line. He sustained such heavy losses that his men began to refer to him as 'Grant the Butcher'.

Next the fighting moved on to Petersburg, through which all railway connections between Richmond and the South had to pass. Grant laid siege to it. In the first month of this conflict he lost 60,000 men, more than Lee had in his whole army, but then the fighting settled down into a desultory trench warfare which lasted until the spring of 1865. The North was horrified. So many losses and Richmond still not taken.

Meanwhile in the south-west Sherman had carried out his

famous march through Georgia and, by Christmas 1864, had reached the Atlantic coast, captured Savannah and was preparing to march northward through the Carolinas and on to Virginia. The last phase of the war was at hand.

Considerably strengthened by forces lately moved in from the western theatre, Grant managed to cut the railway line some ten miles west of Petersburg. That same night Petersburg and Richmond were evacuated and the Confederate government fled to an unnamed destination in South Carolina. Lee ordered his army to march westward, hoping to join up with Confederate forces south-west of Richmond. But the Union army overtook his rearguard and captured his rations. His little army began to melt away. Between 2 and 9 April Lee's army shrank to half its size. He had fewer than 30,000 men, half of whom were not armed.

Lee called a halt at Appomattox. He asked Grant for terms. The two men met in the parlour of a nearby house and Lee, the leader of a now poverty-stricken force that had been unconquerable for more than four years, signed the official surrender. His soldiers wept.

'Gentlemen,' said Grant, 'we are one nation again.' He told Lee his officers could retain their sidearms and that any soldier who owned his horse or mule could keep it and take it home for the spring ploughing. Then, hearing that Lee's men were without rations, he ordered that they be fed from the Federal stores.

Thus ended a war in which Lee had shown himself one of the greatest soldiers in history. He had maintained an army in the field for four years against greatly superior forces, and at times had come close to completely defeating them. He had achieved this through a genius for choosing the right terrain for his battles, by masterly improvization and disguise of his numbers, by uncanny anticipation of his opponents' moves, and by a supreme ability to inspire his troops.

His bust adorns the Hall of Fame of Washington College, now Washington and Lee University, in Lexington, Virginia, of which he had become president after the war. The words inscribed beneath it read: 'Duty then is the sublimest word in our language. Do your duty in all things. You cannot do more. You should never wish to do less.'

Napoleon III

(1808-73)

It is only to be expected that many historians should look askance at Napoleon III. He ought not to be a subject; he ought not to occupy their attention. After all, he was only the nephew of Napoleon, the son of the unhappy marriage between Louis Bonaparte, King of Holland and Hortense de Beauharnais (and, not unnaturally, there was some unfounded speculation as to whether he really was the son of his father). There seemed to be no reason why he should inherit the Napoleonic legend; he was a very ordinary man who had a tendency to reassure his enemies by his apparent lack of distinction and intelligence.

Born in 1808 and brought up mainly in Italy, Switzerland and England, his early attempts to make his mark in France had been failures which aroused ridicule rather than any other sentiment. In 1836 he had tried to suborn army units in Strasbourg, but within a few hours he had been made a prisoner. In 1840 a journey from Gravesend to Boulogne led to a similar fiasco, and to prison in the fortress of Ham (from which he later escaped). And yet by 1848 he seemed to incarnate a great ideal in France. How was this?

The first reason is undoubtedly to be found in the condition of French politics. Ever since 1789 there had been uncertainty in France as to what was the real source of authority in the state. It was difficult to believe that the sovereignty of the people provided stability and efficacy. It became increasingly impossible to accept the divine right of kings. The idea of a monarch who owed his position to a popular vote rather than simply to birth was a way out of this dilemma. And Napoleon had cultivated this position with some skill. *Des Idées Napoléoniennes*, first published in 1839, sought to propagate certain projects of social reform, whilst at the same time he represented the idea of authority.

It is strange to think that the cult of Napoleon, instituted by the *bourgeois* and near-pacifist rule of Louis Philippe, from 1830 to 1848, should not have led to any revival of political Bonapartism. But the fact remains that the growth of the Napoleonic legend was not accompanied by any definite move-

86

ment to hand over the government of the country to Napoleon's heirs. It was only in the unusual circumstance of November 1848, after the February revolution had overthrown the
bourgeois Orleanist government, and after the unsuccessful
popular rising of June 1848, that Louis Bonaparte gained his
enormous majority in the presidential elections (5½ million out
of 7½ million). Those who wanted to protect property and
religion voted for him; those who thought that he intended to
institute great reforms supported him; those who thought that
he provided more than the ordinary politicians voted in his
favour; and there were those individuals who thought they
could make use of him. Thus an untried man carrying a great
but controversial name was elected to a new office, and became
Prince-President in December 1848. It was not surprising that
on 2 December 1851 (the anniversary of Austerlitz) a simply
organized *coup d'état*, with very little opposition, gave him more
permanent power; in November 1852 a plebiscite showed an
overwhelming majority in favour of the President as Emperor.
The next month he became Napoleon III.

Napoleon III was in exactly the sort of position that he had
wanted. There was a system of direct democracy, which added
strength to the principle of Bonapartist authority. A small
Assembly, elected by universal manhood suffrage, had the
power of making laws, and there was also a Senate composed
of nominated or *ex-officio* dignitaries. But the Assembly met
for only short periods, did not have the right to initiate legislation, could not question ministers, debated in private and
could not be reported in the press. It is clear that the working
of the constitution depended entirely upon the Emperor and
upon the administrative system which he controlled. The prefects in the departments had their powers increased and were
entrusted with the task of controlling and guiding the people.

Napoleon III was thus in a particularly strong position; his
uncle, with his incessant need to improvise, never knew such
security. But Napoleon III was always cautious; he made frequent tours of the provinces, and he made every effort to keep
in touch with opinion both at home and abroad. He showed a
constant desire to win over individuals, and he was particularly
skilful in this. He would not allow opposition to organize itself,
and from February 1852 onwards he imposed controls on the
press, whereby a newspaper could be suspended and sup-
pressed after three warnings from the Ministry of the Interior.
A new (although short-lived) Ministry of General Police emphasized the authoritarian nature of the state, which had exiled
or imprisoned its main opponents.

It is curious therefore to reflect on the destiny of the Second Empire. Some historians have suggested that Napoleon had been so determined to come to power that once he had succeeded and had fulfilled the dreams of his youth, he had no clear objective, no idea of what to do with his authority. He therefore, according to this interpretation, allowed himself to drift; a great deal depended upon a single man, but this man was hesitant, confused, secretive and suspicious. In these circumstances, it has been suggested that France lost the leadership of Europe. But others have seen Napoleon III as a connoisseur of ideas, as a man who had a shrewd and realistic understanding of the problems of his times; and undoubtedly under his rule France made remarkable progress in economic and social affairs.

It is difficult, however, to see the Second Empire in terms of a coherent ideology. The Empress Eugénie, a beautiful Spanish aristocrat whom Napoleon III married in January 1853 (and who gave birth to a male heir in 1856) was a devoted Catholic; his cousin Prince Jerome was an anti-clerical; his half-brother, the Duc de Morny, was a liberal; his old companion in exile, Persigny, who became Minister of the Interior, was a fanatic; many of the ministers were self-seeking *bourgeoisie*, anxious to avoid wars and to promote prosperity at home. Perhaps the only group of ideas which seems to provide the Second Empire with any doctrine was the Saint-Simonians. Saint-Simon had died in 1825, but his principal idea, that what counted in society was the organization of production, was developed by his disciples. Since economic ends had primacy over political ends, it was necessary for the state to have an economic programme. Credit had to be organized, the means of transport had to be provided, trade had to be stimulated. Napoleon III appeared as the embodiment of these ideas.

It is true that Napoleon III was fortunate in his timing. The international situation favoured economic expansion. But it is undoubtedly important that the Emperor of France should have been a ruler who understood economic problems and who was attracted by a certain set of economic ideas. Perhaps it is in this characteristic that one can see the significance of Napoleon's unconventional education and his restless, inquisitive intelligence. In 1853 Napoleon appointed Haussmann to the post of Prefect of Paris and, working closely together, they began the rebuilding and the transformation of the French capital.

These were the boom years of the Empire, and although there were areas of discontent and checks to prosperity, success seemed to be symbolized by the Paris Exhibition of 1855. Some five million people visited this memorial to French dynamism and prestige. These were also years of success in foreign affairs. Even before he had become Emperor, Napoleon had shown an interest in reviving the Anglo-French *entente*, and he had welcomed the opportunity of Britain and France fighting together in the Crimean War. When Austria allied herself with England and France (although not participating in the war), Napoleon III could claim to have dismantled the Holy Alliance. The successful conclusion of the war, the holding of the peace conference in Paris and the birth of the Prince Imperial seemed to set the seal on Napoleon's prestige. There was no obvious alternative to his government; for many he was 'the Emperor of Europe'.

It is in 1859 and 1860 that one begins to find the first changes. These affected foreign affairs, economic policy and the constitution of the Empire. The most dramatic of these changes concerned Italy and, as is always the case with Napoleon III, one has to speculate about the explanations for his attitude. It is true that he had a great nostalgia for Italy, where he had spent much of his youth, and for the cause of Italian unification, with which he had himself become involved. It is also true that intellectually he believed in nationalism, and he thought that the emergence of an Italian nation would be one of the more obvious developments of the nineteenth century. At the same time, as a Bonaparte, he was conscious of the need to increase French prestige in the Mediterranean, which his uncle had always thought of as the centre of the world. But it may also be true that he was conscious of some economic difficulty and of the growth of opposition to him in the towns. To meet this opposition it was necessary to have military success.

The attempt on Napoleon's life by the Italian Orsini in January 1858 provided a dramatic opportunity for action. The British-made bombs used caused an estrangement with Britain, but they also provided the occasion for Italian patriots to show that they were appealing to Napoleon (who was pleased to give them maximum publicity). Napoleon had a secret meeting with the Sardinian Prime Minister, Cavour, and agreed to help militarily. After some diplomatic hesitation, the Austrians issued an ultimatum to Sardinia and by April 1859 Napoleon was in Italy, personally directing military operations. He won the battles of Magenta and Solferino, but he in no way destroyed the Austrian forces. He found that he did not like the business of war as much as he had imagined. A rising in the Papal States contributed to making French Catholic opinion worried about what Napoleon III was doing. Many sections of French opinion saw this as a rather unwise adventure, and those who were sensitive to international opinion feared that Russian and British disapproval could lead to complications. Napoleon therefore changed his policy again. On 11 July 1859 he met the Austrian Emperor at Villefranche and agreed to an armistice, which would involve the Austrian evacuation of Lombardy but not of Venetia. In principle Napoleon III had won victories – France had acquired Savoy and Nice – and he was received in France with tumultuous applause. But in reality his position was weaker than it had been.

France was traditionally a protectionist country and since 1815 its protectionism had been increased. Under both the Restoration and the July Monarchy, politicians may have differed over a variety of issues and reforms; but invariably they voted together in order to protect agriculture and industry from foreign competition. Napoleon, however, was attracted towards the theories of free trade; he wanted there to be a greater exchange of goods; he wanted the cost of living to be reduced; and, influenced as he was by Michel Chevalier, he believed that a greater measure of competition would serve as a stimulus. From 1853 therefore he lowered the duties on a number of items, usually on materials used in public works, such as coal and machinery. In 1859 he met the Manchester free-trader, Cobden, and he entered into a series of negotiations with the British government. In January 1860 it was announced that the two countries had signed a trade agreement. In both the textile and the metallurgical industries it became necessary to face up to English competition. Powerful economic interests began to withdraw their support from Napoleon.

It might have been because he realized how, with waning Catholic and *bourgeois* enthusiasm, he would have to look elsewhere for support, that Napoleon decided to modify the authoritarian structure of his government. The fear of socialism had declined and it was reasonable to anticipate a movement for reform. But the decree of November 1860 came as a surprise. It gave a number of powers to the Chambers, such as the right to vote an annual address and the right to debate government bills with the ministers responsible. A later decree gave the Assembly the right to control government expenditure.

These reforms gave a particular importance to the legislative election of 1863. Although the result was a governmental victory, winning all but thirty-two seats in a chamber of 282 deputies, nevertheless the opposition doubled their votes. An anti-Napoleon coalition had been formed and was particularly showing in Paris. It was clear that a period of difficulties had begun.

In 1866 the Prussian army defeated the Austrians at Sadowa, and the balance of power in Europe was decisively upset. Napoleon's Italian policy continued to offend both Catholics and liberals. And from 1865 onwards Napoleon was suffering from a stone in the bladder. As his powers declined it was the Empress who began to have more influence. Since she was often unwise, this was unfortunate.

But Napoleon III showed that he should not be written off too quickly. He responded to unfavourable elections in 1869 by granting a constitution which made ministers responsible to the Assembly, and by inviting a republican, Émile Ollivier, to form a government. In May 1870 a plebiscite approved the new constitution with over seven million affirmative votes. The Empire had achieved a form which might have proved lasting. But Napoleon and his newly-appointed ministers were worsted in their final diplomatic skirmish with Bismarck. In a mood of ill-judged enthusiasm the French government declared war; in a moment of folly Napoleon III took personal command of his army. He became little more than an embarrassing presence, obliged to make an enormous effort of will in order to hide his physical agony and mental anguish. On 1 September 1870 the French suffered the terrible defeat of Sedan. The Emperor was captured, and on 4 September the Republic was proclaimed in Paris.

For some time Napoleon lived in Chislehurst with his wife and son. He took up many of the earlier occupations of his former exile; he wrote, he discussed plans for world peace, he tried his hand at invention. He even plotted a return to France. But on 9 January 1873, after two operations, he died.

Undoubtedly, his dignity in defeat and illness helped to make his reputation. Perhaps there was a tendency to exaggerate his achievement. But he was an unusually perceptive man. His shifts of policy, his changing ideas, his hesitations, even his confusions, probably all came from the fact that he was feeling his way, guessing at public opinion, estimating the effects of his action. In these ways he was a most intelligent and sensitive ruler who fascinates historians as he fascinated his contemporaries.

Abraham Lincoln

(1809-65)

Lincoln's assassination on 14 April 1865, five days after the
ending of the Civil War, and his Emancipation Proclamation
have made him one of the Immortals. The processes of my-
thologizing have been abetted by other factors. One of these is
the rags to riches theme: born to an illiterate and wandering
frontiersman and with hardly any formal schooling, a failure
at forty, he was at fifty-one the President of the United States
at the most critical moment in its history. Another is the
transition in his career from awkward and hesitant westerner,
ill-versed in eastern politeness and in person ugly and ungainly,
to skilful and dexterous politician, the symbol of success in
war and the leader of a reunited country. Still another is the
fact that the war-time President could yet stay firmly civilian-
minded, and that even as he studied military manuals to prepare himself for active command, he remained the humanitarian, prompt to pardon offenders, forgiving towards deserters
and gentle towards the bereaved; the war leader and elect of
the nation had never found it easy even to discipline his own
children.

And most of all, of course, there remains the image of the
man himself, folksy and shrewd and patient, with his tall tales
and rough humour, the brooding figure addicted to melancholy and acquainted with grief; the human figure, bothered
by a shrewish and complaining wife, who in his high office was
untouched by pride or pomp. He was shot on a Good Friday,
sacrificed, it seemed, for the redemption of the Union he loved.
'Now he belongs to the ages,' said Edward Stanton, his Secretary for War, which was one of the first kind things Stanton
said of him. And the ages have seized on his story to make it
the most significant personal saga in American history, and to
see in Lincoln the stereotype not only of the democratic
opportunities offered by the New World but also of its conscience and humanity.

Abraham Lincoln was born 12 February 1809, near Hod-
genville, Kentucky, in a primitive cabin, of undistinguished
parents; he lived in Kentucky for seven years until his father
moved to Spencer County, Indiana. In the frontier life there

he received little education and used his hands to help carve out an existence. In 1830 the family went to Illinois, near Decatur, and Lincoln at twenty-two was on his own. Working in a store and in other jobs in the frontier village of New Salem from 1831 to 1837, Lincoln spent some of his most important and formative years. He served briefly in the Black Hawk War, was postmaster, learned surveying and studied law. He held no job for long, but he came to know people and to be known by them. He was phenomenally strong and striking – however ungainly, well over six feet in height, a wrestler, a captain in the Black Hawk War and a good teller of tales, many of them robust. After one unsuccessful effort he was elected to the state legislature in 1834 and re-elected three times, becoming a leading member of the assembly. He began his practice of law at Springfield in 1837 and in 1842 married Mary Todd, daughter of a prominent Kentucky family. As a Whig he was elected to the national House of Representatives in 1846 and served one rather inauspicious term.

His criticism of the Mexican War and his loyalty to his party lost him the support of his state: he was to many a 'second Benedict Arnold', speaking for the east, where the war was unpopular, and disregarding the west, where it was popular. Although his party won the 1848 election, they did not carry his district. Lincoln resumed his law practice – 'I was losing interest in politics,' he wrote later. The lack of interest remained until the passing of the Kansas–Nebraska Act in 1854 and the repeal of the Missouri Compromise that it carried with it. This, the work of Senator Stephen Douglas of Illinois, made it possible for the settlers in Kansas and Nebraska, before being granted statehood, to vote for the introduction of slavery. It reopened the slavery controversy and brought Lincoln back into politics.

The slavery issue was not only the most perplexing of American – and human – issues. It posed particular problems to the middle western states, as it did to the territories, at a time when American society, already very mobile, was becoming polyglot. And Lincoln faithfully reflected in these years the viewpoint of his section. He lived in an area where slaves were rare; his family hailed from Virginia and, if this did not make him pro-Southern, at least he seems to have shared the contemporary Southern belief that slavery would gradually disappear. He did nothing in the state legislature to interfere with the severe laws that were in force against free slaves; he did not denounce – as so many did – the Fugitive Slave Law, despite the obvious hardships to free Negroes – 'I confess I hate to see the poor creatures hunted down ... but I bite my lips and keep quiet.'

He was slow to condemn slavery as such. He did so now and then, but never formally until 1854, and always accompanying his condemnations by a frank avowal that he did not know what to do about it – 'if all earthly power were given me, I should not know what to do as to the existing institution.' There was, then, distaste for the institution, a firm front against its further extension and a frank avowal of uncertainty how to curb it without offending the South – or the law of the land. But there was something more than this, greatly appealing to Illinois, and that was the theme that the western states, like the territories, were for white men – free men but white men. Alongside every sentence in every speech condemning the wickedness of slavery and stressing the superior merits of a free to a slave society, there is the equal emphasis that the Negro must not be given political or social equality. The Negro was the equal of the white: but he must not be given citizenship. Lincoln was firmly opposed to the spread of slavery but not opposed to the institution itself: it must simply not reach Illinois. He joined the newly formed Republican Party in 1856.

Opposing Stephen A. Douglas of Illinois for the Senate in 1858, he was defeated but added greatly to his reputation through the famous debates (known to history as the Lincoln–Douglas debates) over the expansion of slavery and the theory of popular sovereignty. Lincoln was still a moderate – opposed to the repeal of the Fugitive Slave Laws, opposed to Negro citizenship and to social and political equality of white and black. But in all his dexterity, Lincoln never abandoned the central argument: that slavery must not be permitted to expand.

Throughout 1859 he campaigned, as the leading western Republican, in Ohio and Indiana, Iowa and Wisconsin. When he delivered the Cooper Institute speech in New York in February 1860 – the speech and the photograph that in retrospect he thought gave him the Republican nomination – he held to the same note: denial of abolitionism; distaste for John Brown's radicalism; sympathy for the South – but no support for any proposed extension of slavery to the territories of the United States. This was for Lincoln the central precept, ordained by the Founding Fathers.

Lincoln was nominated at the Republican Convention in Chicago in 1860, due largely to his availability on grounds that he had few enemies and appeared more moderate than other candidates, and because of the shrewd political promises of his friends. In the months that followed he made few speeches, although he talked a great deal to political leaders and delegations. He did little, however, to placate the South. And on 6 November 1860, he was chosen as President by a large electoral majority – (Lincoln 180, Breckinridge of Kentucky seventy-two, Bell thirty-nine, Stephen Douglas twelve) – but with only 40 per cent of the popular vote (Lincoln 1,866,452; Douglas 1,376,957; Breckinridge 849,781; Bell 588, 879). In ten Southern states not a single popular vote was cast for him; he failed to carry his own county in Illinois. But he carried every free state in the North except New Jersey. Moderation paid; the White House awaited him. His silence did not; South Carolina seceded from the Union. By April 1861 ten more states had joined her.

Lincoln won his election not by moral greatness, or by compassion for white or black, but by political skills of a high order. 'If I could save the Union by emancipating all the slaves I would do so; if I could save it by emancipating none I would do it; if I could save it by emancipating some and not others, I would do that too.' He was to reveal greatness in the years ahead, moral as well as political. Earnest he was, with remarkable insight into the essence of the controversy, and firm he was to show himself. But little of this was evident in 1860, least of all to his cabinet. The ill-dressed and awkward figure, with a high nasal inflexion in his voice, was – to Seward as to the country – an unknown quantity, even perhaps a 'Simple Susan'. He had shown uncanny skill in compromising on many questions. He had also shown that there were for him some issues on which there could be no compromise and no surrender. 'Hard as a rock and soft as drifting fog' is Carl Sandburg's phrase.

He fought the war, of course, to defend the Union. The South was never in his eyes a state but a piece of the Union in rebellion. But the war made emancipation possible, and indeed successive Northern defeats made it a valuable, even essential, psychological weapon. This, at first, was indeed its major value; it was the slaves in the states in rebellion who were freed. It was a penal measure. He said he did it as commander-in-chief, not as President. As a result he almost lost the congressional election in 1862. Lincoln was aware that the North fought not to free slaves but to save the Union; four slave states had after all stayed loyal, and he did not wish to turn topsy-turvy the social system of the South. The plan he had favoured was one of gradual compensated emancipation. Yet, however reluctantly, Lincoln had come in the end to emancipate the slaves, although the Thirteenth Amendment was not ratified until eight months after his death.

Throughout the war, he presided over a cabinet in which were some of his rivals for president and his chief critics. He was compelled to extend his executive power until – man of peace as he was – he was accused of dictatorship. His commanders – McClellan, Pope, Burnside, Hooker – were ineffective and sometimes conceited; his chief-of-staff, Winfield Scott, was old, tired and overweight. Lincoln was infinitely patient and infinitely sad. It was a long and bloody war, won in the end only by Ulysses Grant's readiness to spend lives on a colossal scale.

In June 1864 Lincoln was renominated for the presidency, but not without opposition, and he himself despaired of re-election. But victories around Atlanta, the valuable soldier vote and shrewd politics gave him the election over Democrat George B. McClellan. By the time of his second inaugural, Lincoln had formulated basic ideas regarding reconstruction of the South, including a desire to 'bind up the nation's wounds', to form new state governments, to pardon the vast majority of Confederates and to adopt a generally lenient policy which included the constitutional abolition of slavery and reunification of the nation.

The American Civil War ended on 9 April 1865, when Robert E. Lee surrendered his dwindling and now hungry Army of Northern Virginia to Ulysses Grant at Appomattox Courthouse. Both sides were exhausted and one of them was utterly destroyed. The Union dead (360,000) exceeded the number of American dead in World War II; the South had 254,000 dead – and it was estimated that one in five of all its men of military age had been wounded; its cities and many of its splendid homes were in ruins, its railway tracks and rolling stock destroyed; the freeing of its slaves meant a two-billion-dollar loss of 'property', and a new system of free labour had to be introduced. The South's human and physical resources were exhausted; and it has to this day never forgotten the humiliation of defeat, in what was till then the bloodiest war in history, and of occupation by what was to it a foreign army. The years of post-war reconstruction were to be the most demanding in American history; the need for tolerance and statesmanship was never greater. But five days after victory Abraham Lincoln, who alone could have given constructive and magnanimous leadership, was shot.

The President had not wanted to attend Ford's Theatre in Washington that evening; he had suggested to his friend, the reporter Noah Brooks, that he should replace him as a companion for Mrs Lincoln. But in the end he agreed to go. Equally John Wilkes Booth and his fellow conspirators, though they had long planned various amateur attempts to kidnap Lincoln and to hold him as a hostage until Confederate prisoners were released, did not turn to the idea of assassination until Appomattox. On hearing that the President would attend the performance of *Our American Cousin* that evening, Booth alerted his colleagues. He himself entered the President's box, shot him at close range and jumped on the stage shouting '*Sic semper tyrannis!* The South is avenged!' As he fell he caught his foot in the flag draped over the box and broke his leg; but in the confusion he still managed to escape to a waiting horse behind the theatre; he was not found for twelve days, hiding in a barn near Bowling Green, Virginia; and when the barn was burned he was shot as he tried to escape. His fellow-conspirators had struck at other members of Lincoln's cabinet. The affair sent a wave of alarm through the capital and some hundreds of people were arrested on suspicion. In the end four were hanged and four others given life imprisonment.

Mrs Lincoln was almost as much a victim as her husband. She had lost a son, Willie, three years before, her husband was shot at her side in 1865 and in 1871 her favourite son, Ted, died. She was that year declared insane.

William Ewart Gladstone

(1809-98)

More than sixty years a member of the House of Commons, a minister of the Crown in ten cabinets, four times Britain's Prime Minister – in the many hundred years of British politics there is none to surpass the record of 'the Grand Old Man', as Gladstone was familiarly called. He stands out among British statesmen as the man who above all others insisted, and acted on the belief, that political activity is (or should be) the attempt to realize God's will (for His people here) on earth.

William Ewart Gladstone was born in Liverpool on 29 December 1809, the fourth son of John (afterwards Sir John) Gladstone, a Scotsman of sturdy vigour and high character who, from being a corn-dealer in Leith, worked his way up to become a wealthy merchant in Liverpool, with extensive business interests in the West Indies, where he owned sugar and cotton plantations worked by Negro slaves. He also took a leading part in Tory politics in Liverpool, and himself sat in the House of Commons for a number of years. John Gladstone's wife, Anne Robertson, came from Dingwall, so that the future statesman was of Scottish origin on both sides.

Six years at Eton, where William was so happy that he used to look back upon it as 'the Queen of Schools', were followed by three at Christ Church, Oxford, where he performed brilliantly. He was a 'double first', in classics and mathematics; and, more significant in the light of his future career, covered himself with glory as a speaker at the Oxford Union debates. In May 1831, shortly before he left university, he declaimed with such eloquence *against* the Reform Bill that the Duke of Newcastle, father of one of his college friends, offered to bring him into the House of Commons as Tory member for Newark, one of his Lordship's 'pocket boroughs'. Gladstone accepted this dazzling offer, and in December 1832 he was duly elected an MP.

To begin with (and indeed for the next twenty years) he sat on the Tory benches. His first speech of any note was in defence of his father against allegations that the manager of his estates in the West Indies had worked some of the slaves to death. Gladstone did not defend slavery as an institution (it should be noted in fairness), but he maintained that abolition should be gradual, in the interests of the economy and of the slaves themselves. He supported strong measures of repression in Ireland, and voted against the admission of Jews to Parliament, the introduction of the ballot in elections and the abolition of flogging as a disciplinary measure in the army and navy. On the whole he very well deserved Macaulay's description of him at the time as 'the rising hope of the stern and unbending Tories'. In 1834 he had his first taste of office, when for a few months he was under-secretary in Peel's Tory administration.

On Peel's resignation Gladstone retired to the Opposition benches, and occupied himself with writing a book on the relations of Church and State, in which he took an extraordinary High Church attitude, and assiduous attention to his parliamentary duties. He also fell in, and out of, love more than once, until when on holiday at Rome in 1838 he met Catherine Glynne, an altogether charming young lady, about two years younger than he was. They were married in July 1839, in the parish church close by the family seat of the Glynnes, Hawarden Castle, in Flintshire, which was henceforth their country seat and, in later years, became Gladstone's own property.

When Sir Robert Peel formed his second administration, in 1841, he offered Gladstone the post of vice-president of the Board of Trade. Gladstone was deeply disappointed: he had expected something very much more elevated. 'In a spirit of ignorant mortification,' he confessed many years afterwards to John Morley, 'I said to myself: the science of politics deals with the government of men, but I am set to govern packages!' But it was not long before he was discovering that 'governing packages' was not so uninteresting after all. He applied himself with tremendous energy to mastering the details of trade and commerce and Peel came to rely upon him as the most able of his lieutenants in economic affairs. Gladstone followed his chief in his conversion to free trade, and when he had become president of the Board of Trade he did much useful work, notably the removal of restrictions on the exportation of machinery and the passing of the Telegraph Act.

Free trade was carried in 1846, and the Tory party was split down the middle. Gladstone followed Peel when the government fell, and for the next few years was ranked amongst the Tory free-traders as a Peelite. This was a move in the direction of Liberalism, but the transfer of political allegiance was not completed for a number of years yet. In the result it was foreign affairs that gave him the final push.

Always fond of a continental excursion, Gladstone was on holiday at Naples in the autumn of 1850. At that time Naples was the capital of the Kingdom of the Two Sicilies, and its ruler was King Ferdinand II, nicknamed 'Bomba' because of his inhuman bombardment of one of his chief towns when its people revolted against his abominable tyranny. Gladstone was not particularly interested until one day he happened to be in court at the trial of one of the rebel leaders. He was deeply shocked at the travesty of a trial, and even more so at the sentence that was passed – twenty-four years' imprisonment in irons! He started to make inquiries and found that Neapolitan gaols were crammed with political prisoners, men and women alike, existing in conditions of the foulest cruelty and degradation.

When he got back to England he was in a state of truly Vesuvian eruption. On arrival at the station in London he was met by Sir James Phillimore, an old friend of his, who was the bearer of an invitation from Lord Stanley, the Tory leader, to join his cabinet. Gladstone stuffed the letter in his pocket, and although he eventually agreed to meet Stanley he turned his invitation down, ostensibly because Stanley was still in favour of a small duty on imported corn. But the real reason was that he was far too concerned about those poor creatures in the Naples dungeons to take much interest in his own political advancement. He approached Lord Aberdeen, the leader of the Peelites, and begged him to use his influence to obtain some mitigation of the prisoners' lot. Aberdeen was not keen to get involved. But Gladstone was on the boil. In July 1851 he published a pamphlet, a *Letter to Lord Aberdeen*, and a month later followed it up with another. What is this government of the Two Sicilies? he demanded therein; and he gave the answer. 'It is the negation of God erected into a system of Government!'

The sensation caused by the pamphlets was tremendous. True, they did not have any immediate effect on the treatment of the prisoners, who did not obtain their liberty until 1859; but Gladstone at one stroke became a national – indeed, an international – figure. Throughout the world lovers of freedom hailed his name. He had plenty of supporters too on the government benches opposite. Lord Palmerston, the Foreign Secretary in Lord John Russell's Whig (or Liberal) ministry, was specially outspoken. He thought the Right Hon. Gentleman was to be commended, he declared; instead of seeking amusements, diving into volcanoes and exploring excavated cities, he had examined cases of illegality and injustice, and had then sought to arouse the public opinion of Europe against those responsible ...

Gladstone may have shifted a little uneasily in his seat at this encomium from a political opponent, but it is significant that when a Tory (or Conservative, to use the name which had by now become generally accepted) government was formed by Stanley (now Lord Derby), Gladstone declined to join it, and the new Chancellor was Benjamin Disraeli, than whom Gladstone distrusted no man more. Disraeli's budget speech was a splendid effort, and as soon as he sat down Gladstone rose to reply. No-one expected that he could possibly excel Disraeli's performance, but Gladstone did just that. A great storm was raging outside, but Gladstone's marvellous voice rose above the thunder. Disraeli had been clever, but Gladstone spoke in a tone of the highest moral assurance. As *The Times* expressed it the next morning, 'When he concluded, the House might well feel proud of him, and of themselves.'

The Conservatives were defeated in the division that followed, and Derby promptly resigned and was followed by Lord Aberdeen at the head of a coalition of Liberals, Whigs and Peelite Conservatives. Gladstone became Chancellor of the Exechequer, and the budget that he proceeded to introduce was a great parliamentary occasion. Nearly 150 customs duties extinguished, the tea duty reduced, the duty on soap abolished, a prospect of the income tax (then 7d in the pound) being abolished altogether within seven years. Such was the first instalment of Gladstonian finance in action – taxes as low as possible, most especially on articles of general consumption; encouragement of thrift; shackles on private enterprise swept away; government expenditure reduced to the lowest figure possible. 'Economy is the first and great article of my financial creed,' said Gladstone on a later occasion, 'a Chancellor of the Exechequer is not worth his salt if he is not ready to save what are called candle-ends and cheeseparings in the cause of the country.'

The coalition fell in 1855 and Gladstone was once again out of office. He was still a Peelite (although Peel had died years before) and he might have joined the governments that were formed in 1855 and 1858, Liberal and Conservative respectively. He sat with increasing unease on the fence until 1859 when Lord Palmerston formed his second administration. The Italians had risen against their Austrian oppressors and Gladstone was heart and soul with them. Palmerston was a Liberal – but he was a resolute friend of Italian liberation, and when he offered Gladstone any post in the ministry that he cared to name, Gladstone took the plunge. He became Chancellor of the Exechequer again, but this time in a Liberal administration. Henceforth the one-time 'hope of the stern and unbending Tories' was the foremost exponent of a militant Liberalism.

Since 1847 Gladstone had been sitting as one of the two representatives of Oxford University, but his change of party, not to mention the views he had expressed in favour of disestablishing the Anglican Church in Ireland, brought about his defeat at the general election of 1865. He soon found a new seat at Greenwich, however. Now Gladstone was recognized as the leader of the Liberal party. In 1868 the general election resulted in a great Liberal victory, and on a December day when he was cutting down trees in Hawarden Park – his favourite form of physical exercise – he received a telegram from the Queen. He went at once to Windsor and was commissioned to form a government. He did so without difficulty, and was Prime Minister for six years. His chief measures were the disestablishment of the Irish Church; the great Education Act of 1870, which established a system of elementary education throughout the country; the Ballot Act of 1872; and the abolition of the system of purchasing commissions in the army and navy. Another immensely salutary reform was the throwing open of the great majority of civil service posts to those who were successful in passing an open competitive entrance examination.

The Liberals were defeated at the general election of 1874, and Gladstone took the result very much to heart, even to the extent of resigning the leadership of the Liberal party. He retired to Hawarden, and might well have remained there if news had not reached him of the horrible atrocities being committed by the Turks on their Bulgarian subjects. Gladstone was deeply moved. He dashed off a pamphlet, *The Bulgarian Horrors*, which was published in the autumn of 1876.

Gladstone was riding the storm again, just as he had done a quarter of a century before when King 'Bomba' was his target. The public conscience was aroused, and when, having decided to leave Greenwich and stand at the next election for Midlothian, he went to Edinburgh to launch his campaign, he was accorded an overwhelming reception. Vast crowds gathered to see his train go by, and immense audiences were moved to delirious enthusiasm by his tremendous assertions of the moral law in the affairs of nations as of individual men. When the general election was fought in 1880 Gladstone, successful at Midlothian, throughout the country led the Liberal hosts to victory.

Nominally he was still a private member, but the public demanded that he should become Prime Minister – much to the dismay, the disgust even, of Queen Victoria. One reason for her dislike was his habit (so she complained) of always addressing her as though she were a public meeting; but another is believed to have lain in reports that had been conveyed to her of his personal crusade of rescue among the 'fallen women of the metropolis'. This was something he had been engaged in since his marriage, and for more than forty years he devoted much time, and money, to its prosecution.

After standing out against the proposal as long as she could, the Queen at last agreed to accept Gladstone as her chief minister once again. His second administration was not as successful as his first. He was widely blamed – by no one more than the Queen – for General Gordon's death at Khartoum, and there were troubles in Egypt and South Africa. Then Ireland's grievances once again gave rise to a nationalist agitation which under Parnell's leadership brought the country to the verge of civil war. In the summer of 1885 a temporary combination of Conservatives and Parnellites defeated the government in a division.

Gladstone at once resigned, but after a short Conservative administration under Lord Salisbury, there was a general election in which the Liberals were again returned, although with a much reduced majority. In 1896 Gladstone became Prime Minister for the third time, and very shortly announced his conversion to a policy of home rule for Ireland. His action convulsed the political world, and a large and influential section of his party deserted to the Conservatives as Liberal Unionists. Gladstone introduced the first of the series of Home Rule Bills in 1886, and his winding-up speech on the second reading on 8 June 1886 was perhaps the finest he ever delivered. The bill was lost, Gladstone resigned, and at the ensuing general election the Liberals were heavily defeated.

Now in his seventy-seventh year, he might well have decided on retirement, but he chose to become Leader of the Opposition. And after six years, there he was again, sitting on the Treasury Bench as Prime Minister, for the fourth time. A fresh Home Rule Bill was introduced and although it passed the House of Commons, was flung out by the House of Lords. The government stumbled on until 1894. On 1 March Gladstone presided over his last cabinet, and left the room with a hardly heard, 'God bless you all.' Later the same afternoon, he spoke his valedictory in the House of Commons – a fighting speech it was, too, an exhortation to do battle with the House of

Lords... Three days later he had his last audience with the Queen at Windsor, and she was cheerful to the point of rudeness.

Four years were left to the old statesman, and he passed them mostly at his beloved Hawarden. He did not stand for re-election at the general election of 1895, but in the year following he once again felt the call of battle. The Armenians were being brutally slaughtered in their remote valleys by the Turks, and at a great meeting in Liverpool Gladstone spoke for an hour and twenty minutes in denunciation of that 'great assassin', the Sultan Abdul Hamid. In the autumn of 1897 he was afflicted with a cancerous growth behind his cheekbone, but he bore the dreadful pain with religious resignation. Early on the morning of 19 May 1898 he died, his family kneeling round his bed and his son Stephen, a clergyman, reading the prayers for the dying.

When the news was telegraphed to Westminster, both Houses at once adjourned, and on the next day noble tributes were paid to his memory. From all parts of the world tributes poured in, and when his body lay in state in Westminster Hall immense crowds filed past the coffin in homage or simple affection. On 28 May his body was laid to rest in Westminster Abbey, in the north transept, close by the statues of Peel and Disraeli, and the pallbearers included the Prime Minister, Lord Salisbury, the Prince of Wales (Edward VII) and the Duke of York (George V). Two years later Mrs Gladstone was buried beside her husband.

Otto von Bismarck

(1815–98)

When Bismarck was born, 1 April 1815, three months before Waterloo, Germany was – despite Napoleon's reduction of the number of German states – still a congeries of principalities and duchies. In 1789 there had been 300 of them. After Waterloo there were still thirty-eight. Of these the Hapsburg Empire was the largest and included Austria, Bohemia and part of Hungary; it dominated the Germanic Confederation set up in 1815. If Germany had a capital city it was Vienna, and it had been so for over five hundred years. By contrast Prussia was small and seen as a northern and barbarian outpost. By the end of the century Germany was a powerful and united country, perhaps the most powerful on the European continent. There was an overseas German empire. German industry was the most modern in the world, its workers were the best housed in the world and the first to be covered by social insurance. The making of Germany was very largely the work of one man, Otto von Bismarck.

Otto von Bismarck was born at Schönhausen on the river Elbe. The Bismarcks were an old Brandenburg family, indeed as old as the Hohenzollerns – Bismarck once said, 'Not only older than the Hohenzollerns but in no way inferior to them.' His father was a not very efficient farmer and lived like most *Junkers* on his estates. His mother was city-bred and highly intelligent, and descended from the Mencken family, which had provided Brandenburg with some distinguished civil servants. Otto was educated in Pomerania on another family estate and attended school in Berlin with the thought of becoming a farmer like his father. He went to the University of Göttingen in Hanover, studying law, but his attendance was erratic and he was not interested in his studies. He fought no fewer than twenty-five fencing bouts with sabres in not untypical German student fashion. From 1839–49 he managed one of the family estates at Kniephof. In 1847 he married Johanna von Putkammer, a plain and very pious woman to whom he was devoted, but he had a number of affairs with other women – about which his wife was very understanding.

When he learned of the outbreak of the 1848 revolution he

was on his estates in Pomerania, and was outraged at what he thought was a threat to the Prussian system. The system that he considered the ideal was a monarchy built on and supported by a landed aristocracy. In practice this meant a policy of total defence of the *status quo* and the rights of the nobility. These sentiments and his right-wing enthusiasms attracted the attention of the King, Frederick William IV, who invited him to the general surprise to become the Prussian ambassador in the Germanic Confederation at Frankfort. He was only thirty-six and with no experience of politics or diplomacy.

When he appeared on the public stage – and he was to be on it for the next forty years – he was already a man to be reckoned with. The King needed him if the liberal forces were to be checked, but saw him as a reactionary; 'He smells of blood,' he said, 'only to be used once the bayonet rules.' He dressed, it was said, like a gentleman but acted like a boor. He was huge and ungainly in stature, and with a prodigious appetite for food, especially pickled herrings, and drink, especially a concoction of stout mixed with champagne called 'black velvet'.

His years at Frankfort from 1857–59 were decisive. To the national cause, in the shape of German unity under Prussian leadership, he now became devoted. He became not only a critic of Austria but a sympathizer with Russia, and his consistent efforts to keep Prussia neutral during the Crimean War, as later during the Polish revolt of 1863, won him great support in St Petersburg. He was never to change in his view that there must be genuine accord with Russia in order to guarantee the security of Germany's eastern frontier. He was equally determined to try to divert Austrian interests and aspirations away from Germany and towards Roumania and the Balkans, thus imperilling her relations with both Russia and Italy. In 1859 the King asked him to become the Prussian ambassador in Russia. In 1862 he moved in a similar capacity to Paris.

What proved decisive, however, for Bismarck's career was his relationship with the King's brother William, who in 1857 became the Prince Regent on the illness and subsequent insanity of Frederick William IV; William became King in his own right on his brother's death in 1861. In background he was a soldier and an absolutist – on becoming King he declared that he ruled 'by the favour of God and of no one else'. He wanted an increase in the budget for the army, but the Prussian legislature wanted a tightly controlled budget and a small army. In this situation the Minister for War, Albrecht von Roon, persuaded the new ruler to summon Bismarck to guide him, and in 1862 this die-hard *Junker* from his Pomeranian estates was appointed Prime Minister and Foreign Minister of Prussia. He was to rule it for the next twenty-eight years.

For four years, 1862–66, he ruled without legislative consent; he ran the state and paid an army, which was twice successful in war, without sanction of the chamber or the people. But Bismarck's authority was not just the result of his dictatorial methods. It was bound up with the three wars: of 1864, with Denmark, 1886, with Austria, and 1870 with France. Success in each of these made his state and, for his lifetime himself, the dominant forces in Europe. After the Treaty of Vienna in 1815 the two duchies of Schleswig and Holstein, both of which had large German populations, had been united with Denmark in a personal union. From the beginning of his ministry Bismarck intended to annex the provinces to Prussia. 'I have not the smallest doubt,' he said, 'that the Danish business can be settled in a way desirable for us only by war.' On 1 February 1864 Prussian and Austrian armies crossed the frontiers of Schleswig. By the Peace of Vienna, August 1864, Denmark had to give up the duchies to Austria and Prussia. By the convention of Gastein, 14 August 1865, the Austro-Prussian condominium of the duchies was ended by dividing them. Austria was given control over Holstein and Prussia over Schleswig.

The legacy of one two-month war was another: the war with Austria over the spoils. It lasted seven weeks. With speedy communications and superb military organization, and with an alliance with Italy that kept her neutral and held out the hope of gaining Venetia from Austria, the Prussians led by their king in person defeated Austria at Sadowa. It was a quick war; it brought Bismarck immense popularity; it was followed by a peace treaty of remarkable and shrewd generosity. The Treaty of Prague (1866) required Austria to recognize the end of the German Confederation, the incorporation of Schleswig-Holstein with Prussia and the annexation of Venetia by Italy. Austria was to pay a small indemnity of twenty million *talers*.

France, under the leadership of the Emperor Napoleon III, became alarmed at this Prussian dominance in Germany. For his part, Bismarck and his generals, notably von Moltke, believed that in any war with France Prussia would win. His opportunity came with the candidature of a German prince to the Spanish throne, which suggested the encirclement of France by German power. Benedetti, the French Minister, called on King William at Ems, and while indicating his peaceful intentions was rash enough to ask the German government to abandon all claims to the Spanish throne. When Bismarck was sent by the King a telegram describing these discussions, he released to the press a version of it which sounded disturbingly like a French ultimatum. Each side treated it as such, and France declared war at once. In less than two months the French army suffered a series of defeats along its eastern frontier, and was forced to surrender on 1 September at Sedan where Napoleon III was himself captured. From September to January 1871 Paris was besieged and bombed by Prussian guns, and fell mainly because of hunger on 28 January 1871. The peace terms were harsh: she was to surrender to Germany the province of Alsace and most of Lorraine including Metz; Napoleon III went into exile and the Third Republic was proclaimed; and, most bitter irony of all, the new German empire with William of Prussia as Emperor was proclaimed in the Hall of Mirrors at Versailles. Bismarck himself became a prince.

He was undoubtedly the architect of the new empire and of French defeat. Except where France was concerned he acted, and was to continue to act, with remarkable restraint. While he favoured the annexation of Strassburg, the population of which was German-speaking, he was against the annexation of the completely French Metz. He sought to keep France isolated by setting up the Dreikaiserbund, which began as a tacit royal alliance against potential revolutions between Germany, Austria-Hungary and Russia in 1872; but by 1881 it had blossomed into a formal and secret pact, in which each party guaranteed its neutrality if one of the three were to be at war with a fourth power (meaning France). After 1871 peace and diplomacy, not war, were the essential bulwarks of the new empire he had created.

Bismarck was equally successful in creating a constitutional system of autocracy and efficiency. The new empire was a federal union of twenty-five states with a central government in Berlin. The Emperor was commander-in-chief of the army and navy. The Reichstag, which was elected by universal manhood suffrage, could not initiate legislation nor dismiss the Chancellor, and was little more than a debating society. Bismarck was not only federal Chancellor, chairman of the Bundesrat and head of the Prussian delegation in it, but he was also Prime Minister of Prussia. At a time when sweeping social and industrial changes were taking place, he held Germany on a conservative course for two decades.

The acquisition of Alsace-Lorraine brought the resources of iron ore to the coal of the Ruhr Valley, and the Ruhr became the centre of European heavy industry. Between 1860 and 1910 German railway tracks were increased six-fold, and in the same period her coal production increased from 30 million metric tons to almost 200 million. Great iron and steel empires were created by the Krupp and Thyssen families; and two great shipping companies the Hamburg-America line and the North German Lloyd line of Bremen, became among the most powerful merchant fleets in the world. Germany was built not only on blood and iron, but on coal, railways and iron.

But Bismarck struck some false notes. The empire he built had enemies. The first of them in his view was the Pope who, in 1864, in the Syllabus of Modern Errors, had condemned secular education and civil marriage, and who had in 1870 proclaimed papal infallibility on matters of faith and morals. But in 1871 Bismarck launched what his liberal allies called the *Kulturkampf*, the fight for civilization. He expelled the Jesuits in 1872, and by the May Laws of 1872 and 1878 gave the state control over marriage and education, confiscated church property and tightly controlled the Catholic press. One result was the rapid development of the Catholic Centre Party as a force in German politics.

In 1878, however, the accession of the moderate Pope Leo XIII in succession to Pius IX brought a change of policy. Bismarck came to be more alarmed by the rapid rise of socialism than he was by any threats there might be from Rome. By 1887 most of the anti-Catholic laws were repealed, but a campaign was under way against socialists. In 1878 the Chancellor enacted a series of Exceptional Laws which denied freedom of the press to 'socialist machinations dangerous to the common weal'. But it was by no means a policy of hostility alone. Bismarck passed a striking number of measures that were indeed the first of their kind in Europe: Sickness Insurance (1883), Accident Insurance (1884) and Old-Age Insurance (1889). These were seen by many inside and outside Germany as models, and were especially seen as such in Britain by David Lloyd George, who enacted similar measures two or more decades later. Despite these measures the socialist cause flourished in Germany. In 1890, the year of the Grand Old Man's retirement, the Exceptional Laws of 1878 were allowed to lapse.

In 1888 King William I died, to be succeeded by the Crown Prince Frederick who had been brought up in the shadow of Bismarck, even though the two men did not see eye to eye. Frederick III died of cancer, three months after coming to the throne and was succeeded by William II, a young man of the generation which considered that the Bismarck era was over. William II had no respect for the Chancellor particularly as, at that moment, the Reichstag was fairly solidly against Bismarck. The monarch not the Chancellor was the ruler. In 1890 the Prince Chancellor was forced to resign and, as the famous *Punch* cartoon of the day indicated, the German ship of state 'dropped the pilot'. He had not only created the German empire, he had thereafter limited his aims, averted hostile coalitions and never taken on more than one enemy at a time. He was neither a militarist nor an imperialist but a supreme example of a nationalist, who knew at each shift in the international scene exactly what he wanted and when to call a halt. What was supreme about him was neither his ruthlessness nor his lack of scruple, though he had both of these qualities in abundance, but his moderation in success. 'Twenty years after my departure,' said Bismarck, 'Germany will crash to ruins.' He was right. The Kaiser abandoned Bismarck's foreign policy, alienated Russia, quarrelled with Britain. Twenty-eight years after his dismissal, Germany was defeated in a world war, her army broken and her navy scuttled. The Kaiser flew to Holland, discredited, unloved and unmourned.

Bismarck was, as A. J. P. Taylor has described him, 'a clever sophisticated son of a clever sophisticated mother masquerading all his life as his heavy earthen father'. He was half country squire and half urban and revolutionary intellectual, at once both neurotic and decisive; he was capable of great piety, but could equally be swept by waves of rage and resentment (he once said 'I have spent a whole night hating'). He became a legend in his own day, and cultivated the plant warmly. He said that the man who had not drunk 5,000 bottles of champagne and smoked 100,000 cigars could not properly be said to have lived. Certainly he did his best: he smoked fourteen cigars a day; and when he left the chancellorship in 1890 he took 300 crates of paper and 13,000 bottles with him.

He is, then, a figure of astonishing paradox: a gentle, loving husband and devoted father but, to the world outside, a firebreathing autocrat; a gargantuan eater and drinker, but also a hypochondriac; a wily diplomat, but a vigorous and outspoken hater of Poles, Jews and Frenchmen. He was inconsistent, vindictive and mendacious. But, however unlovable to those outside the *Junkers'* world, to some of whom he seemed a monster, intellectually and physically Bismarck was a giant. Most Germans and almost all Prussians see in *der alte Herr* a twin-figure to Churchill: an extension and a prototype of the nation's personality.

Prince Albert

(1819-61)

It was a body of rough, illiterate men – Thames-side labourers
– who coined the title 'Albert the Good' for their Queen's
husband: and meant it from their hearts. Admittedly, they had
special reason for the sentiment. After his appointment as
Master of Trinity House he was appealed to by the ballast-
heavers, desperate to find someone of authority who would
listen to their grievance. Casually employed, they could only
get work through the favour of riverside publicans and middle-
men, who made them spend liberally on drink by way of
commission. The expense was diminishing the men's small
earnings: the drink was ruining their constitutions. Albert
listened, acted, and the abuse was ended.

Perhaps it is a pity for history – not only England's – that
few actual sovereigns have ever borne Albert's stamp. He
combined excellent intentions with high intelligence, sense with
sensibility, qualities for which royal personages have all too
seldom been notable. Yet he could only work his influence at
second hand, as a queen's husband, a foreign-born prince in a
land where foreigners have never been much reckoned. That
he achieved so much in a short life, against great odds, and
managed to gain the affection of ordinary folk, despite a seriousness of mind and Puritan spirit which allowed him no
frivolous meeting-place with them, is a greater tribute to him
than were his widow's decades of obsessive mourning.

He had not always been grave. As a baby he was noted by
his grandmother to be 'quick as a weasel ... lively, very funny,
all good nature and full of mischief'. He had been born in 1819
at Rosenau, in the tiny duchy of Coburg, the second son of the
hereditary Duke of Saxe-Coburg-Gotha. With his elder brother Ernest he was educated by tutors and then at the University of Bonn. His seriousness of mind became apparent early.
He hated to be idle, but refused to resort to superficial pursuits
merely to keep occupied. He like to walk – alone or with a
companion prepared to discuss abstract things. He studied
music, played the organ, composed. He acquired a taste for
art and displayed a sound collector's judgement. In fact, he
showed himself to be quite different in most things from his

brother or their dissolute father, to whom Albert wrote on one occasion, when called to Coburg for Christmas, 'I am afraid we must deny ourselves that pleasure ... Our course of study would be quite disturbed by such an interruption': a sentiment which few students can have been known to express.

Lacking anything substantial in the way of parental influence from his own father or stepmother, Albert came under the influence of two ambitious men – his uncle Leopold, King of the Belgians, and Leopold's shrewd counsellor, Baron Stockmar, a former Coburg lawyer grown wise in the ways of court diplomacy. They were ambitious for both Albert and the house of Coburg, and their ambition centred upon Albert's first cousin, the child Princess Victoria, niece of King William IV of England, whose mother, the Duchess of Kent, was sister to Albert's own mother. A match between the two seemed to Leopold and Stockmar to be the most desirable thing in the world, and in 1836, despite the objections of William IV, who cared nothing for Saxe-Coburgs and had several other foreign candidates on his list, Albert travelled to England and met Victoria for the first time. The impulsive, warm-hearted girl of seventeen fell quickly in love with her handsome cousin. They danced and played piano duets, walked and talked. She wept when he went home. He, dismayed by the emptiness of English court life, admitted that he had found the princess 'very amiable'.

William IV died in June 1837 and Victoria was crowned Queen a year later on 28 June 1838. Albert was still at Bonn University, deeply interested in his studies and apprehensive about his future role. A further meeting with Albert at Windsor in 1839 quite bowled Victoria over. It was his blue eyes, broad shoulders and slender waist that she noticed above all else. They pledged their love. 'I *do* feel so happy! I do so adore Albert!' Victoria wrote. 'Alas my days in my beloved home are numbered,' lamented her bridegroom-to-be. It was his lifelong shyness and introspection speaking: his love and admiration matched Victoria's own.

They were married on 10 February 1840, a wet, miserable day. Albert wore the uniform of a field-marshal of the British Army. It was about all he was entitled to. Under the constitution of England he had no standing; less, in fact, than a peer of the realm. His only predecessor in the role of husband of a reigning queen, Prince George of Denmark, who had married Queen Anne, had been given a peerage. Albert could have had one, but would not take it: it would have prejudiced his inheritance in Coburg. His official allowance had been proposed at

£50,000 a year. The Tories, whom the new Queen made no bones about detesting, forced its reduction to £30,000.

Worse still for him was the knowledge that he was resented at court, suspect in the eyes of the populace and excluded by the Queen from her conferences with her ministers and from taking part in state business. She would not let him read official papers and refused to discuss them with him in private. 'I am only the husband and not the master in the house,' he wrote. However, things began to improve. The Queen tried to get his name included in the liturgy. Parliament passed a bill without debate (though there had been several preliminary attempts to undermine it) appointing him Regent in case the Queen should die leaving an heir under eighteen. He began a course in constitutional law and persuaded Victoria to study with him.

He gave up playing chess – a sober enough game – on Sundays when he learned that it offended Sabbatarians. Word began to percolate to the people that this pale, handsome young man was setting the court and aristocracy an example in moral principles that the rising English middle class heartily approved. Albert, and his wife with him, were seen not as pleasure-renouncing sober-sides, but as exemplars of family conduct. Albert's part in this phenomenon – almost unique in royal circles – was acknowledged and his popularity began to grow. His attitudes did not endear him to the aristocracy, however. They resented the changes at court, where tippling, card-playing and gossip no longer prevailed, and some refused to attend functions rather than pay homage to this foreign prude. But he hunted one day with the Belvoir, and rode so well that he won even their grudging respect.

Undeterred, and sometimes – though not always – encouraged by the Queen, whose devotion to him was quite reshaping her character, Albert pressed on with reforms in the limited spheres accessible to him. His artistic eye had at once recognized the Leonardo da Vinci and Holbein drawings lying neglected in folios in Windsor Castle library. He set about appraising and cataloguing them, together with hundredweights of historic documents with the dust of centuries on them. He had the royal estates put into order, gardens relaid and stocked, trees planted. He introduced domestic economies and labour-saving methods into the royal households, thereby saving so much money in two years that the Queen was able to buy Osborne House on the Isle of Wight for a leisure retreat. It cost some £200,000 and stands as a monument to Albert's efficiency drive in the palaces of England, which had included such seemingly trifling – though actually considerable – economies as ordering that candles be no longer discarded after only one using.

He also began to introduce men of the arts and sciences into court functions. It was one of his regrets that his station in life precluded his attaining distinction as any sort of practising artist. 'It takes the study of a whole life to become that,' he told a dinner partner, 'and we have too many other duties to perform to give the time necessary to any one particular branch of art. Our business is not so much to create, as to learn to appreciate and understand the works of others, and we can never do this till we have realized the difficulties to be over-come.' Following this principle, he acquired enough profi-ciency in several arts to merit genuine compliments from professionals who talked with him.

In science and technology he acquired a grasp of principles and an appreciation of their application to the betterment of modern life akin to that displayed in our own day by Prince Philip, many of whose qualities reflect Albert's. Inspecting a new piece of industrial machinery, he astonished the makers by pointing out a worthwhile improvement which none of them had envisaged. His presidential speech to the British Association for the Advancement of Science, in Edinburgh in 1859, was hailed as brilliant by that large assembly of noted scholars. 'For weeks I have been trying to arrange something popular about science, which is not to be tedious,' he had written to his brother beforehand. This was his brilliance: an ability to see straight through to basic principles and place them in the context of life, rather than let himself be – in an appropriate modern phrase – blinded by science.

In 1847 Prince Albert was elected President of the Royal Society of Arts, whose scope includes the furtherance of man-ufacture and commerce. It was in this capacity that he was visited by a lively-minded civil servant, Henry Cole, with the suggestion that Britain should emulate and outstrip the Paris Exhibition of 1849 with a display that would show the world the superiority of British industry and invention. The Prince reacted with enthusiasm and a royal commission was quickly set up. Leading manufacturers were sounded. To his dismay, both they and the press were similarly against the idea. Big business mistrusted Albert. Had he not, only the year before, chaired a meeting for the Society for Improving the Condition of the Working Classes, and taken the sensational step of castigating capitalists for themselves being the cause of indus-trial unrest and strikes? Now he was asking these same capi-talists to expose their processes and trade secrets for any

foreigner to see and copy! The result would be a flood of cheap
imitations which would ruin Britain's trade, not to mention a
flood of disgusting foreign visitors, whose filthy habits and
loose morals, it was seriously suggested, would deprave and
corrupt London.

Depressed by the response, disturbed by deaths in the family
and by that of 'the strongest bulwark of the Throne', Sir
Robert Peel, and alarmed by an assault upon the Queen by an
ex-officer who had managed to lash her face with his cane,
Albert worked determinedly to prevent his exhibition plan
from being wrecked, or its site forced from Hyde Park, where
he wanted it to be, to some part of the provinces. His determination and that of his well-wishers won through. On 1 May
1851 the Great Exhibition was opened under the vast glass
roof of the Crystal Palace, specially built in Hyde Park to house
it. It was a colossal success, financially as well as in terms of
British prestige. Millions of people visited it throughout that
summer – the Queen and Albert went several times a week.
London was not corrupted; the monarchy was not overthrown,
as had been prophesied: instead £150,000 profit was made
available for the acquisition of seventy acres of Kensington in
which to build and endow the South Kensington Museum
(now the Victoria and Albert) and other institutions, and, in
due course, to pay for scholarships which even today are
helping several hundred outstanding students each year. The
Great Exhibition was the tangible manifestation of Albert's
enthusiasm for his adopted country. The Crystal Palace was
transferred to Sydenham the following year and destroyed by
fire in 1936.

Within three years of this triumph, London mobs were
howling for Albert's arrest and committal for high treason.
Rumour flew that he had been thrown into the Tower of
London, and even the Queen arrested as his accomplice. It
arose from a political storm in which neither of them had taken
part, resulting in the resignation of the Home Secretary, Palmerston, and accusations that this had been forced by Albert
in the interests of Russia and the Coburgs against England.
The vilification lasted for several weeks before news reached
the dismayed Albert and the anxious Victoria at Windsor that
Parliament had officially and firmly cleared his name.

Such anxieties had to take their toll on his health, which had
never been first-class. He was so serious, such a worrier: his
stomach troubled him and rheumatism condemned him to
painful days and successions of sleepless nights. He began to
grumble more in his correspondence and to indulge in self-

pity, which did nothing to improve his condition. Still he kept working on, alive to all sorts of issues. He had much of great value to say and suggest about the conduct of the Crimean War. It was Albert, incidentally, who devised the Victoria Cross for personal valour, in 1855. His counsel was valued in determining a policy for India during the Mutiny. Many amongst the population of Great Britain who had grudged him their respect began to mellow towards him. Some never would. Annoyed by their incivility and by the refusal of some European royalty to grant Albert due precedence as her husband, Victoria urged his creation as Prince Consort. It would have made his way easier if it had been done at their wedding. When at last he received the title, in 1857, he had only four more years to live.

Life gave Albert little kindness for all his good intentions and devotion to duty. His last days were not very happy. Worn by chronic sleeplessness, depressed by continuing criticism of him in *The Times*, which still suspected him of plotting against the country for which he had done so much, worried by the world situation and troubled by family concerns, he fell ill with what seemed to be influenza. It was a fortnight before his doctors realized that he was, in fact, a victim of typhoid fever. He died of it on 14 December 1861.

When one computes Albert's virtues and acknowledges the good deeds he did through them, and the service he gave to an often ungrateful country, one must admire him immensely. His seriousness of mind and high sense of duty, however, made him especially severe in his treatment of his son, the Prince of Wales, later Edward VII, whose frivolous traits accorded not at all with Albert's notions of what an heir-apparent's personality should be, regardless of his genes. Consequently, the young man turned out to be even more pleasure-loving than Albert had feared, and his people, being British, loved him for it. For all his grasp of fundamentals, Albert the Good would never have been able to understand that.

Lord Roberts

(1832–1914)

Of the great soldiers of British history, Lord Roberts of Kandahar is among the most endearing, for his simplicity of character, his friendliness and humility; and when we look at his career it is the man and his achievements which shine forth regardless of whether the wars he fought in were necessary or conducive to the welfare of mankind.

He was born in 1832 at Cawnpore, where his father General Sir Abraham Roberts of Waterford was stationed. Abraham had Irish and French Huguenot blood in his veins, his grandmother's family having settled in Ireland after the Edict of Nantes, and he had married a widow from Tipperary. Besides an adventurous spirit, young Frederick, as he was called, inherited Gallic charm and sparkle. But Cawnpore in those days was not a salubrious spot, and at the age of two the child developed brain-fever which led to blindness in one eye – fortunately for Victorian England not an obstacle at that time to an army career.

Schooling at Eton and Sandhurst was followed by nomination for training at Addiscombe, the military college of the East India Company, and in 1851 Frederick was commissioned in the Bengal Artillery.

Thus opened a career under 'John Company' where promotion was usually slow and went strictly according to seniority. But Lieutenant Roberts was ambitious, soon felt cramped by regimental duties and so cast longing eyes at the staff which consisted in those days of specialized departments which posted qualified officers to units for service in the field. The General Staff had not yet been invented. In the following year the fulfilment of this dream came a little nearer when, on being sent to a field battery at Peshawar, Roberts was made ADC to his father who commanded the Peshawar Division. Here the young man began to show the courage, initiative and organizing ability which were to make him such an outstanding soldier.

After service with his father, Roberts returned to regimental duty with a troop of horse artillery, learning to master unbroken artillery horses with a bunch of tough Irishmen, most of

117

whom could have lifted the small, slim officer with one hand. Then in 1856 he was given a vacancy in the quartermaster general's department where he stayed for twenty-two years, finally becoming head of the branch.

But meanwhile in 1857 the Indian Mutiny had broken out, and Roberts saw the action he longed for in deadly earnest. He had come to India at a time of great change and unrest. The disaster of Chilianwala, when four thousand British troops with their wives and children had been slaughtered in Afghanistan, was only ten years old. Heavy grievances, most of them connected with religion, weighed on the Indians in John Company's Army of Bengal and the issue of cartridges greased with pig and cow fat seemed the final outrage which sparked off the mutiny. Delhi was seized; three thousand British troops were sent to its relief and for three months in the glare of full summer sat on the heights overlooking the city with its milling throng of ninety thousand rebels.

After serving as staff officer to a mobile column which kept order in the Punjab, Roberts was sent to Delhi, to the sunbaked ridge where the would-be besiegers were daily attacked by thousands of mutinous sepoys. After a good sleep on his first night he awoke early – 'scarcely able to believe in my good fortune. I was actually at Delhi and the city was still in possession of the mutineers!'

He was certainly not too late for action. Wounded in a furious *mêlée* outside the gates, he recovered in time to join in the street fighting that came at the end of September; then, when the city was cleared, was sent in charge of an advance-guard to a column hastening by forced marches to the relief of Lucknow and Cawnpore. In savage fighting along the route, two horses were shot under him and near Lucknow he performed a double deed of heroism, saving a loyal native about to be cut down by a mutineer and rescuing a standard from two others about to make off with it. For this action, in which he nearly lost his life, he was recommended for the Victoria Cross.

From 1860 on, Roberts gained a breadth of administrative and fighting experience which no modern British officer could hope to equal. In 1860 and 1861, on the transfer of government from the East India Company to the Crown, he organized the Viceroy's camps on a series of ceremonial tours through north and central India. In 1865 he took part in a campaign on the North-west Frontier against Hindu fanatics. In 1866 he was sent on an expedition to Abyssinia to depose the mad king Theodore who had been maltreating Europeans. 1871 saw him organizing elephant and coolie transport through jungle and mountainous country in the Lushai region between Bengal and Burma where the natives had become a nuisance by raiding tea plantations; in 1874 he was put in charge of famine relief in Bihar and in the following year of the arrangements for the mammoth Imperial Assembly at Delhi, including a tented camp for 20,000 troops, at which Queen Victoria was proclaimed Empress of India.

But so far his fame was confined to India. Now he stepped on to a wider stage. Afghanistan, after several years of difficult relations with the Indian government, had become a potential menace to the North-west Frontier after Russian expansionism, blocked in the Near East at the Congress of Berlin, had turned to the Far East. To counter Russian influence, overtures were made to the Amir of Afghanistan by the British who wanted to send a mission to Kabul. But the mission was turned back at the frontier. Therefore, in order to soften the Amir or bring about his abdication, it was thought necessary to subdue the eastern region of the country. A three-pronged expedition was planned, of which one column of two infantry brigades was put under the command of Roberts.

His first thought was to make good many defects he had noticed on previous expeditions. *His* troops set off fully equipped (most unusual for those days); they were properly fed; plenty of blankets were brought for them against the cold nights; the transport mules were not overloaded; elephants were obtained for the mountain batteries, and the medical arrangements were excellent.

After some days the enemy, well armed and resourceful tribesmen, were found ensconced on a high pass carrying the road to the capital of Kabul. The position was extremely strong and Roberts rejected a frontal attack as too risky. Instead, a flank attack was carried out which found its way round to the back of the pass while a minor assault was made on the front. There were dangerous moments; at times a lesser man would have ordered a withdrawal. But Roberts hung on till the pass was cleared and one fact was established, to be consistently borne out by his later career: here was a buoyant, brave, coolly calculating commander.

The Amir abdicated. A treaty was made providing for a permanent British Resident in Kabul and the Field Force began slowly to withdraw.

Two months later, in September 1879, the Resident, Sir Louis Gavagnari, and his escort of seventy-five soldiers were besieged and murdered to a man in Kabul. An augmented

Field Force was then ordered to about-turn and again under Roberts fought its way through to Kabul. The city was occupied and many Afghans were hanged. Then a dangerous situation arose. Some reinforcements had reached Roberts, but now with winter coming on few more could be expected and hardly any supplies. In the hills 100,000 tribesmen were gathering, aflame with religious and patriotic zeal, thirsty for plunder. Roberts tried to seize a strategic height, was repulsed and, with the enemy now flowing down towards the city, was forced to withdraw to a walled cantonment where the bulk of his troops were stationed. Having put the place in a state of defence – without showing, wrote an eye-witness, 'a shadow of despondency' – Roberts with 5,000 men awaited the onslaught. It lasted for two days – an inferno of whirling arms and scimitars, of dust, heat and concentrated volleys from the walls – till, judging his moment, Roberts put in a flank attack with cavalry and the mob wavered and finally fled.

But another trial was in store, the most famous of all feats performed by 'Bobs' and his men. In the following year a puppet ruler was put on the throne of Afghanistan. In the southern provinces a rival claimant gathered support and advanced with large numbers on Kandahar. A British force sent to stop him was heavily defeated and the survivors, only 2,500 men, withdrew as best they could to the town which was then isolated like a small island in a sea of hostile tribesmen. From Kabul, with 10,000 men, Roberts was sent to its relief.

It was August and the height of summer. Along parched and sweltering valleys, high in the mountains, the column trudged and sweated by day. At night the temperature dropped to freezing point. There were no detailed maps; the column had to find its own route by the compass; no one knew whether Kandahar still held out, and at any moment the triumphant enemy might come surging over the horizon. It was a severe test of morale, and the morale was saved by Roberts. Though sick himself, he watched over the men's comfort, and each night rode back to the end of the column, urging on stragglers by telling them camp was near. The simple truth is that Roberts loved his soldiers. They knew it, and responded.

Anxiously the people at home waited for news, then, having been lost to the world, the column was reported to have reached Kandahar after covering 320 miles in twenty-one days. That night, of the entire force, only sixty-eight had to be admitted to hospital. Twenty-four hours later, having reconnoitred enemy positions on a ridge near the town, Roberts delivered a heavy flank attack and won a complete victory. For this campaign he was made a baronet, given the GCB and received the thanks of both Houses of Parliament.

From then on he was recognized as the leading soldier of the age and high appointments followed: C.-in-C. Madras Presidency Army and, from 1885 to 1892, Commander-in-Chief, India. In these positions he did much to improve the lot of the serving soldier and to raise the standard of fighting efficiency, being one of the first to foresee the need for new training methods to suit the introduction of modern weapons.

Back in England after forty-one years of service in India, the only employment that could be found for him in the following years was as Commander-in-Chief, Ireland. Then, in October 1899, the Boer War broke out and one thing soon became clear: Britannia did not rule the South African veldt. The Boers invaded Natal. Mafeking, Ladysmith and Kimberley were besieged and the British commander, Sir Redvers Buller, committed the error of splitting his forces and trying to deal with the enemy piecemeal. A series of disasters followed - at Colenso in Natal, at the Modder River south of Kimberley, at Stormberg in Cape Colony - and Britain was plunged into Black Week, made blacker still by the universal, nagging doubt: was the whole edifice of Victorian power somehow rotten at the core?

In this crisis Roberts sent a telegram to the cabinet condemning the strategy in South Africa, and it crossed with one appointing him commander-in-chief. With Kitchener as his chief-of-staff he reached the scene of battle in January 1900, a master-plan already in his mind. The besieged garrisons, he saw, were not the primary problem, which was to seize the Boer capitals of Bloemfontein (Orange Free State) and Pretoria (the Transvaal). For this, the British forces must be concentrated and made as mobile as possible by the creation of mounted infantry and a large pool of animal transport.

In the incredibly short space of three weeks the forces were reorganized and moving forward with fresh heart now that the legendary 'Bobs' was in charge. The Boers tried to bar his passage at Paardeberg, but were trapped in their encampment there and 4,000 were forced to surrender. Meanwhile Kimberley was relieved in a wide outflanking movement by a mounted column and in mid-March Roberts entered Bloemfontein.

From Bloemfontein to Pretoria is three hundred miles as the crow flies. Roberts was determined to press on as fast as he could, but a pause was essential to fetch supplies, and it was 1 May before he was ready to move on again with 70,000 men. Within a month, after fighting all the way, Johannesburg was occupied and on 5 June Pretoria fell and President Kruger fled the country.

This was thought to be the end of the Boer War, and in fact was in the sense that from now on the Boers never had a chance of outright victory. So the sixty-eight-year-old veteran was recalled and Kitchener took over command.

For the next fourteen years, as commander-in-chief of the army at home – till the post was abolished – and as the greatest living military expert, Roberts did all he could to ensure that training and reorganization were shaped for maximum efficiency in the field. The new Territorials had all his support; a kind of Home Guard against invasion hovered before his mind and he stumped the country to rouse people to the need.

In November 1914, when he was eighty-two, he went over to France to visit troops of the newly arrived Indian Division. Some were already wounded and in a hospital ship. Dark faces peered from white pillows at the slight, khaki-clad figure. Suddenly he was recognized. In a babel of tongues the word was passed round: 'It is he!' 'Every man,' wrote an eye-witness, 'spoke a benediction. Many wept tears of joy. A single thought seemed to animate them and they voiced it in many tongues: "Ah! Now we shall smite the Germans exceedingly. We shall fight even as tigers for King George. The great Sahib has come to lead us in the field. Praised be his exalted name!"'

Roberts said he was too old.

'No, sahib,' cried one man. 'The body may be old, but the heart is young.'

The old man was deeply moved.

Three days later, visiting more troops in pouring rain, he caught a chill which developed into pneumonia and that evening, to the thunder of the guns from Ypres, he died.

Joseph Chamberlain

(1836–1914)

To millions he was always 'Joe'. For thirty years he rode the storms of politics. He might have succeeded Gladstone as Prime Minister in a Liberal government; he might, not so long after, have headed a Unionist administration. He did neither, but through him each of the two great parties in turn suffered the most grievous shipwreck. Never for long did the spotlight of the most penetrating publicity deviate from the jauntily defiant figure, the smooth, clear-cut features, the inevitable monocle on its cord, the equally inevitable orchid in the lapel of his black velvet coat.

Joseph Chamberlain was born on 8 July 1836, at 3 Camberwell Grove in south London. His father was a boot-and-shoe manufacturer with a prosperous business in Milk Street, Cheapside, which had been in the family for several generations. The Chamberlains, it should be noted, were Nonconformists, staunch adherents of the Unitarian persuasion; and thus from his earliest days the future statesman knew what it was like to be in a minority for conscience's sake.

In 1845 the Chamberlains moved to Highbury Place, Islington, on the other side of London, and for four years Joseph attended a school kept by Rev. Arthur Johnson, to whom in after life he paid tribute as an 'excellent teacher and one to whom I owe much'. When he was fourteen, Joseph was sent to University College School in Gower Street, the most highly regarded of the schools open to the sons of Nonconformist parents. Here he remained for a little more than two years, not particularly distinguished academically but (as one of his intimate friends expressed it), revealing 'a good deal of individuality and a strong will ...'.

At sixteen he left school for good, and spent the next couple of years at a desk in his father's office. Then an uncle of his – John Sutton Nettlefold, his mother's brother – who had a business manufacturing screws by hand in Birmingham, acquired the English rights of an American process for making them by machinery and, since a good part of his capital had been put up by Joseph's father, offered to take the eighteen-year-old youth into eventual partnership. So in 1854 Joseph

Chamberlain moved to Birmingham, the city with which his name was to be ever afterwards indissolubly associated.

For the next twenty years he flung himself with tremendous zest into business activity and, as Winston Churchill put it in his intimate study of Chamberlain in *Great Contemporaries*, 'his business success was as sharp, hard and bright as the screws it made'. With characteristic thoroughness he mastered every detail of the manufacturing process, working with his hands as well as his brain. He drove himself hard and knew how to get the last ounce of effort out of his work people. But he never made the mistake of forgetting that the men at the bench – the women too, the youths and girls – were human beings. He mixed with them on friendly terms. He showed a real interest in their domestic problems, their housing, the education of their children. He had his reward. The dour craftsmen of the Black Country would have sneered and snarled at 'charity', but they responded to his on-the-level overtures with a stolid and undeviating devotion.

By 1874 Joseph Chamberlain was an acknowledged captain of industry. His firm was flourishing – the firm which was the ancestor of the vast Guest Keen and Nettlefold complex of today. He had made a fortune, no less than £120,000. It was enough. 'He had set himself free by his own exertions,' to quote Churchill again. 'Henceforth he was clad in a complete suit of armoured independence.' Money-making interested him no more. What *did* interest him was power.

Nominally he was a Liberal, but he never had much time for Gladstone. He was a radical, fierce in his hostility to everything and everybody smacking of pomp and privilege. The aristocracy, the landed gentry, London society, the established church, vested interests of whatever kind, he whipped them with his scorn, held them up to contumely and hatred. Not even the crown was exempt.

Birmingham began to be proud of him. In 1869 he was elected a city councillor and only four years later mayor; he was re-elected in 1874 and 1875. In this capacity he performed magnificently. What later came to be known as 'gas-and-water socialism' was pioneered by Chamberlain with the most conspicuous ability and success. For generations Birmingham had been one of the most prosperous towns in the country – and also one of the dirtiest, and all that that means in sickness and misery. In the three years of his mayoralty Chamberlain cleaned the place up. A cheap and efficient supply of gas, a pure and plentiful supply of water in place of sewage-infested wells, a vast number of nasty nuisances abated, foodstuffs inspected, a health service inaugurated, insanitary dwellings blacklisted and replaced by healthy homes, and a hugh improvement scheme, in course of which the splendid Corporation Street was created in what had been one of the most disgraceful rookeries of poverty and crime – these were among the principal achievements of the Chamberlain revolution. Until the end of his days he held Birmingham in the hollow of his hand. In 1876 he was elected one of Birmingham's two MPs as the colleague of the veteran John Bright, and notwithstanding the chops and changes of his political allegiance he was returned at every subsequent election.

Chamberlain was forty when he entered the House of Commons, rather late to begin a parliamentary career. He took his seat among the Liberal supporters of Mr Gladstone, for whom he never had a very high regard, feeling (rightly enough) that the 'Grand Old Man' had no real sympathy for the social reforms on which Chamberlain had set his heart. Gladstone returned his dislike, but all the same he felt that he could not exclude him from the government which he was called upon to form in 1880. Chamberlain was appointed president of the Board of Trade with a seat in the cabinet, and as such he introduced some beneficial measures. In Gladstone's third administration, in 1886, Chamberlain was president of the Local Government Board, but he held it only a month, resigning in consequence of Gladstone's sudden conversion to home rule for Ireland. Just why Chamberlain took this momentous step has been much debated, he had no Irish connections and had not displayed any special interest in Irish affairs. Whatever the reason, Chamberlain left his party and was largely responsible for its crushing defeat that ensued.

Bitterly reviled by the Gladstonian Liberals for his desertion, Chamberlain was henceforth among the most prominent of the 'Liberal Unionists' who gave the Conservative Lord Salisbury their general support. In the House of Commons his speeches aroused the fiercest passions, on the one side and the other, and in the country at large he was recognized as one of the foremost politicians of the time. No doubt if he had wished it he could have had some prominent place, but he preferred for the present to maintain his independence. It has been surmised that he thought that Gladstone could not continue much longer in active politics, and that when he eventually retired the Liberal party might be reunited under Chamberlain's leadership. In 1887, however, he did accept Salisbury's invitation to go to America as Britain's representative in a dispute over fishing rights between Canada and US.

Some years passed, and still Gladstone showed no signs of an early retirement. At length when his fourth administration foundered in 1894 he made way for his successor, and the choice fell not on Chamberlain but on Lord Rosebery. Chamberlain cannot have been greatly disappointed, if at all. The Liberal party that he had done so much to smash was still in pieces, and he, for his part, was getting along very nicely with his Conservative allies. When Lord Salisbury formed a new government in 1895 he offered Chamberlain a post, and now Chamberlain broke with his Liberal past and signified his acceptance. He was appointed Colonial Secretary, much to many people's surprise, since the job was not very highly regarded. But 'Radical Joe', thanks in some measure to his experience in Canada, had been transformed into 'Joe the Imperialist'.

Chamberlain was at the Colonial Office for eight years, and his term of office was remarkable for the imaginative vigour with which he pushed the idea and ideal of imperial unity. He had come to a passionate belief in the immense potentialities of the British Empire, and the energies that had transformed the administration of a great provincial city were now directed to a field of world-wide expanse and importance.

Very shortly after he had taken office there came the first rumblings of trouble in South Africa. The degree of his responsibility for the war that broke out in 1899 between Britain and the Boer Republics remains one of the great question-marks in the history of the time, but it is probably safe to assume that he did not over-exert himself to prevent it. When President Kruger of the Transvaal at length appealed to the 'God of Battles', Chamberlain rejoined that 'with all reverence and gravity we accept the appeal, believing that we have our quarrel just'.

War in South Africa meant war in the House of Commons, and for long the Colonial Secretary was exposed to a tremendous barrage of venomous intensity. On the whole he seemed to enjoy the combat, but there were occasions when he complained, not unjustly, of being exposed to a 'dreary flow of petty malignity'. Outside the House it was a different story. The war was genuinely popular with all classes, and Chamberlain's prestige was correspondingly enhanced. When the war had been brought to a victorious conclusion, he made a tour of South Africa which developed into something like a royal procession, but it is significant that he exerted himself to obtain the trust and friendship of the defeated.

Back in England, Chamberlain looked round for ways and

means of strengthening the imperial connection. Sentiment was not enough (he concluded) to hold the far-flung empire together. The colonies and dependencies must be much more closely linked with the 'mother country', and (businessman as he was) he looked to trade and commerce to provide the essential link. In a speech at Birmingham on 15 May 1903 he propounded his scheme of 'tariff reform', proposing the imposition of customs duties on a large variety of imported goods coupled with the grant of preference for colonial products. In this way (he argued) British manufacturers would be assured of a large and rapidly growing market in the colonies, while colonial producers would have a prosperous future as suppliers of the basic raw materials.

This bold advocacy of a return to a system of protection – which Peel had abandoned in 1846 and Disraeli had admitted was 'dead and damned' – had a staggering impact on public opinion. The Liberals were delighted, seeing in the defence of free trade a certain election-winner; the Conservatives and Unionists were deeply divided – in the country, in Parliament, and in the cabinet itself. Balfour, the Conservative Prime Minister, strove dextrously to maintain his position on the fence, but some of his colleagues were not capable of his philosophical detachment. Almost simultaneously, but without knowing what the other side was up to, three free trade ministers and Chamberlain sent in their resignations.

Chamberlain seemed to have recaptured the ardour and energy of youth. He founded a Tariff Reform League, and in a nation-wide platform campaign urged his great audiences to be ready to make some small and temporary economic sacrifices in order to achieve a supremely valuable political ideal. At length Balfour resigned, and at the general election fought in the opening weeks of 1906 the Conservative–Unionist party were almost annihilated. Balfour himself was among the defeated, but Birmingham remained loyal. Joseph Chamberlain and his son Austen were among the few Unionist leaders who survived the massacre.

For the second time Chamberlain had brought ruin to the party he had served. What did the future hold for him? Was there at least a possibility that in the new parliament he might win the leadership of the remnant, with the premiership not altogether out of the question? After all, Gladstone had formed his last government when he was well over eighty ... But Chamberlain's fighting days were almost over.

On 7 July 1906 his seventieth birthday was celebrated with great enthusiasm in Birmingham, and he and his wife drove through eighteen miles of cheering people. On the Monday he addressed a vast audience in Bingley Hall. 'The union of the Empire,' he declared, 'must be preceded and accompanied by a better understanding, by a closer sympathy. To secure that is the highest object of statesmanship now at the beginning of the twentieth century, and if these were the last words that I were permitted to utter to you, I would rejoice to utter them in your presence and with your approval ...'

Two days later Chamberlain had a paralytic stroke, which, while leaving his mental powers almost intact, reduced him to a physical wreck. For eight years he lingered on, still endeavouring to direct from his couch in a darkened room at Highbury, his Birmingham home, the activities of the great campaign he had launched. He remained MP for West Birmingham, and in 1910 even managed to put in an appearance at the opening of the new House; he was unable to sign the book, however, but touched the pen which his son Austen held out to him.

Early in July 1914 he had another stroke. A few hours before his end his wife heard him delivering a speech (while still fast asleep) in reply to one of Asquith's attacks on his tariff reform proposals. On the evening of 2 July 1914 he passed away peacefully. A grave in Westminster Abbey was offered, but his family decided that he should be laid to rest in the city which he had loved, and had loved him, for so many years.

Joseph Chamberlain was three times married. In 1861 he married Miss Harriet Kenrick; she died two years later, leaving two children – a daughter and a son, Joseph Austen, who had a distinguished political career in course of which he, like his father, narrowly missed the premiership. In 1869 Chamberlain married Miss Florence Kenrick, a cousin of his first wife; of this marriage four children were born – three daughters and a son Arthur Neville, who was Prime Minister from 1937 to 1940. Chamberlain's third marriage was to a young American lady, Miss Mary Endicott, who survived him many years.

Thomas Jefferson, third
President of the USA

Andrew Jackson, strong,
vigorous, contradictory

Talleyrand – statesman, wit
and rake

Napoleon in his study

Metternich, brilliant
diplomat and reactionary
statesman

Bismarck, the Iron Chancellor

Prince Albert, Queen
Victoria's consort

Charles Stewart Parnell

(1846–91)

A new force was projected into British political life on the day in 1875 when Charles Stewart Parnell first took his place in the House of Commons as the member for Meath. Combining in about equal measure elements of passion, malice, wit and mischief, it bedevilled the parliamentary scene with the pathos, the savagery and the comedy of what was commonly defined as the 'Irish problem'.

The arrival of Parnell at Westminster demonstrated a fact of history that historians have seldom examined. This is the influence of the English spirit of liberty on Irish affairs and the leadership and inspiration that it provided for a cause that otherwise might have languished for lack of both. For it was true that among the most active promoters of discord in Ireland were men and women who were not of Irish birth or heredity. As St John Ervine, the Ulster dramatist and critic, recorded in his biography of Parnell:

> Many of the leaders of the Sinn Fein rising in 1916 were of English origin, while the more extreme of their successors, those who seceded from the Free State to the Irregular or Republican section of Sinn Fein, were almost all English in origin or English in themselves.

The Parnells had no Irish genes: they were an English family of ancient line adorned with a peerage, that of Congleton in Cheshire. For that matter, most of the outstanding personalities of Ireland's history in modern times have been Anglo-Irish. In that dominating array, which included Swift, Burke, Goldsmith, Sheridan, Wilde, Synge, Shaw and Yeats, by no means the least remarkable was Parnell.

Charles Stewart Parnell was born at Avondale, Co. Wicklow, on 27 June 1846, the son of John Henry Parnell and his American wife Delia Tudor (née Stewart). From childhood he had been impregnated with the prejudice of his American mother, whose anti-English sentiment was often so violent as to suggest madness. Nor was hers the only example of mental imbalance in the family. Several of the Parnells were victims of melancholia in varying degrees of acuteness. One of them

committed suicide. Another was imbecilic, while others were
more than ordinarily eccentric in their behaviour. Parnell himself was a lifelong neurasthenic. His 'extreme nervousness' was
observed as an aspect of his nature from childhood days. One
of his several biographers wrote that he 'terribly felt the burden
of his tormented nerves'.

He was haunted by the spectre of death and a fear of insanity. The woman for whom he finally sacrificed his reputation
and career, Mrs O'Shea, said that 'he would spring up panic-
stricken out of deep sleep, and, without fully waking, try to
beat off the imaginary foe that had pressed upon him'. He
believed in astrology, and had a horror of October, for him a
month of sinister import. It was one of his several superstitious
fears. Passing a churchyard, he was apt to avert his gaze from
it, though he was a member of the Church of England.

At Cambridge, while he was at the university, a shattering
experience helped to confirm him in his mistrust of life, if not
his disgust with it, that seems to have been one of his basic
drives. He 'fell for' a girl of sixteen. She was the daughter of a
fruit farmer who owned apple orchards bordering the River
Cam. Meeting her secretly, he seduced her, fathered her child,
then deserted her. Her consequent suicide haunted him long
after. He would wake in the night shrieking and moaning that
her ghost was standing at the foot of his bed.

Parnell stood for Parliament as a home rule candidate and
was elected at Meath in the spring of 1875. He was so dazed at
the close of his speech of thanks to the voters that the chairman
had to lead him off the platform. Yet within a few years he was
accepted as the political master of Ireland, his leadership also
making him a dominating figure in the House of Commons.
His policy as a parliamentarian was to embarrass the government by obstructive practices put into operation at every opportunity. As soon as a bill was brought in, regardless of its
subject Parnell and his supporters proposed one amendment
after another, all requiring ample discussion. Night after night
members who had never known such proceedings in the House
before were compelled to tramp the corridors and division
lobbies until four or five o'clock in the morning. 'Mr Parnell
unites in his own person all the childish unreasonableness, all
the ill-regulated suspicion, and all the childish credulity of the
Irish peasant, without any of the humour, the courtliness, or
dash of the Irish gentleman.' So wrote Sir Henry Lucy, the
best-known parliamentary journalist of the day. 'He is always
at a white heat of rage, and makes, with savage earnestness,
fancifully ridiculous statements, such as you may hear from

your partner in a quadrille, if you have the good fortune to be a guest at the annual ball at Colney Hatch.'

Endorsing the gospel of the militant Land League, which demanded the destruction of English landlordism in Ireland, Parnell was made its president. In that capacity, he went with John Dillon, MP, on a fund-raising tour of the United States. Stirring up local Irish sentiment from many platforms, together they travelled 16,000 miles, spoke in sixty-two cities and collected £40,000 for the starving poor of Ireland.

In the general election of 1880 Parnell was returned as a member for Cork. Shortly afterwards he was appointed leader of the Irish party in the House of Commons. He was thirty-four. One of his new colleagues in Parliament was Captain William Henry O'Shea. He was the son of a Dublin solicitor who had become wealthy by buying up the properties of impoverished landowners, of whom there were not a few in Ireland in those bitter years. Incurring heavy debts and selling his army commission, young O'Shea married Katherine Wood, the thirteenth child of an Essex parson who was also a baronet. Before his advent into politics, O'Shea and his wife lived for some time in straitened circumstances, involving bankruptcy, in Brighton and London. Parnell was introduced to Mrs O'Shea in Dublin on the occasion of his election as leader of the Irish party. Their meeting was like a move on the chessboard of fate.

The assassination of Lord Mountmorres at Clonbar in the autumn of 1880 evoked from Parnell a denunciation of acts of violence committed for political ends. 'My brother, I know,' wrote John Howard Parnell, the eldest son of the family, 'always set his face strongly against outrage of any kind. The idea of cowardly attacks on individuals, and above all the maiming of animals, repelled him to the last degree.' In 1881 2,589 cases of crime were reported from the Irish countryside, taking the form of threatening letters, cattle killing and maiming, the unlawful use of firearms, and murder. In the same period, there were 10,457 evictions from the land. Before the year was out, Parnell and five other members of Parliament, along with nine activists of the Land League, were arrested and sent to Kilmainham gaol. None of them was tried and sentenced; all were detained at Her Majesty's pleasure as enemies of the state.

A storm of cheering greeted Mr Gladstone's announcement that detentive measures had been taken against the Irish dissidents. He made it at a Guildhall banquet that marked the occasion of his receiving the freedom of the City of London.

'Parnell's arrest,' wrote a well-known editor, 'was hailed almost as though it had been the news of a signal victory gained by England over a hated and formidable enemy.'

There was not much hardship for Parnell in his brief prison sojourn. Far more troubling to his peace of mind was the prospect of a very different category of confinement. He had been a frequent visitor at the O'Sheas' house at Eltham, Kent, while O'Shea himself was away on business in Spain. Now Mrs O'Shea was five months pregnant by him. It was not a matter of passing infatuation. They were profoundly attracted to one another. What tarnished the relationship was the deception practised on the husband, who was skilfully deluded into believing that the child was his. The warranty for that statement comes from the book that Kitty O'Shea subsequently wrote about her life with Parnell.

He was approaching the zenith of his political career. The high esteem that it had gained him among the Irish filled him with the conviction that, alone among men, he was destined to achieve home rule for them. That final triumph might be snatched from him by scandal was a risk that caused him deep anxiety. It was not allayed by the anguished letters smuggled to him in prison from Mrs O'Shea. Largely on Gladstone's initiative, he was released from Kilmainham after seven months, during which time the O'Shea child was born and died. There were resignations from the government, including that of the Chief Secretary for Ireland, W.E. Forster, the Quaker. Those events focused the limelight still more intensively on Parnell. 'If England cannot govern the honourable member for Cork,' said Forster, 'then let us acknowledge that he is the greatest power in all Ireland today.'

His imprisonment had certainly done nothing to modify Irish tensions. Extreme poverty and near starvation were rampant. The campaign of evictions mounted. Lawlessness was rife in many parts of the country, and intimidation ran it close. Arbitrary arrest and detention was obviously no cure for any of those evils. Their gravity was demonstrated with ruthless savagery on 6 May 1882 when Lord Frederick Cavendish and Thomas Henry Burke, the permanent under-secretary for Irish affairs, were struck down while walking together in Phoenix Park. Their assailants were members of a ruffianly group calling themselves the Invincibles, who stabbed them from behind and then cut their throats as they lay helpless on the grass. Murder more foul had rarely been done even in the Ireland of that desperate period.

Parnell was at Blackheath station, waiting for a London

Bridge train, when he read the news. Mrs O'Shea was with him. 'His face was ashen,' she afterwards recalled, 'and he stared, frowning heavily before him, unconsciously crushing the hand I had slipped into his until the rings I wore cut and bruised my fingers.' His brother John said that 'the blow was a terrible one for Charley. He was completely unnerved. For years after, this horrible event preyed on his generous and sensitive nature.'

He had been attacked in the House of Commons as an instigator of the outrage. Parnell replied not from personal inclination but under pressure from his political colleagues. In effect, he expressed indifference to the charges, insisting that an English parliament had no right to sit in judgement on him or his actions. Scorned in the House of Commons, his derisive response produced a new wave of approbation, and more fervent demonstrations of loyalty, from his followers in Ireland and the United States. His words were addressed to them rather than to the benches and galleries at Westminster. It was part of a strategy which even his enemies thought was endowed with the subtlety of genius.

Pursuing his constructive policy, Gladstone introduced the Home Rule Bill of 1886. It caused a political rumpus: schism in the Liberal Party, the foundation of the Unionist Party, the throwing out of the bill, and a general election that in its turn threw out Gladstonian Liberalism. It was also the end of the hopes of the parliamentary Irish group, who could not prevail against the overwhelming Conservative and Unionist majority.

Parnell was beginning to weary of the struggle. Like Ireland herself, he was in need of rest and peace and recuperation. Just then, *The Times* published a series of articles, 'Parnellism and Crime'. Incriminating letters accompanying them were denounced by Parnell as forgeries. As a result, a judicial commission was authorized to investigate the allegations. Its report completely vindicated Parnell. The perpetrator of the letters committed suicide. The affair earned Parnell as much esteem among his enemies as among his friends. He was invited to dinner-tables at which he had never sat before. He stayed with Gladstone at Hawarden, making a good impression on the company. While he was there, unknown to him, Captain O'Shea was seeing solicitors about divorcing his wife. He named Parnell as the co-respondent.

On the day after the divorce decree had been pronounced in the courts, the National League, meeting in Dublin under the chairmanship of John Redmond, MP, reaffirmed its loyalty to Parnell, who was represented at the meeting by Tim Healy,

MP, as 'less a man than an institution'. There could be no question, he declared, of deserting 'the great chief who had led us so far forward'.

Although the Parnell-O'Shea liaison was common knowledge in political circles both in Dublin and London, public opinion reacted unfavourably when the newspapers reported the divorce, in which Captain O'Shea was given custody of the children. That hostility was crystallized in the attitude of the National Liberal Federation, whose Nonconformist leadership decided that it must withdraw its support from the Irish party. As a sequel, Gladstone issued a letter to the press stating that he would feel bound to resign the leadership of the Liberal Party if Parnell persisted in remaining as head of the Irish group.

Parnell responded, some thought unwisely, by composing a long manifesto addressed to the people of Ireland. T.P. O'Connor, MP, thought that it threw 'a very curious light on Mr Parnell's mind, that he should have thought that such a manifesto was likely to bring intelligent, or generous, or honourable men round to his views ...'. As a result, a strong secessionist movement bereft him of many of his most influential followers. A by-election at Kilkenny showed that at last the tide was turning against him. Exerting all his powers of support and persuasion, he failed to make the requisite impression. His candidate was heavily defeated. Significantly, in only one district was the parish priest on his side.

Like a drowning man, he fought desperately to breast the oncoming waves. More by-elections followed, and again his candidates were beaten. In June 1891 he married Mrs O'Shea, by whom he had had two more children. The bishops and priests were displeased, some became actively hostile towards him. At Kilkenny mud, stones and bags of lime were thrown at him. A lime bag burst in his face. For several days after he was beset by excruciating pain in his eyes.

A Dublin doctor, examining him, found symptoms of a rheumatic origin and diagnosed general debility. Ignoring the doctor's advice, he travelled to England. 'I shall be all right,' he said. 'I shall be back.' He died in a high fever a week later, on 6 October 1891.

They took him back to Ireland. Thirty thousand people moved past his coffin as he lay in state. The funeral procession went on its way to Glasnevin in a heavy downpour. As a local historian later recalled, 'no one noticed the rain'.

Sergei Witte

(1849-1915)

In the year 1849 Sergei Yulieyevich Witte, destined to become one of Russia's leading statesmen under the last of the Tsars, was born in the city of Tiflis where his father was a member of the viceregal Council of the Caucasus. This sounded a grand position but the salary it carried was a modest one and the Witte family was brought up to look twice at every rouble. Early in his school days young Sergei developed a habit which irked his companions: instead of joining in their noisy games he preferred to sit on a bench in the playground studying – of all things – a timetable! Since Russia in general and its south-western railway in particular were noted for the inadequacy of their train services the child knew the manual off by heart at six years old and amused himself by inventing more and more trains which would steam across the steppes in some mythical future.

The Witte family was of Dutch extraction, one of their ancestors having come to Russia for either diplomatic or business reasons. Whatever his purpose, this visitor had found favour with the ruler of the day and had been made a count. Neither he nor his descendants had ever returned to Holland but had settled in Russia and married Russian women, with the result that even as a boy Sergei was an ardent Slavophil. Later, while studying at Odessa University, he came under the influence of Katkov, an eloquent leader of the Slav movement, and after graduating became a reporter on a new paper Katkov was starting. The venture failed and at the age of twenty-five Sergei was out of a job, a state of affairs which Count Witte told his volatile son could not be tolerated for a moment. 'Why don't you join the Imperial State Railways?' he demanded, remembering the childish obsession with timetables. Sergei stared at his father. 'That,' he said slowly, 'is a very good idea.'

Within a week he was an assistant booking-clerk at Odessa station. Underneath all his romantic love for Russia Sergei Witte remained, though he did not yet realize it, a cautious Dutchman with a tidy mind. He was genuinely horrified by the waste of time, energy and paper in the booking-office, where his superior was a fussy, ineffectual little man whom he was careful not to offend. Instead he worked unobtrusively in the background, staying on in the evenings long after his querulous colleague had gone home, and by the end of 1876 he had everything under control.

But in 1876 war broke out between Russia and Turkey, and as all troops and supplies for the former were routed through Odessa the volume of work mounted daily. The booking-clerk panicked and collapsed with a nervous breakdown, assistants drafted in from other stations had no idea what they were supposed to do and in desperation the railway directors put Sergei Witte in charge of the office. His efficiency astonished them. Cool and unruffled, he issued orders, interviewed senior officers and kept things running so smoothly that not once throughout two years of warfare was the Russian army kept waiting for anything. It was a remarkable achievement for a young man with little training and it was especially noted by Vishnegradski, Russia's Minister of Finance, who spent much of the war in Odessa. Witte was too good to waste, so the minister had him appointed general traffic manager of the south-western railway, the headquarters of which were in Tiflis. At the age of twenty-nine, after years of pinching and scraping, Sergei was earning an income considerably in excess of his father's.

He also had a railway to run which was far more important, for he was convinced that if Russia only possessed adequate and modern railway communications she could become a great industrial power. Each day on the way to his office he passed through Tiflis market place, that meeting ground of east and west where one stall-owner was a tall Uzbek in robes and skull-cap, the next a wiry, slit-eyed Tartar, the third a Kalmuk with smooth, flat Mongol cheekbones. The transport was as varied as the people: there were superb Caucasian horses and shaggy ponies from the Chinese border, teams of bullocks drawing primitive wagons and goats pulling little carts. Witte looked at them all, thinking of the vast untapped wealth in the places they came from and visualizing the day when it would be brought by rail to Europe.

He saw his dreams come true. On the urging of Vishnegradski an imperial commission was set up in 1880 to study methods for modernizing the railways all over Russia, and Witte was one of its members. He lost no time in putting forward his idea of building a trans-Siberian railway which would not only open up Russia's immense Asiatic resources but bring Moscow within eight days of the Pacific. His fellow members were unanimous in their disapproval. What proof had he that this

fantastic wealth existed? Where was the money for such a
project to come from? Witte produced detailed plans for the
railroad, reports from eminent agriculturists and mining engineers, and schemes for inviting foreign investors, but the commissioners continued to shake their heads.

Fortunately for Witte, Vishnegradski believed in him wholeheartedly and made him controller of the railroad section of
the Finance Ministry, then told him frankly that if he could
conquer the opposition of the two most powerful men in
Russia, Konstantin Pobedonostsev and Vyacheslav Plehve,
money for the trans-Siberian plan would be found. Pobedonostsev was a reactionary diehard and Tsar Alexander III's
closest adviser, who informed Witte scornfully that 'liberty of
any kind is a menace that breeds like a disease and leads to
chaos'. Plehve had been director of the State Police when he
had hunted down the assassins of Alexander II and was now
Minister of the Interior, so he considered that in seeking to
implement his mad notions, Witte was intruding on his
preserves. Both were determined to oust this upstart and they
missed no opportunity to put obstacles in his way.

But Witte was a fighter. Having studied his enemies coolly
he proceeded to play them in such adroit fashion that they
were bewildered. He dropped the subject of the trans-Siberian
and concentrated his energies on augmenting and speeding up
train services between the Volga, the Donetz coal basin and
the Ukraine, and between Baku, Tiflis and the Polish frontier.
Results were swift and astonishing. Many thousands of
peasants in search of higher wages and better living conditions
flocked to the Donetz mines and coal production doubled
within a year. More peasants went to work in the various new
industries which the improved rail services had encouraged to
start in different towns. Exports rose steeply as increasing
numbers of trucks were loaded in Baku sidings with all kinds
of Asiatic Russian produce from lemons to Bokhara rugs.

Naturally, the members of the State Council were delighted.
Perhaps after all there was something in this trans-Siberian
idea...? and at exactly the right moment Vishnegradski put the
proposition to the Council. Only two members, Pobedonostsev
and Plehve, voted against the motion.

The building of the trans-Siberian railway, the largest undertaking of its kind ever attempted, began in 1891. Witte was
made Minister of Communications so that he could keep close
watch over the work which proceeded surprisingly smoothly.
Indeed, by the time he succeeded Vishnegradski at the Finance
Ministry two years later, Russia was already benefiting from it

and every east-bound train on the finished section was filled
with passengers anxious to help develop the new lands.

Now Witte turned his attention to Russia's financial problems, some of which had hitherto been regarded as insoluble.
He was a realist. In his opinion Russia could never take her
proper place in the world until she shook herself free from her
medieval way of life. The peasants must stop picking at the soil
with antiquated tools and be trained in modern methods of
agriculture. The landowners must pay decent wages and keep
their workers' homes in good repair. New industries must be
started and the people encouraged to join them. The lands
through which the trans-Siberian ran were rich in gold,
silver, lead and iron ore, so mining operations must be begun
without delay.

Witte possessed tremendous drive and the valuable gift of
arousing the enthusiasm of others for his many projects. He
was wise too, in that he always had detailed plans ready for
inspection so the arguments about 'wild-cat schemes' which
were put forward by Pobedonostsev and Plehve at council
meetings had little effect. Meanwhile the man they hated
changed the whole face of Russia – for in his ten years as
Finance Minister he did just that.

He was a devoted disciple of the German political economist
Friedrich List, so he believed in moderate protection of industry, and he had remarkable success in persuading investors
from other countries to put capital into Russian ventures. One
thing which had seriously alarmed him when he first took
office was the way in which the value of Russia's paper currency
kept fluctuating. In order to stabilize it he negotiated a huge
loan from France early in the 1890s, afterwards introducing
drastic measures to prevent fluctuations and ruling that all
payments must be made in specie. These actions led to much
grumbling and criticism, but Witte insisted that Russia must
stay on the gold standard. Soon attention was focused on an
even graver matter, his crusade against the evils of alcohol.

When a hard-up young man living in a poor quarter of
Odessa, Witte had seen the devastating effects of vodka on
people who had been oppressed and under-nourished for
generations. They would save kopecks in order to buy a bottle,
for by gulping its contents down at speed they could gain
temporary escape from the miseries of their existence. As a
result their resistance to disease was lessened and they fell easy
victims to the epidemics of cholera, dysentery or typhus.

Personally Witte detested vodka, but one feels that his subsequent actions were motivated less by fears of the havoc it

wrought than by his ambition to make Russia a prosperous state. He instituted searching inquiries into the profits made by the distillers and discovered that these amounted to a colossal sum which was equal to a quarter of the national income! To allow such a state of affairs to continue was unthinkable, so with his usual thoroughness he set about organizing matters, and eighteen months later the Russian government had the monopoly on all sales of vodka.

In 1903 Count Witte (he had now inherited his father's title) became Prime Minister to Tsar Nicholas II, and seldom have a monarch and his leading statesman so disliked each other. Nicholas was weak but possessed the obstinacy of the timid: Witte was strong and resolute, and while he felt compassion for the ruler whose only son was a haemophiliac he despised him for submitting to the demands of the German-born Tsarina and Rasputin – whom he persisted in alluding to openly as 'that horse-coper'.

The Tsarina and Rasputin kept urging the Tsar to get rid of Witte, but he was an extremely difficult man to dislodge. By his efforts over the past decade he had changed the Russian economy out of all recognition and the country was now rich with every prospect of becoming richer, for the trans-Siberian route had opened up many new markets. Witte had persuaded the Chinese to allow them to re-route the railway right through the centre of Manchuria, which saved a journey of six hundred miles round the north of that province and, even more important, made it virtually a Russian possession. Trouble arose in 1903 when a group of businessmen who were close friends of the Tsar obtained a timber and mining concession in North Korea near the Yalu River. The Tsar gave gracious assent to the project, which Witte only heard of when the Russian Foreign Office received an indignant protest from Japan, who said she disapproved of any further Russian penetration into the Korean peninsula. Witte at once sought audience with the Tsar and bluntly demanded that the scheme be abandoned. The Foreign Minister backed him up but Nicholas, fortified by a talk with Pobedonostsev, returned evasive answers. The furious Witte told the Foreign Office to inform Tokyo the concession would not be taken up, whereupon Pobedonostsev told the Japanese the expedition was starting at once. During the next few weeks so many conflicting messages from St Petersburg poured into Tokyo that the Japanese were bewildered, but in August the Tsar found the courage to dismiss Witte. He suffered further humiliation when his beloved railway was used to transport all the equipment and stores to Korea.

In February 1904 the Japanese navy struck at Port Arthur in the Yellow Sea as suddenly and swiftly as they did at Pearl Harbor thirty-seven years later. The ensuing eighteen months of war brought the Russians one disaster after another, and they were finally defeated in May 1905.

The war had cost Russia dear. Both Tsar and country had lost in world prestige, the army and navy had sustained severe damage, the hope of a new empire in the east had vanished. Worse still, the war had crystallized the desire for revolution inside Russia and broken the Tsar's autocratic power. Discontent had first flared on Bloody Sunday, 22 January 1905 when over twenty thousand workers with their wives and children marched to the Winter Palace to present a petition to the Tsar asking for wages of a rouble a day. He was not in St Petersburg, but the Palace guards opened fire, killing over five hundred and wounding several thousand. Since then there had been continual strikes in St Petersburg and Moscow, and growing demands for a constituent assembly. Witte, restored to power, had just negotiated a French loan of £150,000,000, and practically ordered the Tsar to issue the manifesto granting Russia the Duma, the first constitution in her history, but on the eve of its opening in May 1906 at the Taurida Palace Nicholas again removed him from office.

The Duma failed lamentably and for the next eight years Witte, the man who had done so much for Russia, was obliged to stand on the sidelines and watch the country he loved slide back into the stultifying bureaucracy of twenty years earlier. The Tsar, terrified of further demonstrations from the peasants he superstitiously called 'the Dark People', sulked at Tsarskoe Selo and refused to enter St Petersburg for seven weary years: but on the outbreak of the First World War he emerged with a blare of trumpets as the Little Father, the Ruler of all the Russias. In vain the ageing Witte scuttled from ministry to ministry imploring everyone to do their utmost to ensure that Russia remained neutral. 'For Russia war always ends in revolution,' he cried. He was right, though he did not live to see his prophecy come true as he died suddenly on 12 March 1915.

James Keir Hardie

(1856–1915)

Sometimes a political figure arises with such obviously admirable qualities that the line dividing opponents melts in the glow of universal admiration and only the most inveterate party men are left muttering: 'I wish he had been one of ours.' Such a one was Keir Hardie, founder and father-figure of the British Labour Party.

Hardie was a man of strong character able to use even adverse experience as a spur to creativity. Many people would not have survived the hardships he endured as a child, let alone risen to eminence.

He was born on 15 August 1856 at Legbrannock in the Lanarkshire coalfield, the illegitimate son of a farm servant, Mary Keir, who later married and had eight more children by her husband, a ship's carpenter named David Hardie. When the eldest boy, who became known as James Keir Hardie, was five the family moved to Glasgow, suffering great poverty because of the father's frequent unemployment. Though his parents taught him to read, James never went to school but from the age of seven was employed as an errand boy, helping to feed the family. After Christmas 1866, when he was a baker's roundsman, an incident occurred which left a life-long impression on him. One morning, after spending most of the previous night tending his pregnant mother and a sick brother, he was late for work. His employer summoned him to his house and over a breakfast table groaning with delicacies docked a week's wages and sacked him on the spot. 'That night,' wrote Hardie years later, 'the baby was born and the sun rose on the 1st of January 1867 over a home in which there was neither fire nor food.'

Soon, with the father away at sea, the family moved back to Legbrannock and James, aged twelve, went to work in a coal mine, becoming a hewer in his late teens. He attended night school and in the pit practised writing and shorthand at odd moments, scratching the characters on pieces of slate blackened with soot from his miner's lamp. He also read widely and was much influenced by Robert Burns (the democrat), Thomas Carlyle (the pacifist) and tales of the Scottish Covenanters

141

whose fate as a worthy but persecuted minority aroused his admiring compassion. The respect for education and the puritanism of rural Scotland, softened in his case by a strong mystical-romantic strain, were already in his blood.

Concern for the lot of his fellow-miners bit deeply into Hardie and he began to fight for them on two fronts, as a temperance organizer and, in the absence of any effective union, as a spokesman for their grievances before the employers. Morally indignant, highly articulate, he discovered in himself remarkable powers of persuasion, but in 1878 these very qualities brought dismissal from the mine. For a short while he ran a tobacconist's shop and at this time made his entry into journalism as correspondent of a Glasgow radical paper. Then in 1879 (the year in which he married a girl, Lillie Wilson, whom he had met in his temperance work) the Lanarkshire miners appointed him their agent and for the next seven years he was absorbed in mining problems.

The problems were indeed enormous: how to make strike action effective in the face of black-leg labour, how to achieve a statutory reduction in working hours, how to develop strong unions supported by the whole mining community. By 1886 this last objective had been temporarily gained, largely through Hardie's efforts, by the reconstruction of the Scottish Miners' Federation and the Ayrshire Miners' Union.

But the triumph was short-lived. Coal owners reacted savagely to the new developments. Strikes against intolerable wages and dangerous working conditions were broken up by force and at the annual Trades Union Congress at Swansea in 1887 Hardie, representing the Ayrshire miners, stepped on to a wider stage with a bitter attack on lukewarm unionists and sycophants of the Liberals in Parliament. Up to then Hardie himself had been a Liberal who hoped to see industrial reforms achieved through the party of Gladstone, and there were already in fact working-class representatives included under the Liberal umbrella in the Commons. But now Hardie was beginning to see that this was not enough. The problems created by the rapid industrialization of Britain were too urgent, too multifarious to be solved by an overwhelmingly middle-class party whose interests were, to say the least, ambiguous. In an impassioned speech later in that year Hardie pleaded for the first time for 'a party pledged to the interests of labour alone'.

It is difficult today to realize how epoch-making this suggestion was. Working men, in so far as they had the vote at all, voted for one of the major parties, for the people who obviously had power in the land, and even if they could be persuaded to transfer their allegiance, everything to do with a new party would have to be developed from scratch, organization, finance, policy, above all the will and impetus to make it thrive and claim a voice in the nation's affairs. Thus at the time the suggestion seemed dangerous, to some even absurd. That it was ultimately shown to be neither was largely Hardie's achievement.

But progress was inevitably slow. In 1888 he stood as an independent at a Mid-Lanarkshire by-election and came bottom of the poll. This did not discourage him and at a conference he attended in Paris in 1889 for the launching of the Second Socialist International some remarks he made to Friedrich Engels, Marx's collaborator, hinted at the path he would take in future. Speaking of the British, he said: 'We are a solid people, very practical and not given to chasing bubbles' – and by bubbles he meant intellectual ideologies.

Engels referred to him venomously thereafter as 'that super-cunning Scot', but Hardie had revealed one of his strongest and most enduring characteristics, which was to prove of the utmost value to the Labour movement: a pragmatism which worked for practical results in furthering the interests of the working class and avoided political dogma. He was never a man for blueprints, preferring conciliation and compromise. This had two paramount results. First, no potentially divisive section within the movement, of which there were many, was ever allowed by Hardie to take charge of it. A gradualist, evolutionary policy was pursued able to obtain widespread co-operation. Second, and as a result of this, the broad-based Labour movement which he forged was able to enter the stream of national life creatively and not destructively. Class struggle rather than class war was his motto; nor did he hold out a purely material goal to his followers. The reforms he fought for were not seen as an end in themselves but as a means of realizing his mystical, perhaps excessively romantic, vision of the New Jerusalem, a society comprising the whole nation, unified and bound together in Christian brotherhood. But meanwhile there was much to be done, for, in the words of a pamphlet he published in a later year, 'Can a Man be a Christian on a Pound a Week?'

In the general election of 1892 Hardie was elected for West Ham South, the first independent Labour MP ever to sit in the House of Commons. Driven from West Ham in a two-horse brake with a cornet player on the box performing the 'Marseillaise', he dismounted at the Palace of Westminster in an astounding get-up which left his frock-coated, top-hatted colleagues aghast: yellow tweed trousers in flamboyant check ('you could have played draughts on them', said someone), serge jacket and Sherlock Holmes-type deerstalker cap. Labour had undoubtedly arrived, although outwardly at least in questionable shape.

But in the House Hardie proved no eccentric. His stocky build, handsome, bearded face and rich Lowland accent commanded attention, so, too, despite the government's preoccupation with Irish home rule, did his reiterated theme: the problem of unemployment. He spoke earnestly, without rhetorical tricks, suggesting palliatives that were clearly realistic: the banning of overtime in government-controlled workshops, the denial of contracts to foreign firms, the enforcement of maximum working hours, and the setting up of 'home colonies' where the unemployed could work in agriculture. He even persuaded the Liberal government to empower local authorities to acquire land for this purpose.

But in the years 1892–95 the most important step forward was taken outside Parliament in the creation of the Independent Labour Party at the Bradford conference of January 1893. The aim in the first place was modest: the formation of a nucleus round which local labour organizations could gather with the eventual object of setting up a national party. And the organization did in fact become a pilot scheme superseded ultimately by the Labour Party proper (from which it disaffiliated in 1932). But at Bradford it was Hardie, the first chairman, who made the base solid by ensuring that the word 'socialist' (suspect to the working class as of foreign intellectual origin) was not included in the new party's title and, though the nationalization of the means of production, distribution and exchange was mentioned as an objective, heavy stress was also laid on practical industrial aims.

In the following years Hardie became the ILP's main recruiting sergeant and though in the general election of 1895 not one of its twenty-eight candidates was elected and he himself lost his seat, it went from strength to strength. Hardie ceaselessly stumped the country, raising support, worked on a reluctant TUC to sponsor a full-scale Labour Party and took over a monthly journal, *The Labour Leader*, which he converted under his editorship into an important political weekly published in London and Glasgow.

The aim of the ILP, according to Hardie, was to 'blend the classes into one human family', but in fostering the Labour movement it was only too easy to provoke splits. The TUC had to be wooed because many of its members were Liberals to whom the nationalization pledge was anathema. So it was that when the call came in 1899 from the Railway Servants union within the TUC to convene a special conference 'for securing an increased number of labour representatives to the next Parliament' Hardie's pragmatism and tactical skill were again in demand. As a result the conference, which met early in 1900 at the Memorial Hall, Farringdon Street, London, was able to steer between the rocks of 'Lib-Labbery' and Marxism, and set up a broad Labour Representation Committee, consisting of seven trade unionists, two persons each from the ILP and the Social Democratic Federation (Marxist) and one from the Fabian Society. Its purpose was to develop 'a distinct Labour Group in Parliament who shall have their own whips and agree upon their own policy'. Thus the grand coalition came about and the modern 'Labour Party' takes that day, 28 February 1900, as its official date of birth though the LRC did not acquire the new name until 1906, when thirty Labour candidates were elected to Parliament.

Meanwhile in 1900 two further events occurred to push the party on its way. In a famous judgement involving the Taff Vale railway company and its striking employees the House of Lords ruled that unions could be sued for damages by employers. The shattering consequences of this judgement for all unions was obvious and gave urgency to the work of the LRC. In October of that year Hardie was re-elected to Parliament as the ILP-sponsored MP for Merthyr Tydfil, a constituency he continued to represent for the rest of his life.

But now, though he was still only forty-four, pressure of work was beginning to tell on him. There were his endless duties as 'Member for the Unemployed', pressing the government to apply remedies, taking up individual cases of hardship. And there were still hundreds of meetings to be addressed, entailing long train journeys, irregular meals, little sleep, fresh audiences to be gathered to the fold under the spell of his evangelistic fervour. 'Socialism,' he would tell them, 'is much more an affair of the heart than of the intellect.'

He was drained by his own enthusiasm, fell ill, recovered and in 1906 received the supreme tribute of being elected leader of the Parliamentary Labour Party. Soon, with his powerful help, it achieved its first big success by persuading Asquith's government to enact a Labour-prepared Trade Disputes Bill reversing the Taff Vale judgement.

But there was also Hardie the pacifist and Hardie the internationalist, both of a piece with his dream of brotherhood, his hatred of violence and oppression. Soon he was campaigning for women's votes (falling deeply in love, incidentally, with Mrs Emmeline Pankhurst's younger daughter Sylvia). Then, after a mild stroke and an operation, he set off to recuperate on a world tour. But he could not keep out of controversy. Staying for some weeks in India he enraged the establishment and the British Tory press by criticizing bureaucracy and daring to suggest that one day India should be granted self-government.

Back home and now an international figure, he was soon involved in the problem of the party's diminishing support (in the event only temporary) arising from the fact that Lloyd George's social schemes were stealing socialist thunder. And then, as Anglo-German naval rivalry increased, there loomed the hideous danger of war.

Long ago, in 1878, Hardie had become a convert to Christianity and there is no doubt that the most sincerely held of all his dreams was summed up in the phrase: the fatherhood of God – the brotherhood of Man. He had been bitterly opposed to the Boer War, but in a Britain ablaze with jingoistic fervour had reaped vilification for his opinions. Now, in 1910, he not only believed the British people would never succumb to such frenzy again but also that his pacifism was shared by workers throughout Europe. It was a tragic and for him fatal mistake. A resolution he put forward at a meeting of the Second International in Copenhagen, calling for a general strike right across Europe if war became imminent, was not adopted and a manifesto drawn up by him in 1914, only four days before Britain declared war on Germany, one titled 'An Appeal to the British Working Class', was totally disregarded.

He never recovered from this shock. Pathetically, though a sick man, he continued to speak at meetings and in the Commons, suggesting that the more extravagant tales of German atrocities might not be true, drawing attention to the spontaneous Christmas truce on the western front in the first winter of the war, trying to mollify the virulent war hysteria that had once more engulfed the nation. All in vain.

In February 1915, concerned as always for the exploited and oppressed, he made his last speech in the Commons on the subject of child labour in agriculture. Then came a serious stroke, lucidity began to fade and after a long illness he died of pneumonia on 26 September 1915. Said one newspaper: 'The Member for Humanity has resigned his seat.'

Michael Faraday

(1791–1867)

Every year since 1924, with the exception of the war years, the Institution of Electrical Engineers has organized a series of lectures, delivered in major cities throughout Britain on aspects of electrical technology, with the aims of clarifying the role of the engineer in society and explaining to young people the challenge that electrical engineering presents as a career. In recent years the subject of the lectures was the impact of microelectronics on the future of the railways, and the estimated audience was 70,000. In memory of the man whose work underlies the entire field of modern electronics they are called the Faraday Lectures, and a good subject for a future series might well be the story of Faraday himself.

In the year before the battle of Trafalgar we would have found him, aged thirteen, working as an errand boy delivering newspapers from a bookseller's and stationer's shop in Blandford Street off Manchester Square, London. His father James was a blacksmith, his mother Margaret (née Hastwell) a former domestic servant, both from Yorkshire, though the father's family may have come originally from Ireland. They had four children of whom Michael was the third and he, at this time, was barely literate.

But he was fortunate in his employer George Riebau, who soon spotted his intelligence, and within a year promoted him to bookbinder's apprentice, a job which Faraday kept for seven years. Later, Riebau wrote of him with affection and a certain awe, describing how he would soak up the contents of any book that struck his fancy, including one by a Dr Watts called *Improvement of the Mind*, how he seldom drank anything but 'pure clean water' (obviously unusual in apprentices), went for early morning walks 'visiting always some works of art or searching for some mineral or vegetable curiosity ... his mind ever engaged'. Faraday later added to this picture by mentioning among the books he studied the electrical treatises in the *Encyclopaedia Britannica*.

Even as a boy he was obviously a phenomenon, passionately anxious to learn, with growing scientific interests. In the evenings he attended private lectures, writing them out in full from his notes and binding them for future use as text-books. One day, Riebau showed them to a customer who was a member of the Royal Institution and this benefactor gave Faraday tickets for a course of lectures to be given there by the Professor of Chemistry, Humphry Davy. Once more Faraday wrote out the lectures and bound them – so unwittingly preparing for a step forward in his career.

In 1812 his apprenticeship ended and he became a journeyman bookbinder employed by a French exile in London. Gone now was any chance of spare-time study and soon he was writing to a friend, 'I am now working at my old trade, which I wish to leave at the first convenient opportunity.' In desperation he wrote to Humphry Davy, enclosing the summaries he had made of his lectures and asking for an interview, which was granted. Davy was kind and clearly impressed, but advised Faraday to stick to his job. Science, he said, was 'a harsh mistress'. So matters might have rested if chance – or was it fate? – had not taken a hand. Soon after this Davy injured his eyes in an explosion of glass in his laboratory and sent for Faraday to help out, a few weeks later offering him the job of permanent laboratory assistant at a wage of twenty-five shillings a week.

The Institution, founded in 1799 and granted a royal charter in 1800, served the dual purpose of original research and lecturing to the public. Humphry Davy, recently knighted by the Prince Regent, was later to become director of the laboratory. Meanwhile, Faraday was given rooms on the top floor (plus coals and candles), his duties to assist in the experiments: nothing could have suited him better for here, despite his humble background and lack of education, he was privileged to work with one of the most famous men in European science.

It must have been frustrating, then, to hear soon that Sir Humphry was planning a journey of scientific inquiry into Europe and wished to take Faraday with him as assistant and secretary. The young man could hardly say no and they set off from Plymouth heading for Brittany in October 1813 with Sir Humphry's recently married wife in the party. All was not bliss on this journey, largely owing to Lady Davy's snobbish attitude to Faraday and Sir Humphry asking him to act as his valet. But for a youth who had never been more than twelve miles out of London it was an exciting and mind-broadening adventure. They were away for eighteen months, taking in Paris, Nice, Turin, Rome and Naples, meeting many famous European scientists, only abandoning further travels when news came of Napoleon's escape from Elba.

No doubt Faraday returned with those characteristics already appearing that later helped him to fame: intellectual vigour, patience, boundless curiosity, humility in the face of nature's marvels and a deep religious faith that was to sustain him all his life. Now, on that long trip he had shown other gifts which endeared him to Davy, youthful ebullience and humour.

Restored to his former position, Faraday plunged into chemical experiments. But for him this was not enough. In his spare time he and a group of friends met in his rooms to study English grammar and syntax in what they called 'the mutual improvement plan'. He took lessons in 'oratory', had already had some in drawing and joined the City Philosophical Society ('philosophical' in those days including 'scientific'), where in 1816 he delivered the first of many lectures, an art in which he was ultimately to excel.

Meanwhile over a number of years, he succeeded, the first ever to do so, in liquefying a number of gases and isolating benzene, which continues to play an important part in modern chemistry. New chemical compounds were prepared, including ethylene, and a series of arduous, time-consuming efforts were made to produce new alloys of steel. Though Faraday was not entirely successful he was one of the first in this field. He also helped Sir Humphry in the much-needed invention of the miners' safety lamp.

Not surprisingly, in view of this single-minded devotion to work and self-improvement, he professed to have no time for females and in pungent disdain wrote some verses which began:

> What is the pest and plague of human life?
> And what the curse that often brings a wife?
> 'tis Love.

A mutual friend showed these outpourings to the charming, 22-year-old Sarah Barnard, daughter of a London silversmith and already known to Faraday through their joint adherence to a small Protestant sect known as the Sandemanians. Whereupon Sarah decided to capture him. Soon the handsome Michael was violently in love and after the usual ups and downs of courtship they were married in June 1821. Sarah turned out to be the ideal wife. Once, when asked why she did not study chemistry, she replied, 'Already it is so absorbing and exciting to him that it often deprives him of his sleep – and I am quite content to be the pillow of his mind.' Faraday was marvellous with youngsters, but there were no children of the marriage.

The steel experiments continued but already a discovery had been made that would lead to his greatest achievements. In

1820 Professor Oersted of Copenhagen had shown that a magnetic needle was deflected by an electric current flowing through a wire, the current being generated by the only means known at that time, chemical action in a so-called voltaic pile, invented by Alessandro Volta in 1800. From Oersted's discovery the conclusion followed that there was a connection of some sort between magnetism and electricity, and Faraday was quick to follow it up. By ingenious means he was able to show that a magnetic needle would rotate round an electric wire and conversely that the wire would spin round the magnet, so discovering the principle of the electric motor. He even proved that wire would rotate under the influence of the earth's magnetic field alone. When this occurred he was beside himself with excitement, saying 'D'you see, George, d'you see, d'you see?', as his brother-in-law reported. 'I shall never forget the enthusiasm expressed in his face and the sparkling of his eyes.'

But it was to be several years before he resumed these researches. Meanwhile he had become a member of the Royal Society, Director of the Laboratory at the Royal Institution and a famous lecturer particularly effective with young audiences. Then, in 1831, after lengthy experiments to produce improved forms of optical glass, he laid aside other work to concentrate again on electromagnetism. He found a highly confused situation in which a number of European scientists, including André-Marie Ampère, had made experiments and put forward conflicting hypotheses, even to the extent of suggesting that electricity was some sort of fluid. What had been proved was that electricity could have a magnetic effect, and Faraday now began to wonder whether the reverse could be true and a current be generated by magnetic action.

On 29 August 1831 he set up a now famous experiment. Taking an iron ring about six inches in diameter and one inch thick, he wound round opposite sides two coils of fully insulated copper wire, separate from each other. The ends of one coil led to a voltaic pile and the others to a simple galvanometer. When current was passed through the first coil the galvanometer needle moved, then came to rest. When current was disconnected it moved again, but in the opposite direction, then came to rest. What Faraday had done, more by intuition than reason, was to make a powerful electromagnet out of the ring and the coil, and it was its make-and-break effect that had induced the secondary current.

This experiment was to be the origin of the modern transformer. Two months later Faraday made further tests, first proving that induction took place from one insulated coil to another even without the iron core and then, in another famous experiment, he discovered that a magnet placed into and withdrawn from a cylindrical coil of wire also induced a current, but again only when the magnet was in motion. Motion, in short, whether of the magnet or the coil, was the key to producing electricity.

It was only a small step now to generating a constant flow of electricity, and this was done on 28 October 1831 when he rotated a copper disc mounted on an axle, with rubbing contacts attached to each, between the poles of a giant magnet at Woolwich. This time the galvanometer needle was permanently deflected. So was made the first ever dynamo, that vital invention which has made modern civilization possible.

In subsequent years Faraday went on to develop insights into the relations between light and magnetism, originating concepts supporting the modern theory of the electromagnetic field. His discovery of lines of force in electromagnetism was later transformed by James Clerk Maxwell (1831-79) into mathematical equations that underlie all modern theories, and he developed the basic laws of electrolysis (chemical decomposition by electrical action), introducing the terms anode, cathode, electrode. He went even further. Scientists had hitherto concentrated on the effects of electricity and magnetism upon matter; Faraday expanded these studies to embrace the transmission of such forces through space, so instituting a completely new way of looking at physical reality, which was later taken up by Albert Einstein, and laying the ground-work for the modern development of radio and television.

The detail of one experiment alone illustrates the care and ingenuity he used in his work. Two questions obsessed him: what was electricity and how did it work? When it charged a conductor, for instance, did it permeate the whole mass or merely the surface? To find an answer he built an enormous cube, charged it up from a machine and when sparks were flying in all directions climbed inside to test the inner surface – finding no electrical activity.

It seems that Faraday, like many great men, was driven by unconscious forces of which he was the servant rather than the master. Such powers can be ruthless and it is not surprising that, what with his researches, lectures, work as director of the laboratory and many requests for help from public bodies, he began to suffer from mental exhaustion. From 1840 to 1844 he was forced to cut down his activities, then took them up again until, in the last years of his life, he was a semi-invalid, subject to dizzy spells, loss of memory and inability to concentrate.

By then many honours had been bestowed on him, including the Legion of Honour from the Emperor of the French, but he declined the presidency of the Royal Society and a knighthood, saying, 'I must remain plain Michael Faraday to the last.' In 1859 he had accepted from Queen Victoria a 'grace and favour' residence at Hampton Court and it was there, sitting quietly in his chair, that he died at the age of seventy-six.

Certainly a place would have been given him in Westminster Abbey but for his wish to be buried elsewhere. Today he lies in Highgate cemetery, his grave marked by a simple headstone: MICHAEL FARADAY, and then the dates of birth and death: 22 September 1791, 25 August 1867 – the grave of the blacksmith's son and the man whom the latest edition of the *Encyclopaedia Britannica* calls 'possibly the greatest experimental genius the world has known'.

We can see, looking back on his life, that he was no less remarkable as a man than a scientist. Of course he knew his fame was secure, enshrined for posterity in thirty brilliant treatises deposited with the Royal Society entitled *Experimental Researches in Electricity*. But fame was never his concern; he was consumed by a disinterested passion for scientific truth, the truth of God's world, as he called it, and his researches were therefore in his eyes a sacred task involved in the discovery of divine laws.

This spiritual faith found nowhere more moving expression than in a letter he wrote to a scientist friend in 1861, when he was already failing:

I am, I hope, very thankful that in the withdrawal of the power and things of this life, – the good hope is left with me, which makes the contemplation of death a comfort – not a fear. Such peace is alone in the gift of God and as it is he who gives it, why shall we be afraid?

Isambard Kingdom Brunel

(1806–59)

Isambard Kingdom Brunel was the Leonardo of engineering. The range and daring of his imagination were matched by his brilliant talents as a draughtsman and an architect's sense of proportion and landscaping. His restless invention continually threw out ideas which darted into the future and pushed back the frontiers of the possible. Thanks to him a regular steamship service was plying the Atlantic within a generation of the application of steam as a motive power; his sketch-books carried notes for the design of a gyroscopic compass half a century before it was developed for regular use; while his plans for an ironclad, jet-propelled warship and for landing-craft of the type used on the Normandy beaches in 1944 could be entertained as practical propositions by a later generation.

Like Leonardo also, Brunel lived at a time when his chosen field had not yet been mapped out and divided amongst a host of limiting specializations, when the gifted engineer could as well design a marine engine or survey a major trunk railway-line as build a bridge. Brunel excelled in all these enterprises, time and again producing original and brilliant solutions derived from first principles. In one outstanding respect the great engineer differed from his Italian predecessor – he got things done. In the thirty-five years of his working life, I.K. Brunel produced such a plethora of architectural and engineering achievements that here we shall have space for only the greatest and only some of those.

He was born on 9 April 1806, the son of Marc Isambard Brunel and Sophia, daughter of William Kingdom, a Plymouth naval contractor. In his early twenties Marc Brunel had been forced to flee his native France because of his royalist sympathies; and after six years in America, where he established his reputation as an architect and engineer, he at last fulfilled a boyhood ambition and came to try his fortune in England.

For the first fifty years of the nineteenth century, the dynamic of European civilization, that urge to explore, change and improve, was firmly located in the British Isles where a revolution was dawning which was to change the face of European industry and through it the whole fabric of European society. In those years Britain was a fierce competitive world where ambition was the lodestar and ruthlessness a style. Marc Brunel's talent was quickly recognized and he was employed on war contracts; but the coming of peace combined with setbacks in his other enterprises led to bankruptcy and imprisonment for debt in 1821. His release came only after he had threatened to accept an invitation from the Russian government and to leave Britain.

Marc's business troubles must, however, have been amply compensated for by the talents of his young son. Isambard demonstrated from childhood his talent for draughtsmanship and mathematics, mastering the elements of Euclid at the early age of six. He was educated in England and France, passing through the Lycée Henri IV in Paris and being apprenticed not only to the great English mechanic Henry Maudslay, but also to the famous French horologist, Abraham Louis Breguet. To his own natural talents Isambard could add the advantages of a magnificent training and a father now well established in his chosen career; but without the punishing pace at which he drove himself, these advantages would not of themselves have led to the brilliant career which lay before him.

His work as a practising engineer began when, at the age of twenty, he took over the direction of the works on his father's Rotherhithe Tunnel under the Thames. This great undertaking, the world's first underwater tunnel, was completed eighteen years later after many tragic setbacks and the loss of many lives. From the beginning it was obvious that the surveyors had badly misled the Brunels and that the line chosen lay through loose, treacherous shale. In May 1827, when the young Isambard had been in sole charge of the operation for a year on account of his father's ill health, disaster came. The water finally broke through and flooded the whole workings up to the base of the shaft; the setback cost the project a six-month delay.

This delay could well have been longer had it not been for the driving energy and enthusiasm of Brunel. For him, physical involvement with the work in the field was the breath of life, and he spent most of his waking hours inspecting the tunnel itself or taking a diving-bell to the bed of the Thames to supervise the sealing of the numerous fall-ins with clay. But although his capacity for hard work was phenomenal and he drove his men as hard as he did himself, Brunel was quite capable of enjoying the good things of life and delighted in the grandiose gesture. So that when in November 1827 all was set for work to recommence, he threw a dinner in the very tunnel itself, two hundred people – workmen, directors and guests – sitting down to a 'sumptuous collation' at tables lit by gaslight. But the celebrations were soon clouded when, on the night of 12 January 1828, the flood waters invaded again, this time almost claiming the young engineer himself as a victim. He was at the face of the workings when the water broke through, and while struggling as long as possible to bring others to safety, he lost consciousness and was brought to the top of the shaft by the surging flood. As soon as he had recovered Brunel, true to form, worked himself mercilessly in an attempt to reopen the workings. But this time he so overstrained himself that he had to rest and was sent to Bristol to convalesce.

The tunnel itself was closed down, not to be reopened for seven years, and during his convalescence the ambitious young Isambard Brunel was able to reflect that while his rivals were making their names famous he was, at the age of twenty-three, merely a promising if brilliant young man. After his recovery he toured the country unceasingly, undertaking such contracts as came his way. The most important of these, and the one which was to shape his whole career indirectly, was for the construction of the bridge over the River Avon at Clifton.

The Avon Gorge was a wild and romantic site, the high cliffs towering at either side to dwarf the tall sailing ships on their way to the port of Bristol. Brunel's brilliant and beautiful solution of the single-span suspension bridge, which has since become one of the most famous bridges in the world, was typical of every major project which he was to undertake. It was bold; in the length of its span it contradicted the received orthodoxy of what was possible; and it was magnificently vindicated by its performance. The contract was only won after a hard competition in which he triumphed even over the great but ageing Telford, who produced a strange and totally non-functional gothic design. But although his design was formally accepted, Brunel was dogged by bad luck – capital failed and the works on the bridge soon had to be abandoned, the great project only being completed after his death. However, the Clifton Bridge design unquestionably put Brunel's name on the map.

In 1830 he was engaged as chief engineer by a committee of London and Bristol businessmen which had been formed to link the two cities by rail. Immediately Brunel recognized the great possibilities before him. Nevertheless it was typical of him that he was willing to jeopardize even this chance by making it a condition of his acceptance that he should have the sole responsibility in all matters relating to the surveying of the line and of its building. His appointment was confirmed in March 1830 and the committee demanded the preliminary survey of the whole line by May. In two months of astonishingly hard work and hard travelling by stagecoach and on horseback, the deadline was met. The first stage was complete in the building of the Great Western Railway, the proud name which from the outset Brunel gave to this 'the finest work in England'.

The GWR, the only railway to retain its identity from its origins in the reign of King William IV to the time of nationalization more than a century later, was in almost every respect Brunel's personal creation. From the controversial broad gauge of its lines to the very design of the signals, the hand of the chief engineer was to leave its signature. And despite the numerous massive enterprises which Brunel was to undertake, the line from Paddington to Penzance is his enduring monument.

The work entailed not only constant travel in his specially constructed coach, nicknamed from its shape the 'Flying Hearse', not only the survey and design but also, in the initial stages, the diplomatic persuasion of land-owners and the cross-questioning by parliamentary committees. One eye-witness of Brunel's performance in committee said: 'I do not remember ever having enjoyed so great an intellectual treat as that of listening to Brunel's examination.' The opposition came from many quarters, including the governors of Eton as well as the board of the London to Southampton Railway, but eventually the bill was passed and Brunel was free to continue his plans, which now took on a still more ambitious turn, as he began to prepare to extend the line both into South Wales and south-west to Exeter.

In the last days of 1835 his journal has a long and interesting stock-taking in which the twenty-nine-year-old engineer reflected with obvious satisfaction that when all the various enterprises on which he was currently engaged were totalled together, he was responsible for an investment of some £5,300,000.

Brunel's life was, perhaps inevitably with a man of such fiery and determined temper, well filled with battles. His contempt for bureaucracy was complete, and his unconventional approach to everything he took up was calculated to breed enemies. But Brunel's reasons were typically sound. He set himself the clear objectives of faster, smoother running than anything then known or envisaged, and broad gauge presented itself as the answer. Within a few years he was, within terms of reference, vindicated. By 1846 an average running speed of 59 mph was achieved on the Paddington to Swindon run; and the travelling time from Paddington to Exeter via Bristol, inclusive of stops, was four hours twenty-five minutes. Such times were a remarkable achievement less than twenty years after the opening of the first railway in the world and were unmatched by anything Brunel's rivals could produce.

Nevertheless the broad gauge was doomed. The narrow gauge of 4 ft 8½ in, unthinkingly adopted by the Stephensons from the colliery tramways which had formed the prototypes of the new railways, already had over 1,000 miles of track, and the problems of linking broad gauge and narrow gauge systems were bound to bring standardization sooner or later. After Brunel's death the GWR was forced to abandon the broad gauge so as to integrate with the railway network.

During his lifetime enemies accused Brunel of showmanship. At mid-day on 1 September 1857, on the River Tamar between Devon and Cornwall, an event took place which as sheer spectacle must have seemed to warrant their animadversions. It marked the beginning of the second main constructional stage in the building of the great Royal Albert Bridge between St Budeaux and Saltash, a bridge which Brunel himself gave a life of only fifty years but which continues to serve the Western Region line to Cornwall unchanged. The banks of the river were thronged with crowds to watch one of the two spans, a great truss of 1,000 tons in weight and some 500 feet long, being floated into position between the piers just showing above water level. Brunel, who had ordered complete silence, ascended a podium in the centre of the span as the hushed and expectant onlookers strained to see the tiny figure and the actions of the signallers moving at his command. Slowly but without faltering the mighty mass slid soundlessly to its station and, as the tide rose, the ends of the span were fixed to their positions in the piers to within an eighth of an inch. When the final signal was given for completion, the silent throngs burst out into a mighty roar of acclaim.

It was a moment of triumph, but its full savour was embittered for its author who for years had been struggling against mounting odds to build the mightiest of all his dreams, the *Great Eastern* steamship. It was the third of Brunel's steamships, and its predecessors had each in their turn been the largest ship built in any yard in the world.

The first had been laid down as early as 1836. Typically for a Brunel project, it aimed at something viewed as impossible – the crossing of the Atlantic by steam. She was named the

Great Western, and was to ply between Bristol and New York. In April 1838 she made the crossing in fifteen days, and thereafter plied a further sixty-seven times across the Atlantic before being put to other service. This venture of the Great Western Company from Bristol had egged on the rival port of Liverpool to make the crossing first, but their ship, the *Sirius*, designed for coastal waters, although she left Britain three days earlier, entered New York harbour only hours before her rival. The *Great Western* showed that the voyage was not merely a stunt, but was a new commonplace of nineteenth-century life. Five years later the *Great Britain* was launched, a still bigger ship, built in iron and powered by the recently invented screw drive. The ship was true to Brunel's way of doing things in combining many major and revolutionary concepts in one design, and its launch by Prince Albert was another of those grand occasions so characteristic of the style of Victorian England. The Prince travelled down to Bristol from London on a Great Western Express, with Brunel and his chief engineer, the great Daniel Gooch, on the footplate.

The *Great Eastern* was Brunel's last and most ambitious dream, and he laboured night and day for five years to bring her to birth. She dwarfed anything then afloat, and incorporated the revolutionary idea of a double hull – two iron 'skins' three feet apart, one ship within another, a hermetically sealed compartment that extended from the great keelplate up to the water line. But his constitution, undermined by a lifetime of overwork, could not stand the strains and worries imposed by her building and launching. He died on 15 September 1859 without seeing her begin her maiden voyage. However, the *Great Eastern* was to achieve in 1866 the feat of laying the submarine telegraph cable between England and America, thus providing Brunel with a final posthumous triumph.

Charles Darwin

(1809–82)

In 1825 Doctor Robert Darwin, married to a daughter of the famous Josiah Wedgwood, founder of the pottery firm, decided that his sixteen-year-old son Charles should study medicine and from the family home in Shrewsbury Charles dutifully set off for Edinburgh to enter the medical faculty.

From the father's point of view it was somewhat of a shot in the dark for Charles, though amiable and apparently intelligent, had so far shown little sustained interest in anything, either at Shrewsbury grammar school, where he had been a pupil for six years, or at home, except in collecting beetles and gazing enraptured at scenes of nature.

At Edinburgh the collecting passion continued – rocks, plants, insects, worms – and his enthusiasm for *materia medica*, perhaps never strong, began to wane. It was finally destroyed by attendance at an operation on a child, performed in those days without anaesthetic, which left him in a state of horrified shock that scarred his mind for years.

Robert, though himself a 'philosophical deist', now suggested the church, and in 1828 Charles obediently went to Cambridge to study theology. But at that time doubts were in the air which went to the very heart of orthodox teaching and Charles inevitably became involved with them. On the one hand was the accepted belief in the literal truth of the Old Testament, including the story in Genesis of how God created the world in six days with every living thing in it, and man 'from the dust of the ground'. It was even said that the work had begun at 9 a.m. on Sunday, 23 October 4004 BC and this date was printed in Bibles, while the *Encyclopaedia Britannica* felt it right to assert 'the whole account of the creation rests on the truth of the Mosaic story, which we must of necessity accept'.

The fundamentalist belief in a static, once-for-all creation, both simple and reassuring in an age of rapid change, was accepted by many scientists too and it is easy to see its appeal. But other voices had been raised suggesting a different story, including that of Charles's own grandfather Erasmus Darwin (1731–1802), a successful physician and amateur scientist who had written in 1794 of an earth 'millions of years old' and the development of creatures 'possessing the faculty of continuing to improve'.

In his autobiography Charles later admitted that on going to Cambridge he did not 'in the least doubt the strict and literal truth of every word in the Bible'. But an interesting aspect of his career, both at the university and later, is how this orthodox view began to crumble. There were many influences: the writings of James Hutton (1726-97), of William Smith (1769-1839) pointing to continuing change in the earth's crust, above all of Charles Lyell, whose book *Principles of Geology*, published in 1830, was sub-titled *An Attempt to Explain the Former Changes of the Earth's Surface by Reference to Causes now in Operation*. This suggested a new approach to geological study, working backwards from observed fact rather than forwards from biblical myth, and was to guide Darwin's whole life.

But at this stage he was a highly gregarious young man and it was living influences which perhaps affected him most strongly, in particular that of a young professor of botany, J.S. Henslow, with whom he became close friends.

It was Henslow who in 1831 had a hand in an unusual proposition. To Charles on vacation came a letter from a Cambridge professor of anatomy inviting him to become unpaid naturalist on board HMS *Beagle*, a 242-ton, six-gun brig, shortly to sail under her captain Robert Fitzroy to conduct a survey of the South American coast. Charles was very keen to go; his father, on the other hand, doubtless fearing one more dead-end for his son, raised several objections, of which the first, in Charles's words, was 'disreputable to my character as a clergyman hereafter', and the last, 'that it would be a useless undertaking'. Ever the dutiful son, Charles had actually declined the offer when Josiah Wedgwood junior stepped in and wrung from brother-in-law Robert his slow consent. Fortunately the offer was still open and Charles eagerly accepted.

So, on 27 December 1831, after several months' refit at Devonport, HMS *Beagle*, with the 22-year-old Charles on board, sailed for what turned out to be a five-year voyage – and a momentous one for the intellectual history of mankind.

We have the advantage of Darwin's most readable book, *The Voyage of the Beagle*, to tell us what happened. There are two main threads in the narrative; one, his inexhaustible delight in the vast panorama of nature opening before his eyes, his zeal in climbing mountains, collecting specimens, studying rocks, plants, animals; and second, the particular observations which eventually led to his most famous work, that bombshell in the Victorian world, *The Origin of Species*.

Napoleon III, Emperor of the
French

William Lamb, the second
Viscount Melbourne

Sir Robert Peel, prominent
Tory statesman

Benjamin Disraeli, colourful
creator of a more popular
Conservatism

Gladstone introducing his first
Home Rule Bill, 1886

Charles Parnell, leader of the
Irish Home Rule Party, 1880-91

Abraham Lincoln, symbol
of a reunited nation

Meanwhile, heading through the Bay of Biscay towards the distant Cape Verde Islands, Darwin, amid agonizing bouts of sea-sickness, was getting to know his captain, an excellent seaman, but touchy, perhaps a manic-depressive and – ironic touch – a rigid biblical fundamentalist. A television series has shown us the problems in their relationship: but for his amiable, pliant and tactful personality, Darwin, it seems, might shortly have been back on the beach.

In those five years, until return to Plymouth in 1836, the *Beagle* circumnavigated the globe, calling at Bahia in Brazil, Rio de Janeiro, Montevideo, the Falkland Islands, Tierra del Fuego, then up the South American coast to Valparaiso, thence to the Galapagos Islands, across the Pacific to New Zealand, Tasmania, the Keeling Islands in the Indian Ocean, the Cape of Good Hope, to Bahia again, taking in other islands on the way, and so home. At many of these places Darwin was able to make long excursions ashore and in an almost overwhelming mass of material to discover, piece by piece, strong pointers to a new story of the world.

Conflicting with the biblical once-for-all, six-day creation account, for instance, was the evidence of granite rocks along the coast of Brazil. Granite, it was believed, was made from materials heated under pressure. Where had this heating occurred? On the bed of the ocean? Beneath other strata since removed? 'Can we believe,' wrote Darwin, 'that any power, acting for a time short of infinity, could have denuded the granite over so many thousand square leagues?'

Then there were the effects of an earthquake which he observed on the Chilean coast. The level of the land had been raised, in many places with sea shells still clinging to the rocks, and at Valparaiso they were found, due to previous upheavals, at a height even of thirteen hundred feet. Here clearly was evidence of constant change in the earth's surface.

He had already found more dramatic proof of the process in the animal kingdom. At Punta Alta in the Argentine he came on the bones of gigantic land animals embedded in mud and gravel, a giant sloth, a monster like a hippopotamus, the giant armadillo, a wild lama as big as a camel – nine creature in all which, strange though they were, had their equivalents in modern, smaller ones. Here again was evidence of change, and though biblical scholars might say the death of these animals was also evidence of the Flood, the Noah's Ark story did not tally. The present-day species were not the same as the old but had descended from them. There had been 'descent with modification', as it is called, and Darwin was bent on discovering how that arose. This was to be the theme of *The Origin of Species*.

Meanwhile, with unabated zest he was exploring, collecting, observing, sending home specimens pickled in spirit to his friend Professor Henslow – who was not always sure what he was getting: 'for heaven's sake,' he wrote, 'what is No. 233? It looks like an electric explosion.' The gauchos of the Rio Colorado aroused his interest, the swimming habits of ostriches, the coloration of toads, and the charming Spanish ladies of Buenos Aires. But amid all the impressions crowding in on him he never lost sight of the great puzzle: change was the law of nature. What caused it in living creatures? Evidence of the mass destruction of cattle during drought in the Argentine drew from him the conclusion: 'Certainly no fact in the long history of the world is so startling as the wide and repeated extermination of its inhabitants.'

Like a mosaic, the facts to support a theory were beginning to fit together and the Galapagos Islands off the coast of Ecuador supplied some more. There Darwin found new species of birds, plants and animals, including the iguana and giant tortoise, with variations from island to island but none completely different from those on the mainland 500 miles away. Here, clearly, there had been descent with modification. But why? And how?

It was to be three years before Darwin found an answer, and another twenty before he published his findings in *The Origin of Species*.

Meanwhile he had returned home at the end of the voyage, and in 1839 married his cousin Emma Wedgwood, who was to give him ten children of whom seven survived. He was made a Fellow of the Royal Society and in London, where they lived for a few years, worked on an important book about the origin of coral reefs. Then suddenly his health gave way, as an after-effect, it has been suggested, of contracting the rare Chagas's disease in the Argentine, and to avoid the London racket he and Emma moved to Downe House near Keston in Kent where he stayed as a semi-invalid until his death forty years later.

He must have been a strange husband, prematurely ailing at the age of thirty-three and 'haunted', as he said, 'by that mystery of mysteries, the first appearance of new beings on this earth'. But relief was at hand. The year before he married he had read *An Essay on the Principle of Population* (published 1798) by the political economist T.R. Malthus, which stated that population had always tended to exceed food supply and had been kept down by disease, starvation and other causes.

Here Darwin saw the clue to the variations he had observed in living creatures and their course of development. He called it natural selection and allied it to the concept of the survival of the fittest. In brief this meant that in the plant and animal kingdoms the strong, those well adapted to their environment, would survive and multiply while the weak died out, thus producing ever more hardy species through a process of blind, but continuous, evolution.

This was explained in *The Origin of Species by means of Natural Selection*, first published in 1859, but Darwin did not mention man in the book and the public was slow to grasp its implications. Then it dawned: as man was obviously involved like other animals in evolution he must have evolved from a more primitive species and that could only be – perish the thought! – the anthropoid apes. Though Darwin never said or believed this, the idea acted like a fuse on a time-bomb and violent argument broke out. Here was heresy, an insult both to man and his Creator! Churchmen in particular, and some scientists also, were scandalized. In 1860 at a meeting of the British Association in Oxford pandemonium erupted in the course of argument between T.H. Huxley, an ardent supporter of Darwin, and Bishop Samuel Wilberforce, not improved by none other than Robert Fitzroy rising to his feet, waving a Bible aloft and shrieking that here and nowhere else was the eternal truth. Five years later, shattered in his most cherished belief, he committed suicide.

But the breakthrough was there. As we have seen, the idea of evolution had been in the air for some time; now, whatever the opposition, with Darwin's massive documentation from the voyage of the *Beagle*, it had to be accepted as fact that life is not only a going but a growing concern. This is the foundation for the entire structure of modern biology. In that sense Darwin was the pioneer and his insights are still valid. In some other respects his work has not stood the test of time, at least in the opinion of some scientists steeped in modern genetics, of which of course he knew nothing. Notably in *The Descent of Man* (1871) he tried to bring specifically human characteristics under the umbrella of natural selection, even to the extent of believing that acquired skills could be inherited. Here he failed to distinguish between the rest of the animal kingdom, blindly driven by instinct, and the human power of conscious creativity, discrimination and choice; humanity released from compulsion into the realm of responsibility.

But Darwin was no philosopher, had no interest in social questions, politics or education. His strength, leading to his great achievement, was a passionate concern for observed facts, his enormous industry and his courage in proclaiming truths which he knew would put him at the centre of violent controversy. Perhaps it was an anticipation of that, rather than an Argentine bug, which undermined his health at such an early age.

At least he had the consolation of seeing *The Origin of Species* published all over the world in his lifetime, receiving an honorary doctorate at Cambridge and growing public acclaim. Most comforting of all, no doubt, to this gentle, self-effacing man was the devotion of his wife and family. To his five sons and two daughters he was an admirable parent, respecting their separate personalities, their right to be individuals, and they wrote moving tributes to him after his death. One can imagine, then, his horror at the perverted use which has been made in our own time, notably by the Nazis, of the survival of the fittest to justify their theory of the master race and genocide under the guise of 'social Darwinism'.

He had said, 'When I am obliged to give up observation and experiment I shall die,' and he was working until two days before his death on 19 April 1882. He was buried in Westminster Abbey.

Ten years before, at the conclusion of *The Descent of Man*, he had expressed guarded hope for the future of mankind, but then added – and it is an unconscious tribute to himself: 'But we are not concerned with hopes or fears, only with the truth as far as our reason permits us to discover it.'

Louis Pasteur

(1822–95)

It is possible to diminish someone's greatness by concentrating exclusively on some peak of achievement as though it existed in isolation, arrived at almost by accident. In the case of Louis Pasteur, this is a mistake that can very easily be made. His demonstration of the nature of infectious diseases and of their control by vaccination stands out as one of the great landmarks in the history of science. But this was only the culmination of a lifetime's work and dedication to the principles of scientific inquiry, during which he helped found the sciences of stereo-chemistry and bacteriology, did immense work in French industry and agriculture, and virtually saved the silkworm industry from destruction. It is Pasteur's dedication to both the world of pure science and the welfare of humanity which made him, in his own lifetime, a beloved figure to so many.

Louis Pasteur was born on 27 December 1822 in the old French city of Dôle in the Jura Mountains. His parents, of whom he was deeply fond, were peasants, hard-working, religious, honest and patriotic. His father was a tanner, but was adamant that his son should not follow him into the same life of hard, unremitting physical labour. At thirteen Louis entered the secondary school at the Collège d'Arbois, and it was here that he first began to show promise. He attracted the attention of the headmaster, M. Romanet, who was particularly impressed by the boy's capacity for hard work and his powers of concentration. He realized that potentially Louis was more than just an ordinary school-teacher, and suggested that the boy continue his studies in Paris to prepare for entrance to the École Normale. The family agreed, and at sixteen Louis Pasteur set off for the Pension Barbet in the capital. But he was unable to settle in Paris, and soon his father arrived to take the homesick boy back with him.

Pasteur continued his studies at the local school, spending his spare time in drawing and painting. Soon he had to move again, to start working for his degree at the Collège Royal in Besançon. In 1842 he had obtained his Bachelor of Science degree. Ironically enough, his rating in chemistry was 'mediocre'. Now he really was ready to return to Paris. He applied for admission to the École Normale, and came fifteenth out of twenty-two candidates. This was not good enough for the young Pasteur. He withdrew his application, and continued his studies at the Pension Barbet to try to obtain a higher rating.

This time Pasteur was happy in Paris. When he again applied for admission to the École Normale he came fourth, and began to study for his doctorate. His interest in chemistry grew, as he drew inspiration from the great teacher at the Sorbonne, Professor Jean-Baptiste Dumas. M. Balard, professor of chemistry at the École, arranged for Pasteur to become one of his assistants and at the end of 1847 Pasteur gained his doctorate.

In 1848 he began his first important piece of original research when he became interested in the study of tartaric acid. A strange mystery surrounded this chemical. Mitscherlich had found that there appeared to be two forms of the acid, which seemed identical in every way, having the same physical characteristics and the same chemical composition. But they had one important difference: they had different effects on polarized light. Polarized light is light which instead of spreading out in all directions is limited to one specific plane. What Mitscherlich had found was that when he had passed polarized light through one of the tartaric acid solutions, the beam had been bent out of its path, but when he passed it through the other, which he called racemic acid, the beam went straight on. To Pasteur this was illogical. Why should two apparently identical substances react in different ways? He set out to explore this phenomenon.

He examined the tartrate crystals under a microscope and discovered that the crystals were not, as everyone had supposed, perfectly symmetrical, but in each one there was a single facet which spoiled the symmetry. This he thought could be the explanation for the different behaviour. He then examined the racemic crystals, but, to his surprise, discovered that they too had this odd facet. He still had a mystery. He examined the crystals more carefully and then discovered that they could be split into two groups. In one group, the tiny facet was on one side of the crystal and in the second on the other side. He tested the two types. One set of crystals turned the beam of light to the left, the other turned it to the right. Here was the explana-ation that he had been searching for. The mysterious racemic acid must be a mixture of the two types of crystal, and the effects of bending to the left and to the right exactly cancelled each other out. He carefully tested his theory and it worked. He had, for the first time, advanced scientific knowledge.

Pasteur believed that these different crystal structures were somehow related to the actual arrangement of the atoms inside the crystals. He had no way of testing this theory with the apparatus then available, but his research stimulated interest among other scientists, and his investigation led to the formation of a new branch of science – stereochemistry. And many years later Pasteur's theory about the atomic arrangement in crystals was proved to be correct.

At this time Pasteur was not only concerned with crystals. For this was 1848, the year of revolution. He had inherited his father's passionate republicanism and joined in the political upheaval with enthusiasm. When the rioting began, Pasteur volunteered for the National Guard, in spite of appeals from his family to keep clear of the trouble. When Paris was once more peaceful, Pasteur returned to his work.

That autumn he received notification from the Ministry of Education that he had been appointed to a teaching post in Dijon. His sponsors, Professors Biot and Balard, tried to use their influence to keep the young scientist in Paris, but were unsuccessful. Reluctantly, Pasteur travelled south. But his stay in Dijon was short. Only three months later he was appointed assistant professor of chemistry at the University of Strasbourg, where he stayed for five happy years, being soon made a full professor.

At Strasbourg, Pasteur paid his official visit to the president of the university, M. Laurent. He also met the president's daughter, Marie Laurent. Within two weeks of their first meeting he had written his formal marriage proposal and handed it to Marie's father. On 29 May 1849 the young couple were married.

Pasteur himself was still investigating his mysterious racemic acid. Although he now had an explanation for its behaviour under polarized light, he was still not able to prepare the acid directly from tartaric acid. It was May 1853 before he achieved success, and hardly had this occurred before he chanced upon another strange property of racemic acid. One day he found a mould growing on a racemic acid solution. He tested this with polarized light and found the light turned only to the left. To Pasteur this demonstrated that the tiny living organisms had actually selected just one of the two types of racemic acid crystals on which to grow. This extraordinary selectivity began to lead Pasteur away from the study of purely chemical changes to speculation about living matter. However, by the end of the year, the strain of his intense work started to show on Pasteur, and he left for a holiday in Paris. While he was there, news came through of a new appointment. He was to be professor of chemistry and dean of the new science faculty at Lille.

Some of Pasteur's greatest work was done during the years at Lille. His interest in microbes was growing and he was now able to spend a great deal of time in his laboratory. A local industrialist brought a problem to Pasteur. His factory was concerned with manufacturing alcohol from beet sugar, but too often the product turned sour. Pasteur agreed to investigate and did so with his usual thoroughness. He found the cause in tiny rod-like organisms, or bacilli, which gave out lactic acid, thus souring the alcohol. But Pasteur found more than that. He also observed how yeast cells, again living organisms, were actually responsible for the creation of the alcohol from the sugar. This was a revolutionary idea, for here were tiny living creatures actually *causing* chemical changes. This was contaminating nice pure chemistry by that intractable, complicated process – life. The opposition was enormous, but when Pasteur demonstrated that without the presence of microbes no fermentation could take place, his cause was won.

In 1857 Pasteur left Lille to return to the École Normale in Paris as administrator and director of scientific studies. In 1862, at the third attempt, Pasteur was elected to the Academy of Sciences. At this time he again became engaged in practical work for industry. This time it was France's wine-making industry which was in trouble. For a long time there had been trouble from wine which inexplicably soured during the maturing period. Pasteur found that by heating the young wine in the casks to 55 deg. C with a small amount of air present, the microbes that caused the souring were all destroyed. Furthermore this process in no way affected the flavour of the wine. This is the process that became known as pasteurization.

Three years later Pasteur was asked to study a problem in an area which was quite new to him. The French silkworm industry was being ruined by an unknown disease which affected the worms and spoiled the silk threads that they spun. Pasteur knew nothing at all about silkworms, but he agreed to tackle the problem. Two years of careful work resulted in his being able to isolate the causes of the disease. Unfortunately no sooner was that problem solved than he discovered a second disease attacking the silkworms. The whole laborious process had to be repeated before that disease too could be isolated. Meanwhile, Pasteur had become involved in the politics of the École Normale. In a situation familiar enough a century later, Pasteur backed authority against a rebellious student body. As a result he was dismissed, which eventually turned out to be no great tragedy. He was appointed head of the new physiological chemistry department at the École and also professor of organic chemistry at the Sorbonne.

Pasteur's private life had been dogged by tragedy. Two of his daughters had died in infancy, and now he himself, at the height of his career, was a victim. On 19 October 1868 he suffered a paralytic stroke. His left arm and leg were virtually paralysed, but within three months he was back at work. Shortly afterwards he heard that his efforts to save the silkworm industry had been successful: five years of hard work had received their reward.

The following year saw France's declaration of war against Germany. All Pasteur's patriotic fervour was aroused. Unable to contribute actively, he demonstrated his feelings by returning the honorary degree awarded him by the University of Bonn.

After the war, Pasteur began work on the problems of contagious disease. His theory that putrefaction was caused by germs led to the introduction of antiseptic surgery by Lister, which was to save thousands of lives in operating theatres throughout the world. Pasteur now began to study the newly discovered anthrax bacilli which were responsible for a deadly disease in sheep. He demonstrated that the tiny organism, and that alone, was responsible for the disease. But he still had a great problem to solve, how to prevent and cure the disease. The answer came as a result of a fortunate accident. Two of his assistants had been working with chicken cholera and had carelessly left a cholera culture untouched while they went on a short holiday. On their return they injected the culture into a hen and to their surprise the hen lived. They then gave the hen a second injection of a new culture. But still it survived. They were worried about their mistake and confessed their errors to Pasteur. He at once saw the significance. The old cholera culture had aged and died, but had given protection to the hen. Now followed intensive work to produce this effect at will. Eventually Pasteur was successful. He turned his attention again to the anthrax bacilli. He produced a weakened strain and injected it into the sheep. The vaccination worked! The sceptics doubted, so Pasteur arranged a public demonstration. At a farm near Melun fifty healthy sheep were selected. Twenty-five sheep were vaccinated. Two weeks later all fifty sheep were injected with a lethal dose of anthrax culture. Pasteur prophesied that within forty-eight hours all the vaccinated sheep would be alive and well, and all the unvaccinated sheep would be dead. The demonstration was a complete success.

Now Pasteur was ready to move to the greatest problem of all – vaccination of humans. He began to study the terrible disease of rabies. First he had to isolate the microbe, which involved the dangerous work of collecting saliva samples from mad dogs. Initially he was unsuccessful, and not until he had used nerve tissue from the dogs could he be sure he had found the home of the disease. But this was no microbe that would be seen under a microscope. It was far too small for that: it was what we now call a virus. After more work, Pasteur was able to produce a weakened virus which would protect the dogs from rabies. By 1885 he had progressed even further. He had been able to cure dogs by vaccination *after* they had been bitten. That year was to see the biggest step forward of all.

On 6 July 1885 a nine-year-old boy, Joseph Meister, was brought to Pasteur's laboratory in Paris. He had been badly bitten by a rabid dog and unless some treatment could be given he would undoubtedly die. Pasteur agreed to treat the boy. Dr Gracher gave the first injection, but already nearly three days had passed since the boy had been bitten. However, every day the boy became a little healthier. The treatment worked. Soon the word spread and others began to come to the laboratory to be cured. The principle of vaccination had been established.

For the remainder of his life, Pasteur was to receive honours from all over the world, but none can have given him greater satisfaction than the establishment of the Pasteur Institute in Paris, which was to continue his work on contagious disease. The great institute was established in 1888, and it was there that Pasteur spent the last years of his life. His other refuge was his holiday home in the old castle at Villeneuve-L'étang. Pasteur died on 25 September 1895. He was given a public funeral by the French government and memorials were erected in many parts of France. But the true memorials were the Institute that bore his name and the work that still goes forward from the discoveries he made.

Johann Mendel

(1822–84)

A quiet, Augustinian monk, pottering about a monastery garden in Moravia counting peas: not everyone's idea of a man of science. Yet Johann Gregor Mendel was the founder of the science of genetics.

Johann Mendel was born in the part of Silesia that is now part of Czechoslovakia, in the village of Hyncice. His parents were peasant farmers, and the boy was sent to the local village school to begin his education. He at once began to show his ability and, when he reached the age of eleven, his headmaster persuaded the Mendels to send their son to continue his education at the Piarist High School in Lipnik. He stayed there only one year before moving on to the Gymnasium at Opava, where he remained until he finished his schooling in 1840.

The young Mendel was anxious to continue his studies, but the family was far too poor to meet the cost. He enrolled anyway for the philosophy course at the University of Olomouc, and then tried to find work as a private teacher to meet the costs. But in spite of all his efforts, he was unsuccessful. The strain affected his health and he was forced to return home, where he spent a whole year convalescing. When he was completely recovered, his younger sister Theresia gave him part of her dowry so that he could go back to Olomouc. He returned in 1841 and this time he was able to find private tutorial work to help pay his expenses.

For two years he continued at the university, but again and again the strain of trying to teach and study proved too much for him, and his health suffered. Obviously he could not continue this way for very much longer. Friedrich Franz, the professor of physics at Olomouc, suggested a solution. He proposed Mendel as a candidate for the Augustinian monastery at Brno. Most of the members of the monastery were teachers and Brno was the centre for scientific and cultural work in Moravia, so this was an opportunity for Mendel to continue his academic work and at the same time be freed from financial worries. On 9 October 1843 Mendel was accepted as a novice under the name of Gregor. He appears to have entered the religious life of the monastery more from necessity than from conviction, but from the day he joined he served the monastery faithfully and well.

Even in the security of the monastery Mendel's nervous illnesses affected him badly. He had to be taken off all pastoral duties, mainly because he reacted so violently when he had to visit the sick. In 1849 he was appointed as supply teacher to the Gymnasium in Znojmo, and discovered that he had a real talent for teaching and enjoyed the work. He at once applied to sit for the examinations which would enable him to take up a permanent teaching appointment. He took the tests in the summer of 1850, and in the October heard the disappointing news that he had failed. However, he had made a very good impression on one of the examiners, Professor Baumgartner, who suggested that Mendel be sent to the University of Vienna to do extra work in the natural sciences. The abbot of the monastery agreed and in October 1851 Mendel set off for Vienna to begin two years of study that were to lead directly to his great work in the field of hereditary mechanisms.

Mendel was especially fortunate in Vienna, for he came into contact with three great scientists and teachers. The physicists Christian Doppler and Andreas von Ettinghausen taught him the experimental methods of physics and the use of mathematical analysis, and the professor of plant physiology, Franz Unger, aroused his interest in the problems of hybrids and hereditary factors. It was this grounding in both physics and botany that provided the essential basis for Mendel's future experimental work.

In July 1853 Mendel returned to supply teaching at Brno. Two years later, he again applied to sit for the teacher's certificate, but yet again his health broke down under the stress. This time he became so ill he was not even able to complete the first written examination. He never tried again, and remained a supply teacher for sixteen years. But at least he had some spare time and he was able to begin his researches into the problems of plant hybridization.

The basic facts of plant hybridization had already been reasonably well established. It was known that if two plants were crossed, the first generation would resemble one of the parents, but the second generation would be a mixture of the characteristics of the two original parents. For example, suppose two types of pea plant are crossed, one a tall variety, the other dwarf. The offspring may all turn out to be tall. But if we then cross two of these tall, first-generation plants, their offspring will be a mixture of tall plants and short plants. These facts were known, but no one had any explanation for them.

Mendel set to work with edible peas, which he grew in the monastery garden. He selected twenty-two varieties for his experiments. What he was trying to do was test a theory, which he had already worked out, to explain the known facts. He believed that there were two types of hereditary factor for each of the plants' characteristics, and that these were contained in the pollen grain, and that there were a further two factors contained in the 'egg cells' of the female plant. In other words, there were two factors for height, two for colour, two for shape and so on, in each of the parent plants.

He decided to test this theory by statistical methods. He counted the occurrence of different characteristics found in the second generation of plants. For example, he crossed a plant which had round peas with one which had wrinkled peas. In the first generation, he found that all the plants gave round peas but in the second he counted 5,474 plants with round peas and 1,850 with wrinkled peas. In other words, the ratio of round peas to wrinkled peas was almost three to one. He found that this same ratio of three to one held for all the characteristics that he tested. How did this fit the theory? The answer is – incredibly well. This was precisely the result that Mendel had been hoping for, and even he must have been surprised with the exact fit of experiment to theory. To see why, it is necessary to appreciate exactly what Mendel's theory meant.

Suppose we take the characteristics of the peas, round and wrinkled. According to Mendel, one of the plants should carry two factors, which we now call genes, which pass on the characteristic of roundness. The other plant should have two factors for wrinkled peas. Now when the two are crossed, we get one factor for roundness from one plant and one for wrinkled from the other. The round factor is stronger than the wrinkled, so all the plants have round peas. But the plant still carries the two different factors. Suppose we call the round factor, R, and the wrinkled factor, W. Then the factors contained in the new plant will be R and W. Now if we cross one RW plant with another RW plant, what happens? Well, if the plants pass on the different factors in a purely random way, then there are four possibilities. An R factor from the first can join with an R from the second to produce an RR – in other words, the new plant will have round peas. If an R from the first joins with a W from the second, we get RW, but as the R factor is the stronger we still get round peas. If we get a W from the first and an R from the second, we get WR, and again the R is stronger so we get round peas. So the first three possibilities all result in round peas. But if we get a W from the first and a W from the second, the result is WW. So, in this case, all the peas are wrinkled. The final result is that three of the possible combinations result in round peas and one in wrinkled: exactly the ratio that Mendel found in his experiments. Mendel took his experiments a stage further and bred a third generation of his hybrids. Just as he would have expected from his theory, if he bred from the round peas which contained the RW mixture, the results were mixed, but if he bred from the wrinkled peas which contained only the W factors then they went on producing only wrinkled peas. This was magnificent confirmation of his theory, and for the first time the mechanism behind Darwin's newly published theory of evolution could be understood.

Apart from the theory about individual characteristics, Mendel had also demonstrated that each pair of factors acted independently of any other pairs of factors. In other words, even if you could predict exactly whether a particular plant would be short or tall, this in itself would tell you nothing about the colour of the flowers. This part of the theory accounted for the enormous variety of different characteristics found in different plants and animals.

Mendel finished his work with peas in 1863, but he was very well aware that his ideas conflicted with orthodox scientific opinion. So he set to work to produce yet more evidence. This time he crossed French beans with bush beans. The results tallied exactly with those he had found for peas. Next he crossed the bush bean with the scarlet runner, but this time he found one result which did not fit in with this theory. The bush beans and the scarlet runners had different coloured flowers, and the flower colours in the second generation failed to fit the three to one pattern. Mendel was worried by this result, and decided for the first time to make his results public in the hope that someone might come forward with an explanation. He discussed his work on peas at two meetings of the Brno Natural History Society. The society was not a great deal of help, but it did at least publish the two lectures in 1866. Forty copies were printed, and this remarkable discovery of the mechanism of heredity passed virtually unnoticed by the scientific community. Mendel did his best to arouse interest in his ideas, sending out copies to a number of learned societies, but no one seemed interested. It is one of the most curious episodes in the history of science, that a major discovery could be made and be completely neglected in this way. In fact over thirty years were to go by before the monk's work was to be 'discovered'.

The only scientist to take a serious interest in Mendel's work was the highly respected botanist, Carl Naegeli. Unfortunately, Naegeli not only doubted Mendel's results but suggested further work which misled Mendel. After this snub, Mendel made little effort to explain his theories to the world. He continued his experiments, following Naegeli's advice and working with the plant *Hierarcium*. Mendel was not to know when he started that *Hierarcium* was an abnormal genetic type, and he spent a great deal of frustrated effort in producing hybrids from which he could obtain no clear results. In 1866 he started a new series of experiments to repeat the hybridizations carried out by another famous botanist, Carl Gaetner, but he kept no records of this work.

In the spring of 1868 Mendel was appointed abbot of the monastery at Brno. He wrote to Naegeli, telling him of his new appointment, but adding that he would still have time to continue with his experiments. For once, Mendel was wrong. He soon found his new duties taking up more and more of his energies, and within two years he was forced to abandon his work with the plants. One affair in particular occupied the new abbot, and indeed continued to keep him busy until his death. This was a battle with the civic authorities over a new ecclesiastical tax they were levying, which was to amount to 10 per cent of the total value of all the monastic property. Mendel sent in an accurate assessment of the value, refusing to take advantage of various let-outs in the law, but equally refusing to pay over one penny of the tax. The argument went backwards and forwards between the city and the monastery, but Mendel never gave way and at his death it took a long time to sort out the whole tangled affair.

In his last years, Mendel's health again declined. But he remembered past kindnesses. His young sister had given up part of her dowry to help him with his studies, and now he was able to repay her by helping her two sons with their education. In 1884 the abbot finally succumbed to the kidney complaint which had been troubling him for some time. There was no great public mourning at his death. His former students of Brno mourned at the death of a man they remembered as a kind and enthusiastic teacher. The monks of the monastery mourned for the good abbot, who had worked hard for their welfare. Perhaps a few thought of him as a scientist and remembered his experiments. But to most his life and work remained obscure. And there, in one sense, the story of Johann Gregor Mendel ends. But in another sense, the climax had still to come.

The final episode in the story of Mendel takes place sixteen years after his death. In 1900 a Dutch botanist, Hugo de Vries, was ready to publish the results of his years of research into plant hybrids when he received a copy of Mendel's paper of 1865. He must have been dismayed and astonished to discover that his work had already been carried out by an obscure monk in Moravia. Furthermore this monk had produced a complete theory of genetic mechanisms. De Vries went ahead and published his own findings, but had to give the precedence to Mendel. At precisely the same time two other botanists, Correns and Tschermak, had been at work. They had reached the same conclusions as de Vries when they too discovered Mendel's original paper. In England William Bateson, a Cambridge botanist, received word of Mendel's paper and became an enthusiastic proponent of Mendelism. So, within the one year of 1900, the name of Mendel and his theories had become famous in the world of science. His theories were discussed, his experimental results analysed and finally his conclusions were accepted. The mechanism of inherited characteristics of all living things, plants and animals, could now be investigated. The new science of genetics had been born. For thirty-four years the work of a shy, nervous monk who had 'pottered about in the garden, counting peas' had lain unnoticed. Now, at last, Mendel had come into his own. His place among the great men of science was assured.

Thomas Huxley

(1825-95)

Once he called himself 'Darwin's bull-dog', and certainly the progress of the evolutionary theory owed more to his clear and unwearied exposition than to any other cause. Even when he was growing old and tired he was not slow to reach for that formidable weapon his pen, to denounce some folly, expose some humbug, come to the aid of some hard-pressed colleague, propound some new and hopeful truth.

Thomas Henry Huxley was born at Ealing, then a village set among the fields and market-gardens of Middlesex, on 4 May 1825. His father was on the staff of the large semi-public school that had its premises next to the church, and from him Huxley supposed he might have inherited a faculty for drawing, a hot temper and 'that amount of tenacity of purpose which un-friendly observers sometimes call obstinacy'. Physically he owed almost everything to his mother, a woman of an emotional and energetic temperament, with piercing black eyes, whose most distinguishing characteristic was rapidity of thought. This latter quality, he wrote in a personal memoir, had been passed on to him in full strength; it had often stood him in good stead and he would part with most things more willingly than with his 'inheritance of mother-wit'.

For a couple of years, from the age of eight to ten, Huxley went to the school in which his father taught. This was all his regular schooling, for the headmaster died and the school broke up. George Huxley moved back to Coventry, his native town, and became manager of a savings-bank. Tom was left very much to fend for himself, and he spent his time reading everything he could lay his hands on and in pursuing courses of study of his own devising.

This was his way of life until he was fourteen or fifteen. In 1839 two of his sisters married, and both married doctors. Dr Cooke, who married the elder sister, practised in Coventry, and he began to give his young brother-in-law some instruction in medicine with a view to his making that his profession. Early in 1841 it was arranged that the boy, not yet sixteen, should go as assistant to Dr Chandler in Rotherhithe. His experience in London's dockland provided a grim commentary to what he

177

had been reading in Thomas Carlyle. 'I saw strange things there,' he wrote years afterwards, 'among the rest, people who came to me for medical aid, and who were really suffering from nothing but slow starvation . . .' After some little time he was apprenticed to his other medical brother-in-law, Dr J.G. Scott, whose practice lay in north London; and then at the age of seventeen he obtained a free scholarship at the medical college of Charing Cross Hospital. There he remained for three years and, according to his own account, 'worked extremely hard when it pleased me, and when it did not, which was a very frequent case, I was extremely idle, or else wasted my energies in wrong directions'. This must be something of a libel, however, since as early as 1843 he was winning prizes for chemistry, anatomy and physiology, and in 1845 he passed his MB at London University and won a gold medal for anatomy and physiology. Furthermore, in that same year he had published the first of what proved to be a long list of scientific monographs. This appeared in the *London Medical Gazette* under the title 'On a Hitherto Undescribed Structure in the Human Hair Sheath'.

A chance conversation led to the next step in Huxley's career. A friend suggested that he should write to Sir William Burnett, at that time director-general for the medical service of the Royal Navy, with a view to obtaining an appointment as ship's surgeon. He did so, and Sir William summoned him to an interview, with the result that he was entered on the books of Nelson's old ship, the *Victory*, in Portsmouth harbour, for medical duty at Haslar hospital. His official chief was Sir John Richardson, famous for his Arctic voyages, and on his recommendation Huxley was appointed assistant surgeon on HMS *Rattlesnake*, a 28-gun frigate being fitted out for an exploring expedition to New Guinea and the Australian coasts. Early in October 1846 he joined his ship at Portsmouth and on 3 December they set sail.

The whole cruise of the *Rattlesnake* lasted almost four years, and years afterwards Huxley described it pretty scathingly in an article for the *Westminster Review*. One passage runs,

Exploring Vessels will be invariably found to be the slowest, clumsiest, and in every respect the most inconvenient ships which wear the pennant. In accordance with this rule, such was the *Rattlesnake*; and to carry out the spirit of the authorities more completely, she was turned out of Portsmouth Dockyard in such a disgraceful state of unfitness that her lower deck was continually under water during the voyage.

The equipment for her special purpose was altogether inadequate.

But on another occasion he showed that he was by no means ungrateful for the opportunity that the voyage had afforded him.

Life on board was exceptionally rough [he wrote] as we were often many months without receiving letters or seeing any civilized people but ourselves. In exchange, we had the interest of being about the last voyagers to meet with people who knew nothing of firearms – as we did on the south coast of New Guinea – and of making acquaintance with a variety of interesting savage and semi-civilized people.

Apart from experiences of this kind there were the opportunities afforded for scientific work – opportunities of which he took the fullest advantage, collecting a huge store of natural history specimens and writing papers on biology and physiology which he sent home to scientific journals and institutions.

There was yet something more that proved of incalculable importance to his happiness as an individual. In March 1848 we find him writing to his sister that on one of the ship's long visits to Sydney his home there had been the house of his good friend Mr Fanning. And Mrs Fanning had a sister (Henrietta Anne Heathorn), 'and the dear little sister and I have managed to fall in love with one another in the most absurd manner after seeing one another – I will not tell you how few times, lest you should laugh'.

On his return to England in November 1850 Huxley was gratified in being accorded a place in the front rank of naturalists: his zoological collections and scientific papers had made sure of that; and in 1851 he was elected a fellow of the Royal Society at the very early age of twenty-six. But all the same, his future seemed very uncertain. He might have continued in the navy, but he had no wish to do so and retired from the service in 1854. A doctor then? But (so he admits) he had never cared about medicine as the art of healing; he had wanted to be a mechanical engineer, and at Charing Cross hospital 'the only part of my professional course which really and deeply interested me was physiology, which is the mechanical engineering of living machines'. No, what he settled upon was a career in science, and he was soon writing, 'Science in England does everything – but *pay*. You may earn praise, but not pudding.'

Why, the great Professor Owen was receiving only £300 a year, less than the salary of a bank clerk ...

Huxley applied for post after post, and was always disappointed. He was not far off thirty, without a settled job – and the girl he had left behind him in Sydney was eating her heart out in loneliness and longing. But 1854 proved the turning-point – in fact he called it his Year of Victory – as not one job but several tumbled into his lap: an appointment as naturalist to the Geological Survey, a lectureship and then the professorship of natural history, including palaeontology, at the School of Mines (later the Royal College of Science) in Jermyn Street. There also came the glad news that the Heathorns were on their way to England.

At the beginning of May 1855 Huxley met his Nettie again after five years of separation, and he was dismayed at her appearance. Her health had broken down utterly, and she looked at death's door. He took her to one of the best doctors of the day, who told him, 'I give her six months of life.' 'Well,' replied Huxley, 'six months or not, she is going to be my wife.' They were married in July, and embarked upon what was to prove a most happy married life of forty years.

For the next few years after his marriage Huxley was more than busy with his lecturing to students, researches into special problems of zoology and palaeontology that attracted him, and the publication of his results in a long series of scientific papers that won him widespread recognition and distinctions. By the time of the publication of Darwin's *Origin of Species* in 1859 he was becoming known to the general public, and the support that he gave to the promulgation of the evolutionary theory carried great weight. He reviewed Darwin's book in *The Times*, and from the outset of the tremendous controversy performed valiantly. Darwin was modest and retiring; Huxley was vigorously argumentative and loved a scrap.

The famous occasion (30 June 1860) of the British Association meeting at Oxford provided an exciting confrontation. Huxley had another engagement, but when he learnt that Bishop Wilberforce intended to 'smash Darwin' he took his place on the platform. The room was packed to suffocation, since 'Soapy Sam' (as the bishop was nicknamed, on account of his peculiar style of oratory) had a big following. He lived up to expectations. He spoke for a full half hour, to quote one who was there:

with inimitable spirit, emptiness, and unfairness. It was evident that he had been 'crammed' up to the throat, and that he knew nothing at first hand. He ridiculed Darwin badly, and Huxley savagely, but in such dulcet tones, so persuasive a manner, and in such well-turned periods. . . He assured us that there was nothing in the idea of evolution; rock-pigeons were what rock-pigeons had always been. Then turning to his antagonist with a smiling insolence, he begged to know, was it through his grandfather or his grandmother that he claimed his descent from a monkey?

As soon as the bishop had sat down, Huxley – 'a slight tall figure, stern and pale, very quiet and very grave' – rose to reply. There were no reporters present, and the accounts of his actual words are confusing. But there is no doubt about their gist. Another report said there was no reason why a man should be ashamed of having an ape for his grandfather. But if there were an ancestor whom he would feel shame in recalling it would rather be a *man* – a man of restless and versatile intellect – who plunged into scientific questions with which he had no real acquaintance, only to obscure them by an aimless rhetoric and distract the attention of his hearers from the real point at issue by eloquent digressions and appeals to religious prejudice. The effect of his words were tremendous. Some men jumped on their seats in excitement, and at least one lady fainted and had to be carried out.

Henceforth Huxley was in the forefront of the battle. Where Darwin was slow to push his theory to include man, Huxley felt no such hesitancy. A series of lectures on the 'Comparative Anatomy of Man and the Higher Apes' was published in book form in 1863 as *Man's Place in Nature*, whereas Darwin's *Descent of Man*, in which he expounds the same view as Huxley's, that man and the higher apes share a common ancestor, did not appear until 1871. 'There never was book so derided and scoffed at as my first book, *Man's Place in Nature*,' he recalled shortly before his death, 'but it was true, and I don't know I was any the worse for the ridicule.'

This book marks the beginning of his lifelong campaign to 'get science across' to the general public. He was the first and perhaps the greatest – certainly one of the most successful – of 'popularizers', with such books as *Lessons in Elementary Physiology*, *Elementary Biology* and *Physiography*. He loved giving scientific letures to audiences of working men, of which a fine specimen is *On a Piece of Chalk*. When he started on his career 'science' hardly featured in the curriculum of even the highest centres of education; largely because of his splendid advocacy and example, by the close of the century there was not a board school that did not teach it.

But Huxley was not only a scientist; he was a man of the broadest culture, a man of letters in the widest sense, a man who could hold his own with the philosophers and metaphysicians and work havoc among the defenders of Bible orthodoxy, among them the great Mr Gladstone. Huxley was an agnostic; in fact, he coined the word as being the most appropriate title he could think of for those persons who, unlike atheists and pantheists, Christians and free-thinkers, were quite sure that they had not solved the problem of existence and had a pretty strong conviction that the problem is insoluble. Agnosticism, he explained, 'simply means that a man shall not say he knows or believes that which he has no scientific grounds for professing to know or believe'.

Between 1862 and 1874 Huxley was appointed a member of no fewer than eight royal commissions. He was Lord Rector of Aberdeen in 1872, and was the holder of a number of honorary doctorates conferred on him by universities in Britain and abroad. More than once he refused a title in recognition of his services to science and education, but at length in 1892 he accepted a privy councillorship from Lord Salisbury. His last years were spent at his home in Eastbourne, where he found an ever fresh interest in tending his garden. He died on 29 June 1895 and was buried in Finchley cemetery, beside his little son Noel, his first-born, who had died thirty-five years before. And on his tombstone were inscribed, by his special direction, three lines from a poem written by his wife – 'lines inspired' (so Leonard Huxley concludes his 'life' of his father) 'by his own robust conviction that, all questions of the future apart, this life as it can be lived, pain, sorrow and evil notwithstanding, is worth – and well worth – living':

> Be not afraid, ye waiting hearts that weep;
> For still He giveth His beloved sleep,
> And if an endless sleep He wills, so best.

James Clerk Maxwell

(1831-79)

James Clerk Maxwell who, with Newton and Einstein, stands at the summit of the achievements of theoretical physics, was born in Edinburgh on the morning of 13 November 1831. He was descended from the Clerks of Penicuick, a well-known Scottish family, and the Maxwells, whose name his father took when the family came into the Maxwell inheritance, a country estate outside Edinburgh. Here John Clerk Maxwell, the scientist's father, built a pleasant roomy house where the young James passed his childhood years.

He grew up a hardy country boy, but from the earliest years he was asking questions. When he was aged only three his mother wrote to a friend: 'He is a very happy man ... he has great work with doors, locks, keys etc... and "show me how it does", is never out of his mouth.' Maxwell was very fortunate in his father who himself, though a lawyer by profession, was an enthusiastic member of the Royal Society of Edinburgh and a keen amateur of scientific matters. James's questions, about the heavenly bodies and the workings of mechanical things, were all met with a sympathetic interest and intelligent answers which encouraged him to search further.

He and his cousin made their own 'moving pictures', a favourite toy of the nineteenth century; it consisted of a large disc with drawings round the edge which when whirled quickly round gave the illusion of movement. For this James devised an 'animated cartoon', which showed the life-cycle of a frog from an egg. Later, when he was twelve, James's toys showed a precocious sophistication when he began to make models of geometrical solids such as the cube, the tetrahedron, a four-sided figure of equilateral triangles and even the 12-sided dodecahedron.

By this time Maxwell had been at school at the Edinburgh Academy for two years, and had already suffered his first deep tragedy when his mother died in his eighth year. Mrs Maxwell had, like her husband, given the young James the beginnings of an essential trait in his adult character by her conscientious and intelligent introduction of him to religion. When he went to school, James found himself a laughing stock, nicknamed

'Daftie' thanks to his country clothes and provincial manners, and he developed a slight stutter which he never completely shook off. But after a fallow period at school his talents developed rapidly.

At the age of fourteen he produced a paper on the subject of the mathematics of oval curves. After attending a lecture at the Edinburgh Society of Art on mathematics in art, Maxwell went home and did his own experiments which led him not only to equations for the right drawing of ovals of various kinds but also, by a brilliant stroke of intuition, to further equations which linked his geometric figures to the refractive properties of light. His father took the paper to a member of the Royal Society. The mathematician, when convinced that the whole thing was not a hoax, was impressed not only by the brilliance of the young Maxwell but also by the work in its own right, and arranged for it to be read at the Royal Society of Edinburgh. By the time James had been at Edinburgh University for two years the prospects of a brilliant career were assured.

Late in 1850 Maxwell became a member of Trinity College, Cambridge. Again his provincial manners seem to have caused concern, and a private tutor was engaged to help the young man not only in the necessary discipline of expressing himself more clearly on paper but also in improving his table manners. But it must be confessed that Maxwell's reputation for eccentricity was not altogether unearned. Apparently his urge to investigate and experiment led him to some private research into the best time of day for taking physical exercise, and it is recorded that the corridors of Trinity resounded to the thud of his running feet between the hours of two and two-thirty in the morning until direct action from other undergraduates put a stop to it.

Maxwell's determination to find out for himself led him also to investigate at first hand the claims of the spiritualist organizations at the university and the phenomenon of 'electrobiology' or hypnotism. He won second place in the overall markings for the mathematics tripos, although he failed to achieve the distinction of Senior Wrangler. In due course he was elected a fellow of his college and came on to the teaching strength where his work involved him not only in the teaching of undergraduates, but also in voluntary work in classes organized outside the university for workers' education.

Maxwell's talents as a lecturer do not seem to have been outstanding. But his contributions to scientific advance grew in importance with his experiments on the perception of colour by the human eye and his prize-winning paper on the stability of the rings of the planet Saturn.

The problem posed by the strange configuration of Saturn was this: how could such a system remain in equilibrium if the rings, or the planet's gravitational field, or any of the other forces acting in the system, would inevitably tend to be magnified until the system destroyed itself? By brilliant reasoning Maxwell showed that not only were the rings not solid or even continuous, as they could be if liquid, but that they were in fact made up of myriads of discrete particles – 'flying brickbats' he called them. This was not only an important contribution to the astronomy of the solar system, but also prepared the way for Maxwell's pioneering work in statistical mechanics.

In 1857 Maxwell left Cambridge to take up an appointment as professor of physics at Marischal College in Aberdeen. 'No jokes of any kind are understood here,' he wrote to a friend. 'I have not made one for two months and if I feel one coming I shall bite my tongue.' However, there was one consolation at Aberdeen in the shape of the daughter of Principal Dewar. In 1858 James Maxwell and Katherine Dewar were married; a marriage which Maxwell's young disciples and his scientific colleagues seem to have deplored but with which he, as far as we can judge, was perfectly happy. His time at Aberdeen ended when his department was fused with that of King's College, when King's and Marischal were amalgamated to form the University of Aberdeen.

From Aberdeen Maxwell went to London in 1860 to take up the post of professor of natural philosophy at King's College.

Maxwell's career at London did not begin auspiciously when, in the summer of 1860, he went down with an attack of smallpox from which he recovered only thanks to the devoted nursing of his wife. In 1865 he relinquished his post at King's and retired to Scotland. This was probably due to a combination of reasons including health and the need for uninterrupted study for the preparation of his great work on electromagnetism. In 1867 he and Katherine went on an extended continental tour, and then four years later, in 1871, somewhat reluctantly Maxwell accepted the chair of experimental physics at Cambridge University, a new post which carried with it the highly important and, for a man like Maxwell, fascinating responsibility of supervising the building of the new Cavendish Laboratory.

This great research centre was made possible by the munificence of the seventh Duke of Devonshire, Chancellor of the

University. It was named after his ancestor Henry Cavendish, a considerable scientist in his own right whose papers Maxwell himself edited and published. Whatever criticisms of Maxwell's talents as a lecturer, the Cavendish Laboratory is a lasting monument to his exacting standards as a researcher and to his deep understanding of the needs of students. The laboratory was launched on a tradition of greatness which has been brilliantly sustained by a succession of outstanding physicists so that it has remained one of the greatest research institutes in the world. The laboratory was officially opened in 1874, the year after the publication of Maxwell's great treatise on electromagnetism. Within two years signs of the cancer which was to kill him were beginning to make themselves apparent, but Maxwell did not seek medical advice until it was too late. He died peacefully on 5 November 1879.

A contemporary physicist has said of Maxwell that there was 'scarcely a single topic that he touched upon which he did not change almost beyond recognition'. We have already referred to his work on the stability of the rings of Saturn and mentioned his important contributions to the theory of colour; to these should be added researches into the nature of colour-blindness. Not only did he develop a 'colour top', which allowed composite colours to be built up from the three primaries and their exact proportions to be accurately calculated, but he also worked out the typical calculations which have since provided the basis of work in this field. In quite another field he did pioneering studies when he produced 'Maxwell's thermodynamic relations', which describe the behaviour of materials under varied conditions of temperature and pressure.

However, it was in the study of the kinetic theory of gases that Maxwell made one of his greatest contributions to science. This concerns itself with the way in which movements of molecules in gases give rise to their observable characteristics of pressure and temperature. Other researchers before him had come to the conclusion that these characteristics would be most effectively described in terms of the rapid movement of the molecules of the gas, as a result of which they collided with the walls of the containing vessel and with themselves. But without a sound mathematical base the distribution of velocities between the molecules and the frequency of their collisions could not be meaningfully discussed. By introducing the notion of statistical computation Maxwell was able to take account of the fact that the speed of individual molecules would differ, and give valid, mathematically based estimates of the mean distance travelled by individual molecules and of the frequency of their collisions. This was not only a massive advance in the kinetic theory of gases, but opened up a whole new science of statistical mechanics.

To contemporaries this was probably Maxwell's greatest achievement as a theoretician, but for posterity it is above all for his *Treatise on Electricity and Magnetism* of 1873 that his name is listed among the immortals. From the very beginning of his career he had been interested in the electrical researches of the great English physicist Michael Faraday. Maxwell once said: 'Before I began the study of electricity I resolved to read no mathematics on the subject until I had first read through Faraday's *Researches on Electricity*.' The two men were corresponding regularly from the mid-1850s, and on his arrival in London Maxwell was able to meet the ageing Faraday.

It was Michael Faraday who had exploited the known relation between magnetism and electricity to produce the first electric generator with the historic experiments of 1831, and had triumphantly shown that an electric current could be induced in the presence of a fluctuating magnetic field. From this discovery of electromagnetic induction stems the whole of modern electrical technology; without it quite simply electric power would be impossible. But the explanation of the effect force was still to seek. Contemporary science favoured an explanation in terms of action at a distance, analogous to the operation of the force of gravity, but Faraday's intuition led him to the hypothesis that in some way a magnet set up lines of force in the space surrounding it to create a force field.

When Maxwell began his study of electricity then, what was needed was a framework of theory which would adequately unify the observed phenomena of electricity and magnetism, and would provide explanations and grounds for prediction in any imaginable conditions. In an elegant paper published in 1857 he was able to give convincing mathematical grounds for accepting Faraday's lines of force. The significance of this can be appreciated by the layman even if the working is complicated. Indeed Faraday himself wrote to Maxwell in November 1857 as follows: 'When a mathematician investigating physical actions and results has arrived at his conclusions, may they not be expressed in common language as fully, clearly and definitely as in mathematical formulae?'

But the work of the mathematician was by no means finished. The Maxwell Equations, still internationally known by his name, gave quantification to two great principles: first, the continuous natures of electric and magnetic fields; and second, the modes whereby change in one can produce change in the other. But it was the leap of imagination which Maxwell now made that brought the final prophetic touch to his work of genius. For he imagined results of his equations in the condition of outer space. The inspiration is reminiscent of his schoolboy act of imagination when he saw the extension of his theory of ovals into the area of the refraction of light.

The outcome here, however, was infinitely more splendid, for Maxwell found that in the conditions of free space his equations yielded the mathematical equivalent of a typical wave movement; from this he postulated the existence of electromagnetic waves with the property of self-propagation. Furthermore he estimated the speed of such waves, and found to his delight that this was within acceptable margins of error equivalent to the most recently estimated value for the speed of light. Thus Maxwell launched the electromagnetic theory of light, and proclaimed the existence of radio waves some twenty years before their discovery under the inspiration of his work by the young German physicist Heinrich Herz.

Robert Koch

(1843-1910)

In the great pandemics which have periodically swept the world throughout recorded history explanations were anxiously sought and proliferated almost as fast as the bacilli themselves. There was the contagion theory and the miasmic theory: some people believed that pestilence was generated within the human body and conveyed by touch or even glance. The miasmatists held that it came from a noxious vapour sucked from the ground by the stars or breathed out by demons.

But such theories, unprovable as they were, could not stick. None of them answered the demonstrable facts, not even in combination: miasmo-contagionism or contagio-miasmatism; while theologians could not explain why divine wrath often relented when people escaped from plague centres into the countryside. The unknown remained the apparently unknowable.

The truth about disease, or at least vital aspects of the truth, was slow to come and as late as 1665 astrologers were still claiming, in the words of John Gadbury: 'He that hath powerful stars is not only shot-free but plague-free.' But at the same time an off-shoot of contagionism was making ground which was to lead eventually to modern bacteriology. In the sixteenth century the celebrated physician of Padua, Jerome Fracastor, had suggested minute organisms multiplying in the human body as the originators of disease and in the early 1500s, when the magnifying glass came into use, parasitic organisms were first observed, such as the itch-mite and minute 'lumbrici' on the surface of teeth and skin. As time went on the primitive microscope revealed a world of hitherto unknown life in blood, urine, faeces and decomposing matter of all kinds. But as long as equipment and the technique of investigation were primitive, the discovery of so much microscopic life confused rather than simplified the issue.

By the early nineteenth century the advance towards a science of bacteriology was gaining momentum. Evidence of a *contagium vivum*, a living and not a chemical source of disease, was mounting on every side. In 1835 Bassi discovered that the silkworm disease known as muscadine was caused by a fungus;

about the same time Schwann and Kutzing found the living organism in yeast that causes fermentation. Another fungus producing a disease of the scalp was identified in 1839. Semmelweiss proved that the scourge of puerperal fever in childbirth was conveyed by an organism and Pasteur discovered that living germs are at work when milk turns sour, butter rancid and wine goes stale. Of such discoveries a young German doctor practising near Posen was aware and deeply interested. His name was Robert Koch and he has his place in this book as representative of many great names that crowd the pages of late nineteenth-century medical history: Joseph Lister, Paul Ehrlich, Emil Behring, to name only three.

Koch was born in 1843, the third of a family of nine sons and two daughters, the children of a mine inspector in the Harz mountains. At an early age Robert decided he wanted to become a doctor. He studied medicine at Göttingen and qualified in 1866. After short appointments in Hamburg and its neighbourhood he became a general practitioner at Rackwitz near Posen.

Koch's work in this obscure country area was to be, as it turned out, the first rung on the ladder to fame. Everything about the quiet, meticulous young man pleased the Rackwitz farmers: his competence, good humour when they called him out at night, his love of animals and feeling for the country life, his sociable enjoyment of zither-playing and skittles. As for his female patients, they adored him. 'Ah!' wrote one of them later, 'as soon as Dr Koch came into the room you felt better at the mere sight of him.'

When he went off to help with the wounded in the Franco-Prussian War the Rackwitzers raised a howl of protest and before long they managed to get him back as district medical officer centred on the local town of Wollstein.

But at night, sitting on a bale of straw in a farm cart as he was driven over rough tracks to his patients, he was not only thinking of them. Anthrax was rife among the cattle in the neighbourhood and Koch was wondering about the cause. For some years certain facts had been known. A rod-shaped bacillus occurred in the blood of some but not all animals dying of anthrax. Healthy animals injected with blood containing these bacilli had all contracted anthrax; on the other hand, some animals had died when injected with blood that did not contain the bacilli. This confusing picture imposed one conclusion: the rod-shaped bacillus could not be the prime cause of anthrax, which Koch was determined to find.

His wife had given him a microscope for his birthday and

Koch closeted himself in a primitive laboratory, temporarily handing over his patients to neighbouring doctors. To study the bacilli effectively required many innovations in microscope technique, lighting, photography, the preparation of pure cultures and nutritional media, and arrangements for heating the cultures. All these problems Koch solved entirely on his own in a course of research embodying methods still used today.

The results were astonishing. Koch found that anthrax bacilli multiply in the blood of animals by lengthening and subdivision. Leaving the sick animals in blood or other discharges, they then form spores on coming in contact with the air and it is the spores, picked up from the air or ground by healthy animals and growing into bacilli again within the body which cause the disease.

Koch found various ways of killing the anthrax spore and the disease could then be brought under control. But the results of his research went much further. It now seemed probable that every disease of man or animal had its specific originating organism and, in proving experimentally the validity of postulates put forward some years previously by the German pathologist Jakob Henle (1809-85), Koch established the basis of modern advances in bacteriology and a guide to the discovery of the etiological agents in many of the most important diseases of humans, animals and plants. These postulates, or principles, were: (1) A specific organism must be seen in all cases of infectious disease. (2) This organism must be isolated and grown in pure culture. (3) Organisms from pure cultures must reproduce the disease in experimental animals. (4) It must be possible to recover the organism from animals so infected. If these principles are all fulfilled it can then be said that the organism causing a particular disease has been found.

This first great success gained Koch an appointment to the Imperial Board of Health and it was here, as well as later as director of the Berlin Institute for Infectious Diseases, that he obtained government backing for further research on the widest scale. He developed the technique of culture-growth, evolved the method of disinfection by steam rather than by chemicals or dry heat, which has proved such a boon to surgery throughout the world, and in 1882 announced that he had discovered the bacillus of tuberculosis, at that time the first and by far the greatest cause of mortality in civilized countries. Years later, his disciple Paul Ehrlich described the epoch-making scene on 24 March at the Berlin Physiological Society when, quietly and with cogent reasoning, Koch described his researches with visual illustrations. No one present ever forgot that evening, for all realized that a turning-point had come in dealing with the terrible scourge. Tuberculosis was revealed, not as the chronic nutritional disorder that most doctors had supposed, but as an infectious disease that could be cured if the bacillus was destroyed.

Eight years later, in 1890, after much further research, Koch announced the discovery of a substance, called by him tuberculin, which had proved a reliable means of diagnosing tubercular processes. The nature of tuberculin was at first kept secret, but it was in fact a protein substance elaborated by the TB bacillus in artificial culture media, and Koch cautiously forecast that it might prove to be a cure for incipient tuberculosis of all kinds.

But people were not interested in 'mights'. His words released sudden hope throughout the world. Cautious qualifications were swept away and doctors and patients flocked to Berlin for information and treatment. Money poured in for new hospitals and new research, and for months, as a contemporary recorded, Koch's great discovery was on all lips, eagerly discussed in homes rich and poor.

But his caution was, alas, justified. In some cases tuberculin treatment produced improvement, a cure for others and little change in many more. Though tuberculosis is more effectively treated today with streptomycin combined with other drugs, the scourge is still with us, though greatly reduced, and 10,000 people die of it annually in the United States alone. But as a diagnostic agent tuberculin in a modified form is still the most accurate and reliable, better even than X-ray which may reveal other lesions practically indistinguishable from tuberculosis.

But Koch did not rest on these achievements and was busy all his life in tracking down the killer in a number of diseases. In 1883, after discovering the TB bacillus, he travelled to Egypt to investigate cholera at a time, as he wrote later, when practically nothing was known about the cause of the disease and whether it was to be found in the blood or elsewhere. Here again a specific bacillus was found to be the culprit, a comma-shaped bacterium never before identified, which Koch found in the evacuations of sick people and also in the intestinal wall of corpses. Further research in Calcutta, where an epidemic was raging at the time, confirmed the findings and showed that the bacilli could readily be killed with carbolic and infection prevented by the provision of properly filtered drinking and washing water.

Thus cholera could be brought under control, at any rate in Europe where enlightened public health regulations could be enforced, a necessity shown by a cholera outbreak in Marseilles in 1884 where the inhabitants still followed the medieval custom of lighting fires in the streets to ward off the devil.

Koch and the bacteriologists who trained under him at the Berlin Institute, where students came from all over the world to study the new science of bacteriology, were among the first in the world and certainly in their day the most successful in working out the etiology of infectious diseases, their treatment and prevention; and the cloud of ignorance they dispersed is well illustrated by Koch's sight as a young doctor of two young men ill with typhus (and shortly to die) who were being treated in the same room as a wedding party.

As his discoveries piled up, all that was changed and in the later years of his life the ever-modest, scrupulous Koch, an international figure by now, soon to be honoured with the Nobel Prize, was much in demand by governments facing problems of plague, whether it was rinderpest in South Africa, sleeping sickness in Uganda, bubonic plague in Bombay or malaria in Italy and the Adriatic. With seemingly inexhaustible energy Koch studied these problems on the spot with particular attention to the cases of immunity which he often found, so contributing to the development of protective vaccines and sera so much in use today.

When he died in 1910 the world was unanimous in eulogy, praising the weapon of bacteriology which he had given humanity in the battle against disease, praising his extraordinary imagination controlled by a razor-keen analytical brain, praising, not least, his humility, what Joseph Lister called his 'beautiful character'.

Yet Koch, in his spare time an ardent student of philosophy, would, one feels sure, have listened attentively to those voices raised today which warn us against splitting our view of life by over-concentration on scientific analysis, which urge us to unglue our eye from the microscope from time to time and see nature as part of a creative whole where an infinity of factors, some already understood, others barely glimpsed, are influences on our totality, over bodies, minds and souls, in sickness and in health.

Alexander Graham Bell

(1847-1922)

He was a complex, volatile character, a genius who invented one of the most important electrical devices we possess - and yet, in the words of a rival, Alexander Bell knew nothing of electricity and 'never could have invented the telephone if he *had*'. For, by all the teaching of the day, it was impossible.

He can hardly have imagined, as a boy, that one day he would be considered a scientist. Nothing, to young Alexander Graham Bell, could have seemed less likely, for he had already started in the illustrious footsteps of his father and his grandfather; he had discovered that he shared their great gift for teaching the deaf to speak. It was a calling - and he would not refuse that call. Right up till the end of a long and incredibly active life, Aleck Bell was busying himself with the problems of the deaf and the dumb.

To put this genius into perspective we must go back for a moment to the closing years of the eighteenth century and to the chilly, bracing seaside town of St Andrews. The Bell family had been shoemakers there for more years than anyone could remember, when Aleck's grandfather, another Alexander Bell, was born in 1790. He made the startling transition from cobbler to actor, and it was while he was declaiming Shakespeare to a puzzled, happy audience and noting their various expressions of understanding or incomprehension, that he realized exactly what God had in mind for him. He, ex-cobbler Bell, was moving these simple people not by the magic of Shakespeare, which few of them could understand, nor by the handsome regularity of his features, but by the all-important quality of his voice. With a well-trained voice a man, any man, could perform miracles; and from this day on, Alexander Bell would forget about the theatre and teach men to speak. And in particular he would concentrate on those unfortunates, deaf from birth, who had never heard the human voice and thus could not reproduce it. Within a very few years Alexander Bell, 'Corrector of Defective Utterances', was a rich man.

As fame and riches came to him, Bell moved and set up schools successively in Edinburgh, Dundee and London. It was while he and his wife were residing in Edinburgh that their

second son was born – and almost as soon as he was able to
speak, young Melville Bell showed that he had inherited his
father's ability and his ambition. But before he could make
anything of them he fell seriously ill and had to be rushed out
to Canada to stay with family friends and recover his strength.
The bracing air of North America had the desired effect. In
due course Melville returned to Scotland fully restored to
become a lecturer on elocution in the University of Edinburgh.
It was at Edinburgh that Alexander Graham Bell (Aleck) was
born in 1847.

Early in life Aleck evinced a desire to follow in the footsteps
of his father and grandfather. He was educated in the universities of Edinburgh and London, but in 1870 his health deter-
iorated. Both his brothers had died of tuberculosis, and
Melville decided to emigrate to Ontario with his wife and the
surviving Aleck. Canada had healed him once and he was
confident it would do the same for his son.

But before we join them there, a last, revealing glimpse of
the entire family in Edinburgh before death had stolen Aleck's
brothers. Melville had just invented his 'Visible Speech', a
system of phonetics whereby any sound discernible by the
human ear can be written down, and he is giving a demonstration of it to a few friends in his rambling old Edinburgh house.
The three sons are assisting him, and for a description of what
happened here is the Reverend David Macrea, Melville's good
friend.

When Bell's sons had been sent away to another part of the
house, out of earshot, we gave Bell the most peculiar and
difficult sounds we could think of, including words from the
French and the Gaelic, following these with inarticulate
sounds as of kissing and chuckling. All these Bell wrote
down in his Visible Speech alphabet and his sons were then
called in. I well remember our keen interest and astonishment as the lads – not yet thoroughly versed in the new
alphabet – stood side by side looking carefully at the paper
their father had put in their hands, and slowly reproducing
sound after sound just as we had uttered them. Some of
these sounds were incapable of phonetic representation with
our alphabet. One friend in the company had given as his
contribution a long yawn sound, uttered as he stretched his
arms and twisted his body like one in the last stage of
weariness. Of course, Visible Speech could only represent
the sound and not the physical movement and I well remember the shouts of laughter that followed when the lads, after

studying earnestly the symbols before them, reproduced the sound faithfully, but like the ghost of its former self in its detachment from the stretching and body twisting with which it had originally been combined.

The new world smiled on the Bells, welcomed them with enthusiasm and all the highly paid work Melville could accept. They arrived on the first day of August 1870. Back in Europe the Franco-Prussian War was just beginning, but this new, exciting life drove all thought of that from their minds. Melville at the age of fifty-one was starting all over again, but he had one great advantage: he had already been invited to come from Edinburgh, all expenses paid, and give a few lectures to the Lowell Institute in Boston, and it was only a matter of getting used to the prospect of not seeing Britain again. He talked of 'giving the climate a two-year trial', but he knew that if Aleck recovered they would never risk going back.

The Boston lectures were a huge success, but so great was the fame of Melville Bell and his Visible Speech that he was snapped up to give more lectures in Canada and could not agree to a second series south of the border. He suggested that Aleck go to Boston instead. The lad was now twenty-three, making an astonishing recovery from his galloping consumption, and 'qualified in every way to deputize for his father'.

In the first week of April 1871 Alexander Graham Bell moved to Boston: its School for the Deaf had voted five hundred dollars toward his lecture fees, and already teachers were gathering in that sedate New England town to find out what he had to say. So successful were these first lectures that Aleck was prevailed upon to leave Canada and settle in Boston as teacher of 'vocal physiology'.

And now life rushed on. In quick succession he met and fell in love with a beautiful deaf girl, Mabel Hubbard; and conceived the novel idea of a 'multiple telegraph'. Soon he was burning his candle at both ends, giving speech lessons all day and dashing back home in the evening to work on his telegraph. He had two reasons for his devotion to the idea of sending more than one message at a time along the same pair of telegraph wires: the idea had come so suddenly, so naturally, from the experiments he was making with speech that he was certain it must be successful; and if it *were* successful, he would be rich enough to ask for Mabel's hand in marriage. Mr Hubbard, for his part, thought the idea brilliant and commercially promising. He urged the young man to work hard at it.

Aleck had hit upon the principle while he was trying to make a speech that was, literally, visible. If he could get the vibrations of the human voice to trace a pattern across a piece of smoked glass, a deaf pupil could experiment, make sounds with his own voice and by trial and error reproduce the pattern and thus the sound. He found, when using a reed to trace the pattern, that it vibrated in response to one pitch of voice and no other. Reeds of different length were affected by sounds of a different pitch. So, Bell reasoned, might one make a telegraph sounder to respond to one pitch of electric 'buzz' and to no other. In this way it might be possible to send six or more messages each at a different pitch, down the same pair of wires, and have each message read only by the instrument tuned to the correct pitch.

It was a promising idea and experiments were encouraging, but never quite conclusive. But it was during the course of them, working with a young assistant, Thomas Watson, that Bell hit upon the idea of sending the various notes of the human voice down a wire the same way and having them vibrate reeds at the far end.

As we have seen, it was said that if Alexander Graham Bell had known the first thing about electricity he could never have invented the telephone. He hoped piously that he might get some form of electric switch to turn on and off at the speed of a vocal vibration. With middle 'A', the familiar tuning of 'A' of the musician, for example, Bell's 'switch' would have to turn itself on and off 440 times in each second. It stubbornly refused to, refused to operate even at the much lower speeds demanded by the bass notes of a piano. And yet, though the switch was palpably not operating as a switch, Bell and Watson fancied, when they shouted their heads off at it, that they could hear a faint humming from the reed to which it was linked by wires and a battery.

Bell's interest mounted and soon he became so excited by the discovery which seemed to lie just round the corner that he began to neglect his work on the multiple telegraph. His prospective father-in-law grew angry and said that unless he gave up the time-wasting nonsense of this 'electric speech' and concentrated on the telegraph, he would have to give up all thought of marrying Mabel. Convinced he was on the threshold of some great discovery, Bell faced his dilemma. He went on, doggedly, with electric speech. And as he spent more time on it, and made no progress with the multiple telegraph which had been intended to make his fortune, his clothes grew threadbare, his face haggard. Mr Hubbard grew more and more exasperated.

In June 1875 there was a breakthrough. Watson, adjusting one of the several reeds, each with its own switch contact, that comprised his 'transmitter', accidentally plucked it. There was a roar of delight from the next room: the note had been carried, somehow, and the appropriate reed in the 'receiver' was vibrating faintly to it. Still this was not human speech. Yet, as Watson wrote many years later, 'The speaking telephone was born at that moment. Bell knew perfectly well that the mechanism which could transmit all the complex vibrations of one sound could do the same for any sound, even that of speech.'

Bell, that very evening, wrote to Mr Hubbard: 'I have accidentally made a discovery of the greatest importance. . .' Mr Hubbard was unimpressed. No one was impressed. But Bell knew he had found the secret of electric speech, even though that metal larynx obstinately refused to utter.

The months dragged on. And then, on 10 March 1876, the voice spoke. The faithful Watson was listening, ear hard against the receiver. Suddenly – perfectly, frighteningly, clear – came the words:

'Mr Watson, come here! *I want you.*'

The words had come, not through the air, but along the pair of wires, and Watson, whooping with delight, tore into the next room. An agitated Bell was mopping at his trouser leg, but when he blurted out his news, all thought of trousers vanished from Aleck's mind. Like children playing some game, a vocal musical chairs, they pranced from one room to the other, reciting poems to each other along the wire, singing snatches of song. Bell had spilt battery acid down his clothes and being a poor man, unable to buy more clothes, he had been appalled. Forgetting his electric device he had shouted for Watson to come in with water to help him save his trousers.

Within two years Bell was demonstrating his invention in England to Queen Victoria. Before that, he astonished people at the United States Centennial Exhibition. Transmitter and receiver were separated by one hundred and fifty yards of wire, and the distinguished visitors, helping to commemorate the hundred years which had passed since Independence, were astonished at hearing Bell's voice squeak down the wire with 'To be, or not to be, that is the question. . .' The foremost scientist of the day, Sir William Thompson, soon to be Lord Kelvin, gasped when he heard the voice. A visiting Japanese asked whether the machine spoke his language as well and was delighted to be shown that it did.

By now Bell realized exactly how his machine worked. His contacts, his 'switches', did not operate at all, but the mere vibration of the metal reed near an electromagnet generated a fluctuating current which was sent down the wire and made the electromagnet at the receiver set a sympathetic reed dancing to the same note. His transmitter and receiver were identical.

Still Mr Hubbard was sceptical. But after Bell had made improvements to his machine, and the Post Office in England had written and asked him to design them a 'telephone system', he relented and allowed the young Scots inventor to marry his daughter. Their honeymoon was spent, partly, in designing a telephone system in England and Scotland. Aleck was delighted to be back in his native land, to show it off to his young and beautiful wife, but he had become too much of an American to want to stay there. A few months was sufficient before he went back to Boston. In 1882, just six years after the first anguished telephone call, he became an American citizen.

He lived a long and active life during which he discovered how to transmit sound along a beam of light, made the first practical 'gramophone' as we know it today, with a flat record, and designed a number of successful aeroplanes. The Wright brothers had flown a few years before, but it was only with the public demonstrations of Bell's various aircraft that men and women realized that flight was at last a fact. The gramophone was eagerly seized upon as being a vast improvement on Edison's 'phonograph' with its little waxed cylinder; though Bell gave Edison full credit for having improved his own telephone out of all recognition by the invention of a carbon-granule microphone. The amazing concept of a voice along a beam of light was more than the last years of the nineteenth century could accept; and only now, with the development of laser beams, is the idea being used.

Bell died on 2 August 1922 at his American home. To the last hour of his life he was puzzling over a new improvement to an old invention. We may have been deprived of it forever.

Georg W.F. Hegel

(1770-1831)

Georg Wilhelm Friedrich Hegel was born in 1770 at Stuttgart, the son of a revenue officer, and studied theology at Tübingen, where he became a friend of Hölderlin and Schelling. He was more interested in the classics than in theology, however, and the theological certificate he obtained in 1783 stated, ironically in the light of his later career, that he was deficient in philosophy.

After a spell as a private tutor in Berne and Frankfurt, he became a *Privatdozent* or lecturer at Jena in 1801. From 1802 to 1803 he was joint editor with Schelling of the *Kritisches Journal der Philosophie*, to which he contributed many articles. Hegel was appointed to a chair at Jena, just before Napoleon's victory in 1806 which closed the university, and he had to spend the following decade as a newspaper editor in Bamberg and as a headmaster of a *Gymnasium* in Nuremberg. He married Marie von Tucher, twenty-two years younger than himself, in 1811. In 1816 he became a professor at Heidelberg, and in 1818 he succeeded Fichte in the chair of philosophy in Berlin, where he remained until his death in the cholera epidemic of 1831.

Hegel was, then, a professor of philosophy. He described his books as an attempt 'to teach philosophy to speak in German'. His first major published work, *Die Phänomenologie des Geistes* [The Phenomenology of the Mind] appeared in 1807. In his second work, *Wissenschaft der Logik* [The Science of Logic] (3 vols., 1812, 1814, 1816), he developed his system fully for the first time and, in particular, his famous view of the dialectical process. Every truth, he held, is a synthesis of two contradictory elements; the formula of thesis, antithesis and synthesis was clearly spelt out. The book made his reputation and brought him the offer of three chairs. In 1817 he produced his *Encyklopädie der Philosophischen Wissenschaften* [Encyclopedia of the Philosophical Sciences]. His views on political philosophy were expressed in his *Philosophie des Rechts* [Philosophy of Right] in 1821. His lectures on art and aesthetics and the philosophy of history were published after his death, as were his proposals for the German constitution, from the collated lecture notes of his students.

His collected works extend to nineteen volumes (1832–40)

and were the basis of his influence, especially on German education and on later philosophers – especially F.H. Bradley, T.H. Green, R.G. Collingwood and Benedetto Croce. The two-hundredth anniversary of his birth in 1970 was marked by the publication of a twenty-volume edition, and there is an impressive Hegel Archive in the University of Bochum.

But no philosopher, least of all so academic a figure as Hegel – who never intervened directly in politics – can be understood merely as a writer and teacher. Indeed as teacher and personality Hegel was dull and unimpressive. The reason for his importance lies in part in his doctrines, but even more in the coincidence of the man and his times. For Hegel's career spanned the end of the *ancien régime* and years of revolution. In the year of his birth, Marie Antoinette of Austria married the Dauphin of France, James Cook was sailing round the world and discovering Australia, and British troops fired on a mob in Boston, causing five Americans to die – for a 'country' none of them knew. In the year of his death, Napoleon had been dead ten years, the United States was now an independent republic reaching the western ocean, and Karl Marx was thirteen. Hegel's death took place a few months after the revolutions of 1830 and thus his life spanned the years of hope passing through dictatorship to the emergence of nationalism. And he died four years before the first German railway was opened in 1835.

The dominant influences on the young and theologically-minded student were the French Enlightenment, the Revolution and Napoleon. Hegel began by believing, with the *philosophes*, in the ruthless application of reason to all the affairs of men. 'What is real,' he said, 'is rational.' Like Kant he saw the facts of history as in themselves devoid of meaning; the only way to grasp and understand the past was, he believed, by the application of reason, for order rests not in the chaotic world around us but in the mind of man. And what he particularly admired in France was that the ideas of the *philosophes* were put into action – they now appeared to be the cause and the instrument of political change. It was possible for philosophers to be, in measure, kings. Bliss was it, indeed, in the dawn of 1789 to be alive.

The first and strongest note in Hegel's philosophy, however, is that of change, of challenge and response, of progress as a central fact in history and as the product of the constant clash of opposites. Hegel began, then, like Goethe, as a man of the Enlightenment. It was the spread of knowledge that gave meaning to history. But in contrast with the *philosophes* he never divided men into good and bad; early on, he accepted that even those who opposed progress conditioned its course and direction, by the very fact of opposition. To him the essence of history is the dialectic of struggle and conflict. The historical consciousness was strong in him. As with Herodotus, whom he greatly admired, his philosophy is a philosophy of challenge and change, and the method - the dialectic - owes much to Heraclitus. Moreover, he was influenced as much by German mysticism as by French rationalism. This, and the romanticism of his youth, reinforced his strong sense of change and mutability.

But what the revolution also did for him was to make him aware that the world could be changed, and by philosophers. Philosophers and poets became increasingly concerned with politics. Hegel himself abandoned the study of theology for philosophy because he said theology could save souls but not the body politic. Philosophy's task was to demonstrate the unity and rational order behind the material world, but it was also to be, to him as to Bacon, a guide to statesmen.

Second, change and turmoil were not always welcome. Hegel felt acutely the sufferings of his country under the impact of the revolution. In *The German Constitution*, written when he was thirty-two, but not published, he bewailed German feebleness. He saw the essence of her weakness in the absence of statehood; it was this, he believed, that gave France and Britain their unity and hence their power and wealth. Moreover, by 1802 the excesses of the revolution were all too clear. Order, he believed, is essential to society. 'A settled government is necessary for freedom.' What he most admired and envied in the Napoleonic Empire was its strong central government, its sense of order and Codes of Law. The alarms of German weakness in 1802-6 were redoubled after 1815. Such was Hegel's prestige that he was called on by the Prussian Minister of Education, Von Allenstein, to lecture to students and army officers, to act as guide and counsellor, a philosopher made king indeed. Against this unrest he wrote his *Philosophy of Right* in 1821, and here the essential political conservatism of the man is most clearly expressed.

Hegel became an admirer and defender of the state, and the idealization of the state is the third and most characteristic feature of his philosophy. He saw the state as sacrosanct - it is 'the Divine Idea' as it exists on earth. For the sovereignty of numbers, the rights of man and other such abstractions and universals he had the same scorn as had Burke. Cynics have said that for him the kingdom of Prussia and the kingdom of heaven were one and the same.

This is a basic part of the Hegelian doctrine. *Freiheit* is not liberty, not freedom from restrictions, but freedom to fulfil oneself in society, to become part of a larger whole, and in doing so to escape from the limitations of self. There is here something of St Augustine, and something of Plato, and much that is later found in T.H. Green. But the whole which offers an individual escape and salvation is for Hegel not God but the state. Differences between states must be settled by war; and war is a fact of life, not a matter for moral judgement. He saw in Machiavelli and Richelieu the two heroic figures in modern politics. This was not a glorification of war but a plain recognition of the facts of life and history.

All of this suggests the steady remorseless evolution of an arch-conservative and an authoritarian. But much as Hegel admired the German state and saw in it the actualization of an idea, his awareness of the constancy of change and of the dialectic operating in history meant also an awareness that there was no final form. At the end of the historical process when the state has fully realized itself, a global state of universal reason would be attained. The origins of Marx's vision is here.

Hegel's conservatism was in any event counterbalanced by his belief in freedom and in progress, by the remorseless working of the dialectic through history. For him history gradually replaced reason, or in measure became its voice. History, he says, 'is the development of Spirit in Time, just as Nature is the development of the Idea in Space'. The spirit, Hegel contends, enters a certain people for a time and then leaves them. When the spirit is most intense, the individual is fused with the state and absorbed in it. It is this spirit – at once mind or reason or God and also energy or will – that is the creative force through history.

Much of this sounds, and is, like the language and approach of the *philosophes*. Robespierre also saw progress as the march of reason. But to Hegel, reason and God are one – he never quite escaped the grip in the formative years of his youth of the mystic Christian tradition going back to Meister Eckhart of the thirteenth century. Whereas to Diderot and the Encyclopedists the advance of reason and enlightenment was episodic, a series of inexplicable and little-related events, Hegel sees progress as a universal force. But it is the work of people, who must will it and struggle for it. Reason means effort and will and conflict, not just the revelation of great truths. And it is in the struggle that we perfect ourselves. We are part of history by willing ourselves to be so. Here Hegel is the forerunner of Marx.

In the last decade of his life Hegel wielded immense influence. He helped to make Berlin a rival to Vienna as an intellectual centre. His colleagues were equally influential as scholars – and as myth-makers. Friedrich Karl von Savigny, the friend of the Grimms, taught law and was for a time a Prussian minister; he preached the importance of German rather than French law, and founded a new system of jurisprudence to match the new doctrine of the folk-nation. And the young Leopold von Ranke, who began that collection of source material that marks the beginning of scholarly history, infused with this an acceptance of the Hegelian view that the power struggle is the most important theme in history.

Hegel began as a Romantic and ended up as a conservative. It is by no means an unfamiliar course, as one's experience widens. But unlike Savigny, and despite his own influence and renown, he was an ivory tower philosopher. He was first and last a metaphysician and a system builder, interested not in men but in mankind and what he called 'absolutes'. Like Kant he dealt in generalizations; some of his concepts are elusive and they are not always clearly presented. Yet he was through it all a rationalist, not a dreamer; a conservative, but not a Hitlerian.

Thus the two striking features of Hegel's writing are his method – the dialectic – and the result, the nation state as idea and ideal. To him they were inseparable. But in the end they became distinct. His notion of progress as dialectic was used by Marx to become the economic interpretation of history and as the intellectual instrument of socialism; in the end therefore it became internationalized and assumed the withering away of the state. Nationalism for its part gradually lost its radicalism and became conservative in essence. In his method and in the content of his writing Hegel can be seen as the author of the two dominant political philosophies of the twentieth century.

Hegel, and still more the school of his disciples, are responsible for developing that worship of the idea of the state to which late nineteenth-century and early twentieth-century Germany and Europe fell victim. His lectures, though delivered without style or oratory, were treated in contemporary Europe as the work of a sage. As the proponent of will and power, his name was invoked by Bismarck and Wilhelm II. His notion that progress is the consequence of a dialectical process of thesis and antithesis working out through history has been one of the great seminal ideas in European philosophy and sociology; it was taken over in different form by Marx. Consesequently, Hegel is at once the founding father of European conservatism and the unwilling grandfather of European communism.

Stendhal

(1783-1842)

Stendhal, whose real name was Henri-Marie Beyle, was born at Grenoble in 1783 of a comparatively well-off *bourgeois* family. He adored his mother, who died when he was seven. He detested his father, whom he had heard say 'It is God's will' when his mother died. He had an unhappy childhood and developed strong anti-religious feelings at an early age, augmented by the lack of understanding of a priest who was for a time his tutor. In 1792, when Louis XVI was guillotined (Henri Beyle was nine), he records in the autobiography of his early years 'a shock of pleasure'.

He studied at Grenoble to enter the École Polytechnique in Paris, the elite school for soldiers, engineers and administrators; but when, aged sixteen, he went to Paris for his examination he failed to present himself to the examiners. Why? The charm of Paris – and the fact that he arrived on the day before General Bonaparte, already his hero, overthrew the Directory and became First Consul – the 18th of Brumaire (9 November) 1799. Stendhal found work in the military administration through a relative, Pierre Daru. Later he obtained a commission in the 6th Dragoons in Bonaparte's army in Italy.

He was in love with the gospel of revolution, and deeply impressed by the hope which this army commanded by young men brought with it and which seduced the Italians of the north. Stendhal at seventeen began his most permanent love affair – that with Italy. The tombstone that he designed for himself had the inscription 'Enrico Beyle – Milanese'.

He served as a soldier until 1814, when he was thirty-one, though there was a break in 1805 when he followed a woman to Marseilles and opened a grocer's shop. He may have exaggerated his fighting experience and probably did not fight at Marengo, at Jena or at Wagram. But he certainly took part in the Russian campaign of 1812, in the terrible retreat from Moscow, and he remained with Napoleon during the last desperate battles in France. In 1814 Napoleon abdicated and retired to Elba. Stendhal returned to Italy. The lone-wolf trail had begun; the empire was over, and he had no profession.

He stayed in Italy from 1814 to 1821, when the Austrian

police hounded him out as a dangerous 'liberal'. But this liberal was above all a lover of the beautiful. He wrote a great deal to live – a history of Italian painting, several books of Italian travels and chronicles, the lives of Haydn and Mozart. In 1821, when he returned to France, he began writing regularly on literary subjects for English magazines – *The London Magazine* and *The New Monthly*. He was a devotee of Shakespeare. He frequented the literary *salons* of Paris – a strange man, a *poseur* to some people, with his caustic tongue, love of logic and his enthusiasms. He treated women as though they were intelligent, which many men of letters did not. In conversations he would deliberately take the opposite side to that generally adopted. To acquaintances, he was a disquieting figure.

From the age of fifteen, when he first fell in love with more than usual adolescent violence, until the end of his life, Stendhal was occupied and preoccupied with 'the greatest and for me almost the only thing which matters'. Apart from prostitutes, with whom he sometimes slept, and innumerable short affairs, the catalogue of his loves is impressive in its length. It was not until he went to Milan in 1814 that his preoccupation with sex became a preoccupation with love. In 1800, during his first visit to Milan, he had admired Angela Pietragua, the mistress at that time of a French officer. He met her again during a short visit in 1811, reminded her of their meetings and said he had been in love with her. 'But why didn't you say so?' she asked him. She was an impulsive amorist, bold, energetic, with a strong love of drama and intrigue. Stendhal was only one of her lovers, but for a long time the one who pleased her and satisfied her most. With her, he forgot Waterloo and the tragic end of the Napoleonic epic. Angela Pietragua delighted and tormented him. His next love, Methilde Viscontini-Dembrowska, like Stendhal a liberal intriguing against the Austrians who now held northern Italy, rejected him outright. By 1824 he was cured of Methilde by the Countess Curial for whom he also had a passionate love. This affair lasted two years, the usual period for the Countess to keep a lover being six months. After the Countess came, in 1829, a short passionate affair in Paris with Alberthe de Rubempré, an intellectual French woman.

Stendhal, in his late forties, had the good fortune to be captured, in his turn, by a woman of thirty from Siena, Giulia Ranieri. 'I've seen for a long time that you are old and ugly,' she said to him, kissed him and declared her desire to be his mistress. She was the only woman to whom he proposed marriage. Alas, her relations decided otherwise and, whilst Sten-

dhal was attending to his duties as consul in Civitavecchia, the
seaport near Rome, Giulia was hastily married off to a cousin.

At the age of fifty-six he fell in love again twice. To the end,
even after he had had a first stroke in Civitavecchia, the pursuit
of women transported him out of his worries and out of a
world which was gradually growing drab.

Stendhal considered that love was more important than
literature, and it was therefore logical that he should consider
his treatise on love published in 1824 after his return to France,
his most important work. In 1825, when he learnt of the death
of the beautiful Methilde Viscontini, he wrote in the fly-leaf
of his copy of *De L'Amour*, 'Death of the author'. It was a
hopeless love which had made him seek to understand the
torments he had suffered. *De L'Amour* is a collection of short
reflections and anecdotes written without any sentimentality
or romanticism. He divides love into passionate love – the
greatest, most dangerous and most enthralling; love which
desires strongly the beautiful and exquisite, but which doesn't
go beyond bounds (Angela Pietragua); physical love; and
love-vanity, a very common form of love by which a woman is
desired as an object of luxury like a horse (or today the most
fashionable car). The best-known passage in this book is the
likening of the way love grows in the mind of a man or woman,
unconsciously, after the first sight of the loved object, the way
a branch of a tree left in a salt mine is gradually covered with
salt diamonds. Stendhal calls it a process of crystallization, the
necessary prelude to passionate love, by which the loved one is
invested with every perfection. *De L'Amour* interested Goethe,
as did Stendhal's essay on Racine in which he mocked at the
seventeenth-century French classical tradition.

It was not until 1827, at the age of forty-four, that he wrote
his first novel *Armance*; and then, in 1830, *Le Rouge et Noir*
[Scarlet and Black]. *La Chartreuse de Parme* [The Charterhouse of Parma] followed in 1839. Much of his other work
appeared posthumously, including his memoir on Napoleon.
In 1830, when the Bourbon monarchs disappeared and the
so-called liberal monarchy of Louis Philippe began, Stendhal's
friends managed to get him what he appeared to want, a job in
Italy. He became consul in Civitavecchia. With typical Beylian
perversity, Stendhal seems never to have so much loved Paris
as when he was supposed to be living and working in Italy. He
performed the bare minimum of his diplomatic tasks and only
remained in Italy because of Giulia Ranieri.

So let us sum up this man. In his attitude towards religion
he belonged to the eighteenth century, to the Voltairian tradi-

tion of mockery. Attracted by Napoleon, his fervour faded somewhat when Napoleon made himself emperor in 1805. Stendhal was a 'liberal', which in those days meant something near a conspirator. His fifteen years as a soldier deeply marked his outlook. It gave him an admiration for energy, a quality which he looked for in men and women. His attitude towards women was a blend of opposites. He was at once a Casanova or a Don Juan, a professional seducer in whom the finer feelings are not a predominant characteristic, and the most sensitive and idealistic of lovers. This did not make for happiness, but it gave him an uncommon understanding. This paradox in his attitude to women is that too of his attitude to life. He conceives his heroes as men of will but also of a good-natured ingenuousness and sincerity; or, in the case of Julien Sorel in *Scarlet and Black*, of passion which only finds complete expression in surrender of life.

'I have taken a ticket in a lottery, the first prize of which is to be read one hundred years from now,' said Stendhal about the time he wrote *Scarlet and Black*. Although his works on history, painting and music were widely known, his novels were scarcely known at all during his lifetime. He took not the slightest notice of this, not even searching for the few reviews, generally supercilious, which appeared. There was one major contemporary exception. Ten months after *The Charterhouse of Parma* had appeared, the great Honoré de Balzac wrote an immensely long article about this novel, which he declared was the greatest work of its time. It was a very generous and inspiring article. It is strange that Balzac had never read *Scarlet and Black*, although he mentioned some other of Stendhal's works, such as *De L'Amour*.

Public taste in the early nineteenth century was no doubt alienated from Stendhal's novels by their style. In France more even than in England, the taste of the early nineteenth century was for long descriptions of landscapes, houses, appearances of people; for evocative, emotionally charged prose. Stendhal never went in for long descriptions; his points are made quickly and briefly, almost negligently. On the other hand, he is much more to the taste of our time, and André Gide noted of him with pleasure that 'he insists so little'.

The nineteenth century was essentially moralistic and moralizing. Balzac, who certainly never feared to touch the seamy side of life, draws his good and bad characters in sharp black and white. Flaubert, a rebel against social conventions, a hater of the *bourgeoisie*, shared the Victorian moral code; and what else is *Madame Bovary* but an indictment of moral laxity and vice? Neither Sainte-Beuve, the French critic who was a contemporary of Stendhal, nor Flaubert could abide him. Sainte-Beuve, for example, was deeply shocked by the fact that in *The Charterhouse* the beautiful Gina, Duchess of Sanseverina, had poisoned the Prince of Parma; and that Count Mosca, whose mistress the Duchess was, had arranged her marriage to the Duke for his own purposes. Sainte-Beuve even suggested that Balzac must have been bribed to praise *The Charterhouse of Parma* so highly. Times change. The philosopher and writer Alain, who, at the end of the nineteenth century, had an influence extending far outside literary or political circles, expressed the view of today: 'The exterior rules of morality I despise; and on this I follow close in the footsteps of Stendhal. The force of a soul, its truth to itself, that is virtue.'

Stendhal was no preacher of amorality or of 'a new morality' as Nietzsche was. Because he avoided hypocrisy, because he never muffled his mind or intoxicated himself with words, all that he wrote has the quality of freshness and naturalness. He certainly lacked any kind of moral prejudices. His heroes are most imperfect viewed from a pulpit, but he casts no stone at them; nor does he, on the other hand, emphasize the perfect moral beauty of Madame de Rénal. He answered his critics:

Is it the author's fault if his character, seduced by passions which he, unfortunately for himself, by no means shares, descends to actions which are profoundly immoral? It is true that things of this sort are no longer done in countries where the only passion which has survived all others is that for money. . .

Stendhal is the least 'literary' of novelists. He hoped, as he said, to be read by posterity; but his was not the ambition which 'scorns delights and lives laborious days'. He 'scribbled away his bits of nonsense in a garret' because he liked doing so, he gave his friends to understand. He didn't, in Oscar Wilde's phrase, 'put his genius into his life'. It is rather that Stendhal tended to live like a character of fiction himself – hence his frequent changes of pseudonym and habitat. In his own life the boundaries between fact and fiction were never totally clear. Did this help him to give his characters, often complicated, always exceptional, that quality of being so human that their triumphs delight, their misfortunes and deaths appal? All one can say with certainty is that his three most successful novels fulfil Berenson's definition of the greatest works of art – 'they enhance life'.

Stendhal died of a stroke in Paris in 1842.

Percy Bysshe Shelley

(1792–1822)

He was the eldest son of the eldest son of a wealthy landowner. His future was assured: Eton, Oxford, a rich inheritance of land and money, a sound marriage, a seat in Parliament in the Whig interest. For some time, that was the way it went: then it all went wrong.

Percy Bysshe Shelley was born at a country house near Horsham, Sussex, on 4 August 1792. He developed almost feminine good looks, belied by boyish mischievousness and temper and accompanied by astonishing gifts of imagination and literary memory. As a child he could recite back whole poems after only one reading and spin strange stories around made-up experiences. At the age of ten he was sent to his first boarding school, Sion House, Isleworth. Inevitably, he was unhappy there, for he was the type for whom – then as now – boys' boarding school life was least suited. His sensitivity and tendency to day-dream made him a choice target for bullying, which, bad as it was at Sion House, proved far worse at Eton, where he went after two years. There he was known as 'mad Shelley' and goaded unremittingly. He would not seek refuge in conformity, refusing to be anyone's fag, a revolt against hallowed custom that was not to be countenanced. He would spend his life in similar rebellion, and would never escape the bullying which is as prevalent amongst adults as amongst schoolboys.

Shelley left Eton in 1810, headed for University College, Oxford. So far, his career had accorded to pattern and his parents were pleased enough to let him get engaged to his cousin Harriet Grove. The arrangement lasted only for a few months. Shortly before leaving Eton, Shelley had read the book *Inquiry Concerning Political Justice*, whose startling advocacy of the overthrow of authority and the abolition of marriage had brought both fame and infamy to its author William Godwin, philosopher, novelist and widower of the feminist Mary Wollstonecraft, who had died giving birth to their daughter Mary. Godwin's views had impressed Shelley deeply and his letters to Harriet had begun to reflect them, to the justifiable alarm of her parents. Then, at Oxford, he met his future biographer Thomas Jefferson Hogg, a like-minded anarchist whose endless arguments with Shelley helped to cement his views.

Shelley's marriage hopes crumbled after the publication in December 1810 of his Gothic romance *St Irvyne*. Though he was only eighteen this was not his first publication. While still at Eton he had completed an equally lurid work, *Zastrozzi*, and in 1810 had had published a small volume of poetry 'by Victor and Cazire', himself and his sister Elizabeth respectively. The publisher of *St Irvyne*, a devout Christian, began to have misgivings about some of the novel's passages which seemed to him to reveal deistic beliefs. He wrote to Shelley's father, a conventional-minded man, who swiftly threatened to remove his son from Oxford if he did not abandon his 'detestable principles'. This paternal bullying achieved the same effects as that of Shelley's antagonists at Eton. His engagement to Harriet now firmly broken off from her side, he allowed himself brief despair, talked of suicide, then waded resolutely from the shallows of deism to the deeps of atheism. He wrote and had privately printed a pamphlet, *The Necessity of Atheism*, got an unsuspecting Oxford bookseller to display copies in his window and also sent ones to the vice-chancellor and college heads. Quickly identified, Shelley refused to admit authorship or account for his action. He was sent down. Hogg protested on his behalf and was similarly dealt with swiftly enough for him to join Shelley in the London coach.

They took lodgings together in Poland Street where they studied, wrote and argued as of old. Much of the writings took the form of letters asking their parents for money, without result. They took long walks, some of which brought them to Clapham, where two of Shelley's sisters were at school. It was a practical form of taking exercise, for the girls willingly handed over part of their pocket money to their poor brother. He was able to see something of one of their fellow pupils, Harriet Westbrook.

After only a few weeks at Poland Street, Hogg succumbed to his father's urging and went to York to study law. Lingering for another month in the lodgings, Shelley was visited increasingly by Harriet Westbrook, bringing him the money from his sisters. She invited him several times to the house in Grosvenor Square where she lived with her father and her older sister Eliza. He saw Harriet as fertile soil in which to sow his views. Eliza saw him, a landowner's heir and grandson with expectations of inheriting the baronetcy which his grandfather had been granted, as a splendid catch for her schoolgirl sister. For her part, Harriet was much impressed by the vigour of his

opinions. No doubt prompted by Eliza, she took the initiative
and wrote to Shelley, throwing herself on his protection.

He did not love her and was astonished and alarmed to
receive such a proposal from a sixteen-year-old girl. But he
was sorry for her and afraid that if rebuffed she might kill
herself. He carried her off in the Edinburgh coach and married
her there in August 1811. He was nineteen.

Unable to reconcile himself with his father and equally unsuccessful in persuading the old man to make him a comfortable financial settlement, Shelley remained desperately hard
up. Then, suddenly, his father granted him £200 a year and
Harriet's father promised her a similar amount. Shelley, who
had by now entered into ardent correspondence with his mentor, Godwin, determined that he would make use of this comparative affluence to enable him to further the principles he
had admired in *Political Justice*. He settled upon Ireland as
ripest for the preaching of anarchy and went there with Harriet
and Eliza, armed with supplies of a pamphlet written by him,
Address to the Irish People, which they proceeded to distribute
to anyone who looked likely to respond to its message. The
campaign was a dismal failure.

The trio re-crossed the water to move restlessly between
several residences in Wales and England. At one of these, in
Bristol, Shelley began to write his poem *Queen Mab*, with its
revolutionary message. It was too outspoken against conventions of religion and morals to be produced by a publishing
house, so he had it privately printed and issued in May 1813.
Ianthe, its heroine, provided the name for the Shelley's daughter, born the following month. Shelley was pleased to become
a father, but the birth marked the beginning of the end of the
marriage. Harriet, much influenced by Eliza, who still lived
with them, gave up her efforts at scholarship and became all
woman, interesting herself in things which her husband found
merely trivial. All the same, he cemented their Scottish marriage by undergoing another ceremony in London in March
1814. Eliza left them, and Shelley saw the way to reawakening
his wife's lost interests. Her response was to leave him, perhaps
more to register a protest than with permanent intentions.
Fatefully, it was just at this moment that Shelley, visiting
William Godwin, met his sixteen-year-old daughter Mary.

They fell in love immediately. Godwin, aware of their feelings, forbade them to meet, but they did so secretly. Only four
months after remarrying his wife, Shelley eloped to the Continent with Mary Godwin.

After spending a week in Paris trying to borrow money, they

set off on a six-week tour of France and Switzerland, poor but joyous. Shelley, in a rush of impractical enthusiasm, wrote affectionately to Harriet urging her to come and join them. She did not accept. When they arrived back in London, owing the price of their boat fare, he managed to borrow £20 from Harriet to pay it.

Shelley was now so poor that he and Mary had to live apart, the better to avoid pursuing bailiffs. They met briefly on weekdays in St Paul's Cathedral, where they could not be approached.

In November 1814 Harriet bore a second child, Charles Bysshe Shelley. A death soon afterwards proved more consequential. When Sir Bysshe Shelley died in Sussex, his grandson became heir to the entailed property inherited by his father, the new baronet. He at once offered to sell his father his interest in the estates for cash. Agreement was reached and Shelley found himself entitled to £1,000 a year. It was far more than he needed and, characteristically, he gave it away freely, paying Harriet's debts, settling an income on her and sending William Godwin the first of many sums.

Mary's first child was born prematurely in February 1815 and died in March. Shelley was ill and a doctor assured him that he was dying rapidly of consumption. He was not, but his health would always remain indifferent. He began to write *Alastor, or the Spirit of Solitude*, his fine verse study of the driving force within him, and published it in the spring of 1816. It was ignored. He enjoyed no public success in his lifetime with any of his works and knew only the contempt and detestation his unorthodox thought provoked.

In May 1816 Shelley and Mary visited Switzerland again and met Byron, the beginning of a notable friendship of two great men of utterly different character and with only their poetry as common ground, yet whose association would prove of deep significance to them both. While the two talked for hours on metaphysical themes, Mary listened silently. One night, having heard them arguing the possibility of the nature of life being discovered and the means of creating it achieved, she had a strange vision of 'the hideous phantasm of a man', created by a 'student of unhallowed arts'. Next day she could not wait to start writing her book *Frankenstein*, the prototype of a fictional convention familiar now to far more people than ever read Shelley's verse. As Byron said when he had read it complete, it was a wonderful work for a girl not yet nineteen.

In that same year birth and death again obtruded on Shelley's life. In January Mary's second child, William, had been born. In October her half-sister Fanny committed suicide. It has been suggested that she loved Shelley and killed herself because she could not have him. The idea is unlikely, but her death caused him much anguish. A more personal blow struck him towards the end of the year. Harriet, his wife, was found drowned in the Serpentine.

The practical result of the tragedy was that Shelley and Mary were able to marry at once, despite his continued view on the artificiality of the state of matrimony.

Now living at Great Marlow, Buckinghamshire, Shelley returned to work. He completed the long, partly autobiographical poem *Laon and Cythna*, a work of political prophesy which also has a theme of incest between a brother and a sister. Again, Shelley disclosed the gap between his romantic idealism and the realities of life by glorifying a state of love which he saw as a sort of heroic protest against convention. The teaching of Godwin's philosophy and his own head-in-the-clouds nature enabled him to see life in terms of theoretical abstractions rather than of actuality. It did nothing to endear him to the public.

Incest was also the theme of his play *The Cenci*, based on an account he read in an old manuscript of the relationship between Count Cenci, a Renaissance Italy devil-figure, and his daughter Beatrice. It is the most down-to-earth of his works – 'a sad reality', he termed it – powerfully written and unpleasant in its effect.

By 1819 the Shelleys had left England for good, drawn towards Italy and Byron. Shelley was in debt again, ill and feeling the cold. The Italian climate and scenery restored him partially, though he often thought wistfully of England. His infants were now dead, but another baby was born in this year. It restored the spirits of both Shelley and Mary and he was able to write to a friend that he was in good health, 'ready for any stormy cruise'. It was a fateful metaphor.

In 1819 he completed his masterwork, the verse play *Prometheus Unbound*, which gives the poetically finest and most mature expression of his belief that mankind, having allowed itself to be fettered by religious orthodoxy and dogma, had lost its essential identity as part of nature's order of things, and that only by casting off the chains could the human mind regain its rightful freedom. It was published in 1820, followed in 1821 by *Epipsychidion*, the love poem inspired by his brief infatuation for a beautiful young noblewomen imprisoned in a nunnery, and *Adonais*, his lament for the lot of misunderstood poets inspired by the death of Keats, whom Shelley had tried to help in his last illness.

In August 1821 he turned twenty-nine. He was still a 'mild-looking, beardless boy', tall and slightly stooped, his long hair become grizzled, his voice, as ever, high-pitched, hoarse and the least attractive of his physical attributes. Most of the year was spent at Pisa, much caught up with Byron, whom Shelley admired intensely as a poet but little as a man. By the summer of 1822 he was glad to get away from his fellow poet and move to a remote little house on the Gulf of Spezia. Sharing the summer with their friends Edward and Jane Williams, 'serene people', the Shelleys led an uneventful life, she pregnant again and disliking the solitude, he reading and dreaming aboard the small sailing vessel *Ariel* which Williams, his co-owner, made ineffective efforts to teach him to handle.

On 1 July Shelley and Williams sailed their craft to Leghorn to meet Mr and Mrs Leigh Hunt from England, and try to smooth the way to a relationship between them and Byron in the founding of a quarterly journal. A week later *Ariel* sailed for home on a day of oppressive heat, fog and impending storm. Edward Trelawny, who had intended to sail with them in his own boat but had had to turn back, watched as the storm broke with great violence and the boat vanished.

The bodies of Shelley and Williams were washed ashore some days later and the remains of their craft found. It did not appear to have capsized, but seemed to have been rammed. A story got about later that this had been a deliberate act by some Italians who believed that the *Ariel* had Byron and a large sum of money aboard.

The bodies were buried in the sand until mid-August when, with Byron and Leigh Hunt looking on, Trelawny supervised their burning on funeral pyres on that desolate beach over-looked from afar by the Italian Alps, a proceeding which Shelley would have found satisfyingly romantic; especially that part of it in which Byron, seeing that his fellow poet's heart would not burn, snatched it from the flames. Shelley's remains were buried in the English cemetery at Rome, near those of Keats.

Shelley was the archetype of a classic poet: a master of words and their rhythms; a dweller amongst the clouds, or, rather, the stars; a romantic idealist, 'always in love with something or other', as he put it. 'The error,' he admitted, 'consists in seeking in a mortal image the likeness of what is perhaps eternal.' Several women suffered because of this hopeless search, and he suffered because they did. It provided rich material from which to make exquisite verse.

Thomas Carlyle

(1795-1881)

Thomas Carlyle was a man of contradictions. In his early years he was a radical; later he preached a doctrine of totalitarianism and rejected his earlier beliefs. He was honoured and idolized by his countrymen, who listened carefully to what he said, read his books and rejected or ignored his conclusions. His background was of the strictest and most rigorous Calvinism, yet he rejected the Christian faith, although he held to a somewhat obscure belief in deism.

Looking back on his life and work over the distance of a century it is sometimes difficult to appreciate his significance to the intellectual life of nineteenth-century Britain. It is possible, however, to see that his contemporaries' views were substantially right. Carlyle was a historian who could brilliantly recreate the personalities and events of the past, and for this he was rightly admired. He diagnosed the ailment of Britain at the height of a fever of materialist optimism, and many saw that he was right. He proposed remedies, and his remedies were ignored. The experience of totalitarianism in the twentieth century suggests that his contemporaries were again wise in their judgement. One side of Carlyle which meant much to his friends we can never recreate in its fullness – the brilliance of his conversation and rhetoric. We are left with glimpses, so that now we can only guess at the force of his personality: a dimension has been removed. It is worth bearing this in mind when trying to appreciate why a whole generation accepted him completely as one of the world's great men.

Thomas Carlyle, the eldest of nine children, was born on 4 December 1795 in the village of Ecclefechan in Dumfries. His father was a stonemason, and both his parents shared the same fiercely Puritanical faith. They had left the kirk, which they considered too lax, to join a secessionist sect, the Burghers. The family in which Thomas Carlyle was raised was warmly affectionate but deeply serious; and their code of conduct was based on an unquestioning acceptance of biblical truth. They were poor but frugal, and able to save enough to give the eldest son a good education. After finishing school, Carlyle was admitted to Edinburgh University and set off in November

1809 to walk to the capital. He was a raw, awkward youth and the university was not unduly impressed by the young scholar. Equally Carlyle was not unduly impressed by the university, only Sir John Leslie, the professor of mathematics reaching his exacting standard.

In 1814 Carlyle completed his studies, the most valuable of which had been those he had undertaken for himself in the university library. His original plan had been to enter the ministry as his father had always wished, but already he was beginning to question the absolute truth of the Bible. In the meantime he got a job as mathematics master at Annan, then two years later moved to another school at Kirkcaldy. It was here that he first became friendly with Edward Irving, three years his senior and obviously already destined for a brilliant future as an ecclesiastic. Irving was a strong influence on Carlyle, and the two young men spent many hours discussing literature and philosophy together. But the life of a schoolmaster was becoming more and more irksome to Carlyle, and his growing doubts about Christianity ended in rejection of the faith, though he retained a firm belief in the moral teaching. In 1818 Irving resigned his post and Carlyle left with him for an uncertain future.

Having abandoned all idea of entering the ministry, Carlyle for a time tried studying law, but found this even less congenial than teaching and quickly abandoned the attempt. He did a little private teaching and wrote articles for the *Edinburgh Encyclopedia*. His financial struggles were matched by mental stresses, for since turning away from Christianity he was searching desperately for a new form of faith. The idea of atheism horrified him. The conflict was not resolved until one summer day in 1822 when, walking down to the sea, he suddenly experienced what he later described as 'spiritual new-birth'. This gave him back a God to believe in, though the precise nature of the new belief was never very clearly expressed.

The years after the abandonment of teaching brought other changes besides the spiritual new-birth. First, he began to study German and German writers. Second, his friend Irving introduced him to Jane Welsh. His study of German led him to the writings of Goethe, which completely captivated him. He set to work on a translation of *Wilhelm Meister* and began a life of Schiller. He rapidly acquired a reputation as an expert on the German Romantics. Unfortunately the German Romantics found little favour among the British reading public and the demand for translations and critical appraisals soon

died away. Carlyle, however, did receive kind words from
Goethe which he greatly appreciated and which gave encouragement at a time when encouragement was badly needed.

The second event, the meeting with Jane Welsh, led to one
of the most curious courtships of the time. Jane Welsh lived at
Haddington with her widowed mother. The Welsh family was
a good few rungs up the social ladder from the Carlyles.
Further, Jane herself was a witty, highly intelligent girl, who
attracted many admirers including, in spite of his engagement
to be married, Edward Irving. Carlyle, poor and awkward,
must have thought his chances of capturing Miss Welsh slim
indeed. He succeeded by flattery, not of her beauty but of her
intellect. After the first meeting, the correspondence between
the two consisted mainly of German lessons and literary criticism. Jane came to recognize Carlyle's genius and eventually
agreed to the marriage. The wedding took place on 17 October
1826.

The Carlyles set up home in a small house at Comely Bank,
Edinburgh, where they quickly attained something of a reputation among local intellectuals for the brilliance of their conversations. Carlyle was able to earn some money by writing
occasional articles for the *Edinburgh Review*, although his
views differed widely from the accepted editorial line of the
journal. He applied for a professorship at St Andrews but
was turned down, and financial worries became even more
pressing.

Carlyle's brother, Alexander, took over a lonely, remote
farm belonging to Mrs Welsh at Craigenputtock. In 1828 the
Carlyles moved into a nearby house. Carlyle began work on
Sartor Resartus, an extraordinary book, written rather in the
style of Sterne, in which he expressed his radical ideas about
politics and his mystical ideas about religion. He also canni-
balized his proposed history of German literature to produce
articles for journals. But life at Craigenputtock was hard. They
were short of money and the strain of trying to keep house in
that desolate spot began to tell on Jane.

In the autumn of 1831 Carlyle accepted a loan of fifty pounds
from Francis, Lord Jeffrey, the editor of the *Edinburgh Review*,
and set off for London to try to find work and a publisher for
Sartor Resartus. He was unsuccessful at both and returned
to Scotland. Jeffrey continued to offer help, which Carlyle
rejected for as long as possible. Jeffrey, however, remained
sympathetic and was able to find a job for Carlyle's brother,
John, who, with Carlyle's help, had just finished his medical
training. In 1832, Carlyle approached Jeffrey about a post at

the Edinburgh Observatory, but Jeffrey turned him down and the two men quarrelled. *Sartor Resartus* was at last being published in serial form in *Fraser's Magazine*, but with so little success that the publishers cut Carlyle's rate of payment. He had now begun work on a new project – a history of the French Revolution. The stay in Edinburgh was short. The Carlyles preferred London, and the material for the new work was mostly to be found there. So in the summer of 1834 the Carlyles moved again.

The house they moved to was 5 Cheyne Row in Chelsea, and here they remained for the rest of their lives. Their old friend Irving was in London, but his brief popular success as a preacher was now over. He had become more and more strange in his ways, illness had overtaken him and now he was dying. But there were new friends in London who recognized Carlyle's genius. Foremost among these was John Stuart Mill who welcomed Carlyle as a fellow radical, although Carlyle's radicalism was of a very different order from his own. Mill had been responsible for introducing Carlyle to Ralph Waldo Emerson, and the Scotsman and the American kept up a lively correspondence for many years.

Mill also helped with the work on the French Revolution, and it was to Mill that Carlyle first sent the completed manuscript of the first volume. Mill took it to his friend Mrs Taylor and the manuscript was left overnight on a table. The next morning a servant was looking for waste paper to start the fires. She decided Carlyle's manuscript would do admirably and almost the whole work was burned. A horrified Mill brought the news to Carlyle, who took it surprisingly calmly. Mill offered £200 in compensation, but Carlyle would only accept half, his actual living expenses when writing the lost volume. Nevertheless the loss was a real hardship to Carlyle. His health had always been wretchedly bad, and he found the task of rewriting almost unbearable. But in January 1837 the work was finished. Six months later it was published.

The French Revolution was an immediate success. Thackeray wrote a fine review in *The Times*, Dickens carried it around everywhere and praised it to everyone. Carlyle had arrived. For many this remains his finest work. Certainly, for the first time, he found a framework suitable for expressing his philosophy and developing his style. Lacking modern facilities, the research behind the work is impressive, but more striking is his ability to bring the characters to life, to set off their personalities in a few phrases and to capture the vividness of events. His own remarks to his wife when the work was complete are a fair summary: 'You have not for a hundred years any book that came more direct and flamingly sincere from the heart of a living man.'

Success brought an easing of financial worries, lectures, pamphlets and a new circle of admiring friends. But Carlyle was changing. He wrote an article on Chartism that pleased his radical friends, but in subsequent work, such as *Past and Present*, he began to shift his philosophical ground. His new stand is best summed up in the title for a series of lectures he gave in 1840 – *Hero Worship*. He began to attack Mill's ideas, and soon broke with him entirely. He scorned the idea of universal suffrage as mere head-counting, and instead put his faith in the hero, the strong ruler, a new aristocracy. In his diagnosis of nineteenth-century liberalism's inability to effect significant social change he showed undoubted accuracy, but his solution was very like totalitarianism. In many of his views he was remarkably modern. Even his religion, which his contemporaries found totally unintelligible, seems familiar today with its mysticism and half-defined spiritual force diffusing through all nature. The two sides of Carlyle's thoughts, the political and the religious, determined the future direction of his writings. He concentrated on historical biography, where he could examine the lives of heroes and the workings of the spiritual force in man. In 1845 he published his next major work, the *Life and Letters of Oliver Cromwell*. It is almost totally uncritical of Cromwell, and shows little awareness of social and political factors beyond the individual. As a vehicle for Carlyle's ideas it is perfect.

While Carlyle's literary work prospered and his reputation grew, his domestic life was far from happy. He had always suffered from very bad stomach troubles and now he was a victim of insomnia. The least noise was so disturbing to him that he had a special sound-proof room built at the top of the house. His wife too was always ill, often on the verge of a nervous breakdown. The pair often quarrelled, particularly over Jane's jealousy of her husband's friendship with Lady Ashburton, though this was in fact purely platonic. In spite of all these difficulties the Carlyles' home was full of visitors who came to talk to the great man. In later years these conversations became little more than monologues by Carlyle, who impatiently dismissed all dissenters.

After the publication of *Cromwell*, Carlyle wrote little for some time. He made two trips to Ireland, where he travelled the country with a young Nationalist leader, Duffy, who acted as Carlyle's Boswell, carefully recording conversations and comments. In 1849 he wrote a racist pamphlet on slavery which enraged his old liberal friends; and the following year he produced the *Latterday Pamphlets* which denounced practically everybody and everything and, not surprisingly, enraged most people. In 1851, in more tender and mellow mood, he wrote a charming biography of an old friend, the theologian Sterling. In 1851 he began work on his monumental *History of Frederick the Great*, whom he had chosen to epitomize the hero. It was an immense labour for Carlyle, which lasted for years during which he made two trips to Germany to inspect the sites of Frederick's battles. The five volumes appeared between 1858 and 1865, and were an immense success. The battles were superbly recreated and the writing was touched with real humour. The sheer hard work in producing such a mass of material was greatly admired. If the work is not a complete success, it is because Carlyle was never quite able to fit Frederick into the heroic mould he had prepared for him.

In 1865 Carlyle was elected Rector of Edinburgh University. The voting is an indication of the esteem in which he was held: Carlyle 657 votes, Disraeli 310. While he was still in Scotland, Jane died. Carlyle became more and more withdrawn. He wrote his *Reminiscences* and occasional political articles on topics such as the Reform Bill, which of course he opposed. As he grew older his view of Britain's future grew gloomier, and the rejection of his own solutions deepened the gloom. He lived on, but wrote little, and finally on 4 February 1881 he died. His last wishes were observed and, instead of being buried in Westminster Abbey, his body was taken back to Scotland to lie beside his parents.

At his death Carlyle was revered by his countrymen as a genius, but the ideas of the genius were ignored. Yet he saw the faults of society with a clearer eye than many of his countrymen, and he left behind him a volume of work that contains some of the finest writing in the English language.

John Keats

(1795-1821)

Here lies one whose name was writ in water.

At once the humblest and the proudest line in English literature, so Keats wrote his own epitaph – not so much in despair
as in ambition disappointed with the little achieved, the greatness intended. Harrowing details of Keats's long journey to
tragic death have moved the world's compassion for generations. The poetry gathers poignancy from the tragedy; in the
light of the poems, that premature, tortured death becomes the
bitterest waste. Both are recorded in letters which show that
Keats was not only a good poet and a great letter-writer but
more – he was a great and a good human being.

Little recognized and less loved by the literary world of
London and Edinburgh, he was virtually deserted with polite
excuses by his friends who left him during his last illness in the
inexperienced but, as it turned out, staunch and loving care of
the young painter Joseph Severn, his companion-attendant to
Italy, Rome and death. Keats had delayed too long for the
warmer climate to benefit him: the consumption was well advanced. A fragment of verse overpoweringly records the ter-
rorizing anguish of his mood:

> This living hand, now warm and capable
> Of earnest grasping, would, if it were cold
> And in the icy silence of the tomb,
> So haunt thy days and chill thy dreaming nights
> That thou wouldst wish thine own heart dry of blood
> So in my veins red life might stream again,
> And thou be conscience-calmed – see here it is –
> I hold it towards you.

Born in Moorfields, Finsbury on 31 October 1795 he was by
23 February 1821 lying dead in Rome. Yet in those twenty-five
years in 'the vale of soul-making', as he called life, he had
crammed more experience, wisdom and intensity than many a
nonagenarian. 'The coarse-bred son of a livery stable-keeper',
in Yeats's unfair words, he was the eldest of three brothers; his
beloved sister Fanny was the youngest in the family. His father

died in 1804 and his mother soon married again. Keats was sent to his grandmother Jennings at Edmonton. He was educated at Mr Clarke's school in Enfield from 1803 till 1810. Here he became friends with the master's son, Charles Cowden Clarke, who fostered his interest in poetry and in 1816 introduced him to Leigh Hunt, the radical journalist and sentimental poet, and also to Benjamin Haydon, the grandiose painter.

Keats's mother died in 1810. He had nursed her and cooked for her during her illness, and the shock of her death turned him from boisterous schoolboy to pensive youth. The powerful description of Moneta's face from *The Fall of Hyperion* is possibly a memory of her dying face that haunted him.

From Clarke's school he went in 1811 as an apprentice to Thomas Hammond, a surgeon of Edmonton, to learn a safe profession. His guardian, Richard Abbey, businessman as he was, saw little future in poetry. During the course of Keats's money problems, he suggested the unlikeliest professions for the poet: hatmaking, bookselling and, oddest of all, tea-brokering. He quarrelled with Hammond, and in 1814 moved to study at St Thomas's and Guy's Hospitals. Two years later he was appointed dresser at Guy's and also passed with credit as a licentiate at Apothecaries' Hall – well on the way to a career he never entirely rejected.

Yet poetry absorbed more and more of his time. He had already written in 1814 a sonnet that was to become one of his most anthologized poems: *On First Looking into Chapman's Homer*. His first book of poems, largely derivative of eighteenth-century practice, appeared in March 1817. Nothing spectacular, at least it introduced him to a circle of friends: Charles Wentworth Dilke, Charles Armitage Brown, Benjamin Bailey and the young painter Joseph Severn. They, with Leigh Hunt and Haydon, gave him considerable encouragement and appreciation – though whether either were of the right type may be doubted. Keats had the finest five senses – and sometimes a sixth – of all poets, except perhaps Shakespeare. The circle encouraged an indolent expression of these at the expense of parallel development of Keats's powerful and original mind. It was an emphasis he himself was rather prone to at that stage. Ambitiously, he set out to write a sizeable poem – *Endymion*. The object was to 'make 4,000 lines of one bare circumstance and fill them with poetry ... in which the images are so numerous that many are forgotten and found now at a second Reading ...'

He soon realized the structural weaknesses of *Endymion* – even before publication. Later he remarked: 'In *Endymion* I leaped headlong into the Sea, and thereby have become better acquainted with the Soundings, the quicksands, and the rocks ...' Published in April 1818, the poem was treated savagely by reviewers, mainly opponents of Hunt whose protégé they regarded Keats as being. Jeffrey of *The Edinburgh Review*, however, judged it squarely on its faults, merits and promise.

Keats had already moved on by then. Thrown back even more on his own resources, he searched for better guides. His achievements were a miracle of self-education. He asserts, 'I will have no more of Wordsworth or Hunt in particular ...' But Hunt had directed his attention to Boccaccio and Italian; those briefer verse-tales gave Keats the chance to concentrate more on structure and technique. In the same month, he finished *Isabella*, a verse-tale written in octava rima. Morbid and mawkish the tale: two brothers murder their sister's lover to preserve their control of her estates. She digs up the body and keeps the head in a pot of basil which she waters with tears. The poem contains some promise of a better Keats, especially in its natural descriptions now subordinate to plot, and the occasional concision in narrative. Characteristically, Keats dismissed it as a 'weaksided poem'.

Sidetracked by even greater ambitions, the epic form, Keats spent the winter of 1818–19 on *Hyperion*, his guide here being Milton. Though he modulates Milton's style, both methods and theme are too derivative to succeed. Contemporaries, however, were impressed. Again by the autumn, he had discarded the poem, unfinished. 'Life to him [Milton] would be death to me.'

Even while engaged on this, he wrote the first narrative that is stamped in every part with his own poetry: *The Eve of St Agnes*. One quotation must suffice to illustrate its perfection:

> Full on the casement shone the wintry moon,
> And threw warm gules on Madeline's fair breast,
> As down she knelt for heaven's grace and boon:
> Rose-bloom fell on her hands, together prest,
> And on her silver cross soft amethyst,
> And on her hair a glory, like a saint ...

The strong colour of stained glass softened by moonlight; seldom in English verse such subtle hues. Keats here finds his real master, the Shakespeare of *Romeo and Juliet*.

In the July of 1819 he reverted to the extended narrative: this time Dryden is guide in developing the heroic couplet. The poem, *Lamia*, described how a serpent-woman entices Lycius, a student, to fall in love with her. The sensuous again

momentarily masters Keats. The escape from it is shown as
entailing death, so powerful its hold.

But knowledge of the world, 'the burden of the mystery',
was thrusting itself upon Keats. He nursed his brother Tom
during the autumn and winter of 1818 until he died of consumption in December. The sensuous could not alleviate the
sorrows of life: 'Poor Tom – that woman – and Poetry were
ringing changes in my senses ...' That woman was Fanny
Brawne for whom he developed a crazing, insatiable love.
Signs of his own likely fate were becoming increasingly
apparent in his sore throat.

Yet 1819 was the year in which his greatest poetry was
written. He had begun with *The Eve of St Agnes*, continued
with *Lamia*, written the great odes and even attempted with
Brown a verse-drama *Otho the Great*. Indeed, in November he
wrote: 'the writing of a few fine Plays – my greatest ambition'.
This play gives no indication that he would have achieved it,
despite the fact that Shakespeare was, as he put it, his 'Presi-
dor'. Speculation here is useless. What is clear is that the odes
with the rewritten induction to *Hyperion* are his maturest and
greatest work.

In *Ode to a Nightingale*, he is tempted again to reject harsh
reality and escape in the ideal beauty of the bird's song which
he could pursue in 'poesy'. Even death seems tempting. This is
finally rejected:

> Still wouldst thou sing, and I have ears in vain –
> To thy high requiem become a sod.

He returns to the 'verdurous glooms': the bird flies on: the
problem is unsolved: 'Fled is that music:– Do I wake or sleep?'

The *Ode to Autumn* is perhaps his greatest achievement.
Here is that resolution he was seeking, 'a more thoughtful and
quiet power', sensuous and profound:

> Then in a wailful choir the small gnats mourn
>   Among the river sallows, borne aloft
>   Or sinking as the light wind lives or dies;
> And full-grown lambs loud bleat from hilly bourn:
>   Hedge-crickets sing; and now with treble soft
>   The red-breast whistles from a garden-croft;
>   And gathering swallows twitter in the skies.

This was the greatest work that Keats finished. Though it is
useless to speculate upon his potential greatness, it would
perhaps have been in the direction of this or the mature and

responsible humanism of the *Fall of Hyperion* that he would have developed.

Legend soon sprang out of his death. In *Don Juan*, Byron – not one to waste affection on poets contemporary with himself – assumed that Keats's ailing health had finally been undermined by damning reviews his books had received. Keats became the symbol of the outcast, abused Romantic poet. Accordingly, imprecations were called down upon the heads of the reviewers supposed responsible for the tragedy. Keats joined 'the inheritors of unfulfilled renown'.

Yet Keats was not so readily fixed in amber. The legend was eventually exploded by the publication of his letters in 1848. They were letters full of poetry and affection, wisdom and humour, tempered with tolerance and keen intelligence, steeled with ambition and determination. They record how he was obliged to borrow money for his bills – and for his friends; how he helped his young sister Fanny with her schoolwork, entertained her with amusing poems and concerned himself with her health: 'George has been running great chance of a similar attack ... You must be careful always to wear warm clothing not only in frost but in a Thaw ...'

A maturity and natural wisdom is movingly drawn upon: 'Reynolds and Haydon retorting and recrimating [*sic*] – and parting forever – the same thing has happened between Haydon and Hunt – It is unfortunate – Men should bear with each other – there lives not the Man who may not be cut up, aye, bashed to pieces on his weakest side. The best of Men have but a portion of good in them ...'

Time and again his thoughts return to poetry, and with such perception that his correspondents probably could not immediately follow him. T.S. Eliot remarked somewhere that what he says about poetry in the letters was right. He admires Wordsworth, and then we see him grope his way to a criticism of this contemporary giant: 'But, for the sake of a few fine imaginative or domestic passages, are we to be bullied into a certain Philosophy engendered in the whims of an Egotist?'

Sometimes he doubts poetry itself: 'I am sometimes so very sceptical as to think Poetry itself a mere Jack a lanthen [*sic*] to amuse whoever may chance to be struck with its brilliance.' (Keats's thoughts came so fast he had little time for spelling or punctuation.) At other times he is sure of his own powers: 'I feel it in my power to become a popular writer – I feel it in my strength to refuse the poisonous suffrage of a public.' Such hesitancies and certainties, the graspings and gropings, create a vivid impression of a fine, original mind and personality.

Through all this, the note of sadness sometimes breaks: 'Life must be undergone ...'; 'Everybody is in his own mess.'

These letters present us with a man no review could kill. Matthew Arnold was right to insist 'the thing to be seized is, that Keats had flint and iron in him ...' Keats's life shows how much will-power and endurance he must have had to have come through at all, let alone to have written great poetry as well.

The world has rightly preferred Shelley's epitaph on Keats, rather than his own:

> He is made one with Nature: there is heard
> His voice in all her music ...
>
> *Adonais*

Heinrich Heine

(1797–1856)

At home, in the beer garden or hiking with their rucksacks over hills and dales, generations of Germans have sung the famous *Lorelei*, the poem that tells of the Rhine maiden who combs her golden hair on the Drachenfels and lures fishermen to a watery grave.

Most of us know it, too, and many of Heine's other poems set to music by Schubert, Schumann, Liszt, Mendelssohn and Wagner, poems that express for us in the simple form of the folk-song some of the deepest human emotions: delight in nature, the joys and miseries of love, the wonder of fragile innocence.

Though Heine was a Jew and his works were banned by the Nazis, *Die Lorelei* could not be expunged from popular memory and was published with the fatuous note: 'author unknown'. Then as soon as the war was over his most famous collection, the *Buch der Lieder*, was brought out again and amid the chaos of defeat Germans could pick up the silver threads of their heritage. It was not the granite of Hitler's Reich Chancellery that had survived, but flowing verses with clear rhythms and simple rhymes, so poignant in their directness that after years of Teutonic froth they seemed almost to come from some depersonalized spirit of humanity.

Among German poets especially Heine was unique and no one had written such lines before. Lesser men had escaped to some childhood paradise of nature, but sentimentality had engulfed them and not even their tears, as they wept over gravestones in moonlit churchyards, were wholly sincere. But Heine had to be realistic. Life and his own temperament imposed genuine suffering with the result that, seeing the dark, he could also revel in the light and his poems are shot through with real lyricism, real grief, as well as with a spectrum of intermediate feelings, flippant, satirical, tender, sometimes even coarse and spiteful. It has been said that in his rich vocabulary, artistry of form and close association of nature with all his moods, Heine carried romanticism to its ultimate conclusion; and it is true that no German poets, other than imitators, have since followed in his footsteps.

As a lyric poet Heine is placed by Germans second only to Goethe, yet he had a very different life and background from the Olympian of Weimar. Money problems dogged his youth and being a Jew brought many difficulties as anti-semitism was rife in Germany after the Napoleonic wars.

But his early years were idyllic. His father had been a quartermaster in the Hanoverian army and settled in Düsseldorf in 1796 as a cloth merchant. His origins were humble and, presumably to further his career, he had changed his Jewish name of Chajjim to Heinemann and subsequently to Heine. In Düsseldorf he married Peira (usually called Betty) van Geldern whose Jewish ancestors had originally come from Holland. To this oddly assorted couple – Betty being as hard-headed as her husband was soft and dreamy – were born four children, the first, Heinrich, in December 1797.

Heinrich, or Harry as he was called after an English friend, found plenty in Düsseldorf to stimulate his imagination. Capital of the duchy of Jülich, the little town had been occupied by the French in 1795 and was enjoying a new-found freedom under the Napoleonic Code. Everyone, even Jew and former serf, was technically equal and all lived under the protection of the law. The great watchwords of the revolution seemed to have become fact, and as Harry gazed at French veterans sunning themselves in the market-place, and later at Napoleon himself on a visit to the town, his heart nearly burst with admiration. It seemed to him like the spring-time of mankind.

To his mother, however, dreams were always suspect. For her first-born she planned a brilliant practical career and the first step was a good education. So he was sent to a Jewish private school and later to a lyceum run on French lines where Catholic priests confused his mind by mingling orthodox piety with free-thinking liberalism.

Harry did not do particularly well, but his mother was the driving force and after an interval at a business school, where he failed miserably, he found himself at eighteen in Frankfurt, apprenticed to a banker. Within a fortnight he was home again, disgusted with figures and deeply upset by the anti-semitism rising in Frankfurt as French control began to weaken.

His mother found him scribbling verses, of which she highly disapproved, and concocted another plan. Her husband's brother Solomon was a Hamburg banker and one of the richest men in Germany. Harry should stay with him and under his personal supervision work his way into a banking career. Solomon agreed and Harry spent the next few years in Hamburg with fateful results. Solomon was kind, but a self-made man who felt he knew what was best for his nephew and was furious when Harry disagreed. To him finance was still a crushing bore, its operations for ever mysterious: he knew he would never be a banker. On the other hand, Solomon's *Schloss* on the banks of the Elbe, the rose-filled gardens and, above all, Solomon's daughter Amalie were entrancing. Amalie was sixteen, with Grecian features and cool and disdainful ways, and with her Harry fell hopelessly in love, as though with his very soul.

Many of his early poems are concerned with Amalie and for the rest of his life Heine was to be preoccupied with the eternal feminine, with the positive inspiring angel and the negative destroying witch; and though it seems strange in view of his immense creative output, he was always very conscious of this treacherous Lorelei-figure in himself. Amalie was her first focus; how happy he might have been if she had proved warmly understanding, calling forth all his masculine protection, instead of taunting and cold!

But Amalie was never within reach and, being strongly sensual, Heine consoled himself with Hamburg prostitutes while pouring into poetry consoling dreams of Amalie:

> Im stillen Traum, bei stiller Nacht,
> Da kam zu mir mit Zaubermacht,
> Mit Zaubermacht die Liebste mein,
> Sie kam zu mir ins Kämmerlein ...

Rejected by Amalie and useless as a bank clerk, Heine became truculent with his uncle, but Solomon, with creditable patience, gave him another chance and set him up as a shopkeeper in Hamburg selling English textiles. This too was a failure and within a year Harry was bankrupt.

He did not deserve it, but his uncle now paid for him to study law in Bonn: a great lawyer could also fit in with his mother's ambitions. The next six years until 1825, when Heine finally became a Doctor of Law and then abandoned the law for ever, are a kaleidoscope of study, amorous adventures, dreams and political enthusiasms. It was his fate never to fit in anywhere for long, never to join permanently in the game of life, but to oscillate to and fro, impelled by his hypersensitive nature to seek friends and then to revile them, to take up a cause and then fall into disenchantment.

All this time he was writing: a novel and two dramas as well as poems, and with the publication in 1822 of his first volume he was becoming known as a poet. Schlegel, the translator of Shakespeare, had befriended him and many famous literary people in Berlin were interested in his future. Yet he could not feel at home in Germany, and not merely because of his race.

Long ago he had written a poem, 'The Two Grenadiers', which breathed admiration for Napoleon. But now throughout the country the ideals of the revolution were being swept aside and 'freedom' – something which Germans had never known – acquired on the lips of students a lowering ferocity reminiscent of the Goths and Vandals.

Disgusted and racked with headaches – they were, in fact, the herald of syphilis – Heine spent some months at his uncle's expense by the sea on the island of Nordeney, there writing a series of poems, later published in the volume *Die Nordsee*, which show him to be among the finest sea poets in any language. Already as a student he had written of forests and mountains, the conventional loves of German romanticists, in a brilliant prose narrative, *Die Harzreise*, a hitherto unknown blend of luxuriant fantasy, brisk realism and satire.

But frustration dogged him. He yearned to strike a blow for freedom, yet by writing he could do painfully little. Many people were stirred by another travel book, *Reisebilder*, which contained a moving eulogy of the revolution and sold well, partly because it was banned by every state in Germany. But in the fatherland cruder chauvinistic feelings were rife and it was not Heine but a certain bull-necked 'father' Jahn who was the hero of the day, an ex-peasant who taught gymnastics to young people, harangued them about their glorious German-hood and sent them marching with shouts and banners through peaceful village streets.

So Heine fled again, this time to London, where the ant-heap atmosphere appalled him; then he tried to get a professorship in Munich or alternatively in Berlin, went to Italy, wrote about Italy and by 1830 was still undecided what to do. Then the July revolution in Paris burst like a bomb; he was carried to the seventh heaven of optimism for the human race and dashed off more travel pictures which contained a call to the German people:

> You are the true emperor, the real power in the land. Your will is sovereign and far more legitimate than any divine right ... Your own right must triumph ... Liberation will come ... The long night is over; the red dawn gleams; the new day is at hand.

This brought him a threatened prosecution for sedition and released the springs of action. Still racked with headaches, Heine, in May 1831, packed his bags and made for Paris, the home of liberty. Except for one brief visit he never went back.

The first years in Paris were probably the happiest of his life.

Though his poetry had not yet crossed the Rhine, he was accepted at once in literary circles for his sparkling conversation and made many friends, among them Théophile Gautier, Dumas and Balzac. His Jewish embarrassment fell from him like a cloak and he was entranced by everything French.

Soon, though as yet he knew little about France, he set himself the task of interpreting Frenchmen and Germans to one another. To a Berlin newspaper were sent articles about French art, social life and politics, while in France were published books on German romanticism, religion and philosophy, all easily digestible, very subjective in tone and alive with wit and intuitive brilliance. Understood, applauded, spending money – including his uncle's – like water, Heine was on the crest of the wave and there, appropriately, dabbling in the foam, he met a woman, a siren figure, a Lorelei.

Crescence Mirat was her name, nineteen years old, an illegitimate child of a peasant mother, sprightly, laughing, with animal spirits and a skin that glowed like satin. In her mundane moments she served in her aunt's glove shop in the Passage Choiseul; with the aunt Heine had a financial transaction and then took Crescence home with him, rechristening her Mathilde.

After several months of delirious love-making Heine took a sober look at his girl: mentally she was a child and a rather backward one at that: pleasure loving, rumbustious, lazy, spendthrift, possessive. She lived for the moment and nothing touched her very deeply. She did not even know and would not have cared anyway that her 'Henri' was a poet. And for these very reasons he loved her dearly and protectively, could never let her go. 'Little lamb,' he wrote, 'I am the shepherd meant for thee ...'

But Heine suffered, all the same. Mathilde was too stupid to be accepted by his friends and went out dancing when he visited them. Dancing ... Heine grew jealous, watched over her, shut himself up with her and soon was lost to society. When he emerged it was to quarrel with his fellow-*emigrés* and then write excoriating attacks on them. Years passed in these futile pursuits: the poet was lost.

Then in 1841 he married Mathilde and began writing poetry again: 'Atta Troll', a romantic story with political overtones, a collection called *Zeitgedichte* which included 'Deutschland, ein Wintermarchen' a savage attack on Prussia and its king, Frederick William IV. He met Marx in Paris and listened fascinated to the theory of communism which his reason could not upset though his heart was prophetically disturbed.

'Anxiety and terror fill me,' he wrote, 'when I think of the time when these grim iconoclasts will come to power.'

But there was another reason for his disquiet. In these years his terrible disease was developing and in his weakened state all thoughts of upheaval were disturbing. By 1847 he was blind in one eye and both legs were paralysed; in 1848 he took to his bed where he lay until his death in 1856.

In his 'mattress tomb', as he called it, he bore his sufferings with great fortitude and the clarity of his mind was never affected. Some poetry was written, including the grimly impressive 'Romanzero' and, towards the end, his last love lyrics, addressed to a mysteriously anonymous woman who visited him, later identified as Camille Senden who became the mistress of Thiers. Mathilde nursed him with high-spirited indifference. Literary friends called. Street noises came up through the window, and Heine the scoffer, neither Christian nor Jew, thought about God, apparently with satisfaction for when someone asked him, a few days before the end, whether he had made his peace with the Almighty he replied: 'Oui, Dieu me pardonnera,' then added with the trace of a smile: 'C'est son métier.'

On the morning of the funeral, in February 1856, Mathilde vanished from the house and could not be traced for a month. Then she came back to claim her rights and royalties as his widow. How he would have laughed, and indeed he could afford to, for each year has made him more secure in the world's esteem as a great romantic poet and as a prophet, too, whom we in the twentieth century should have read more closely. For it was Heine who wrote:

Christianity has occasionally calmed the brutal German lust for battle, but it cannot destroy that savage jog. And when once that restraining talisman, the Cross, is broken, then the old combatants will rage with the fury celebrated by the Norse poets. The wooden talisman is fast decaying; the day will come when it will break in pieces. Then the old stone gods will rise and rub the dust of a thousand years from their eyes, and Thor will leap to life at last. Do not smile. This is no mere fantasy. German thunder is truly German; it takes its time. But it will come ... A drama will be performed which will make the French Revolution seem like a pretty idyll. Never doubt it; the hour will come.

It was this hatred and fear of nationalism, coupled with a longing for universal brotherhood, which made Nietzsche call him the European of the Future.

Honoré de Balzac

(1799–1850)

A young man living in a garret in Paris in 1818–19 writes to his sister: 'Never, never will I be a lawyer – count me as dead if I let myself be stifled by such a life. Dearest Laure, my two great and immense desires – to be famous and to be loved – will they ever be satisfied?' The young man with heavy features, a mass of tangled hair, a large forehead and black eyes was then engaged in writing a tragedy – *Cromwell*.

Balzac was luckier than many other young men attempting to win fame from garrets. He produced his tragedy, and read it at home to the family circle and some literary friends; but he himself knew, from his reading, that it was unconvincing – in fact, a complete flop. However, he was encouraged by his parents to live at home at Villeparisis in the country. His father, the son of a peasant from south-west France, had changed his name from Balsa to Balzac; he had just retired from an important post in the civil service, having pursued his career peacefully through all the changes of the revolution, the empire and the restoration. It was Honoré who added the 'de' to Balzac.

'To be loved.' Balzac in the country met the first of his loves, a Madame de Berny, aged forty-five when she met Balzac who was then twenty-four. She had eight children and didn't care for her dull husband who, fortunately, did not mind her friendship which soon turned into a liaison. Her greatest effect on Balzac was in an unexpected direction. Madame de Berny encouraged him to embark on various commercial ventures to make his fortune. Balzac all his life had dreams of becoming rich quickly. Twice he set himself up as a publisher and twice failed. Madame de Berny supplied money for certainly the last and far the most costly of her young protégé's schemes – that of becoming a type-founder and publisher combined, on a large scale. It was from these attempts to grow rich that Balzac acquired debts which steadily grew larger all his life as he made new debts to repay old ones.

At the height of his success, Balzac, the Parisian celebrity, was watched by creditors to whom he was forced to hand over money hot from a publisher's advance. He wrote, in fact, with the duns at the door. He used to refer jokingly to 'my floating debt'; it did not worry his robust character nor did it prevent him enjoying all the pleasures of life and of rich living. But the chain fate pulled round his legs with, as it were, Madame de Berny's aid, enriched his genius. Balzac's novels are full of crooks, usurers and misers; full of the shifts which men resort to at times on account of money troubles and which easily become crimes; rich with a side of life which had never before appeared in literature – the world of high respectable finance, the money-lender's parlour and the bucket-shop. Karl Marx, whose favourite author was Balzac, said one learnt more about society from Balzac's novels than from any treatise on sociology.

In this early period he wrote and published seven novels of no particular value and, as late as 1829, it seemed it was his power of work rather than his genius which appeared the more remarkable. Even then love and business were secondary to his work. It was from 1830 that the great flow of novels grouped under the title *La Comédie Humaine* began to pour in a steady stream from his pen until his death in 1850. He wrote close on one hundred novels in all. The stream began to flow when he had left the quiet of his parents' house and Madame de Berny's affection and had found his way into Paris society.

He had a liaison with the Duchesse de Castries, who wrote to him under a pseudonym to praise one of his first novels. He had many mistresses – addresses and demi-mondaines – and he rushed helter-skelter from balls, theatres, ballets and every sort of respectable and unrespectable form of amusement. For months on end, he would visit the provinces, not to write but to live in another atmosphere. Balzac never appeared like a man-of-letters who goes round with a notebook and listens; nor in fact was he a writer of this kind. The world of Paris and its underworld, the life of the small towns with their priests and doctors and gossipy old women, were observed unconsciously and absorbed.

In the length of time he would concentrate, in the ferocious energy with which he wrote and rewrote for long hours, not even Sir Walter Scott could equal him. He would begin work an hour or so before midnight, wearing a monkish robe and writing with a candelabra of seven candles with a green shade in front of him in a workroom at the top of the house furnished like a comfortable monastic cell. Sometimes he would continue writing until the next afternoon, drinking cups of black coffee; a favourite food during those hours was heaps of sardines mashed up with butter piled high on bread. Often, at the end of these vigils, he was speechless and half blind. He could keep

up this life for a long time. He wrote the whole of *La Cousine
Bette*, certainly among the greatest of his creations, in six
weeks. Then, after his work was over, he would go back to his
financial intrigues, his loves and his amusements.

Théophile Gautier has described him at the height of his
career:

> A fine, vast, noble forehead, considerably whiter than his
> face which was totally without wrinkles except for a deep
> one at the base of his nose. His hair was abundant, long,
> thick and jet black, usually thrown back from his head like
> a lion's mane. As for his eyes, they had a life, a light and
> inconceivable magnetism. In spite of his nocturnal habits,
> the white of his eye was limpid blueish like that of a child or
> a virgin and it surrounded two black diamonds ... They
> were eyes which would make eagles close their eye-lids, eyes
> which saw through walls and breasts, which could strike
> down a wild beast, eyes of a monarch, a mystic or an animal
> trainer.

La Comédie Humaine is not an architectural structure as is,
to a large extent, the work of Proust. It is unfinished. You
could read most of the novels which compose it without being
aware that they form part of the structure. Yet it has a very
real unity. This comes about not so much because the characters, whole families, appear and reappear in different parts of
the *Comédie*, nor because it is a portrait of French society,
Parisian and provincial, from the time of the restoration to the
period of Louis Philippe. The unity lies in Balzac's vision of
humanity and the society he paints. His originality, which
makes him the father of the realistic novel, was to see his
characters in their social relationships; and so money, dowries,
investments, wills, police, even secret police and lawyers, figure
a great deal throughout the *Comédie*. He is interested in the
struggle for money and position, in the efforts we make to
satisfy our desires. So inevitably the view of humanity at which
one arrives on reflection after reading Balzac is a pessimistic
one, not one of human nature at its best. All writers have to
select, to focus their view of life, to exclude some aspect of the
human being. Many fail, as a result of this selection, to give
the impression that what they are describing is so significantly
a part of life that it is totally satisfying in itself. One feels this
great defect in writers who have a 'message', and very often in
the realistic social novel which rarely escapes a whiff of propaganda. Balzac's selection, the choice of looking at people in
their social relations, is convincing, the core of his world

vibrates with passionate life. One believes in the total reality of Balzac's world, and this in spite of his extravagant notions and his love of melodrama which sometimes intrude.

Balzac's world satisfies because all the several hundreds of characters in the *Comédie* are conceived as individuals and not as types. One can feel that all the misers in the world are summed up in Molière's Harpagon, that Molière has created the archetypal miser and that nothing more remains to be said. Balzac creates Gobseck, Grandet and many others, all misers and all different. His young fops and adventurers who seek rich marriages – Lucien de Rubempré, for example, and Rastignac, with the same outlooks on life, using their charms in much the same manner, are as different as chalk from cheese.

The *Comédie* is a highly seasoned dish that can put off people with delicate digestions. But it cannot be dismissed as the subjective, even if great, creation of an abnormal mind. Far from it; Balzac writes of men and women everyone has met. There is a consistent Balzacian view of humanity which the French critic Emile Faguet sums up as that of creatures 'composed of a collection of passions and wants, served by organs and intelligence, and struggling with circumstances'. In the *Comédie* Balzac created a number of characters who stand out like gigantic statues. Their differentiation from the rest of the world is in the intensity of their passions or desires, and the single-mindedness with which they pursue them. The intensity gives these characters a sort of genius and uniqueness, and it also causes tragedy for them and those around them.

Grandet is not a miser like the terrifying Gobseck, a money-lender, a man with a 'lunar' face, who dies in the odour of rancid food which he obtained in payment of bad debts and has not sold because he could not get the price he wanted. Grandet is not the conventional miser at all, but a man solely devoted to the acquisition and saving of money, the richest wine-grower in the region of Saumur, before whom bankers and lawyers crawl and humble neighbours tremble. He makes money because of his knowledge of crops and markets and his cunning; part of his armoury in life's battles is his stutter and his pose as a poor provincial. Grandet is not radically different from the majority of peasants and *bourgeoisie* around him, all of whom worship money. He is merely infinitely cleverer and more ruthless in the pursuit of gain. Grandet has genius but it has taken possession of him. As mystics for the love of God, so Grandet for filthy lucre.

Baron Hulot was a good soldier-administrator, and for twelve years a loving husband. If he had had a mistress or two,

nothing could have troubled his family nor even his sensible
and understanding wife. But he goes out for expensive young
girls and lives ever more and more beyond his means. Then
he has the ill-luck to fix on Valerie Marneffe, a superficially
attractive young married woman, with airs and graces, who
completes his financial ruin. He has to raise large sums in a
hurry; is dismissed from his government post after being found
out in fraud. From every quarter, disgrace comes on him.
There is more to this book – *La Cousine Bette* – than Hulot's
incapacity to resist his obsession. Evil pervades the soul of the
old maid, his cousin Bette, who helps to ruin the Hulots. In
Valerie Marneffe, Balzac has drawn the epitome of all that is
fundamentally base and corrupting in human relations. The
theme of the book is not only the downfall of Hulot but the
contagion of corruption. It spreads to Hulot's children who
lose all respect for him. Madame Hulot's love for her husband
begins to sap her own integrity. She wants to learn to practise
the attractions which 'these women' have for her husband. Her
son-in-law, who hears Valerie so constantly talked about in
the family circle, is ensnared by her, and so Baron Hulot's
daughter loses her husband to Baron Hulot's mistress.

What can be more admirable than paternal love? Jean-
Joachin Goriot, former manufacturer of pasta, sacrifices himself for his daughters, both of whom have made aristocratic
marriages, spoiling them just as, at the age of fifteen, he gave
them carriages of their own. He abets them in their adulteries,
though one has a passable husband and has fallen in love with
an appalling type of gigolo. He loves them so much that he can
refuse them nothing. As time progresses he becomes to them
merely a sugar-daddy – they know his advice will only be what
they want to do. On his deathbed, an already ruined old wreck,
he wants to see them. 'No, they won't come,' he murmurs, 'I
have known that for ten years.' The excess of Goriot's love for
his daughters has become what is, for others, a meaningless
passion.

Love of money, love of girls and paternal doting do not
necessarily lead to disaster; on the contrary there are over-fond
parents in Balzac's novels, plenty of reasonably good-hearted
lechers and many men far too much concerned with money.
But they do not meet with disaster. It is the excess, the excess
which gradually destroys any form of discrimination, which
ends in the defeat of life and sanity. These three characters
which are drawn in astonishing detail and with consummate
skill convey the basic message of the *Comédie*.

The main experience of Balzac's private life began in 1833,

when he was famous already, and was to last to his death in 1850. It began with his correspondence with a highly intelligent rich married Polish woman, Madame Hanska. Balzac fell in love with Madame Hanska and loved her more than anyone, or more than anything except his work. Apparently she returned his affection. In 1841 her husband died. They met frequently in Russia, in Italy and in Germany, and once Madame Hanska came to Paris. Yet it was not until nine years after her husband's death that they married. Balzac went to Russia to marry in spite of poor health. His health got worse, then improved somewhat, and in joy and hope he brought his wife to the house in Paris which he had luxuriously furnished for her.

Balzac had worn out his robust constitution and he suffered from congestion of the lungs, as it was called then, and heart trouble. Shortly after his return to Paris he took to his bed and after a few weeks, on 18 August 1850, he died. There is an element to the end of mystery in Balzac's relations with Madame Hanska. He died in the arms of his aged mother, he and his wife having probably, though not certainly, quarrelled. His funeral was attended by all literary and social Paris. 'A very distinguished man,' said the Minister for the Interior. 'Sir,' said Victor Hugo, 'He was one of the very greatest geniuses.'

Lord Macaulay

(1800-59)

Among the great names of English literature there is none more honoured or better remembered than Lord Macaulay. His *Essays*, his *History of England*, and the *Lays of Ancient Rome* are among the best-known works in the language. But what of the man himself? Did he do anything else but write books?

Let us begin with the child who became the father of the man. Born on 25 October 1800, Thomas Babington Macaulay was the son of Zacharay Macaulay, who came of a line of Scottish ministers and spent most of his life in forwarding the anti-slavery movement. He was a precocious child, although his parents did their best to hide the fact from him. His first home was a house in Clapham High Street and from the age of three he read incessantly. Before he was eight he had written a Compendium of Universal History, which gave (so his mother declared) 'a tolerably connected view of the leading events from the Creation to the present time, filling about a quire of paper', and, when he had just come across Scott's *Marmion*, he produced a romance in three cantos called *The Battle of Cheviot*. A little later he was accumulating a vast pile of blank verse dealing with one of the Scandinavian heroes and, to quote his mother again, 'he has composed I know not how many hymns'.

While he was still the merest child Macaulay was sent to a day school at Clapham. At the age of twelve he went to a boarding school at Little Shelford, near Cambridge, which a couple of years later was removed to Buntingford, in Hertfordshire. Here he remained until he was just eighteen, when he went into residence at Trinity College, Cambridge. As an undergraduate he revelled in the possession of leisure and liberty, enjoying to the full the most agreeable company and endless opportunities for reading. He became a sound classical scholar, but he detested mathematics, with the result that he did not do at all brilliantly in his finals. But he succeeded in winning a prize – a fellowship at Trinity – which in his eyes was the most desirable of all the prizes that Cambridge had to give.

On leaving the university Macaulay established himself in

London and was called to the bar in 1826. He went on the northern circuit for a time, but his heart was never in the law, and he got very few briefs. So he went back to London, where he was soon made more than welcome in society drawing-rooms and the clubs of St James's. Now we meet Macaulay the brilliant conversationist, the splendid talker.

I had a most interesting companion in young Macaulay [wrote Crabb Robinson, celebrated man of letters, after a dinner-party at a friend's country house some time in 1826], one of the most promising of the younger generation I have seen for a long time. He has a good face – not the delicate features of a man of genius and sensibility, but the strong lines and well-knit limbs of a man sturdy in body and mind. Very eloquent and cheerful. Overflowing with words, and not poor in thought. Liberal in opinion, but no radical. He seems a correct as well as a full man. He showed a minute knowledge of subjects not introduced by himself.

Even as a very young man, 'nine people out of ten liked nothing better than to listen to him: which was fortunate, because in his early days he had a scanty respect of persons, either as regards the choice of his topics, or the quantity of his words.' So we are told by Sir George Trevelyan, in his life of his uncle – a book, incidentally, which has been ranked by good judges only a little below Boswell's *Johnson* and Lockhart's *Scott*. Those who met him for the first time might be put off by his vehemence, his over-confidence, his apparent inability to recognize that there were two sides to a question. 'I wish I was as cock-sure of anything as Tom Macaulay is of everything,' remarked Lord Melbourne once. But better acquaintance usually stifled all criticism. He always, or nearly always, managed to keep his temper, and so far from being conceited he really thought that other people knew as much as he did.

His memory was most extraordinary. To the end he could read books more quickly than other people skimmed them, and skimmed them as fast as anyone else could turn the leaves – and yet he seemed never to forget anything that he had read. Against Crabb Robinson's grumble, 'The greatest marvel about Macaulay is the quantity of trash that he remembers,' may be set Macaulay's own claim that, if by some miracle of vandalism, all copies of *Paradise Lost* and the *Pilgrim's Progress* were destroyed from off the face of the earth, he would undertake to replace them from his own recollection whenever a revival of learning came.

Macaulay the essayist is the next to claim our attention. In

1825 the *Edinburgh Review*, the most influential organ on the Whig side in politics was on the look-out for 'some clever young man who could write for us'. Macaulay's name was suggested, and in the issue for August 1825 appeared his essay on Milton. The effect on his reputation was tremendous (writes Trevelyan); like Lord Byron, he woke one morning and found himself famous. John Murray, publisher of the Tory rival, *The Quarterly*, declared that it would be worth the copyright of Byron's *Childe Harold* to have Macaulay on their journal's staff. The essay on Machiavelli followed in 1827, and altogether Macaulay contributed twenty-seven essays to the *Edinburgh*, of which the most important and perpetually readable are those on Burleigh and his times, Boswell's Johnson, Lord Bacon, Lord Clive, Warren Hastings, and two on William Pitt, Earl of Chatham.

Next, Macaulay the politician. As one of the chief of the 'Edinburgh reviewers' Macaulay was brought into contact with the leaders of the Whig party, whose social centre was Holland House in Kensington, and it was only natural that his thoughts should turn in the direction of a career in politics. Early in February 1830 Lord Lansdowne, who had been favourably impressed by his articles on James Mill and the Utilitarians in the *Edinburgh*, offered to nominate him for Colne, one of his Lordship's 'pocket boroughs'. Macaulay gratefully accepted the offer and was duly returned, entering the House of Commons when the great struggle over the Reform Bill was about to begin. He took his place among the Whigs (although his father was a staunch Tory) and supported the Bill with speeches that aroused intense admiration.

But while he was making a big name for himself in Parliament and the country, his family at home was falling on hard times. When Macaulay was at Cambridge his father believed himself to be worth £100,000 but his business ventures proved disastrous and Macaulay became entirely dependent on his own exertions. He made about £200 a year by his writing, and had a salary as a member of the Board of Control, the government department concerned with Indian affairs. As a bachelor – he never married – he might well be able to keep himself comfortably enough, but as the years passed it became increasingly evident that his two sisters would have no provision other than what he could make. In these circumstances he jumped at the offer of a seat in the supreme council of India that carried with it the princely salary of £10,000 a year, out of which he estimated that he should be able to save in five years a capital of £30,000. His sister Hannah accepted his proposal that she should accompany him, and in 1834 brother and sister sailed together for Calcutta.

The performance of Macaulay the Indian administrator was masterly. The part he took has been described as 'the application of sound liberal principles to a government which until then had been jealous, close and oppressive'. He vindicated the liberty of the press, maintained the equality of Europeans and Indians before the law and, as chairman of the committee on public instruction, inaugurated a system of national education through which European literature and science were introduced to the people of India. But his greatest service was rendered when he drafted a penal code which became the foundation of the legal system of the Indian Empire.

When he and his sister (now Mrs Trevelyan) returned to England in 1838 he was financially secure, and he immediately re-entered political life. He was elected Whig, or Liberal, MP for Edinburgh in 1839, and entered Lord Melbourne's cabinet as Secretary at War. After two years he went out of office when Peel supplanted Melbourne, but in Lord John Russell's administration in 1846 he received the appointment of Paymaster-General. He lost his seat at the general election in the following year, but he sat again for Edinburgh from 1852 to 1856, when he definitely retired from political life. His health was already beginning to break down, but he applied himself with great vigour and enthusiasm to literary tasks on which he had been engaged since his return from India.

These led, in the first place, to the emergence of Macaulay the poet. The description may be objected to by those who are of the opinion that good poetry cannot possibly be popular. No doubt about it, Macaulay's *Lays of Ancient Rome* were immensely popular when they were published in 1842 and they have been hardly anything else in all the years since.

And now we come to Macaulay the historian. The first germ of his *History of England from the Accession of James II* may be discovered in a prize essay on William III, written when he was at Cambridge, but the idea did not begin to take shape until just after his return from India in 1838. For a time his parliamentary duties kept him from his desk, but as soon as he was out of office he hurried back to his chosen task. It would seem that one of the reasons for his defeat at Edinburgh in 1847 was, as Lord Cockburn put it, that 'Macaulay, with all his knowledge, talent, eloquence and worth, is not popular. He cares more for his *History* than for the jobs of constituents, and answers letters irregularly and with a brevity deemed contemptuous.' More and more, as the work grew on him, he withdrew from society and spent delightful hours in the dusty spadework of research. His composition was slow, his corrections of matter and style endless. Nor was he content with what he got from books on his own heavily-loaded shelves and at the British Museum library: he sought for facts 'on the ground', tramping over the sodden marshlands of Sedgemoor, exploring Glencoe – 'the very valley of the shadow of death', he describes it – penetrating into every corner of Londonderry where there still lurked a vestige of the past and calling upon any inhabitant who might have a tradition worth the hearing. The toil was worth the effort. The famous third chapter, which gives a view of the condition of England at the death of Charles II, 'may challenge comparison' (to quote Professor Saintsbury) 'as a clearly arranged and perfectly mastered collection of innumerably minute facts sifted out of a thousand different sources, with anything in history ancient or modern'.

Soon after he had really got started on his *History*, Macaulay was confessing, 'I shall not be satisfied unless I produce something which shall for a few days supercede the last fashionable novel on the tables of the young ladies.' Seven years later, a few weeks before publication date of the first two volumes, he told his sister, 'The state of my mind is this: when I compare my book with what I imagine history ought to be, I feel dejected and ashamed; but when I compare it with some histories which have a high repute, I feel reassured.' He need not have worried. The book was published by Longmans in December 1848 and within a matter of hours its future was assured. There were a few critics, but their voices were drowned in the storm of popular applause. The sale was enormous. Edition after edition appeared, and the success the book enjoyed in England was equalled in the United States – in April 1849 Harper's of New York were advising Macaulay that they had already sold 40,000 copies, and that probably within three months the sale would amount to 200,000.

Volumes 3 and 4 of the *History* were published in November 1855 and on the last day of February 1856 Macaulay noted in his journal: 'Longman called. It is necessary to reprint. This is wonderful. Twenty-six thousand five hundred copies sold in ten weeks!' And a week later,

Longman came, with a very pleasant announcement. He and his partners find that they are overflowing with money, and think that they cannot invest it better than by advancing to me part of what will be due to me in December. We agreed that they shall pay £20,000 into Williams's Bank next week. What a sum to be gained by one edition of a book!

The *History* is still one of the most popular works in its class. In the spring of 1856 Macaulay quitted his rooms in Albany, just off Piccadilly, in which he had spent fifteen happy years, and went to live at Holly Lodge, on Campden Hill in Kensington. In the following year he was raised to the peerage under the title of Baron Macaulay of Rothley. 'It was one of the few things that everybody approved,' wrote his sister Lady Trevelyan; 'he enjoyed it himself, as he did everything, simply and cordially.' With rapidly failing health Macaulay pressed on with his *History*, although well aware that he would never be able to continue it, as he had originally intended, to a date within the memory of living men.

The end came on 28 December 1859 as he sat in his easy chair in his library at Holly Lodge, dressed as usual, with the book he had been reading lying open on the table beside him.

He died as he had always wished to die, [wrote his nephew in his concluding page] without pain; without any formal farewell; preceding to the grave all whom he loved; and leaving behind him a great and honourable name, and the memory of a life every action of which was as clear and transparent as one of his own sentences.

Ten days later he was buried in Westminster Abbey, beside his peers in Poets' Corner; and with a truth that no one will question, his grave was inscribed with the words:

His body is buried in peace,
But his name liveth for evermore.

John Stuart Mill

(1806–73)

Thomas Woolner's bronze in the Thames Embankment Gardens shows him every inch the expression of the Victorian philosopher. His head is finely sculptured, and the broad brow is made broader by the bald crown. His frock-coat is closely buttoned, his collar high and stiff, his cravat gracefully flowing. In his right hand he is gripping a book – his *Logic*, perhaps, or his *Principles of Political Economy*; it is much too big for the *Liberty*, since that is one of the smallest of the world's great books that have ever been written.

John Stuart Mill was born in London on 20 May 1806. He was the eldest son of James Mill, the hard-headed and hard-natured son of a poor Scottish shoemaker who, abandoning the idea of a career in the Scottish kirk because he could not preach what he had come to believe was untrue, took the road to London, where he made himself into one of the most influential of 'intellectuals'. Jeremy Bentham, the Utilitarian philosopher, took him under his wing, but James Mill was no unquestioning disciple. He ploughed his own furrow, and his experience as a struggling man of letters did nothing to soften his temper or take the cutting edge from his intellect.

From the beginning John Stuart (his second name was bestowed as a kind of tribute to Sir John Stuart, who had given a helping hand to James Mill in his youth) was marked out for great things. His father was resolved on rearing him to become the model of all that a thinking man ought to be, a kind of reasoning machine, free from all disturbing emotions, a man without passions and almost without heart. With this end in view he subjected the boy to a course of education that has been taken as the most dreadful example of parental tyranny.

John Mill never went to school, but was trained by his father as his daily companion and pupil. He was learning Greek when he was three; at least, so he was told – he had no remembrance of the time when he began it. In his eighth year he was launched into Latin and shortly afterwards he was initiated into logic and political economy. What he learnt during the day as he sat on his stool beside his father's desk he was expected to pass on to his brothers and sisters who were even younger than he was.

246

By the time he entered his teens he had read and mastered all
the classics of the ancient literatures besides a vast quantity of
the moderns. There was only one subject in the customary
curriculum that was never taught him. As he puts it in his
Autobiography, the most illuminating and perhaps the most
generally interesting and valuable of all his works:

> I was brought up from the first without any religious belief,
> in the ordinary acceptation of the term ... I am thus one of
> the very few examples, in this country, of one who has, not
> thrown off religious belief, but never had it: I grew up in a
> negative state with regard to it. I looked upon the modern
> exactly as I did upon the ancient religion, as something
> which in no way concerned me.

When he was about fourteen this extraordinary system of
education came to an end: he was the finished product, as
nearly as possible a replica of his father's mind. So successful
had the process proved, the victim had not the least idea of the
way in which he had been victimized. In the book just mentioned he has nothing but good to say of his father, and he
congratulated himself with having started out in life with a
mental equipment far in advance of that possessed by any
other man of his own class and age.

After a year in France staying with the family of General Sir
Samuel Bentham, Jeremy's brother, at seventeen John was
given a desk in the London offices of the East India Company,
on whose staff James Mill (on the strength of a *History of
British India*, which he had written without ever having been
to India or knowing anything much about the country or its
people) had been appointed to a responsible and well-paid
position. His job in the India House gave Mill his bread and
butter for the rest of his life. From the first he had responsible
work to do, and from 1836 he wrote nearly 'every despatch of
any importance that conveyed the instructions of the merchant
princes of Leadenhall Street to their pro-consuls in Asia'.

For several years Mill was happy enough. With just enough
work at the office to keep him occupied and with plenty of
spare time in the evenings, he helped Bentham in preparing his
MSS and contributed to the Benthamite organ, the *Westminster Review*. At that time he had what must surely be held to be
a most worthy object, nothing less than 'to be a reformer of
the world'. But in 1826, when he was twenty, he (not surprisingly) fell into a dull state of nerves, 'unsusceptible to enjoyment or pleasurable excitement', and a most awkward question
began to pester him. 'Suppose that all your objects in life were

realized: that all the changes in institutions and opinions which you are looking forward to, could be completely effected at this very instant: would this be a great joy and happiness to you?' And to his deep surprise he found himself replying, 'No!' At this all his happiness seemed to collapse. The end had ceased to charm. 'I seemed to have nothing left to live for ...'

Months of misery ensued. There was no one he could go to for help or advice. He was driven in upon himself, and at length relief came. He was reading a passage in a book of memoirs in which the author narrates his father's death, and suddenly he was moved to tears. From this moment the burden grew lighter. 'The oppression of the thought that all feeling was dead within me was gone. I was no longer hopeless: I was not a stock or a stone!' He turned to poetry, and Wordsworth's nature poems completed his cure. 'What made Wordsworth's poems a medicine for my mind, was that they expressed, not mere outward beauty, but states of feeling, and of thought coloured by feeling, under the excitement of beauty.'

The excitement of beauty! Before many more months had passed he was experiencing another manifestation of that excitement, not coming now from the pages of a book but through 'great dark eyes, flashing unutterable things' (Thomas Carlyle's description) that first met his across the dinner-table in the house close by Finsbury Square of his acquaintance, Mr John Taylor, wholesale druggist. The eyes were those of Harriet Taylor, *Mrs* Taylor, his host's young wife.

This was the beginning of one of the strangest of Victorian love affairs.

Harriet was the daughter of Thomas Hardy, a medical man with a successful practice at Walworth, in south London, and she was eighteen in 1826 when she married John Taylor, who was getting on for thirty. When she first met John Mill she was already the mother of two sons, and a girl (Helen) was born the following year. John Taylor was an excellent fellow, solid, thoroughly reliable, completely respectable – but a trifle dull. His wife was certainly not that. She was good-looking, intense, strongly intellectual, a woman full of ideas and not afraid of expressing them.

What her husband lacked, she was quick to discover in John Mill and she made him her devoted slave. Read what he writes about her in his *Autobiography* and we may well rub our eyes in amazement. He compares her with Shelley, 'but in thought and intellect, Shelley was but a child compared with what she ultimately became'. With her gifts of feeling and imagination she might have been a consummate artist – a great orator; if

such a career had been open to a woman she might have
become eminent among the rulers of mankind. Furthermore,
'her intellectual gifts did but minister to a moral character at
once the noblest and the best balanced which I have ever met
with in life'.

All this sounds impossibly exaggerated, the sort of thing
that a young man with next to no experience of women might
write when he falls in love for the first time. Surely no such
paragon of a female could ever have walked this earth! But
Mill was penning this ecstatic description years afterwards,
when Harriet had been long dead, and to the end of his days
he never ran out of superlatives when referring to her. And the
evidence that has accumulated since leaves one with the feeling
that after all he may not have been so very far wrong in his
evaluation of the woman who had won his heart and ruled his
mind.

From the date of their first meeting in 1830 to John Taylor's
death in 1849, John Mill and Harriet were – it is still not
quite clear what. They met every day whenever possible.
They exchanged long and tenderly intimate letters. They
went abroad on holidays together, and he was a regular visitor
to the country house at Walton-on-Thames that she kept,
chaperoned only by her young daughter. Of course the
tongues of gossip were soon clacking. Carlyle jested at John
Mill's 'Platonica', and his wife's sharp voice mimicked
Harriet's little mannerisms.

To read some of their letters one might suppose that they
were lovers in the physical sense, but the supposition would
almost certainly be wrong. Mrs Taylor never left her husband,
and Mill seems to have always held him in high regard; certainly they remained on friendly terms. Mill's own account of
his relationship with Mrs Taylor is that it was 'one of strong
affection and confidential intimacy only', and we may believe
him. If it had been otherwise – if theirs had been a conjunction
of bodies as well as of minds – should we have had the books
which did so much to create the intellectual climate of the last
century, whose effects are still not without influence in the
thought – political, economic, social, moral – of our own times?

Mill's first really important book was his *System of Logic*,
which appeared in 1845. He tells us that this book owed little
to Mrs Taylor 'except in the minuter matters of composition,
in which respect my writings, both great and small, have largely
benefited by her accurate and clear-sighted criticism'. But her
share was 'conspicuous' in his next work, *Principles of Political
Economy*, not so much in the first edition, published in 1848,

as in the third of a year or two later. One chapter in particular, that on the 'Probable Future of the Labouring Classes', was (he asserts) entirely due to her; and since this is the chapter in which what may be termed socialistic ideas were mentioned with something like approval, it may be claimed that Harriet Taylor has a right to be included among the founders of the British socialist movement. 'What was abstract and purely scientific' in the book, Mill informs us, 'was generally mine', but 'the properly human element came from her: in all that concerned the application of philosophy to the exigencies of human society and progress, I was her pupil, alike in boldness of speculation and cautiousness of practical judgment.'

John Taylor died of cancer in May 1849; and two years later, in April 1851, John Mill and Mrs Taylor were married at a register office. In the following September they set up house together in Blackheath Park. Here they worked on what was intended to be the definitive edition of the *Political Economy* and on the short essay *On Liberty* which has proved (as he himself expected) Mill's most enduring work.

The *Liberty* was more directly and literally our joint production than anything else which bears my name, [he wrote
in the *Autobiography*] for there was not a sentence of it which
was not several times gone through by us together, turned
over in many ways, and carefully weeded of any faults ...
The conjunction of her mind with mine has rendered it a
kind of philosophic text-book of a single truth – the importance, to man and society, of a large variety in types of
character, and of giving full freedom to human nature to
expand itself in innumerable and conflicting directions.

The book was about to receive its final revision when – just after Mill had retired from the India House on a pension of £1,500 a year, and they had gone to spend the winter in the south of France – Mrs Mill was taken suddenly ill with acute bronchitis. She died in an hotel bedroom at Avignon on 3 November 1858 and was buried in a cemetery there.

For seven years only had they been husband and wife, and Mill was desolated by this 'most unexpected and bitter calamity'. He wrote a fulsome tribute to be inscribed on the stone above her grave, and to the *Liberty* (1859) he prefixed a dedi-
cation, 'To the beloved memory of her who was the inspirer, and in part the author, of all that is best in my writings – the friend and wife whose exalted sense of truth and right was my strongest incitement and whose approbation was my chief reward ...' Henceforth, 'Her memory is to me a religion, and

her approbation the standard by which I endeavour to regulate my life.' With a view to feeling 'her still near me' he bought a cottage at Avignon near where she was buried, and lived there for a portion of each year.

Fifteen years were left to him after Harriet's death, and they were filled with achievement. *On Liberty* was followed in 1860 by his *Considerations on Representative Government*, a classic of democratic theory, *Utilitarianism* in 1861 and, after long preparation, *The Subjection of Women* in 1869. Every page of this last bears the impress of Harriet's personality, and it lives as a standard presentation of the case for the political and social emancipation of the female sex. From 1865 to 1868 Mill was Liberal MP for Westminster, and as such he introduced an amendment to Disraeli's franchise bill which proposed that the word 'person' should be substituted for 'man', thus opening the door to women as parliamentary voters. The amendment was rejected by 196 votes to seventy-three, but the result was taken as a great encouragement to the women's cause.

At the general election of 1868 Mill was defeated by W. H. Smith, the Conservative candidate. He took his reverse with philosophic calm and retired to his home at Avignon. And there the 'Saint of Rationalism', as Gladstone once called him, because of his single-minded love of truth, his humanity, his passion for justice, died on 8 May 1873. The next day he was buried in the marble tomb beside his wife.

Alfred Tennyson

(1809-92)

In his Sussex home at Aldworth the poet lay dying. He had
been ill for some weeks and was prepared for the end. Two
days ago he had looked at his doctor steadily and said one
word: 'Death?' When the doctor silently bowed his head the
old man murmured: 'That's well.'

Now during the last hours of daylight he would see – it was
Wednesday, 5 October 1892 – he asked for his well-thumbed
Shakespeare and though he could not read, held it in his hand,
saying faintly: 'I have opened it.' Soon after, he spoke for the
last time, words of blessing to his wife, his son and daughter-
in-law who were beside his bed.

After dark the moon rose, flooding the room with light and
shining full on the poet's magnificent head. His family, the
doctor and two nurses who had been tending him waited for
the end. It came in the early morning of the 6th, a final short
breath, and in the room still suffused with reflected moonlight
all knelt in prayer.

'Lord Tennyson,' said the vicar of the local church who
came a few hours later, 'God has taken you, who made you a
prince of men.'

These words were echoed by the whole of Victorian England.
After sending her sympathy, the Queen noted in her journal:
'He was a great poet and his ideas were ever grand, noble and
elevating.' The press too stressed the ennobling example of his
life and poetry; in many households the slim volumes of *In
Memoriam* and *The Idylls of the King* had a place second only
to the Bible and for nearly fifty years men and women in all
walks of life had found Tennyson's lines on their lips in
moments of stress or joy.

There was not an aspect of life which Tennyson had not
touched, not a corner of the great Victorian tapestry where the
golden thread of his genius did not shine. We are inclined to
think of that age as sedate, but with rapid industrialization
and the march of science thinking people were deeply disturbed
by the feeling that everything traditional was crumbling into
the melting pot – religion, morality, social standards, the age-
old view of humanity's place in the universe. There was a sense

that evil was growing, a sense that Britain was rushing head-long towards a future which we might find hard to control or shape. In all this Tennyson became the lode-star of positive faith, almost the incorporation of Newman's 'kindly light', a seer and guide of seemingly superhuman proportions.

He was born at Somersby in Lincolnshire, the fourth of twelve children, in 1809. Early in life he was confronted with tragedy amidst idyllic rural surroundings in the heart of a family he dearly loved. His father George, an eldest son, had been cut off in favour of his younger brother by an ambitious parent and relegated, as being unlikely to establish the fame of the Tennysons, to the rectorship of two small places totalling less than a hundred souls. To the talented and versatile George this spelt continual frustration and despite the efforts of his devoted wife he eventually succumbed to gloom, embitterment and the bottle. Though only by indirect reference, his son's poetry reflects terrible scenes of violence, insult or degradation in the home and a nameless guilt seems to have attached itself to Alfred's soul, as to a boy called on too often to take sides between parents he loved.

But, aged five, the same boy had already received the mystic call. One day in a gale he cried: 'I hear strange voices in the wind,' and with his brothers and sisters he was soon shouting lines of verse on their rambles through the wolds, by copse and reedy marshes, by the shores of the wild North Sea – meaning-less lines, but full of *something*, as yet he hardly knew what: 'a thousand brazen chariots rolled over a bridge of brass' or 'with slaughterous sons of thunder rolled the flood'.

Then, as he was devotedly tutored by his father from the large rectory library, ancient myths, the magic of Shakespeare, the charm of the Lincolnshire countryside began to weave together in his mind. Whole poems came forth, powerful and controlled, and at times he had strange experiences when the world fell away and he was free in a fourth dimension:

> All sense of time
> And being and place was swallowed up and lost
> Within a victory of boundless thought.
> I was part of the Unchangeable,
> A scintillation of eternal Mind,
> Remix'd and burning with its parent fire.

With his feet on firm ground again, he saw the beauties as well as the ugliness of life more clearly, as well as the dualism in his own nature and that reverence was born for small things like flowers and birds which was never to leave him.

He grew into an impressive youth, tall, broad-shouldered, black-haired, sallow-complexioned, with strong aquiline features. 'That man must be a poet,' said the Master of Trinity College, on seeing the new undergraduate.

At Cambridge in argument with a group of brilliant friends, Tennyson left the Somersby backwater for the broad stream of contemporary life, exulting in the new vistas opened by the natural sciences and eager 'to follow knowledge like a sinking star beyond the bounds of human thought'.

But the deepest influence was that of his friend Arthur Hallam, two years younger than himself, strikingly handsome, exceptionally gifted. A profound affection developed between them, partly due perhaps to the fact that each felt somewhat isolated from his fellows by his outstanding talents. Hallam became engaged to one of Tennyson's sisters and a lifetime of fruitful friendship seemed to lie before the two young men. Then, in 1833, after they had known each other for five years, Hallam died at the age of twenty-two while on a continental trip.

Tennyson felt the loss of this kindred spirit for the rest of his life, but it gave rise to the poem *In Memoriam* which grew over a period of years and expressed in agonized tones the doubts of bereaved and sorrowing people everywhere. By the time it was published in 1850 Tennyson was loved both as man and poet by many intellectual friends, but it was *In Memoriam* which brought him nation-wide fame and after the death of Wordsworth caused Queen Victoria, at the Prince Consort's suggestion, to offer him the laureateship, which he accepted.

Of this poem of over 700 stanzas 60,000 copies were sold in the first few months and upwards of twenty editions printed in Tennyson's lifetime. It appealed not as a prop to orthodox religious faith, in which it was singularly lacking, but as a humble search for a personal answer to a tragic situation which confronts people in all ages. The poet groped as people are forced to do, despairing and sincere, for some inner conviction which would enable him to go on living, and he found it in an intuitive belief that the spirit of love created the universe, that the human soul in this world and the next is upheld by it and that there is a purpose in life, 'one far-off divine event to which the whole creation moves'. In the words of Granville Bradley, later headmaster of Marlborough, the poem 'is a journey from the first stupor and confusion of grief through a growing acquiescence, often disturbed by the recurrence of pain, to an almost unclouded peace and joy'.

Meanwhile, after Cambridge where he did not take a degree,

Tennyson had lived precariously on his inheritance and what he could eke from his poetry. Forthright in his ways, utterly unaffected and sincere, spiritually intense, he became known as a man apart, a natural phenomenon. It seemed that with him every experience of life sank down and emerged in some new combination in the form of verse.

But these years also laid a burden on him. In 1836 he had first met and fallen in love with his future wife, Emily Sellwood, but it was fourteen years before her father's opposition was overcome and they did not marry until 1850, by which time Tennyson felt that he must 'find love and peace or die'.

Emily proved the perfect wife for him and for forty-two years devoted her whole self to serving his genius, both being humbly convinced that his gifts were God-given, to be used for the public good, and that a great responsibility was laid on him. Three years after their marriage, when his collected poems were already going through their eighth edition, they moved to Farringford near Freshwater Bay in the Isle of Wight to escape the attentions of hero-worshippers and find peace by the sea he loved so much.

Year by year grew *The Idylls of the King* and other long poems on spiritual themes, sonnets and ballads illustrating the Tennysonian message, as well as lyrics which returned again and again to the sense of mystery in nature:

> O hark O hear! how thin and clear,
> And thinner, clearer, farther going!
> O sweet and far from cliff and scar
> The horns of elfland faintly blowing!

At night, when the breakers crashed on Freshwater beach, he watched the ebb and flow and thought of Arthur Hallam. He wrote 'The Charge of the Light Brigade', 'The Revenge', humorous verse in Lincolnshire dialect, and in verse abjured Gladstone, who was a fervent admirer, to be careful about electoral reform. He wrote 'Enoch Arden', a moral tale, patriotic poems answering the threat of Napoleon III's France, sent charming verses to his living friends, wrote poignant epitaphs on friends who died. And one summer evening, when he was crossing the Solent as an old man, sixteen lines rose without effort to his mind, the most famous of all, and he jotted them down on an envelope: 'Sunset and evening star, and one clear call for me ...'

His output was prodigious, many more verses, as he said, going up the chimney with the smoke of his pipe than he ever wrote down. And reading his poetry today we are still stirred by the dogged faith it expresses, which appealed so strongly to his contemporaries. Yet, disliking the over-ethearialized element in much of his work, several of his friends thought him greater as a man than as a poet. 'He is humble and true,' wrote the dramatist Henry Taylor, 'incapable of disguising a single weakness or fault, simple as a child, naked as a statue.' Edward Fitzgerald, Robert Browning, Edward Lear, Dr Jowett, the Master of Balliol – all lifelong friends – Gladstone, even Lord Acton who blamed the airiness of his metaphysics, were deeply moved by his simple heart, his sincere and questing mind. At the same time he was a rugged individualist. 'Angularity,' said another friend, 'was his dominant characteristic,' and added: 'In Tennyson we find the man who cannot be identified with any one of the many tendencies of the age, but has affinities with all ... He is the mirror in which the age contemplated all that is best in itself.' And the best, as Tennyson and leading Victorians saw it, was Britain's imperial mission, Britain as a shrine of freedom and justice, of domestic virtue, of progress linking a glorious past with a yet more civilized future. The smoking slums of the industrial cities might belie this – then it was that people turned with gratitude to Tennyson and his message.

So he became established as a national institution. Two sons were born, Hallam and Lionel, and Farringford became a 'little Athens' where scientists, theologians, poets and musicians conversed with the bard, tramped with him about the island downs and in the evenings listened spell-bound to tempestuous recitations of his own poetry. 'It was enough,' wrote Edward Lear, 'to make you stand on your head.'

He formed a close and touching friendship with the ageing Queen and in 1884 was created a baron, the first poet to be so honoured. He was already the only one in Britain ever to earn a substantial income from his work – 'Enoch Arden' alone made him £6,000 in one year – and in the 1860s he built another house for himself at Aldworth.

The tall figure with the cloak and wide sombrero could not move anywhere unrecognized. But though outwardly he became somewhat harsh and imperious, the core of simplicity remained. Perplexed like many contemporaries by the challenge of science and materialism, he preserved faith in the spirit which he sensed to be the only true reality, 'like a great ocean pressing round us on every side'. He bore witness to this faith in his life and poetry, and even if it were possible to reject his work entirely Tennyson the man would still be there, majestic, vulnerable, earnest, kindly, the man who thundered

Charles Darwin, author of the controversial *Origin of Species* and *The Descent of Man*

Thomas Huxley, the foremost exponent of Darwin's theories

Louis Pasteur, pioneer of chemistry and bacteriology

Isambard Kingdom Brunel,
versatile engineering genius

Michael Faraday, best known
for his research and discoveries
in electromagnetism

Alexander Graham Bell,
inventor of the telephone

at doubters that there *was* a God, the individuality *did* endure, there was 'something which watches over us', the man who fell on his knees one night in the moonlit park at Farringford and called to a companion: 'Violets, man, violets! Smell them and you'll sleep the better!', the man who wove the best minds of his age in a shining net of friendship, of whom they said after his death: we are grateful to him merely for having existed.

William Makepeace Thackeray

(1811–63)

The future critic and chronicler of English life was born in India. The Thackerays, of good Yorkshire stock, had gone out during the eighteenth century as servants of 'John Company', and it was in Calcutta in 1810 that young Richard Thackeray, holder of an important post there, married Anne Becher, a local beauty. Their son, young 'Billy Boy', enjoyed a happy, cosseted life for his first six years. Even his father's death, when William was four, cannot have disturbed him greatly, so beloved and petted was he by his mother and the native servants. Then, at the age of six, the inescapable change came. The Indian climate and the lack of educational facilities made it imperative that a boy-child must be sent 'Home' as soon as he was old enough to travel.

It is impossible to transplant without disturbance either a flower or a child. The young Thackeray missed his mother bitterly, and the elderly, amiable aunts and formidable Great-grandmamma Becher were inadequate substitutes. His first school, at Southampton, was a nightmare of canings, bullying, starvation, strange penances, cold and chilblains. His family soon rescued him: but the school at Walpole House, Chiswick, was not much better and in his first term he ran away, only to be deterred from reaching his relatives' home by the frightening traffic in Hammersmith Road. One day, in the distant future, Miss Becky Sharp was to take a vindictive farewell of the school where she had suffered – also in Chiswick.

In spite of unhappiness, William grew into a big, hearty boy. He was bright at school, conspicuous even when he reached Charterhouse: though his family could not decide whether he was going to be an author or an artist, for he showed equal skill at writing stories and illustrating them. His mother had come home from India, bringing with her a second husband, Captain (later Major) Carmichael-Smythe, who had been her sweetheart before she had met and married Richmond Thackeray. William was entirely happy in this gentle, quiet man who had been one of his favourite playmate 'uncles' in India, and who was to be immortalized in one of his greatest characters – Colonel Newcome.

Charterhouse gave way to Cambridge. He enjoyed it but came away with unremarkable honours and the feeling that his studies were to be of life, not letters. So he stands alone for the first time: a young giant of six feet three, with a good-natured, rosy face, a ridiculously small flattened nose (a legacy from a school bully), weak eyes and 'a heart susceptible and true'. As ready for play as an amiable puppy, pleasure-loving and affectionate, he is inexorably marked down as a victim of life's harshness.

He travelled abroad, fell in and out of love, drank into the night with friends, read for the law and joked about becoming Lord Chancellor, neglected his studies to join in glee-singing parties at such rendezvous as the Eagle Tavern or the Cider Cellars in Maiden Lane. He was drifting into literary Bohemia, polishing his wits, veering between art and authorship as a career. In Paris he studied art and felt that he could become a second Hogarth. In London he joined eagerly in the new sport of satirizing popular novelists such as Bulwer, using as his weapons articles written under a pseudonym for *Fraser's Magazine*. With him as contributors were Carlyle, the old Coleridge and Harrison Ainsworth.

In 1836 Thackeray became Paris correspondent of a journal floated by his stepfather, the *Constitutional and Public Ledger*. He had received a blow in his ambitions to live by art, for a somewhat cocky young man called Charles Dickens had dismissed as unsatisfactory Thackeray's drawings for *The Posthumous Papers of the Pickwick Club*. However, literature would keep him and his bride – for he had met and married Isabella Shawe, a gentle, pretty creature of seventeen with a formidable Irish mother. When in later years he wrote the strange, crypto-autobiographical book *Lovel the Widower*, his mother-in-law was savagely caricatured in it. The Thackerays were certainly happy at first, in their Bloomsbury home, where their first daughter, Anne Isabella (known as Annie), was born.

He began to develop as a satirist, writing *The Yellowplush Papers* under the nom-de-plume of Mr Charles Yellowplush, a footman, and *Strictures on Pictures* as a Mr Michael Angelo Titmarsh. Social climbing, the vulgarity of the *nouveaux riches* of the middle classes, sentimentality, 'romanticophobia', and the Gothick horrors of 'dead bodies, coffins, and what not' – all were fodder to him. He was enjoying life. Another daughter had been born. To her mother he wrote, '. . . two years married and not a single unhappy day . . . I feel in my heart a kind of overflowing thanksgiving.'

He spoke too soon. Jane, the second child, died in infancy.

He bore the blow philosophically. Soon another baby was on the way and the Thackeray fortunes were improving when, in 1840, Minny was born. Her mother's nerves had been strained throughout the pregnancy, and after the birth she was slow to recover. Thackeray decided to see what a holiday in her native Ireland would do. They set out hopefully on the three-day sail to Cork. After a few hours of it, Isabella climbed out of a porthole and jumped into the sea. A frantic rescue operation succeeded. Better if it had failed, for her reason had gone, never to come back. After two years Thackeray reluctantly gave up his attempts to care for her at home, and she was consigned to a private hospital in France. Her sad, wasted life lingered on until 1894. The young husband was left to bring up his two little girls alone: unable to divorce his wife and marry again, forbidden by convention and scruple from taking a mistress, shocked by what had happened into deep fears for his own sanity.

These fortunately were unfounded. Basically sane and sensible, he pushed away his sorrows and anxieties and turned to work. A new periodical, called *Punch*, had just been started. Thackeray became first a contributor and then a member of the staff. He began his first novel, *The Luck of Barry Lyndon*, a picaresque story with a quality of brilliance soon discerned by its readers. Deprived of a normal home life, he travelled, sometimes with Annie, sometimes alone in the East, the Greek Islands, the Holy Land, using his travels as material for later sketches. In London he threw himself into tavern conviviality. There was wine, beer, beefsteaks, pipe-smoke and good company. But for Thackeray, a man with a nature as domestically gentle as his character as a satirist was violent, it was not enough; he craved feminine company.

Among his friends at Cambridge had been William Henry Brookfield, who had taken holy orders and was by 1842 a highly popular young clergyman, famous for his dramatic colourful sermons. He had recently married Jane Octavia Elton, tall, beautiful, intelligent without being a blue-stocking. The young couple mixed freely in the intellectual circles of London: one might meet them in Cheyne Row, at one of Mrs Carlyle's soirées, or in the drawing-room of Alfred Tennyson or Walter Savage Landor. The lonely Thackeray was invited to dinner by his old friend's bride, and instantly fell in love with her. That she did not fall in love with him is clear. She gave him for some five years the feminine friendship he so greatly needed, was the recipient of his letters – the only safety valve for his emotions, was flattered by his open admiration, rapturously expressed. She seems to have regarded him with a tinge of mockery, and she repelled smartly any move of his to increase the intimacy between them, such as it was.

Eventually Thackeray expressed himself too warmly in a letter, and Jane replied that unless he could write 'in more commonplace style' she would find herself unable to answer him at all. The painfully sensitive Thackeray retreated. He was a realist: he had got himself into an impossible situation. There were to be no more women in his life, other than his beloved daughters.

When, in 1846, he followed his *Punch* series 'The Snobs of England' with the novel *Vanity Fair*, Jane was written into it as Amelia Sedley. It is difficult to see any resemblance between the sentimental, feeble, yet irritatingly pig-headed Amelia and the cooly sardonic, cryptic Jane of the letters and reported speeches. Nor is she to our eyes particularly apparent in Lady Castlewood of the later book *Henry Esmond*, a character into which its author put his frustrated love and longing for the woman who, when he wrote *Esmond*, was almost lost to him. 'This fair creature ... an angelical softness and bright pity ... the tone of her voice, though she uttered words ever so trivial, gave him a pleasure that amounted almost to anguish.'

Vanity Fair was a success. He had ventured to think that this book, the first written under his own name, might make him, and it did. Into it he put much of his own life: his Anglo-Indian background, his unhappy schooldays in Chiswick, his Irish in-laws, friends, enemies and public figures. His avowed and sincere intention to castigate society resulted in a novel superbly entertaining, witty, dramatic, moving even by the standards of today. The would-be satirist and reformer had emerged as a story-teller whose brilliance rivalled that of the noonday sun of his rival, Dickens.

The years that followed were good ones for Thackeray, by material standards. He was comfortably settled in his handsome Kensington home: Annie and Minny ('my dearest little women') made excellent, loving companions to their father. He followed *Vanity Fair* with *Pendennis*, another semi-autobiographical novel. Then came *The English Humourists of the 18th Century*, *Esmond* (followed six years later by its sequel *The Virginians*), and *The Newcomes*, a development and extension of the *Pendennis* theme. Clive Newcome has much of his creator in him. Colonel Newcome in an affectionate portrait of Thackeray's stepfather, and Rosey Mackenzie who dies young resembles Isabella. Thackeray moved among the great, became editor of *The Cornhill*, travelled on the Continent and in America, lectured, dabbled in politics and was nearly elected as Whig member for Oxford, and enjoyed something like rich living. The house in Onslow Square acquired a butler and a footman; Thackeray, proudly if somewhat ineptly, rode in Rotten Row, and kept a carriage and a brougham.

Yet he was not happy. For many years he had been dogged by ill-health. He suffered from painful 'spasms', which became more and more frequent. His hair whitened early. Doctors advised abstinence from smoking, hearty eating and drinking. Thackeray defied them; after all, he had few enough pleasures. At forty-seven he wrote that there was 'no incident, no character, no go left in this dreary old expiring carcase'.

His late novel, *Lovel the Widower*, is a final burst of self-expression, rambling and uncontrolled, a blend of bitterness, self-pity and self-depreciation, nostalgia for what might have been. The enigmatic 'heroine', Elizabeth Prior, governess and ex-ballet-girl, is the last fictional guise of Jane Brookfield. It is a rueful 'little comedy', all in all.

One fulfilment was possible. Thackeray had always been at heart a man of the eighteenth century. He belonged to it spiritually, loved its robustness, its realism of outlook, so contrasted with the sentimentality and hypocrisy of his own time – with which, to his secret shame, he had been forced into alliance. A commission to continue the dead Macaulay's *History of England* through the reign of Queen Anne decided him to identify himself solidly with the period he loved by building a fine house in Queen Anne style. There, on Kensington Palace Green, he would live and write his book, an eighteenth-century dweller at one remove. The house rose, a materialized vision, and delighted him. But from the spacious mansion, the new library, there only emerged the inferior novel *Philip* and the early scenes of a story based on his seafaring ancestors, *Denis Duval*. His daughter Annie was also writing a novel, *The Story of Elizabeth*. The harsh review it received in *The Athenaeum* hurt Thackeray more than its author. He was too tired, too ill to take many more blows from life.

On the eve of Christmas 1863, Thackeray was found dead in bed.

Carlyle, who had given him a grudging and qualified friendship, had once described him as 'a big, fierce, hungry man; not a strong one', It was a shrewd analysis of the literary giant who for all his humour, wordly success, riches and lionization, remains a figure of pathos.

Charles Dickens

(1812–70)

There was a solid middle-class background to the baby Charles John Huffam Dickens, born on 7 February 1812, in the Portsea district of Portsmouth. His grandfather William Dickens had been a footman and steward, his grandmother a housemaid, then housekeeper; their son, John Dickens, a clerk in the Navy Pay Office, had married a girl, Elizabeth Barrow, who was related to the second secretary of the Admiralty.

But of middle-class security and steadiness there was nothing. John Dickens was a cheerful, feckless man, hopelessly inept at providing for his large family. The original of Wilkins Micawber, his imprisonment in the debtors' prison, the Marshalsea, imprinted shame and horror on the mind of the young Charles, who wrote it out of his system many years later in *Little Dorrit*.

Charles's early childhood was happy. His father was employed at the Pay Office of Chatham Dockyard. The lively atmosphere of Chatham, combined with good schooling and his own immense capacity for reading and learning, enriched the child's mind and fed his imagination. Then, in 1823, when he was eleven, his happiness was shattered: the family removed to London, to Bayham Street, Camden Town, an unlovely district made uglier by the Dickenses' poverty. Charles, the bright scholar and romantic dreamer, became the family drudge and errand-goer. His education ceased, his precious books, even his bed, were sold to bring in a little money. His one pleasure was the discovery of London – nineteenth-century London, sordid, foggy, frowsty and evil, yet full of riches and excitement to a mind such as his.

When finances were at their lowest, Charles was offered a job. A cousin volunteered to take him on at Warren's Blacking Factory, at Hungerford Stairs, Charing Cross, for the princely wage of six shillings a week. It was a place of horror to the delicate, clever child: a crazy, tumble-down old house on the noisome river, swarming with rats. The blacking factory was to haunt Dickens's mind as long as he lived. It is impossible to overestimate the effect of it and the humiliation it caused him on his character, his attitude to security and wealth, his relationships and his writings.

Within a few months he was freed. A legacy cleared his
father's debts and a family quarrel had the result of taking
Charles away from the factory. His mother tried to send him
back. He never forgot that, nor forgave her.

He resumed the education he had longed for. At his new
school he began to write tales and circulate them among his
fellow-students, and became a leader in school dramatic performances. In 1827 he left to work as an office-boy to a solicitor, occupying his spare time in learning shorthand, intending
to follow in the footsteps of his father, now a parliamentary
reporter. Being Dickens, he worked with tremendous application and enthusiasm, qualified himself to be a reporter for a
legal office and acquired that knowledge of the law, its delays,
humours and horrors, which permeates his books.

At this 'unsubstantial, happy, foolish time' he fell in love.
Maria Beadnell was the daughter of a bank manager, pretty,
flirtatious and empty-headed. Some sort of secret engagement
seems to have been agreed, but Maria's family were not
anxious for her to marry a struggling young reporter. Maria
herself rejected him; and on that violently impressionable
nature another scar was deeply graven, never to fade. Dickens
the novelist portrayed Maria as the delicious, useless Dora
Copperfield, and later, cruelly, after meeting her in fleshy
middle age, as the silly Flora Finching of *Little Dorrit*.

He was a successful parliamentary reporter before very long;
now, in his travels, learning of social abuses and their need for
reform in that England of the early 1830s in which injustice,
oppression and the growing black shadow of the Industrial
Revolution were overlaying the old pastoral scene. And he was
writing – in 1836 he began to collect into two volumes some
sketches he had contributed to periodicals, which he called
Sketches by Boz (Boz being the nickname of a small brother).
Approached by the firm of Chapman and Hall to provide copy
to accompany some sporting sketches, he agreed; and *The
Times* of 26 March 1836 gave notice of the first shilling number
of *The Posthumous Papers of the Pickwick Club*.

It became the most ebullient, irresistible comic book ever to
have been written by an Englishman, and it swept the country.
Two days after its publication Dickens was married. His bride
was Catherine Hogarth, daughter of a colleague on the *Morning Chronicle*, an amiable, pretty, somewhat languid young
woman. She was the eldest of three sisters; Georgina, the
youngest, was still a child, but Mary was sixteen and charming.
'So perfect a creature never breathed. She had not a fault,'
Dickens said of her. When the young couple and their baby

son moved into a house in Doughty Street, Bloomsbury, Mary went with them, and domestic happiness reigned. But it was short-lived, like Mary herself. One night after returning from the theatre she was taken ill and died the next day. It was the third traumatic experience of Dickens's life, a sorrow suffered over and over again, reflected in his letters and his novels. His relationship, innocent yet passionate, with Mary, in her life and death, is one of the great puzzles presented to his biographers.

After *Pickwick* came *Oliver Twist*, a cry of anger against the terrible workhouse system and the Poor Law; and as it ended he began *Nicholas Nickleby*, in which Dickens the reformer campaigns against the notorious Yorkshire schools where unwanted boys were farmed out and kept under miserable conditions. The campaign succeeded – the schools were closed down. And the public had incidentally been treated to a picaresque novel full of the sort of fresh, bubbling fun which Dickens was perhaps never again to equal. We see him as he was then, in his glorious prime, in Maclise's portrait of 1839, picturesquely clad (he loved bright colours): his face of a vivid sensitivity, almost feminine in its delicacy, the eyes brilliant with intelligence, the mouth charming and sensual.

The growing family now lived at 1 Devonshire Terrace, Marylebone, in increasing prosperity. There Dickens wrote *Barnaby Rudge* and *The Old Curiosity Shop*, two novels built into the framework of *Master Humphrey's Clock*, a collection of otherwise unremarkable stories. The author and his public fell in love with the heroine of *Curiosity Shop*, Little Nell, the child whose weary travels with her old grandfather end in her death. She appears today a sentimentalized, characterless doll; but to Dickens she was Mary Hogarth over again, and his own grief brought floods of tears on both sides of the Atlantic.

In 1841 he was on the farther side of it, enjoying a working holiday in America at his publishers' expense, being lionized, wined, dined and fêted. The classlessness of the United States appealed to him, but he found much to dislike, and in *American Notes* and *Martin Chuzzlewit* he attacked these things freely, adding to his unpopularity in America with his strenuous propaganda for international copyright. But he had given the world Mrs Gamp, the drunken midwife, possibly the most quoted of his characters at least during his own lifetime; Pecksniff, the arch-hypocrite; and Mercy Pecksniff, his nearest approach so far to a real woman among his gallery of simpering wax figures.

He was rapidly maturing as a writer, his humour rich and

fertile, his satire sharp, his social criticism biting, but in the portrayal of the characters he cared for most he could not rise above the sentimental – as with the children Paul Dombey, of *Dombey and Son*, and Tiny Tim of *A Christmas Carol*, and he was wholly bound in freedom of expression by the repressive conventions of the time. Victoria and Albert had imposed their own extreme respectability upon their kingdom, and Dickens, born a full-blooded Georgian, was forever to be thought of as a Victorian, upholder of the family, the English Christmas and the strict morals supposed to be entertained by all classes. His own situation made an irony of his public face. In 1848 his eighth child was born and his newest novel, *David Copperfield*. For the first time the story was told in the first person: much of it his own story, translated into fictional terms. Here was the sad child of the blacking factory, the feckless Micawber, the shallow Maria/Dora and, in his own words, 'the old unhappy loss or want of something'. Maria/Dora is killed off, because by now she is Maria/Dora/Catherine. He was tired of his wife, exasperated with her gentle laziness, impatient of her frequent pregnancies. Disappointed in her as a chatelaine, he had replaced her as such by her sister Georgina, in whom he saw a likeness to the lost Mary and a domestic capability not possessed by Kate.

It was not until 1857 that he found any personal fulfilment. He had founded the journal *Household Words*, had written the rest of the Christmas Books and *Bleak House, Little Dorrit* and *Hard Times*, and had moved to Tavistock House, Bloomsbury. He had travelled widely, become a cosmopolitan; the youthful, bright-faced Charles had turned into a patriarchal figure with a flowing, grizzled beard. He had begun the public readings from his own works which increased his fame and gave him an outlet for the dramatic instinct which had always been strong in him.

In 1857 he produced and acted in *The Frozen Deep*, written by himself and Wilkie Collins. Three professional actresses took part, a Mrs Ternan and her two daughters. For Ellen Ternan, eighteen years old, he developed an infatuation that changed his life. The affair – secret, furtive, guilt-laden – led to his separation from his wife and the splitting-up of their family. It also led to his maturing as an author, for Ellen is reflected in three girl characters verging on reality and humanity – Bella Wilfer of *Our Mutual Friend*, Estella of *Great Expectations* and Rosa Bud of *The Mystery of Edwin Drood*. A darkness looms over these late novels, dominated by their themes: the emptiness of riches, snobbery and bureaucracy, the degradation of the debtors' prison, London's filthy, fascinating river, the farce of the divorce laws and, in *Bleak House*, the tragic fatuity of the law itself. In *Great Expectations* Dickens reaches maturity. It is an immensely adult novel, tinged with the intimations of mortality which were overtaking its author.

He lived now in a house which had been the dream-place of his Kentish boyhood, Gad's Hill Place, between Rochester and Chatham. Even there, as happy as it was possible for him to be, with his three females, Georgina and his daughters Mamie and Katey, his inner fires, his demon, compelled him to rush up and down giving his dramatic readings and travelling for pleasure and stimulation. On a journey back from Paris in 1865, possibly in company with Ellen, he was involved in a serious railway accident at Staplehurst, Kent, which permanently weakened his nerves and constitution. Two years later he went to America on a reading tour. It was immensely successful and financially rewarding, but his health was rapidly breaking and the tour worsened it. On 15 March 1870 he gave the final reading and returned to Gad's Hill to work on his last book, *The Mystery of Edwin Drood*.

Much has been said of the mystery, unsolved because he did not live to finish the novel – too little of the novel's quality. Nearly all his old faults are gone, giving place to a lovely clarity of style. The scene is the Rochester of his childhood, but Rochester bathed in an unearthly light. It is ostensibly a story of mystery and murder, revenge and detection, but the overall atmosphere is one of strange peace. *Edwin Drood* is the twilight of a god, more beautiful than his dawn. On 9 June 1870 Dickens died at Gad's Hill, struck down by a paralytic seizure.

They buried him, against his express wishes, in Poets' Corner, Westminster Abbey, not in the peaceful Kentish churchyard where he wanted to lie. 'A vast hope has passed across the world,' wrote Alfred de Musset. Visiting that spot, it is difficult to believe that anything of Charles Dickens lies under the plainly-inscribed stone, incongruously surrounded by the bewigged monuments which amused him so much in life. He was, and is, and will be, with the rest of the immortals.

Samuel Smiles

(1812–1904)

Samuel Smiles is known best for his writings rather than for his other activities, and in recent years his writings have been re-examined and reassessed. Some of them were bestsellers and one of them, *Self-Help*, published in 1859, has appeared in many different editions and in many languages. Its message was simple and unoriginal. ' "Heaven helps those who help themselves" is a well-tried maxim, embodying in a small compass the results of vast human experience,' the book begins.

> The spirit of self-help is the root of all genuine growth in the individual; and, exhibited in the lives of many, it constitutes the true source of national vigour and strength. Help from without is often enfeebling in its effects, but help from within invariably invigorates. Whatever is done *for* men or classes to a certain extent takes away the stimulus and necessity of doing for themselves; and where men are subjected to over-guidance and over-government, the inevitable tendency is to render them comparatively helpless.

> Yet simple and unoriginal though the message was, it has to be studied in the context both of Smiles's own life and, above all, of his times if its relevance and its appeal are to be appreciated. Smiles lived for long enough to see his own society and the world change profoundly. He admired energy and he believed in progress. What he called 'energetic individualism' would generate new wealth. He had little respect for inherited privilege and he feared the unruliness of large crowds as much as he disliked expensive measures of state intervention in economic life. By the end of his life, however, there were many signs that some of the energy was going out of the British economy, that democracy was generating a new kind of radicalism which demanded increased action on the part of the state, that 'mass culture' was producing new kinds of social conformity. Further changes which have taken place since his death have widened the psychological distance between Smiles and most of his readers. They have also challenged the 'cheerful optimism' which pervades most of his work.

> Samuel Smiles was born in 1812 in the small town of

Haddington in Scotland, eighteen miles from Edinburgh, the first coach stop on the journey from Edinburgh to London. He was one of eleven children, and his father was a paper-maker and general merchant. He was educated at local schools and at Edinburgh University, although he was expected to work as a 'half-timer' as well. After qualifying as a doctor he returned to Haddington, where he wrote his first book *Physical Nurture and Education of Children* (1835). He also served on the town council. Yet, like the heroes in the books he was to write later, he was dissatisfied with the limitations of local life and dreamed of bigger things.

'How are you getting on?' his old teacher Dr Mackintosh asked him one day.

'I'm not getting on. I'm going off,' was the reply.

'How's that?' Dr Mackintosh went on. 'Remember a rolling stone gathers no moss.'

For once Smiles was not impressed, as he usually was, by a proverb. 'Since I have been settled in Haddington,' he retorted, 'I have gathered nothing whatever, so I think I had better begin to roll.'

In 1838, therefore, he sold his stock, settled his accounts and set off, like many ambitious Scotsmen before him, for a European tour. He then went to London, 'a new world, unlike anything I had before seen or even imagined'. Finally, towards the end of the most exciting year in his life, he accepted the job of editor of the *Leeds Times*, a radical newspaper in one of the most thriving communities in the still-developing industrial north of England.

Perhaps the word 'thriving' gives the wrong impression of Leeds as it was just at the moment when Smiles arrived. There was no doubt about its bustle or its potential, but an economic depression was creating unemployment and generating political unrest. Businessmen were pressing for the repeal of the Corn Laws, which they felt were handicapping commerce; and workers, stimulated by fiery platform speakers, were demanding the vote. Leeds was a centre of discontent, a city where people met to exchange ideas, and obviously a newspaper editor was in the thick of the argument. Smiles was an enthusiastic radical at this formative time of his life. He felt considerable sympathy with workers' desire to win the vote, although he did not favour any reliance on violent methods to try to secure it. He was an enemy of the Corn Laws and had made the acquaintance of Ebenezer Elliott, the 'Corn-Laws Rhymer', who lived in Sheffield and whose moving verses were capable of stirring the crowds.

Smiles's political interests reached their climax in 1841 when he joined with his friends in backing the candidature of Joseph Hume, the well-known parliamentary radical, as a member of parliament for Leeds. Hume was defeated, but Smiles was later to pay a warm tribute to him in *Self-Help*:

> The motto of his [Hume's] life was 'Perseverance', and he well acted up to it.... To be outvoted, beaten, laughed at, standing on many occasions almost alone, to persevere in the face of every discouragement, preserving his temper unruffled, never relaxing in his energy or his hope, and living to see the greater number of his measures adopted with acclamation, must be regarded as one of the most remarkable illustrations of the power of human perseverance that biography can exhibit.

Smiles's critics were often to argue that he was interested only in material success. Nothing was further from the truth, as this comment on Hume shows. Hume's failure at the general election of 1841, however, deflected Smiles both from journalism and from politics. Editing a newspaper, he wrote later in his *Autobiography*, 'seemed to lead to nothing'. For a time, therefore, he returned to medical practice in Leeds, and in 1845 he hitched himself to the most profitable business operation of the age, railway construction and operation, when he became secretary of the Leeds and Thirsk Railway. During the 1840s railways were regarded as symbols of progress and Smiles was to remain directly connected with their planning and administration, first in Leeds and then in London, until the 1860s.

He continued to write in his spare time, and in 1859 published what was to be the book by which he is always remembered, *Self-Help*. The book was a link between his Leeds and his London years, for it was based on lectures given to a group of hungry but enthusiastic Leeds workers in 1845. In the meantime his railway interests turned him more and more to the study of engineering, particularly civil engineering. He published a life of George Stephenson, the railway pioneer, in 1857 and his famous *Lives of the Engineers* in 1861. These books, dealing vividly and readably with the triumphs of the age, are concerned not only with the drama of man's conquest over nature but with the self-discipline, skill and drive of the individual engineers that made progress possible. In other words, they need to be set alongside *Self-Help* since they are pervaded by the same philosophy.

Self-Help was merely one, albeit the most successful, of a whole range of books concerned with the possibilities of

individual advancement in society, which were published
around this time, not only in Britain but in the United States.
Smiles himself acknowledged his debt to George Craik's *The
Pursuit of Knowledge under Difficulties*, which was published
in 1830 before he left Scotland. There was obviously a demand
for books of this kind. Victorian England prided itself on the
new opportunities it offered to men of independent spirit
whoever their parents were and whatever initial difficulties they
had had to face. There was still no formal system of national
education, and men had to make their own way not only by
their abilities but by their character. Smiles played down the
importance of innate genius, just as he played down the importance of luck. Diligence, hard work, self-control – these
were the human qualities which counted for most.

In later books Smiles was to dwell at length on such qualities
and their most effective development and deployment. *Character* (1871), *Thrift* (1875) and *Duty* (1880) were the most important of them. *Thrift* is particularly significant within this
cluster. For Smiles thrift was 'an acquired principle of conduct ... the subordination of animal appetites to reason, fore-
thought and prudence'.

Society consists mainly of two classes – the savers and the
workers, the provident and the improvident, the thrifty and
the thriftless, the Haves and the Have-nots. The men who
economize by means of labour become the owners of capital
which sets other labour in motion.

Smiles was completely out of sympathy with all socialist
theories. He believed that working classes and middle classes
should work closely together, the former learning from the
latter. He was inclined to argue throughout his long life, however much social conditions changed, that if people were poor
it was somehow or other their own fault. He was not alone in
pursuing this line of argument. He always qualified it, moreover, first by stressing the need for the successful to do more
than make money, and second by identifying social evils which
needed redress. 'The individual is required under pain of being
stunted and enfeebled in his development if he disdains to carry
others along with him in his march towards perfection.' Society
could go wrong if economic *laissez-faire* (allowing the individual to make money on his own without interference from the
state) were confused with social *laissez-faire*, just letting things
be. In one of his most striking passages Smiles attacked people
who were uninterested in social betterment or stood in its way.
'Before the age of railroads and sanitary reforms, the pastoral

life of the Arcadians was a beautiful myth. The Blue Book men
[the compilers of the great official inquiries into social conditions in Britain] have exploded it for ever.'

> When typhus or cholera breaks out [Smiles went on] they
> [he did not identify who they were] tell us that Nobody is to
> blame. That terrible Nobody! How much he has to answer
> for! More mischief is done by Nobody than by all the world
> besides. Nobody adulterates our food. Nobody poisons us
> with bad drink ... Nobody leaves our towns undrained.
> Nobody fills jails, penitentiaries and convict stations. No-
> body makes poachers, thieves and drunkards. Nobody has
> a theory too – a dreadful theory. It is embodied in two words
> – *laissez-faire* – let alone. When people are poisoned with
> plaster of Paris mixed with flour, 'let alone' is the remedy
> ... Let those who can, find out when they are cheated: *caveat
> emptor*. When people live in foul dwellings, let them alone,
> let wretchedness do its work; do not interfere with death.

Self-Help sold 20,000 copies in the first year, 55,000 by the
end of five years, 150,000 by 1889, and over a quarter of a
million by the time of Smiles's death. As it went round the
world, the gospel of self-help and the gospel of work which
went with it sometimes fell on stony ground, but more often
they took root. Japan, a country which embarked upon a
programme of industrialization during the 1870s and 1880s,
gave them a particularly warm welcome. *The Lives of the
Engineers*, recommended to his fellow-countrymen by Gladstone, was another great success. Smiles was especially popular
in Italy, where he was received both by the Queen and by
Garibaldi in 1879. 'Amongst contemporary English authors,'
one Italian member of parliament wrote to him, 'there is no-
one better known or more heartily admired in Italy than yourself'. The King of Serbia bestowed a decoration upon him, and
the Khedive of Egypt placed texts from *Self-Help* upon the
walls of one of his palaces. The professor of philosophy who
taught Mao Tse-tung had been deeply influenced by Smiles.

All Smiles's books were used as guides to the young and as
prizes for the diligent. Yet as Smiles grew older, the number of
critics of what he had to say greatly increased. Robert Blatch-
ford, the *Clarion* socialist, who admired Smiles, added nonetheless that many socialists spoke of him as 'an arch-Philis-
tine' and of his books as 'the apotheosis of respectability,
gigmanity and selfish grab'. Some critics complained that he
had nothing to say of failure: others that he was wrong about
thrift. In 1889, for example, A. F. Mummery and J. A. Hobson

set out to show in their book *Physiology of Industry* that excessive savings were responsible for under-employment of capital and labour in periods of bad trade.

It was the criticism that Smiles was too respectable that cut deepest. One of his granddaughters has written tersely, 'among the insults hurled at Samuel Smiles in histories of Victorian England, there is one thoroughly deserved. He is accused of being "aggressively respectable". He was.' By the 1880s and the 1890s respectability was ceasing to be praised, and even the gospel of work was being attacked as a defence of drudgery. For the most part Smiles clung to his old values and continued to advocate them as cheerfully as he could. Although he had a stroke in 1871, which paralysed his right hand and robbed him of his memory for names, he taught himself how to write and how to remember again. The follies of politicians bothered him more than his own possible limitations. Thus, when Gladstone made a second effort to carry home rule for Ireland during the 1890s, Smiles wrote in unexpectedly forthright language,

> I am quite appalled at that wretched hound, miscalled states-man, throwing the country into a state of turmoil. I cannot understand how so many persons in this part of Britain follow that maniac like a flock of sheep. He is simply burst-ing with conceit. Alas! Alas for Liberalism!

Smiles was a great family man. He had married in Leeds, and he was proud both of his children and of his grandchildren, even though some of them let him down. It was a great tragedy when his wife died in 1899. He lingered on himself until 1904. His *Autobiography*, an engaging book, was unfinished and was published posthumously. He was buried in Brompton Cemetery, and his gravestone bore the simple words 'Samuel Smiles, author Self-Help'.

The Brontë Sisters

Charlotte (1816–55) Emily (1818–48)
Anne (1820–49)

By 'the Brontës' one tends to mean those of them with their names on the spines of books: Charlotte, Emily and Anne. But others share their remarkable story: their brother Branwell (1817–48), their father, the Rev. Patrick Brontë, and their mother.

The latter, alas, has the least part to play in the chronicle. The former Maria Branwell, of Penzance, died of cancer many years before her children's genius emerged, moaning, 'Oh, God, my poor children! Oh, God, my poor children!'

There were six children in all – Maria and Elizabeth were the other two – and none over eight years old. She took her leave of them in a cold, depressing stone house, exposed and high on the edge of the Yorkshire Moors, where the wind blows and it rains a good deal. The cheerless Haworth Parsonage looked on to what might have been a causeway of gravestones: flat, grey-green, all too often telling of life cut short. The average age at which death occurred in that district was about twenty-five.

The dying Mrs Brontë must have known how ill-equipped this husband and father would prove to care for six children without her. He was forty-five and the energy, ambition and good looks which had attracted her to him as a curate had left him as a rector. He was a gifted man who had written verse and essays and he liked his children well enough. But he did not love them with a warmth comparable to a mother's. After Mrs Brontë's death he made two or three dutiful attempts to marry again for their sake, failed, and had to settle for the presence of a rather forbidding sister-in-law to run the home and bring up his family, while he spent more and more time in the solitude of his study.

Within four years the Rev. Brontë found himself with two less children to concern him. A school for clergymen's daughters had been opened in a former mill at Cowan Bridge, not far away, and Maria and Elizabeth were sent there to board, followed by Charlotte and Emily. Conditions at the school were spartan and it was unhealthily situated. Both Maria and Elizabeth were delicate girls. Depressed by the harsh discipline, they declined progressively until, too late, their condition was recognized, they were rushed home and died of consumption within a fortnight of each other.

Charlotte, who, with Emily, was hastily withdrawn from the school, maintained in later life that the precocious Maria was the true family genius, and wrote her with pity into *Jane Eyre* as Helen Burns.

Apart from a year spent by Charlotte in a school at Dewsbury, the rest of the children's learning was acquired at home. They had few of the normal childhood contacts, but showed no sign of missing them. The three girls and their brother were content amongst themselves, reading almost anything they could find, from respectably garish Methodist magazines belonging to their aunt, to the classics of literature. The drama of real life was brought to them by the kindly forthright servant Tabitha Aykroyd, who sat for hours with them beside her kitchen fire, embellishing half a century's experience and hearsay into fascinating tales. The greatest wonder of the Brontës' writings is that these narrowly-educated girls who grew up and lived in such isolation from 'life' and the world at large should have been able to depict relationships and convey passions of which they had no experience.

The Rev. Brontë was neither a harsh disciplinarian nor a neglecter of his family. Like many men before and since, he was not at ease with his children *as* children, but he did his best for them according to his lights. On one notable occasion he succeeded by accident. A simple present brought home for Branwell contributed astonishingly to the content of all their lives.

The present was a box of wooden soldiers. It was Charlotte who excitedly seized one, declaring him to be her hero, the Duke of Wellington, thus giving spark to the game of the kingdoms Angria and Gondal which would supply, in imagination, all that the children were missing from the real world and occupy them happily for years of leisure time. Perhaps most importantly their invented people had to have newspapers and books, which the children set about writing for them. They wrote thousands of words, in handwriting so minute that one needs a magnifying glass to read some of it, and bound their 'publications' in the form of pages measuring two inches by one. Many of these incredible productions still exist at Haworth Parsonage, which has been preserved as a Brontë museum.

Charlotte spent some time away from Haworth in her late teens, teaching at a school in which Emily and then Anne were briefly among her pupils. Brought home again by ill-health, she sent some verses to the Poet Laureate, Southey, for an opinion. After a long delay he replied, 'Literature cannot be the business of a woman's life.' Disappointed but not discouraged, she turned to other means of making money to supplement her father's small stipend. She planned to establish a small school in which she and Emily would teach. Needing greater proficiency in French, the two girls took the enterprising step of spending some months studying in Brussels. Their tuition was cut short by the death of their aunt, who had agreed to put up the money for their school. However, she left them enough to carry on with the plan and Charlotte returned to Brussels alone in 1843. The outcome was an unhappy one. She conceived a passion for her married teacher, M. Heger. Though it was not reciprocated his wife became understandably jealous. Charlotte went back to Haworth, from where she was artless enough to send him a series of agonized letters – love-letters in all but intention, for her puritanical nature would have been shocked to learn what she almost certainly did not know, that her fixation upon this married man was not the pure, ideal thing she believed it to be. She was left bewildered by this, the only passionate episode in her life, to which she would return in part in her novels *Villette* and *The Professor*.

The need for money was now pressing, especially since Branwell's instability, which at times seemed to be something more, had got the better of him and he was increasingly spending his time with a brandy bottle at the Bull, in Haworth. Branwell had tried his hand at literature and had partially studied art, but had succeeded in neither. A job with the Leeds and Manchester railway ended with the sack. A post as tutor with a family Robinson collapsed abruptly when Mr Robinson found that his wife and Branwell – seventeen years her junior – had been having an affair for months. Deprived of Mrs Robinson, Branwell gave up all effort to resist his ruin and spent his last years at Haworth in drunken misery.

In 1845 Charlotte found some poems which the reserved Emily had been secretly writing. She was transfixed by their obvious quality and risked her sister's fury by saying so. Anne chimed into the quarrel to admit that she, too, had been writing poetry. Anger gave way to excitement as the girls discussed the notion of publishing the works of all three in one volume. Several publishers were approached in vain before the sisters fell back on a firm which would publish works at their authors' expense. At a cost of thirty guineas, the volume of poems appeared in 1846. Just two copies were sold.

Of the few reviewers who noticed the poems, two or three discerned quality in Emily's contributions to the collection. Only it was not Emily Brontë whom they mildly praised, but 'Ellis Bell'. Wishing to hide under *noms de plume*, the sisters had retained only their respective initials and adopted the masculine names Currer, Ellis and Acton Bell.

They were unbowed by the failure of the venture. As well as poems, each had been quietly writing a novel. Now they put their novels into circulation amongst the London publishing houses, and experienced that agonizing sequence shared by so many authors of submission, rejection, re-submission, rejection again ... But one day, Charlotte received along with her returned manuscript a courteous letter from the firm of Smith, Elder telling her that they had found some things to admire in *The Professor*. They did not wish to publish it, but would be happy to consider another work, if she had one. She had. Hastily writing the final chapters, she put it in the post. It was *Jane Eyre*.

She had written it at great speed, completely possessed by the passionate story of the fulfilment of a heroine in her own mould, insignificant and plain, yet with inner fires for the stoking. Smith, Elder's chief reader, William Smith Williams, took it home to read one evening and had to sit up all night, unable to put it down. The firm's senior partner, George Smith, spent a whole Sunday in his study, refusing even to come out for meals, utterly engrossed in the rags-to-romance tale which would become a bestseller in its author's lifetime and a classic thereafter.

It was published in 1847 – by 'Currer Bell' – and became an immediate success. But one of the most remarkable features of the Brontë story is that the same year saw publication also, by another firm, of *Wuthering Heights* by 'Ellis Bell' and *Agnes Grey* by 'Acton Bell'. While it is perhaps true that more people today are familiar with *Wuthering Heights* than with *Jane Eyre*, it was the latter alone which made forceful impact on the Brontës' contemporaries. Its passion proved irresistible; the former was regarded until a quarter of a century after its author's death as a tale not fit for decent households.

Inevitably, with such success attending *Jane Eyre*, the moment had to come when its author must reveal her true identity to an unsuspecting publisher. With Anne, Charlotte took a night train from Leeds to London and an historic

interview. Prim, shy, unfashionably dressed and almost faint-
ing with apprehension, the sisters presented themselves without appointment at the offices of Smith, Elder in Cornhill.
They asked to see Mr Smith, giving the names 'the Misses
Brown'. After some delay they were admitted. Tongue-tied,
Charlotte could only hand the publisher one of his own letters
to her. He glanced at it, puzzled, and asked, 'Where did you
get this?' 'I am Currer Bell,' she replied.

From that moment, Charlotte's and Anne's lives were temporarily transformed. For the next two days they were whirled
by Smith and his colleagues from one place to another, beginning every evening with the opera. 'They must have thought us
queer, quizzical-looking beings,' Charlotte wrote to a friend,
'especially me with my spectacles. I smiled inwardly at the
contrast which must have been apparent between me and Mr
Smith as I walked with him up the crimson-carpeted staircase
of the Opera House and stood amongst a brilliant throng.'
When the girls returned to Haworth Charlotte looked in a
mirror and thought herself grey and old after this first taste of
celebrity.

The happiness which overlay her tension was short-lived.
Branwell's wasted life was clearly drawing to its close. Drunken, often drugged, raving by night in delirium tremens in the
bedroom which his elderly father insisted on sharing with him,
he was beyond all saving and died in convulsions a few hours
after murmuring, 'In all my past life I have done nothing either
great or good.'

Charlotte was too prostrated by a nervous attack to attend
his funeral. His sisters went and Emily caught a chill in the
piercing hill-top wind. It persisted, with pains in her side and
constant coughing. Urged to see a doctor, she refused. She
would not even rest, but got out of bed every day at the
customary early hour and went about her household work,
retiring as usual at 10 p.m. for a sleepless night of fever and
coughing. Her family could only look on helplessly as she
drove herself to death, furious at any attempt to help her, her
mystical nature insisting that her illness was unreality and
would disappear if ignored. She wrote:

> No coward soul is mine,
> No trembler in the world's storm-troubled sphere:
> I see Heaven's glories shine,
> And faith shines equal arming me from fear.

On 19 December 1848 the pain was so intense that she agreed
at last to see a doctor. She died within hours. But the chain of

disaster was not yet broken: the next day, the quiet, gentle Anne fell ill with the same all-too-familiar symptoms of tuberculosis. In less than six months she, too, was dead. She was buried at Scarborough, where she had been making her last bid for recovery, leaving Charlotte and her old father alone in that grim house where no one ever visited, nothing ever happened outside a rigid daily routine, and almost no sound was heard except the ticking of clocks and the moaning of the wind as the two sat alone in different rooms.

Anne had published *The Tenant of Wildfell Hall* a year before her death, and now Charlotte, taking refuge in work, added to the small total of Brontë works with *Shirley*, again scoring an immediate success. It took her to London once more, where she suffered more agonies of nerves at dinner parties, receptions and theatres. Driven by her shyness and the consciousness of her sexual unattractiveness into that least admirable of northern qualities, forthright utterance, she proved a prickly person to meet, displaying no tact or finesse and blurting out ruthless criticism to the faces of well-wishers. George Smith recalled later that she was

> very small, and had a quaint old-fashioned look. Her head seemed too large for her body. She had fine eyes, but her face was marred by the shape of the mouth and by the complexion. There was little feminine charm about her; of this fact she herself was uneasily and perpetually conscious ... Perhaps few women ever existed more anxious to be pretty than she, or more angrily conscious of the circumstance that she was not pretty.

It is a good summing-up of Charlotte Brontë's character, and it must account a great deal for her tart rejection of the men who did wish to pay court to her: she had made up her mind that no one could really love her in that way, and sent them about their business. One at least proved irresistible, though not in the usual sense of the word. Arthur Bell Nicholls, her father's curate, suffered the usual rejection, was ostracized by Mr Brontë to the point of seeking another curacy, then fell into such an alarming decline that Charlotte, moved by his grief, eventually defied her father and married him.

They had seven happy months together before Charlotte, now pregnant, became bed-ridden after a winter cold and chill had brought on the unmistakable signs of consumption. She died on 31 March 1855 and was buried in Haworth church beside her mother, Branwell and Emily. The Rev. Patrick Brontë, who had seen his entire family come and go, lived on for six more years in that northern fastness which had helped to kill them all and in which some of the greatest works of all literature had been astonishingly wrought.

Karl Marx

(1818–83)

Karl Marx was born in 1818 at Trier, in the Rhineland, the
son of a Jewish middle-class lawyer, Hirschel Marx. The date,
the family and the region are all significant. Europe was just
beginning to recover from the dislocations of the Napoleonic
wars. The Rhineland was the most prosperous part of Germany and Jews were accepted to a degree impossible in the
ghetto-bound world of eastern Germany. Rhinelanders saw
themselves as culturally superior to the Prussians; to them
Prussia was a land of backward *Junkers*, the Siberia of Germany. This sense of superiority made Rhinelanders very sensitive about Prussia's political control after 1815, especially
when the Napoleonic reforms were reversed by Prussian
officials. Marx's father found it more and more difficult to
practise his Jewish faith, and was converted to Christianity
when his son was six. Thus the young man was conscious of
being in part German, in part Rhinelander and in part a Jew.
His world was comfortable and cultured. It seems unlikely that
he was ever much influenced by religious ideas. When in his
old age he visited Ramsgate he described it as being 'full of
fleas and Jews'.

Almost as a matter of course he looked towards a university
career and studied primarily in jurisprudence and history at
Bonn, Berlin and Jena. But while busy with his thesis for a
doctorate at Jena there came the Prussian conservative reaction of 1841, of which he became a savage critic. After his
father's death in 1838 he needed money. In any event he was
never – unlike Hegel – an ivory tower philosopher; he always
sought to combine the theory of politics with organization and
action; he was always a man of two worlds, the study and the
forum. By nature combative, he turned towards politics and
journalism and abandoned his dream of becoming a university
teacher.

He was, until the paper was banned, on the staff of the
Rheinische Zeitung which had been founded by a group of
young followers of Hegel to counter the influence of the conservative *Kolnische Zeitung*. In 1843 he moved to Paris, accompanied by his bride, Jenny von Westphalen, the daughter of a
well-born Prussian official. Until her death forty years later,
and despite all the trials and turmoils of his public life, it was

a marriage of utter happiness. There were to be four daughters and two sons, but both sons and one daughter died in infancy.

Paris was at this time a hot-bed of socialist activity and discussion. He met Proudhon and, in particular, Friedrich Engels, who became his life-long friend. Expelled from Paris in 1845, he moved with other exiled German socialists to Brussels, where he wrote in collaboration with Engels *The Communist Manifesto*, published in 1848. The *Manifesto* was drawn up as the platform of the Communist League, originally a German workers' association. In it he set out in popular form the main points of his doctrine and the way in which the more practical parts of his teaching might be applied. Having defined the principles of communism, it advocated a series of immediate reforms, all of which appeared to the bourgeoisie of 1848 the peak of revolutionary madness. They included: the expropriation of landed property; a high and progressively graded income-tax; the abolition of the right of inheritance; the centralization of credit and of transport in the hands of the state; universal obligation to work; and the public education of all children.

Expelled from Brussels in 1848, Marx spent a month in Paris. When he returned to Germany in that year, the year of the revolution, it was as a fully-fledged and convinced socialist. He found employment as editor of a radical paper, the *Neue Rheinische Zeitung*, but in 1849 had to escape again, this time with a threat of high treason hanging over him. And so, aged thirty-one, he moved to London, and it was in and around 28 Dean Street, Soho, Haverstock Hill and the British Museum that he spent the rest of his life.

For the first few years his circumstances were darkened by poverty and ill health, and he survived only by work as a journalist and with an allowance from Engels. By 1855, however, his circumstances were improving, and he was endlessly engaged with pamphlets, addresses and newspaper articles. In 1864 he helped to found the First International Working Men's Association, whose programme he helped to draft, and which he led through a series of faction-ridden squabbles, especially with Proudhon, until its dissolution twelve years later. Of its death, as of its birth, he was the author – he had a rare capacity to make enemies. But by this time his reading in the British Museum was beginning to bear fruit, and the first volume of *Das Kapital* was published in 1867. His last eight years, 1875-83, however, were embittered and sad. The task of finishing *Das Kapital* proved too great; the next two volumes were prepared by Engels from notes Marx left uncompleted at his death. His wife died in 1881. His health declined. The small group – no more than a dozen in number – who attended his funeral at Highgate cemetery, now a place of pilgrimage, heard an oration by Engels in which Marx was hailed as the 'provider of the key to social change'.

At the personal level, Marx was infinitely unlikeable: there was the tense relationship with his father, his inability to complete things; his hopeless and contemptuous attitude to money; his anti-semitism; his fathering of an illegitimate son by Helene Demuth, the maid who served the family for forty years, often without wages; his indifference to the world around him, and the plight in which his wife and children were placed. He survived and became a full-time scholar entirely because of the generosity of Friedrich Engels, yet he always found it hard to say 'Thanks'. Yet he was a fond and devoted father to his children and the warmth of his relationship with them is striking – he was to them 'dear Devil', the 'Moor' because of his coal-black eyes and hair, and in later years 'Old Nick'. Yet for at least six years – the years at 28 Dean Street, Soho, living in two little rooms on an upper floor in what was then the quarter for the poorest of foreign refugees – they lived in poverty, depending on friends, money-lenders, and pawnbrokers.

However, it is not his life but his thought and writing that is central. Marx sought to adjust the thinking of men to the constancy of change. 'In our time, change is upon the world and cannot be stopped or channelled as we wish. The thing now is to understand it.' None of his immediate predecessors – the idealists, Fichte and Hegel, from whom he drew some of his basic principles, the positivist Comte, with his laws of society, or his contemporary the liberal John Stuart Mill – regarded themselves as social revolutionaries. Marx considered the socialist thinking that preceded his own – especially that of Proudhon and Blanqui whom he sharply criticized in *The Communist Manifesto* – as utopian, whereas he claimed, or Engels claimed for him, that his own was scientific. Socialism with him became a body of doctrine resting firmly on an economic base.

His ideas were rooted equally firmly in a special materialist interpretation of Helegian philosophy. 'The history of all hitherto existing society is the history of class struggle.' So began *The Communist Manifesto*. Seeing all history as a struggle not of ideas, as Hegel had done, but of classes, he held that reconciliation could come only from the abolition of classes, and this gave him an agenda for political action as well as an economic and philosophical system. He not only recognized class-hatred as a central fact in history, he saw it as a conscious instrument of revolution. Only through revolution could progress take place. 'Force,' he wrote in *Das Kapital*, 'is the midwife of every old society pregnant with a new one.' The state he regarded as an executive committee of the dominant economic class. Its character was exclusively coercive. It was in no sense a social-welfare agency or an instrument for maintaining and promoting general prosperity. It was a police agency, an organization of force to maintain the supremacy of a dominant class. Marx's theory of the state is in the end a theory of force and his interest is in action. As the eleventh thesis on Feuerbach asserts, hitherto philosophers have thought about the world, now it is time to change it.

Marx was also the creator of the theory of surplus value. The value of all marketable commodities, he held, is determined by the quantity of labour power necessary to produce them. Capital creates nothing, but is itself created by labour. However, the worker does not receive a just share of the value that his drudgery or skill creates. Instead he receives a wage, which ordinarily is just enough to enable him to subsist and reproduce his kind. The bulk of the remainder flows into the pockets of the capitalist in the form of interest, rent and profits. Properly speaking, it is these three elements which constitute *surplus value*. Since the capitalist creates none of them, it follows that he is a thief who confiscates the fruits of the labourer's toil.

In no sense, however, did Marx regard the destruction of capitalism as the end and goal of the workers' efforts. Instead it would be the prelude to other developments of greater importance. Of itself it would merely establish the *political* supremacy of the proletariat, who must then, by degrees, wrest all capital from the bourgeoisie ('expropriate' the 'expropriators'), centralize all instruments of production in the hands of the state, and increase the total productive forces as rapidly as possible. To accomplish these aims, it would be necessary to establish a temporary despotism or dictatorship of the proletariat. This would then give way to communism, the perfect goal of historical evolution. The state would wither away; it would be relegated to the museum of antiquities, 'along with the bronze axe and the spinning wheel'.

It is, of course, possible to point to the many contradictions in his philosophy. First, if it is possible to read history in terms of thesis and antithesis, why will this dialectical process halt with the coming of communism? And in any case does the thesis hold throughout history that society is stratified into two classes, and that the oppressed class can perceive its interests and has the necessary wisdom to promote them? There is no record of a class struggle marking the collapse of a primitive communism and the arrival of slavery. Throughout the history of Greece and Rome there are many stories of group clashes, but there is no evidence that the downfall of Rome was the result of the struggle between two classes, one basically pro-slave and the other basically pro-feudalism; nor is there any evidence that feudalism was necessarily a higher order of civilization than the society of ancient Greece or Rome. As late as 1848 Marx expected a bourgeois revolution in Germany, which in *The Communist Manifesto* he likened to the revolution of the seventeenth century in England and of the eighteenth century in France. No such bourgeois revolution ever came in Germany. Nor was the October Revolution of 1917 in Russia a contest between a feudal class and a new bourgeoisie. As history, the doctrine of the class struggle is impossible to sustain.

Again, the striking feature of the late nineteenth century in the advanced countries, and of the twentieth century throughout much of the world, is precisely that the working class has acquired greater and greater privileges and much economic and political power. The state, far from being the instrument of capitalism, has moved in with laws to provide social and health insurance, to recognize trade unions in law and indeed to foster factory and industrial development on a considerable and very healthy scale. The same Blue Books and Public Health Reports on which Marx drew to compile, in *Kapital*, his vivid picture of the contrast between rich and poor in capitalist England led governments to act.

Societies have been transformed not by cataclysm but by law, and peacefully. Moreover, the whole development of the managerial revolution has separated the ownership of industry from its technical management, so that neither the story of the recent past nor any agenda for present action can be based on a picture of the wicked capitalist risking his own resources and exploiting everyone else's; and there has been a vast development of workers' participation at all levels of industrial society. The petty bourgeoisie has not identified its interest with that of the working class. Marx did not indeed forsee the extent to which the salariat would grow, nor expect it to be so hostile to the proletariat. His view of the class struggle proved to be altogether too simple. Proletarians, Marx said, had nothing to lose but their chains. In fact they had much more to lose than their chains, and they did not really want to unite.

Again, Marx's indifference to ethical questions, to the fundamental question of what is the public good, is a sharply limiting mental question of what is the public good, is a sharply limiting factor in his work. In all his writing, production is seen as the major and indeed sometimes the sole criterion. There is no acknowledgement that non-economic factors do play a formative part in life. Nor is there any emphasis on the interaction of intellectual and spiritual factors with those that are purely economic. There are political, social, racial and religious barriers among work-people, as among employers, which have not always been overcome by economic factors, and have sometimes, as in 1914, prevented consistent unity of action by the working class. A major phenomenon in recent history has been the bid for power by an army or a totalitarian party concerned less with social justice than with power-mania. Fascism revealed the elements that were missed in an interpretation that was based purely on economic man. In other words, there are many omissions from Marx's contribution.

It is equally easy to attribute his interpretations and his opinions to a brusque temperament, to ill-health, to a sense of unfulfilled ambition, to a long and hard life in London and to his almost total personal failure to win friends and friendship.

But few of these things really matter. For many people in many countries came to accept his views, and to act politically on that acceptance. He was more than a thinker, he was a prophet. If he was less gifted as a prophet than many Marxists have imagined, the concepts of historical materialism, surplus value and the nature of the dialectical process have been of immense value to philosophers and sociologists. His idea of the power of the proletariat makes him far more significant a figure than either Gladstone or Bismarck. His faith in class-hatred as a factor in history, allied to a doctrinaire temperament, made him the great advocate of revolution. Foreseeing the age of the masses, he is scornful of classical liberty as a chimera. He described the age of *laissez-faire* capitalism as the age of 'liberty, equality, property and Jeremy Bentham'. For the whole generation brought up in the late nineteenth, and to many others in the twentieth, century, Marx was the great visionary figure and it is impossible to assess the role played by Lenin or Jaurès or a host of socialists and communists in France, Italy and Germany without a study of Marx. He said of himself that he was not a Marxist, but Marxism has dominated and conditioned the political thinking of twentieth-century Europe. He was, if not the greatest, certainly one of the most influential thinkers of the nineteenth century or indeed of all time.

Ivan Sergeyevich Turgenev

(1818-83)

On a misty autumn evening in the late 1840s a young man strode up and down an upstairs room at 37 Ostrozhenka Street, Moscow, expounding his political views to a group of friends. 'I do not believe in the autocracy of the Tsar,' he cried passionately, 'nor in the bureaucracy which is slowly choking our beloved country to death. I do not even believe in this new Narodnik movement whose members think that if they go down among the people, appeal to the instinctive communism within them, the peasants will immediately unite together to form a new state. I do not believe in anything, anything at all.' He paused, then held out his hands, palms upwards. 'I am a – a *nihilist!*'

There was a momentary silence followed by a burst of applause as the listeners surged forward to congratulate the speaker. 'Bravo, Ivan Sergeyevich!' they chorused, and one called loudly, 'Bless you, my friend, you have invented a word that will live long in the Russian language. From henceforth we, the apostles of freedom, shall be known as the nihilists!'

The young man shook his head. 'Freedom calls for more than a mere name,' he cautioned. 'In order to win it you must fight a long crusade in which you must be prepared to sacrifice all you hold dear, perhaps even life itself. Only thus can you achieve your aim – the total destruction of constitutional authority. You sweep the broken pieces into a heap and set them alight; *then* you call modern science to your aid and begin your real task, the building of a new Russia on the ashes of the old ...'

Ivan Sergeyevich Turgenev was born in 1818 at Orel where his mother, a member of the powerful Litvinov family, had inherited large estates. His father was a colonel of a crack cavalry regiment so was seldom at home, and since he was an ardent sportsman he filled the days of his rare visits with hunting, shooting and fishing. In consequence Ivan and his elder brother Nikolai never really grew to know this parent. Their lives were dominated by their mother, a woman of strong personality who held rigid views on the upbringing of young aristocrats. From a very early age the boys were taught to use their own language only when addressing serfs and to speak French at all other times.

Nikolai, a docile child, accepted their mother's rulings without demur: Ivan, who had an eager, questing mind, was irked by them. Why should Russian be regarded as an inferior language? Why was he not allowed to mix freely with the servants? Why should he and Nikolai have good food and warm clothing while the peasant children were half-starved and in rags? His persistent questions met with evasive answers from his tutors and severe lectures from his mother, so he resorted to guile and by the age of seven was adept at disappearing from under the very eyes of his mentors to enjoy happy hours talking to two serfs of whom he was particularly fond.

One was the librarian in charge of the large collection of books which were seldom opened except by the tutors. The shrewd Mme Turgenev had noted this serf's intelligence and paid for his education. His years of schooling brought him no financial reward, but he was a true bookman and delighted to share his knowledge with Ivan, reading aloud to him the long epic poem *Rossiak*, by Kheraskov, which described the appalling conditions endured by the peasants. The second serf was different, a rugged soldier who had served under Colonel Turgenev during the war against Napoleon and now worked as a gardener. He told how Tsar Alexander I had exhorted his troops in their valiant struggle, promising all manner of reforms once the French were driven from Russian soil; and how, after signing the Treaty of Tilsit, he had promptly forgotten all his fine words. This had led to the formation of a right-wing revolutionary group joined by many young officers and the result had been the 1825 Decembrist mutiny which had lately taken place in St Petersburg.

As he grew to adolescence Ivan learnt much from these two men and developed a passionate interest in all problems connected with the deplorable poverty suffered by the mass of the Russian people.

Ivan was sixteen when his father died suddenly, leaving his possessions to be equally divided between his two sons. This was wonderful news, for while Turgenev's fortune was modest by Litvinov standards, it was sufficient to provide both boys with comfortable incomes. Ivan felt grateful to the parent he had barely known, but was careful to betray no emotion. The mutual distrust between him and his mother had lately flared into open antagonism and there were still five years before he attained his majority and his inheritance. If he flouted her authority openly he knew full well that she would devise some swift and subtle revenge which might put his future at risk.

He was by all accounts a singularly unattractive youth of

Thomas Carlyle, influential man of letters

John Keats portrayed by his friend Joseph Severn

Keats's grave

Honoré de Balzac, author of
the *Comédie Humaine*

William Makepeace
Thackeray, prolific
novelist and
journalist

Henrik Ibsen,
outstanding pioneer of
social drama

seventeen when he was sent to Moscow University, and any hope of escape from his mother's surveillance was quickly dispelled as he had to live with Litvinov relatives who kept a vigilant watch on his acquaintances, his professors, even his books. His only solace was writing and under the plea of study he spent his evenings in his room filling notebooks which were kept hidden in his trunk. He scraped through his examinations then moved on to more Litvinov kinsmen in St Petersburg, as the last thing Mme Turgenev wanted was his presence at Orel.

The result was that when Ivan reached his twenty-first birthday he was a frustrated, embittered creature totally unable to use his new-found freedom. For months he fumbled with this or that idea and was near despair when, as he recalled afterwards, the pieces of the puzzle suddenly began to fall into place. It all started when some short sketches he had written were accepted by a magazine and won praise from Bielinski, foremost critic of the day, who sought him out and not only urged him to go on writing but introduced him to several young intellectuals. Under their stimulus the youth the Litvinovs regarded as an inarticulate boor changed into a fiery being with a remarkably eloquent tongue.

One might say, indeed, that Ivan Turgenev was reborn at the age of twenty-two. This new Turgenev moved into rooms of his own, studied so vigorously that he graduated with honours from St Petersburg University, became a professional revolutionary and, at the close of 1842, made the journey to Orel to tell his mother that he was about to go to Berlin. A lamentable scene followed, in which she accused him of betraying a long line of statesman and soldiers by submitting his paltry writings to criticism in the newspapers, and he retaliated by vowing that his life was dedicated to the destruction of her and her kind.

By the late 1840s Turgenev was living in Moscow busily engaged in training recruits to the revolutionary cause: but strangely enough for a man of his literary gifts, his published work was still limited to a few short sketches. Not until he was thirty-four did his first book appear. It was called *The Papers of a Sportsman* and it won instant acclaim in Europe as well as in Russia itself, where it greatly influenced the man who was to ascend the throne in 1855 as Tsar Alexander II. His second book was *A Nest of Nobles* (1859) followed a year later by *On the Eve*, while his masterpiece on nihilism, *Fathers and Children*, was published in 1862.

Turgenev achieved far greater international renown during his lifetime than any other contemporary Russian writer because through his morbid, penetrating psychological insight he gave the reader extraordinarily vivid portraits of his characters. His actual writing too was beautiful, filled with what Bielinski called 'the still, sad music of humanity'. People who had hitherto thought of Russian peasants as half-wits in sheepskin coats suddenly discovered they were sensitive creatures with the ability to love, hate and suffer as intensely as themselves, and the knowledge that they were forced to exist under conditions which would not have been tolerated elsewhere in Europe roused public indignation.

Within Russia itself the authorities were alarmed by the rapid growth of the new cult fathered by this troublesome author. The secret police kept discreet watch over the house in Ostrozhenka Street where Turgenev sat writing his story *The Threshold*, which put into words the Russian revolutionary's mania for extremism, perfection and martyrdom. The police unobtrusively tailed his visitors, and grew a little bolder every day. Before he had finished his story Turgenev realized he faced an agonizing choice. Should he stay in Russia, live a furtive underground existence in constant fear of arrest and a life of exile in Siberia; or should he leave his country voluntarily and continue his work in another land?

His passionate love for Russia had to be stifled, for it was his duty to do what would most help his countrymen, not to consider his own feelings, and in his heart he knew that he could be of far more practical use to them if he remained at liberty outside the borders of his homeland. He made his arrangements quickly and efficiently, and three days later was on his way to Poland. It was a bright spring morning in 1855, and as the coach jolted towards the frontier and he gazed out at the birch trees showing green against a milky sky, Turgenev felt his heart would break.

On arrival in Berlin he was greeted by the celebrated singer Pauline Viardot, with whom he had been in love for years. They decided to live openly together in future, and it was her steadfast devotion which saved him from melancholia. She now taught singing, having retired from the operatic stage, and had one house in Baden Baden and another outside Paris. Turgenev continued to correspond at length with his nihilist friends inside Russia, exhorting them to further efforts and organizing their work. He wrote too, of course, though few Russian publishers had the courage to produce his work. With the exception of *Smoke* in 1867, and *Virgin Soil* ten years later, no further novels of his after the famous *Fathers and Children* appeared openly in his own country.

There was, however, a most useful journal called *Viestnik Evropi* [European Messenger] which was run by a group of revolutionaries and enjoyed a wide circulation all over the continent. Large quantities of copies were smuggled into Russia, so it was an ideal medium for such stories of Turgenev's as *The Diary of a Useless Man* and *Clara Milish*.

With the accession of Tsar Alexander II Turgenev began to have new hopes for Russian reform. Unlike his predecessors this Tsar was a man of intellect and possessed the zeal of the reformer. When he decreed the abolition of serfdom in 1861 it seemed that at last the way to victory lay clear. All that was needed now was for the peasants to rise in massive revolt, as they had done under the Cossack Pugachev in the reign of Catherine the Great, and destroy the masters who had tyrannized over them for so long. Turgenev and his fellow revolutionaries waited tensely for the first sign of action, but the weeks crawled into months and the months into years and still nothing happened. Centuries of existence under the leaden weight of oppression had sapped the mental and physical strength of the Russian people, and they had neither the spirit nor the muscle to fight.

There was nothing anyone could do to help them, and the knowledge that this was so caused Turgenev to fall back into a melancholy pessimism from which he never recovered. Now Turgenev moved listlessly among his old friends, scarcely heeding the ideas they expounded so valiantly, shaking his head when they strove to awaken his interest in their schemes. The nihilism he had planted and nurtured with such care had grown into a monstrous misshapen thing which sucked the very life blood from his veins. Almost mechanically he continued to write, to lecture to university students, to converse with other authors, but the fire had gone from speech and pen. He moved restlessly between Baden Baden and Paris and paid several visits to England, being given an honorary degree at Oxford in 1871.

In the year 1881 Turgenev's physical state began to decline and although Pauline nursed him devotedly he grew steadily weaker over the next two years. On his death in 1883 his body was taken to St Petersburg and buried there in the Volkov cemetery close to the grave of Bielinski, the mentor to whom he owed so much. He did not know that in a few years' time a boy named Vladimir Ilyich Ulianov was to read his books with avidity and learn from them much that was to help him, as Lenin, to create the new Russia dreamed of for so long.

Leo Tolstoy

(1828–1910)

At 3 a.m. on 28 October 1910 at his home at Yasnaya Polyana, 130 miles south of Moscow, the 82-year-old Count Leo Tolstoy got up, put on warm clothes and told a doctor friend that he meant to abandon his wife Sonya and his family. He was not sure where to go, maybe to Turkey, maybe to Bessarabia, maybe to a peasant hut somewhere he could live out his days in peace and solitude. All he knew was, he had to get away.

He set out, first by coach, then by train, but Tolstoy was very weak and at the little wayside station of Astopovo he could go no further. He was put to bed in the stationmaster's cottage and there Sonya, a son, a daughter and the press caught up with him, for he was world-famous. Sonya, in her sixties now, married to him for forty-eight years, who had borne him thirteen children, was not allowed to enter for fear of upsetting him. The hours dragged on, the milling crowds increased – journalists, police, idle onlookers – until early on 7 November he died.

Years before he had been excommunicated by the Orthodox Church so there were no priests at the funeral. But a fervent, deeply moved throng of well-wishers, including peasants from his own estate, watched as he was buried on the edge of a ravine in a forest near his home, in a spot where he had asked to be, where long ago in childhood his brother Nikolai had said there was a green stick buried, engraved on it the secret of universal love, a secret that in his later years Tolstoy had been searching for, but never found.

In part the green stick symbolized the idyllic life he had known as a boy. Born on 28 August 1828, the youngest of four sons, his mother a Volkonsky, descended from an illustrious general and captain of Catherine the Great's Guards, his father Count Nikolai Ilich Tolstoy claiming descent from a Lithuanian knight, young Leo's main characteristics were superabundant energy and an intense, almost overwhelming delight in the physical world including the beauties of nature that surrounded the family home, a large wooden house with a comfortable carefree life sustained by hundreds of serfs.

But his mother had died in 1830 and after his father's death when he was nine the idyll began to disintegrate. By then the family had moved to Moscow so that Nikolai could attend the university and Leo found himself confronting a world disconcertingly ugly, squalid and incomprehensible. With amazing precocity he sought refuge in ideas, the question of reincarnation, of appearance contrasting with reality, writing later in *Boyhood*, 'I often imagined myself as a great man discovering new truths for the benefit of mankind, and I contemplated other mortals with a proud awareness of my own worth'.

But the proud awareness was sharply deflated when in 1841 the family transferred to Kazan on the middle Volga to be cared for by an aunt. Here, as the grandchildren of an ex-governor, they moved in elegant, sophisticated circles and Leo discovered he was little better than a country bumpkin. He stared at himself in a long mirror, noted thick lips, protruding ears, small, close-set eyes, big hands and feet, and was in despair.

In 1844 he entered Kazan University, studying first oriental languages then law, and failing miserably. His mind was in chaos. Conscious of tremendous energy and willpower, he longed to excel. But in what? In diplomacy perhaps, the army, or as a philosopher and leader of men? He wrote out for himself rules of conduct befitting the role, but his life was getting caught up, in fact, in the loose student world revolving round girls, drink and gambling.

He cursed and swore at himself, wrote out more rules quickly broken, read Descartes and decided that 'I think, therefore I am' must be changed to 'I want, therefore I am'. This *want* was to encapsulate the theme of his life, an almost absolute egotism and in later years a determination, at war with reality, to make the world conform to his wishes.

Meanwhile in 1847 he had left the university as being too restrictive and returned to Yasnaya Polyana (Ash Glade) which he had inherited with its 4,000 acres and 330 serfs. He intended to be a model overseer and also to study, a vast programme embracing medicine, languages, agriculture, the natural sciences, mathematics, statistics. But after eighteen months of a solitary life, apart from the company of amenable servant girls, he fled to Moscow in disgust at the bovine stupidity of his workforce and his own indolence.

There and in St Petersburg in 1849 gambling again took hold of him, more seriously than before, and other aspirations. 'Get into the highest society,' he told himself in his diary, 'find a good position ... under certain conditions, marry.' But only the gambling losses were real, so serious that he jumped at the

chance offered by Nikolai, home on army leave, to accompany
him to the Caucasus where there was sporadic fighting with
tribesmen.

Tolstoy set off in April 1851 a raw youth living on impulse
and returned nearly five years later as a writer of brilliant
achievement, lauded by the Russian literary world as probably
a genius. The vast and varied scenes of nature, of military life,
of excitement, danger and death witnessed in the Caucasus and
later in the Crimean War at Sebastopol silenced his inner
conflicts for a while and released what had always been
latent in him, a rare creative talent and the most acute and
joyous powers of observation.

But first, while on campaign, he wrote a gravely beautiful
book called *Childhood*, greatly acclaimed, reflecting his delight
in the paradise of his early years, and this was followed at
intervals by *Boyhood* and *Youth*, and, with a flavour of inspired
reportage, by *The Raid* and *Sebastopol Sketches*. But the
dichotomy in his nature had already broken through again,
idealism on the one hand, sordid self-indulgence on the other.
At one time he was cursing himself with the familiar words,
'... laziness ... stupidity ... despair ... lust', at another he
wrote of a 'grandiose, stupendous idea ... it is the founding of
a new religion ... the religion of Christ, but divested of faith
and mysteries, a practical religion, not promising eternal bliss
but providing bliss here on earth'. It was the typical romantic
dilemma, the contrast between what might be and what is, with
the added ingredient, peculiar to Tolstoy, that he never could
stand mystery but wanted paradise in the here and now.

Having shown great bravery in the war and been gazetted
second lieutenant, he left the army in 1856 and went to St
Petersburg where he succumbed to debauchery again and
agonized reproaches, this time directed at the female sex that
he found irresistible. It was women's fault, he decided, they
shouldn't be so attractive, shouldn't corrupt men, sap their will,
undermine their courage. After a visit to an amusement park
he let out a positive howl in his diary: 'Disgusting. Girls, silly
music, girls, mechanical nightingale, girls, heat, cigarette smoke,
girls, vodka, cheese, screams and shouts, girls, girls, girls ...'

He had to get away and after extensive travels in France,
Germany and Italy he returned home intending to give his
serfs their freedom (not achieved in fact till official emancipation in 1861). But they were suspicious, disliked the plan he
put forward and, baulked of the set-piece he no doubt imagined
– ancient *mushiks* on their knees in gratitude to the benevolent
master – he turned to their children and decided to set up a

school for them with himself as teacher. There would be no set tasks, no discipline, no learning by rote; the children could attend or not as they liked, and surprisingly the scheme was a great success.

But after a few months he became restless and, on the pretext of studying educational systems abroad, went to Europe again, including England, returning strongly convinced that his teaching method should be applied to the whole of Russia. Always extreme in his ideas, he now saw the peasants and their children as a pure, unsullied elite, the hope indeed of mankind, and wrote '... though we are all products of civilization, we must not contaminate the common people with this poison; instead, we must purge ourselves through contact with them.'

He collected a band of student teachers around him and set up more schools. But the tsarist police, ever suspicious of educated youth, were watching and in the spring of 1862, while Tolstoy was away taking a cure, they ransacked his home, looking for subversive documents, and found nothing. When Tolstoy returned he was almost beside himself with rage and demanded redress from the Tsar, which was eventually forthcoming. Whereupon he decided not to kill himself as he had threatened and instead got married.

Tolstoy was thirty-five, his bride, Sonya Behrs, daughter of a Moscow doctor, eighteen, an attractive, clever, artistic girl, strongly practical, but jealous by nature and somewhat unstable. Tolstoy found her fascinatingly childlike; to her he was a god, though tarnished by his youthful promiscuity which he obliged her to read about in his diary. For some years he at least was blissfully happy.

Within a year, in 1863, secure now in his domestic paradise, Tolstoy began to write *War and Peace*, while Sonya ran the house, bore children, made fair copies of his drafts. By 1869 all 2,000 pages of the unique and formidable epic had been completed and published, receiving awe-struck acclaim and establishing Tolstoy as the greatest writer of the age. *Anna Karenina* followed, in some ways an even greater masterpiece, and was published in 1877.

But already, while still writing, Tolstoy was getting bored with the work. A new phase was opening for him, revolving round the obsessive questions, 'Who am I? Why am I here?' Only with this knowledge could he face what he believed to be the awful truth, that death was the end of everything. But he also knew, or thought he knew that the questions could never be answered, so he decided on the next best thing, a life of simplicity, the propagation of universal love.

Tolstoy was a man of power, ruthlessly determined that the world should agree with him in all his thoughts, all his doctrines, and first of all, of course, his own family. Naturally they rebelled, particularly Sonya, who now saw her husband performing weird rituals, pumping water, chopping wood, making boots, living the earth-bound peasant life in a dream-world of his own while she struggled with the endless chores of running the family. Long since they had started to wrangle, Sonya deploring his selfishness, Tolstoy adamant to mould her to his heart's desire.

Sonya (December, 1862, on his past debaucheries): 'If I could kill him and create another person exactly like him, I should do so with pleasure.' Tolstoy (1884): 'To the day I die she will be a stone round my neck, and the necks of my children.' Tolstoy (aloud to Sonya, 1885): 'You poison the very air around you!' Sonya (1886): 'He does not have one drop of love, either for his children or for me or for anyone except himself.' Sonya (1903): 'The passionate husband is dead, the friendly husband never existed.'

Sonya knew him better than anyone and saw through his teaching of Christianity without Christ as simply the Great Escape: rejection of the world, of sex, marriage, of all authority including that of the Orthodox Church.

In fact the ageing Tolstoy was a deeply tragic figure, never able to bridge the gulf between his magnificent ability as a creative artist, celebrating and rejoicing in the human scene, and the sour, puritanical, slightly ridiculous sage, pouring out 'religious' tracts advocating chastity, vegetarianism, non-violence and universal love when he could not even love his own family. For years in later life he scorned art as frivolous, but nevertheless between sermonising wrote his third major novel, *Resurrection*, set in an urban middle- and lower-class world, his great play, *The Live Corpse*, and the deeply moving, marvellously written story, *Hadji Murad*, a legendary tribesman who deserted his people, went over to the Russians and, returning later to see his son, was killed by the people he had betrayed.

It has been said of Tolstoy that, amazingly for one so gifted, in part of himself he longed to get back to the womb, or at least the nursery, and there is much to support this view. Perhaps then the betrayal of Hadji Murad was really his own as he regressed more and more towards an evasion of reality until, on that bleak October morning in 1910, he put on warm clothes and abandoned for ever his family, his last remaining anchor in the human world.

Jules Verne

(1828–1905)

Few writers have been gifted, in addition to superb technical skill, with prophetic powers capable of seizing the imagination of their contemporaries, lifting them out of themselves and carrying them on breathtaking expeditions into a seemingly fantastic future, which, if they live long enough, they will eventually see becoming reality. H.G. Wells was one of these: Jules Verne was another.

His imagination was in play from his earliest days in Nantes, the Breton port on the Loire, where he delighted to watch the sailors and fishermen on the quays at which the 'San Domingo planters' had once landed their rich cargoes from the Indies.

When he left the *lycée* at Nantes Jules would have liked to go to sea, not least because he had been disappointed in his first love, for his cousin Caroline, and wanted to get away from it all. M. Verne had other plans for him: he must qualify in law and then take over the family practice. Luckily for Jules, it was to Paris that he was sent to study in 1848. Amongst his baggage were the manuscripts of a number of plays he had been writing.

With a friend, he settled into rooms in the university quarter on the Left Bank of the Seine and began to experience for the first time the hardships of having to live on an inadequate allowance. He and his friend Bonamy had one set of evening clothes between them, so only one could go into society in the evenings while the other took his turn at staying in. And there was society awaiting them, for two of Jules's uncles introduced him to some of the leading salons. One of the earliest acquaintances he made in this way was Alexandre Dumas the elder, a great host to hard-up students, freely dispensing good food and talk. More importantly to Jules Verne, Dumas was manager of the Théâtre Historique; and it was there in June 1850 that he presented the first of his young friend's plays to reach the stage, *Broken Straws*, a marital comedy. It went well enough, running for twelve nights. Jules was praised by several critics and honoured by his new circle of friends. It was a good beginning.

He passed his law finals, read to Dumas a vaudeville sketch he had written and reduced the older man almost to helpless laughter with it, collaborated with a composer in writing an operetta, and submitted two stories, which were promptly accepted, to a journal. Weighing these successes in the balance, he felt able to tell his father, 'I may become a good writer, but I would never be anything but a poor lawyer, since I habitually see only the comic or the artistic aspect of things.' His mind teemed with 'thousands of projects that I'm not yet able to put into shape'. This intangible stock-in-trade, he felt, would serve him better than his degree in law. The immediate difficulty was financial – he offered to marry any wife his mother cared to choose for him, so long as she brought enough dowry. The necessity did not arise: he was appointed secretary of the Théâtre Lyrique.

The salary was scarcely enough to live on – 'The meat which I put up with must have dragged a good many omnibuses through Paris,' he wrote to his father – but it helped. Experience was what mattered. He still saw himself as a humorous writer, but critics found warm praise for his historical novel of racial conflicts in Peru, *Martin Paz*, with its impressive literary style and, to some, even more impressive use of geography and anthropology for dramatic purposes. Since his childhood days on the quays at Nantes, Jules had been keenly curious about geography in all its aspects and in more recent years his chief reading had been in the associated fields of science. His perceptive father urged him to give up the theatre for the novel. Jules realized that his ill-paid job was absorbing the time and energy he might have been using for writing. He decided to cut loose and took a fateful trip to Amiens, to attend a friend's wedding. It was to lead to his own.

During the festivities he met the bride's sister Honorine, a handsome young widow of twenty-six, and fell in love with her. But how could he marry without an income? The inspiration came from Honorine's brother, a stockbroker. Excitedly, Jules listened to his account of the pickings to be had on the *bourse*. He could scarcely wait to write and ask his father to buy him a partnership in one of the Paris stockbroking firms. Hesitating, but finally swayed when his son assured him that the scheme would be only a means to an end, and that he would never give up literature, M. Verne consented. Jules entered a business partnership in 1856, and into domestic partnership the following year when he married Honorine.

His new state of relative prosperity and domestic happiness suited him well. He quickly settled into a routine of rising at five, writing and reading until ten, then, after breakfast, changing into his city clothes to hurry to the Exchange. Even there he did not have to divorce his mind from literature entirely. Several brokers had literary and theatrical backgrounds and they formed a jolly clique, exchanging banter and ideas in between dealings, with Jules Verne at their centre. Yet those who were not admitted to his friendship found him disturbingly hard to know.

In 1859 one of his friends, a shipping agent, made the welcome offer to Jules and his seafaring brother of a free trip to Scotland and back. They went eagerly, Jules with a notebook ready to be crammed with impressions – practical and poetic – of Scotland, the Hebrides, Liverpool and then, for a few days, of London, where he saw the giant steel ship *Great Eastern* being built and swore he would cross the Atlantic in her when he had attained wealth and fame.

But it was an interest in another form of transportation which brought both those desired objects. Soon after the birth of a son, his only child, in 1861, Verne called on the publisher Hetzel with the manuscript of an episodic account of a flight over Africa by balloon. Having read it, Hetzel summoned the author to him again. Jules Verne's face fell as he heard the work being rejected, but brightened with hope when the publisher went on to suggest that he rewrite it into a complete novel. Dashing back to his desk, he finished the work in two weeks and gave it the title *Five Weeks in a Balloon*.

Hetzel at once saw the new version for what it was: a compelling narrative, beautifully written and bubbling with unique inspiration, while full of wholly plausible detail. He began to make publication plans and meanwhile summoned Jules Verne for a talk about further projects. Hitherto only half-envisioned, these ideas sprang into form under the stimulus of the publisher's interest, with the result that a contract was signed for forty books in twenty years or less at a generous fee for each. Verne promptly resigned from the stock exchange. At thirty-five he now had the security he needed to work uninterruptedly at the writer's craft.

The grandiose project which Verne had outlined to his publisher with increasing confidence as it grew from his words was a study in fictional form of the universe and the elements through contemporary eyes. He had begun with Air, in the terms of ballooning – and his book had proved to be an immediate success. Next he considered the phenomena of the eternal icefields, the aurora borealis and the magnetic eccentricities of the North Polar region in *The Adventures of Captain Hatteras* and *The Desert of Ice*, and proceeded to take his readers, young and old, on an exhilarating trip into unknown regions: the infinite space of the heavens, the dark depths of the earth, the strange world of the ocean bed. Yet in *Journey to the Centre of the Earth* and *Twenty Thousand Leagues under the Sea*, as in his ballooning tale, the scientific and technical details were so convincing as to seem true.

He wrote *Twenty Thousand Leagues under the Sea* after achieving his ambition to cross from Liverpool to the United States in the *Great Eastern*. During the voyage he had spent much time staring across the empty sea and questioning in detail members of the crew who had earlier taken part in laying the transatlantic cable. Everything he saw and heard was noted for future use, along with the details he had absorbed on attempts to build an undersea craft, and worked up into the adventure of that prophetic submarine, *Nautilus*. Much of the book was written aboard a boat of his own, the *Saint Michel*, a former fishing-smack to which he escaped whenever he could to write and daydream.

He was awarded the Légion d'Honneur in 1871 and almost immediately conscribed, at the age of forty-two, as a coast-guard, to serve for the duration of the war which had broken out between France and Prussia. By the war's end he had four more books in manuscript; but his money was gone. Hetzel's publishing works in Paris had been unable to go on operating during the siege and the Commune. No payments had been forthcoming. Verne had had to live off his capital. He went back to the stock exchange; but he had not been there long when he chanced one day to pick up a Thomas Cook's leaflet suggesting the feasibility of a round-the-world tour in less than three months. The *bourse* was forgotten as his mind raced ahead to the Eccentrics' Club in London where Phileas Fogg would accept a wager and set off with his willing companion, Passe-Partout, on a journey *Around the World in Eighty Days*.

It began to appear late in 1872 as a serial in *Le Temps*. The journal's circulation rocketed from the first instalment and Phileas Fogg seized hold of the public imagination in a way that would only be equalled, a few years later, by Sherlock Holmes. Every stage of his journey was reported as though it were real news. Wagers were made that he would or would not achieve his task. Jules Verne was offered enormous sums by steamship companies anxious that the world-traveller should be said to have made the last, dramatic dash of his trip in one of their ships.

He made a fortune without them. Two years after the serial, and with the book version selling in huge quantities, *Around the World in Eighty Days* was given a spectacular stage production in Paris. It was a terrific hit. Jules and Honorine were made as rich as they would ever be. They took a big town house; the old *Saint Michel* was supplanted by a specially-designed yacht; they gave a ball of Hollywood proportions, attended by hundreds.

He was now world-famous. Yet he continued to produce several novels a year, at the same time working on a mammoth study of geographical discovery through the ages, *The Discovery of the Earth*, an eight-year task which gave the lie to the inevitable critics who claimed that the detail which characterized his stories was largely made up.

Another huge success ushered in the 1880s, the stage version of his novel *Michael Strogoff*. It ran for a year in Paris, with a further long run later, and was reproduced in many other countries with equal acclaim. Now he bought a third *Saint Michel*, a nobleman's super-yacht going cheap, engaged a crew and began to voyage in earnest with his master-mariner brother Paul. They visited the North African ports, to be fêted wherever they landed; Norway, Ireland and Scotland; Holland and Germany; the Mediterranean. All the time, Verne was acquiring fresh material, fresh ideas to embroider. He set *The Survivors of the Chancellor* in the Sargasso Sea; *Child of the Cavern* in the Scottish coalfields. In *The Begum's Five Hundred Millions* he presaged the German menace to France; in *Castle of the Carpathians* he gave his readers a preview of the sound film and television.

Astonishingly to his friends, he went into local politics in Amiens, where he had settled, on the left-wing ticket, explaining that he had done so to make himself useful, regardless of any party label. But life was beginning to lose its zest for Jules Verne. Although he could write with great humour a novel *The Floating Island*, and one of his liveliest tales, *Before the Flag*, a stirring adventure of terror on the high seas, he suffered from increasingly recurrent lapses into melancholy.

His publisher and friend, Hetzel, died; his mother died; his brother Paul, his only deep intimate, died. Becoming deaf, part-blinded by cataract, yet still working hard - too hard - Jules Verne burnt his letters, his notebooks, his unpublished manuscripts, as though symbolizing his readiness to begin the exploration that would take him into regions more wonderful and unknown than any he had envisaged in his tales. On 25 March 1905 he set off from Amiens on that Greatest Journey.

Henrik Ibsen

(1828–1906)

Ibsen, the greatest playwright of the nineteenth century and one of the greatest of all times, was a man of contrasts. He was an ardent nationalist who lived half his life in voluntary exile from his native Norway. He became one of the most famous and successful writers of his day, yet spent his first forty years in miserable poverty while his work was ignored. He was the founder of a whole new school of writing, yet he himself deserted that school to move off into new directions. He was a master of prose styles, but beneath everything he wrote lay a deep, poetic use of imagery.

Ibsen was born at Skein in Norway on 20 March 1828. His family was rich, and when Ibsen was four they moved to a new house, larger and altogether grander. There Ibsen's father entertained his friends lavishly in a style which he felt fitted his new surroundings. But the family fortune was not equal to his generosity, and within two years he was bankrupt. Taking with them the bare necessities of life, the Ibsens moved to a small farmhouse outside Skein. For Ibsen the life of luxury could never have been more than a dim memory.

Ibsen's childhood was an unhappy one. He was the eldest child of a large family, for whom he never felt any real affection. He would shut himself away for hours to draw cruel caricatures of the family or to play with his toy theatre, and any interruptions would send him into a wild rage. Only his sister Hedwig, whose name he was later to use for the heroine of *The Wild Duck*, received any love from the young boy. At the age of sixteen, he was sent fifty miles away to Grimstad to be an apprentice to an apothecary.

Life at Grimstad was no happier than life at home, but at least it was a break with the family, and soon the break was to be made final. At first Ibsen returned to Skein on visits, but these soon stopped and shortly after that he stopped writing home as well. Ibsen loathed the tiny town. He was too poor to afford a room of his own and was forced to share with the chemist's young sons. He despised the local gentry and they in their turn despised him. He was, however, able to find some consolation during this time with his young literary friends.

302

Ibsen began writing poems, satirizing life in the small provincial town, and in 1849 he wrote his first full-length play. This was *Cataline*, a verse play set in ancient Rome. The Oslo theatre rejected the play, but had some kind words to say about it. Ibsen tried to get the play published, but the publishers too rejected it. Eventually Ibsen's friend Ole Schulerud paid for it to be published, and it was quite well received by the critics.

Full of optimism, Ibsen and Schulerud set off for Oslo, dreaming of the riches that would flow to the successful young writer. Forty-five copies of the play were sold. His next play, however, was more successful. *The Warrior's Tomb* was actually put on and ran for three performances. A year later Ibsen was offered a job at Ole Bull's theatre in Bergen. He joined the company as a 'theatre director' at a salary of about thirty shillings a week. He was an efficient stage manager, but his shyness made him a very bad director. He was always too nervous to talk to actors. He continued writing plays, but none of them were successful, except for *Feast at Solhaug*, a bright and cheerful little piece that made Ibsen popular with the students.

In 1857 Ibsen was offered a post at the National Theatre in Oslo. This new theatre was founded to develop Norwegian drama, and the thirty-year-old Ibsen plunged into this work with enormous enthusiasm. Norway had for centuries been dominated by her neighbours, Denmark and Sweden. The cultural domination by Denmark had been so complete that it was only in the nineteenth century that there had been a revival of the native Norwegian language, inspired by a group of ardent nationalists. Politically, Norway had been taken from Danish control and placed under the rule of the Swedish crown by the Treaty of Vienna in 1815. But the movement towards independence was steadily growing with each year.

Ibsen was a passionate nationalist, and he threw himself into the task of helping to create a truly Norwegian theatre. His plays at this time are all historical works which dwell on the period when Norway was free and independent. This effort culminated in the early masterpiece *Kingmaking*, where we see the first portents of Ibsen's genius. But his main efforts during his years at the National Theatre were spent in writing poetry. His poems were mostly political and brought Ibsen a great deal of praise but, unfortunately, very little money. And Ibsen needed money. For in 1858 he had married Susannah Thoreson, and the family was beginning to run into debt. In 1862 Ibsen was forced to abandon his efforts at the National

Theatre. For some time the theatre had been limping along from crisis to crisis, until finally it had to close. The Ibsens were deep in debt, and only a small grant from the university enabled them to keep going.

By the end of 1862 Ibsen's new play, *Love's Comedy*, had been published, to be greeted by a storm of controversy. Ibsen was denounced from the pulpits of Norway for his views on marriage, and no producer could be found who would risk facing such a wall of hostility. The controversy was probably responsible also for the government's refusal to grant Ibsen a poet's stipend, so that the family was constantly besieged by debt. Ibsen must have felt that things could get no worse, but the following year was to show otherwise. It was to be the year that his exile began.

In April 1864, thanks to the help of his friend Bjørnson, Ibsen was awarded a grant for foreign travel, and he set off immediately for Copenhagen. There he became passionately involved in the Danes' struggle with Prussia. In poems and articles he exhorted his countrymen to unite to fight this threat to fellow Scandinavians. But the governments of Norway and Sweden decided to remain neutral and the Danes were defeated at Dybbøl. Ibsen was overwhelmed with shame for his country, and in his bitterness turned his back on Norway. With the aid of a grant, and a private subscription raised by his friends, he left for Rome.

The departure from Norway was to prove the great turning point in Ibsen's life. At first life seemed no better than it had in Oslo. He was still desperately poor, and his wife and young child frequently went hungry. But creatively the move proved a great success. Away from the cold light of the north Ibsen began to write the play which was to change the whole course of his life – *Brand*. It was an immediate success. Within the first year of its publication, the play had run into four editions, and at last the government granted Ibsen his poet's stipend. The years of poverty were over, Ibsen was a success at last. But he was now thirty-eight, and the years of hardship had taken their toll. He had not only had to fight the constant hardships of poverty and the worries over debt, but he had also had to fight to find a style. For Norwegian was a new language, difficult to work on, and Ibsen was only just finding his own unique style.

Success brought many changes into Ibsen's life. From now on he had no life outside his work. It was almost as if the years of hardship had drained him of everything except the will to write. In terms of events in his life, very little more was to happen to Ibsen, except the plays. But those plays were to place him at the very forefront of the literary life of Europe.

Brand, the play that established Ibsen's reputation, was an intensely emotional, autobiographical work. Brand, the religious fanatic, believes that everything must be sacrificed in the face of his drive for the truth, much as Ibsen himself had sacrificed the welfare of his family to pursue the truth of his own writing. The play is also concerned with Ibsen's great disappointment over the Danish–Prussian war. It is, too, a play which vividly conjures up the country he had left, as if he needed to leave before he could see Norway clearly. With *Brand* completed, Ibsen began to work on the last and greatest of his verse plays, *Peer Gynt*. It was published in 1867, and was again an immediate success. It was a complete contrast to the harsh, oppressive *Brand*. The gay, feckless Peer travels through his world of trolls and adventure with a marvellous vivacity and a perfect credibility. Ibsen had captured the fairy-tale of Norway for all time, but had given it a new and deeper significance. When he sat down to write again, he would move to a very different style and a very different subject.

In 1868 the Ibsens went to live in Germany, where they stayed for the next ten years. *Brand* and *Peer Gynt* were both written at great speed, but now Ibsen began a two-part history of Julian the Apostate, which was to be 'a Great Play'. It took six years for Ibsen to complete this long and tedious work. Perhaps he felt that after the flippancy and humour of *Peer Gynt* he should turn to more serious things, but, whatever the reason, the result was a monumentally dull work. In 1869 he took time off from the Great Play to write a satirical play, *The League of Youth*. It attacked the Young Party in Norwegian politics, and led to many years of conflict between the young progressives and Ibsen's supporters.

With his historical play finally completed, Ibsen returned to prose drama and contemporary Norway in *Pillars of Society*, the first of the great plays of his middle period. The respectable society of the play is firmly based on Grimstad, and the citizens are attacked with a ferocity that had not been dimmed by the years that had passed since he had left the small town. From *Pillars of Society* he turned to the play which for many is the quintessence of Ibsenism and which established Ibsen as a European dramatist – *A Doll's House*. All over Europe the play was discussed with a vehemence and partisanship which was astounding. In Britain, George Bernard Shaw emerged as the champion of Ibsenism, defending Ibsen as a great moral dramatist, whereas his critics found him a shocking libertine.

But more important than the immediate controversy was the long-term effect of the play, for it proved to be the forerunner of the modern drama.

To Ibsen the controversy was very disturbing, but he continued working. Two years later, in 1881, his new play, *Ghosts*, was finished. The controversy surrounding *A Doll's House* was as nothing compared with the storm unleashed by *Ghosts*. But now Ibsen could relax. He knew that whatever might happen his success as a dramatist was assured. International honours were starting to pour in to him, and he launched himself into the battle with enthusiasm. In 1878 he had returned to Rome, a very different person from the poor ragged creature who had first come there over ten years ago. His success and his affluence gave him the confidence to hit back at his critics, and he did so, typically, by way of another play – *An Enemy of the People*.

By now, Ibsen had a whole army of disciples, the Ibsenites. They preached his virtue as a great writer on social themes all over Europe. But Ibsen was a true original. No sooner did the public think they had pinned him down than he was off in a new direction. In *The Wild Duck*, he turned from the problems of society to the problems of the individual personality, and wrote one of his greatest works in doing so. His followers still spoke of him as the great social reformer, but he had left them far behind.

A year after the completion of *The Wild Duck*, Ibsen returned to Norway for his first visit for twenty-one years. Back in Germany he produced over the next four years three more of his great dramas of the human condition – *Rosmersholm*, *The Lady from the Sea* and his ironical masterpiece, *Hedda Gabler*. Then in 1891, at the age of sixty-three, he returned to Oslo, but this time to stay.

In his last years Ibsen again confused his supporters by changing direction. His work became more mysterious, dealing in symbols rather than plot and story. He seemed to be wrestling with the problems of personal conscience, problems which lay at the very depth of his own soul. In his last play, *When We Dead Awaken*, this process has been completed, though the finished work bears more resemblance to his earlier poems than to a work for the theatre.

The play was finished in 1899. A year later Ibsen had a seizure and collapsed. He never fully recovered, and in 1906 he died at the age of seventy-eight, the fame which had always meant so much to him assured for all time.

What are we to make of the Ibsen of his exile? He is an

unattractive figure – irritable, vain, uncommunicative. For hours each day he would be shut away in his room, writing, and even when he emerged he was a lonely self-centred man. Not an attractive person at all, but Herr Doktor in his top hat and frock coat was more than just the public figure. He was also the greatest dramatist of the century. In part his greatness comes from his influence; he has been called the father of modern theatre. In an age where melodrama was more common than drama, Ibsen's realism introduced a whole new concept of theatre. He was concerned with ordinary, provincial men and women, and men and women who were firmly placed in their social context. It was this aspect of Ibsen's work that so appealed to Shaw; the mixture of rounded, complex characterization and social criticism. But this is only part of Ibsen's greatness: he may have been the apostle of realism in terms of the subject matter of his plays, but as years went by this became allied to a rich, poetic style which probed deep into human problems. It is this richness which ensures that the plays of Ibsen are still performed, not as museum pieces which set a trend, but as masterpieces in their own right. In the final analysis, the works justify the man.

William James

(1842-1910)

In the present crisis of humanity our view of ourselves, our nature, our place in the universe is a crucial factor; hence the science of psychology and the road it takes is of great importance. Science, with its staggering achievements in so many spheres, has unsurpassed prestige and has become a dominating factor in our lives. What science says has authority, and in a sense, may be incontrovertible; we tend to live in its grip.

But in psychology this holds great danger. Scientists would not be scientists if they did not seek to systematize their knowledge and reduce mysteries to equations; similarly psychologists may try to explain the totality of people and come to believe they can succeed. This has the evil effect of cutting people off in the eyes of the ignorant – who include many psychologists themselves – from the unknowable creative forces of the universe.

So on its negative side – which too often is interwoven with the positive – psychology may diminish respect for people and teach how they may be manipulated instead of how they may live. Hence it is very desirable that this necessary science should have among its leaders people big enough to accept the fact that we are part of something unknowable which is greater than ourselves, and that when we turn to study ourselves science is not enough. Fortunately there have been such leaders in the past, and one of them was William James, who has been called 'the unsystematic psychologist *par excellence*'.

James's importance depends not only on what he propounded, but when. Psychology as a science dates from the early nineteenth century and, when James was a young man, was becoming more and more deterministic. Empirical studies had revealed so-called laws of association; physiology seemed to suggest that knowledge comes only through the senses; German philosophy added its quota of dogmatism and the belief was held that reason alone would solve the riddle of people and reveal them as a kind of mechanism.

Darwin shook this belief with his *Origin of Species* (1859) and James, combining to an unusual degree artistic and scientific abilities, toppled it with powerful attacks on what he called 'the iron block universe'; while in books and lectures he propounded his doctrines of pragmatism, pluralism and radical empiricism, anti-doctrines really, boiling down to the view that truth is eternally relative and consists of what *works* in any field at a given time, until it is enlarged and superseded by another truth. In simple terms: the proof of the pudding is in the eating and absolutes are mere airy inventions.

When we look at ourselves and see how prone we are to adopt systems of belief for the sake of safety and convenience, we realize what courage is needed to embrace wholeheartedly the view that all is flux and nothing certain. But temperamentally James was always on the razor's edge between chaos and life, and he could not afford to fool himself about the insights which gave him real stability and conceptual ideas which did not.

He was born in New York in 1842, the eldest of five children (the second was to be Henry James the novelist) to parents with English, Scottish and Irish blood in their veins, descended from middle-class farming and merchant stock. In 1789 grandfather James had emigrated to the States from Ireland with a Latin grammar instead of money in his pocket and proceeded to make a fortune in business and real estate. To his son and grandchildren he bequeathed ample means for them to live without working for the rest of their lives and also, by way of reaction to his strict Calvinism, an open-minded approach to religion.

William James's father, a delightful, tender-hearted man, had had the misfortune when a boy to suffer a leg amputation after being badly burned in a fire, and later compensated for this by restless travelling in Europe and by immersing himself in a personal brand of Swedenborgian mysticism which visualized all evil as automatically leading to good.

Trailing in the wake of his affluent parents across Europe, William as a child had a scrappy education which ranged from New York to Boulogne and Geneva. Papa was a dabbler and William dabbled, too, picking up languages, trying his hand at art, making chemical experiments. At eighteen back in the States he took up art studies in earnest under William M. Hunt, but abandoned them for ever in the following year when he entered the Lawrence Scientific School at Harvard where he took courses in chemistry and anatomy.

But William had been delicate as a child and throughout life was to suffer from psychosomatic disorders of which the physical symptoms were severe back-ache and heart trouble. With him it was not a straightforward question of choosing a career;

somehow his activities had to help towards a better understanding of himself and when, in 1864, he entered Harvard
Medical School he already had misgivings: 'My first impressions,' he wrote, 'are that there is much humbug therein.'
In the result, he became an MD in 1869, but never practised
as a doctor.

Meanwhile, medicine was interspersed with philosophical
and psychological studies, especially in the works of the French
philosopher Renouvier, whose main themes were a refusal to
theorize about the unknowable and a belief in the validity of
personal experience. This chimed exactly with James's growing
convictions and Renouvier proved a lasting influence. Soon it
was reinforced by a drastic discovery.

Before qualifying as a doctor James had been to Bohemia to
take the waters at a spa, and succumbed there to a mood of
terrible depression. On his return there was an incident –
mentioned only in a letter to his brother Henry – about taking
an overdose of chloral. Then, in the spring of 1870, came the
experience.

He had been to an asylum and seen an epileptic youth,
virtually an idiot, sitting on a bench with his knees drawn up
under his chin. One evening, when he was alone in a darkening
room, James was suddenly overcome by a horrible fear of his
own existence; and almost at the same moment a vision of the
epileptic rose before him and he realized with terrible clarity
that the idiot youth was part of himself. Against that other
being he felt utterly defenceless:

> There was such a horror of him, and such a perception of
> my own merely momentary discrepancy from him that it
> was as if something hitherto solid within my breast gave way
> entirely and I became a mass of quivering fear. After this
> the universe was changed for me altogether ...

This visitation by a ghoul from the unconscious led him for
once and for all away from determinism in two senses: to
escape the fate that seemed to lie in wait for him he had to
assert the freedom of his own will; at the same time no me-
chanistic view of humanity could explain the horror in the
depths of his mind or in life itself. To retain freedom and abide
by the fruits of personal experience were in future the twin
poles of his striving and thought. All his later views on
psychology were coloured by this necessity, which also dictated
an open-minded approach to mental, spiritual and psychic
phenomena.

After this, two years were spent as a semi-invalid at his

father's house; then he became a lecturer, first in physiology, then in psychology at Harvard where he was to teach for the next thirty-five years – a much-loved teacher, sympathetic to his pupils' ideas, full of wit and vitality. He never wielded the stick of authority and some students took advantage of this.

> I confess [wrote one of them later] to having always trespassed upon him and treated him with impertinence, without gloves, without reserve ... I used occasionally to write and speak to him in tones of fierce contempt; and never failed to elicit from him in reply the most spontaneous and celestial gaiety.

At Harvard in 1876 he set up the first 'psychological laboratory' in America where body-mind relations were studied, a very crude affair to start with, consisting of a tiny room under a stairway. Though James disliked laboratory work – in fact he said it 'stuck in his gizzard' – he recognized its importance and over the years it became increasingly sophisticated.

All this time, travels to Europe, partly for health, partly for study, were interspersed with the job at Harvard, while unbeknownst to James, a young American, Miss Alice Gibbens, whom he was soon to marry, was also touring the Continent with relatives. The two cosmopolitans made an admirable pair. They reared four sons and a daughter and in the years ahead they were often seen in Rome, Paris or London, coping as long-suffering parents will with their travel-sick, food-sick or over-excited progeny. With James would go the manuscript of a book he was writing, which had been commissioned by Henry Holt in 1878 but did not appear till 1892 – *The Principles of Psychology*.

The *Principles* burst like a bomb on the scientific world, and paradoxically because of their very absence of dogmatism. The two thick volumes, with their brilliant passages of description and analysis on such subjects as perception, the emotions, will, the stream of thought (an expression coined by James) and necessary truths, were the first to be published on psychology in any language which attempted no systematization. Here was no flimsy conceptual structure, but something evolutionary and dynamic which laid bare, on a strictly empirical basis, what seems to be a basic clue to life: it is subject to law yet irrational, regulated yet unpredictable, meaningful and meaningless – and the master-word which we should never forget is paradox. As Einstein, Russell and Bohr have since taught us in physics, so in humanity, James thought, the seemingly impossible may happen and we are at bottom unfathomable. 'What has concluded that we should conclude about it?'

One may well think that the life of this humble, humane and open-minded man, battling for his own truth, is an illustration of the unpredictable result. But for the sinister figure in the unconscious, his artistic and analytical gifts might not have been used in psychology and the stream of modern understanding would have been impoverished. Throughout life his first and most important pupil was his buried self.

Meanwhile, James had finally sickened of laboratory psychology – 'a nasty little subject' – and turned to studying religion. Religious experience never seems to have come to him directly, but he was fascinated by mystics; in his unprejudiced way he was interested enough to attend seances and examine psychic phenomena; and he did reach certain conclusions about the spiritual life which he embodied in his Gifford Lectures on Natural Religion, delivered in Edinburgh in 1902. Later the lectures were published in book-form under the title *The Varieties of Religious Experience*. The book represents a milestone in the psychology of the religious life and – even more important, one may think, for distracted people today who crowd the consulting rooms of atheistic psychiatrists – it illumines the problem of the mentally sick as essentially a spiritual one, a cutting-off from the roots where the spirit dwells.

But James's researches into religious experience did not lead him to accept either popular Christianity or scholastic theism. There seemed to be something altogether more strange and multifarious that came into the conscious mind than a kind of orthodox spirituality. 'The phenomenon is that of new ranges of life succeeding on our most despairing moments', so new, in fact, and unexpected that in a later book, *A Pluralistic Universe*, James argued in favour of polytheism and in his famous *Essays in Radical Empiricism*, which enshrined the pragmatic proof-of-the-pudding rule, he chose the word radical to contest the idea of an eternally uniform and unchanging divinity.

All this was, and is, anathema to those priests, philosophers and psychologists who theologize and theorize with the hidden object of keeping the unconscious at bay. In his day James was condemned for being a 'popular philosopher', which in fact meant merely that people could understand him and say 'yes' from their own experience. But, unlike his learned *confrères*, he did not believe in final truth.

Vital and lively to the end, James certainly lived out the validity of his pragmatic rule. Summers were often spent in

Europe, sometimes visiting his brother Henry in London. There was a country home surrounded by wild nature at Cambridge, Massachusetts, where he walked, climbed and swam. There were innumerable friends for whom he kept open house. There were his students at Harvard who, in a unique tribute, gave him a loving cup after his last lecture and there was the family: grown-up, devoted children and an adoring wife, practical, patient and sharing his interests.

Perhaps the most startling outward event in his life was the 1906 earthquake at San Francisco where he happened to be at the time. 'This is an earthquake,' he said to his wife as the bedroom began to rock at 5.30 in the morning. 'Are you afraid? I'm not!' Otherwise life was lived more in thought, writing and lecturing than in memorable activity. He died in 1910 of angina, unhappy only that he could not write one last book, to be entitled *A Beginning of an Introduction to Philosophy*.

But his last words may be taken from an earlier work, as they seem to summarize the man: 'There is no conclusion ... There are no fortunes to be told, and there is no advice to be given. Farewell': words curiously similar to those written near the end of his life by James's great successor, C. G. Jung: 'There is nothing I am quite sure about. I have no definite conclusions – not about anything, really. I only know that I was born and exist.'

Oscar Wilde

(1854-1900)

When he was born on 16 October 1854, the parents gave their second son the names Oscar Fingal O'Flahertie Wills Wilde. Though in later years he was to declare that nothing succeeds like excess he dropped the three middle names and even toyed with the idea of being known simply as 'The Oscar' or 'The Wilde' – 'just as a balloonist when rising higher sheds unnecessary ballast'.

Meanwhile, as he grew up the sturdy child, dressed in some of his mother's cast-off, cut-down clothing, he had much to interest him in Dublin. His father, descended from a Colonel de Wilde, a Dutch immigrant to Ireland in the seventeenth century, was the leading eye and ear specialist of his day, a physician of international repute and the inventor of the operation for cataract. Wilde's mother, Jane Francesca *née* Elgee, of half-Italian descent, had been before her marriage an inflammatory partisan of the Young Ireland Movement, hotly anti-English and given to exhorting her countrymen in sensational verse. A good head taller than her husband, stately, massive, emotional, eccentric, clever, kind, she became a famous hostess, entertaining in a home described as disorderly though picturesque. After Sir William's death in 1876 she moved to London where, flamboyantly dressed and heavily scented, she gave receptions for Oscar, exploding sometimes into vibrantly oracular statements: 'I have come to the conclusion that nothing in the world is worth living for except sin.'

Oscar was sent to Portora Royal School, Enniskillen, where he dreamed away the lessons and discovered a permanent dislike of all knowledge that did not stimulate his imagination. Later he was to dismiss conventional education in one sentence: 'We teach people how to remember, we never teach them how to grow.' But at school he found his own nourishment, the classics, the pagan world that gave wing to fantasy, and this passionate interest which never deserted him gained him an entrance scholarship at Trinity College, Dublin. Though he only started to work when his parents dangled the carrot of university before him, more honours were to descend on him at college, a Foundation Scholarship, a Demyship at Magdalen

College, Oxford and, most useful against hard times, the eminently pawnable Berkeley Gold Medal for Greek. In view of folk memory which trivializes and distorts, it is well to remember that Wilde was intellectually brilliant and, far from being weak, had a punch like a sledgehammer.

At Oxford, when he went up in 1874, he discovered 'the dangerous and delightful distinction of being different from others'. The river, the gymnasium, the football field were not for him, 'I never liked to kick or be kicked', nor the life of the fox-hunting gentlemen, 'the unspeakable in full pursuit of the uneatable'. Nor could he be bothered to condescend to the academic expectations of the dons whom he heartily despised. His problem was of a different kind; he found it difficult, as he said, to live up to the blue china he had installed in his rooms. The remark became so famous that a university divine felt it necessary to preach against this 'heathen' aestheticism in church, and of course Oscar was delighted.

Not that he had the distinction of being totally different. Aestheticism, by which is meant the cult of the beautiful, was indeed to be the golden thread of his existence, but it was already in the air as a development of the Pre-Raphaelite Brotherhood, founded about 1850 as a protest against existing conventions in the arts, and its more extravagant aspects were to be satirized by Gilbert and Sullivan in *Patience* soon after Oscar left Oxford. The essence of his own creed, which was to be a view of art as almost entirely divorced from life or nature, 'remote from reality', ignoring ugliness and evil, was to be propounded in his essay, 'The Decay of Lying', first published in 1889. Meanwhile at Oxford his ideas were being fertilized by two dons in no way donnish, John Ruskin, then Slade Professor of Art, and Walter Pater, Fellow of Brasenose. Ruskin fulminated against materialism and machines, movingly described the nobility of man and the necessity of beauty and later, in *The Soul of Man under Socialism* (1890), Oscar reflected some of his political ideas. Pater's *Studies in the History of the Renaissance*, in which he propounded his gospel of the senses, of living with a 'hard, gem-like flame' and 'exquisite passions', expressed in lapidary prose what Oscar was already beginning to feel and he took this 'golden book', 'the very flower of decadence', everywhere with him.

'Golden ... decadence', an ingenious paradox. But nothing that Oscar ever said in high spirits should be taken literally and this was one of the keys to his provocative success when, on leaving Oxford, he set out to conquer London. The phrase sounds like a cliché, but in this case is accurate. He planned his strategy with care. In his pocket he had a first-class degree in the Humanities and the Newdigate Prize, awarded annually, for his poem 'Ravenna'. But for an impoverished son of an Irish knight (who had left him property worth only £4,000) something much more than academic distinction was needed to get into high society. He had to make a splash and get himself talked about, and these aims well suited Oscar's temperament. He would wear extravagant clothes, knee-breeches, buckled shoes, velvet coats edged with braid, floppy wide-necked shirts with flowing ties, carry a jewel-topped cane and lavender coloured gloves, all this often enough to get caricatured in *Punch*. As for being talked about, he would achieve that objective by talking, for which indeed he was magnificently equipped.

Those who heard him were unanimous on one point: Wilde was the most brilliant conversationist of his time (today we hardly know what a conversationist is). Bernard Shaw called him incomparably great as a raconteur and personality. Lily Langtry, Edward VII's mistress, spoke of 'one of the most alluring voices I have ever heard'. A friend, Robert Sherard, wrote how his whole nature seemed to change in the company of Oscar, who had actually saved him from suicide. 'If he had taught me nothing but the great value and happiness of life, I should still owe him an incomparable debt.' Max Beerbohm said he was 'hypnotic', and Winston Churchill, asked whom he would most like to meet in another world, replied instantly: 'Oscar Wilde.'

Oscar captured the citadel and soon was the darling of society, or rather one should say a smiling *agent provocateur*, complex, unfathomable, half-man, half-boy, challenging, stirring up moribund imaginations, but always with good humour for, as his best biographer Hesketh Pearson says, he possessed 'that rarest of virtues, an unqualified joy in making people happy'. Women were on his side almost immediately, and he well knew how important this was for his future. Men were harder to ensnare. Quite a few loathed and resented him as an effeminate mountebank, and who can blame them for catching their breath at such statements as : 'I would sooner have fifty unnatural vices than one unnatural virtue'; or 'What people call insincerity is simply a method by which we can multiply our personalities'; and at his talk of the 'seven deadly virtues' and the beauty of profiles rather than of philosophy. 'Outrageous,' muttered the men, but the women were charmed and hurried to issue their invitation cards: 'To meet Mr Oscar Wilde.'

Early in 1882, having accepted an invitation from Rupert D'Oyly Carte to lecture in America, he arrived in New York. The idea was for him to make a lucrative addition to the profits from *Patience*, shortly to be produced there and in which the character of Bunthorne was believed by the public to be himself. At the customs when he landed came that famous remark: 'I have nothing to declare except my genius', and from that moment an extraordinary relationship developed between Oscar and Americans. By the press he was vilified, by women – as usual – adored, by some men respected for his intellect and vastly superior knowledge of art. Oscar swam through it all with beatific serenity, gave eighty lectures east and west, including one on, of all things, Florentine art to some tough Colorado miners whom he then quietly drank under the table, and returned to England famous and richer by several thousand pounds.

In London doors were opened to hear his comments on America, which were not favourable. 'In America life is one long expectoration.' Americans had no manners, no appreciation of art and were obsessed with machinery. After some months in Paris, Oscar returned to expand on these views in provincial lecture tours where he would appear in tight Regency trousers with his chestnut hair dyed amber.

It seemed he could get away with anything, even marriage, for a while. In 1884, Constance Lloyd, the beautiful daughter of an Irish barrister, became his wife. They produced two sons whom Oscar adored, but by 1891, bored by domesticity, he was already drifting away and in that year his latent homosexuality flared when he met the handsome young poet son of the Marquis of Queensbury, Lord Alfred Douglas, known to his friends as 'Bosie'.

Meanwhile, Oscar's literary career had been developing. Early poems had been published in 1881, then six years later came the first interesting prose work, the charmingly improbable story, *The Canterville Ghost*, followed, amongst others, by *Lord Arthur Savile's Crime* and a collection of fairy-tales, delightful mixtures of romantic fantasy and satire, which included 'The Happy Prince', 'The Selfish Giant' and 'The Remarkable Rocket'. 'The Decay of Lying', full of wit and paradox, reappeared in 1891 with other prose works, 'Pen Pencil and Poison', 'The Critic as Artist', 'The Truth of Masks', under the general title of *Intentions*. By and large, society swallowed these dishes without indigestion. But in 1890 a novel appeared, *The Picture of Dorian Gray* and the long essay, *The Soul of Man under Socialism, and hatred of the all-too-successful*

Oscar, always potential, leapt into flame fanned eagerly by the press. The extraordinary novel, which almost seemed to preach diabolism, aroused hysterical reactions, while the essay trumpeting youth's eternal revolt against inherited values sent deep shudders down aristocratic spines. But what could anyone do? Wilde was irrepressible and triumph was just around the corner where the world would meet Oscar the dramatist.

Lady Windermere's Fan (first produced in 1892), *A Woman of No Importance* (1893), *An Ideal Husband* (1895): these social comedies with a somewhat serious import – one has to say 'somewhat' – were an immense success. Nothing like them had been seen since Sheridan. And, a month after the last, on 14 February 1895, that unique masterpiece *The Importance of being Earnest* was produced at the St James's Theatre, to be greeted with rapturous applause. Oscar, the wonderful, the glorious, had now reached the pinnacle of fame.

But now Greek tragedy was to be enacted in his own life, with its essential ingredient, the *peripeteia*, or sudden change of fortune. On 28 February he found a card from the Marquis of Queensbury waiting for him at his club. On it was written 'To Oscar Wilde posing as a somdomite' (this was the spelling). By this time Oscar and Bosie had become inseparable and urged on by the boy, who for good reason hated his father, he very foolishly took out a prosecution against Queensbury for criminal libel. The 'scarlet Marquis', as Oscar called him on account of his mad and aggressive temperament, found plenty of incriminating evidence against Oscar with which to defend himself and at his trial was acquitted. The same evening, after the evidence had been surveyed by the Director of Public Prosecutions, Oscar was arrested and charged with homosexual offences under an Act unique to Victorian Britain.

At his first trial the jury failed to agree and a second was ordered, amid a furore in which the hypocritical moralism of the English public was shown at its worst. The brilliance of Wilde in the witness-box, his sparring matches with Sir Edward Carson who was prosecuting, the 'absurd and silly perjuries' he later confessed to have uttered, the ruthless determination of the Crown to secure a conviction*, all this obscures the more interesting question of whether he felt guilty in morals as well as in fact. Probably he did not.

But on 25 May he was sentenced to two years' hard labour, and served the full term at Wandsworth and then at Reading. The labour involved shredding tarred rope with his bare hands

---

* For full treatment see *Trials of Oscar Wilde*, H. Montgomery Hyde, London, 1962.

for caulking the decks of ships and turning a metal drum against an inbuilt resistance by means of a handle, 10,000 times a day. Solitary confinement. One hour's exercise in twenty-four. Sanitation, a chamber pot. Meals, mostly gruel, suet, water and greasy cocoa, with consequent chronic diarrhoea. No talking with other prisoners. No conversation with warders. No books except a Bible and, to start with, no visitors. Some friends stood by him and obtained relaxations eventually. But surely no plunge into the abyss has ever been more drastic and terrible. What it meant to him is described in his long letter to Alfred Douglas, 'De Profundis', and in 'The Ballad of Reading Gaol'.

But incredibly he survived, to face new sorrows on his release in 1897. He was a declared bankrupt, his household goods had been sold, his wife had obtained a separation and a legal guardian had been appointed for his children, whom he was never to see again. As for England, there were no white cliffs there for him, but only ostracism. He could not go back so he lived in Paris with occasional trips elsewhere, not a broken man quite, but fading, though still with some of the old wit. Marvellously he was able to overcome resentment, and sensed a necessity about what had happened, which gave him comfort.

He knew he was dying – 'I am dying beyond my means,' he said, and his most devoted friend, Robert Ross, was with him at the end which came, from cerebral meningitis probably complicated by syphilis, on 30 November 1900, in a dingy room in a second-rate Paris hotel. Oscar had made him promise to bring a priest, 'when I am no longer in a fit condition to shock one'. This was done and, already beyond the power of speech but with his gestured affirmation, he was received into the Catholic Church.

Today he rests in the cemetery of Père Lachaise, beneath a hideous monument designed by Jacob Epstein. But people still bring flowers. Perhaps they are paying tribute to a supreme individualist, like the conversationist, a species now almost extinct.

Hugh Bourne

(1772–1852)

The assertion that the British Labour movement owes more to Methodism than to Marx derives somewhat from the attraction of alliteration, and as a generalization it is too simplistic. Nonetheless it is a valuable observation and increasingly persuasive as it is broken down into more detailed elements. The life and work of Hugh Bourne gives precise effectiveness to this claim that the most significant political development in Britain during the last hundred years is not so much a refraction of continental socialism mainly promoted by Marxist thinking, but the reflection of a religious movement deriving its impetus from the Methodist revival as a whole, and the 'Primitive' expression of that revival in particular.

The founder and chief architect of Methodism was of course John Wesley, though the hymns composed by his brother Charles also played a vital part in the spread and vigour of the Methodist societies. One of the dominant characteristics of early Methodism was the appeal it made to the poor and the care it engendered for the needy. Wesley himself was a profound humanitarian, but politically he was no radical in the accepted modern sense of that word. Ecclesiastically his commitment was 'high church'. Politically he was a high Tory, and he was certainly no friend of socialism. What is more, the 'Wesleyan Methodist Connection' in the nineteenth century maintained, and in some instances even deepened, the gulf between personal piety and political radicalism.

However, as with other religious movements, the central impetus tends to carry with it implications and developments which go beyond and often contrary to the original intentions of their founders. The story of Methodism is no exception. The emphasis on moral earnestness, the assurance of personal salvation, the 'priesthood of all believers', created in many who were affected by these gospel messages a new sense of dignity; and, what is more, it offered a standard by which they came to judge the society in which they lived. Alongside the experience of personal salvation came the vision of a new sort of world in which these personal blessings found their expressions in a Kingdom of God which Jesus insisted was first in importance and foremost to be sought and found. It is in this context that Hugh Bourne epitomizes the development of Primitive Methodism. It came to be called 'primitive' though, strictly speaking, in the time sequence this was historically not so; but from the wider standpoint Bourne was expressing the essential nature and necessary consequence of the religious convictions of the Methodist spirit – the imperishable value of everyone in the sight of God, and by His grace the equality of all to inherit God's promises. In that sense Hugh Bourne was the founder and exponent of Primitive Methodism.

He was born in 1772 in the parish of Stoke-on-Trent at a remote farm, to a father who was an irascible churchman and to a mother who, like Wesley's mother, taught him to read and write before he went to an endowed school at Bucknall, from which his father removed him at the age of twelve to take up work on the farm and in the wheelwright's shop. From his earliest years he was concerned with, and often plagued by, religious matters, as he himself records, while he 'did not cease from study', beginning to learn from the arts and sciences and 'resolving for the present to be circumspect as possible'. He passed, as so many do, through an adolescent period of waywardness and theological uncertainty, but acquaintance with the Quakers and more particularly the Methodists led to a Welseylike conversion experience in the spring of 1799.

From that time forward, despite sundry periods of doubt, Hugh Bourne's was a 'guided life' and his employment as a carpenter in coal-mine timber became the immediate *milieu* in which to fulfil his calling 'to preach and pray'. In 1800 he purchased a quantity of oak timber at Mow Cop near Bemersley, and there he began a ministry of open-air preaching and revivalist evangelism which soon distilled a wine too new and potent for the older bottles of contemporary Methodism in which it was first set. Mow Cop became the *rendezvous* for a series of 'camp meetings' which attracted widespread attention and were the occasion of many dramatic conversions.

Such evangelical enthusiasms were not to the liking of some of the local Methodist churches, which paradoxically enough had lost the crusading fervour of their founding fathers. They even resented this form of mission as alien and theologically dubious. Misunderstanding was followed by disapproval, and in 1808 Hugh Bourne was put out of the Methodist Society at Burslem by the circuit quarter-day meeting. The result was all too predictable. The society at Mow Cop and other societies created by Bourne became over the years a new connection, as did the original Methodists (though the various separated Methodist connections came together again in 1932).

Apart from one visit to the USA Bourne travelled incessantly in Britain, as did John Wesley, and like his predecessor he wrote and argued on a thousand theories, kept a journal and administered an organization. Unlike John Wesley he was never a priest, and he does not appear to have had amorous problems. He never married. He died 'in full connection', as Methodists say, in 1852.

Studying the story of his leadership (which he shared with his friend Clowes) of this Primitive Methodism does not immediately substantiate the claim made at the beginning of this article. The radical trends within nineteenth-century English society were not the specific projects to which he and his followers were originally committed. Nevertheless they were the manifest effects that followed the movement which he led. He was a layman and under his leadership the priesthood of all believers took on a new significance. It enfranchised ordinary men and women from the sense of unavoidable separation from the seats of power. It was the somewhat belated fruit of the French Revolution and claims to equality, and persuaded those who had been indoctrinated with a sense of inferiority just because they belonged to a 'working class' that they were not only as valuable in the sight of God as their superiors in church and state and class, but could be just as capable in religious and political affairs as the 'establishment'.

The British trades-union movement owes a debt to Bourne and his friends even if at the time neither side was fully aware of its size. Then again this lay movement, for such it was, had a profound influence upon the overall relationship of church and state. It democratized ecclesiasticism (if that is not too portentous a phrase) for a generation of church and chapel goers; and by its insistence on the role of the congregation, in contrast with the primacy of the clergy, facilitated the development of social thinking about the Kingdom of God and indeed fostered what is now known as the ecumenical movement. Strong evidence of these things emerges when the story of Hugh Bourne is seen across the seas.

The impact of this Primitive Methodism was by no means confined to the country in which it was born. The continuing story of Methodism itself became a blend of Wesleyanism and its various 'connections' – organizations which broke away from the parent body but still contributed to a spiritual impulse which was distinguishable, indeed identifiable as Methodist. Hugh Bourne, almost as much as Wesley himself, was the founding father of this blended spiritual impetus which crossed the seas. It would be impossible in any exact sense to quantify the extent to which the trades-union movements generally in the non-communist world were influenced by the radicalism of nineteenth- and early-twentieth-century Methodism, but no one could seriously question the assertion that the Tolpuddle Martyrs, for example, inspired proletarians in many a country who knew little or nothing of the spiritual and theological beliefs of these Dorset heroes, yet revered them as pioneers and sought to follow where they had led.

However, this more diffuse outcome and development of Methodism is by no means the whole story. In Australia and in the USA there is precise evidence of profoundly important developments in the life and times of both these countries testifying to the influence of men like Bourne and the religious movement which he inherited and did much to transform. The Australian story begins in Cornwall and the tin mines of St Agnes, Redruth and Helston. Many of their skilled craftsmen were converted to Christianity through the Methodist witness. Their individual lives, though changed for the better because of their vibrant faith, became progressively more precarious and economically difficult because of the overall decline of the tin-mining industry. Forced into unemployment and without hope of returning to anything like full employment in Cornwall, many of them found their way to the colonies and dominions, in particular Australia. They took with them their mining skills and the name of 'Jack', and dug for gold where previously they had dug for tin. They also took with them their belief in the dignity of workers and the vision of a new society in which capitalism no longer operated a class society but was replaced by socialism. The Australian Labour Party for the first half of the twentieth century owes an immense debt to these Jacks and to their children. Ben Chiffley, the first Labour Prime Minister of Australia and himself a Roman Catholic, acknowledged this debt to the Methodist Jacks from the other side of the world but, as he also said, 'from the same side of truth'.

In regard to America the story is somewhat different but equally definite. The United Methodist Church of the USA carries with it the unmistakable marks of nineteenth-century Methodism. In fact the tradition of American Methodism has shown how naturally Coke and Asbury, its co-founders, prepared the way for developments in which one of the important aspects of Hugh Bourne's evangelism acquired and maintained a vital role. Though Primitive Methodism has never been anti-clerical, it has from the beginning emphasized the role of the laity and looked with suspicion on any hierarchical pretensions on the part of the ministry. Nowhere has this explication of the 'priesthood of all believers' found a more fertile soil than among the eight to ten million Americans 'of good standing' in the Methodist Church of the USA. In view of the fact that, unlike British Methodism, their sister Church is episcopally governed, it might appear that the foregoing claim is suspect; but in fact the American Methodist bishops are administrators rather than prelates and the organization which they help to administer is a democratic body in which no prescriptive rights belong, as they do in other episcopal churches, to the higher ranks of the clergy.

The question of whether the laicization of Christian organizations is sufficient of itself to become 'the body of Christ' goes far beyond the terms of reference of this article. Certainly the Roman, the Anglican and the Eastern Communions have always insisted that certain powers must be reserved for the *sacerdos*. What can be claimed is that men like Hugh Bourne, by this questioning of priestly authority, as if it were automatically justified, and this contempt for lay servility, as if ordinary men and women must regard themselves as under the tutelage of their spiritual betters, have tended to make religion more relevant to the world in which today it has to express itself. The Kingdom of God is both up in Heaven and down to earth. The best aspects of American Methodism testify to this and have inherited at least some of the promises explicit in the work of men like Hugh Bourne.

It is a golden truth that whenever the insistence is upon 'doing the will', those who thus obey God tend to know more and more of the Gospel. Bourne helped to spread that goodness which leads to the 'unity of the spirit in the bond of peace and righteousness of life'. The splendour of his faith, the power of his preaching especially in the open air, the movement he promoted, and the breadth of his personality would in themselves warrant his place among the giants of the nineteenth century. Hugh Bourne left no evidence that he had ever heard of the Karl Marx who said, among other things, that 'man makes his own history'. Had he been told of this dictum he could surely have commented that only when man seeks to make his own history in obedience to God's will as revealed in Jesus Christ will that history be worth while.

Pius IX

(1792–1878)

Committed men in matters of faith must always be controversial figures in a world which is not sure what to believe.
Among the most committed, and therefore the most controversial, are the popes of Rome. Among the most controversial
of these in the nineteenth century was Pius IX. His early life
gave little indication of his ultimate destiny.

Giovanni Maria Mastai-Ferretti was born at Sinigaglia,
near Ancona, on 13 May 1792, the fourth son of Count Jerome
and Countess Catherine Volazzi. He was educated at the College of Piarists in Volaterra with a view to joining the pontifical
guard as an officer. However, he suffered an epileptic attack
while studying, and the military career was ruled out. He
eventually overcame his illness and was ordained priest in
1819. Only eight years later he was consecrated Archbishop
of Spoleto. No doubt the promotion owed something to his
patrician blood. On the other hand, his father and mother, for
all that they were patricians, were regarded as 'enlightened', at
that time not a complimentary term on every tongue. Napoleon was defeated; but the spirit of the French Revolution lived
on in Italy as elsewhere in Europe. The restoration of the old
dynasties meant the return of better times to some and relapse
into tyranny for others. The Church had temporal power in
the Papal States, and had to become involved in purely political
issues. The popular aspirations for a more equitable share of
the good things of life went hand in hand even in the Pope's
kingdom with a desire for political responsibility.

Outside Italy, the existing régimes, centred in great families
and restored after the Napoleonic era, had long been a traditional bastion of the Church, law, order and civilization as
they had always been understood. As a responsible organization, the Church could not simply repudiate them and march
with the *sansculottes* towards new revolution. In the event the
revolutionaries marched without it and blamed its abstention
with anything from mild disapproval to out-and-out hatred.
Archbishop Giovanni had to deal with the problem at close
quarters in 1831, the year of revolution throughout western
Europe. By force of an engaging personality and sheer courage

he had persuaded a group of Carbonari in armed rebellion to lay down their arms and disperse peacefully. His rule in his diocese could be described as firm but mild. His superiors did not overlook his success.

Mastai-Ferretti was translated to Imola in 1832, and in 1840 was created cardinal. His zeal, always without zealotry, and his evident humanity and goodwill continued to win him friends among the liberals. Indeed, some even thought he had been won over completely to the radical Father Gioberti, a fiery Turinese priest, very much involved in popular politics. In 1846, the Cardinal went to Rome for a papal election. He emerged from the conclave as the new Pope on 16 June. He took the name of Pius; but from the first his task called for more than the piety with which he was plentifully supplied.

His predecessor, Gregory XVI, and Gregory's Secretary of State, Cardinal Lambruschini, in their anxiety to avoid anarchy, had brought the Papal States close to being the ideal setting for Puccini's *Tosca*. Pius IX immediately showed where his own sympathies lay by declaring an amnesty for political prisoners, establishing liberty of the press and introducing gaslighting and railways in the Papal States. In 1847 a consulta, or advisory council of laymen, was set up to assist with the task of government. The city of Rome was given municipal government. In the international sphere, an agreement was reached with the Ottoman Empire in 1847, which allowed the re-establishment of a Latin Patriarch in Jerusalem about the same time. A fairly favourable concordat was concluded with Russia. The year of success was followed by a year of stark failure. 1848 was another year of revolution. But for Pius this was no repetition of 1831 in Spoleto. The papal prime minister, Rossi, was assassinated by the radicals, and by November the Pope himself was in full flight to Gaeta. In his absence Mazzini and his friends proclaimed the Roman Republic.

Mazzini's escapade or triumph was short-lived. With the support of European diplomacy and French arms, the Pope returned to Rome as a restored sovereign on 12 April 1850. Modern historians do not agree that the Pope returned to rule henceforward as a disillusioned reactionary. Undeniably, he had learned caution and, in the new beginning, perhaps used too much caution. He was now suspicious of politics, but he had by no means done with reform.

Prince Metternich of Austria, a man sometimes more clever than wise, once dismissed Pius as 'warm of heart' but 'of feeble intelligence'. Metternich was surely wise as well as clever when he said that although the Pope undermined the foundations of his temporal power by his liberalism, his spiritual office would ensure his survival. Certainly, whatever may be said for or against Pius's politics, the next few decades saw considerable expansion in the spiritual influence of his Church. Indeed, although the Pope's worst difficulties arose from his temporal sovereignty, already the world was being prepared for a Vatican whose influence was to be almost entirely in the moral order.

Pius was well fitted for the spiritual role. He was genuinely a man of prayer; he hated cruelty and the meaner shifts of politicians whether of the right or left. He was genuinely anxious to be all things to all men. His real danger was to be too many things to too many men. Hence disappointments; but he enjoyed genuine successes. On 30 September 1850 the hierarchy was formally restored in England. In spite of a vociferous no-popery campaign, it marked a new point of departure for the development of the Catholic Church in England. Not that Pius was ever quite forgiven in English government circles. An Act of August 1851 invalidating the restoration remained a dead letter; but the resentment which led Palmerston, for example, to dismiss Pius's régime as the 'worst of governments' remained a living force in English politics until the end of the century. Undeterred, the Pope issued a similar Bill of Restoration for Holland in May 1853. This was followed by the 'April Agitation' on similar lines to the popular reaction in England. Utrecht was no more palatable to the Dutch than Westminster to the English as the seat of a Catholic archbishop. Nevertheless, the Dutch reaction died down much more quickly than the English.

The next year Pius turned to a purely spiritual topic, and on 8 December the doctrine of the Immaculate Conception was solemnly proclaimed. Some Catholics found it inopportune, and blamed it on the Jesuits. In fact, the initiative came from the body of the nave, so to speak, rather than the sanctuary. The Catholics of France, in particular, were anxious for the further mark of honour to the Madonna. They seemed to be extraordinarily vindicated when the apparitions took place at Lourdes in 1858 less than four years after the definition.

The Pope's more pressing difficulties on the spiritual front, however, did not arise from the demands of simple faith but from those of a more complicated kind of belief as well as complex unbelief. Augustine Bonnetty, it seems, claimed too little for reason and too much for tradition in Catholic thinking. Anthony Guenther, on the other hand, seemed to attribute too much to the power of human reason in understanding matters of faith, while James Frohschammer conceded too much to the principle of scientific liberty. The abuse of 'natural magnetism' and 'mesmerism' drew Pius to comment in 1856. All of this amounted to skirmishing over detail, however. It became increasingly evident to the Pope that the Catholic Church would need to define its position before the growing body of non-Catholic, anti-Catholic and secularist thought, all of which underwent great elaboration and development in the nineteenth century.

This accorded with growing competence and knowledge in the fields of science and history. The encyclical *Quanta Cura* was issued with this end in view on 8 December 1864 – just ten years after the definition of the Immaculate Conception. *Quanta Cura* was accompanied by a 'syllabus of errors' which rejected some eighty propositions of pantheism, rationalism, indifferentism, communism, protestantism and many other 'isms' opposed to the 'ism' represented by the Pope. The syllabus did not amount to a solemn definition, but the canons of the First Vatican Council of 1870 certainly did. God, faith, revelation, the relation between faith and reason, and the Catholic Church itself, were all the subject of decrees. The most significant, or at least most remembered, definition, however, was that on the subject of papal infallibility.

The spiritual question continued to complicate the political issue and *vice versa*. A man of Pius IX's ability could not fail to see the problems, even if he could not see all the answers. It was impossible in practice to distinguish between the Pope as the spiritual head of Catholic Christendom and the Pope as head of the Papal States. The Catholic Church is not a democracy, and could not become one. Christ's promises, as Catholics read the New Testament, were to Peter and his successors, and the apostles' teaching in harmony with the Pope. This was the doctrine solemnly reiterated by the Second Vatican Council. As a spiritual head, then, the Pope's powers could not be shared or delegated. As head of a temporal state he was bound to find himself in opposition to the general trend of western political aspirations towards rule by the people. The Pope would only have surrendered enough power when he had surrendered everything. This was impossible. But clinging to the possible made the papacy unbearable on more than one count. The Pope could scarcely act as supreme pastor of Catholics and countenance armed opposition to a Catholic power. As an Italian patriot, he might secretly have wished the Austrians out of Italy. As Pope, he could not take active part in a peninsular war of independence against the Habsburgs. The antagonism between the temporal and the spiritual order in these years seemed to be symbolized by the hurried collapse of the Vatican Council before the oncoming Piedmontese soldiers in 1870.

But if the principal goal of Italian democracy could not be allowed, there could be vast concessions on the kind of detail that affected everyday life. Pius might not accept Cavour's concept of 'a free Church in a free State', but he could make the government of benevolent despotism much less irksome. This he did. Rayneval, the French ambassador at Rome, summed up Pius's achievement in a dispatch of May 1856:

> There is in truth, misery here as elsewhere, but it is infinitely less heavy than in less favoured climates. Mere necessities are obtained cheaply. Private charity is largely exercised. Establishments of public charity are numerous and effective . . . Important ameliorations have been introduced into the administration of hospitals and prisons. Some of these prisons should be visited, that the visitor may admire – the term is not too strong – the persevering charity of the Holy Father.

At this time, the average Roman was paying rather less than half of what the average Frenchman paid in taxes. Rayneval, as it happened, was transferred elsewhere for his truthfulness.

Cardinal Antonelli, secretary of state, was not only benevolent but effective. In 1860, however, the Romagna and the Marches were taken from the Pope in the onward march of Italian unity. Now only the depleted Papal States, to all intents and purposes, lay outside the new and rising kingdom of Italy. Pius IX continued to resist the future, but only for another ten years. The protecting hand of France was removed to protect herself in the Franco-Prussian War of 1870. The Piedmontese lost no time; Rome was occupied on 20 September 1870, and the Pope became the 'prisoner of the Vatican'. Ironically enough, this resolution of the problem imposed by the anti-clericals proved in time to be the ideal solution. The Roman pontiff, freed from preoccupations with drainage and popular elections, was able to concentrate on his other task of being Vicar of Christ. The proprietor of a not very vast estate – some 109 acres – he was still independent of sovereigns, presidents and plain despots, at least in theory. He was able to grow in the stature of his spiritual role.

This was not immediately apparent; certainly not to the Pope himself. But time which had brought the solution would win approval for it. The last few years for Pius were rather years of anticlimax, notwithstanding the lively opposition put up by the anti-clerical politician Agostino Depretis. However, the Italians generally had no desire to push things à outrance with the papacy. In November 1870 the Italian parliament passed the Law of Guarantees. This recognized the sovereignty of the Pope with all the rights pertaining thereto. He was declared immune from arrest and protected by the same treason laws that sheltered the King of Italy. This arrangement was not substantially modified before the mutual agreement between State and Church reached by the Lateran Treaty of 1929. Meanwhile, the Pope continued to preside over what was and continued to be a very real revival of Catholic faith and practice. The Church in Germany successfully withstood Bismarck's Kulturkampf. The blows of the secular hammer only drove the nail deeper into the wood. Pius IX, courageous, good, fervent, if not inspired in all his dealings with his own generation, had proved no unworthy successor to the Apostle by the time of his death on 7 February 1878.

Not even in death, however, did Mastai-Ferretti know peace for long. In 1881 it was decided to move his body to San Lorenzo for final interment. Although it took place by night to avoid incident, an anti-clerical mob attacked the funeral cortège and threw mud at the coffin. A great deal of mud has been thrown since; and it cannot be denied that for all Pius IX's obvious merit, he suggests himself as a target for progressive abuse. However, surprisingly little of the mud has managed to stick after a century. Even his enemies realized that however little they had in common with him as a man, they could accept the fact that as a man he tried to be true to himself and the best ideals of his Church.

John Henry Newman

(1801-90)

Before me as I write lies a wisp of yellowish grey hair and a stout, little volume of letters written in a small, neat and extremely regular hand in black ink: a precious souvenir, especially the letters, of one of the greatest churchmen of the nineteenth century. Cardinal Newman, from whom they came, is an important bridge-figure of two interpretations of Christianity, and one of the finest minds of his age.

John Henry Newman was born in the City of London on 21 February 1801. His early years were peaceful and serene. From the first, his context was a religious one. His father, a prosperous London banker, was tolerant in religious matters, but unmistakably Protestant. His mother, descended from a French refugee Huguenot family, imbued her son with her own deep piety and knowledge of scripture. Both were devout Anglicans, but there was nothing narrow in their views. Playgoing and reading, music and the arts were encouraged in the family circle.

As a boy at an enlightened private school in Ealing, he emerged already as editor of a magazine and president of a club. But if Newman was precocious, he was never priggish. The breadth of his tastes prevented the danger of imbalance in his development: classics, mathematics, geology and the violin all held some part of his many-sided attention.

Meanwhile, the waters troubled by Napoleon in which the Emperor himself found shipwreck brought disaster to Newman's family. In 1816 the bank in which John's father had been a partner failed. The boy was flung prematurely in collision with new problems. He turned with a new intensity from the failure of his material support to the spiritual. The process was hastened by an adolescent illness and subsequent years at Oxford, which began when he took up residence at Trinity College in June 1817. At Oxford, Newman was something of a prodigy, if only because he worked – he himself once described his own college, Trinity, as 'a very dear place, but a very idle one'. All the same, through nerves and overwork he failed to get honours in his first important examination, taken in 1820. He soon retrieved this failure by being elected a Fellow

331

of Oriel on 12 April 1822, an appointment which not merely raised him from obscurity but brought him an income. To Newman this was important not so much for himself as his family. At the end of 1821 his father had been declared bankrupt.

Newman was by now not only a scholar but a convinced Christian. His real bent was to be exercised for some years in the Anglican ministry for which he was ordained on 29 May 1825. A zealous pastor, he soon acquired a reputation as a preacher. Newman started to move away from his original evangelical position. Edward Hawkins, Vicar of St Mary's, the University Church, and Richard Hurrell Froude were the most important influences drawing Newman to High Church views.

In January 1828 Newman succeeded Hawkins at St Mary's. The parish included Littlemore near which Newman's mother and sister came to live. Here Newman was often glad to retire for rest from the city and another kind of pastoral work than that exercised among the sophisticated students of the University. On the latter, Newman exercised a great influence not only by the reasoned forcefulness of his teaching but by the holiness of his life. Although liberal churchmen were becoming estranged, he was asked to preach a number of official sermons, and was select preacher to the University from 1831 to 1832.

Newman's life had taken a new turn through material disaster. It was to take another as the result of physical misfortune. In 1832 Newman went with Hurrell Froude on a Mediterranean cruise. Encouraged by this experience, he decided to return the following year to an island which had captured his imagination more than any. It was while travelling in Sicily that he contracted typhoid. A long and dangerous illness began. Once more the kaleidoscope in his agitated soul began to revolve. In his earlier illness, Newman emerged convinced not only of God but that God willed him to live a life without the consolation of women. During convalescence after his second illness, however, Newman visited a number of Catholic shrines and churches. He returned to England in July 1833 and summed up the stage he had reached in his spiritual odyssey in the words of a hymn, 'Lead, kindly light amid the encircling gloom'.

Newman seriously began to question the foundations of his Anglican faith when Parliament thrust the question unavoidably upon him. Parliament had presumed to abolish a number of redundant Anglican bishoprics in predominantly Catholic Ireland. For Newman and his friends, it brought up the whole vexed question of the ultimate authority of and in the Church Established. Newman was not simply defending the bishoprics, but the right of the Church of England to put its own house in order in its own way. John Keble preached in St Mary's on the 'national apostasy' on 14 July. Newman, perhaps too modest in his own regard, considered this the beginning of the Oxford Movement. The question of disestablishing the Church of England now came up, and with it the thorny problem of Church-State relations. Newman, Froude, John Keble and others began to publish *Tracts for the Times* in December 1833. Over a quarter of them were written by Newman. Deepening his roots in the early Church Fathers, in whom he had been interested since boyhood, the idea of a Church in which the State had much, or even any, direct authority became increasingly repugnant.

The average modern reader, used to the idea that one church is probably as good as another, and the morality of Parliament is at least no worse than that of any other public body, will find it difficult to appreciate Newman's difficulties. Certainly Newman's generation found much of interest in the sermons which began to be published in 1834, and from this time the local divine moved steadily towards a national reputation. The Tractarians were already becoming a movement known nation-wide, and by 1839 Newman's influence was at the highest point it ever reached in the country as a whole. Early in the Tracts, Newman had been accused of popery. Few even of his friends could remain unperplexed when with Tract 90, published on 27 February 1841, he seemed to be interpreting the 39 Articles as if they were part of the code of the Roman Catholic Church rather than basic principles of the Church of England. Ironically enough, his principal aim was to show how unnecessary it was for Anglicans to become Catholics. He was censured not only by the University authorities but by twenty-four bishops as well.

Newman, at the end of the year, retired from Oxford to neighbouring Littlemore to think – and, of course, to suffer. He fasted, as well as prayed, in accordance with very ancient tradition, in order to get his mind clear. Even now, although his interpretation of the 39 Articles in a Catholic sense had been rejected for the most part by his fellow Anglicans, there could still be no question of joining Rome. There were still too many points of difference, above all in the matter of honour to be paid to the mother of Jesus and the Saints. From October 1842 Newman made Littlemore his permanent residence. There among his books, members of his family and a few intimate friends he thought his way forward methodically and painfully.

In September 1843 Newman preached his last sermon as an Anglican divine; but not until 1845, when he produced his famous *Essay on the Development of Christian Doctrine*, did he decide finally to join the Roman Church. He was received by the Italian Passionist, Dominic Barberi, on 9 October in Littlemore Chapel. It was not the end of a struggle, only the beginning of a new phase in Newman's wrestling with and for truth. And, of course, he did not cease to suffer. It meant becoming estranged, in the circumstances of the times, from many old friends. Keble, Pusey and Newman's own family found it impossible to understand or follow his example. His reception by Barberi symbolized another inevitable clash of spirit between the intensely English Newman and the essentially Italian Passionist, who was passionate for his peninsula as well as his faith.

Rome was at least accommodating in what it demanded before Newman was ordained – it was scarcely thinkable, especially by now, that Newman could have been other than a priest. After a short time at Oscott College, Newman went to Rome in the autumn of 1846. He studied in the College of Propaganda, and was ordained priest of the Roman rite on Trinity Sunday 1847. In the capital of Catholicism Newman found a promising seed to transplant to one of the world capitals of commerce. It would have taken a Newman to see the promise and make a success of its fulfilment. On 1 February 1848 Father John Henry established the first Society of the Oratory at Oscott. The following year the Oratory moved to Birmingham.

The Oratorians were founded by St Philip Neri in the sixteenth century. They were a loose-knit organization of secular priests joined not by vows but by common interest and fraternal charity. Allowing considerable liberty within the system, they appealed to Newman's spirit of independence and corresponded to his need to live intimately with people of like mind. Pius IX gave him permission to establish Oratories in England and to adapt St Philip's rule for his own time and environment. Frederick Faber, another convert from Anglicanism, established an equally distinguished Oratory in London in April 1849 under Newman's original direction and influence. By this time the forces of Protestantism were beginning to take up what they took to be the challenge.

The establishment of the Roman Catholic hierarchy in 1850 marked the beginning of a vehement no-popery campaign. It was in this year that the Privy Council overruled the decision of the Bishop of Exeter not to institute the Reverend G. C.

Gorham as a vicar in his diocese because his view on baptism
seemed unsound. Many thought this only underlined the
soundness of Newman's judgements, that the Church of England was no more than a puppet of the state. In 1851 another
group of Newman's friends, Archdeacon Manning, James
Hope and Robert Wilberforce, became Catholics.

Of great interest to Newman in his day, and to posterity,
was the Oratorians' concern for education. Over the next few
years Newman worked on his magnificent study, *The Idea of
a University*. For a long time it seemed that the idea might be
realized. The Irish bishops asked him to found a Catholic
University in Dublin, and in May 1852 Newman delivered five
lectures related to the subject in the fair city itself. These
became the nucleus of his essay. The University opened on 3
November 1854 with good prospect of success, but the Irish
bishops were divided among themselves and Archbishop Cullen of Dublin scarcely trusted Newman.

There was plenty to divide the Catholics of Newman's day:
the ultramontanes versus the cisalpines; those who supported
the papal prerogative, which led to the definition of the first
Vatican Council in 1870, as opposed to those who adopted
more insular attitudes; the old Catholics, still blinking in the
catacombs, versus the newly enlightened who felt they could
teach everybody everything. Newman's adversaries of his own
side were to be found less among the 'old Catholics', who were
used to the idea of tempering their distinctive faith with the
tradition of their own country, than among the recent converts
whose zeal and enthusiasm, like Faber's, sometimes outran
discretion. Indeed, after 1855, relations became so strained
between the two Oratories that thereafter it seemed better that
they should pursue their separate ways.

As time went on, the figure of Newman began to emerge and
grow patriarchally; a figure of reason and understanding as
well as faith. Indeed, the rationalists hated him for his faith
just as the emotionalists distrusted him for his reason. But in
the long run no one with any insight could fail to respect him,
and the ecclesiastical politicians had to acknowledge him. Certainly Newman was far ahead of his day in envisaging lay
participation in church institutions. Only five of his thirty-two
professors at Dublin were priests, and he himself wanted a lay
committee to manage finances. Thwarted by Cullen, Newman
resigned his rectorship in November 1858 and returned to the
Birmingham Oratory.

In May 1859 he founded the Oratory School and became
editor of *The Rambler* in succession to Richard Simpson. The

appointment was short-lived. Newman was asked to resign over an article in the July issue 'on consulting the Faithful in Matters of Doctrine'. It was quite orthodox, but capable of unorthodox interpretation. Newman's article was delated to the Congregation of Propaganda for heresy. The affair blew over but it left Newman under a cloud for some years at Rome, and at variance, if not exactly loggerheads, with Manning. It was Cullen who eventually put the record right with the Vatican, so that Rome, in 1867, vindicated him completely.

Meanwhile, Newman could not share the interest of many Catholics, including the Pope himself, in maintaining the temporal power in the form which was then being fought over. By 1864 Newman's influence with all parties had shrunk to negligible proportions. It swayed back on a new tide when he produced an answer to an unfair attack by Charles Kingsley in a review he wrote of J.A. Froude's *History of England*. Kingsley, a professor at Cambridge and tutor to the Prince of Wales, did not scruple to accuse Newman of indifference to truth and truthfulness. It provoked the great *Apologia pro Vita Sua* which was published between April and June 1864 in weekly parts. Many former Anglican friends renewed acquaintance with him, feeling he had vindicated himself.

Newman avoided any personal commitment in the proceedings of the Vatican Council of 1870, and that year published *A Grammar of Assent*. He was far from overjoyed at the definition of papal infallibility. Nevertheless, when in 1874 Gladstone, nettled by a recent political setback, produced a pamphlet to show that Catholics could not be loyal citizens, Newman produced a reply at the end of the same year to refute him. *A Letter addressed to the Duke of Norfolk . . .* had something also to say about Catholic extremists as well as Protestant. This work was well received, not least by Gladstone himself. Newman's dry comment was that 'the rock of St Peter on its summit enjoys a pure and serene atmosphere, but there is a great deal of Roman malaria at the foot of it'.

In 1879, shortly after the accession of Leo XIII, Newman was created Cardinal. He appreciated the compliment but not the pomp attached to his new dignity, and was well content to live on at the Oratory in a palace consisting of one room, overcrowded, over-painted, over-furnished but only with simple things and objects precious for their association rather than themselves. His life continued to be his writing, although by the mid-eighties the stream was already flowing past him to influence the future. Active to the end, he died on 11 August 1890.

Perhaps when the last sub-atomic particle has been found, and the farthest attainable planet colonized, and we have exhausted the possibility of further great discoveries in natural science, we will turn once again to the exploration of the spirit. The future will look for old points of departure for new destinations; for pioneers in the past pointing the way to the future. It is then that Newman may be rediscovered. Not that he has yet been lost.

Joseph Smith

(1805–44)

Among the founders of modern religions Joseph Smith must be given a high place. Although he was only thirty-eight when he was brutally murdered, he had lived long enough to start the Mormons – or the Church of Jesus Christ of Latter-day Saints, as they are properly styled – on their career of almost uninterrupted expansion and prosperity.

At the outset he was no favoured child of fortune. He was born in 1805 at Sharon, Vermont, in the USA, where his father, Joseph Smith, worked a small farm. When he was ten the family moved to Palmyra, in New York State, and four years later they were on the move again, this time to a small place with the imposing name of Manchester. As the years passed they sank deeper into a morass of debts and mortgages, and there was no money to spare for schooling. Young Joseph's education was what he could pick up, and no doubt he read every book he could lay hands on. Long afterwards he wrote, in reply to some accusations of youthful wrong-doing, that 'during this time, as is common to most or all youths, I fell into many vices and follies', but he strongly denied that he had been guilty of 'wronging or injuring any man or society of man'.

He was a young man who saw visions and had spiritual communications. We have this on his own authority, and we may read his account in the opening pages of the *Book of Mormon*, the holy scriptures of the Mormons for which he was so largely responsible. On the night of 21 September 1823 (he tells us) he had 'sought the Lord in fervent prayer' when a brilliant light shone in his room, till it was lighter than at noonday, and at his bedside appeared 'a personage, standing in the air, for his feet did not touch the floor'. The angel proceeded to inform him that

> there was a book deposited, written upon gold plates, giving an account of the former inhabitants of this continent, and the source from whence they sprang . . . Also, that there were two stones in silver bows – and these stones, fastened to a breastplate, constituted what is called the Urim and Thummin – deposited with the plates; and the possession

338

and use of these stones were what constituted *Seers* in ancient or former times; and that God had prepared them for
the purpose of translating the book ...

He was told where the plates were deposited in the ground,
and from the description he had no difficulty in finding the site.
'There indeed did I behold the plates, the Urim and Thummin,
and the breastplate, as stated by the messenger.' Smith would
have taken them out, but he was forbidden to do so by the
angel, as the time for that had not arrived, and would not
arrive until four years had passed. During those four years he
visited the site on each anniversary of the message, until on 22
September 1827,

> the same heavenly messenger delivered them up to me with
> this charge: That I should be responsible for them; that if I
> should let them go carelessly, through any neglect of mine,
> I should be cut off; but that I would use all my endeavours
> to preserve them, until he, the messenger, should call for
> them, they should be protected.

The plates are described as being nearly 8 inches long by 7
inches wide, made of gold a little thinner than ordinary tin,
and bound together by three rings, forming a volume about 6
inches thick. They were engraved with characters, letters or
hieroglyphics of a language which Smith described as 'Reformed Egyptian'. The 'Urim and Thummin' found with them
are said to have been something like ordinary spectacles, and
by their aid Smith set about the work of translating the text
into English.

This was done in the house at Harmony, Pennsylvania,
which Smith's father-in-law had made available, for Smith was
now a married man: his wife was Emma Hale, a pretty,
serious-minded woman of twenty-one, and she was his first
scribe. She never saw the plates: Joseph kept them on the table
carefully covered with a cloth. But she was soon pregnant, and
other scribes had to be enlisted. A blanket was rigged up across
the room; on one side sat Smith staring through his stone at
the plates, while the other scribe took down what he dictated.
When the translation had been completed, Smith agreed to
show the plates to a select few, and at the beginning of the
Book of Mormon there is printed the 'Testimony of Three
Witnesses', of whom two had been scribes, and also the 'Testimony of Eight Witnesses', who bore witness that

> Joseph Smith Junior, the translator of this work, has sworn
> unto us the plates, which have the appearance of gold; and

as many of the leaves as the said Smith has translated we did handle with our hands; and we also saw the engraving thereon, all of which has the appearance of ancient work, and of curious workmanship.

This was the manner in which The *Book of Mormon* was produced, and the first edition (of 5,000 copies) was published at Palmyra, New York, in 1830, the expenses being met by Martin Harris, who believed in Joseph Smith sufficiently to mortgage his farm for the purpose. After the book had been published, the gold plates were 'returned to the messenger' as had been arranged.

The *Book of Mormon* professes to give the history of America from its first settlement by a colony of refugees from among the crowd dispersed by the 'confusion of tongues' at the Tower of Babel down to the first quarter of the fifth century A.D. The original colonists bore the name of Jaredites, and for long they were highly favoured by Heaven; but they degenerated and became so wicked and corrupt that their civilization collapsed in a period of bloody strife. For some hundreds of years the record is almost blank, until about 600 B.C. a man named Lehi, with his wife and four sons, and ten friends, all from Jerusalem, landed on the coast of South America in Chile. While Lehi was alive all went well, but on his death Nephi, his youngest son, was appointed by the Lord to take his place, and this aroused the jealousy of the other brothers. They rebelled, and in consequence the Lord condemned them to have dark skins in future: these Lamanites, as they were called, were the ancestors of the American Indians or Redskins. Between the good Nephites and the bad Lamanites war continued for centuries; then the former likewise fell away from goodness, and the Lord allowed them to be nearly annihilated by their dark-skinned foes in about A.D. 385 in a battle fought at the Hill of Cumorah. Among the handful who escaped the slaughter were Mormon and his son Moroni, the former of whom collected the sixteen books of records that had been kept by successive kings and priests, into one volume, which on his death was supplemented with some personal reminiscences and buried by him in the hill of Cumorah – he having been divinely assured that in due time the book would be discovered by God's chosen prophet. Joseph Smith was that prophet.

Unschooled as he was, Smith was not unlettered; he had not read many books, but he knew his Bible from cover to cover. And only a man who knew his Bible could possibly have composed the *Book of Mormon*. Another book that it seems likely he had read was Ethan Smith's *View of the Hebrews, or the Ten tribes of Israel in America* (published in 1823), in which the view is propounded that the American Indians were descended from the 'lost ten tribes of Israel' who were taken into Babylonian captivity and never returned to Palestine. Some of these Hebrews (Ethan Smith argued) on securing their release crossed the seas to America, where the great burial-mounds that dot the plains of New York and Ohio were their handiwork. Joseph Smith knew those mounds well and had heard the legends about the buried treasure they contained.

Taken together, these things, these hints and suggestions, may well support the view that the material for the *Book of Mormon* lay ready to Joseph Smith's hand. But even so, it was the raw material only: he would have shaped and amplified it, enriched it with his powerful imagination, given colour and texture to the narrative. And there will be plenty even of non-Mormons who will insist on leaving the door ajar for something in the nature of religious inspiration and mystical experience.

Upon its publication, copies of the *Book of Mormon* were hawked round the country by Joseph Smith's agents, with the result that many people were convinced that here was an authentic revelation. On 6 April 1830 what was subsequently called the Church of Jesus Christ of Latter-day Saints was legally organized at Fayette, in Seneca County, New York, and numerous branches were soon established in the adjoining states and also across the border in Canada. Intense opposition was aroused by this success, and in 1831 the 'prophet', as Joseph Smith was now called, directed the migration of the Mormon colonists to Kirtland, in Ohio. Later in the same year a colony migrated from Kirtland to Missouri and established themselves at a place called Independence which had been revealed to the Mormon prophet as the chosen site for the City of Zion.

At both Kirtland and Independence the Mormon settlers throve tremendously, buying land, starting businesses, banks and printing presses, building temples and so on. But in both places they encountered fierce opposition from those who had been there before them and who regarded their religion with abhorrence. Eventually Smith and all his followers, numbering between twelve and fifteen thousand people, were allowed to cross the Mississippi into Illinois, where they formed a fresh settlement near Commerce, in Hancock County.

As before, they were soon going ahead. The land was richly fertile, and on the banks of the Mississippi they built a new

city, to which they gave the name Nauvoo (Hebrew, 'beautiful'). The city was laid out in neat squares, surrounding a
mound on which the Mormon temple was soon rising. Within
a year there were several hundred houses built or building, and
the population numbered some 15,000, many of whom had
come over from Britain, where Mormon missionaries had been
active for some years. A charter was granted, which made
Nauvoo almost independent of the Illinois state government,
and Joseph Smith enjoyed wellnigh dictatorial powers. He
organized a body of troopers, called the Nauvoo Legion, of
which he constituted himself commander with the title of
lieutenant-general, and he was also president of the Mormon
Church, mayor of the city, judge of the municipal court, owner
of the principal store, hotel and steamboats, and a good many
other things. Then in the spring of 1844 he declared himself a
candidate for the presidency of the USA and issued a 'platform' which included a drastic reform of the penal laws and
the abolition of Negro slavery.

All this was not achieved without its giving rise to a great
deal of jealous resentment among the earlier settlers, but
Joseph Smith might perhaps have continued in his successful career if his precept and practice of 'plural marriage' had
not given rise to nation-wide scandal.

When he was pursuing his Biblical studies at Kirtland he
had been greatly impressed by the polygamous relationships
of the Hebrew patriarchs, and he soon persuaded himself that
polygamy had divine sanction. In January 1827 he had married
Emma Hale, and for a quite a time he was able to keep her in
ignorance of his successive 'marriages'. The first of his additional 'wives' is supposed to have been Fannie Alger, an or-
phan girl of seventeen whom his wife had taken into their
house. In the next few years he slowly added to the number of
his brides. Altogether about fifty women are listed as his
'wives', and of these forty were 'sealed' to him – the Mormon
term for marriage – in 1842-44. The youngest of his brides was
fifteen and the oldest nearing sixty.

The prophet's example was followed by many, but not all,
of his immediate followers; and although at first every effort
was made to keep the matter secret, news of it leaked out. At
first Smith took refuge in denials, but on 12 July 1843 he let it
be known that he had received a 'revelation' sanctioning 'plur-
ality of wives'. The non-Mormons in Illinois were highly indignant, and even among the Mormons there were many who
demurred. A disgruntled former intimate mounted a bitter
attack on the prophet, not on this ground only but also because

of his political ambitions; he was chased out of Nauvoo, but got a great deal of support outside. So strong was the storm of opposition that Smith seriously contemplated getting his community on the move again, in search of a haven in the far west.

For the present, however, he was still presenting a bold face; and when some of his most violent attackers launched a rival newspaper, the *Nauvoo Expositor*, in which he was assailed with venomous vigour, he sent his legionaries to destroy the paper's printing-press and offices.

This act of high-handed aggression raised the surrounding country against the Mormons, and Nauvoo was threatened with imminent sacking. Joseph Smith and his elder brother Hyrum, who for years had been his most trusted lieutenant, escaped across the river into Iowa, but returned to Nauvoo when appealed to do so by Joseph's wife and other friends in the city. Here they were arrested under orders issued by Governor Ford, and were charged at Carthage, the county seat, with inciting to riot, in the attack on the *Expositor* office, and treason, in that they were alleged to have conspired to establish an independent state at Nauvoo. They were then imprisoned in Carthage gaol – for their own protection, said Governor Ford – with two friends, John Taylor and Willard Richards, to keep them company.

Meanwhile the mob in Carthage had been gathering; Governor Ford was suspected of being too weak to give the Mormons their deserts, and it was resolved to have resort to the time-honoured custom of lynching. In the afternoon of 27 June 1844 a crowd of 150, all heavily armed, approached the gaol and pushed aside the guards. The most daring of them fired through the door of the prisoners' cell. Hyrum was the first to fall, and next Taylor. Joseph Smith, after emptying his six-shooter into his attackers, tried to escape through the window, but was shot from behind and in front. His body crumpled and fell through the window on to the ground below.

The next day the bodies of Joseph and Hyrum, the 'Mormon Martyrs', were taken back to Nauvoo, and 25,000 of the prophet's followers filed past his coffin in reverence. Then he was buried with his brother in a secret grave. Before long the history of Mormonism proved the truth of the saying, that 'the blood of the martyrs is the seed of the Church'.

Soren Kierkegaard

(1813-55)

Soren Kierkegaard was born in Copenhagen in 1813. His father, Michael Pedersen Kierkegaard, had risen from being a poor shepherd-boy on the heaths of Jutland to prosperity as a wool-merchant, and on his retirement from business some years before, having made a substantial fortune, he bought the big house on the Hytorv (New Market) where his son was born. Soren was the youngest of seven children, and when he was born his father was fifty-six and his mother forty-five.

The word *kierkegaard* in Danish means churchyard or cemetery, and from the beginning there was someting melancholy and morbid in the surroundings and associations of the future philosopher. His father was a patriarchal figure, intensely introspective, gloomy in outlook, severe in his attitude even towards those he loved most dearly, and taking his profoundest pleasure in the most abstruse problems of philosophy. Soren's mother was his father's second wife, and he married her a year after the death of his first, by whom he had had no children. This second wife had been his wife's maidservant, and she gave birth to a daughter four months after their wedding. Seven children were born to them, but by 1835 these were all dead save Soren and his brother Peter Christian, who was older by seven years. Of the five who died none lived longer than thirty-three, and it became the family's superstitious fancy that neither of the surviving sons would reach the age of thirty-four and that the father would outlive them both. The old man accepted this as part of the price being exacted for an act of juvenile blasphemy.

Soren Kierkegaard left no autobiography, but his books are filled with material which has been generally taken as autobiographical. When he was five he was sent to school, and after two years was transferred to the high school – the school of Civic Virtue, as it was quaintly named. As regards his religious upbringing, he was baptized and confirmed in the State Church of Lutheran Protestantism, rigidly orthodox in doctrine and severely practical in its conventional ethic. In 1830, when he was seventeen, he matriculated at Copenhagen University and put his name down among the theology students, as his brother Peter Christian had done some years earlier.

On becoming a university student Kierkegaard enrolled as a volunteer in the Royal Life Guards, but after only three days was discharged as 'unfit for service'. He suffered from a physical disability which is sometimes described as spinal curvature and sometimes more bluntly as hunchback. He himself attributed it to a fall from a tree when he was a small boy. It had the effect of giving an irregularity to his movements, so that, as one friend explained, 'one could never keep to a straight line when walking beside him, but was constantly being pushed against the houses or cellar stairs or over the curb'. When he was gesticulating with his arms or waving his cane about, as he usually did, progress became 'still more like an obstacle race'. It was this disability that gave Kirkegaard the bent-back appearance which is so noticeable in some of the pictures drawn or painted of him.

Kierkegaard was at the university through all the 1830s. To begin with, he found the intellectual atmosphere stimulating, intoxicating even. He had become aware of the perpetual conflict between the aesthetic and ethical, and being a young man just released from parental leading-strings he naturally preferred the first. It was not long before he was neglecting his theological studies, and not much longer before he had decided that the Christianity that he had been taught was not to be reconciled with philosophy and must therefore be rejected. He became quite a young man-about-town, tending to foppishness and as near a dandy as his awkward shape would allow; he absented himself from home, choosing to dine in restaurants where there were cheerful music and good companions and pretty faces; in the evenings he was a frequent visitor to concert-rooms and theatres, and he tried to make himself agreeable to actresses and opera-singers and literary people. And of course, dependent as he was on the allowance that his father made him, he was soon running into debt.

So far we may suppose him to be successful in keeping clear of the more vulgar vices, but there came an occasion – it was probably in May 1836 – when he joined some of his young friends in a drunken spree and was taken to a brothel. In the morning he was filled with disgust, and it was quite a time before he could get it out of his head that as the result of the squalid encounter 'another being might owe its life to him'. Although this fear proved groundless, he could not forget, still less forgive, his lapse into sensuality, and this may well have been the 'secret sin' with which it is known that his conscience was burdened.

Perhaps his feeling of guilt would not have been so intense

and long-lasting if his father (now over eighty and near his end) had not at about this time felt obliged to unbosom himself of those recollections that had weighed down his spirit – his boyish blasphemy, and some discreditable aspects of his sexual relations with his second wife, Soren's mother. The young man was appalled at the revelations. Taken in conjunction with his own 'fall', he came to suspect that there was a strain of sensuality in his family; and such was his revulsion that henceforth the sexual side of life carried with it associations of shame and outrage.

Old Pedersen Kierkegaard died in 1838, and Soren was left very well off. A few weeks after his father's death he published the first of his books, a critical study of Hans Christian Andersen. Already he may have had in mind a literary career, but for the present he went back to his theological studies. In the summer of 1840 he passed his final examination, and then went off on a holiday trip to his father's birthplace in Jutland. He returned in August and forthwith plunged into a love affair, the only love affair of his life – and a very unsatisfactory one it turned out to be.

The girl was Regina Olsen, the youngest daughter of State Councillor Olsen, a rather high-ranking official in the Treasury. He first met her at a friend's house in 1837 when she was fourteen, and for him it was a case of love at first sight. For three years he saw her only occasionally, but as soon as he had completed his university course and had come back from his trip to Jutland he presented himself with all due formality as her wooer. Her father was non-committal, but quite willing to let her follow the instincts of her heart. She was attractive and intelligent and at least one suitor had already put in an appearance. But when Soren asked her for her hand she had not the least difficulty in making up her mind. After a courtship of only a month they were engaged in September 1840 and exchanged rings. And the very next morning Kierkegaard was wishing that her 'yes' had been 'no'.

What had gone wrong? Why this sudden change of heart? A lovers' quarrel, perhaps? Nothing of the kind, it seems; Regina appeared to be perfectly happy in her choice, she was in high spirits – he says that he had never known her to be in such high spirits – and her endearments spoke of her affection warming into passionate love. All the same, a great change had come over their relationship, and the change was in him, and him alone. He had suddenly realized that he was not the marrying sort; he had recalled his 'wildness, lusts, and excesses' (although he hastened to add that 'these were yet perhaps not so heinous in the sight of God'); the thought of a sexual relationship (associated as this had become in his mind with what was nasty and degrading) with a pure young girl, shook him with its inconceivability; and finally, he had become convinced that he had received a divine injunction not to marry.

When he saw Regina again, he was morose and ill at ease, and she was quick to spot the difference. He raised the question of their engagement, and she was aghast at the suggestion that they might have made a mistake. Before long he was asking to be relieved of his vow, and she 'fought like a tigress' to keep him. With tears she implored him not to desert her, and Kierkegaard only obtained his release at length after he had adopted the disreputable tactic of pretending that he had never been in earnest, that he had been trifling with her affections all along. Deeply wounded and humiliated, the girl agreed in August 1841 to accept her ring back.

Kierkegaard had behaved abominably, and to escape the scandal he fled to Berlin, where he busied himself in writing what was to prove his most popular work, *Either/Or: A Fragment of Life*, which was published in 1843. The *either* in the title is the aesthetic way of living and the *or* the ethical, and the contrast is developed with a good deal of personal detail. When the storm had blown over somewhat he returned to Copenhagen, but in church at evensong on Easter Day in April 1843, he happened to catch Regina's eye and she nodded to him in apparently friendly fashion. So she was still thinking of him! All his efforts to prove himself an imposter had gone for nothing! Filled with fright, he went off again to Berlin, and wrote among much else the book called *The Repetition*, the story of a love affair wrapped round in philosophy. It did not end as he intended originally, however, with the 'hero' killing himself because he could no longer live with the thought that his loved one had been rendered desperate by his desertion. Just in time he heard that Regina had becomed engaged to another man! Really, the perfidy of women! If Regina Olsen had married Kierkegaard she must have been unutterably miserable, and she married Fritz Schlegel, a former suitor, who had a good post in the civil service. In 1855 she accompanied her husband to the Danish West Indies, of which he had been appointed governor.

Kierkegaard never got her out of his system. Even after her marriage he followed her around and – since Copenhagen was such a small, close-packed place – met her quite often. He even seems to have had some idea of reaching a sort of platonic relationship with her, but this was, of course, out of the question. Their last meeting was just before her departure for the West Indies; they passed one another in the street, and she said in a low voice, 'God bless thee. May it go well with thee.' Kierkegaard raised his hat.

For a time Kierkegaard played with the idea of becoming a parson, but in the end he decided against it; henceforth he was a writer, a man with a message which he felt bound to proclaim. His literary output was impressive: between forty and fifty titles are listed in the synopsis of his works. He is an exceptionally difficult writer to classify, but in the main, and particularly in his later years, he wrote on religious and ethical subjects, expressing a viewpoint that was peculiarly his own.

Once he would not have hesitated to deny his Christian faith; and although in the maturity of his genius he was an outstanding preacher of the Christian gospel and the Christian ethic, he never returned to the grim theology of his father, and for the Christianity preached and practised by the State Church he had nothing but contempt and bitter hostility. The church of which Bishop Mynster was the primate was, he exclaimed again and again, nothing but a swindle, and the clergy were hirelings, concerned for their places in the Establishment. 'Christendom,' he once wrote, 'is a conspiracy against the Christianity of the New Testament.' What he took upon himself was the restatement of the Christian message, a reaffirmation of the Christian ethic, such as he conceived them to have been in the beginning. The doctrine was formidable, while as for the ethic it was hard and uncompromising, very far removed from the comfortable attitudes of official Christianity. Those who would follow in Christ's footsteps must be prepared to give up all in the process, and it need hardly be said that in his vision one of the first things to be forgone was the expression of human relationships through the medium of sex.

In our own day Kierkegaard is widely accepted as a religious teacher, but he is also recognized as one of the founders of the existentialist philosophy, because of his insistence that all philosophy and all knowledge must be drawn from the facts of human existence.

Among the more important of his later works were: *Stages on Life's Road* (1845), another look at his unhappy love affair; *The Book of Adler* (1847), written round the case of a Danish pastor who had been deposed for claiming divine inspiration in his writing; *The Works of Love* (1847); and *Training in Christianity* (1850). His last production was a periodical, *The Instant*, of which nine numbers appeared in the summer of

1855. Many of his later works were paid for out of his own pocket, and in this way the last of the fortune he had inherited from his father was dissipated. He had just drawn out the final balance at the bank when, on 2 October 1855, he collapsed in the street. He was carried to Frederick's Hospital, where on 11 November he died, apparently from an attack of paralysis. A funeral service was held in the cathedral, at which Kierkegaard's brother delivered the oration; but at the cemetery, where Kierkegaard was buried beside his father, his nephew Henrik Lund protested against the dishonesty of the Church in thus appropriating to itself a man who had so decisively rejected its teaching.

William Booth

(1829–1912)

Britain's most famous general ... Who is most worthy of the title out of the host of bemedalled warriors who march across history's pages? Name after name springs to mind, and indeed the choice is a difficult one. But steadily narrowing it, we may well come to a man whose name never featured in the Army List, who never held the royal commission, never wore a red coat or a khaki, never waved a sword or fired a gun, and at the end of his long day found no grave among the great ones in St Paul's Cathedral. But to millions of people all over the world he was the General, and the Army that he founded and captained through so many years of constant struggle still goes marching on.

William Booth was born on 10 April 1829 in a small terraced house in Sneinton, then a suburb of Nottingham. He came of Derbyshire stock not in any way distinguished. His father Samuel Booth started out in life as a 'nailer', or maker of iron nails, in Belper, but at an early age he moved to Nottingham, where the new lace industry was thriving. He developed his own business of building houses for the industrial workers, and later invested largely in tenement property. His story was concisely summed up by his son. 'My father was a Grab, a Get,' William Booth once said. 'We had been born in poverty. He determined to grow rich; and he did. He grew very rich, because he lived without God and simply worked for money; and when he had lost it all, his heart broke with it, and he died miserably.'

Booth's mother, born Mary Moss, was Samuel Booth's second wife and considerably younger. She was the daughter of a well-to-do farmer, and bore her husband five children, of whom William was the middle one. He drew more than one portrait of her. In one he calls her 'a good mother, so good that I have often said that all I know of her life seemed a striking contradiction of the doctrine of human depravity. From infancy to manhood I lived in her. Home was not home to me without her.'

As a child Booth was sent to a village school, and then to an academy for young gentlemen in Nottingham, until the time came when his father could no longer afford to pay his school fees. In his home there was no one who gave him a helping hand with his school books, and no one told him anything about religion. He was popular with his school-fellows and took the lead in the usual boyish pranks. His prominent nose won him the nickname of 'Wellington', and in the game of 'soldiers', which they played more than any other, he was generally 'the captain'. But his family was going steadily down in the world and in 1842, at the age of thirteen, when his father had gone bankrupt – he died a few months later – William was pushed out into the world to earn his living.

He felt the change exceedingly. He had been at a school for young gentlemen and now, suddenly, he became a pawn-broker's apprentice! To the end of his days he found it difficult to speak of his first job in any detail; always he referred to it as being something 'in trade' or 'business'. Yet he was not ill-treated and it had its advantages. It provided him with an opportunity of 'getting on' in the world, and this was something he was quite capable of doing, since he had inherited his father's business sense. Furthermore, it gave him an insight into the daily life of the poor, often the very poor, which proved of immeasurable value to him in after years.

On his father's death, his mother was left in such poor circumstances that they had to leave the small house in Sneinton and move to Nottingham, where, in one of the poorest quarters, Mrs Booth opened a small shop in which she sold children's toys, needles and cotton, tape, and suchlike household necessaries.

Nottingham in the 1840s was a storm-centre of radicalism. Young Booth was among the great crowd that gave a boisterous welcome to Cobden and Bright, the Anti-Corn Law agitators; and he was a frequent attendant at Chartist meetings. He cheered Feargus O'Connor's fiery oratory when that most popular of the Chartist leaders came to Nottingham, and was quite prepared to shoulder a musket if the cause should come to blows. 'The Chartists are for the poor,' he reasoned, 'and therefore I am for the Chartists.' As he passed along the streets on his way to and from the shop he was deeply affected by the sight of little children, ragged and shoeless, crying for bread.

What might have been Booth's future if he had entered politics is an interesting question, and one that has often been asked; but in fact his heart was never in politics, and in later life he became one of the most hardened conservatives of his generation. His real and abiding interest was in religion. As a matter of course, he had been baptized into the Church of

England, but its services never had much appeal for him. He hungered after something more emotional, more personally demanding and absorbing, and as a youth he became a regular worshipper at Wesley Chapel in Nottingham. He had an instinctive belief in God, but for a time he found it beyond him to make the public confession of faith and all-out surrender to the claims of Christ that was generally expected among the Methodists. Something held him back – the knowledge of a sin that he had committed.

Years afterwards he disclosed the circumstances.

In a boyish trading affair [he said], I had managed to make a profit out of my companions, whilst giving them to understand that what I did was all in the way of a generous fellowship. As a testimonial of their gratitude they had given me a silver pencil-case. Merely to return their gift would have been comparatively easy, but to confess the deception I had practised upon them was a humiliation to which for some days I could not bring myself.

But his guilty conscience nagged him into action.

I remember, as if it were yesterday [his account continues], the spot in the corner of the room under the chapel, the hour, the resolution to end the matter, the rising up and rushing forth, the finding of the young fellow I had chiefly wronged, the acknowledgment of my sin, the return of the pencil-case – the instant rolling away from my heart of the guilty burden, the peace that came in its place, and the going forth to serve my God and my generation from that hour.

This was the way of William Booth's 'conversion', on a never-to-be-forgotten evening in 1844, when he was a youth of fifteen. Immediately afterwards (so he says, although in fact it was a couple of years later) he had a bad attack of fever, which brought him 'to the edge of the River'. When he was slowly recovering he received an invitation from a young companion, Will Sansom, to join him in starting a mission in a slum quarter of the town. As soon as he was out and about again he hurried off to join Sansom, and the two seventeen-year-old evangelists might be seen preaching from a chair at the roadside, singing hymns, reading the Scriptures and visiting the sick.

At nineteen his 'weary years' of apprenticeship came to an end, and for a year he tried to find some employment more congenial than pawnbroking. At last he went to London, and in his autobiography he sums up his first impressions in the one word, 'Loneliness!' The places of worship he found depressing, museums and art galleries and libraries interested him not at all, and he spent days tramping the streets looking for work. Finally he got a job at a pawnbroker's in Walworth, 'where it was work, work, work, morning, noon, and night. I was practically a white slave.' But he somehow managed to continue with his preaching, wherever one of the London chapels could be persuaded to lend him their pulpit. Very often he found the congregations dull and lifeless, but there were some who were favourably impressed with his efforts; and in 1851 a Methodist layman named Rabbits, a prosperous boot-manufacturer, made him an offer of twenty shillings a week to enable him to devote his whole time to mission work. Booth jumped at the offer and at once gave in his notice to his employer, who was very incensed at losing such a good employee as he had proved to be. Three things marked the next day. 'The first day of my freedom was Good Friday. It was also my birthday. Most important of all, on that day I fell over head and ears in love with the precious woman who afterwards became my wife.'

Catherine Mumford was her name – a young woman a few months older than Booth, the daughter of a carriage-builder in Clapham; intelligent, cultured, educated, living with her parents in a middle-class home in Brixton. She was thus considerably above Booth in social status and upbringing, but this 'suburban blue-stocking', as Harold Begbie describes her, was also a 'true child of the dissenting chapel'. She shared to the full Booth's evangelical faith and sternly puritanical outlook, and after she had heard him preach a couple of times they became engaged. Booth by this time had become an itinerant preacher on the roll of the Methodist New Connection and his duties took him to all parts of the country. For several years they saw each other but seldom, but they kept in touch by correspondence. In June 1855, when they were both twenty-six, Catherine Mumford and William Booth were married at a chapel in Stockwell; and after a week's honeymoon in the Isle of Wight they set off together on a preaching tour of Guernsey. Their first child – William Bramwell, who in due time became the successor of his father as General of the Salvation Army – was born in 1856.

For a number of years Booth worked with the Methodists, at first as a lay preacher and then as a minister at Brighouse and Gateshead. But he was uncomfortable in a settled pastorate. His congregations were mostly composed of 'respectable people', and more and more he felt drawn to those who were far otherwise, the poor and destitute, the vicious, those who had fallen into evil ways and criminal courses. His preaching tended to be violent, shocking to the conventional-minded, and his theology was forthrightly crude and uncompromising. For those who made a public confession of Christ as the one and only Saviour – Heaven; for those who, for whatever reason, remained outside the fold – Hell, and a very real Hell at that, a place of horrible torments that would last for ever.

His was indeed a grim, a terrifying gospel – but it was inspired not by hate or disgust but by the sincerest and deepest pity for those whom he was firmly persuaded were heading for eternal damnation. And this pity went hand in hand with a profoundly exercised social conscience.

There came a time when he was asked by the Church authorities – at the Conference of 1861, held at Newcastle – to compromise, to 'go slow' in his revivalist teaching and methods. 'Never!' he shouted to the astonished platform and, waving his hat in farewell, strode out of the chapel, embraced his wife at the foot of the gallery stairs and went off with her to face a very uncertain future.

Never again was he to place his neck in a ministerial collar. He was an independent missioner, and at first things were hard. After a campaign in Cornwall that for revivalistic scenes recalled the visits of John Wesley a century before, he established himself in July 1865 in the East End of London, where a former drinking-saloon was converted into his headquarters. His mission was named, to begin with, the East London Christian Revival Society, and he himself was the General Superintendent. When the work extended beyond London the name became the Christian Mission, and at Christmas 1878 this gave place to the Salvation Army and Booth assumed the title – and dictatorial powers – of 'the General'. The year following the first issue of *The War Cry* was published, and the first Salvation Army band blared and boomed.

For years 'the Army' met with fierce hostility, and 'the General' was pelted with mud and hooted, and what was worse, perhaps, laughed at and ridiculed. But Booth kept on his way, beating his showman's drum, insisting that 'the Devil should not have the best tunes', fanatical for righteousness, shattering the somnolence of Victorian orthodoxy. Thousands upon thousands were 'converted' – drunkards, besotted gamblers, wife-beaters, child-pursuers, pimps and prostitutes, men and women who were so low as to be quite beyond the reach of church or chapel.

Booth had his faults, plenty of them; he was dogmatic in the extreme, largely ignorant, indifferent to culture and learning and, above all, intensely autocratic. No 'general' could ever have demanded more unhesitating obedience – and he got it, although from time to time 'the Army' was torn by dissension and some of his own family were among the rebels. But it must be allowed that he displayed superb powers of generalship, and under his leadership the Salvation Army invaded almost every country of the world. Only once did his spirit wilt, when in 1890 his wife, who by her labours had well earned the title of 'Mother of the Salvation Army', died of cancer after months of agonizing pain.

As a national figure Booth's acceptance may be dated from the publication in 1890 of his book *In Darkest England and the Way Out*, in which he outlined plans for dealing with the vast problems of social distress and demoralization. He asked for £100,000 within a year – and he got it. Of course he was unable to do all he had schemed to do, but he showed the way and (however much he would have disliked some of its features) he may be justly hailed as a pioneer of the welfare state.

In his latter decades the gaunt old figure with the patriarchal beard, the still passionate voice and the magnetic personality became one of the best-known, and one of the best-loved, men of his day and generation. The great ones of the earth – among them King Edward and Queen Alexandra – delighted to do him honour; governments at home and abroad gladly furthered his work of social redemption. At length, half blind and weighed down by his eighty-three years, he died. Outside the Army's headquarters in London's Queen Victoria Street there appeared on 20 April 1912 the notice 'General Booth has laid down his sword'. Messages of grief poured in from all parts of the world; and as the body of the old warrior was borne through the London streets to his grave at Abney Park, millions lined the route to pay a last tribute of affection.

Charles Haddon Spurgeon

(1834–92)

Charles Haddon Spurgeon was born on 19 June 1834 at Kelvedon in Essex; he was one of seventeen children of an Independent or, as we should say, Congregational preacher and Eliza Jarvis, a god-fearing wife and mother who held religious household meetings for her children every Sunday evening. Six years of Charles's early childhood were spent with his grandparents. His grandfather, whom he greatly loved, was minister at Stambourne Meeting House and a preacher of wide local repute. At Stambourne Manse the child became acquainted with *Pilgrim's Progress* and other Puritan classics, and when he was still only ten he was earnestly spoken with about the state of his soul at six o'clock one morning by Richard Knill, a visiting missionary from India.

In short, Spurgeon's upbringing took place in surroundings where heaven, hell and the Day of Judgment were regarded as literal and imminent realities. His mother once told her children that she would witness against them at the Last Assize if they persisted in their sins, and Charles repeated to himself again and again, 'If God does not send me to hell, then he ought to do it.' He was indeed 'a very sinful child', capable of such atrocities as defying his father at chapel by singing the last line of every verse twice instead of once. At the age of fifteen he was busy writing a book of 295 pages called *Antichrist and her Brood, or, Popery Unmasked* as a competition entry.

Spurgeon's inheritance of Calvinistic Puritanism, like all varieties of Protestantism, taught that no one could win God's approval by religious or moral activities: in order to gain eternal life the one thing necessary was not faith in one's own efforts, but faith in a crucified Christ – 'Nothing in my hand I bring, Simply to this cross I cling.' This religious tradition differed, however, from other forms of Protestantism, such as Methodism, by strongly emphasizing that such faith could not be obtained by an act of the will; rather it was reserved for those to whom the Almighty's inscrutable decree chose to give it. One Sunday morning, instead of visiting his usual place of worship, Spurgeon was caught in a snowstorm and so driven into the Primitive Wesleyan Chapel in Artillery Street, Colchester, where the preacher addressed the tiny congregation on the text, 'Look unto me and be ye saved all the ends of the earth.' After speaking for ten minutes he addressed Spurgeon directly. 'Young man,' he said, 'you look very miserable. You always will be miserable in this world and the next if you don't obey my text.' That morning Spurgeon found faith in Christ and experienced the sovereign love of God: 'I felt I could dance all the way home'. The snowstorm had been no chance event, but part of the Almighty's plan for Spurgeon's salvation. The date, 6 January 1850, was decisive for his future.

Spurgeon's study of the New Testament and, ironically enough, of the Church of England's catechism, convinced him of the necessity of adult baptism, and in April he was baptized in the river at Isleham; thus he was lost to the Congregationalism of his forefathers and entered into the ranks of the Baptists. In August he moved to Cambridge to finish his education with a family friend who was a schoolmaster, and he taught in the Sunday School of St Andrew's Street Baptist Church. He delivered his first sermon in the nearby village of Teversham, though he was wholly unprepared to do so, since he supposed that the friend who accompanied him was due to preach. He made such an impression that he was soon in great demand for chapel pulpits; he became well enough known for the Mayor of Cambridge to dispute with him on the subject of whether angels possessed pockets; and from 1851 to 1855 he was resident preacher at Waterbeach for £45 a year.

One of Spurgeon's Cambridge audiences included a Mr Thomas Olney, deacon of New Park Street Chapel, one of London's leading Baptist churches, though at that time in a run-down state and without a pastor. Olney enthusiastically persuaded his fellow-deacons to invite Spurgeon to preach before their dwindling congregation. The nineteen-year-old country lad, with his white-spotted blue handkerchief, got an inhospitable reception, but the sceptics soon revised their opinions of him once they had heard him preach. The evening congregation happened to include Miss Susanna Thompson, whom he married in 1856. In April 1853 Spurgeon was offered the pastorate of New Park Street, and so not yet twenty, without formal theological training, and with no experience of London life, began his work at this important chapel.

Although the chapel had seats for 1,200 it had to be enlarged in 1855. But it was still too small, and in 1856 it was resolved to build an entirely new chapel, which was to be 'the largest in the world'. During the periods of reconstruction Spurgeon preached in Exeter Hall, in the fields at Hackney and in the Surrey Music Hall. Traffic came to a standstill. Crowds of 20,000 were reported, half of them unable to get in. On the first

night of the Surrey Music Hall services word went round that
the place was on fire, and in the following panic seven persons
were killed and twenty-eight badly injured. Spurgeon fainted
and was carried out like a corpse. His friends regarded the
uproar as the result of a malicious hoax, but it ensured Spurgeon's fame – or notoriety – all over London.

The press was often hostile: 'This hiring of places of amusement for Sunday preaching is a novelty. It looks as if religion
were at its last shift.' Bishop Samuel Wilberforce of Oxford
was amusingly contemptuous; when asked if the Established
Church envied the Nonconformists their Spurgeon he replied,
'Thou shalt not covet thy neighbour's ass.' And even admiration could be double-edged; one listener wrote: 'He preached
for about three-quarters of an hour, and to judge by the use of
handkerchiefs and audible sobs, with great effect.'

Nevertheless the crowds still came. There was a popular
London song, 'Oh my sweet, my rosy Spurgeon'. A cartoon
was published portraying Spurgeon as the driver of a railway
engine called the 'Fast Train' with a bishop at the reins of a
carriage and pair called 'The Slow Coach'. In 1857 *The Times*
came out in Spurgeon's favour: in an article which made the
Church of England look incredibly silly, it suggested to the
Archbishop of Canterbury that 'this heretical Calvinist and
Baptist, who is able to draw 10,000 souls after him' should
preach in St Paul's or Westminster Abbey:

> at any rate, if he preached in Westminster Abbey, we shall
> not have a repetition of the disgraceful practice now com-
> mon in that church of having the sermon before the anthem,
> in order that those who would quit church when the sermon
> begins may be forced to stay it out for the sake of the music
> which follows.

The services in Surrey Music Hall ended in December 1859,
since the proprietors wanted the building for sabbath concerts.
It was noted with gratification that they went bankrupt shortly
afterwards. Spurgeon's new chapel, the Metropolitan Tabernacle, was opened with a three-week feast of services in 1861.
It had seating for nearly 5,000, though it appears to have held
8,000 on occasion. Admission was by ticket, the general public
being permitted to rush into the building five minutes before
service time. The chapel was built in 'the Grecian style' on the
rather curious grounds that a Baptist should be Greek not
Gothic, since Greek is 'the sacred tongue', that is, the language
of the New Testament. It was the centre of Spurgeon's work
until his death, though he travelled to Scotland and Ireland,

preached from Calvin's pulpit in Geneva, and met the Queen of the Netherlands. His publications flooded the market. They included a massive seven-volume commentary on the Psalms and sixty-three books of sermons. A Latin-American Jesuit read every sermon by Spurgeon that he could get hold of, and the Archimandrite of Moscow authorized a selection for use in the Russian Orthodox Church.

Spurgeon's message was also spread across the globe by preachers trained in his Pastors' College. The College began in a small way with one student, Thomas Medhurst, in 1855. The earliest classes were held in rooms under the Tabernacle, and a proper building was not opened until 1874. However, as early as 1866 the College trained one-third of all Baptist preachers in England. Spurgeon called it 'my firstborn and well-beloved', and it sent men as far as the Falklands and South Africa.

Spurgeon's concern with souls did not blind him to bodily needs: 'What is the use of the best gospel sermon when a man is starving?' On the strength of a surprise legacy of £20,000 he founded a boys orphanage which opened in 1869; a girls wing was added ten years later. Like most religious social reformers he believed in philanthrophy rather than social revolution. On the other hand he was not afraid to speak out on social and political issues. He condemned war; he denounced the opium traffic; he attacked the slavery system of the United States, much to the distress of his American sermon-salesmen; he voted Liberal and told everybody so. Nevertheless, his attitude on such issues was essentially ambiguous; the ambiguity sprang from a conflict between his genuine desire for social improvement on the one hand, and on the other his rooted conviction that all improvements were useless unless people believed the gospel. 'Where the grace of God is put in the hearts of men, then will come an end to slavery, tyranny, war and class legislation.' Society cannot change until individuals are changed.

Spurgeon probably foresaw that Nonconformity would lose the allegiance of the working classes. He did his best to stave off their defection. His impact on the urban poor was greater than most preachers'. Bricklayers and carpenters worshipped at his Tabernacle. He addressed gatherings of coalmen. In 1877 he enthralled a grateful congregation of clerks employed in a biscuit factory. But he realized that most of the artisans who attended his church were not Londoners born – they were immigrants from the provinces. He knew of street after street from which nobody went to Sunday service. 'London will never be reached by ministers – the people will not come to hear them.'

His perceptive mind also spotted something else: that such fundamental Puritan doctrines as the literal accuracy of Genesis and the everlasting agonies of the damned were being undermined, not only by the scepticism of unbelievers but by scepticism inside the Baptist Union itself. In 1887 he argued in defence of traditional dogma by publishing two articles called 'The Down-Grade' – 'We are going downhill at breakneck speed.' Attempts at conciliation failed, and the controversy ended with Spurgeon leaving the Baptist Union. Twenty years earlier he had quitted the Evangelical Alliance following a paper war over Baptism. If he felt sure of his ground he could not compromise.

The fact is that Spurgeon never really debated; he asserted. He was inadequate for reasoned argument and he knew it: 'The logical faculty in me is too small.' But though this deficiency made him weak in controversy, it gave strength to his preaching. The force of his appeal rested on the annunciation of great certainties in simple English, livened by humour and clarified by illustration. He smiled the smile of one who was sure of ultimate victory. 'We must talk of such things as sin and death and judgment and heaven and hell and Christ and his blood. Yes, the blood. We must have that, and disgust the hypocrites till they go their way.' It was after all a matter of life and death. 'In your office,' he told the London City Missioners, 'earnestness is above all things necessary.' It is a surprise to learn that he enjoyed smoking a cigar 'to the glory of God', though he disapproved strongly of the theatre.

There is no doubt that Spurgeon was a kind of genius and, by common consent, the greatest of all the great Nonconformist preachers of the nineteenth century. In February 1892 some 60,000 persons filed past to do homage at his coffin as his body lay in the Metropolitan Tabernacle. At his birth the Baptist Dissenters were hardly out of the cold religious twilight of the eighteenth century; at his death thousands of little brick chapels marched across the towns and countryside of England. For this advance Spurgeon himself had provided much of the motivation, the means and the manpower. Bishop Randall Davidson of Rochester, later to be Archbishop of Canterbury, described him as a stalwart champion of Christianity, a great preacher and a good man, and also pronounced a benediction at his funeral in Norwood cemetery: he sleeps there now awaiting the Resurrection and the Day of Judgment. 'At the Judgment Bar,' Spurgeon had declared, 'how shall we hear it said, I sent you to perishing sinners, and you sought not to save them? Fetch them in! Gather them in! Drive on! Farewell!'

St Bernadette

(1844–79)

Sir Arthur Conan Doyle, former Catholic and ardent spokesman for spiritualism, made Sherlock Holmes say, 'It is an old maxim of mine that when you have excluded the impossible, whatever remains, however improbable, must be the truth.'

As a principle of detection or research, it is admirable and frequently applicable; but not in the case of Bernadette. Even if one cannot believe with Catholics and many others, and rejects as impossible that what she saw in the grotto near Lourdes was indeed the Virgin Mary, the remaining field of the improbable is too vast to be narrowed to anything so precise as the truth. We had better stick to telling Bernadette's story, leaving readers to interpret it according to their own beliefs and prejudices.

She was born in 1844, the daughter of a miller François Soubirous and his wife Louise Castérot, living at the foot of the Pyrenees which divide south-western France from Spain. She was frail from infancy, puny and asthmatic, but fun-loving and as energetic as her constitution would allow, especially when it came to trying to help her harassed mother. For life was increasingly harassing to the Soubirous. Their fortunes had been going down year by year as milling failed to pay and their small capital dwindled. Eventually when Bernadette, the eldest of the four children surviving out of seven, was twelve, they had to leave their country mill and move their few belongings into one slum room in Lourdes. François had no work. He and the children would range the town and neighbouring country, looking for sticks for a fire and rags and bones to sell for the few sous that would buy them bread and the makings of broth.

Bernadette went to school in Lourdes. On Thursday, 11 February 1858, a day's holiday was observed; it was a day that was to prove extraordinary.

Bernadette had a cold, so was ordered to stay indoors while her sister Toinette and a friend went out with a basket to look for kindling. She begged successfully to be allowed to go with them and they went off into the country to the south of the town. It was cold, but the sun shone hazily and the air was quite still. Their way took them along a forest track to a meadow with poplar trees and as many suitable twigs as they would be able to carry. A mill stream bordered part of the field. Across it was an overhanging rock mass, known as Massabielle, topped by an ancient, straggling rose bush. Thousands of years before a grotto had been naturally gouged into the rock. Toinette and the other girl waded the shallow stream and ran off amongst the trees, leaving Bernadette to wonder whether she dared follow, at the risk of making her cold worse. She had never been to the grotto, which the stream separated from her by only a few feet, and a child's curiosity drew her to it.

While she was standing uncertainly, the midday Angelus sounded from Lourdes. Almost simultaneously, Bernadette heard something else: a sound like the rushing of wind from the mountains; yet she felt nothing and noticed that the trees were quite still. But the undergrowth about the grotto stirred visibly as a brilliant light started to shine from the cave. As the child stared, the light resolved into the form of a girl of about her own height. She was young, very pale and radiantly beautiful, with large blue eyes and a delightful smile. She wore a white robe of some material too exquisite for Bernadette to recognize and a blue sash, had golden roses on her feet, and carried a white and gold rosary.

The figure extended its arms as if to welcome Bernadette. All she could do, instinctively, was to take out her rosary, fall to her knees and pray, her eyes never leaving the vision. She saw it begin to tell its own beads, its lips moving soundlessly, until, seeming to have reached the end of the prayer, it bowed, smiled again, then vanished.

Bernadette remained kneeling beside the stream, no longer afraid as at first, but overwhelmed. She did not hear the other girls return, nor feel the pebble which one of them threw at her. When they came close and saw how still and pale and staring she was, they were alarmed; but she suddenly came out of her fixation and without hesitation crossed the stream to them.

On the way home Bernadette told the others what she had seen, requesting her sister not to tell their mother, who would be angry with her for making up so fanciful a tale. But Toinette did tell, and Bernadette's parents duly scolded her. Toinette's friend, too, blurted out the story to all her friends. Next day in school, the teacher, a nun, persuaded Bernadette to tell her the story in detail. So the story began to gain currency, and after Sunday Mass Bernadette was pressed by a little crowd of friends to go with them to the grotto and see if anything further would happen. They went; and although the others saw nothing there they witnessed a remarkable change come over Bernadette herself after she had cried out, kneeling and holding her rosary, that the lady had again appeared. Her face turned deathly pale, her upward-looking eyes, grown large and incredibly beautiful, seemed transfixed on something invisible to the other girls, and a tear ran down each cheek.

She stayed so still for so long that one or two of the more frightened girls cried out that she had died. Someone touched her: she took no notice. They shook her: she paid no attention to them. Thoroughly frightened, they decided they had better carry her home. To their astonishment and fright, they could not even lift her. It took some adults, anxiously summoned from the town, to get her away. Her mother, frantic and uncomprehending, scolded her. Bernadette, pale but calm, told quietly of what she had seen, and by nightfall the news was all round Lourdes and its district.

Three days later a rich woman called at the Soubirous slum to ask permission to go with Bernadette to the grotto. Very early on the cold morning of 18 February the woman, her dressmaker and Bernadette went back to Massabielle. It was still dark when they got there. The woman lit a blessed candle, the first ever to flicker where untold numbers have since been placed. They all knelt, holding their rosaries. Suddenly Bernadette indicated that the vision had again appeared to her. She did not go off into the so-called state of ecstasy this time, and the other women, who could see nothing were able to speak to her, giving her writing materials and telling her to get the 'lady' to write down her name. Bernadette obeyed, going further into the grotto, but, not surprisingly, the vision's response to the absurd request was a laugh. Then, for the first time, she spoke, though Bernadette alone could hear her. In a voice of great delicacy, and using the Lourdes dialect, she asked the child to do her the favour of returning to the grotto every day for fifteen days. Bernadette answered that, with her parents' permission, she would. Then the lady added, 'I do not promise to make you happy in this world, but in the next' – and vanished.

Bernadette kept her promise, but it was not an easy task. Increasing numbers of people began to accompany her to the grotto. Many were devout, aching to share the child's vision. Some were mockers, ready to jeer at the others' gullibility. Some were the idly curious. A few, in uniform, were police; for if the clergy were carefully refraining from becoming involved, the authorities were not. There seemed to be a danger of disorders breaking out between the believers and the sceptical.

Soon after seeing her sixth vision, Bernadette was brought before the local prosecutor, who asked her questions framed to discover whether the whole affair might be a money-making deception planned by her desperately poor parents. Bernadette's ingenuous answers and the simplicity of her nature convinced him otherwise. He sent her home and wrote a puzzled report.

But that same day Bernadette was catechized by another awesome functionary, the local police chief, in the presence of witnesses. This was a tougher interview, full of traps, tricks and accusations; yet the child remained calm, kept to every detail of her story and insisted in the face of a threat of being sent to prison that she must obey 'that one' (*aquéro*, as she always named her vision in the local patois) and continue to go to the grotto. Unable to break her down, the policeman dismissed her, but gave orders for a guard to be mounted on the grotto.

Bernadette continued to visit the grotto, undeterred by the presence of the police and crowds. Sometimes she saw her vision; sometimes she did not. No one else saw anything, but the moving state of ecstasy into which the ignorant child fell in their presence was enough to convince many that they were in the presence of something miraculous. Then, late in February, a more tangible event occurred. According to Bernadette's own account, 'that one' told her to drink at the spring and wash herself there. When Bernadette moved obediently towards the stream the lady indicated another spot in the rock itself where there lay a little muddy water. Hesitantly, the child tried to drink some, but could not. She scraped at the place, and at length there began to trickle out some beautifully clear water, evidently from an underground spring. Again in obedience to her vision, she plucked some of the herb growing in the rock and tried to eat it. Having seen her try to drink mud and now to eat an uninviting herb, which she promptly spat out, some of the crowd jeered; but they had just witnessed the discovery of the healing spring which has since drawn millions of people to that spot.

The first healing by the water took place a few days later. A woman with an injured hand went to the grotto with her children and several other witnesses and plunged the hand into the new fount, praying hard. When she withdrew it the fingers that had been deformed and pronounced incurable by her doctor were normal again and free of pain.

The time had arrived when the clergy could remain aloof no longer. The *curé* of Lourdes, Abbé Peyramale, an essentially kindly man, though dauntingly authoritarian, subjected Bernadette to as withering an examination as any she had had from the police. He too failed to shake her story, and was himself somewhat shaken to be quietly told that 'that one' had instructed Bernadette to request the building of a chapel at the grotto. He demanded the vision's name: Bernadette could not tell him. He told her to go and find out.

Bernadette's account is that she passed on this challenge to her vision: the lady merely smiled.

Early in March Bernadette made the last of the fifteen promised visits to the grotto. Then something seemed to have left her. For several weeks the call to go there had been compelling within her: now she felt it no longer. She became ill with her accustomed asthma and stayed in bed. A local newspaper named another form of sickness – catalepsy, a disease characterized by a state of trance; but doctors who examined Bernadette not long afterwards, when the 'catalepsy' had begun to manifest itself again, found that apart from chronic asthma she was a perfectly normal child, especially mentally.

For twenty days she received no call to the grotto. It troubled her greatly. Crowds, from increasingly far afield, continued to go to the place, and there were reports of further healing 'miracles'. Then, on 25 March, before dawn, Bernadette felt herself called again. She hurried to the grotto and found 'that one' apparently waiting for her. Once more Bernadette asked for a name. The reply, she reported afterwards, came at length: 'I am the Immaculate Conception.'

Bernadette hurried to the *curé* to tell him that the lady had given her name. Incredulous, he questioned her keenly. The case and the medical report on Bernadette were passed to the Bishop of Tarbes and Lourdes, who had been maintaining a watchful silence. Now he would go so far as to admit that he could not rule out the possibility that something supernormal was afoot.

In June Bernadette was at last able to make her long-desired first Communion. Then in July she saw the vision for the eighteenth and last time. At the end of the month the bishop announced that a commission of clerics, scientists and even geologists would sit in enquiry into the so-far inexplicable sequence of events. The investigation lasted nearly four years. When it ended the bishop made the unreserved declaration, 'We are convinced that the apparition is supernatural and divine . . . Rejoice, inhabitants of the town of Lourdes!'

For whatever reason, the inhabitants of Lourdes have been rejoicing ever since, for their little town, its nearby grotto and the chapel that was soon built, as 'that one' had commanded, has for over a century been a kind of Mecca for Catholics from around the world and for many others who have gone there out of interest or curiosity, or with a last hope of finding a cure for the 'incurable'. Whatever it was that Bernadette saw, or thought she saw, her vision began something which has proved beneficial to many more than one small peasant girl who believed she had been in the presence of something wondrous.

The special trains from Bordeaux to Lourdes which have since carried such multitudes of pilgrims began running in April 1866. Less than three months afterwards Bernadette left the town for good. She had entered a religious order and was given the new name Sister Marie Bernard.

'That one' had intimated that she could expect no great happiness in this world. In material and physical terms, the prophecy was correct. Bernadette suffered a good deal at the hands of superiors, no doubt jealous of her experience. Her faith weakened at one stage – understandably enough, since spectacular witness had given way to the monotonous and seemingly unrewarded routine of religious discipline. She regained it, but the period of doubt was made no easier by her deteriorating health. Severe illness began to possess her. There came no miraculous cure for the girl who had led so many others to a place of curing. She died on 16 April 1879, aged thirty-five.

In 1908 an enquiry into the possibility of her beatification began and her coffin was opened. Her body was found to be completely incorrupt. In 1933 Pope Pius XI named her Saint Bernadette.

Francis Place

(1771-1854)

Among the national archives in the British Museum are some hundreds of volumes in which are bound letters and other literary leavings of a London tailor, together with a great number of newspaper cuttings, pamphlets, manifestos and other printed papers which he collected in the course of a long life and thought worthy of preservation in the interests of posterity.

The tailor's name was Francis Place, and he was in his prime in the earlier years of the last century. By all accounts he was an excellent tailor – it might have been hard to find a better for a well-fitting coat or pair of buckskin breeches – and he did a thriving business at his shop at Charing Cross. But he was something more than a tailor, something more and very different.

Francis Place was a Londoner, born on 3 November 1771 on the premises in Vinegar Yard, off Drury Lane, in which his father Simon Place, a bailiff of the Marshalsea Court, kept a 'sponging-house', a temporary lodging for arrested debtors awaiting trial. As might be expected from his occupation, Simon Place was a ruffianly fellow, intent on squeezing as much as he could out of the unfortunates and worse committed to his charge. According to his son,

> he was a resolute, daring, straightforward sort of a man, governed almost wholly by his passions and animal sensations, both of which were very strong ... He never spoke to any of his children in the way of conversation; the boys never ventured to ask him a question, since the only answer which could be anticipated was a blow.

He was also an inveterate gambler, and more than once the home was broken up because he had lost practically his all in the state lotteries. Then he would absent himself for months at a time, while his poor wife was left to keep the family on the pittance she might earn by needlework.

When old enough Francis went to some sort of school but he got most of his education in the streets and alleys of Drury Lane, one of the most disreputable areas in the metropolis. He was a leader in the boys' gangs, took his part in many a squalid scuffle, mixed on the easiest terms with criminals, street-women and vagabonds. He had the makings and the opportunities of what today we would style a juvenile delinquent, and he might well have turned to crime and met a criminal's fate if he had not been taken in hand by a kindly schoolmaster, who lent him books to read and gave him a lot of good advice which he was sensible enough to heed.

A few months before he was fourteen his father took him into the inn parlour – he had given up the sponging-house some years before and was now keeping the King's Arms public-house in Arundel Street, Strand – and offered him to anyone who would be prepared to take him off his hands. The successful bid was made by a breeches-maker, and 'I was sent the very next morning on liking for a month to learn the art and mystery of leather-breeches making.'

After four years he was a fully qualified journeyman breeches-maker; and in March 1791, when he was nineteen, he married Elizabeth Cladd, a girl who was not quite seventeen, and they went to live in one room in a court off the Strand. Their combined earnings were under 17 shillings a week, and after paying 3s. 6d. rent and 1s. 6d. for coals and candles they were left with only 12s. a week for clothes and everything else.

As the trade of making leather-breeches was in such a poor way, Place turned his hand to making stuff breeches, for which there was a bigger demand. Several master tailors gave him work to do at home and he was doing fairly well until in the spring of 1793, soon after the birth of their first child, he became involved in a strike called by the Breeches-makers Benefit Society and was sacked. Although he had had no part in starting the strike, Place joined the strike committee and by good management helped to make the strike funds spin out for four months. Then the strike collapsed. Most of the men drifted back to employment, but Place was a marked man and could not get a job anywhere. For eight months (he tells us)

> we suffered every kind of privation consequent on want of employment and food and fire. As long as we had anything which could be pawned, we did not suffer much from actual hunger, but after everything had been pawned 'but what we stood upright in', we suffered from actual hunger.

To add to their distress, their baby died of smallpox soon after the strike began; during the child's illness they lived and slept in the one small room that was their home.

He was able to borrow a few books for a trifle from a

bookshop in Covent Garden – this was long before there were public libraries – and their landlady lent him volumes from the chambers of the lawyer in the Temple she 'did for'. He tackled Adam Smith and Locke and Hume's *Essays* (which, with Thomas Paine's *Age of Reason*, made him something of an unbeliever), and while he was out of work he taught himself the rudiments of algebra and geometry.

So the months passed, and the dauntless pair continued their struggle to survive. They might have gone under if their landlady had not discovered their plight and forced bread, soup, coal and candles upon them. Place was just about to accept the post of overseer of the parish scavengers at 18 shillings a week when one of his former employers sent for him. He feared a trap and his wife went in his stead. 'In a short time she returned, and let fall from her apron as much work for me as she could bring away. She was unable to speak until she was relieved by a flood of tears.'

For some time husband and wife worked sixteen hours a day, sometimes eighteen, Sundays and all. 'I never went out of the house for many weeks, and could not find time for a month to shave myself. We turned out of bed to work, and turned from our work to bed again.' As soon as they could they repaid their debt to their landlady and then moved to a better room. They bought clothes, bedding, a good bedstead 'and many other things which made us comfortable'. They had never been so well off, and Place was even able to spare something to help his mother, his father having decamped again.

But even now it was not plain sailing. Before long Place was out of work again. He then reorganized the Breeches-makers Society under the guise of a sick club (thus evading the ban on trade unions), became its secretary at a tiny salary and obtained without a strike the advance in wages which the strike a year or two before had been unable to secure. This small success won him favourable notice among the politically conscious workers, and he was given a seat on the committee of the London Corresponding Society and sometimes acted as chairman. The society's programme included such radical proposals as manhood suffrage, annual Parliaments, and payment of MPs, but before long Pitt's government clamped down on all such activities as being seditious. The society collapsed in 1798 but Place had left it the year before, partly because he had formed a very poor notion of his colleagues' ability but more because he had determined upon a complete change of his way of life. The dreadful experience of being unemployed had left its mark. Never again should such a thing happen to him and his. There was no future in journeyman tailoring. He would put himself beyond the reach of a master's tyranny by becoming a master himself.

To begin with, he set up as a middleman in drapery and dress goods, but in the spring of 1799 he entered into partnership with a fellow workman nearly as poor as himself and opened a tailor's shop at 29 Charing Cross. The shop was stocked entirely on credit, and the two partners had only 1s. 10d. in the till when they opened for business. They worked tremendously hard, however, and soon they were doing a fine trade. Then a terrible thing happened. Place's partner, having obtained some financial backing, got control of the business and Place was turned out into the street. 'This was the bitterest day of my life,' he records; while Mrs Place never recovered from the shock and until the end of her days could not get the prospect of ultimate ruin out of her head.

But now Place once again showed the sort of man he was. With obstinate courage he set about starting afresh but this time on his own. His good name and business connections stood him in excellent stead. Offers of credit poured in and on 8 April 1801 – only three months after his ejection from the first shop – he opened a better one at 16 Charing Cross, only a few doors away. With solid pride he records that it had plate-glass windows, the largest and perhaps the first ever to be seen in London.

Then for a number of years he was completely absorbed in his business. 'I never lost a minute of time,' he records; 'never spent a shilling, never once entertained any company. The only things I bought were books, and not many of them.' Often he was dispirited and disgusted. To be a really good tailor, 'a man should be either a philosopher or a mean cringing slave. He who is neither the one nor the other will never be anything but a little master, and will probably end in debt.'

Three things he kept constantly in mind:

> The first, and far the most important, was to get money, and yet to avoid entertaining a mercenary, money-getting spirit; to get money as a means to an end, and not for its own sake. The second was to take care that the contumelious treatment I had to endure should not make me a sneaking wretch from principle to those above me, a tyrant to those below me. The third was to beware of presumption, that I did not become arrogant ...

One thing he was very careful about: never to allow any of his ordinary customers to penetrate into the room behind the shop in which he kept his library. It would never do to let them know that the 'fellow' who took their measurements for a suit not only collected books but knew quite a lot of what was inside them. They would have considered that 'an abominable offence in a tailor, if not a crime'.

As his bank balance grew, however, he began to assert his independence; he enlarged his circle of friends, so that it included such men as Jeremy Bentham the Utilitarian philosopher, Sir Samuel Romilly the penal reformer, and Sir Francis Burdett the radical politician, and he also ventured to play an increasing part in public affairs. As early as 1807 he was largely instrumental in securing the return of Burdett as MP for Westminster, which had one of the most democratic franchises in pre-Reform Bill days. Then in 1817 he handed over the management of the now highly successful tailoring business to his son, leaving him free to concentrate on those political activities which won him the title of 'the radical tailor of Charing Cross'.

From now on it is not too much to say that the room behind the shop was the headquarters – power-house might be a better term – of British radicalism.

> My library [he wrote in 1834] was a sort of gossiping shop for such persons as were in any way engaged in public matters having the benefit of the people for their object. No one who knew me would hesitate to consult with me on any subject on which I could either give or procure information.

There from six in the morning to eleven at night he sat – 'the philosophic sage', as one writer describes him, upon 'a three-legged stool, gowned in wholesome grey, with an absolute avalanche of schemes, scraps and calculations around him' – pronouncing and pushing the schemes which his pupils and disciples proclaimed in Parliament and the world at large.

This writer goes on to say that 'the singular part of the business is that the others should get all the merit'. But Place did not mind that in the least: it was just how he liked it. He was not afraid of the limelight but he preferred to work in the background. The bitter experiences of his early years had taught him the art of the possible, which is about the most valuable thing that a politician can learn. He knew just how far you could go and get away with. He was a wire-puller of consummate tact and resource. He was a dab hand at writing a letter, framing a manifesto and drawing up a petition. He loved power, but it was the reality that he was concerned with, not the outward show. When we delve into the mass of documents that constitute the 'Place collection' in the British

Museum we begin to appreciate the extraordinary extent of his influence and achievement.

More than any man it was Francis Place who obtained the repeal of the Combination Acts in 1824-5 that had hamstrung trade-union activity. At the height of the Reform Bill agitation it was Place who invented the cry 'Go for gold!' that stopped the Duke of Wellington from forming another Tory government. He gave powerful support to Joseph Lancaster's 'schools for all' movement. He drafted the 'People's Charter' in 1838, and in his seventies aided Cobden in the Anti-Corn Law campaign. Nor should we forget to mention that in 1822 he published, under the title *Illustrations and Proofs of the Principle of Population*, the first book in the English language in which birth-control or contraception was openly advocated, and in the year following caused to be published, and probably himself wrote, those 'diabolical handbills' (as the critics called them) which gave the first instruction in contraceptive technique.

That gallant woman who was Place's wife died in 1827; he married a second wife a few years later and far less happily. He lost much of his money and spent his last years with a married daughter in Hammersmith and Earl's Court. Almost to the end he was busily occupied in sorting through the mass of papers he had accumulated in a half-century of political and social agitation and pasting them into 'guard-books'. He died on 1 January 1854 and the newspapers were far too occupied with the preparations for the Crimean War to give much space to his passing. But the old radical, Joseph Hume, who had worked with him in many a good cause, spoke a memorial tribute at a meeting of the Parliamentary Reform Association. Francis Place had been, he said, 'the most disinterested reformer he ever knew, valuable in council, fertile in resource, performing great labours; but he never thought of himself. Honours and advantages he might have commanded, but he preferred assiduous and private service, which he rendered of his own zeal, and defrayed out of his own wealth.'

Robert Owen

(1771-1858)

If we search through the volumes of biography to find a
companion-piece for the traditional American 'log cabin to
White House' story, we should find it in the chapter on Robert
Owen. With nothing to back him in the way of birth or education, with no influential friends or connections to push him
up the ladder, this spry little Welshman became the leading
figure in the new race of manufacturers, a wealthy capitalist, a
great and highly successful captain of industry, the intimate of
royal dukes and politicians of every shade of opinion.

He has been called the founding father of the socialist movement in Britain, and just as surely it was he who provided the
inspiration and impetus for the Co-operative Movement in its
earliest days. Factory legislation found in him a constant supporter. He was a pioneer in educational advance, especially in
the matter of infant schools.

Robert Owen was born on 14 May 1771 in the village of
Newtown, Montgomeryshire, just over the border from England in north Wales, where his father was a saddler and iron-
monger. He started at the village school when he was four and
did so well there at reading, writing a legible hand and the first
four rules of arithmetic that at the age of seven he applied for,
and was given, the post of usher and assistant.

Owen's school-days came to an end when he was nine and a
year later his parents agreed to his urging that he should be
allowed to join one of his brothers in London, where he had a
saddlery business. In 1781, when he was ten, he made the
journey alone on the top of the coach. On arrival in London
he was welcomed by his brother but after a few weeks was
offered a job at Mr McGuffog's, a draper at Stamford with a
very successful line of business. McGuffog, a canny Scotsman,
taught him the business from the bottom up, and Owen's three
years of apprenticeship behind his counter were very well
spent. Going back to London, he was taken on as an assistant
at Flint & Palmer's old-established drapery business on London
Bridge, where everything was rush and ready money. Before
long 'the work and slavery of every day in the week' threatened
to undermine his constitution, and he was more than glad to

accept an offer of '£40 a year, besides board, lodging and washing', made to him from a Mr Satterfield, wholesale and retail draper in Manchester. This was in 1786, and he remained with Satterfield until 1789, when at the age of eighteen he felt capable of striking out on his own.

To begin with he joined another young fellow in the then rapidly developing trade of cotton-spinning. They were doing well enough when one day Owen happened to read in the newspapers that Mr Drinkwater, one of the biggest Manchester merchants, was advertising for a manager. On the spur of the moment he put on his hat, walked round to Drinkwater's counting-house and asked him for the job. Proving to Mr Drinkwater that he was already earning in his own business the £300 a year salary he was asking, he was appointed to the vacant position forthwith.

But when he arrived at the factory on his first morning, he must almost have wished he had not been. 'How came I here?' he said to himself, as he looked round on the busy factory with its machinery, much of which he had never seen before, and five hundred men, women and children; 'and how is it possible I can manage these people and this business?' Almost the whole of his experience had been in a retail shop. He was extremely sensitive, very retiring, and could seldom speak to a stranger without blushing, especially to one of the other sex.

For six weeks he was at the mill first thing in the morning and locked up the premises at night. He kept a grave look on his face, said as little as possible, merely 'yes' or 'no' as the question might be and not giving a direct order about anything. But at the end of that time there was precious little about the place and its inmates that he did not know. As time passed he revolutionized the processes of manufacture and became recognized as the most knowledgeable and go-ahead cotton-spinner in England.

Perhaps he would have stayed for good with Mr Drinkwater if the manufacturer had not gone back on his offer of a partnership. As it was, Owen was not content with a managership but left to become a partner in the Chorlton Twist Company. This led to his making business trips to Glasgow, and on one of these he fell in love with Miss Anne Caroline Dale, daughter of David Dale, who in 1785 had joined with Richard Arkwright in establishing cotton-mills on the Falls of Clyde, at New Lanark, which had become justly celebrated as one of the best of the kind. Miss Dale suggested that he might like to see the mills. He said he would be very glad to do so – he had already taken a preliminary peep – and as a result he persuaded his

Manchester partners to join him in buying the place. This was in 1800, the year after he had married Miss Dale.

Owen assumed the managership of the works and went to live at New Lanark. He was surprised – shocked – by much of what he found. Mr Dale was supposed to be a good employer but the place was in a terrible state. Connected with the mills were about two thousand persons, five hundred of whom were children brought, most of them, at the age of five or six from the poorhouses and charitable institutions of Glasgow and Edinburgh. The children had been well treated by Dale, but the general condition of the work-people was deplorable. Many of them were the dregs of the population, since no respectable folk would submit to the long hours and demoralizing drudgery of the factory. Thieving went on almost unchecked, drunkenness was general, sanitation was hardly thought of, the homes in which the people lived were mostly one-roomed hovels in the shanty town at the mill gates.

For the next sixteen years Owen devoted himself to the mills' transformation. New Lanark was his laboratory, in which he carried out what he described as 'the most important experiment that has as yet been carried out at any time in any part of the world'. The claim may seem absurdly far-fetched, but Owen did not think it at all out of the way. Quite early on, as a boy in fact, he had arrived at the conclusion that man's character is not made by him but for him, it has been formed by circumstances over which he has no control; and this being so, the only right and sensible thing to do is see that, from his earliest years, he is placed under the proper influences, physical, moral and social.

One of the first things Owen did was to open stores where the work-people might buy their groceries, clothing, etc., on very favourable terms; the good effects of this were soon apparent for all to see. He built new houses and put a second storey on the existing ones, thus doubling their accommodation. He arranged for the women to be taught the elements of good housekeeping and child care. He imposed severe restrictions on the sale of strong drink and put an effective stop to pilfering by instituting an efficient checking system.

As soon as he was able, Owen recruited no more pauper children for his labour force and the hundreds of 'free' children whom he employed were required to spend part of their day in the schools that he provided. This provision has earned for him the honour of having been the first to start infant schools in Britain. His establishments were in fact nursery schools, since children of one year old or who had learnt to walk were admitted. It is on record that at first parents were dubious about sending their infants, but after a time they were begging to be allowed to send them even before they had arrived at their first birthday. The school fees were fixed at 3d. a month; and although the cost to the firm was £2 per head per annum Owen was positive that they were getting their money's worth. As for the children who were trained in his schools, Owen declared that they were the most attractive, the best and happiest human beings he had ever seen. He insisted that all the school lessons should be made interesting, and he absolutely forbade the use of the tawse, or leather strap, and cane.

All these things cost money, and although the business continued to be highly profitable, Owen's partners grumbled at spending money on schools and such-like that might have gone into their pockets. At last he got so fed up with their complaints that in 1813 he very cleverly bought the business over their heads with the aid of a fresh set of partners, including the old philosopher Jeremy Bentham.

By this time New Lanark had become one of the showplaces of the British Isles, and between 1815 and 1823 nearly 20,000 persons signed the visitors' book. Owen was in great demand as an expert on all matters connected with trade and industry and labour relations. In 1813 he published his first book, *A New View of Society, or Essays on the Principle of the Formation of the Human Character*, which was very favourably received; Lord Liverpool, the Prime Minister, accepted a copy, and 'superiorly bound' copies were sent to all the sovereigns of Europe and to Napoleon, then in his exile on Elba. At Owen's prompting, Sir Robert Peel (father of the future Prime Minister, and one of the most important of the 'cotton lords') agreed to sponsor a Factory Bill; Owen's evidence in support before the House of Commons Committee created quite a stir and in 1819 the Bill became law, although it had been much watered down in committee.

Just after the 'great war' with France ended in 1815, Owen was at the peak of his influence. There was widespread unemployment and social distress, and Owen was invited to give his views on how the crisis should be met to the House of Commons Committee on the Poor Law over which the Archbishop of Canterbury presided. In due course he presented his report. The immediate cause of the general misery and stagnation was, he argued, the termination of the long struggle with France, but more important, because it was permanent, was the competition of machinery with human labour. To meet this chronic situation, 'advantageous occupation must be found for the poor and unemployed working classes, to whose labour mechanism must be rendered subservient, instead of being applied, as at present, to supersede it'. Then he proceeded to recommend the establishment of 'villages of co-operation', modelled on the plan of New Lanark, each to consist of about 1,200 souls living all together in a single range of buildings and maintaining themselves by their labour in workshops and factories and the thousand or fifteen hundred acres of surrounding land.

This in brief outline was 'Mr Owen's Plan', and it is hardly to be wondered at that this first expression of Owenite socialism should have met with a cool reception in official circles. When the Archbishop's committee turned it down, Owen decided to make his appeal to the general public. He organized two big meetings in the City of London at which he explained his proposals. The first was not too critical, but the second brought a distinct rebuff. For some reason not properly explained, Owen included in his speech an exposition of his hostile attitude towards all forms of organized religion, with the result that the man who (according to his own account, and he was writing in all seriousness) 'was by far the most popular individual in the civilized world', when he stepped down from the platform was on the way to becoming a social outcast.

This public association of 'Owenism' with 'infidelity' deprived him of a great part of his support among the governing classes and for the future he directed most of his propaganda – political, social and moral – to the workers.

In 1828, following increasing dissension between the partners, he severed his connection with New Lanark. From 1825 to 1829 he was in America, trying to establish one of his social communities at New Harmony, in Indiana; it failed, as did similar ventures elsewhere, and they cost him most of his fortune. Henceforth he was a chronically hard-up visionary, making some sort of a living out of his books and platform appearances. His numerous ventures into newspaper publishing were likewise disappointing and costly. But among the working classes his name still cast a spell and he was the acknowledged leader of the trade union revival that marked the early 1830s. He was the inspirer and leader of the pretentious Grand National Consolidated Trade Union which, formed in the spring of 1834, collected almost a million members and was dead by the end of the year – killed by poor generalship, internal disputes, strikes not properly prepared for and lock-outs that were, and the infamous sentence passed on the six poor Dorchester labourers, the 'Tolpuddle martyrs', whose 'crime' was having taken 'illegal oaths' in forming a local branch of the Consolidated Union.

This disaster ended Owen's connection with organized trade unionism, but there is yet another wing of the labour movement that owes him a great debt of gratitude: nearly all the twenty-eight poor weavers who in 1844 constituted the Rochdale Pioneers, the first practical 'Co-op', were socialists of the Owenite persuasion. Indeed, the word 'socialist' first became current in connection with the Association of All Classes of All Nations that Owen founded after the collapse of the Grand Consolidated.

In the more than twenty years that remained to him, Owen occupied himself chiefly with educational and moral propaganda. His wife died in 1830 and his sons settled in the United States and became American citizens. He spent some years with them, but returned finally from America in 1847 and lived on a farm at Sevenoaks.

In February 1858 he managed to attend the Chartist conference in London and later in the year the conference of the National Association for the Promotion of Social Science held in Liverpool. There he was taken ill and was in bed for a fortnight but he rallied and decided to return to Newtown, his birthplace. He was arranging a series of meetings on education when he died on 17 November 1858. He was buried beside his parents in the churchyard, and many years later the Co-operative Movement erected a memorial over his grave.

Thomas Arnold

(1795-1842)

In 1828 Thomas Arnold was ordained as an Anglican priest, took his doctorate in divinity and took up his appointment as headmaster of Rugby School. These three events point to the main elements of his character and his life; he was a priest, a scholar and a teacher; and in a letter to his friend John Tucker in 1827 Arnold revealed how closely they were integrated into his conception of what his life's work should be.

> With regard to reforms at Rugby, give me credit I must beg you, for a most sincere desire to make it a place of Christian education. At the same time, my object will be if possible, to form Christian men, for Christian boys I cannot hope to make; I mean that from the natural imperfect state of boyhood they are not susceptible of Christian principles in their full development upon their practice ...

The Provost of Oriel College, Oxford had said that if Arnold were chosen as headmaster, 'he would change the face of education all through the public schools of England'. This he did, not in fact through any radical reforms of the existing system, but by giving his school a new conception of what its aims should be, which in the later nineteenth century gave other schools a fresh impetus towards the central preoccupations of imperial Britain. Arnold was given the credit – and the abuse – for the emergence of the public schools from the casual chaotic aristocratic institutions of the eighteenth century into the Victorian nurseries for future rulers of the empire. But many of Arnold's ideals were distorted and simplified by their adaptation to other schools. He could never have been so influential had he been a prominent figure in areas other than schoolmastery. It had been a profession with little status until Arnold's prestige gave it dignity and, more important to the Victorians, a sense of its necessity to the moral welfare of the nation.

Thomas Arnold was a serious man in the Victorian sense – a man concerned with the serious matters of life. The twentieth century finds him solemn and ponderous – he would have found it trivial and barbaric. He was born in 1795, the son of

379

William Arnold, a customs officer, in the Isle of Wight. He
passed his childhood there, during the Regency period when
the careless extravagance of the eighteenth century was culminating in one final fling before new needs and concepts
imposed themselves on the old order. His father and two elder
brothers died when he was still a child, and after preparatory
schooling in Wiltshire he was sent off to Winchester in 1807,
where he gained a scholarship and stayed till he was sixteen
years old. Winchester had never lost its ancient reputation for
scholarship, even during the lean eighteenth-century years
when most public schools were teaching decayed remnants of
Renaissance classical learning under a corrupt and indifferent
administration. Thomas Arnold learned a good deal from the
forceful personality of the headmaster Dr Goddard, who had
tried to deal with the perennial public-school problem of an-
archic and brutal behaviour among the boys by introducing a
prefect system. In 1811 Arnold went up to Corpus Christi,
Oxford, as a scholar, to read classics, *Literae Humaniores*. He
took first-class honours but his friends felt even then that he
did not share their interest in the predominantly eighteenth-
century concern with elegance; his friend J. T. Coleridge wrote:

> This arose in part from the decided preference which he gave
> to the philosophers and historians of antiquity over the
> poets, coupled with the distinction which he then made,
> erroneous as I think and certainly extreme in degree, be-
> tween words and things, as he termed it.

Already the moral preoccupation is there, outweighing the
niceties of style; Arnold's awareness of the need to cut the dead
wood from classical and ecclesiastical learning in order to
make them live again in a new age shapes his approach to
teaching and preaching. When his first volume of sermons was
published in 1828 he wrote: 'If the sermons are read I do not
care one farthing if the readers think me the most unclassical
writer in the English language.' And characteristically he
merged the office of school chaplain and headmaster to make his
Sunday sermon in Rugby chapel a climax of the school week.

> My object has been to bring the great principles of the
> Gospel home to the hearts and practices of my own coun-
> trymen in my own time ... I have tried to write in such a
> style as might be used in real life in serious conversation with
> our friends ... the language, in short, of common life.

That this objective would involve Arnold in a storm of
controversy becomes clear when one remembers that nothing

upset the eighteenth century so much as 'enthusiasm', and the first decades of the nineteenth century were very close to the previous age. Here was a man who threatened to take serious matters too seriously, who saw life as a moral battlefield on which he, and his pupils, rode out to fight the good fight. The eighteenth century would have thought him vulgar; the twentieth century finds him unhealthy. But Arnold's faith was forged in the fires of the religious revivals of the 1830s. He fought the corruptions of the eighteenth-century Anglican Church as he did those of the public schools. He also turned against the fanatical dogmatism, as he saw it, of the Oxford Movement, which sought to reinvest the Anglican church with medieval grandeur and authority. Arnold was so horrified by this that he quarrelled permanently with his close friend John Keble. Keble was a Fellow of Oriel College when Arnold was made a Fellow in 1818; when Arnold moved to Laleham in Middlesex and married Mary Penrose, the daughter of a Nottingham parson, in 1820 Keble was a constant visitor. He became godfather to Arnold's most gifted son, Matthew, born one of nine children in 1822.

The nine or so years spent at Laleham were among the happiest of Arnold's life. He tutored young men for university, preached at the parish church (he had been ordained deacon at Oxford); he read German historians and Thucydides; travelled on the Continent; and swam and boated and played with his children and pupils. His strenuous mental activity was matched by extraordinary physical energy. His friend James Martineau remarked that his vitality was essential to his personality: 'Its beauty is not of form, like a statue, or of colour, like a picture, but of *movement* like – what he simply was – a man.'

But Keble's sermon of 1833, defending the established Anglican Church in Ireland, shocked Arnold and shattered his peaceful existence. He had not always preferred the historians to the poets for nothing, and his public stand against the illiberal rigidity of the Oxford Movement shows the kind of awareness that he brought into the classroom.

> What I mean then by the original error of the political creed of many good men is the principle that in all questions of political alteration the presumption is against change. Now on the contrary the presumption is always in favour of change, because the origin of our existing societies was an unjust and ignorant system.

Arnold knew that change would come and that the *status*

quo was not invariably right. When he came to Rugby in 1828 he found 'an unjust and ignorant system', where the strong tyrannized the weak and where physical prowess was highly prized, where masters were despised by the young aristocrats who dominated schoolboy life, with their aristocratic code of honour among friends and contempt for the rest. Arnold did not try to impose a new system on so conservative a group as schoolboys; what he did, remembering Dr Goddard, was to incorporate the most resistant elements of the old order into his conception of how things should be. Such was the prefect fagging system where the youngest boys were forced to act as servants to the eldest. Arnold created a legitimate hierarchy, with himself as head, his masters next and his prefects as lieutenants, thus enlisting their allegiance and prestige on the side of authority, instead of against it, and also protecting the little boys from indiscriminate brutality.

But Arnold did not rely on administrative alterations. He transformed the school by his personal faith. This was not the civilized rational dogma of the eighteenth century, still less was it the Oxford Movement's medieval celebration of an established eternal truth. It was an achievement won by scrupulous personal examination, by struggling with doubts and evil desires and by moulding the will to believe in absolute moral values. On this kind of personal commitment Arnold based his reforms of schoolboy life. Obedience was not imposed; it became a matter of individual conscience based on self-respect. Arnold wanted his boys to hold the right moral values and exerted psychological pressure on them not to become unthinking conformists. He saw as an evil of the old system '... too much one of fear and outward obedience, the obedience of the heart and the understanding were little thought of'.

Independence and the ability to stand on one's own feet were to be encouraged once the moral ground work had been laid. Only then could the oldest boys be entrusted with power and authority, and Arnold made it clear that the responsibility was a heavy one. 'You should feel like officers in the army, whose want of moral courage would be thought cowardice. When I have confidence in the sixth there is no post in England for which I would exchange this, but if they do not support me, I must go.'

Arnold moralized the schoolboy code of loyalty, generosity and a sense of solidarity with one's fellows, adding the emotional attraction of self-sacrifice to a principle and to God. If he required these standards from his boys, he naturally looked for exceptional qualities in his teaching staff, whom he placed in control of the boys' houses of residence. A master should be in holy orders and should have the same ideal of teaching as Arnold himself: 'He should devote himself to it as the especial branch of the ministerial calling which he has chosen to follow ... I think our masterships here offer a noble field of duty.' He himself demanded complete freedom of action from the school trustees and influential parents; if a boy was a bad influence and Arnold felt that Rugby could not help him, he went, no matter who his parents were.

Arnold would probably not have been so successful if he had not made learning important to the schools again by bringing his vigorous approach to classical literature into the classroom, relating it to his moral concepts and thereby giving them intellectual strength and range. The classical curriculum was being challenged; it was too narrow, it did not meet the needs of the industrial nineteenth century. Arnold answered all these charges:

> The knowledge of the past is valuable, because without it our knowledge of the present and the future must be scanty: but if the knowledge of the past be confined wholly to itself: if instead of being made to bear upon the things around us, if it be totally isolated from them and so disguised by vagueness and misapprehension as to appear incapable of illustrating them, then indeed it becomes little better than laborious trifling ...

As Lionel Trilling in his biography of Matthew Arnold says, 'he undertook to make the classics useful by making them broad'. He did not despise other fields of learning; he overhauled the teaching of mathematics, he introduced modern history into the curriculum of the upper forms; and he felt that boys should be able at least to read German and French. He was not, like so many of his contemporaries, against scientific studies for theological reasons; he simply did not see their usefulness. The classics were useful for their moral teaching; they represented the balance between individual freedom and social obedience that the Victorians sought; to Arnold's eyes they reflected the heroic virtues extolled by the historian Carlyle: courage, devotion to duty, nobility of mind.

When Thomas Arnold died suddenly of heart failure in 1842, his achievement had been recognized by his appointment in 1841 to the Regius Professorship of Modern History at Oxford, which he never took up. His success influenced new and old public schools in the 1850s, like Harrow and Haileybury. But by the end of the decade opinion had changed. First of all the dangers and contradictions in Arnold's ideals became apparent when his energetic personality and impressive personal faith were no longer there to uphold them. There were those who felt that it was pernicious as well as foolish to burden adolescents with a sense of heavy moral responsibility:

> It's all Arnold's doing; he spoilt the public schools ... Not that I mean that the old schools were perfect, any more than we old boys that were there! But whatever else they were or did, they certainly were in harmony with the world, and they certainly did not disqualify the country's youth for after-life and the country's service.

That is the voice of opposition in Arthur Hugh Clough's dialogue on Arnold in *Dipsychus*. Clough was one of Arnold's most faithful supporters and most brilliant pupils. Once Clough was at Oxford, away from Arnold's bracing certainty, his early promise crumbled under the stress of finding that the realities of good and evil were not as clear cut as Arnold had made them. The liberals could not forgive Arnold for failing to perceive such possibilities inherent in his ideals. Lytton Strachey says that Arnold's prefect system merely substituted a more insidious kind of conformity for the old brutal autocracy.

Arnold's public school, in short, depended on Arnold's high moral conception of duty and faith, humanized and broadened by a commitment to intellectual activity. Once he had gone the structure remained but the ideals became simplified and vulgarized, as in *Tom Brown's Schooldays*, written by a former Rugby pupil, Thomas Hughes. As far as most boys were concerned, Arnold simply added one simple moral quality to the old code of honour: decency. One learnt to know one's place and also to be determined to win that place; loyalty and self-sacrifice were social virtues. But whereas for Arnold the school was a place for nurturing these, for Hughes the school became their focus and embodiment. Tom Brown's father sums up Arnold's aims as they were popularly understood: '... if he'll only turn out a brave, helpful, truth-telling Englishman, and a gentleman, and a Christian, that's all I want.'

There had been a spiritual fineness about Thomas Arnold himself which his later followers and critics had forgotten. Such a quality was, perhaps, out of place in wealthy imperial Britain; but it gave his work a kind of splendour possibly more valuable than any of its more tangible achievements.

Alfred, Lord Tennyson, the popular Victorian poet laureate

Charles Dickens, photographed the year before his death

Anne, Emily and Charlotte Brontë painted by their brother Branwell

Count Leo Tolstoy,
philosopher, moralist, mystic
and novelist

The flamboyant Oscar Wilde,
poet, wit and dramatist

Tolstoy in his study at
Yasnaya Polyana

Edwin Chadwick

(1800-90)

When Edwin Chadwick was at the height of his career in the civil service there was hardly anything too bad to be said about him, and when at length he was given the sack there was a pretty general sigh of relief. But looking back over the century that has passed since then he appears in a very different light. Notwithstanding his faults, his many errors in judgment and performance, Chadwick is seen to have deserved well of his generation and of the generations that have come after.

Born at Longsight on the outskirts of Manchester in 1800, he was the son of James Chadwick, a journalist of advanced liberal opinions, and what little he remembered of his mother was summed up in the phrase, she was 'a sanitarian, *pur et simple*'. As a boy he went to school at Longsight and Stockport and then, after the family had removed to London in 1810, he continued his education with private tutors. At an early age he was given a stool in an attorney's office and was entered as a student at the Inner Temple; he was 'called' as a barrister towards the end of 1830. But already he had started writing for the papers like his father before him. Social topics attracted him most, and it was when getting material for an article in the *Westminster Review* on life assurance that what he was to call 'the sanitary idea' first formed in his mind. Throughout the rest of his long life this idea never left him.

In 1829 an article of his in the *London Review* on 'Preventive Police' attracted the notice of Jeremy Bentham and so impressed that very practical-minded old philosopher that he invited Chadwick to join his small circle of intimate disciples. For some time Chadwick lived under Bentham's roof in Queen's Square, Westminster, and made himself useful in the compilation of Bentham's 'administrative code'.

When he was still without a settled job and hesitating about his future course, Chadwick received the offer of an appointment as an assistant commissioner on the staff of the Poor Law Commission that had been set up in 1832 by Lord Grey's Whig government. He performed his duties so capably that in the next year he was promoted to a chief commissionership and in 1834, when the Poor Law Board was constituted, he was appointed its secretary.

Nothing could surpass the energy with which Chadwick went about his new duties. In Whitehall he organized the Board's offices with businesslike efficiency, and from one end of the country to the other there was not a workhouse master who did not learn or dread his approach on one of his numerous visits of inspection. His colleagues were soon complaining that he was a very difficult fellow to work with.

Chadwick seemed to be quite unconcerned about the number of toes he trod on, the noses he put out of joint. He had been given a job to do and he was determined to do it to the very best of his ability. For generations the administration of the Poor Law had been a by-word for waste and extravagance, and as a result the labouring population to a very large extent had become demoralized and vicious. There was no incentive to honest labour. Wages had been kept below subsistence level, and the gap had been filled by doles in the form of out-relief granted by the parish overseers. Now, however, a new policy had been decided upon. The 'workhouse system' had been devised, and what that meant may be gathered from Chadwick's own statement.

> By the workhouse system [he explained] is meant having all relief through the workhouse, making this workhouse an uninviting place of wholesome restraint, preventing any of its inmates from going out or receiving visitors, without a written order to that effect from one of the Overseers; disallowing beer and tobacco, and finding them work according to their ability; thus making the parish fund the last resource of a pauper, and rendering the person who administers the relief the hardest taskmaster, the hardest that the idle and dissolute can apply to.

No wonder that the new-model workhouses came to be denounced by Carlyle as 'Bastilles of the poor'. Chadwick was not responsible for their invention, but he did his best to make them work, and with them his name became indissolubly associated. From that time the workhouse was regarded by the decent poor as the ultimate indignity, something to be avoided until the last possible moment, at the cost of who knows what pain and penury.

By virtue of his position at the Poor Law Board, Chadwick was well placed to further the public health agitation that may be said to have had its rise in the 1830s. Here his record makes much more satisfactory reading, even though his defects of character are still painfully obvious. The initial impetus came from an auditor's surcharge. The Poor-Law guardians at

Shoreditch were faced with epidemics of typhus and influenza, which cost them a great deal of money in sickness relief. They concluded, reasonably enough, that a main cause of the epidemics was the insanitary living conditions in their area, and they took steps to improve the housing, drainage, etc. in the worst spots. Whereupon the government auditor stepped in and surcharged the guardians, on the ground that such activities were outside their powers.

Chadwick took the view that the guardians had acted quite properly and he obtained the appointment of a committee of inquiry composed of three medical men of unquestioned standing in their profession and known to hold enlightened views on sanitary matters, viz. Dr James Phillips Kay (later Sir James Kay-Shuttleworth), Dr Neil Arnott and Dr Southwood Smith. Arnott and Kay explored Wapping and Stepney, while Southwood Smith investigated Bethnal Green and Whitechapel. In due course the three doctors laid their reports on Chadwick's desk and he had them appended as a special supplement to the Fourth Report of the Poor Law Commissioners, published in 1838. They made horrifying reading, these plain descriptions of thousands of human beings living in the most disgusting conditions on the fringe of the greatest and most wealthy of the world's cities. Why did they do so? Because they couldn't help it; they had nowhere else to go, and besides, they had to live near their places of work. Need it always remain so? No, declared Chadwick's doctors, and he echoed their claim; all these shocking evils could be prevented, by such simple remedies as light, fresh air, plenty of clean water, soap, refuse collection, street sweeping, house drainage.

There was nothing new in the revelations, not much in the remedies proposed; but now Chadwick had come on the scene and that made a difference. In the House of Lords the Bishop of London (who, as chairman of the Poor Law Inquiry Commission, had come to appreciate Chadwick's calibre) moved that Chadwick should be called upon to undertake an inquiry into sanitary conditions of the country as a whole. Very possibly Chadwick had put the bishop up to it; he certainly seized the opportunity with both hands. The result was the *Report on the Sanitary Condition of the Labouring Classes* (1842) that is one of the great public documents of the century and a milestone in the history of social progress. Every page of it bears the impress of Chadwick's character, but the General Report at the end is most distinctively his.

'Such is the absence of civic economy in some of our towns,' he wrote in an outburst of righteous indignation, 'that their

condition in respect to cleanliness is almost as bad as that of
an encamped horde, or an undisciplined soldiery'. In an army
the strictest rules were enforced as regards sanitary arrangements, but

> the towns whose populations never change their encamp-
> ment, have no such care, and whilst the houses, streets,
> courts, lanes and streams are polluted and rendered pestilen-
> tial, the civic officers have generally contented themselves
> with the most barbarous expedients, or sit still amid the
> pollution, with the resignation of Turkish fatalists, under the
> supposed destiny of the prevalent ignorance, sloth, and filth.

Then he proceeded to outline a programme of action. 'The
primary and most important measures, and at the same time
most practicable, are drainage, the removal of all refuse of
habitations, streets and roads, and the improvement of the
supplies of water.' And he urged that these measures should be
carried out at the public expense by 'responsible officers qualified by the possession of the science and skill of civil engineers'.

In retrospect it may seem that Chadwick's case was unan-
swerable and that nothing remained but to put his proposals
into execution. But in point of fact he met with strong opposition from the various vested interests involved, which might
have undone a man of thinner skin and more sensitive nerves.
Notwithstanding his report's hundreds of fact-filled pages, it
was decided that even more evidence was required before Parliament could be expected to take action. In 1843, therefore,
Sir Robert Peel's Conservative administration set up a royal
commission to inquire into the state of large towns. The commissioners appointed included Southwood Smith and Neil
Arnott, but not Chadwick. He had, however, proved himself
so indispensable that he was left to run the commission. The
first report was published in 1844, covering fifty of the largest
towns in the country, in most of which the housing conditions
were shown to be deplorable and the drainage and water-
supply shockingly deficient; most of this report was written by
Chadwick. The commission's second report followed in 1845
and provided further pictures of urban mismanagement and
neglect. As a direct consequence the first Public Health Act was
passed in 1848, under which a central board of health was set
up and provision made for the establishment of local boards of
health responsible for sanitary arrangements in their districts.

The central board consisted of three members. One of these
was Lord Morpeth, who sat *ex officio* as the Commissioner of
Woods and Forests in the government; the second was Lord

Ashley, the noble-spirited philanthropist who is better known as the seventh Earl of Shaftesbury; and the third was Chadwick, who was the full-time and salaried member. Upon Chadwick fell the main responsibility for making the Act work.

For the six years that the board was allowed to continue, he was the driving-force behind this first attempt to make Britain's towns and cities clean and decent places to live in. He had immense obstacles to encounter. He had many of the doctors against him, many of the civil engineers and most of the town councils, whose members were chiefly concerned with keeping down the rates. He rode rough-shod over the highly placed and well connected. He was as unsparing of his subordinates as of himself.

One of the many gibes at Chadwick was that no one had ever accused him of having a heart. It was untrue of course, but only his closest friends and co-workers knew how the hard and rough exterior belied the real man. Friends and enemies alike were agreed, however, that what he most certainly possessed was a brain, one of the keenest, most critically constructive and richly inventive brains in England. There was something else he had – a will of tempered steel, without which he would never have been able to ride the storms that his revolutionary ardour had provoked.

Of course he made mistakes, plenty of them, and among the worst was when, at the height of the cholera visitation of 1849, he was responsible for flushing the London sewers with water that discharged into the Thames. In his defence it should be remembered that Chadwick, no more than anyone else in those pre-Pasteur days, had any knowledge of germs; he thought, as all his advisers thought, that disease was engendered by something in the atmosphere – *miasma*, it was called – which was particularly virulent in conditions of dirt and squalor.

But if his errors were great there are splendid achievements to be recorded on the other side of the account. Throughout his career he was the principal preacher of that 'sanitary idea' which had come to him as a young man. Above all competitors he must be regarded as the 'father' of the public health movement in this country (from which it spread into all parts of the world); thanks to him, millions of people have been enabled to lead healthier and happier lives.

When he was desperately busy in getting the public health network established throughout the land, he could yet find time to prepare a *Report on the Practice of Interment in Towns* which led to the closing of such appalling accumulations of human remains as the churchyard off Chancery Lane that

Dickens described in *Bleak House*. It was Chadwick who was responsible for the insertion in the great Registration Act of 1836 of the clause providing for the registration of the causes as well as the numbers of deaths. It was Chadwick who protested against the abominable housing conditions of the railway navvies; who urged local authorities to provide open spaces for public recreation and enjoyment and preserve the footpaths on which the workers might take a stroll with their families on Sunday afternoons; who advocated the opening of museums and art galleries on the only day on which they might be visited by the mass of ordinary folk. And (to mention one of those vastly important things which so seldom get into the history books) it was Chadwick who pushed the use of the newly-invented glazed earthenware pipes for drainage in place of the brick tunnels that got so easily clogged with filth.

What more he might have accomplished remains a matter of conjecture, for in 1854 the Board of Health was merged with the Local Government Board and Chadwick was retired – on the by no means inconsiderable pension of £1,000 a year. In a lively article *The Times* commented on the change. Under the Chadwick régime it had been a 'perpetual Saturday night', in the course of which Master John Bull had been 'scrubbed and rubbed and small-tooth-combed till the tears ran into his eyes, and his teeth chattered, and his fists clenched themselves with worry and pain'. Now it was ended and it was shown that 'we prefer to take our chance of cholera and the rest, than to be bullied into health'.

So this bold, vigorous, strongly opinionated, fiercely quarrelsome hard-as-iron bureaucrat, who was also one of the most profoundly gifted and enlightened men of his generation, went into retirement. But many more years remained to him, and to the end he was untiring in his labours in the great cause of public health. When we survey his magnificent record, the knighthood conferred on him by Queen Victoria in 1889, the year before his death, seems not only tardy but almost petty.

When Napoleon III was engaged in rebuilding the centre of Paris on broader and more spacious lines he heard that Chadwick was on a visit to the city and invited him to an audience. The Emperor inquired what he thought of the improvements. And Chadwick replied: 'Sire, they say that Augustus found Rome a city of brick and left it a city of marble. If your Majesty, finding Paris stinking, will leave it sweet, you will more than rival the first emperor of Rome.' Chadwick did not succeed in making England sweet but he reduced the stink. He would have liked to have that inscribed on his tombstone.

John Bright

(1811–89)

John Bright, the best known of all Victorian radical politicians, was born at Rochdale in Lancashire in 1811, a troubled year in English social history when industrialists were complaining of the burden of the wars against Napoleon and workers were complaining of the burdens of factory industry. He was born in a small redbrick house next to the cotton mill which his father had opened two years earlier. Rochdale depended upon cotton: it was already a factory town. Yet the Bright family depended for its vitality not on economics but on religion. It was a solid and conscientious Quaker family, and John was educated somewhat sketchily in a number of northern Quaker schools. Throughout his life he was to relate economics and politics to religion. His speeches, like many nineteenth-century speeches, had a biblical ring about them. He thought in terms of great moral causes. He looked back to the seventeenth-century Puritans, above all to Milton who was one of his earliest heroes.

At the age of fifteen he began to work in his father's mill. Yet his future was to lie not in money-making but in politics. Rochdale was a good place to provide a political apprenticeship. Bright made his first public speech in 1830 on the question of temperance, an issue which divided Rochdale voters. Soon afterwards he was drawn into an even more dramatic local contest. In 1834 the Vicar of Rochdale, who had been the chairman of the Lancashire County Magistrates at the time of the 'massacre of Peterloo' in 1819, attempted to increase the church rate which was levied on all local parishioners whether they were churchmen or not. Bright took a prominent part in the anti-church rate agitation. It involved what he called, Quaker though he was, 'a stand-up fight'. Not surprisingly, given the social pattern in Rochdale, he was on the winning side. He was also active in the Rochdale Literary and Philosophical Society which was founded in 1833.

In concerning himself with such local issues Bright always emphasized principle rather than interest, and he looked beyond Rochdale to those national issues which also involved principle. He made his first visit to London in 1832, the year of the passing of the Great Reform Bill, a measure which seemed to him to open up national politics. Privilege had begun to give way to popular agitation. With a wider franchise which included middle-class and some working-class voters there were new possibilities of radical action.

At a by-election in 1837 he seconded the nomination of the Liberal candidate, urging a further extension of the franchise and the introduction of voting by ballot. He also interested himself increasingly in an issue which was to dominate politics in the 1840s – free trade. The Rochdale Literary and Philosophical Society was unanimous in believing that 'laws for restricting the importation of grain are impolitic', and when he seconded the Liberal nomination Bright spent considerable time attacking the Corn Laws both on economic and on moral grounds. The bread taxes, he argued, were particularly hard on the poor. At the same time they impeded the growth of British commerce. They were designed to protect the privileges of the aristocracy. Bright knew little at first hand of the aristocracy, but from his youth onwards he was to dwell on aristocratic self-interest. The country would prosper only if it were to pass under new management.

Bright first met Richard Cobden, who was to play such a big part in his early life, in 1837, when he invited him to address a Rochdale meeting. Their close association did not begin, however, until 1841 two years after the Anti-Corn Law League had been founded in Manchester. It was a somewhat unequal association, since Cobden was already a well-known public figure and Bright was only on the threshold of his career. Nonetheless Bright had qualities which Cobden admired, and he quickly established his reputation as a forceful and popular speaker. All the themes which had appealed to him before were suddenly forced into focus as the Anti-Corn Law League mobilized support throughout the country, carrying the campaign into the enemy's camp.

'The Anti-Corn Law League,' Bright told a Manchester audience three years after the Corn Laws had been repealed in 1846, 'will henceforth stand before the world as a sign of the new order of things. Until now, this country had been ruled by the class of great proprietors of the soil. Everyone must have foreseen that, as trade and manufactures extended, the balance of power would, at some time or other, be thrown into another scale. Well, that time has come … We have been living through a revolution without knowing it.'

There were to be many moments in Bright's long political life when he was to be far less optimistic than this, when he was to doubt, indeed, whether there had been any revolution at all. For the moment, however, there seemed to be ample reason for exhilaration. Bright wanted to use the forces which had united to secure the repeal of the Corn Laws to secure further changes – extension of the suffrage, lower taxation, a cheaper foreign policy. In 1847 he became an MP for Manchester, 'the centre and heart of the greatest and most remarkable industry that the world has ever seen'. He had high hopes of leading new crusades, confident in the belief that 'we live in an age of agitation'. Manchester seemed to be a good base, and he had now passed out of his period of apprenticeship into a period of leadership.

While he never lost the enthusiasms which stirred him at this time, he was, in fact, about to begin a period of sustained trial. He had enemies in Manchester, manufacturers who felt that he went too far both in his rhetoric of denunciation and in his advocacy of further radical causes. In Parliament he was in a tiny minority, out of sympathy with some of the people who called themselves radical. Yet his personal stature grew in Parliament during the Crimean War (1854-6) which he attacked as stupid and un-Christian, just at the time when he was most under challenge in Manchester. Bright hated an expensive foreign policy. He also hated war. He had no wish to support the Turks against the Russians. Popular though the Crimean War was, not least with the largest section of the radicals, he did not hesitate to condemn it. It was in relation to the war that he made what still stands out as the greatest of all his parliamentary speeches. 'The angel of death has been abroad throughout the land,' he told his hushed fellow-members, 'you may almost hear the beating of his wings. There is no one, as when the first-born were slain of old, to sprinkle with blood the lintel and the two side-posts of our doors, that he may spare and pass on; he takes his victims from the castle of the noble, the mansion of the wealthy and the cottage of the poor and the lowly, and it is on behalf of all these classes that I make this solemn appeal.'

Even Bright's political opponents in Parliament were moved by this great speech, although they were not persuaded. Bright himself was worn out by his efforts so that he became a kind of war casualty himself. He was still convalescing when he lost his seat at Manchester in the snap general election of 1857. His friend Cobden also lost his seat, and the so-called 'Manchester School', to which they were both said to belong, was described by *Punch* as having been converted into 'the School of Adversity'. During the course of the election campaign Cobden had told a Manchester audience that he and Bright 'lived ... in the most transparent intimacy of mind that two human beings ever enjoyed together. I don't believe there is a view, I don't believe there is a thought, I don't believe there is one aspiration in the minds of either of us that the other is not acquainted with.' It was a remarkable tribute. The two men were, in fact, partners, and the experience of being partners in tribulation was as deep as or even deeper than the experience of being successful partners during the golden years of the Anti-Corn Law League. Cobden, however, was to die in 1865: Bright was to live on until 1889. During the years after Cobden's death there were to be far-reaching changes both in politics and in society, and Bright was to establish a distinctive position of his own as a radical leader who was more interested in principle than in power. He turned his own brand of radicalism, indeed, into a kind of creed. It was not an intellectual creed, for he was in no sense an intellectual. It drew rather on the same kind of moral earnestness which inspired religious loyalty. Increasingly after 1865 Bright was to turn to Gladstone, the maker of a new Liberal Party, as the one politician of his generation who could best ensure that morality and politics were never separated from each other.

Having been rejected by Manchester in 1857, Bright was elected MP for Birmingham in the same year. This was a critical switch in his life, for he was to remain MP for Birmingham until his death. Undoubtedly Bright found Birmingham a more effective political base than Manchester, not least because there was a far less wide psychological and economic gap between manufacturers and their workers. Yet he remained essentially a man of the north and he never identified himself fully with his new city. In his speeches – and he was to deliver many of them on Birmingham platforms – he always referred not to 'our city' but to 'your city'. Between 1857 and 1867 he built up ever-increasing support in Birmingham and in other English cities for a further extension of the franchise to include working men. He believed that the vote was a right, and although he was dogged by bad health he made every effort to impel his fellow citizens to recognize this simple proposition.

It was during the 1860s that he became perhaps the most familiar national figure on any liberal political platform. Everyone knew what he looked like as well as what he had to say. An American journalist who listened to him in 1866 described how the rather irregular but powerful features gave you at first sight an impression of singular force and firmness of character. So did the whole man. The broad shoulders, the bulk of the figure, the solid massiveness of his masterful individuality, the immovable grasp of his feet upon the firm earth, his uprightness of bearing, the body knit to the head as closely as capital to column – all together made the least careful observer feel that here was one in whose armour the flaws are few.

This was the public image of Bright. The fact that it was an American who drew it was a tribute to Bright's interest in the United States. He was the most active British supporter of the cause of the North during the American Civil War (1861–5) and he corresponded regularly with Lincoln whom he greatly admired. His political enemies in Britain sometimes referred to him as the Member of Parliament for the United States, and he certainly had the highest respect for American democratic institutions.

Yet the image, like all images, did not fully correspond to the truth. Bright was not quite as masterful as he looked. Nor were his reactions quite as simple. His frequent illnesses revealed psychological strain. His will often faltered. His radicalism concealed conservative tendencies which appeared more openly in the last years of his life.

In 1867, however, he had the great satisfaction of seeing the suffrage extended and in 1872 the country also secured vote by ballot. When Gladstone formed his Liberal ministry in 1868 Bright accepted his invitation to become a minister. He accepted office reluctantly, for he preferred to use his influence outside rather than inside the central circles of power. He was not interested in the details of administration, but he was proud to work closely with Gladstone and he believed that the ministry in which he served was perhaps the greatest administration that there had ever been in English history.

Bright accepted office again in 1880 when Gladstone returned to power in a blaze of glory. This time it was as Chancellor of the Duchy of Lancashire, where his departmental duties were minimal. Yet his stay in office was short. In 1882, when he was already over seventy years old, he resigned from the government in protest against Gladstone's decision to intervene in Egypt and to bombard Alexandria. No one was surprised when Bright resigned on this issue. He had always advocated a non-interventionist foreign policy, and he was disappointed to see Gladstone acting in what seemed to Bright to be a Palmerstonian way. Palmerston had been Bright's arch-enemy in politics not only during the last stages of the Crimean War, when he was Prime Minister, but earlier when he followed what both Bright and Cobden felt was a policy of glory and gunpowder, and later when he opposed any further extension of the suffrage. His views were accorded deep respect in the country, even by those who disagreed sharply with them. 'Could any veteran statesman, in the autumn of his days, desire a more noble record?' the *Illustrated London News* asked in 1883.

There was a further and this time more bitter break with Gladstone in 1886 when Bright opposed his policy of home rule for Ireland. This time Bright felt himself 'outside all the contending sections of the Liberal Party'. He ended his life isolated not only from Gladstone but from new spokesmen of radical opinion. His inherent distrust of what seemed to him newfangled ways of thinking and acting led him to defend 'the constitution, which has come down to us from our forefathers, with such amendments as circumstances and our own experiences seem to warrant'. When he died in 1889 he received almost universal praise.

Bright was buried very simply in the graveyard attached to the Friends' Meeting House in Rochdale. He thus returned to his roots. He was the first Quaker in English history to become an aggressive platform speaker. He was the most vigorous advocate in his age of an end to privilege. He tried to appeal not only to the middle classes but to the working classes and to preach their common interests. Yet he was as strongly opposed to active and expensive policies of social reform at home as he was to active and expensive foreign policy. Both, in his view, entailed a degree of state intervention and power which he was not prepared to accept. However great his renown, few Englishmen followed Bright consistently or without qualification. He died towards the end of a decade of upheaval in politics and society as intense as the upheaval in the decade in which he had been born.

Benjamin Jowett

(1817-93)

His funeral, on a serene October afternoon, was 'one of the most impressive ever seen in Oxford'. There were eight pall-bearers – seven heads of Oxford colleges and the Provost of Eton: they had all been his pupils. So had the Viceroy of India, who telegraphed his profoundest regrets, deputing his son, the Earl of Kerry, then an undergraduate, to represent him. Statesmen and schoolmasters, country clergymen and archbishops, judges, journalists, scholars and administrators – 'leaders' great and small – thronged the funeral procession of their teacher and friend. The special train that ran from Paddington at noon was crowded. When Benjamin Jowett, Regius Professor of Greek, Fellow, tutor and Master of Balliol, died Victorian England mourned one of its greatest architects, 'the mentor-in-chief of its golden age'.

These were not the last rites of aristocratic privilege and inherited rank, nor did they celebrate a primrose path of success. His career spanned a century of unprecedented social revolution: the bitter pangs of expansion to industrialism and empire; the agony of the established church, wracked by reasoned doubt and declining secular influence; the challenging tide of educational and scientific advance; God, Mammon and Darwin reconstituting the fabric of society; the triumphant era of the self-made man. Jowett's story mirrors the age.

It was a forlorn start. He was born in Peckham, the son of 'trade' – and unsuccessful trade at that. Through his father's neglect and mismanagement, what had been a flourishing family business for two generations – Benjamin Jowett and Sons, Furriers, of Bermondsey, handling beaver skins from the Hudson's Bay Company – collapsed. A pious evangelical and incompetent day-dreamer, his father turned to job-printing and hack journalism, and dabbled with the vision of his New Metrical Version of the Psalms. His mother suffered dutifully. Nine children had been produced in twelve years, years of ever-increasing financial doubt and insecurity. Benjamin, born in 1817, came third.

His mother's brother-in-law was a wholesale stationer. Through him in 1829 she luckily secured the nomination of a place for 'clever, curly-headed Ben' at St Paul's School, at that time still huddled in the churchyard of Wren's mighty cathedral. It was the beginning of everything for him, but far from a joyous dawning. He loved his brothers and sisters; the children at least had been happy together. But his settlement at school precipitated the long-threatened crisis between the parents. Gathering her other children about her, his mother fled from London and her husband's failure to provide, and took refuge with a widowed sister in Bath.

From the age of twelve the future Master of Balliol was left to trudge into school from mean and solitary lodgings in the City Road; they were not even shared by his father, who preferred his latest printing-press and the 'Psalmody versification' to the company of his bright young son. This went on for six years – his entire adolescence. There was no money for holiday reunions at Bath; cousins at Clapham and Blackheath took him in. Filial piety compelled occasional visits to his father, but even to think of him loosed disturbing feelings of shame and near-contempt; nothing escaped the clear eyes of the precocious child. It was vital not to be a failure in life: this was the deepest and bitterest lesson of Jowett's youth.

At school he applied himself earnestly to his books. In 1835 'the best Latin scholar' that old Sleath, the High Master of St Paul's, had ever seen, won a brilliant Open Scholarship to Balliol College, Oxford; it was, he wrote later, the greatest joy of his life. Money, however, was still a problem. The scholarship he had won was the most highly prized at Oxford, but was worth only £30 a year. Although Jowett had learned to live on little, not even he could manage on that alone. The Mercers' Company was finally persuaded to supplement his award, but there was still nothing for extras.

A fellow student sent him an anonymous gift of £20 to ease the strain of his first-year studies and subsidize extra tuition for the approaching Hertford Latin Scholarship exam. Jowett won the Hertford in the spring of 1837. Grasping at every straw, he also won a £10 College book-prize for English composition. At the end of his second year at Oxford, Jowett had his first ever holiday, a steamer-trip from Bristol to Ilfracombe and a fortnight walking along the beach.

When he returned to Oxford for his third and final year, there were four fellowships vacant. At that time, appointment was by examination. Undergraduates were eligible, but only one successful attempt was traditionally on record, the Old Master of Balliol himself, the freakish Dr Jenkyns. Jowett was reluctantly persuaded to sit by one of the two Balliol tutors in

Classics - Scott, of *Greek Lexicon* fame. When news of his election was announced in the quad, Jowett's initial disbelief gave way to an enormous leap in the air - he was normally, according to his very first pupil, 'absolutely devoid of athletic propensities' - and it was some considerable time before he felt able to meet the fellows assembled in the chapel to congratulate him.

His public career was now launched, an outwardly glittering parade of successes. In 1842 he was appointed one of the three Balliol tutors, upon whom the main burden of the college teaching fell. He held the post for twenty-eight uninterrupted years. His pupils were the best that Eton, Harrow and Rugby could produce - which was talent indeed after Arnold's reforms: for Dr Jenkyns, who remained Master until 1854, could pick a winner, and in the 1830s and 1840s confined his annual hunts for fresh Balliol blood almost exclusively to these three schools.

A familiar biographical pattern began to establish itself: public school - Eton, Harrow or Rugby in particular; Oxford - Balliol and Jowett's tutelage in particular; public service, pre-eminence in whatever profession, renown. Jowett completed at university the educative processes, in the broadest sense, which Arnold established in the schools.

In teaching as in all things, Socrates was the inspiration. Jowett taught his pupils how to work with disciplined regularity, how to order their lives to the best individual advantage, how to fulfil themselves beyond their own imaginings, above all how to think for themselves. There was no attempt to preach a given point of view or convert pupils to his own way of thinking; for Jowett, 'the only results of value are those which a man reaches for himself: truth cannot be seen with the eyes of another'. The best and brightest of the era thus acquired an independent maturity of outlook and a social and intellectual versatility that eminently suited the rising demands of public service and empire, and their influence inevitably came to permeate society.

In 1855 Jowett was appointed to the Chair of Greek; in 1870 he became Master of the college and ruled it like a monarch for twenty-three years; from 1882-6 he was Vice-Chancellor of the University, 'an outstandingly good one'. He played a leading part in Lord Macaulay's commission on the selection of candidates for the Indian Civil Service - a turning point in the century's imperial history; and he was at the forefront of the movements for university extension and reform. These led to the royal commissions of 1850 and the 1870s and 1880s and to the establishment, principally in the 1870s, 1880s and 1890s, of two-thirds of the universities in England today. When Jowett began his undergraduate studies at Oxford in 1835, there were only two universities in the country (Scotland had twice the number!) and both were the 'clerical incubators' of the established church: every undergraduate had to sign the Thirty-nine Articles, every fellow had to be ordained within four years of election and remain unmarried, as befitted the clergy. Nonconformists and Catholics either went to the Continent or Scotland or were denied a university education altogether. When Jowett died, the foundation colleges of most of the great provincial universities had already been established; Oxford and Cambridge were no longer Anglican seminaries; and religious conformity was nowhere demanded of a student – the university world as we know it had been born. No one individual produces social movements of such massive constructive significance; Jowett was one among many, but his was a lion's share, and the University College of Bristol, founded in 1876, was a direct and personal beneficiary.

Greek philosophy and philosophy in general were his chief academic loves. His lectures on Plato drew capacity audiences, and his pioneer explorations of the pre-Socratic Greek philosophers attracted even greater attention in their day. He devoted the last thirty years of his life to a huge undertaking, the translation and analysis of all Plato's dialogues (the poet Swinburne helped him with an early draft of the *Symposium* – he is on record as gleefully announcing 'Another howler, Master!' to which Jowett would meekly reply, 'Thank you, Algernon, thank you!'). But no full-scale commentaries or major interpretative studies were produced (the analyses are merely condensed summaries of the text and the introductory essays are general in scope and essentially lightweight productions). The same applies to his work on Aristotle's *Politics* and the greatest of the Greek historians, Thucydides. Jowett was not a scholar in the traditional or the modern sense. He concentrated more on teaching and its needs as he understood them; the fact that he published no 'definitive' study of Platonic thought or Thucydidean historiography is characteristic, and reflects his educational theory and practice; give a man the basic tools – good reliable tools – but let him build his own structure to his own specifications. The translations, however, are standard works of reference still, monuments of felicitous expression.

There are fascinating accounts of him indomitably at work, even on holiday:

He used to begin immediately after breakfast and work on till dinner at four o'clock. He then went for a walk, and on coming in retired again and worked, I believe, till about twelve o'clock ... He worked harder and longer with his mind than most workmen with their hands.

'What matters', he once said to a lackadaisical pupil, 'is the sense of power which comes from steady working.' It was a cardinal doctrine both of his teaching and his life.

His most significant academic achievement however, was the introduction of Hegelian philosophy into England. At the age of twenty-seven he visited Germany with his lifelong friend and confidant, A.P. Stanley, the future Dean of Westminster; his luggage contained Liddell and Scott's recently published *Greek Lexicon* and Kant's *Critique of Pure Reason* in the original German (these, by mutual agreement, were studied for three hours each day!). At Dresden Jowett met Hegel's leading pupil, Erdmann of Halle. The difficulties of Hegel's thought, which he mastered in the original, fascinated him: it was the 'greatest stimulus' in his life, he said later.

By January 1849 he had almost finished a translation of Hegel's *Logic*; the work was never published and the manuscript is now lost, but, like his influence generally, it was the personal experience transmitted through his teaching that counted. After his return from Germany he taught and lectured on Hegel as a matter of course. Both T.H. Green and Edward Caird were pupils of his; inspired by their introduction to Hegelian idealism, they began that 'idealist revolution in late nineteenth-century English philosophy of which Bosanquet (another Balliol man) and Bradley at Oxford and McTaggart at Cambridge became the mature apostles.

A still more living memorial is that legendary university course, Oxford 'Greats', extended under Jowett's direction to include *all* philosophy, ancient and modern. It was and is the sternest intellectual challenge to the minds of the young that the world has ever seen.

But there were difficulties he never resolved and bitter failures too. Problems of ideology and world peace dominate the intellectual scene today; in Jowett's day the burning issues were theology and the role of the Church of England; Newman, Pusey, John Colenso and Wilberforce were names on every tongue – so was Jowett for a time. In the middle of the century he was one of the most prominent new 'broad' churchmen – those who held firm to a belief in God, but opposed all unreasoning fundamentalism in the interpretation of Holy Writ and exercised a fearless critical intelligence on what they regarded as the essentially human dogmas and institutions of the Church. The liberalizing attempt of the 'Oxford Movement' to reconcile reason and faith met with fierce resistance from the High and Low Church alike.

He was one of the seven contributors to the notorious *Essays and Reviews*, which appeared in 1860. Newman's Tract 90 and secession to Rome caused no greater uproar. *Essays and Reviews* caught the popular imagination and became a bestseller: some said 'Seven against Christ' would have been a better title. Jowett's essay 'On the Interpretation of Scripture', the last and best in the volume, is a classic statement on the critical analysis and reasoned assessment of scripture and, as such, represents the accepted orthodoxy of modern biblical scholarship and theological debate. Things were very different then. Three of the contributors, including Jowett, were prosecuted for heresy (a fourth died before the charge could be presented; the remainder, for one reason or another, were technically immune). His whole livelihood was at stake – this barely a century ago; the situation fraught with dismal irony. The case was called in 1863. The legality of the court was successfully challenged (*The Times* had denounced it as a 'rusty engine of intolerance') and Jowett's acquittal was hailed as a victory for liberal opinion within the Church of England. But Jowett never again published or spoke publicly on controversial theological questions.

The silent inner struggles were the worst. He never married: 'The great want of life', he wrote at the age of sixty-three, 'can never be supplied, and I must do without it.' Fits of deep depression troubled him all his days. Even in the years of greatest worldly acclaim, his self-doubts were so great that on one of his frequent visits to Florence Nightingale, the one woman in his life, he broke down and cried like a child.

He never knew the warmth of family life. Behind all the masks he presented to the world, there stretched a desolating loneliness of spirit. His private notebooks, filled – pages at a time – with lists of the names of his pupils and friends, tell the same sad story. 'I have no doubt he is passing in review a procession of all his friends,' said Florence Nightingale, when news of his final coma was brought to her. Friendship was his one crutch against the haunting terrors of the soul's abyss. The Balliol undergraduates of 1881 celebrated the learning and renown of their revered Master in a verse that became his unofficial epitaph.

First come I, my name is Jowett,
There's no knowledge, but I know it.
I am Master of this College,
What I don't know isn't knowledge.

What they did not know, what nobody knew, was the paradox
of the man: he lived and died an essentially lonely man.

Julius de Reuter

(1816-99)

In the early nineteenth century there lived in Kassel, capital of the old Electorate of Hesse in western Germany, a prosperous Jewish family of high intellectual attainments. The father, Samuel Levi Josephat, was provisional Rabbi of Kassel and his father had been judicial adviser to a neighbouring Jewish community. Two cousins were university professors, one of them the distinguished Sanskrit scholar, Theodor Benfey of Göttingen, and a nephew was a banker in the same town. Samuel had two sons and in July 1816 a third was born and named Israel Beer.

When Israel was thirteen his father died and the boy was sent to his banker cousin for whom he worked during the next ten years. But in 1833 something happened to arouse a new interest: the famous physicist Karl Friedrich Gauss arrived in Göttingen, set up an electric wire on the highest tower in the town and transmitted signals to a neighbouring village. Israel met Gauss and the gracefully spoken youth with his dark intelligent eyes much impressed the older man, particularly, it is said when Israel pointed out to him a serious error he had made in a money transaction. Together they discussed telegraphy and from this time Israel's imagination toyed with its future.

He is next heard of in Berlin, in the 1840s, where he was baptized, choosing the Christian names Paul Julius and a surname so familiar to us now: Reuter (perhaps from the German *Reiter*, a horseman). He was still in the banking world and married a banker's daughter, Ida Maria Magnus, a young lady whose buxom good nature and dreamy temperament contrasted amusingly with his own slim precision. Soon after, helped by capital from his father-in-law, he took a share in a Berlin bookshop and publishing firm which was renamed Reuter and Stargardt. Under the latter name it still exists in Hamburg today.

In publishing Reuter was successful, in fact too successful, for during the reaction after the 1848 revolution certain political booklets issued by the firm attracted official attention and, like many other democratically minded intellectuals at that time, he thought it advisable to emigrate to Paris.

In Paris Reuter worked as a translator for a wealthy merchant from Oporto, Charles Havas, who had just bought one

of the few 'news bureaux' then in existence, the Correspondence Garnier. In that turbulent age there was a tremendous
demand in all the continental capitals for news of European
events and Havas made a good income by selecting items from
newspapers and selling them to the press in Paris and abroad,
where he established correspondents.

This set-up attracted Reuter immensely and he could not
rest till he had tried to run a news agency of his own. But this
proved a failure, partly perhaps owing to lack of capital, and
a picture is drawn by a friend of Reuter and his wife slaving
away, translating, printing and dispatching in a single squalid
office-cum-living-room with half-eaten crusts thrown in the
fireplace and the floor littered with paper. In the summer of
1849 they vanished from this gloomy scene to follow a chance
which was opening up in Germany.

Across the border, growing industrialization, the development of the railways and the unsettled aftermath of the
attempted revolution were producing wild financial speculation offering good prospects for an efficient commercial news
service. In October 1849 a telegraph line was opened to the
public from Berlin to Aachen and – the Berlin end being
quickly monopolized by a rival named Bernhard Wolff (origin-
ator of Wolff's Bureau) – Reuter sped to Aachen and set up an
office there to supply customers as far afield as Amsterdam
with the latest market prices from Berlin. All were treated with
strict impartiality and their agents were locked in the office so
that they could receive 'Mr Reuter's prices' simultaneously
before taking them to their destination by train.

This rather awkward system worked for some months until
a telegraph line was opened from Paris to Brussels and Reuter
saw a chance to improve it. Between Paris and Berlin, the two
main centres of continental commerce, there was still a gap of
one hundred miles not spanned by the telegraph which took
nine hours to cover by train while carrier pigeons would do it
in under two. From a certain Herr Geller in Aachen – brewer,
baker and pigeon-fancier – Reuter arranged to hire forty pigeons and in a silken bag tied to their feet dispatched the Berlin
prices to Brussels while an agent in Brussels did the same thing
in reverse, with a pigeon-post to Aachen.

In this way throughout most of 1850 Reuter had an edge on
all competitors for speed and he began to appoint correspondents in the main European centres to send him political as
well as commercial news. But as the months passed the telegraph was steadily extended and by the end of the year not
even a five-mile gallop on horseback was necessary to link

Berlin and Paris. Reuter was out of business, but by no means in despair. He decided to try his luck in London.

It was in 1851, the year of the Great Exhibition, that Reuter and his faithful Ida rented rooms in Finsbury Square and an office in the Royal Exchange Buildings and began to explore possibilities for a news service. He had his agents and well-satisfied customers on the Continent, a certain amount of capital (including perhaps something from his father-in-law) and introductions to leading English businessmen. In that year, too, the first submarine telegraph was laid between Dover and Calais. The field was wide open. All the same, it must have taken all Reuter's considerable talents to break down English reserve and be accepted as an unknown foreigner and it would be interesting to trace his efforts in this period. But the records are silent and all we know is that, within a couple of years, he had made an agreement with the Stock Exchange to supply a twice-daily service of news from continental Bourses in return for a fixed annual sum and was also sending London prices to Amsterdam, Berlin, Vienna and Athens.

But years passed before he managed to make contacts with English newspapers to supply political news and this was a much more difficult breakthrough. The conservative *Times* came absolutely first in the world of journalism and already had a large force of correspondents abroad with its own channels of news transmission. To start with, its manager called the new Channel cable 'a great bore' and dismissed offers from Reuter with bleak refusal.

But events were moving in Reuter's favour. *The Times* was soon forced to see the advantage of the telegraph and in a leading article protesting against attempted government influence propounded the view: 'The first duty of the Press is to obtain the earliest and most correct intelligence of the events of the time, and instantly by disclosing them to make them the common property of the nation.' There was also a demand for cheaper newspapers carrying less comment and more news; now provincial dailies like the *Manchester Guardian* and the *Liverpool Post* were starting up; the world telegraph system, overland and under the oceans, was being steadily extended.

Well aware of these factors and already supplying most of the leading continental papers with London news, Reuter in 1858 abandoned frontal assaults on *The Times* and approached the *Morning Advertiser*, no longer as an alien but as a naturalized British subject, which he had been since the previous summer. Years later, when Reuter had become famous, the editor described the interview.

'Have I,' began Reuter in good English but with a German accent, 'the pleasure of speaking to Mr Grant?' I said that Grant was my name. 'Would you favour me with a few minutes of your time, as I have what I regard as an important proposal to make to you?' 'Oh, certainly,' was my answer. 'Take a seat,' and so saying I handed him a chair. 'My name,' he continued, 'is Reuter. Most probably you have never heard of it before.' I said I had not that pleasure.

After these courteous preliminaries, Reuter arranged with Grant to supply him for a trial period of a fortnight with exclusive political news from Europe, after which, if satisfied, Grant agreed to give him a contract.

It was the most important interview of Reuter's life. Grant was fully satisfied with the service supplied, which proved better and cheaper than competitors, and took it up at the price of £30 a month. He was followed by all the other London dailies, including *The Times*. So was born the great news agency which we know today. Its first telegram, headed ELEC-TRIC NEWS, dated 8 October 1858 from Berlin, reported that Frederick William IV, King of Prussia, had appointed his brother William as regent during his illness.

Seldom, as Julius Reuter's career shows, has a great need found the right man to fulfil it so quickly and satisfactorily. For the extension of a world cable network – the Atlantic was crossed in August 1856 and India linked to Ceylon two months later – meant that someone of impeccable integrity had to take up the collection, dispatch and distribution of international news. For the state to have done so would have risked partiality, and competing newspapers would not form their own organization. So it had to be a private individual and Reuter from Kassel admirably filled the part.

The story of Reuters then entered a new phase in which the aim was to extend the service while maintaining accuracy and increasing speed. The last factor is illustrated by Reuter's first big scoop when in 1859, amid growing tension between France and Austria, he made special arrangements to get early reports of a speech by Napoleon. While the Emperor was still speaking his text was being telegraphed to London and an hour after he had finished special editions of the newspapers carrying translated extracts were on sale in the London streets. Forty-odd years before, it had been considered a record for Wellington's victory at Waterloo to be published within four days.

The Franco-Austrian war followed and Reuter was faced with a new challenge. To keep the press fully abreast of world events meant employing a vast number of agents and his first action was to send correspondents to report on the activities of both sides. Their success in getting information from military commanders, their brief and factual reports, enhanced Reuter's reputation and in 1859, thanks to the reduced terms he offered the press for publishing his name, it was becoming a household word. But how to pronounce it? A versifier in one of the weeklies offered advice:

> I sing of one no Power has trounced,
> Whose place in every strife is neuter,
> Whose name is sometimes mispronounced
> As Reuter.

> His web around the globe is spun,
> He is indeed the world's exploiter;
> 'Neath ocean, e'en, the whispers run
> of Reuter.

Two years later, the American Civil War posed harder problems. Reuter sent out a special agent to organize a body of reporters on the spot, and the Atlantic cable having inconveniently failed, went to desperate lengths to be first in getting the war news to London. Mail boats were intercepted off the Irish coast, the news picked up in canisters thrown overboard, then flashed by a special line which Reuter had laid from the south-west tip of Ireland to Cork, and from there to England. By this means Reuter beat rivals who were now in the field and when the famous Trent case arose, involving the interception on the high seas of two Confederate commissioners bound for London, he was able to give Palmerston personally the news of a northern climb-down.

But the cost of all this was enormous and the need to expand as against rising costs posed a delicate problem. Newspaper subscriptions were doubled and in time trebled, but the load could not be borne by them alone. An arrangement to supply foreign news direct to the provincial press, hitherto dependent on the national dailies, was a help, but Reuter found a bigger source of new revenue in a private telegram service to the public, undercutting high post office rates.

Meanwhile as the years passed, agreements were made with continental agencies, notably Havas of Paris and Wolff of Berlin, for an exchange of services and a division of world 'empires', Wolff monopolizing northern Europe and Russia, Havas the French empire and Mediterranean countries, Reuter the British empire and the Far East.

By the time these agreements were signed, a Reuter representative was already established in Egypt and in 1866 Henry Collins, a young man of twenty-two, had been sent to India, now linked to Britain by overland cable, to set up branches throughout the country. In India there was a ready market for home news, commercial and political, and by the end of the year Collins, who to start with had only one white assistant, was firmly established in Bombay and planning to open offices in Calcutta, Madras and Rangoon. The laying of submarine cable from Ceylon via Bombey to Aden opened up immense possibilities of news exchange with Australia and the Far East, finally fulfilled in 1873 when cables were extended to Singapore, Japan and Port Darwin.

That Reuters should link up with New Zealand, penetrate South America and come to terms with the big agencies in the United States was only a matter of time. Meanwhile within twenty years of his start, Julius the founder had set up a framework and established the efficiency of an organization which today still thrives as one of the four great agencies of the world.

Five years later, after long and finally unsuccessful attempts to obtain a railway-building concession from the Shah of Persia (an enterprise which had little to do with the news agency), Julius handed over day-to-day management to his son Herbert. Already in 1871 the Duke of Saxe-Coburg-Gotha had conferred a barony on 'Paul Julius Reuter of London in acknowledgement of his extraordinary services', and in 1891 Lord Salisbury was to draw Queen Victoria's attention to his deserts. Graciously and willingly – for in those impassioned notes she was fond of sending to her premiers she had often referred to the reliability of Reuter's news – she gave Baron Reuter and his heirs the privileges of the foreign nobility in England.

So Baron Julius retired full of wealth and honour, to die in Nice in 1899, while his news agency, 'dignified, conservative, omniscient', as an American admirer called it, marched forward into the trials and perils of the modern world. Today it is owned by the British and Commonwealth newspapers under a trust which guarantees its independence from any form of government control and ensures the objectivity of its service. For this we have great reason to be grateful, and to the quiet-spoken genius from Kassel who ruled his staff like a patriarch and built for us one of the bulwarks of our freedom, a news agency, as the *Daily Telegraph*, 'conducted with an impartiality and integrity that are beyond praise'.

Florence Nightingale

(1820–1910)

She could so easily have been neither Florence nor Nightingale. Her father William Edward Shore inherited in 1815 the rich estate of Peter Nightingale, his great-uncle, and perpetuated his legator's name at the expense of his own, becoming William Edward Nightingale. He was a man of culture and lost little time in making for the Continent with his wife Frances. Their first child born in 1819 at Naples, was christened Parthenope, the city's classical name. The second was born the following year at Florence: hence Florence Nightingale.

The Nightingales returned to England to live between London and the two estates, Lea Hurst, near Derby, and Embley Park, near Romsey, Hampshire, at both of which Florence found plenty of scope for carrying out Good Works. Her parents and sister were not pleased by these unfashionable inclinations, correctly ascribing some of them to the influence of the feminist Mary Clarke with whom Florence had struck up an immediate friendship when they had met in Paris. Like 'Clarkey', her friend for many years, Florence recognized the emptiness of the kind of life which her position seemed to make inevitable: a rich marriage and the preoccupations of child-bearing and entertaining. When she suggested that she enter the nursing profession her parents and sister were appalled.

'Profession' is scarcely the term for nursing at that time. It was, as it had long been, a degrading, disgusting job. Most nurses were illiterates from the lowest classes, unfitted for much else and, if not corrupt to begin with, quickly made so by a system which did little to discourage drunkenness and sex relationships between nurses and patients, not to mention doctors. The nurses' squalid conduct matched the insanitary conditions prevailing in most hospital wards, where a large proportion of patients died from sheer filth and neglect.

A doctor associated with Salisbury Hospital agreed to take Florence as a probationer. She told her family: her plan was squashed, there and then. But the opposition merely served to strengthen her resolve. She had already heard of the Kaiserswerth institution, near Düsseldorf, and had recognized in it the very training ground she wanted for herself.

410

The institution had been established experimentally by a Lutheran pastor named Fliedner, who had been influenced by the English prison reformer Elizabeth Fry. From caring for discharged female prisoners, he had moved on to training nurses, known as deaconesses, on a five-year basis which also included reading, writing and domestic duties.

She got her way in the end. In 1851, Parthe, as they called her sister, was ordered to Karlsbad for treatment and Mrs Nightingale, thinking that experience might prove the best cure, allowed Florence to go with her sister and then to Kaiserswerth where Pastor Fliedner would let her share for a few months the life and training of his deaconesses. The spell at the institution only strengthened Florence's resolution, in which she was encouraged, to Mrs Nightingale's surprise, by several notable family friends, such as the rising politician Sidney Herbert and his wife. She felt, at the age of thirty-three, that she could delay no further. She applied for, and was appointed to, the position of superintendent of the Hospital for Invalid Gentlewoman in Upper Harley Street, London. Relieved that her daughter would at least be dealing purely with gentlewomen, Mrs Nightingale gave in grudgingly.

The chief duties at the Home concerned administration, fund-raising and – once Florence had insisted that Catholics as well as Protestants should be admitted as patients – supervising visits by Catholic priests, at her committee's insistence, to ensure that they did not start trying to make converts. The work suited her perfectly, teaching her much about the diplomacy of handling opinionated superiors, and she managed to gain experience in the practical work of nursing. That year, 1854, was not three months old before the Crimean War began.

The war, like most, was expected to be short. Confident in the army, whose soldiers and leaders included some of the victors of Waterloo, the British government scratched up a force from overseas garrisons and landed it, in summer kit, some thirty miles from the vital port of Sebastopol. The army and its French allies won a useful victory over the Russians at the River Alma, but failed to storm on at once to Sebastopol and so found itself committed to a long winter siege for which it was totally unequipped. The men were without warm clothing; supplies of necessities for fighting and living were inadequate and inefficiently organized; and arrangements for moving the wounded to hospital and treating them were scandalously poor, the few doctors lacking stores and equipment and the 'nursing' done by rough-handed, often callous, old-soldier pensioners, helped by partly-recovered patients.

The British public was not kept in ignorance, thanks to the indignant despatches of the first war correspondent William Howard Russell of *The Times*. Again and again, in his fearless reports of the bungling of the British military authorities, Russell returned to the plight of the wounded, as compared with the French. The French had ambulances and well-organized base hospitals staffed with nuns. The British wounded faced an agonizing journey from the front to Turkey, followed by the likelihood of death from neglect. *The Times* took up its correspondent's appeal: 'Are there no devoted women amongst us, able and willing to go forth to minister to the sick and suffering soldiers ... in the hospitals of Scutari?' There was one: Florence Nightingale.

Two days after the newspaper's plea she wrote to Mrs Sidney Herbert, whose husband was now War Minister, offering her services. Her letter crossed one from Herbert to her: 'There is but one person in England that I know who would be capable of organizing and superintending such a scheme ... My question simply is, Would you listen to the request to go out and supervise the whole thing?'

Using an office in Herbert's own London house, Florence and a friend set about trying to recruit the forty nurses she was permitted. It proved difficult. Most applicants were hospital nurses in the bad old mould, or eager, educated ladies who had never set foot in a hospital and would clearly prove unequal to the grim experience. There were complications of religion. Florence's instructions were to ensure that nurses did not 'tamper with or disturb' the religious opinions of patients. When she sought ten trained Catholic nurses there was argument about whether she, a Protestant, ought to have control over them. Protestant organizations able to contribute a few nurses tried to insist that although she was of their following, Miss Nightingale should defer to a specially-appointed representative. She won all these disputes, but still had to face attack from politicians and military men who argued that women would undermine discipline, prove unable to stand up to the Crimean climate and need nursing themselves.

The 'Nightingales', as they quickly became known, arrived at Scutari in early November to find a scandalous situation facing them.

Ten nurses were appointed to the General Hospital. Florence and the remaining twenty-eight moving into a leaking, ill-equipped and verminous tower of the Barrack Hospital, an unfinished barracks which had been crammed with wounded and sick. Men with every sort of wound shared wards with

sufferers from cholera and other highly infectious diseases.
There was little evidence of measures to prevent the spread of
infection and every sign of its encouragement, if filthy bedding,
unwashed floors and crude sanitary arrangements were anything to go by. Most patients lay on the ward floors and in
corridors: there were no beds for them. Perhaps some were
luckier for it – a bed was a death trap for a wounded man if its
previous occupant had just died of cholera and the sheets had
not been changed.

On the day that the 'Nightingales' stepped ashore, hundreds
of wounded began to arrive after a nightmare sea voyage from
Balaclava. In a way, the tragic battle helped the women. The
hospital doctors and officials, ready to show resentment at the
intrusion, were overwhelmed with work. By the time things
had eased a little, the nurses, briskly supervised by Florence,
had shown much worth, even if there remained those among
the men too stubborn to recognize it. Whatever the doctors
felt, the patients knew only gratitude. The British soldier then
was as tough, uncouth and ignorant a specimen as it was
possible to find, resigned to appalling hardship and the contempt of his officers and the people for whom he was fighting;
yet there were many who wept at the gentle treatment they
now received. Their chief affection went out to Florence herself. With a little lamp, she patrolled every night the grim, dark
corridors and wards, jam-packed with groaning, restless forms,
pausing at every few paces to make someone easier or whisper
a few words of encouragement. Some kissed her shadow as it
fell across them.

After the most hectic days were past she was able to concentrate on transforming chaos into good order, knowing that
every move she made would be scrutinized by jealous eyes in
the hope that she would make a mistake which, gloatingly
reported to London, would result in the women's recall. But
although she was aware of enemies at her elbow – among them
the Chief Medical Officer, Dr John Hall – and had to fight
daily against deliberate obstructionism, the conditions against
which she railed were not all the fault of the officials on the
spot. England's part in the Crimean War was incompetently
played at all levels.

Supplies of all kinds were desperately short. Urgent requis-
itions for more were delayed by slow-moving bureaucratic
processes at home, a shortage of shipping and gross errors of
handling. Food reached the Crimea too rotten to eat; medical
supplies for Scutari were stowed underneath vast cargoes for
the Crimea, so could not be unloaded until after the ship had

been to Balaclava and back again; an eagerly-awaited consign-
ment of boots proved to consist only of ones for the left foot.
Florence Nightingale bombarded Sidney Herbert with reports,
complaints, suggestions, meanwhile taking every measure she
could to make life in her hospitals more sanitary and tolerable.

From funds raised by the British public, she bought scrubbing brushes and soap and had the filthy wards scoured. She
provided thousands of shirts when the official commissariat
would not, with which to replace the stinking bloodstained
ones in which many patients slept and would not give up
because they had none other and feared they would never get
them back. She revolutionized the mass catering which had
resulted in some men not getting their meals until several hours
after they had been dished out, partly cooked, from greasy
vats. She made proposals about the planning and organization
of military hospitals in general. In most things Sidney Herbert
gave his powerful support.

Florence herself was criticized. She was accused of wilful
interference; of exaggerating her reports of shortcomings and
of mollycoddling her patients so that they would become too
soft to return to the fighting; of employing too many Catholics
and taking part in a papist plot to undermine the Church of
England.

She wrote, 'There is not an official who would not burn me
like Joan of Arc if he could.' A letter from Queen Victoria
which was cheered by the hospital patients when it was read to
them silenced many of the critics; but more effective still were
some undeniable statistics. In February 1855 forty-two
patients out of every hundred in the Scutari hospitals had died.
By June only two deaths per hundred were occurring and these
were from medical causes. Florence Nightingale and her handful of women had transformed the hospitals and the whole
conduct of nursing.

Early that year the British government fell and Sidney
Herbert lost office. Had it happened before, it might well have
wrecked Florence Nightingale's efforts, for he had been her
untiring advocate. Even now he remained outspoken on her
behalf.

Outbreaks of cholera and typhus, which claimed some
doctors and nurses as victims, recurred and kept Florence
under constant pressure, on her feet for as many as twenty
hours a day. Visiting the hospitals at Balaclava she caught
'Crimean fever', lingering on the threshold of death for nearly
a fortnight. Her health, undermined by overwork and anxiety,
would never be the same, doctors assured her, and urged her

to go home. She refused, returning to Scutari to work as hard as ever until the end of the war and the British evacuation in July 1856.

The government wished to pay its tribute to Florence by sending a man-of-war to bring her home. She refused, preferring to travel as an ordinary passenger in a French ship under the name 'Miss Smith'.

Personal recognition meant nothing. What she desired, and demanded as her right, was that official heed should be paid to every proposal she might put forward for the training of nurses and the administration of hospitals, both military and civil, and for the reform of certain aspects of the British army itself. She wrote endless memoranda for Sidney Herbert and other supporters to use in their often frustrating campaign against reactionary officialdom. Her 800-page document, *Notes Affecting the Health, Efficiency, and Hospital Administration of the British Army*, formed the basis for a royal commission's inquiries. Her *Notes on Nursing* proved an immediate bestseller. The public had subscribed £50,000 in recognition of her services: she used it to create a training scheme for nurses at St Thomas's Hospital, London, the prototype for many similar schemes.

Her health would never recover, and she would spend the greater part of the last fifty years of her life in bed, or shut up in her room, in a curious state of self-induced invalidism. However much she chose to remain out of sight, she did not cease to make herself heard. The exhortations, suggestions, criticisms and plans poured from her pen, their subjects ranging from the training of nurses for Liverpool workhouses to land reform in India.

But gradually she began to feel herself a failure, and was deeply hurt when the Queen did not respond actively to some of her schemes and when leadership of the growing nursing profession moved into other hands.

She spent her last fifteen years at her home in Park Lane, never going out except for an occasional early-morning drive when the streets were empty, and receiving only a few favoured visitors. Congratulations reached her from every part of the world on her eightieth birthday. In 1907 King Edward VII made her the first woman ever to be appointed to the Order of Merit. She died aged ninety on 1 August 1910 and was buried as she had insisted not in Westminster Abbey but at East Wellow, Hampshire, beside the parents who had striven so hard to prevent her remarkable career from materializing.

Elizabeth Blackwell

(1821-1910)

'A pretty little specimen of the female gender' is how Elizabeth Blackwell was described by an American medical journal when in 1848 she began to attend lectures in a medical college in a small township of New York State. 'She comes into the class with great composure,' the report continues, 'takes off her bonnet and puts it under the seat, exposing a fine phrenology. The effect on the class has been good, a great decorum is observed while she is present.'

The 'pretty little specimen' was an Englishwoman, born in 1821 in Bristol, where her father, an Independent (or Congregationalist) in religion and an ardent reformer in politics, was in business as a sugar refiner. Elizabeth was the third daughter in a family of nine and, like her brothers and sisters, she was educated mainly at home. In 1832, when she was eleven, her father's refinery was burnt down and, rather than attempting to rebuild his fortunes in England, Mr Blackwell resolved to emigrate to the United States, taking the whole family with him. They sailed from Bristol in August and seven weeks later they arrived in New York. There they lived until 1838,when, following some business losses, Mr Blackwell decided to remove to Cincinnati, then a small but promising town of the American West. The family made the seven-hundred-mile journey by stage-coach and canal boat, and hardly had they arrived when he was taken ill and shortly afterwards died, leaving his family entirely unprovided for.

Elizabeth was now almost eighteen and with her two elder sisters (Anna, who was twenty-three, and Marion two years younger) she started a day and boarding school for young ladies. Her eldest brother, aged fifteen, got himself a post in the Court House as a clerk where he was soon able to find a place for the next youngest boy. For the next few years, so Elizabeth writes in the 'autobiographical sketches' which were published in 1895 under the title *Pioneer Work in Opening the Medical Profession to Women*, 'until the younger children grew up and were able gradually to share in the work, we managed to support the family and maintain a home'.

She joined her sisters in their religious activities – they all

Soren Kierkegaard,
progenitor of modern existent-
ialism

Cardinal Newman,
theologian and author

William Booth, founder of the
Salvation Army

Robert Owen, Welsh social
reformer

Francis Place, self-educated
champion of radicalism

Benjamin Jowett,
celebrated Master of Balliol

Florence Nightingale,
reformer of nursing and
hospitals

Octavia Hill, housing reformer
and founder of the National
Trust

became members of the Episcopalian church in Cincinnati –
and in supporting the anti-slavery movement. Together they
read Emerson and Thomas Carlyle, and were ardent advocates
of the wider education of women which was a subject just
beginning to be discussed. In 1842, when the younger boys had
started earning, the school was given up. For a short time
Elizabeth took private pupils, and then she was invited to take
charge of a district school for girls about to be established
at Henderson, in western Kentucky. When she arrived there
she found Henderson, although styled a 'city', to be a small,
very uninteresting country place and the schoolhouse was not
much better than a shed. The people however, were friendly
enough.

> I believe they are a little afraid of me [she wrote home]
> particularly when they see me read German. I am amused to
> learn accidentally how I have been talked about in every
> direction, and my teeth particularly admired in peculiarly
> Kentucky style. 'Well, I do declare she's got a clean mouth,
> hasn't she!' – white teeth seeming remarkable where all use
> tobacco!

But Kentucky was a slave-state and soon she was writing in
her diary that she 'disliked slavery more and more every day'.
She heard no mention of a whipping-post and saw no instance
of downright cruelty,

> but to live in the midst of beings degraded to the utmost in
> body and mind, drudging on from earliest morning to latest
> night, cuffed about by everyone, scolded at all day long,
> blamed unjustly, and without spirit enough to reply, with
> no consideration in any way for their feelings, with no hope
> for the future, smelling horribly, and as ugly as Satan –
> to live in their midst, utterly unable to help them, is to me
> dreadful ...

At the end of the first term of her engagement she had had as
much as she could stand and handed in her resignation.

Returning home to the family in Cincinnati, she busied
herself in studying music, German and metaphysics, and in the
ordinary interests that social life presented. But before long
she began to feel the need for something more engrossing.
Then one day a friend who was suffering from a painful disease
that eventually killed her made the suggestion that was to
change her life. 'You are fond of study, have health and
leisure,' this lady said; 'why not study medicine? If I could

have been treated by a lady doctor my worst sufferings would
have been spared me.'

At first Elizabeth repudiated the suggestion as being quite
out of the question. She told her friend that she hated everything connected with the body and could not bear the sight of
a medical book; she recalled an incident of her schooldays
when the master, intent on interesting the class in the wonderful structure of the eye, produced a bullock's eye resting on its
rather bloody cushion of fat and she had been horrified. But
before long her attitude began to change. 'I must have something to engross my thoughts,' she confided in her journal;
'some object in life which will fill this vacuum and prevent
this sad wearing away of the heart.' Until at length what
had seemed repulsive presented itself as the necessary, the
inevitable, answer to her problem. 'I determined to become
a physician.'

Easier said than done, however. She had not the slightest
idea of how to set about it. She wrote for advice to several
physicians known to the family. They all replied that the idea
was an excellent one but quite impossible to carry out. There
was no way in which a woman could obtain a medical education and even if there were it must prove long and expensive.
The difficulties placed in her way served only as a challenge. 'A
force stronger than myself, then and afterwards, seemed to
lead me on; a purpose was before me which I must inevitably
seek to accomplish.'

Thrown entirely on her own resources, in 1845 she accepted
a teacher's post in a school at Asheville, North Carolina, where
the principal, who had been a doctor, helped her in her medical
studies. After eighteen months she moved to a school at Charleston, South Carolina, where she taught music in a fashionable girls boarding-school and in her spare time studied medicine along the lines suggested by a local practitioner. Then in
1847 she took a boat to Philadelphia, which was then considered the chief seat of medical learning in America.

There were four medical colleges in the city; she applied for
admission to each one in turn and each one turned her down.
She then applied to the medical schools in New York with the
same result. Still undaunted, she obtained a complete list of all
the smaller medical schools in the northern USA – 'country
schools' they were called – and wrote to twelve that seemed the
most promising. For a time there was no answer but in October
1847 there came a letter from the Dean of the Faculty in the
medical college at Geneva, a small town in western New York
State, informing her that the faculty had thought it desirable

to put her application before the medical class of students and that the students had discussed it and had adopted unanimously the following resolution:

That one of the radical principles of a Republican Government is the universal education of both sexes; that to every branch of scientific education the door should be open equally to all; that the application of Elizabeth Blackwell to become a member of our class meets our entire approbation; and in extending our unanimous invitation we pledge ourselves that no conduct of ours shall cause her to regret her attendance at this institution.

With an 'immense sigh of relief and aspiration of profound gratitude to Providence' Elizabeth instantly accepted the invitation and hurried off to Geneva. She arrived there late at night on 6 November and on the next morning was duly inscribed on the list as Student No 130 in the medical department of the Geneva University.

To begin with, things were far from easy. As she walked from her boarding-house to the college and back again, the ladies in the street stopped to stare at her, 'as at a curious animal'. Later on she found that she had so shocked Geneva propriety that it was generally agreed that she was either a bad woman, whose designs would gradually become evident, or that, being insane, an outbreak of insanity would soon be apparent. But she soon felt perfectly at home among her fellow students. 'The behaviour of the medical class during the two years that I was with them was admirable,' she writes; 'it was that of true Christian gentlemen.'

'My place in the lecture-rooms was always kept for me, and I was never in any way molested. Walking down the crowded amphitheatre after the class was seated, no notice was taken of me.' At first she was required to absent herself from some of the anatomy lectures, but when she wrote in a note to the class that the study of anatomy seemed to her a most serious one, exciting profound reverence, and the suggestion that she should absent herself from any lectures seemed a grave mistake, they at once accepted her point of view and she quietly resumed her place.

After little more than a year, Elizabeth took her 'finals'. In her diary for 22 January 1849 we find the entry: 'Our examinations came off successfully. Hurrah, 'tis almost over!' And the day following: 'The day, the grand day ... 'twas bright and beautiful and very gratifying ...' The graduation ceremony was held in the Presbyterian Church, a large building but not large enough to hold all who wished to see 'the full and equal diploma of Doctor of Medicine' conferred upon a woman. One of Elizabeth's brothers had come to Geneva for the occasion, and his vivid account is worth quoting.

> After a short discourse by Dr Hale, the President, the diplomas were conferred – four being called up at a time – the President addressed them in a Latin formula, taking off his hat, but remaining seated, and so handed them their diplomas, which they received with a bow and then retired. Elizabeth was left to the last and called up alone. The President, taking off his hat, rose, and addressing her in the same formula, substituting *Domina* for *Domine*, presented her the diploma, whereupon our Sis, who had walked up and stood before him with much dignity, bowed and half turned to retire, but suddenly turning back replied: 'Sir, I thank you; by the help of the Most High it shall be the effort of my life to shed honour upon your diploma'; whereupon she bowed and the President bowed, the audience gave manifestations of applause ... and our Sis, descending the steps, took her seat with her fellow-physicians in front.

Many of the newspapers recorded the event and the fame of it spread across the Atlantic. In London *Punch* published a delightful set of verses 'in honour of the fair MD'.

Although she had realized her ambition of becoming the first woman doctor Elizabeth Blackwell recognized the necessity of obtaining much more experience before she ventured to set up in practice. She continued her studies in Philadelphia, but opportunities for further study in America were so limited that in spring 1849 she returned to the England she had left when a girl of eleven. At Birmingham she was shown over the hospitals and in London made a tour of St Thomas's under the guidance of the senior surgeon. But she had been told by all her teachers and advisers that Paris was the place to go to find unlimited opportunities for study in any and every branch of the medical art, and so after a few weeks she crossed the Channel, 'with a very slender purse and few introductions of any value'.

Arrived at Paris, she was permitted to enrol at La Maternité, the great state institution at which French midwives received their training. Her six months there proved extremely trying, what with the strict discipline, the harsh living conditions, the long hours, the almost constant labour. On the other hand, she quite enjoyed watching the frolics of the bouncing country girls, and a pleasant comradeship developed between her and one or two of the young doctors. She qualified as an obstetrician, but towards the end of her stay what she describes as a 'very grave accident' befell her. When syringing the eye of one of her tiny patients for purulent ophthalmia some of the water spurted into her own eye. For three weeks she was in bed with both eyes closed, and in spite of the most devoted attention she lost the sight of one eye completely.

Thus obliged to abandon her hope of becoming a surgeon, she went back to London and obtained permission to study practical medicine at St Bartholomew's Hospital. Every ward and department was thrown open to her, except the department for female diseases! It was during this second stay in London that she made the acquaintance, which ripened into life-long friendship, of such notable workers in the cause of women's emancipation as Bessie Rayner Parkes (later Mme Belloc, mother of Hilaire Belloc), Barbara Leigh Smith (Mme Bodichon) and Florence Nightingale.

In July 1851 she went back to America and for the next seven years was fully occupied in promoting medical education among women. When she was refused admission as a physician at a large dispensary in New York, she set about establishing a dispensary of her own, which developed into the New York Infirmary and College for Women. Then in 1857 she opened a hospital in New York conducted entirely by women, in the running of which she was ably supported by her sister Emily, who had qualified as a doctor at Cleveland, Ohio, and Maria Zackrzewska, who was the third woman to qualify. During the American Civil War a number of Blackwell-trained nurses rendered valiant service.

Twenty years after her graduation as MD, Elizabeth felt that the early pioneer work in America was ended and returned again to England. For some years she practised medicine in London and when the London School of Medicine for Women was opened in 1875 accepted the chair of gynaecology. She lectured and wrote on health matters until advancing years caused her to retire. She died at her home in Hastings on 31 May 1910 and was buried in the churchyard at Kilmun, the Argyllshire village where she had spent happy holidays with one of her sisters.

Josephine Butler

(1828–1906)

From hotel to hotel she went, trying in vain to get a room for the night. At the next on the list she gave her maiden name and this time she was successful. The porter took her bag and she was shown up to her room. She was in bed, trying to sleep after an exhausting day, when there came a knock at the door. It was the hotel proprietor. She bade him come in and he was very apologetic but all the same insistent. 'I am sorry, madam, I have a very unpleasant announcement to make,' he said. 'I find you are Mrs Josephine Butler, and there's a mob outside who have found out that you are here, and they are threatening to set fire to the hotel unless I send you away at once.' Then, seeing how tired she was, he said that he would get her away under another name to some lodging in the neighbourhood, where she would be quite safe. He was as good as his word, and Mrs Butler passed what was left of the night in a little cottage down a side street.

This was in 1870, in the town of Colchester, when Mrs Butler was one of the most unpopular women in England – 'hated' might not be too strong a word to use. And yet this same woman, although her name may not be as well known as, say, Florence Nightingale's, has long been sure of a place in the portrait-gallery of 'great Victorians'.

Mrs Butler was Josephine Elizabeth Grey, born at Milfield Hill in Northumberland on 13 April 1828. The Greys have long been one of the most distinguished of the Border families, and Earl Grey of the Reform Bill struggle and Sir Edward Grey, Foreign Secretary at the time of World War I, were distant cousins. Her father John Grey was also a man of great public spirit, an ardent co-worker with Clarkson and Wilberforce in the anti-slavery movement and supporter of parliamentary reform and other liberal measures.

With her sister Harriet, Josephine had two years of schooling at Newcastle but for the most part she was taught at home, where she learnt to ride at an early age, becoming an expert horsewoman, and developed a love for horses and dogs (especially dogs) which persisted through her long life.

Early in 1852 she became Mrs George Butler. Her husband,

nine years her senior, was a member of a highly distinguished scholastic family; his father had been headmaster of Harrow and eventually became Dean of Peterborough, and his brother Henry Montagu Butler also became Headmaster of Harrow and later Dean of Gloucester and Master of Trinity College, Cambridge.

After a brilliant career at Cambridge and also Oxford George Butler was appointed to a tutorship at the University of Durham, and it was during his residence at Durham that Josephine first met him. Shortly after their marriage they settled in Oxford, where Butler had an examiner's post, but also did a good deal of lecturing. He was the first who brought into prominence the study of geography, Josephine Butler tells us in her book *Recollections of George Butler* (1892), and he was one of the first who introduced and encouraged the study of art in the university.

The five years she and her husband spent in Oxford left many happy memories, but there was also what she called a 'shadow side'. She had come from a large family circle, and from free country life to life in a university town – a society of celibates, with little or no leaven of family life. There was much good talk in the social gatherings in her drawing-room of an evening, serious and weighty, witty and brilliant, ranging over many subjects. But often she 'sat silent, the only woman in the company, and listened, sometimes with a sore heart; for these men would speak of things which I had already revolved deeply in my own mind, things of which I was convinced, which I knew, though I had no dialectics at command with which to defend their truth.'

On one evening (so she recalled years afterwards) they were discussing the latest novel of Mrs Gaskell – it must have been *Ruth*, published in 1853. Judgments were expressed, judgments which seemed to her false, fatally false. 'A moral lapse in a woman was spoken of as an immensely worse thing than in a man; there was no comparison to be formed between them. A pure woman, it was reiterated, should be absolutely ignorant of a certain class of evils in the world, albeit those evils bore with murderous cruelty on other women. One young man seriously declared that he would not allow his own mother to read such a book ...' On another occasion she was distressed by what she considered a bitter case of wrong inflicted on a very young girl. She ventured to raise the matter with one of the wisest men – at least, so he was esteemed – in the university, in the hope that he would suggest some means not only of helping her but of bringing the young man who had wronged

her to a sense of his crime. The sage sternly advocated silence
and inaction. 'It could only do harm to open up in any way
such a question as this,' he opined; 'it was dangerous to arouse
a sleeping lion.'

Already 'every instinct of womanhood' within her was in
revolt against certain accepted theories in society and 'I suffered as only God and the faithful companion of my life could
ever know'. Her feeling of the unfairness of men's, some men's,
attitude towards women was fortified and intensified by certain
incidents that occurred. There was in particular the case of a
young unmarried mother who was in Newgate charged with
the murder of her infant. The father of the child, 'under cover
of the death-like silence prescribed by the Oxford philosophers', had perjured himself to her, forsaken and forgotten
her, and fallen back, with no accusing conscience, on his easy
social life and possibly his academic honours. Mrs Butler had
the urge to go to speak to the poor woman in prison 'of the
God who saw the injustice done, and who cared for her'. Her
husband suggested that they should write to the chaplain at
Newgate and ask him to send the woman to them when her
sentence had expired. 'We wanted a servant, and he thought
that she might be able to fill the place. She came to us. I think
she was the first of the world of unhappy women of a humble
class whom we welcomed into our home. She was not the last.'

George Butler – by now he had taken holy orders in the
Church of England – was invited in 1857 to become vice-
principal of Cheltenham College and they were glad to accept
the invitation since Oxford had a very bad effect on Josephine's
health. Thus Butler was launched on his career as a schoolmaster that was to continue for the next twenty-five years. It
was while they were at Cheltenham that they suffered the tragic
loss of their little daughter Eva. They had been to some function in the town and returned home about seven. Eva, in her
haste to greet them, rushed out of her bedroom, leaned too far
over the banisters and fell headlong on the stone floor of the
hall. She was killed instantly. 'Never can I lose that memory,'
wrote the grief-stricken mother; 'the fall, the sudden cry, and
then the silence ... Would to God that I had died that death
for her!'

A year or so later (in 1865) Butler was appointed to the
headship of Liverpool College, a school with eight or nine
hundred boys drawn from a great variety of homes and many
of them belonging to other races and different religions. The
move did Josephine a world of good. She almost forgot her
personal sorrow in the openings for service that presented

themselves. As she put it, 'I became possessed with an irresistible desire to go forth and find some pain keener than my own
... to find other hearts which ached night and day, and with
more reason than mine.' She soon learnt that it was not difficult
to find misery in Liverpool. There was the immense workhouse, containing five thousand persons – a little town in itself.
On the ground floor there was a bridewell for women, consisting of huge cellars, the so-called 'oakum sheds' to which came
women and girls driven by hunger, destitution or vice, begging
for a few nights' shelter and a piece of bread, in return for
which they were allotted a portion of oakum to pick. Mrs
Butler went down to the oakum-sheds and begged admission.
She mixed with the girls, tried to pick oakum herself, and when
the girls laughed at her clumsy efforts she joined in their laughter and then tried to give them the gospel message. She also
visited the hospital where some of the seaport's thousands of
prostitutes, many of them ranked as 'incurables', were rotting
their lives away, and she walked the quays in the hope of
reclaiming a woman here and there not too far gone in vice.

The result of these efforts was 'to draw down upon my head
an avalanche of miserable but grateful womanhood'. She and
her husband let it be known that they had a dry cellar and an
attic or two in which friendless girls would always be sure of a
welcome. So many applied that they were soon obliged to take
a house nearby for the purpose, and when this 'House of Rest'
proved insufficient they, aided by a number of generous
Liverpool merchants and their friends, took another and larger
house where women might not only find shelter but be taught
some useful trade. An envelope factory was one of their
projects.

Now we come to the period when Josephine Butler embarked on the great work of her life, her crusade against the
state regulation of vice. This system had its rise in France
under Napoleon in 1802 and was copied in other European
countries. Several attempts were made to introduce something
similar into England but without success until 1864 when,
following a scare about the increase of venereal disease among
the men in the army and navy and also in the civilian population in industrial centres, an Act of Parliament was passed,
with the minimum of publicity, 'for the prevention of contagious diseases at certain naval and military stations'. This was
a temporary measure but it was renewed in 1866, and in 1869
its operation was extended to about twenty seaports and military towns in England. The main features of the CD Acts were:
registration and police supervision of prostitutes; their com-

pulsory medical inspection for the purpose of detecting cases of VD; and the compulsory detention for treatment in special hospitals of those found to be so suffering. It was understood that in due course the operation of the Acts would be extended by degrees to other parts of Britain.

To begin with, very little notice was taken of the CD Acts; many people may have supposed that they were something to do with animals. Mrs Butler, who had made a personal investigation of the operation of the system in Europe, was among the few who took alarm, although for the time being she kept quiet. But before long disquiet became widespread. In the autumn of 1869 a National Association for the Repeal of the CD Acts was formed and almost simultaneously a Ladies Association for the same purpose. Mrs Butler was thereupon urged to take the lead in the coming agitation.

If she had only herself to consider she would have had no hesitation, but there was her husband to consider. Mr Butler was a highly esteemed clergyman, and at that time almost the full weight of public opinion was in favour of the CD Acts as being the best means yet devised of meeting and controlling sexual vice. Mrs Butler, after much thought and prayer, laid the invitation she had received before her husband and asked his advice.

And that good and noble man [she wrote in her *Memoir of George Butler*], foreseeing what it would mean for me and himself, spoke not one word to suggest difficulty or danger or impropriety in any action which I might be called upon to take. He did not pause to ask: 'What will the world say?' or 'Is this suitable work for a woman?' He had pondered the matter, and looking straight, as was his wont, he saw only a great wrong, and a deep desire to redress that wrong, a duty to be fulfilled in fidelity to that impulse, and, above all, he saw God ... his whole attitude in response to my words expressed, 'Go! and God be with you.'

From that time Mrs Butler was, as one of her principal coadjutors put it, 'the head and front of the movement; her beauty, her grace, her eloquence and indomitable courage won adherents on every side and secured the victory for us at last'.

But it was a hard fight and it brought down upon her head intense opprobrium. Between June 1869 and June 1870 she addressed ninety-nine public meetings and four conferences, and travelled more than 3,700 miles. An outstanding incident in the campaign was the National Association's opposition to the Liberal Government candidate Sir Henry Storks at a by-election in Colchester in autumn 1870. Storks was a prominent advocate of the CD Acts and the abolitionists made a determined effort to prevent his return to the House of Commons. The Liberals were infuriated at Mrs Butler's intervention, and she was set upon by hired roughs and even her life was threatened. Her meetings were broken up and she was denied rooms at the hotels. So fierce was the opposition that her friends insisted that she should not stay in the town to hear the result of the poll. It was conveyed to her by telegram, 'Bird shot dead', Storks having been defeated by a big majority.

The struggle continued for years and always Mrs Butler was in the thick of it. At length in 1886 the obnoxious CD Acts were repealed. For the rest of her life, however, Mrs Butler continued to inspire and guide the activities of those who wanted the achievement of women's equality not only in the sexual but in the educational, professional and other fields. As a platform speaker she was in constant demand and the list of her writings runs to several pages. Particular value attaches to her *Personal Reminiscences of a Great Crusade* (1896), in which the story of the fight against the CD Acts is told as only she could tell it.

In 1882 her husband gave up teaching when Gladstone appointed him to a canonry at Winchester. They moved to Winchester, where one of her earliest actions was the establishment of a 'House of Rest' similar to the one at Liverpool. Dr Butler died in 1890 and Mrs Butler's last years were spent at Wooler, near to her birthplace at Milfield. There she died on 30 December 1906, peacefully in her sleep, and was buried among her ancestors in the churchyard of Kirknewton.

Richard Norman Shaw

(1831-1912)

'An architectural Picasso', 'pioneer of modern design' or, in domestic architecture, 'a bridge between the gross grandeur of Barry's generation and the "simple life" of Voysey and the Garden Cities'. So Richard Norman Shaw has been described in the twentieth century. To the late Victorian there was little doubt. This was the man to commission to build your house. The successful architect of the 1870s and 1880s, an Associate of the Royal Academy when he was only forty, Norman Shaw's career covered a span of nearly fifty years.

His early life had been relatively modest. He was born in Edinburgh in 1831. His mother was a Scot; his father, who died when he was only two, is described as an Irish Protestant 'with a Huguenot strain'. His formal education was scanty. He attended a local school in Hill Street, Edinburgh and never went to public school or university. He showed little interest in scholarship and one of his masters, questioned about the advisability of his studying classics, replied, 'There is something in him, but it is not Greek.'

When he was about fifteen his family moved to London, and there his bent for architecture was recognized. Still in his early teens, he entered the office of William Burn, a Scot who had built up a most successful practice designing Jacobean and Scottish mansions for the aristocracy. During his seven years with this very competent man, Shaw must have laid the foundations of his interest in domestic architecture while being trained in the clean clear draughtsmanship for which he became noted. This draughtsmanship probably stood him in good stead at the Royal Academy where he attended lectures. In 1853, when he was twenty-two, he won the Academy's Silver Medal, and in the following year won the Gold Medal and Travelling Scholarship. For eighteen months he travelled in Italy, France and Germany and, sharing the contemporary interest in Gothic, concentrated on sketching French cathedrals.

In the middle of the nineteenth century it was customary for an architect to publish a work which would, it was hoped, establish its author as an artist and a scholar and, by bringing him to the notice of the public, lead to some lucrative com-

428

missions. After his travels Shaw, in 1858, followed the pattern and published a most attractive Victorian Gothic source-book *Architectural Sketches from the Continent*. Possibly on the strength of this he was taken on as chief draughtsman in the office of G. E. Street, one of the most serious and conscientious architects of the Gothic revival.

In 1862, still almost unknown, Shaw went into partnership with W. Eden Nesfield, an architect he had known in Burn's office and with whom he had travelled. The two young men were close friends and shared an intense interest in Gothic art. They travelled together, in England and abroad, enthusiastically sketching and measuring genuine medieval buildings and revivals such as Pugin's Houses of Parliament. Even on holiday Shaw showed an extremely singleminded devotion to architecture. While Nesfield's diaries are full of little notes about pubs, food and so on, Shaw stuck to the subject. He was not so much concerned with producing 'beautiful' drawings as with noting down vital structural features and he did not hesitate to add notes in writing when these more concisely covered a point.

Although Shaw was the elder, the partnership was known as Nesfield and Shaw, possibly because Nesfield was the more wealthy of the two. As the son of the leading garden designer of his day, he was able to introduce aristocratic clients. It was a loose partnership in which little of their work was signed jointly. As Nesfield was a retiring character and hostile to all publicity, his work has tended to be overlooked until recently. There is little doubt, however, that many ideas later developed and made famous by Shaw show the influence of Nesfield. Although the formal partnership was brief the two men shared an office until 1876, by which time Shaw was well launched in his career. He had already designed country houses such as Leyswood, Sussex, Boldre Grange, near Lymington and Wispers, Midhurst.

In 1867 Shaw had married Agnes Haswell Wood. In 1876 he moved with his wife and three children to a new house he had built for his family in Ellerdale Road, Hampstead.

The 1870s and 1880s were the years of Shaw's greatest success. By then the nature of patronage was changing. The most lavish houses were as likely to be for rich industrialists as for the aristocracy. In Shaw's case many were designed for successful fellow academicians who wanted 'artist' houses in South Hampstead or Kensington; houses in which the large studio took the place of the hall which was a feature of his country houses. His first client was the painter, J.C. Horsley, RA. Frank Holl, Marcus Stone and many other other academicians followed. A house built for Kate Greenaway, the illustrator of children's books, still stands in Frognal.

The lavish scale of many of these houses shows just what a golden age it was for the painter as well as the industrialist. Shaw seems to have been quite clear-headed and aware of the unnatural affluence of the period. When questioned over some extra cost on an artist's house, he commented, 'Oh, he can paint another nose.' A story of Henry Tate, of Tate Gallery fame, gives some picture of the attitudes of the time. In 1887 Tate offered a Norman Shaw house to any member of his family who was not contented with his current home. Four were built, one in Frognal and three in Liverpool. Even in 1887, each cost £10,000.

Apart from Pugin, Shaw had more effect on the English scene than any other architect since Robert Adam. In London his work has fared fairly well. At 170 and 196 Queen's Gate, in Melbury Road, Kensington and in Hampstead many of his houses still stand, proof of the brilliance and variety of his invention. Yet apart, perhaps, from the so-called Queen Anne always linked with his name, it is impossible to pin down a typical 'Norman Shaw' style. Nor can progressive development in his style be traced. Like Picasso he leapt easily from style to style. In the theatrical verve of a country house such as Leyswood at Groombridge, Sussex, a vast half-timbered tile-hung house, drawing on picturesque old English Sussex rather than any specific period style, one sees the Shaw 'manorial' mode. With its fantastic tall chimneys, mullioned and transomed windows, gables and bays amassed round an open courtyard, Leyswood was one of the best known of the houses in which Shaw combined the wealthy-looking with the homely-looking. It was a combination of great appeal to affluent Victorians of the next twenty years.

In 1875 Shaw built Cheyne House, Chelsea Embankment. The balance and symmetry of its facade suggested a return to the calm simplicity of Georgian style. In the same year, however, at 196 Queen's Gate he built another house which shattered the by then rather sterile unity of a neighbourhood in which stucco-fronted houses were still being erected in builders' 'renaissance' design. With its brick and terracotta of brightest red, its large mullioned windows and asymmetrical composition, this tall gabled facade totally ignored its surroundings. It made such an impact on other designers that for the next fifteen years such houses sprang up all over Chelsea, Kensington and Earl's Court. Shaw built some of them such as 62, 68 and 72 Cadogan Square; Sir Ernest George built

Collingham Gardens (1881–87); Stevenson developed the so-called Pont Street Dutch; and the builders followed the vogue, turning red brick and terracotta into the most popular West End style of the period.

In 1888, with 170 Queen's Gate, which he built for an American diplomat, Fred White, Shaw returned to a quieter, more classical style. Possibly White had some choice in the design for he had originally commissioned Philip Webb. He only turned to Shaw when alarmed by Webb's demand for a completely free hand in all questions of design. Wrennish in style, a simple rectangular block of red brick unornamented apart from the pedimented doorway and a central dormer window, White's house seems a direct forerunner of the English domestic neo-Georgian of 1910 onwards.

It is Shaw's final 'Baroque' phase in a building, such as the Piccadilly Hotel, with its vast colonnade on massive arcades, that brings him the most criticism today. After the sensitive handling of some of his earlier work it is sad to see him lead the way to the vulgarity of Edwardian-Imperial Baroque. On the other hand, how typically Victorian is the confidence of this man, who, although nearly seventy-five, was able to design a building of such vitality. It was to be only one part of a design (unexecuted) for the rebuilding of the Regent Street Quadrant.

Although certain aspects of Shaw's work have won him mention as a pioneer of modern design it is wrong to think of him as consciously striving to be 'modern' or ahead of his time. He showed little sympathy with the innovators of his period. There is no reason to believe that he did not like the lush Victorian paintings of his academician clients. He was capable of dismissing William Morris as 'just a tradesman posing as a socialist'. When the two men worked together as they did on Old Swan House it must have been in uneasy partnership. Not surprisingly, Morris did not really like Shaw either. When writing about him on one occasion he mentioned the 'elegantly fantastic Queen Anne houses in Chelsea' and the 'quaint and pretty architecture' of Bedford Park. In Morris's vocabulary elegant, pretty and fantastic were not words of praise.

Norman Shaw was one of the most eclectic of architects. He was greatest, however, when the artist overcame the historian and his debt to the past became more an understanding of the function, materials and beauty of a period rather than an imitation of its style. He had many different manners and only ever completely dropped his first love, High Victorian Gothic. Looking back in 1902 he wrote: 'Until recently we were all intensely Gothic and intensely wrong ... I was trained in the older Gothic lines ... I admire it in the abstract but it is totally unsuited to modern requirements.' Together with his partner Nesfield, with his fellow architect Philip Webb and with William Morris in textile design, Shaw led the revolt against the pomp and grossness of High Victorian Gothic. In its place we see the sensitive balance of a building such as Old Swan House, Chelsea, whose delicate elegance puts it far ahead of its time.

Shaw's open-minded experimentation applied as much to new materials and methods as to style. If the twentieth century looks back in judgement on his use of sham half-timbering at Leyswood, they must also consider that as early as 1874 he was using the still new material, concrete, in a convent he built at Boscombe. A little later he did a series of designs for constructing cottages from patented prefabricated concrete slabs. As a rule, his desire for freedom in his plans and a wish to design each floor as an independent entity led him to using steel girders to carry weight rather than making the walls of one floor support those of the floor above. At Old Swan House the internal iron skeleton above the bold cantilever on the front is in effect 'skyscraper construction', for the skeleton carries the complete weight of the brickwork of the upper walls. Yet this was built in 1876, a decade before the 'invention' of that type of construction in Chicago.

In other ways, too, Shaw showed himself as an innovator. He was one of the first to realize the dangers of out-of-date indoor plumbing and to devise a safer method. His Albert Hall Mansions of 1879 is said to be the first great block of flats in London. Bedford Park at Turnham Green, for which Shaw did the overall design but not all the individual buildings, is also outstanding. Although it was built some thirty years before Hampstead Garden Suburb, Bedford Park is much closer in spirit to a new town or garden suburb than to the stockbrokers' Gothic or white stucco renaissance which had been going up in London earlier in the nineteenth century.

Shaw, having attained his youthful ambition of becoming a Royal Academician, seems to have been uninterested in further honours. Later in life he was offered and declined a baronetcy. He twice turned down the Royal Institute of British Architects' Gold Medal. While his relations with the Royal Academy were always very cordial, the same cannot be said for his attitude to the RIBA. Apparently he had resigned his membership some years before because, he said, the meetings were dull. He believed that their wish to improve professional standards meant that they were looking at architecture from a purely business rather than an artistic viewpoint. In the rather muddled arguments which he put forth in the heated controversy of 1892, 'Architecture, a profession or an art?', Shaw clearly showed himself as an artist rather than a scholar.

Shaw's ready understanding of his clients' requirements made him popular but he could be quite adamant if he did not agree on any point. On one occasion a client wanted a house with french windows opening on to the garden. Shaw, who had a curious dislike of this style, is said to have replied tersely, 'I will not make your windows open to the ground. When I have quite finished the house and left it you can call in the village carpenter and do what you want.' But apparently that client was a hostess of considerable beauty, and for the same house Shaw took the trouble to design the doors with handles high up so that her sleeve would fall back to reveal an elegant forearm as she opened the door.

Richard Norman Shaw died in 1912. Unfortunately while he was alive he discouraged the idea of anyone writing his biography. Nothing appeared until Sir Reginald Blomfield's work in 1940. This covers Shaw's buildings thoroughly but does not give us much of a picture of his character. As a man he remains a mystery. We are repeatedly told of his charm, friendliness and modesty, but not much about the toughness and courage which he must also have possessed to have fought so hard for some of his designs and also to have been capable of putting up a building such as New Zealand Chambers, Leadenhall Street, undaunted by the fact that its lively facade was quite at variance with the sombre pompousness of its city neighbours.

Of all Victorians Shaw alone founded a school, and it is to his credit that it was his office which turned out men of such various and original talents as Edward Prior, Ernest Newton and William Lethaby. Perhaps it is right in an architect that in the end one can only see the man through his influence and through his buildings. It is of these that Nikolaus Pevsner, in writing on the Domestic Revival in England, says: 'If one looks for brilliance, fecundity of invention, and sheer joy in novelty, one has to go to Richard Norman Shaw.'

Robert Applegarth

(1834–1924)

The life of Robert Applegarth spanned almost a century of unprecedented change which began with Britain's rise to industrial predominance and ended with the world economic crisis that followed World War I. Born in Hull in 1834, the year of the Tolpuddle Martyrs and the hated New Poor Law, he died in 1924, when the first Labour government came to office. His early years were neither remarkably poor nor especially eventful. The son of a sailor who rose to be a whaling captain, Robert at the age of ten went to work as an errand-boy: afterwards he moved to the workshop of a joiner and cabinet-maker and, unapprenticed, picked up the trade as best he could. In 1854, now married, he emigrated, as many of his countrymen were doing, to the United States but returned three years later as his wife's health had not allowed her to join him there. In Sheffield in 1858 he joined the local Carpenters' Union and quickly became its leading member: the important public period of his life lasted only from then until 1871, though he was to live on after this for another half-century.

Applegarth entered into a trade-union world which was weak, dispirited and split within itself. Unions were by no means new in 1858 – some indeed had existed among skilled workers for a hundred years and more – but a 'union' still implied an association of local trade clubs rather than a national organization, a fragile combination which could be easily broken by an unsuccessful strike or an employer's lock-out. Earlier attempts to organize powerful national associations of workers, like Robert Owen's Grand National Consolidated Trade Union, founded in the year before Applegarth's birth, had been defeated partly through their own financial and administrative weaknesses, partly because of the savage hostility of employers and the law. Applegarth would not have remembered the trial and transportation of the Dorchester Labourers the next year, though he grew up with what quickly became a working-class legend: he would certainly have remembered the Chartist agitation of the 1840s, the mass meetings by torchlight on the Yorkshire moors, the passionate talk of revolution, the haggard looks on the faces of starving men.

434

The collapse of Chartism in 1848 marks an important turning-point in the history of English labour. Up until then the great working-class movements – radicalism, Luddism, Owenism, Chartism – had aimed at social revolution, at some sudden overthrow or transformation of the industrial system which would give the worker immediate and powerful control. Capital and labour seemed to be locked in a deadly conflict, the only resolution of which would be the total surrender of one or the other. But during the 1850s Britain began to move into a period of new prosperity, and capitalism began to bestow some of its fruits more equitably over the population: employment, if not full, was fuller than it had been for decades past, real earnings were rising and the price of some foods falling. In these new circumstances, newer, gentler relationships began to develop between masters and workers, and some forms of labour organizations, once regarded indiscriminately as dangerous and revolutionary, came to be tolerated, even encouraged.

At the time when Robert Applegarth returned from America a new trade-union movement was already beginning to be built. The reconstruction involved new policies, new procedures and new men, a renunciation of violence and militancy, an acceptance of industrial capitalism but a firm belief that through powerful combination it could be made to yield ever greater rewards to those who had only their labour to sell. The prototype of this 'New Model' unionism was the Amalgamated Society of Engineers, founded in 1851 by men who were widely regarded as the aristocrats of labour. The ASE amalgamated many small local unions into a national association, concentrating power in the centre: it was a craft union, open only to skilled men who could afford to pay a subscription of a shilling a week out of a wage of around 35 shillings: membership gave important Friendly Society benefits against sickness, unemployment and for dependants. Above all, the New Model unions were determined to demonstrate that the worker was respectable and responsible, that skill was a scarce commodity and worthy of a better reward, that the common interests of capital and labour lay in an expanding market out of which both could profit. Strikes, disputes and lock-outs only constituted impediments to the expansion of wealth: conciliation should therefore take the place of conflict, co-operation that of anarchy.

During the third quarter of the nineteenth century, then, the trade-union movement was being rebuilt along new lines of caution, moderation and financial strength. To a large extent this reconstruction was the personal achievement of a handful of young men who were the general secretaries of the new unions – William Allan (b. 1813) of the Amalgamated Society of Engineers, Daniel Guile (b. 1814) of the Ironfounders, George Odger (b. 1820) of the Shoemakers' Society and Robert Applegarth (b. 1834) of the Amalgamated Society of Carpenters and Joiners. All were self-educated men who had imbibed one philosophy more than any other – that of 'self-help' – the simple yet striking idea that one could be the instrument of one's own advancement, that through education and skill, hard work, thrift and sobriety one could raise oneself from poverty and obscurity to riches and fame. It had been a message well known for centuries past, the principle on which not a few middle-class fortunes had been raised in the earlier stages of industrialization. What Applegarth and his colleagues did was to apply this essentially individualist philosophy collectively to the whole body of workers in a particular trade. At its foundation in 1860 the Amalgamated Society of Carpenters and Joiners counselled its members to 'become respectful and respected': another New Model union advised, 'Get knowledge instead of alcohol: it is sweeter and more lasting.'

In Sheffield in the late 1850s, a town noted for the militancy of its labour movements, Robert Applegarth enthusiastically accepted the principles of the new unionism. He was largely instrumental in bringing his small local union into the Amalgamated Society of Carpenters and Joiners when it was founded in 1860: two years later he became its general secretary, holding the office for ten years. It was during this comparatively brief period that he made his outstanding contribution to the labour movement. At first he stood in the shadow of William Allan, whose Amalgamated Engineers had already existed for a decade. There was close personal friendship between the two men, Allan advising on the constitution and organization of the Carpenters and Joiners, and lending the rules of the engineers as a model. But under Applegarth the Carpenters and Joiners quickly grew in membership, status and accumulated funds and became second only to the engineering aristocrats. Moreover, Applegarth's evident ability quickly raised him to a position of power and influence in the trade-union world as a whole.

He made of the secretaryship a new kind of position quite unlike that of the demagogues and agitators who so often had controlled unions in the past. He was concerned, in the first place, to bring efficient administration into the running of his

union, to see that contributions were regularly collected and
invested, that meetings were democratically and soberly conducted, that insurance benefits were properly paid to those
members entitled. This was all mundane, almost trivial, work,
though vitally necessary in demonstrating that national
unions, with thousands of pounds of public money in their
control, could run their affairs on sound business principles.

But, more than this, Applegarth had a vision of what organized labour might achieve, wider than any immediate concern
over wages, hours and conditions of work, important as these
things were. His ultimate interest was the social improvement
of the working classes as a whole, through education and
political participation to raise their status and give them equality with the rest of society. In the year that Robert Applegarth
was beginning work as an errand-boy, Disraeli had published
his *Sybil, or the Two Nations* –

> between whom there is no intercourse and no sympathy;
> who are as ignorant of each other's habits, thoughts and
> feelings as if they were dwellers in different zones, or inha-
> bitants of different planets; who are formed by a different
> breeding, are fed by a different food, are ordered by different
> manners, and are not governed by the same laws.

It was these kinds of inequality that Applegarth was determined to suppress and by so doing to bring the working classes
into political and social competence.

Together the New Model leaders formed a close and powerful group which contemporary observers referred to as 'the
clique' and later historians as 'the junta': from their headquarters in London, and the leading part they came to play in
the London Trades Council, Applegarth, Allan, Guile and
Odger in effect composed an inner cabinet which largely dominated the trade-union world for a decade. Their evident integrity and liberal philosophy precisely suited the needs of the time
and commended them alike to middle-class employers and
politicians. This was, no doubt, partly because in the purely
industrial field their objectives were limited and reasonable – to
raise wages and conditions of work in particular trades to what
had already been conceded by the best employers. 'Self-help'
perhaps had this selfish characteristic, that it was more concerned with the interests of engineers or ironfounders than it
was with the improvement of labour as a whole.

Applegarth himself, though he derived much of his philosophy from self-help, was not bounded by such narrow hori-
zons. Trade unions to him were not to be ends in themselves,

but the instruments of working-class emancipation – political, legal and social – and his greatest achievements lay beyond the direct interests of his own union members. In its long-term effects, the most important of all was the leading part he played in the achievement of the 1867 Reform Act, which extended the franchise to the majority of urban workers and so began to break the monopoly of political power which the middle classes had formerly enjoyed. He had the difficult task of convincing the unions that an interest in national politics was their proper concern and a necessary condition of their advance in status. In 1864 he had been one of the committee which welcomed the democratic hero Garibaldi to England, a visit out of which developed the Reform League to press for universal suffrage: with the support of middle-class radicals like John Bright it quickly became a highly influential pressure-group and won wide trade-union backing in London, Birmingham and Manchester. The achievement of the working-class franchise and the involvement of so many trade unionists in the campaign for it were radically to change British political life and ultimately to result in the creation of a new political party primarily concerned with the promotion and furtherance of working-class interests.

Had he chosen to remain in active public life, Applegarth might well have become himself one of that small group of working men who began to infiltrate the House of Commons after 1868. As it was, his political interests brought him into close touch with leading members of all parties: his advice was often sought on a wide variety of social issues and in 1870 he was selected to sit on the Royal Commission on Contagious Diseases, so becoming, as the Webbs have pointed out, 'the first working man to be styled by his Sovereign "Our Trusty and Well-beloved"'. This honour came at the most active phase of his career when, in addition to his trade-union work, he was playing a leading part in the National Education League campaigning for the introduction of universal state education, and was also chairman of the General Council of the International Association of Working Men. Although he was thus in close contact with leading European socialists and had considerable sympathy for their ideas, his own political beliefs remained solidly liberal: when invited in 1870 to become a parliamentary candidate for Maidstone, he retired in favour of the official Liberal candidate, Sir John Lubbock, and canvassed for him successfully.

At this same time Applegarth was making an even more direct contribution to the working-class movement by the part he played in legalizing the status of trade unions. During the late 1860s the trade-union movement went through a period of crisis which might easily have resulted in permanent disability, or even early death: that it emerged stronger than before, and with a legal position guaranteed by the state, was quite largely to the credit of Applegarth. The victory of New Model principles and precepts had never been complete. In parts of the country, especially in the north, the earlier type of aggressive unionism, dedicated to industrial conflict, had persisted and in 1866-7 there was a series of 'outrages' in Sheffield which had involved intimidation, violence and an explosion of gunpowder. A royal commission was set up to investigate the incidents and to report on trade unions generally. Applegarth was the most important trade union witness and, as Asa Briggs has said, 'soon became the star of the proceedings'. Even the originally hostile members were ultimately persuaded that unions like the Carpenters and Joiners were beneficial not only to workers but to the economy as a whole, that through such powerful national organizations collective bargaining could take the place of strikes, that it was smallness, not size, that made for 'union tyranny' and oppression of members. Three commissioners were completely won over by Applegarth's arguments, and signed a minority report which became the basis of the legislation of 1871: by this, trade unions could no longer be regarded as criminal in restraint of trade and by a simple process of registration they could secure protection of their funds. The right of peaceful picketing was also granted by a later Act in 1875.

The legalization of the status of trade unions was Applegarth's greatest and enduring contribution to the labour movement. In the longer term his part in the struggle for the suffrage and for universal education were even more important, though in these his was only one voice among others. It remains true that in the short period of his active public life – between 1862 when he took over the secretaryship of the Carpenters and Joiners and 1871 when he joined an engineering firm of which he later became the successful proprietor – he was instrumental in transforming the British labour movement, raising immeasurably the power and prestige of trade unions and bringing the worker into the ambit of political and social competence. That respectable middle-class Victorian society could identify with Applegarth's reasonable ambitions for his fellows was one of his greatest assets, though he never abandoned his own deeply-held convictions in order to seek such an alliance.

Octavia Hill

(1838-1912)

'Octavia Hill? I've heard the name somewhere. It's an open space in Kent, isn't it?' This remark, reputedly made at the time of Octavia Hill's centenary celebration, would have delighted Octavia, so much of whose time and effort were spent in preserving the countryside for the benefit of the people. But it is significant of the comparative neglect of this particular Victorian figure, a neglect that is thoroughly undeserved.

Born in 1838, Octavia Hill was the middle of the five daughters of James Hill, a corn merchant in Wisbech, and his wife Caroline Southwood Smith, who was the daughter of that Dr Southwood Smith who was one of the pioneer 'sanitarians' in the earlier part of the last century and a worthy colleague of Edwin Chadwick in the creation of a public health system in Britain. Soon after Octavia was born her father got into financial difficulties and went bankrupt. For a few years he struggled unsuccessfully to retrieve his position but at length became a physical and mental wreck, with the result that the care of the young family devolved on Mrs Hill. Fortunately Dr Southwood Smith came to the rescue, and established the family in a small cottage at Finchley. Here, in what was then a charming country district, the little Octavia spent the happiest years of her childhood.

The predominating influence in her young life was her grandfather. As she stood beside his chair Dr Southwood Smith told her of his experiences as a young doctor when he was attached to the London Fever Hospital, and his stories of East End life made an indelible impression on her mind. It was probably then that she formed the ambition of doing something when she grew up to improve the living conditions of the poor.

Like the other Hill girls, she never went to school but was taught by her mother at home. Since they were so poor, it was necessary that they should go out into the world as soon as possible to earn their keep, and in those mid-Victorian times there were few opportunities for a girl of the genteel class to get paid employment. Teaching was the most obvious choice and Miranda, the eldest sister, went as a pupil teacher to a private school at the age of thirteen. Octavia was the same age when she made her first venture into employment, as an assistant in a glass-painting workshop established by some good people for the employment of ladies in distressed circumstances. This was in 1851, the year of the Great Exhibition, when 'arty-crafty' had become quite the rage. Shortly afterwards her mother was put in charge of the workshop in Russell Place, Fitzroy Square, and the family moved to the living accommodation provided on the premises.

From the glass-painting establishment she soon moved on to another workshop in which children drawn from the Ragged Schools of the neighbourhood were employed in making toy furniture, and then obtained a position as clerical assistant to the classes for young women which the Christian socialist parson F. D. Maurice had formed as an adjunct to his Working Men's College at St Pancras. Maurice took a kindly interest in her and through him she made the acquaintance of John Ruskin. At this period she had dreams of becoming a great artist. Ruskin encouraged her art studies and invited her to his home at Camberwell where he gave her painting lessons and put her to work copying old masters and doing illustrations for his *Modern Painters*, for all of which he paid her a small fee.

By this time Mrs Hill had ceased working with the Ladies' Co-operative Guild which had been running the glass-painting concern and had moved the family to a house in Nottingham Place. Here in 1862 she and her daughters opened a day and boarding school for young ladies. The schoolroom was a converted stable, the living accommodation was sketchy and only one of the girls was a qualified teacher. But in those days there was no government inspector and the deficiencies were soon repaired. In 1864 Octavia wrote triumphantly that she had passed the qualifying examination for teachers and had her certificate to that effect from Queen's College.

In her successive employments Octavia had always got on well with the poorer folk, the children in particular, and her grandfather's example had inspired her to take a practical interest in their welfare. She threw open the kitchen of the house in Nottingham Place as a place for tired housewives of the neighbourhood to repair for a cup of tea and an hour or two of pleasant relaxation, combined perhaps with a lesson in simple dressmaking. One evening when one of the mothers collapsed from fatigue Octavia insisted on seeing her home and was not a bit surprised to find that this was in a damp and unhealthy basement. She resolved to see if she could find better accommodation and searched all over Marylebone but without success. Sadly she came to the conclusion that dwellings for poor families, especially families in which there were small children, at rents which they could afford, were impossible to obtain. Whereupon she decided that she would go into the landlord-business herself.

Her idea was for a model lodging-house where families with small children would be welcome and at once she set about carrying it out. A number of houses were offered her by estate-agents, but when they heard of the use to which she proposed to put the property they assumed a very different tone. Especially when she mentioned the small children.

'Where *are* the poor to live?' she inquired in desperation of one agent. 'I don't know,' came the reply; 'but they must keep off the St John's Wood Estate.'

Disappointed but far from discouraged, the young woman turned to her friend John Ruskin for assistance. He was rich and she knew that recently his father, a wealthy wine-merchant, had died, leaving him with more money than he knew what to do with. Ruskin agreed without hesitation to finance her scheme, making only the one stipulation that he should receive 5 per cent on his investment – not that he cared about the money but because he was hopeful that Octavia's enterprise should become an example which other people would be glad to follow, which they would not do if they thought they were not going to get a fair return. Octavia thought this only reasonable. 'A working man *ought* to be able to pay for his house,' she declared firmly.

The first properties Ruskin bought for her were three houses in Paradise Place, one of the worst courts in Marylebone; a year later he purchased 'a row of cottages facing a bit of desolate ground, occupied with wretched dilapidated cowsheds, manure heaps, old timber and rubbish of every description'. That sounds pretty horrible, but Octavia was filled with such happiness that she could 'hardly walk on the ground'.

How she started out on what was to prove her life's work is best gathered from a magazine article that she wrote a year or two later. The first thing to be done was to put the properties in decent tenantable order, and Octavia tried to make sure that they should be kept in that good order in future.

Those tenants who would not pay, or who led clearly immoral lives, were ejected. The rooms they vacated were cleansed, [and] the tenants who showed signs of improvement moved into them. The rooms, as a rule, were re-let at the same prices at which they had been let before; but tenants with large families were counselled to take two rooms, and for these much less was charged than if let singly. Incoming tenants are not allowed to take a decidedly insufficient quantity of room, and no sub-letting is permitted. The elder girls are employed three times a week in scrubbing the passages in the houses, for the cleaning of which the landlady is responsible. For this work they are paid, and by it they learn habits of cleanliness. It is, of course, within the authority of the landlady also to insist on cleanliness of wash-houses, yards, staircases and staircase-windows; and even to remonstrate concerning the rooms themselves if they are habitually dirty.

Like the good business woman she was, Octavia went on to say that 'the pecuniary result has been very satisfactory'. Five per cent had been paid on all the capital invested, a fund for the repayment of capital was accumulating, a liberal allowance had been made for repairs and funds had permitted the erection of a large assembly room, in which classes were held for boys and girls and married women. Then a piece of ground in front of the houses had been made available as a drying ground for clothes and also as a playground in which the children could play in safety.

Hitherto, games at trap, bat and ball, swinging, skipping, and singing a few Kindergarten songs with movements in unison, have been the main diversions. But I have just established drill for the boys, and a drum and fife band ...

Mr Ruskin, to whom the whole undertaking owes its existence, has had trees planted in the playground, and creepers against the houses. In May, we have a May-pole or throne covered with flowers for the May-queen and her attendants. The sweet luxuriance of the spring flowers is more enjoyed in that court than could be readily believed...

There follows a paragraph in which the essentials of Octavia Hill's system are clearly indicated.

Week by week, when the rents are collected, an opportunity of seeing each family separately occurs. First, there is the outside business – rent to be received, requests respecting repairs to be considered; sometimes occasions touching the behaviour of other tenants to be made, sometimes rebukes for untidiness to be administered. Then comes the sad or joyful remarks about health or work, the little histories of the week. Shall a daughter go into service? Shall the sick

child be sent to hospital? Sometimes violent quarrels must
be allayed.

Careful selection of tenants; overcrowding guarded against;
prompt and efficient attention given to repairs; scrupulous
cleanliness insisted upon and supervised; rents to be paid when
due, no arrears allowed to accumulate; accounts to be kept
with the utmost strictness and properly audited: these are the
outstanding features of the system of housing management
that Octavia Hill devised and directed for so many years with
outstanding success. There is one thing more, however, to be
mentioned, and not the least important, that may be called the
personal approach. She insisted on treating her tenants as
individuals, not just as units in a nice, tidy, bureaucratically
administered scheme; and, deeply and sincerely religious as she
was, in a broad, unsectarian sense, she was equally insistent
that, while material welfare was important, what may be called
spiritual welfare was much more so. Hence she was sternly
opposed to that indiscriminate charity with which the rich
hoped to secure their own peace of mind, regardless of the
effect that it might have on the recipient's self-respect.

This was Octavia Hill's philosophy of thought and action,
and it is hardly surprising that it met with strong opposition in
some quarters. Among the people she hoped to benefit there
were not a few who complained that she was an interfering old
busy-body, fellow workers sometimes found her bossy and
opinionated, some of those with a vested interest in public
charity stigmatized her as harsh and self-righteous, and her
emphasis on self-reliance ran counter to the rising tide of more
or less socialist opinion.

On the whole, however, she met with far more approbation
than hostility. From its establishment in 1869 the Charity
Organization Society (now the Family Welfare Association)
lent its aid to one who was a highly valued co-worker. John
Ruskin's example was followed by other benevolently disposed
wealthy and Octavia was able to extend her activities to other
parts of London. Housing schemes in the East End were given
her to manage and in 1884 the Ecclesiastical Commissioners
appointed her manager of a large part of their Southwark
estates. She invented a new profession for women as social
workers: a young woman who could say that she had trained
under Miss Hill might be sure of a job. Housing schemes on
the Octavia Hill model were carried out in other cities at home,
in Europe and in the USA. In 1885 she was accorded a measure
of official recognition when she was invited to give evidence

before the Royal Commission on the Housing of the Working Classes. This was when she was at the height of her influence. As the century neared its close the housing question became far too vast and complex for private enterprise and (much to Octavia's disgust) local authorities assumed the responsibility of building 'council houses' for the workers at subsidized rents.

But great as was her achievement in housing, of even greater importance may have been her unremitting advocacy of open spaces in which the pent-up urban populations might have room for healthful recreation and exercise. She insisted on the provision of a playground for the children in her very first housing scheme. As a young woman she and her sister Miranda joined in establishing a society for the 'diffusion of beauty' in the East End of London. Before long she was taking a leading part in the struggles which resulted in securing for the public Parliament Hill Fields at Hampstead, Vauxhall Park and Hill Fields at Lewisham. Many a derelict churchyard was converted into a pleasant garden through her efforts, many a country footpath was kept open and, long before the term had been coined, she was urging the creation of what is now known as the 'green belt' round London. Then in July 1894 she moved at a meeting presided over by the Duke of Westminster at Grosvenor House, 'that it is desirable to provide means by which landowners and others may be enabled to dedicate to the nation places of historic interest or natural beauty'. So the National Trust was launched, and Octavia Hill shares with Sir Robert Hunter and Canon Rawnsley the proud distinction of being the founders of this eminently worthy and successful enterprise.

With voice and pen Octavia laboured to get the Trust on its feet. The first property was the cliff at Barmouth, the second Barras Head at Tintagel, a place very dear to Octavia. The first building acquired was the medieval Clergy House at Alfriston in the Sussex downland. 'A song of thankfulness seems to be singing on in my heart for having been given power to have some hand in devoting some of the lovely places to the people for ever,' she expressed herself in a letter to her mother in 1902.

Octavia Hill died on 12 August 1912 and was buried in the churchyard of Crockham, the Kentish village in which she had shared a home with her sisters. Three years later some hundred acres of heath and woodland at Hydon's Ball and Hydon Heath, south of Godalming, were bought by the National Trust and dedicated as her memorial.

W. T. Stead

(1849–1912)

On 15 April 1912 'the ship that could not sink', the monster liner *Titanic*, went down in the Atlantic on her maiden voyage, her great body split by an iceberg. She took with her a man who died as heroically and dramatically as he had lived: W. T. Stead, great journalist, champion of the oppressed, crusader and mystic, a loud voice of truth in a world of hypocrisy and ignorance.

William Thomas Stead was born in 1849 in the north, the traditional home of British plain-speaking. His father, a Congregationalist minister, was a tremendous influence on him – 'The most interesting man I ever met ... my teacher, my story-teller, my universal encyclopedia of knowledge and my greatest playmate' – and the daily life of the Stead children in the Northumberland manse was very happy, though ruled by stern Puritan principles. Stead's solace during his first unhappy days at boarding school was the Bible, but in time he was rejoicing in the benevolent rule of the headmaster of Silcoates, Dr Bewglass, a hero-figure in the same mould as his father.

The crusader's zeal was in him from the beginning. There is a story that he exclaimed, while still a tiny boy, 'I wish that God would give me a big whip that I could go round the world and whip the wicked out of it!' When he left school in 1863 and became office boy in a Newcastle merchant's counting-house he gave his leisure time to charity work and helping to educate the ignorant. At the back of his father's church was a notorious slum, disregarded by the authorities. Stead wrote them a stinging letter. To his surprise it appeared as a leading article in a local newspaper. The slum was reformed and Stead encouraged to fire freelance articles at the *Northern Echo*. He received no payment but much valuable advice about journalism, and when the editor left it was Stead, aged twenty-two, who was approached to replace him. Full of confidence and impatient to begin the social reforming which he had no doubt was his vocation, he accepted.

In 1873 he married Emma Jane Wilson, a childhood playmate. Three years later he met Mrs Josephine Butler, with whom his name was to be linked in a very different way. An

446

ardent campaigner for downtrodden women, she had organized a petition for the repeal of the Contagious Diseases Acts,
which provided for the compulsory examination of prostitutes
in English garrison towns, viewing this as an outrage against
the women's modesty and private rights. Stead had read her
book *The New Abolitionists* and thought a follow-up to it was
needed. In several years' time he would provide that follow-up
in a way that would take him beyond any reformer in terms of
sheer dramatic impact.

Meanwhile, outspoken and unafraid, he made the *Northern
Echo* a forum for his startling opinions and original attitudes
of mind. His pro-Russian articles, at a time when that country
was unpopular in England, attracted the attention of another
woman, Olga Novikoff, an ardent campaigner for Anglo-Rus-
sian friendship. The 'Member for Russia', as Disraeli called
her, invited the lively young editor to her Mayfair salon, his
first introduction to the high places of London's political–
intellectual society. Before long he was receiving warm encouragement from such men as Gladstone, who expressed a
wish that the whole British press might aspire to the *Northern
Echo*'s standards of 'justice, heartiness and ability'.

More tangibly, Stead was invited in 1880 to become chief of
staff to John Morley, editor of the *Pall Mall Gazette*. He found
himself already known by reputation in Fleet Street. He and
Morley became good friends, though Stead thought Morley an
intellectual aristocrat with no eye for news, not an atom of
journalistic instinct and interested in the newspaper merely as
a pulpit.

In 1883 Morley left the paper and Stead became editor.
Under him the *Gazette* became the liveliest publication ever to
have appeared up to that time, widely discussed and argued
over, dominated by Stead's personality, a compound of inspired evangelist and, it sometimes seemed, fraud and maniac.
He even looked the part: his eyes visionary, 'un-English', his
beard flowing like an Old Testament prophet's, his dress dis-
gracefully shabby and awry. With Stead came what Matthew
Arnold described as 'the New Journalism'. Stead introduced
the personal interview, made a feature of extra editions, published declarations of policy more sweeping and humanitarian
than had ever before been made – and kept to them. From
1883 to 1885 a series of milestones marked his progress. In
1883 a Congregational clergyman had published anonymously
a penny pamphlet, *The Bitter Cry of Outcast London*, drawing
attention to the horrors of slum life. Stead published excerpts
in the *Pall Mall Gazette*. His readers were shocked by the

brutal and disgusting details; but the articles led to the appointment of a royal commission on the housing of the poor. This
first great coup of Stead's was followed by a more sensational
achievement, his interview with General Gordon which resulted in Gordon's mission to Khartoum.

When, at the height of national anxiety about the revolt in
Egypt, Gordon was said to be about to take an administrative
post in the Congo, the *Pall Mall Gazette* had complained that
this would be a waste of a great leader in time of need. Stead
followed this up with a visit to Gordon's home at Southampton. After listening keenly to the enigmatic Gordon's exposition of his Congo project, he neatly turned the conversation to
Egypt, extracting from him a masterly plan for the defence of
Khartoum against the Mahdi. The next issue of the *Gazette*
carried a headline: 'CHINESE GORDON ON THE SOU-
DAN', and a leader headed 'CHINESE GORDON *FOR* THE
SOUDAN'. A few days later Gordon was summoned to the
War Office and despatched to Egypt 'to report upon the best
means of effecting the evacuation of the Soudan'. It was the
first time that a newspaper had changed a government's policy.

On 6 July 1885 the *Pall Mall Gazette* exploded a bombshell
under the noses of unsuspecting readers: a bald account of
what had happened to a girl referred to as 'Lily', in real life
Eliza Armstrong, the guinea-pig in an extraordinary test-case
which shocked the country and changed the law.

Once again Stead had met Josephine Butler, who had long
been struggling to promote a Bill to deal with two major evils in
Victorian society, white slave traffic and juvenile prostitution.
He learned that a girl even one day over thirteen was in law
a woman, of the age of consent; and that a very young child
might not accuse her violator unless she could be shown to understand fully the nature of an oath. He sought out a man who had
been head of the Criminal Investigation Department and learned
the facts of the black world of procurers and child-dealers.

'I will raise hell!' Stead vowed; and did so in a manner that
justified an old colleague's description of him as a mixture of
Barnum and Don Quixote.

He began conventionally enough by approaching three
eminent churchmen – the Archbishop of Canterbury, Cardinal
Manning and Dr Frederick Temple, Bishop of London, to
support a practical demonstration of the evil conditions which
demanded a Criminal Law Amendment Bill. The Archbishop
recoiled on hearing Stead's plan in detail. The Cardinal and
Dr Temple agreed. So did Bramwell Booth, later to become
head of the Salvation Army. Through him Stead was intro-

duced to Mrs Rebecca Jarrett, now 'saved' but once a notorious brothel-keeper. Between them, Stead and Josephine
Butler persuaded her to take part in a daring scheme.

Pretending to have reverted to her old ways, Mrs Jarrett
went to a Mrs Armstrong and offered to buy her daughter
Eliza, just turned thirteen, ostensibly for Stead to use for his
pleasure. Young Eliza having been bought for £3, Stead conducted her to a brothel where her virginity was ascertained and
certified by Madame Mourez, who kept the house and also
practised as a midwife. Then Eliza went to bed and was left
alone. In half an hour Stead entered the room. He, whose
Puritan conscience would not even permit him to enter a
theatre, approached the bed. Eliza woke and screamed.

Stead immediately went out and Eliza was taken by a woman
Salvationist to a doctor, who declared her still *virgo intacta*.
Next morning she was taken to Paris to live under the wing of
the Salvation Army and subsequently to marry happily and
become the mother of a large family.

Stead's account of Eliza's adventure, under the title 'The
Maiden Tribute of Modern Babylon', had precisely the effect
he had hoped. Mr Cavendish Bentinck, an enemy of the Criminal Law Amendment Bill, asked the Home Secretary whether
the author and publishers of these objectionable articles could
not be subjected to criminal proceedings. The *Pall Mall Gazette* was banned from railway bookstalls, and eleven newsboys
were tried for causing an obstruction and selling indecent
literature: but on the Friday of the same week, five days after
the first 'Maiden Tribute' article's appearance, the Criminal
Law Amendment Bill galloped through its second reading in
the House of Commons.

Victory was won: yet public opinion was shocked, not by the
revelation of vice but by Stead's exposure of it. There was
general agreement that such filth as juvenile prostitution was
best swept under the carpet and ignored. The *Weekly Times*
prophesied: 'The evil will spread, till there will be scarcely a
boy or girl in England whose ignorance will not be displaced
by forbidden knowledge ... A plague worse than any Egyptian
plague has visited the homes of England!'

Although Eliza Armstrong's mother had willingly sold her
daughter into prostitution, when her neighbours started taunting her with it she went to the police. An inspector saw Bramwell Booth and advised him to try to get the mother's consent
to keep the child where she was, as she was much better off
with the Salvation Army than in a Marylebone slum. Mrs
Armstrong refused, whereupon Mrs Jarrett, the 'procuress',

was arrested. Returning from holiday abroad as soon as he learned of this, Stead too was taken into custody, along with Bramwell Booth, Madame Mourez and other conspirators.

Stead soon saw how the trial would go. Again and again he reiterated the motive for what he had done: again and again it was pushed aside by the prosecution. In conducting their ruse, Stead and his associates had overlooked a technical point: they had obtained Mrs Armstrong's consent to her daughter's being bought but they had not thought to approach her husband as well. The prosecution seized on this, a misdemeanour in the eyes of the law; the judge favoured the prosecution; and the jury followed the clear direction of the judge. The Salvationists were acquitted. Madame Mourez, Rebecca Jarrett, a Greek accomplice and Stead were found guilty. Stead was sentenced to three months' imprisonment.

He refused to appeal. He had written years before, 'all my ideals end in martyrdom'. As he entered his cell, he wrote later,

> my first sensation was one of pleasant satisfaction ... From all parts of the Empire rained down upon me every morning the benedictions of men and women who had felt the unexpected lift of the great outburst of compassion and indignation which followed the publication of the 'Maiden Tribute'. I had papers, books, letters, flowers, everything that my heart could wish. Twice a week my wife brought the sunlight of her presence into the pretty room. On the day after Christmas the whole family came, excepting the little two-year-old, and what high jinks we had in the old gaol with all the bairns!

On 18 January 1886 the rested, confident Stead emerged from the strange paradise of Holloway Prison to embark at once on a new crusade to clean up London. The next few years also saw him take a leading part in the great struggle for Irish home rule and campaigning for, and winning the war against the Contagious Diseases Acts. He went to Russia in 1888 (horrifying Paris en route by his dreadful tweed cap and suit, which gave him the air of a dog-stealer), shook hands with a surprised Tsar, who was not used to that form of greeting, and, after a trenchant discussion on several burning questions, graciously dismissed an even more surprised Tsar from his presence.

In 1889 he left the *Pall Mall Gazette* to found the *Review of Reviews*, intended to circulate throughout the English-speaking world with connections in every town and correspondents in every village. As well as giving his readers a month-by-month chronicle of the world's progress, Stead offered them his services as a sort of father confessor. Always, his superb editorship, his news sense, his political acumen were dominated by a driving passion. It shocked some, it amused others (who referred to the *Review* as *Fagin's Miscellany*), but it gave him that power over readers' minds which mere brilliant journalism could not have given.

For his own needs, Stead knew that neither his native Nonconformism nor the Romanism to which he was partly attracted could satisfy him. One answer was given to both: the new religion of spiritualism.

He had started cautiously, sceptical but curious. Before long he was involved with the Society for Psychical Research, investigating haunted houses, attempting spirit photography. He found that he had the gift of automatic writing, his hand transmitting involuntarily messages from the living or the dead. The death of his son Willie in 1908, followed by numerous communications from him, convinced him of the truth of spiritualism.

His last major campaign was for international peace. No longer imperialistic, he had launched in 1899 an international peace crusade and a new weekly, *War Against War*. When the South African war broke out he had attacked Chamberlain for warmongering, got up a memorial to the Queen to stop hostilities, bellowed wrathfully against the apathetic clergy. The war went on and Stead was abused by some for supporting the Boers, admired for it by others.

He continued to work for peace throughout the first eleven years of the twentieth century. There was more of the prophet to him than mere appearance: his eyes saw into the future as 1914 drew nearer. In March 1912 an invitation reached him from New York to speak alongside President Taft in Carnegie Hall on the subject of world peace. He cabled at once that he would leave by the *Titanic* on 10 April.

He was last seen standing alone on the deck of the sinking liner in an attitude of prayerful meditation, having done all he could to help his fellow passengers.

A tribute typical of countless others was paid to him by Admiral Lord Fisher, his friend for a quarter of a century:

> Stead was a consummate journalist – he was an honest man – and, thank God, he possessed the 'insanity of genius' which will hand him down to posterity as a famous man. He was a lover of his country and, like John the Baptist, he 'constantly spoke the truth, rebuked vice and patiently endured for the truth's sake'.

Sir John Franklin

(1786-1847)

John Franklin was born on 16 April 1786 in the market-town of Spilsby in Lincolnshire. He was the youngest of a large family of four boys and six girls and, as with so many youngest sons of that period, his parents hoped that he would become a clergyman.

Spilsby, however, is only some ten miles from the sea and the French wars were on. By the time John was twelve years old England was fighting for her life against Napoleon. Franklin decided that above everything else he wanted to be a sailor. Hoping to cure him of this craving for a sea life his parents sent him on a trip to Lisbon and back in a small merchant ship. It only served to make him more determined.

When John Franklin's parents realized they could not dissuade him from a sea-faring life they obtained an appointment for him as midshipman in HMS *Polyphemus*. Franklin joined the ship at Chatham on 9 March 1800. He was fourteen years old. On 2 April 1801 the *Polyphemus* took part in the battle of Copenhagen under the command of Lord Nelson.

His next ship was the *Investigator* which had been commissioned for a voyage of discovery to the Southern Hemisphere. Her commander was Lieutenant Matthew Flinders, an officer who had already made a name for himself as an explorer and navigator. Flinders was also a Lincolnshire man and a distant relative of the Franklins. It was due to him that John Franklin developed his love of geographical research and navigation and acquired valuable experience in surveying and exploring.

Franklin next joined the *Bellerophon* which under Lord Collingwood was engaged in blockading the French fleet in the harbour of Brest during the winter of 1804. On 21 October Franklin was made signal-midshipman of the same ship. Probably it was he who reported to his captain, John Cooke, Nelson's famous signal at the onset of the battle of Trafalgar which finally established Britain's mastery of the seas.

When the end of the war came in 1815 immediate cuts were made in naval personnel. Franklin, like many other officers, found himself discharged on half pay.

Since the time of Columbus men had been searching for a

North-west Passage to the Pacific. Queen Elizabeth had commissioned Sir Martin Frobisher to seek such a route in 1576; Henry Hudson's voyage in 1607, in which he discovered the east coast of Greenland, led to the establishment of the lucrative whale-fishing industry. Several subsequent expeditions were sent to ascertain how far navigation was practicable in the direction of the North Pole. In 1818 the government decided to send two more expeditions: one commanded by Lieutenant John Ross in search of a North-west Passage; and a second commanded by David Buchan to the North Pole. Lieutenant John Franklin was appointed second in command to Buchan.

The vessels selected for the trip were the *Dorothea* which Buchan commanded and the *Trent*, a brig of 250 tons, with Franklin in command. Captain Buchan's instructions were to try to force his ships northward between Spitzbergen and Greenland and thence to the North Pole. The ships crossed the Arctic Circle on 10 May 1818 and rendezvoused as arranged in Magdalena Bay in June. Here, finding the ice to the north impenetrable, they stayed for some time, making various scientific observations and investigations. By August the two ships were so battered by constant encounters with the ice that they sought refuge in Fair Haven and, after repair, sailed for home.

Although the expedition achieved nothing concrete it did provide Franklin with valuable experience which the government decided to put to good use. In 1819 Franklin was placed in command of an expedition whose object was to penetrate to the Arctic Sea by land and if possible to join a second expedition headed by Commander Parry who would endeavour to reach the rendezvous by sea. At this time the northern coast of North America, from Icy Cape north of Bering's Strait as far as Hudson Bay to the east, was practically unknown. Franklin's instructions were to proceed to Hudson Bay and thence to travel northward overland to the mouth of the Coppermine River. From here he was to work his way along the coast eastward to meet Parry.

The expedition sailed from Gravesend on board the Hudson's Bay Company's ship *Prince of Wales* in May 1819. They landed at York Factory in Hudson Bay Territory on 30 August. From here they travelled in a 'York' boat, the kind used by the Hudson's Bay Company for the transport of their goods on the rivers and lakes. They reached the trading port of Fort Chipewyan on 26 March 1820 and hired canoes and French-Canadian *voyageurs*.

In July the expedition headed towards the Great Slave Lake,

proceeding through country never before visited by Europeans. They constructed a house which they named Fort Enterprise in which to pass the winter. Franklin spent the long winter months writing detailed reports on the flora and fauna of the area. The following June the party set out again and on 20 July they sighted the Arctic Ocean. The next day they emerged at the mouth of the Coppermine River and launched the canoes on the Arctic seas. Each moment expecting the frail craft to be crushed to pieces by the masses of solid ice that rose and fell with every motion of the rough seas, they sailed on, naming the most prominent points, until they reached a headland which Franklin named Point Turnagain.

The return journey, mostly on foot and carrying the canoes on their backs, was even more hazardous. At one point the party survived only on *tripe de roche* and a few old deer skins. On 11 December they reached Fort Providence and by October 1822 they were back in England.

On his return Franklin was promoted to the rank of captain and elected a Fellow of the Royal Society. His detailed account of the expedition was published the following year and provided much information about the geography, geology and natural history of the northernmost parts of North America.

Captain Parry's voyage in search of the North-west Passage by way of Lancaster Sound had meanwhile ended in his ships being marooned in the Arctic ice for the winter. He had, however, reached a longitude of 110°W and thus gained half of the government reward of £10,000 for the discovery of a North-west Passage, half of that sum to be paid if the expedition reached 110°W longitude.

Franklin was now eager to implement the information gained from his last expedition and in 1825 persuaded the government to send him back to the Arctic. This time he was better organized. Instead of relying on *voyageurs* he took volunteers from the Navy. He divided his expedition into two parties. One led by himself travelled to the Arctic Sea by way of the Mackenzie River and mapped 340 miles of coastline from there westward. The second party successfully surveyed the stretch of coastline 863 miles eastward from the Mackenzie to the mouth of the Coppermine. In all Franklin's second expedition mapped over a thousand miles of the north coast of the American continent.

Franklin's tireless leadership and patient hard work were appreciated both in France and England. When he returned he was presented with the Paris Geographical Society's gold medal for having made 'the most important acquisition to geographical knowledge' during the year, and on 29 April 1829 he was knighted. But Franklin was not so satisfied with the results of his expedition. He had not found the North-west Passage though he was by now firmly convinced of its existence.

But the government had neither the money nor the inclination to spend more on polar exploration. In 1830 Franklin was appointed to the command of the frigate *Rainbow* and later was the senior naval officer in Greece. On his return from Greece Franklin was offered and accepted the lieutenant-governorship of Van Diemen's Land or Tasmania.

During his absence in Tasmania polar exploration had not been entirely neglected. In 1829 a privately-financed expedition commanded by Sir John Ross in a small vessel named the *Victory* sailed up Lancaster Sound into Prince Regent Inlet and made winter quarters on the east coast of Felix Boothis. Learning from some Eskimos that Boothis was in fact a peninsula, James Ross, nephew of the commander, set out to explore the neighbourhood with sledges. He became convinced that King William Land was connected with the Isthmus of Boothis and marked it so on his chart. Little did he know that by this error he had sealed Franklin's fate.

The *Victory* finally had to be abandoned after being stuck in the ice for three winters. The members of the expedition eventually escaped overland and were picked up by a whaler after the world had given them up for lost. The Rosses had not found the North-west Passage but their voyage had kept alive interest in the search. The gap to be closed had narrowed considerably. The Royal Geographical Society and other bodies urged the government to complete the work. At last in 1844 it agreed that yet another attempt should be made to find the channel.

To Franklin there was still nothing 'dearer to my heart than the completion of the survey of the northern coast of America and the accomplishment of the North-west Passage'. He persuaded the First Lord to give him the job. He was fifty-nine.

Two ships, the *Erebus* and the *Terror*, lately returned from an expedition to the Antarctic, were made ready for Arctic service. They were overhauled, strengthened, provisioned and outfitted for a three-year expedition. They sailed down the Thames on 19 May 1845 with the good wishes of the nation to see them off. At Disko on the west coast of Greenland the men wrote home telling their friends to reply to Petropavlovsk, so confident were they of reaching the Bering Strait. In July a whaling captain reported that he had seen them about to enter Lancaster Sound. That was the last the civilized world saw of them.

When by the next summer there was no news of Sir John's expedition there was no great alarm in Britain. Everyone knew that the ships were well provisioned and expected to spend at least one winter in the ice. But when by 1847 still nothing had been heard the government became worried. Three expeditions were organized to try to find Franklin. Not a sign of the explorers or their ships was found. During the next ten years forty search parties were sent out, most of them government sponsored. Lady Franklin outfitted four different ships at her own expense to search for her husband.

As time passed a revolution in polar exploration took place. It was pioneered by a young lieutenant, Leopold McClintock. A technique of sledging, based on Eskimo methods, was developed. Small parties on sledges traversed mile upon mile of coastline searching for wreckage or cairns where records might have been deposited. The search stimulated interest in the Arctic as nothing else had ever done. Vast new regions were surveyed and mapped. Franklin had contributed much in his lifetime to filling in blanks on the map; the mystery of his disappearance was to contribute even more and, ironically enough, to solve the problem of the North-west Passage for which he had sought so long.

In 1853 Dr John Rae of the Hudson's Bay Company travelled up the western side of the Boothis Peninsula and discovered the strait that now bears his name and the fact that King William Land was an island. Quite by accident he stumbled on the first traces of the missing men. From some Eskimos he learned that some six years before forty Europeans had been seen dragging a boat and some sledges southward along the west shore of the island and that a number of corpses had been seen on the mainland. Proof was provided when the Eskimos sold Rae some relics which were obviously of the expedition.

In 1857 Lady Franklin, anxious to know more of the fate of her husband, bought and outfitted the steam yacht *Fox* which, with Leopold McClintock in command, sailed on yet another expedition. McClintock reached Bellot Strait in 1858 and was forced to winter at Port Kennedy Bay. During the winter he organized sledging parties to King William Land and Prince of Wales Land. Between them these parties filled in the last gaps left in the mapping of the north-east corner of Canada. They did more. At Point Victory on the north-west corner of

King William Land they found a cairn of stones under which was the following note written on an Admiralty form:

28 May 1847, H.M. Ships Erebus and Terror wintered in the ice in lat. 70N. long 98° 23/W having wintered in 1845–46 at Beechey Island. Sir John Franklin commanding the expedition. All well. Party consisting of two officers and six men left the ship on Monday 24th May 1847
Wm. Gore, Lieut.
Chas. F. Des Voeux, Mate.

To this had been added in another hand:

April 25th, 1848. H.M. ships Terror and Erebus were deserted on 22nd April, 5 leagues NNW of this, having been beset since 12th Sept. 1846. The officers and crews, consisting of 105 souls, under the command of Captain F. R. M. Crozier, landed here in lat. 69°37 42N., long. 98°41 W.

Sir John Franklin died on the 11th June, 1847. And the total loss by death in the expedition has been to this date 9 officers and 15 men.
James Fitzjames
Captain H.M.S. Erebus.

Along the west coast of King William Land a skeleton was found; later a boat containing two skeletons. Eskimos told McClintock that the men they had seen 'fell down and died as they walked along'. Other skeletons found later corroborated this statement and the dreadful fact that all of the 105 men who left the Erebus and Terror had died from exposure and starvation.

Franklin's probable route was pieced together from the meagre evidence found. In the summer of 1846 he must have sailed down a channel on the left of Cape Walker (Cape Sound) being unable to pass to the right because of ice. He passed southward through the channel separating Prince of Wales Island and Boothis, now called Franklin Strait, but was brought to a halt by ice just north-west of King William Land. Here the ships were inextricably marooned. Franklin did not realize that King William Land was an island for the chart of James Ross marked it as joined to Boothis. If he had known of the existence of Rae Strait he might well have sailed down the *east* coast of King William Land instead of the west. In doing so he would have avoided the permanent ice flow which engulfed him and in fact would have discovered the North-west

Passage. For McClintock, in his search for Franklin, made the circuit of King William's Island, on sledges, trekked down Rae Strait to Montreal Island and found the only feasible passage to the west.

McClintock judged that 'to Franklin must be assigned the earliest discovery of the North-west Passage'. He had been the first to sail on the Arctic Ocean and the first to map its coastline. Years later he had tried to finish the job and virtually accomplished it. His resolution, daring, hard physical work and determination to succeed have been recognized by later generations who have linked his name inseparably with that of the North-west Passage.

David Livingstone

(1813-73)

When the Napoleonic wars ended, worsening trade forced many factory owners to sack their adult workers and take on children in their place. One such child was David Livingstone, son of a grocer who lived in Blantyre in Scotland. In 1823 when he was ten years old he entered the employment of Messrs Monteith and Co. of the Blantyre Cotton works near Glasgow. His working day began at six in the morning and went on until eight in the evening.

With his first earnings he bought a copy of *Ruddiman's Rudiments of Latin* which he propped up on the spinning-jenny at which he was working. After work, from 8 p.m. to 10 p.m., David attended evening school. He spent from 10 p.m. till midnight reading and studying. Sometimes his mother had to confiscate his books in order to get him to bed. By the time he was sixteen David had read *The Philosophy of Religion* and *The Philosophy of a Future State* by Thomas Dick. These works confirmed his belief that 'religion and science are not hostile', and he determined that one day he would become a medical missionary. His increased wages earned in the summer months of 1832 enabled him to attend medical and theological classes at Glasgow University during the winter.

In September 1838 he was accepted by the London Missionary Society as a candidate and in November 1840 he took his medical degree in the Faculty of Physicians and Surgeons in Glasgow. The young doctor's primary ambition had been to serve in China but the outbreak of the opium war in that area forced a change of plan. The Society sent him to South Africa. A mission station had been opened at Kuruman in Bechuanaland some twenty years earlier by Robert Moffat, and it was there that Livingstone was sent in December 1840 with orders to establish a new mission further to the north.

During his first few months at Kuruman Livingstone acquainted himself with the Bechuana tribes, learned their language and saw how Robert Moffat and his associates worked. He spent the next two years exploring the country to the north in search of a suitable place to establish his own mission. Eventually he fixed upon the valley of Mabotsa on one of the

459

sources of the Limpopo River, two hundred miles north-east of Kuruman. Here in 1844 Livingstone brought his wife Mary, the daughter of Robert Moffat.

The tribe to which the Livingstone mission was attached was the Bakwain. The chief, Sechele, was a remarkable man. He was so eager to learn to read that he acquired a knowledge of the alphabet in one day. He became a Christian, somewhat to the disgust of his tribe, who were inclined to blame all the misfortunes which befell them afterwards on their chief's renunciation of the old medicine and incantations. Nevertheless, although only a few of the tribe were converted, Livingstone and his wife were well loved by the Bakwains.

In 1849 Livingstone started on the first of his exploratory journeys. With two English sportsmen, William Oswell and Mungo Murray, he crossed the Kalahari Desert (of which he wrote the first scientific account) and reached Lake Ngami on 1 August. When he returned to Kolobeng he found that Sechele and his tribe had been attacked by the Boers. The mission had been sacked, men and women carried away as slaves and Livingstone's own house plundered. His books and stocks of medicine were destroyed.

Livingstone's next resolve was to travel as far as the land of Sebituane, chief of the Makololo, who lived some two hundred miles beyond Lake Ngami. Sebituane was a powerful and intelligent chieftain. He had conquered most of the tribes in the country of the Zambezi River. He realized that to open up trade and communications with the whites would be to his tribe's advantage. However, before he could give Livingstone much help, he was stricken with inflammation of the lungs and died. His son Sekeletu, who succeeded him, was equally friendly and became one of Livingstone's closest friends and supporters. With Sekeletu Livingstone ascended the Leambye River to look for a healthy spot to establish a mission. Swampy land and the prevalence of the tsetse fly made it impossible to find a suitable site. At last Livingstone was forced to return to Cape Town without having attained his objective.

But perseverance was one of the doctor's great qualities. From Cape Town he shipped his wife and children back to England and then returned by himself to Linyante, Sekeletu's capital. Still finding no suitable land free from tsetse fly, he determined to open up a route from Linyante to the west coast. This would involve him in a longer journey than any he had attempted so far. Sekeletu was eager to help him in this project. It would enable his tribe to trade with the west. Twenty-seven of his best men were assigned to accompany Livingstone.

The expedition started out on 4 November 1853. They travelled by canoe along the Chobe River, then up the Leambye and the Leeba. They stopped at the villages of many different tribes on the way and were received in a friendly way by all. Livingstone carried among his supplies a magic lantern. It was a never-failing source of interest to the Africans and did much to increase their friendship.

Livingstone felt well satisfied with his journey. Up till then the region across which he had travelled was believed to be a vast barren desert. He had proved it to be a populous and fertile region, watered by splendid streams, navigable for hundreds of miles and inhabited by tribes 'capable of benefitting from the civilizing and humanizing influences of honest commerce and the teaching of the Gospel'. The party arrived back in Linyanti in September 1855. There were great rejoicings among Sekeletu's people who had given the expedition up for lost. Livingstone's thoughts ran now to the Zambezi River and a route to the east. He decided his next journey would be to follow the Zambezi to its mouth.

This time 114 Makololos accompanied him. The faithful Sekeletu provided oxen and ivory to help Livingstone to pay his way. The party set off on 3 November 1855. Livingstone had heard many stories from the Makololo of 'the sounding smoke', rising up several hundred feet into the sky and visible for over twenty miles. None of the tribe had ever dared venture very near to the phenomenon. Livingstone was determined that this time they would. In his company, as a result, they discovered the Victoria Falls. The expedition reached Quilimane on the coast on 20 May 1856.

On 12 December Livingstone was back in England. He had been away for sixteen years. In 1857 he published a straightforward account of his experiences in his *Missionary Travels and Researches in South Africa*. As a result of his lengthy journeys a great part of the almost blank map of central Africa could now be filled in. His geographical and scientific data were abundant and accurate, but it was the character of the man himself which aroused the enthusiasm of the British press and public. Livingstone became a national figure. He accepted an appointment to be 'Her Majesty's Consul at Quilimane and Commander of an expedition for exploring Eastern and Central Africa' and returned to Africa to carry out his government project.

On 16 September 1859 he discovered Lake Nyassa. While encamped near the lake he came into direct contact with the slave trade. Some Arab slave-hunters encamped close by offered Livingstone some young children for sale. On hearing that the expedition was an English one, however, they seemed afraid and struck camp during the night. Several great slave paths or trails crossed the upper valley of the Shire. The chiefs, Livingstone thought, who dealt in this terrible business were ashamed of it and excused themselves by declaring that they 'did not sell many and only those that have committed crimes'. Many tribes had no ivory with which to buy foreign goods. Their only saleable 'article' was slaves. The Arabs, who were the great slave agents, encouraged the use of human beings as 'currency' in return for cheap cloth. The price near Lake Nyassa was four yards of cotton cloth for a man, three for a woman and two for a boy or girl.

By the time Livingstone returned to England in July 1864 he had explored much of the territory which became the British protectorate of Nyassaland. His last great journey, therefore, was undertaken with two main objectives: the suppression of slavery by means of civilizing influences, and the ascertainment of the watershed in the region between Nyassa and Tanganyika.

Livingstone left England in August 1865 and arrived at Zanzibar on 20 January 1866. He was landed at the mouth of the Rovuma on 22 March and started for the interior on 4 April. His party consisted of thirteen sepoys, ten men from the island of Johanna and several boys from the Shire region. From the south end of Lake Nyassa, Livingstone headed north-north-west towards the south end of Lake Tanganyika. A dispatch, dated 18 May, informed the British Government that he was on the threshold of previously unexplored territory. And that was all that was heard of him until a man named Moosa, one of the ten men from Johanna, and his companions returned with the story that Livingstone had been slain by a band of hostile natives. Livingstone's friends did not believe the story and immediately organized an expedition whose aim was to follow Livingstone's trail and discover the truth.

During the next two years nothing very definite was heard. Rumours were rife. Livingstone was dead. Livingstone was ill. He had been captured by slavers. In May 1870 the shroud of mystery regarding his fate resulted in the government sending £1,000 to the consul at Zanzibar to be spent on efforts to find him. The mystery of Livingstone's whereabouts caught the imagination of newspapers both in Europe and America. The council of the Royal Geographical Society organized an expedition which was to march to the interior for news.

These relief expeditions gained much publicity in the British press and the public felt that everything possible was being done to find the famous explorer. No one gave much thought to another expedition which had been organized by the proprietors of the American *New York Herald*. They sent their correspondent, Henry Stanley, to Africa with orders to find Dr Livingstone or bring back news of his safety or his death at whatever cost.

Stanley was determined to reach Ujiji, an Arab station on Lake Tanganyika towards which Livingstone had reportedly been heading before the British expeditions got there, but he found a war had broken out between the Arab settlers and a powerful chief named Mirambo. Mirambo's country lay in the direct line of march from Unyanyembe to Ujiji. Mirambo routed the Arabs who fled in confusion and left Stanley's expedition open to attack. However, at Kwihara the indefatigable Stanley ran up an American flag on a pole, got his men to dig fortifications and successfully defended the village.

Stanley and his party entered Ujiji with hundreds of its people milling around them.

> As we move, they move; all eyes are drawn towards us. The expedition at last comes to a halt. There is a group of the most respectable Arabs and as I come nearer, I see the white face of an old man among them. He has a cap with a gold band around it; his dress is a short jacket of red blanket cloth; and his pants – well I didn't observe. I am shaking hands with him.
>
> We raise our hats and I say: 'Dr Livingstone I presume?' and he says, 'Yes.'

Livingstone had reached Ujiji in March 1869 weak and emaciated with fever. He recrossed Tanganyika in July and reached the town of Nyangwe in March 1871. Here a party of Arab slavers assembled one day when the market was busiest and without warning or provocation began shooting the women. Hundreds were killed or drowned while trying to escape. Livingstone had the 'impression that he was in hell' but he was powerless. 'The massacre filled me with such intolerable loathing,' he wrote, 'that I resolved to return to Ujiji, get men from the coast and try to finish the rest of my work by going outside the area of Ujijan bloodshed.' But when he reached Ujiji after a march of between 400 and 500 miles under a blazing sun he thought he was dying and could not put his plan into action. He had no provisions, no money and was sick and weak from fever.

Stanley's timely arrival filled the doctor with new vigour and

enthusiasm. Together they explored the north end of Tanganyika. In August 1872 the doctor started for Lake Bangweulu
in a vain search for the 'fountains' of Herodotus. In January
1873 in the spongy jungle on the east of the lake he went down
with dysentery. By the middle of April he could not walk and
had to be carried on a litter. On 1 May his boys found 'the
great master', as they called him, kneeling by the side of his
bed, dead.

His faithful followers preserved his body and carried it with
his instruments and journals across the continent to Zanzibar.
Thence it was taken to England and on 18 April 1874 it was
buried in Westminster Abbey.

Livingstone, during thirty years of exploration, did more to
fill in the map of Africa than any other man; yet perhaps his
work as a missionary was more important. Almost without
exception the tribes he visited cherished his memory; even the
Arab slave traders whom he opposed admired him and called
him 'the very great doctor'. His example and his death inspired
others to follow in his footsteps and his exposition of the slave
trade aroused such indignation in Britain that the government
made strong and partially successful efforts to get the Sultan
of Zanzibar to suppress it.

Many years after the death of the great explorer Stanley
wrote:

In the annals of exploration of the dark continent we look
in vain among other nationalities for a name such as Livingstone's. He stands pre-eminent above all; he united in himself all the best qualities of other explorers. Britain excelled
herself even, when she produced the strong and perseverant
Scotsman, Livingstone.

Sir Richard Burton

(1821–90)

In 1853 a struggling throng of Moslems set out from the
southern gate of Cairo on the annual pilgrimage to Mecca.
With them was an Englishman in disguise, 32-year-old Richard
Burton. In all history only eleven Europeans had set eyes on
the birthplace of Mohammed and lived to tell the tale.

After a nightmare voyage down the Red Sea and encounters
with marauding tribesmen, the pilgrims reached Medina,
where the prophet had died, and burst into paeans of praise at
the sight of its gardens and orchards. Burton, too, was momentarily carried away but his enthusiasm was tempered with
caution. He had come with the blessing of the Royal Geographical Society with the ultimate aim of exploring the blanks
on the map of central Arabia and had survived so far thanks
to his acting ability and a detailed knowledge of Moslem rites
and customs. But a single slip in religious observance, doubly
strict now the pilgrims were on holy ground, might lead to
detection and that would mean certain death. Meanwhile,
carefully concealing his writing materials (of which Arabs
were very suspicious) he noted meticulously all he saw and
experienced.

Some days later he was following, with seven thousand
pilgrims, the inland route to Mecca through the parched Nejd
Desert, as yet untrodden by white men. In Mecca Burton was
in even greater danger. Here was the *Kaaba*, the sacred shrine
towards which all Moslems pray and even in the twentieth
century infidels defiling the precincts have been torn to pieces.
But after he had kissed the famous black stone let into one of
the walls – judging it to be a meteorite – Burton actually gained
admission to the building and under the eyes of watchful
guards dared to make a rough sketch on the sleeve of his robe.
In the intervals between religious duties he also wrote copious
notes on the whole colourful, ecstatic scene in Mecca, crowded
with Moslem pilgrims from all over the world.

From this daring journey Burton returned safely to Egypt
by sea from Jedda. Three fascinating volumes, *A Pilgrimage to
El-Medinah and Mecca*, resulted and if he had gone back to
London at once he would have been fêted as a famous man. But

he lingered in Cairo and then sailed for Bombay, leaving a
vacuum at home in which rumour and scandal grew about this
strange person – for strange indeed he was.

Born in 1821 of upper-class English stock – his father was a
colonel who had seen service under Sir John Moore and his
mother came from a wealthy family named Baker – Richard
lived with his parents at Tours in France till he was ten.
Practically the only surviving record of these years is of fighting: Dick and a younger brother attacking their nurse, smash-
ing the windows of a confectioner's shop, shooting at gravestones in the churchyard and breaking stained-glass windows.
When the family returned to England Dick fisticuffed his way
through a short period of schooling. Back in France again
there were more violent escapades, followed by several years
accompanying Burton senior on peregrinations in Italy, during
which Dick learned fencing (he was later one of the best
swordsmen in Europe), found a macabre fascination in helping
to bury dead from a cholera outbreak in Naples and, at
the age of fifteen, discovered the pleasures of drinking and
whoring.

But there was another side to this handsome, athletic boy: a
gift for languages and drawing, a brilliant analytical brain,
courage, stamina and an unflagging zest for new scenes, new
experiences. As long as he lived he would compensate by travel
and observation for his inner lack of balance.

Fatuously, father Burton intended this youth for the Church
and in 1840 sent him to Trinity, Oxford where his only relief
from misery was in fencing, boxing and studying Arabic. News
of the Afghan revolt in 1842 revived his desire to be a soldier
and, having managed to get himself sent down from Oxford,
he persuaded his father to buy him a commission from the
East India Company in the Bombay Native Infantry.

In the next seven years Dick Burton served as a very untypical soldier, identifying himself with the ruled rather than the
rulers. There was plenty of leisure for officers in those days and
Burton used his to study native languages, history, customs
and religions, wearing native clothes, dying his skin with henna
and even running a street stall in Karachi so that he could mix
with the inhabitants. His regiment never saw action but after
Sir Charles Napier's conquest of Sind he was appointed a
member of the Survey and extended his studies.

As a result Burton passed top in six interpreter's exams,
became probably the best linguist in the British Army in India
and collected a mass of anthropological information, later to
be published in book form, which he passed to the Bombay

government. By 1848 his prospects seemed excellent and he applied for the job of chief interpreter to the army about to fight the Second Sikh War.

But then a time-bomb, as it were, exploded and shattered his career. Three years before, being anxious about the morals of his soldiers stationed in Karachi, Napier had asked Burton to investigate three notorious homosexual brothels. This Burton did, in disguise, and sent in a report which left nothing to the imagination. Napier himself was not shocked, but after he had left India the report was maliciously sent to the Bombay government with the result that Burton's application for the interpretership was refused. Under this heavy cloud he fell ill, was granted sick leave and sailed for England, leaving the wreck of his military career behind him.

But he had not been cashiered and after the Mecca pilgrimage and his return to Bombay he devised a scheme which won the approval of the East India Company: the exploration of little-known Somaliland, centre of the slave trade and a source of troublesome raids on the Red Sea coast. In 1854 Burton set off, disguised as an Arab merchant, while Lieutenant John Speke and two other white officers were given jobs on the adjoining African coast and told to wait for his return.

Somaliland was a hermetic country from which strangers were rigorously excluded and Burton's plan – almost certainly not understood by his superiors – was to penetrate the capital, the Moslem missionary centre of Harrar, as yet untrodden by any white man. 'I could not suppress my curiosity about this mysterious city,' he wrote, and was bent on 'breaking the guardian spell'.

The xenophobia, the topography, the climate, the tribes, the wild animals made the journey as dangerous as the pilgrimage to Mecca. But Burton reached Harrar, boldly presented himself to the Amir as an Englishman bringing the friendship of his government, got him to sign a meaningless treaty and returned, nearly dying of thirst on the way, to his friends on the coast in January 1855. With him, stored in a phenomenal memory, came a mass of facts about the city, the country, its people and a 1,000-word vocabulary of the unknown Harrari language.

Soon exploiting a request from the Amir for medicine, Burton planned another expedition with his three white friends, this time 'Nilewards via Harrar', which his superiors grudgingly allowed. But bandits attacked their tents while they were still on the coast; one officer was killed; Speke was badly wounded and Burton was forced to run three miles to a friendly ship with a javelin through his cheeks before it could be extracted.

On returning to England Burton found that his account of the Mecca pilgrimage had been published and well received, but officials were too preoccupied by the Crimean War to show much interest in himself. Disgruntled, he volunteered for the front and finally was appointed as chief-of-staff to General Beatson, training Bashi-Bazouks at the Dardanelles who in fact never saw action and spent most of their time fighting the French.

In England again after this fiasco, Burton now found influential support for a new expedition with Speke to look for the great lake, the 'Sea of Ujiji', reputed to exist in the interior of Africa and cited in myth and legend since the days of Ptolemy as the source of the White Nile. Thrilled by the prospect of new adventure, before leaving for Africa he left some verses with a young lady to whom he had just become engaged, verses which throw light on his temperament:

> I were thine image, Fame,
> Within a heart well fit to be thy shrine;
> Others a thousand boons may gain –
> One wish was mine.
>
> The hope to gain one smile,
> To dwell one moment cradled on thy breast,
> Then close my eyes, bid life farewell,
> And take my rest ...

On 1 July 1857 Burton and Speke, with porters, native guards and enough baggage for a two-year journey, left the coast south of Zanzibar to follow a trail leading roughly west and used by Arab slave traders. This was the same route taken by Stanley twenty-four years later in his search for Livingstone. But the trail was by no means a path. For seven and a half months the straggling column plodded slowly on with many long halts for rest, through dense jungle, across rivers, swamps and head-high savannah, over formidable hills, in burning sun and clammy, miasmic cold. Fever struck again and again till both white men were almost too weak to stand. Porters deserted with their baggage; local chiefs demanded ruinous tribute; marauding tribesmen hovered like menacing clouds.

But still they struggled on, till they came at last – the first white men ever to see it – to the longest lake in the world, the Sea of Ujiji, Lake Tanganyika. Speke by now was almost blind with fever and Burton's hands and legs were half paralysed. But the great prize lured them on, the source of the Nile, and they decided to explore the north end of the lake where the natives said there was a river.

They hired canoes and were paddled by smelly, yelling, drum-beating boatmen for a hundred miles to the village of Uvira. A river? Oh, yes, said the locals, but flowing into, not out of, the great water. Burton and Speke wanted to inspect and in fact only twenty miles separated them from the River Ruzizi, which did flow into the lake. But warlike tribes were said to be ahead; no one would accompany them and so exhausted they turned back to Ujiji. From there, soon after, they started the long march eastwards to the coast.

At Tabora, 150 miles from Ujiji, Burton then made the great mistake of his life and threw away a chance which he would regret to the end of his days. A story was heard of another great lake north of Tabora. Speke volunteered to find it. Burton, for reasons which each described differently later on, chose to stay behind. Speke said Burton claimed he was exhausted; Burton alleged he had wanted to have a rest from Speke. The real reason probably was that, being an anthropologist first and an explorer second, Burton found enough to interest him at Tabora. But whatever the truth of this, the unknown lake was Lake Victoria and from its northern end flowed the Nile.

In sixteen days and easy marches, Speke reached the southern shore, stayed long enough for intuition to tell him that this was, indeed, the fabulous source, then hurried back jubilant to tell Burton the news. Burton said 'nonsense', and from then on, as they finished the march back to the coast, the word 'Nile' was never mentioned between them.

Back in London in May 1859, a fortnight before Burton, Speke announced that he had discovered the source of the Nile and was believed and acclaimed. In disgust and a sick man, Burton at once set off on a trip to visit the Mormons in Salt Lake City, carefully recording his experiences in a book, *The City of the Saints*. On his return he found himself, owing to his prolonged absence, dropped from the roll of serving officers under the East India Company and so deprived at one stroke of pay and pension.

This was a watershed in his life. He was about to marry the well-connected Isabel Arundell; he was almost penniless and at once had to secure a settled job. This he found as consul at the miserable, fever-ridden port of Fernando Po off the coast of Biafra.

For the next thirty years the baleful Burton, with his brilliant mind poised above chaotic emotions, obsessed with pornography, rabidly anti-Christian, 'more barbarous', as one biographer says, 'than the barbarians', lived a love-hate existence with a devout Catholic who adored his diabolism and at the same time tried to save him from the devil. Married, he fled, note-books at the ready and bearing messages from the Queen, from Fernando Po to the West African kingdom of Dahomey and recorded sexual practices, the dimensions of the king's Amazon warriors and the horrific annual 'customs' when a hundred natives were slaughtered in pious ceremony.

From Africa he was sent as consul to Santos in Brazil and after five years there to Damascus and finally, in 1872, to Trieste. In all these years his consular duties were relegated to a subordinate position while Burton travelled, studied and translated works of legend and eroticism from rare languages. As his books poured from the press – forty-seven were published in his lifetime and five years after his death – he became recognized as the leading anthropologist of the age, and in 1886 he was made a KCMG.

Fame had at last smiled, but irony was the other power that ruled his life, and it was not as a man of science that he finally became a household word. A fumigated and sentimentalized version of *The Arabian Nights* was already known to Victorian children, but in his last years Burton set about translating the entire collection of tales, unexpurgated, from the Arabic. The result, published in sixteen volumes, was a shocking, fascinating, highly instructive masterpiece, universally read, critically applauded, which made him £16,000. 'Now I know the tastes of Victorian England,' he told his wife, 'we need never be without money.'

Yet the final years were sad. Not all his learning, his multifarious gifts could bring him peace and to the end a kind of savagery possessed him. When he died in 1890 the loyal Isabel brought a priest to his bedside and persuaded the man to give him extreme unction, though she knew that Burton was no Catholic and was already dead. Today he rests in Mortlake cemetery under an overgrown and crumbling tent of marble at either end of which Isabel, hopeful to the last, erected a cross and a crescent.

Heinrich Schliemann

(1822–90)

Behind the royal palace in the centre of Athens is a huge house built in the late 1870s, its flat roof adorned with twenty-four marble statues of the leading deities of Greek antiquity. Schliemann designed it himself and lived there with his second wife and family for the last twelve years of his life. It was a remarkable establishment. The servants, like his children, Andromache and Agamemnon, were given names from the Greek myths. Around the house and at meals Schliemann spoke ancient Greek and required the same of others. There were no curtains, and it cost his wife months of tearful entreaty before she was permitted a sofa and two easy-chairs in her private boudoir – such creature-comforts were considered un-Homeric and therefore undesirable.

Strings of quotations from ancient Greek literature ran round the walls of most rooms. The decoration of the bare and draughty ballroom was modelled on the ruined Roman villas of Pompeii, but the naked *putti* of the blue and white frieze re-enacted Schliemann's archaeological triumphs, one of them in horn-rimmed spectacles being Schliemann himself. In three rooms on the lower floor a great wealth of ancient gold ornaments and vessels was set out on display – treasures unearthed by Schliemann at Troy. The same objects were represented in mosaic on the marble floors. Upstairs was his 'study', the heart of the house. Here Schliemann would spend the day, alternately reading his favourite bits of Greek literature, digesting the latest stock exchange reports from London, Paris and Berlin and dispatching business telegrams all over the world.

He called his house Iliou Melathron, Homeric Greek for 'Trojan Palace'. It was as bizarre an affair as the whole anecdotal life and career of its master, the millionaire entrepreneur, eccentric dilettante and archaeologist extraordinary who 'discovered' Troy.

Schliemann was born on 6 January 1822 in Mecklenburg, one of the Baltic German states. His father's irresponsibility with money and women deprived him of an education. It also drove his mother to a premature death in 1831. Removed from school at the age of fourteen, Schliemann was forced to earn his living as a grocer's assistant. After several years he finally broke loose and walked to Hamburg. He wanted to get to

America, the New World where the streets were rumoured to be paved with gold. By selling his one and only overcoat he scraped enough money together to buy a passage on a small vessel bound for Venezuela and a Spanish grammar to study on voyage. Off the Dutch coast on the night of 11 December 1841 he survived a dramatic shipwreck. By a miracle – his life was full of them and many were pure fantasy – the tin box containing his few belongings was washed ashore. He ended up in Amsterdam, coatless, in borrowed wooden sabots. He was twenty and totally without prospects. He had reached rock-bottom.

But within four years he was prosperously installed in Russia as the agent of the world-wide Dutch trading enterprise B. H. Schroeder and Co. Languages proved his salvation, just as later his acquisition of ancient Greek was the key to the career that made him 'immortal'. He had a mania for languages and ultimately claimed to be fluent in eighteen. First he taught himself English in six months, perfecting the method that he practised and preached the rest of his life. Twice each Sunday he went to the English Church in Amsterdam and, without intitally understanding a word, repeated aloud the sounds the preacher made, and every spare moment of the day and half the night learnt prose passages off by heart, including, he said, the whole of *Ivanhoe* and Goldsmith's *Vicar of Wakefield*. French was next, then Dutch, Spanish, Italian and Portuguese, each in the henceforth statutory six weeks. (Ancient Greek, which he approached immediately after mastering modern Greek in 1856, took him twice as long – the only exception.) Armed with these qualifications he was taken on by Schroeder's as a clerk. Some of their business was with Russian merchants, so Schliemann learnt Russian and was appointed their resident representative in St Petersburg. His half per cent commission was soon doubled. Over the years he acted for more and more firms, receiving anything up to fifty per cent of the profits.

The first twenty-odd years of his adult life were devoted to amassing money with fanatical zeal. He was a born genius when it came to business and figures. He made several fortunes: one out of indigo, for which he became one of Europe's chief importers; another in the Californian gold-fields, as an opportunist private banker buying up prospectors' gold-dust and selling it again, mostly to the Rothschild banking company. He made yet another fortune out of tea and cotton, and a further one – claimed to be the largest – by the ruthless exploitation of saltpetre, sulphur and lead during the Crimean War.

In the early 1860s, at the height of his prosperity and success but prompted by unnecessary fears of ruin, he retired. After three or four years of indecision and a trip round the world he then took up archaeology – fulfilling what he afterwards claimed to be a childhood ambition, the discovery of Homeric Troy. It was for this alone, he asserted in later years, that he had worked and slaved so long, acquiring the wherewithal to finance archaeological expeditions. He was an arch-mythomaniac, however, and a cooler appraisal of the pattern of his existence indicates that if any one thing dominated and directed his life, it was not an interest in archaeology or Greek antiquity – his love of Homer became a fetish – but a consuming passion for money and riches. The pursuit of modern gold was to be matched by the romantic quest for ancient gold. Had not Homer sung of the riches of Priam, king of Troy, and the fabulous wealth of Mycenae, the royal seat of Agamemnon who led the armed might of Greece against Troy to rescue Helen? If Homer was 'true', a successful treasure hunt could net his biggest and safest fortune yet.

In 1863 Schliemann cashed his business interests, arranged solid investments in America, Cuba, Germany and Russia, and bought property in Paris. His dozen or so archaeological expeditions and wide travels, as well as his house in Athens, were to be an enormous drain on his financial resources, but when he died he was still estimated to be worth over twelve million francs. Yet all this was achieved virtually without the benefit of formal schooling and in the teeth of adversities that would have crushed a less exceptional being.

Personal relationships, including marriage, were handled like business deals. His sister, who once accused him of 'icy coldness', was invited to choose his first, Russian wife for him. The marriage produced a son and two daughters (the latter, he prided himself, 'stolen' from their 'frigid' mother) but was a complete disaster. To obtain a divorce he became a naturalized American citizen in 1869, and carefully filed the suit in Indiana where the divorce laws offered speediest hopes of freedom. In the middle of all this he asked the man who had taught him modern Greek in Russia, now a Greek Orthodox bishop in Athens, to find his second wife. She proved an ideal victim. Sophia Engastromenos was just seventeen when they married in September 1869. She was vetted before acceptance – she had to answer three questions correctly: Would you like to go on a long journey? When did the Emperor Hadrian visit Athens? Can you recite some Homer by heart? And then write him a proposal of marriage, like a business contract. She was hustled

off to Paris, forced to learn French and German simultaneously, plus two hundred lines of Homer a day: within three
months she was seriously ill. Undoubtedly their return to
Greece in 1870 to hunt for buried treasure in the Troad saved
her life.

Sophia actively participated in almost all of Schliemann's
excavations, digging and organizing the workmen, and on the
day of their discovery was decked in the 'Golden Ornaments
of Helen' from the 'Treasure of Priam', while her husband,
feverish at the fulfilment of his dreams, was furtively plotting
how to flout the terms of his *firman* – his official permit to dig
on Turkish soil – and keep it all to himself.

He began excavating Hissarlik in April 1870. Neither the
naive fundamentalism of his belief in Homer nor his selection
of Hissarlik as the site of Homeric Troy were new or original.
The theory had first been proposed in 1822 by the English
archaeologist Charles Maclaren, and independent support had
followed. But Schliemann's predecessors lacked his resources
– and motives. Now, armies of workmen drove enormous
trenches through the hill. Roman, Hellenistic and classical
Greek remains standing in their path were ruthlessly broken
apart. Unimpressed by the immense scholarly potential of
what he was uncovering – the successive occupation of the site
by civilization after civilization had left what Carl Blegen in
the 1930s finally teased apart into forty-six separate strata –
Schliemann decided, in April 1873, to have done with archaeology that June. He was disillusioned by the lack of gold and
anything he could confidently label 'Homeric' to the outside
world.

Then came the discovery that restored his faith in 'archaeology' for the rest of his life. 'At the end of May' – the date
remained a mysterious trade secret – he was digging near
'Priam's Palace' when he uncovered a broken copper container
about three feet by eighteen inches with something glinting
dully inside. Avarice reared in triumph. He immediately
ordered his wife to clear the whole site of workmen. The
treasure was removed when they were alone and he placed it
carefully in the red shawl his wife held. Behind locked doors
they examined it in detail. He was unshakeably convinced that
he had found the 'Treasure of Priam'. Within a few days it had
been smuggled out of Turkey and dispersed in hiding among
his wife's relatives in Greece. On 17 June he followed his hoard
to Athens and informed the world of his discovery. He also
announced, significantly, that he would never return to Troy.

Mycenae offered even more dazzling prospects. A secretive

start without official permission was halted in 1854. Two years later – having won the Greeks over by the astute offer to remove an eyesore on the Acropolis, the ruins of a medieval Venetian tower, at his own expense – he unearthed graves at Mycenae and a haul of gold diadems, ornaments and death-masks far richer than his 'Treasure of Priam'. One of the masks, with traces of flesh still clinging to the skull, Schliemann wishfully identified as Agamemnon's. This time there was no possibility of evading the vigilant authorities; the treasure went straight to the Greek nation. Thus ended a disgruntled Schlie-mann's interest in the site: he never went back.

In 1878 he abandoned excavations on Ithaca after only a fortnight – Mycenae had made him impatient for quick results – and returned after all to Troy. The influence of his admirer Gladstone (who had contributed a lengthy preface to his typi-cally doubtful report on Mycenae) secured him a *firman*, though the cautious Turks this time supplied an official super-intendent with ten policemen. Troy was kind. After only two months he discovered another smaller hoard and two more the following April – the last gold he found in the earth. In 1880 he tried Orchamenos, the third richest city in Homer, and in 1884–5 Tiryns. At both he brought to light great quantities of the same grey monochrome pottery which he had found all over Hissarlik and Mycenae. It was the distinctive pottery of 'Homeric' civilization. This, and not his 'Treasure of Priam' and 'Mask of Agamemnon', was to prove the vital clue to the Bronze Age culture of prehistoric Greece. But Schliemann never realized it – he lacked the real archaeologist's interest in mere potsherds, and their interrelated significance passed him by.

In England especially, Schliemann was lionized during his lifetime as the father of classical archaeology. (Oxford made him a DCL in 1883 and an honorary Fellow of Queen's Col-lege, although Jowett for one remained loftily unconvinced that Schliemann had discovered the world of Homer.) It is not a reputation that has stood the test of time. The faults in method and procedure and the inaccurate sensationalism of Schliemann's hasty pronouncements were not the pardonable failings of the true pioneer. He loses out on the profoundest levels of all – motives, intent, seriousness and 'truth'. This is what crucially distinguished him from his dedicated profes-sional German contemporaries excavating Olympia. It was they, not Schliemann, who devised the patient and meticulous techniques of modern archaeological scholarship. Schliemann was intellectually sham.

Strip away the drama and Schliemann's archaeological significance is minimal, an accidental by-product of his hunt for treasure. When even Troy was no longer indulgent, he talked wildly of Mexico and a search for Atlantis. The real work, the true honours belong to others. At Troy his young assistant Doerpfeld took over in the late 1880s, followed by Carl Blegen of the University of Cincinnati in the 1930s. Chrestos Tsountas in 1889-90 and Wace in the 1920s did important work at Mycenae. In 1900 Sir Arthur Evans began to unlock the secrets of Cnossos on Crete. A scientific perspective was gradually achieved on the 'Homeric' world of Mycenaean civilization, culminating in the 1950s with the dramatic decipherment of its language, Linear B, by Ventris and Chadwick. The 'Burnt City' in which Schliemann found his 'Treasure of Priam' was an early Bronze Age settlement, a millenium earlier in date than Homeric Troy. His Mask of Agamemnon and the Royal Grave Circle at Mycenae is at least three centuries earlier than Homeric Mycenae. Troy VIIa and not Troy II – for convenience sake, Doerpfeld's classification of nine strata was retained by Blegen but sub-divided – is most probably Homeric Troy.

Few men of renown and still fewer scholars invite more suspicions than Schliemann. His reports were produced in extreme haste: there was always an impressive parade of figures, but grave doubts about their reliability and wild theorizing. Emile Burnouf, the distinguished French archaeologist, had paid Schliemann a visit at Hissarlik and criticized his failure to keep detailed records of all finds and accurate measurements; and without these, as Burnouf rightly insisted, archaeology was nothing.

Despite such contemporary criticisms, Schliemann succeeded in convincing his generation of the validity and importance of his work, and in doing so establishes himself as one of the most brilliant *poseurs* of the nineteenth century. The paradox remains, however, that despite his unscrupulous methods and intentions it was Schliemann who insisted upon the historical reality of Homeric Troy and proved it.

Schliemann died in Naples on 26 December 1890 on his way from Germany to Athens. He had been walking across a square on Christmas Day when he fell down, dazed, his powers of speech paralysed, and deaf from a recent operation on his ears. No one knew who he was. He was mute and the hospital refused him entry. As always, he was shabbily dressed, and alone, but there was a wallet full of gold in his pocket. He died in his hotel the following day. It was like a final surrealist comment on the nature of his existence.

Henry Walter Bates

(1825-92)

The Victorian naturalists, with their butterfly nets, collecting boxes, sun helmets and specimen jars, have often been ridiculed in cartoons, films and music-hall sketches, but it was their patient work which provided the world's museums with thousands of hitherto unknown specimens of flora and fauna and, in many cases, opened the way into the interior of continents previously unexplored by white men. Wherever they ventured in their quest for knowledge these explorer-naturalists were invariably welcomed by the native populations. They were accepted because they were seen to carry only the tools of their trade and not, as so often happened, military weapons and other instruments of oppression. Thus they were permitted to penetrate areas where later adventurers, with more questionable motives, were greeted with hostility and armed resistance.

The prototype of the professional Victorian naturalist was Henry Walter Bates. Before his time all naturalist expeditions had been sponsored by kings, states or wealthy aristocrats. But Bates, in collaboration with his friend Alfred Russel Wallace, was the first naturalist to make his expedition pay for itself. He managed this by selling duplicates of his collections to museums and private collectors.

Bates was born at Leicester in 1825. He became interested in natural science while at school and was early filled with a desire to go to the Amazon to collect insects. Bates's interest in South America had been fired by Alexander von Humboldt, a German baron who, early in the nineteenth century, spent five years in South America, coursing its rivers, climbing its mountains and collecting its plants. Humboldt's writings acted like a magnet on the botanists and naturalists of the world. They flocked to South America to see the wonders Humboldt had described so vividly. Among them was the young naturalist Charles Darwin. He left England for South America in 1831 on the HMS *Beagle*.

Thirty years later in 1861 Darwin heard Bates deliver a paper on the Insect Fauna of the Amazon Valley to the Linnaean Society. He was so impressed that he persuaded Bates to publish a connected narrative of his travels. The result was one of the most fascinating travel books ever written: *The Naturalist on the River Amazon.*

Bates first set foot in South America in May 1848. It was to be his home for the next eleven years. He landed at Para (officially called Belem do Para), seventy miles up the mouth of the Amazon. Para was the headquarters of all navigation on the great river and the principal commercial city of northern Brazil. Bates and his friend Wallace lived there for a year and a half. They made short excursions into the forest which surrounded them and found themselves in an entomologist's dream world. Just how entrancing Bates found it can be judged by the fact that within one hour's walk of Para he found 700 different species of moths and butterflies. (There are only 321 known species for the whole of Europe.)

Bates was painstakingly thorough and unceasingly active. His mornings were spent rambling through the dense forests for specimens; in the afternoons (when most local inhabitants were sleeping) he dissected, analysed and annotated his catches or packed them for shipment to England. This work often went on until midnight.

In September 1849 Bates embarked on his first trip up the Amazon. In those days all communication with the interior was by means of small sailing vessels. Steamships were not introduced on the Amazon until 1853. When the regular east wind blew all was well but when this failed the boats had to proceed by means of the *espia*. In this method a small canoe called a *montaria* was sent ahead with a couple of men who fastened the end of a rope attached to the main vessel to some strong bough or tree-trunk. The crew then hauled the vessel up to this point after which the men in the canoe re-embarked the cable and paddled forwards to repeat the process.

On 19 November Bates embarked in the schooner or *cuberta* owned by a trader from Obydos, named Penna. He was taking merchandise to the Rio Negro, stopping frequently on the way to trade with the scattered settlements along the river. Bates's luggage was extensive. He took with him 'all the materials for housekeeping – cooking utensils, crockery and so forth'. It was his habit to stop at various settlements along the rivers, find some kind of house or cabin in which he could set up home for a while and then spend weeks or months investigating the surrounding forest. He also carried 'ammunition, chests, store-boxes, a small library of natural history books, a hundred-weight of copper money and a stock of groceries for two months' consumption'. One wonders how it all fitted into the little schooner. 'Penna gave up part of the *toldo* or fore-cabin,' wrote Bates, 'and here I slung my hammock and arranged my boxes so as to be able to work as we went along.'

Throughout his narrative Bates's delight, curiosity and enthusiasm for all aspects of his new way of life shine through. The dangers and difficulties of the voyage are glossed over. Bates is much more interested in describing the habits of foraging ants or the Indian tribes than the tropical storms which often threatened to swamp the small boats.

He stayed several weeks at Barra, at the mouth of the Rio Negro, making daily excursions into the forest. Then he set out for Ega, some 400 miles up the Solimoens (or Upper Amazon) River, in a small *cuberta* manned by ten Cucama Indians. He spent twelve months in Ega before returning to Para, but his main accounts of Ega are concerned with his second visit in 1855 when he spent three and a half years exploring the area.

From Ega back to Para is 1,400 miles. Bates made the voyage in twenty-nine days in a heavily-laden schooner filled with turtle oil, Brazil nuts and a great pile of sarsaparilla. When he arrived at Para he found the city had been desolated by two terrible epidemics of yellow fever and smallpox. Bates himself contracted yellow fever. As usual he met the crisis with calm common sense and the minimum of fuss:

> I wrapped myself in a blanket and walked sharply to and fro along the verandah, drinking at intervals a cup of warm tea made of a bitter herb in use amongst the natives called *pajemarioba*. About an hour afterwards I took a good draught of a decoction of elder blossoms as a sudorific and soon after fell insensible into my hammock. I did not wake until midnight when I felt very weak and aching in every bone of my body. I then took as a purgative a small dose of Epsom salts and manna. In forty-eight hours the fever left me and in eight days from the first attack I was able to get about my work.

From Para Bates shipped off his collections to England. In return he received a fresh supply of funds. He then spent several weeks preparing for his second journey. He planned to make his headquarters at Santarem, a small town at the junction of the Amazon and its tributary the Tapajos.

He arrived at Santarem in November 1851 and spent six months exploring its environs. In June 1852 he set off up the river. This time he travelled in a vessel of his own as he wished to explore districts out of the ordinary track of traders. He had hired a two-masted *cuberta* of about six tons and adapted it for his use. Every bit of space was used for his chests, store-boxes, specimen trays, useful books, guns and game-bags, boards and material for skinning and preserving.

Their next stop was at the village of Aveyros where Bates rented a house and stayed for a few weeks to make collections. A few years before his visit Aveyros had been deserted on account of the fire-ant and the inhabitants had only recently returned to their houses thinking its numbers had decreased.

Wherever the landing place was sandy [wrote Bates] it was impossible to walk about on account of the swarms of these terrible fire-ants whose sting is likened by the Brazilians to the puncture of a red-hot needle. The soil of the whole village is undermined by it. The houses are overrun with them; they dispute every fragment of food with the inhabitants and destroy clothing for the sake of the starch.

On 2 August they left Aveyros and ascended a branch river, the Cupari. A new insect pest plagued them here: a large brown fly with a proboscis half an inch long and sharper than the finest needle. 'It settled on our backs by twos and threes at a time and pricked us through our thick cotton shirts, making us start and cry out with the sudden pain.' Along this river they were startled one night by a crashing blow on the side of the boat. In the morning Bates discovered a large rent in the bottom of the hen coop which hung over the side of the vessel and two of the fowls missing. The Indians told him that the depredator was a *sucuruju* (the Indian name for the anaconda, or great water serpent), one of which had been haunting that part of the river for several months and carrying off ducks and fowls from the settlements. A few days later some of the young men organized a hunt for the serpent and eventually killed it with harpoons. It measured 18 feet 9 inches in length, 16 inches in circumference. Bates later measured the skin of an anaconda 21 feet long and 2 feet in girth.

On 7 August they reached the house of the last civilized settler on the river, Senhor John Aracu. Many species of fish, reptiles, monkeys and insects were added to the collection during Bates's expeditions from here.

On 26 August Bates resolved to start on his return journey. By 21 September they had emerged from the confined and stifling gully through which the Cupari flowed, into the more refreshing atmosphere of the broad Tapajos. The relief, however, was short-lived. The descent of the Tapajos at the height of the dry season proved most hazardous. They could travel only by night. During the day such strong winds raged from down river as to make progress impossible. The perilous journey back towards Santarem was made against the difficulties of contrary and furious winds, shoaly water and rocky coasts. It was the beginning of October before they finally arrived safely at Santarem.

Bates obviously had the knack of getting on with everybody he met and with all the Indians and half-breeds that worked for him. During the course of his journeys he visited many Indian tribes and described them in the same detail and with the same interest as he gave to his entomological studies. Whilst at Ega he attended a saint's day festival (Roman Catholic holidays were kept with great spirit, Indian sports being mingled with the ceremonies introduced by the Portuguese missionaries). A large number of men and boys disguised themselves as different grotesque figures, animals or persons, in a kind of masquerade. Bates was much amused when one Indian boy appeared rigged out as an entomologist with an insect net, hunting bag and pin-cushion! 'To make the imitation complete, he had borrowed the frame of an old pair of spectacles and went about with it straddled over his nose!'

For four and a half years Bates made Ega on the Upper Amazon his headquarters. From there he made many excursions into the neighbouring regions. In between he led a quiet life in the settlement in his little cottage. Bates's worst inconvenience at Ega was the lack of letters, reading material and news from home:

I got on pretty well when I received a parcel from England by the steamer [which started operating in 1853] once in two or four months. I was worst off in the first year, 1850, when twelve months elapsed without letters or remittances. Towards the end of this time my clothes had worn to rags and I was barefoot, a great inconvenience in tropical forests.

Every page of Bates's 500-page narrative is filled with fascinating details of his experiences with Indian tribes, scarlet-faced monkeys, owl-faced night-apes, toucans, electric eels, umbrella birds, ant-eaters, humming birds, mining wasps, mason wasps and countless other species of birds, insects, butterflies and moths. His notes on foraging ants take up a whole chapter and were the result of long and patient observation. He found ten distinctive species, nearly all of which had a different system of marching.

The only cannibalistic tribe with whom he had any contact were the Majeronas who lived on the Jauari River, a tributary of the Upper Amazon. Four months before Bates's arrival at St Paulo, the nearest settlement to Majerona territory, two young half-castes went to trade on the Jauari. Soon afterwards news came that they had been shot with arrows, roasted and eaten by the savages. An expedition was sent to the Majerona village to make inquiries but the whole village had been evacuated, with the exception of one girl who had been in the woods when the rest of her people had taken flight. The guards brought her back to St Paulo where Bates saw her.

She was decidedly the best-humoured and, to all appearance, the kindest-hearted specimen of her race I had yet seen. Her ways were like those of a careless laughing country wench. I heard this artless maiden relate, in the coolest manner possible, how she ate a portion of the bodies of the young men whom her tribe had roasted. But what increased greatly the incongruity of this business, the young widow of one of the victims, a neighbour of mine, happened to be present during the narrative and showed her interest in it by laughing at the broken Portuguese in which the girl related the horrible story.

Bates was finally forced to abandon his work because of ill health. He had exposed himself too much in the sun, worked too hard for too long and suffered from bad and insufficient food. Reluctantly he abandoned his plans for continuing up the river to the foot of the Andes. When the steamer came up river to St Paulo in January 1858 he was persuaded to return to Ega and thence to Para.

On 2 June 1859 he embarked from Para in a North American trading vessel, having divided his extensive private collections into three portions and sent them by three separate ships.

Bates was in a precarious way when he returned to England. His health had been undermined and his finances exhausted. Luckily, however, he obtained the post of assistant secretary to the Royal Geographical Society, a job which he retained until his death in 1892. He never returned to his beloved Amazon. His collections, particularly of the insects found around Ega, attracted considerable attention in the scientific world. He had gathered upwards of 7,000 species of insects from the Ega district; 550 distinct species of butterflies, including eighteen species of true Papilio (the swallow-tail genus). Altogether Bates discovered 8,000 insects new to science. His most memorable contribution to biological science was his paper, 'Insect Fauna of the Amazon Valley' in which he clearly stated and solved the problem of 'mimicry', or the superficial resemblances between totally different species and the likeness between an animal and its surroundings.

John Brown

(1800–59)

John Brown was a classic product of the American frontier. He was a direct descendant of Peter Brown, carpenter, who crossed the Atlantic in the *Mayflower*. Like his ancestors he was deeply religious, some would say fanatically so, and he believed God guided his every thought and action.

He was born in 1800 in Torrington, Connecticut but in 1805, when the great American westward migration was just beginning, his father Owen Brown moved himself and his family to the remote frontier town of Hudson, Ohio. In 1805 Hudson was about as far west as you could go. In those days too the frontier was literally jumping with religion. Fervent missionaries were busy reforming frontier farmers to such strange cults as Shakerism, Millerism and Campbellism. Within the next three decades some two hundred new sects were to appear along the frontier. Very few remain today.

The Browns were fervent Nonconformists, favouring the Calvinist sect. They seem to have been converted to Calvinism in 1798, two years before the family moved west. They attended religious revivals and camp meetings in which ministers preached the uncompromising doctrine of the Old Testament with great emphasis on hellish punishment and torment for sinners.

The young John Brown was reared on the very edge of the frontier. He learned to ride as soon as he could walk and to fire a gun as soon as he was strong enough to lift one. He tended his father's cattle and roamed, often alone and unafraid, in the wild new country. He received virtually no official schooling. He learned to read at home with the help of a friend who also guided him through the Bible, Aesop's *Fables*, *Pilgrim's Progress* and other edifying reading matter.

John Brown was not the first of his family to become an abolitionist. His father had described himself as one as early as 1790, after listening to denunciations of slavery by Calvinist preachers. The frontier town of Hudson had been founded by the Calvinist, David Hudson, who was also an abolitionist. John Brown, therefore, grew up in a fervent religious anti-slavery atmosphere.

His wife bore him six sons and one daughter. She died in childbirth in 1832. The following year Brown married again. His second wife bore him thirteen children, seven of whom died in early childhood.

Until 1825 he worked in Hudson as a tanner and land surveyor. He then moved to Richmond, Pennsylvania and in 1835 to Franklin Mills, Ohio where he became a shepherd and later a wool merchant. Indeed he seems at this period to have dabbled in many trades being at various times a 'lumber-dealer, stock fancier, land speculator, farmer, orchardist and woolfactor'; but as the years went by became convinced that his real 'calling' was to emancipate the Negro slaves. Finally he resolved to devote his life solely to this purpose.

His resolution coincided with the period when that most militant abolitionist, William Lloyd Garrison, published the first issue of his anti-slavery newspaper, *The Liberator*. In the same year, 1831, a slave insurrection broke out in Virginia. The South blamed the abolitionists for the uprising. Henceforward there was no hope of moderate views prevailing. Northern abolitionists began deliberately to help slaves escape. The famous 'Underground Railroad' was organized to help runaway slaves find their way to the North and freedom.

The Railroad helped thousands of slaves to freedom but it did not solve the problem of slavery. Brown became convinced that slavery could be overthrown only by the spilling of blood. John Brown junior recalls that the first time he ever saw his father *kneel* in prayer was just after he communicated to his older children his intention to make *active war* upon slavery. He then got down on his knees and asked the blessing of God upon his undertaking, justifying his action by the text, 'Without the shedding of blood there is no remission of sins.'

In 1846 he moved to Springfield. In that year Gerrit Smith, the agrarian emancipationist, offered to give one hundred thousand acres of the wild land he owned in New York State to such coloured families or fugitive slaves as would occupy and cultivate them in small farms. John Brown visited Smith and arranged to settle in the same region where he would supervise, employ and direct the labour of the ex-slaves. So in 1848 Brown bought a farm and moved with part of his family to North Elba in northern New York State. The farm became his headquarters and was manned by his family during the period when Brown was engaged in carrying on his war against slavery in Kansas, Missouri and Virginia.

John Brown continued to plan, scheme and save for the furtherance of his life's work. He read all the books he could find about guerilla warfare from Roman times to his own. It was about this time that he propounded his ideas to several of the men who were later to follow him to Harper's Ferry. His basic idea seems to have been to enlist a sufficient number of slaves and free Negroes of the North as soldiers, without inciting a general insurrection, and then to establish his armed force where it could best annoy the slaveholders. He believed that upon the first intimation of a plan formed for the liberation of the slaves they would immediately rise all over the southern states. But before these plans could be given any concrete form, John Brown's activities were directed to another field.

The Territory of Nebraska, acquired by America at the time of the Louisiana Purchase, had been declared 'free soil' by the Missouri Compromise of 1820. In 1854, however, Senator Douglas of Illinois proposed that the territory should be divided into two states, Kansas and Nebraska, and that their status regarding slavery should be settled by popular sovereignty. Douglas, in the face of great opposition from the free-soil members, drove his act through Congress. The South was jubilant at the possibility of Kansas, which lay west of slave-holding Missouri, becoming another slave state. Northern free-soilers, on the other hand, regarded the repeal of the Missouri Compromise as an intolerable breach of faith. They decided to prevent the creation of another slave state at all costs. The struggle which followed widened the breach between North and South and paved the way to civil war.

Most of the emigrants who had settled in Kansas had belonged to the ordinary stream of westward-moving pioneers. Now, however, anti-slavery organizations, such as the New England Emigrant Aid Company, began to send their supporters into the area to counteract any plans the South might have of settling more pro-slavers in the territory. Among the Northern emigrants were five of John Brown's sons.

In March 1855 the first state legislature was to be elected. On election day pro-slavery 'border ruffians' poured over the line from Missouri to vote. There could not have been more than 3,000 legal voters in Kansas at the time. Yet the vote actually counted was 6,307 of which 5,427 were for the pro-slavery candidates. The slavery men proceeded to set up a puppet government at Shawnee Mission. The free-soil men set up an extra-legal regime of their own in Topeka. Tension mounted. Clashes between pro-slavery and free-soil men grew frequent. John Brown bought arms and ammunition and, concealing these under conspicuously displayed surveying implements, arrived in a covered wagon to join his sons in Kansas.

Posing as a surveyor he struck his tripod just outside the slavers' camp, sighted a line through the centre of it and, with the help of one of his sons, began 'chaining' the distance. The Southerners took him to be a pro-slavery government surveyor and spoke to him freely of their plans. These included going over to Pottawatomie Creek to drive off all the free-state men and to 'clean out' Brown's settlement on North Middle Creek. When asked who had volunteered information about the Browns and of other free-state families, the names given were Sherman, Doyle, Wilkinson and Wilson.

Soon after this an armed force from Missouri entered Lawrence, the headquarters of the Emigrant Aid Society, destroyed its printing offices, wrecked buildings and generally pillaged the town.

John Brown exacted a terrible revenge for this episode. At the head of a little company of six men he murdered, in cold blood, five pro-slavery men of Pottawatomie. The victims were from the families of Doyle, Wilkinson and Sherman. The weapons used were short cutlasses or artillery sabres which John Brown had brought into the territory. Controversy has raged ever since about the 'Pottawatomie executions'. It seems clear that John Brown directed the operation although he probably did not effect any of the executions with his own hands.

This action lost him the support of many moderate anti-slavers and resulted in ever-increasing violence and retaliation by the pro-slavers. John Brown and his sons were declared to be murderers and conspirators by the territorial government. They became virtual outlaws. In the ensuing months they took part in many skirmishes. Both sides raided settlements, burned down houses, killed and plundered. Two of Brown's sons were imprisoned, another killed in battle.

Brown spent from March until June of 1858 in a sustained effort to organize funds and followers for his next big foray. He had decided that this should be an attack on the arsenal at Harper's Ferry. Few of his supporters knew his actual plan of campaign. They probably would not have agreed with it if they had. Even amongst the men who followed Brown to Harper's Ferry there was much dissension as to the wisdom of such an attack. Brown's personality, however, seems to have been such that no one could dissuade him once his mind was made up.

The little town of Harper's Ferry on the junction of the Shenandoah and Potomac Rivers in West Virginia was originally chosen as a site for an arsenal and armoury by George

Washington. The village was originally named after an English millwright, Robert Harper, who ran a ferry across the river at this spot. In John Brown's day, however, a bridge spanned the Potomac.

In July 1859 Brown rented a farm from an unsuspecting slaveholder on the Maryland side of the river near Harper's Ferry. The farmer believed Brown to be a plain Yankee farmer and cattle-drover. Calling himself Isaac Smith, Brown settled in this farm with three of his sons and a henchman named Jerry Anderson. Here he made his final plans.

The rifles and ammunition originally canvassed for the Kansas campaign were brought to the farm and hidden. By the middle of October twenty-one faithful followers had joined him. At eight o'clock on the evening of Sunday 16 October Brown mustered eighteen of his men; five of them were Negroes. His horse and wagon were brought to the farmhouse door and some pikes, a sledge-hammer and a crowbar placed inside. 'Men, get on your arms! We will proceed to the Ferry!' cried Brown, as he put on his 'old Kansas cap' and mounted the wagon.

Two men were sent on ahead to tear down the telegraph wires on the Maryland side of the Potomac. The rest followed the wagon. They met no one. As they approached the bridge they halted, fastened their cartridge boxes outside their coats and brought their rifles into view. They crossed the river. On the Virginia side they overpowered the sentinel and, leaving two men to guard the bridge, marched on to the armoury gate. Breaking open the gate with the crowbar they rushed into the yard and seized the watchman. Within a short while the arsenal was in their hands and some sixty leading citizens of the town had been taken prisoner. Brown's intention was to use them as hostages.

If Brown had retreated from the town at this point his adventure might well have been successful. As it was he delayed too long, in spite of repeated urgings from his men. The free citizens were given time to organize some resistance and by the evening Brown and six of his men were penned up in the engine-house near the armoury gate, the remainder killed or captured. When a small force of United States Marines commanded by Colonel Robert E. Lee arrived from Washington, Brown was easily overpowered and taken prisoner. By the time Lee had gained control ten of Brown's men (including two of his sons) had been killed, seven had been taken prisoner and five had escaped.

Brown was committed to Charlestown jail. At his trial he

was convicted of 'treason and conspiring and advising with slaves and other rebels, and murder, in the first degree'. He was found guilty and on 2 December 1859 he was hanged at Charlestown. Sixteen months later the American Civil War began.

Why didn't Brown leave Harper's Ferry when he had the chance? One reason was his reluctance to desert the men who had been taken prisoner. Another was that Brown believed that all that had happened had been ordained. 'All our actions,' he said, 'even all the follies that led to this disaster, were decreed to happen ages before the world was made.' Soon he began to believe that his 'actions' were leading him to his most glorious success – a victory such as he might never have won in his own way. To his brother he wrote from prison on 12 November: 'I am quite cheerful in view of my approaching end – being fully persuaded that I am worth inconceivably more to hang than for any other purpose ... So far as I am concerned I count it all joy. I have fought the good fight and have, as I trust, finished my course ...'

John Brown's death had made him a martyr in the eyes of Northern abolitionists. His name, however, might well have been forgotten but for a song, a song sung by the troops of the Massachusetts 12th Regiment as they marched through New York City:

> John Brown's body lies a'mouldering in the grave
> But his soul goes marching on.

This song was not originally about John Brown the abolitionist. It referred to Lieut. John Brown, US Army, stationed at Fort Warren. When news of the abolitionist's death reached the fort the Regimental Glee Club improvised a few verses about John Brown being dead as a joke against Lieut. John Brown. The tune they used was an old camp meeting hymn composed in 1856 by William Steffe of North Carolina. However, when abolitionists in New York heard the song they thought it referred to the martyred John Brown and took it up with enthusiasm.

In April 1861 when the Northern armies first went to war their most popular marching song was 'John Brown's Body'. By then it was the favourite hymn of all abolitionists from Maryland to Maine. At the end of the war all slaves *were* free, and John Brown's life ambition had been realized. However misguided may have been his actions, this was the end to which he had worked. His death helped to speed up events that finally resulted in emancipation.

Charles Bradlaugh

(1833–91)

When the newly elected MP advanced towards the door of the
House of Commons with a view to taking his seat, he was met
by several officials who barred his passage. 'I am here in accordance with the orders of my constituents,' he said, 'and any
person who lays hands on me will do so at his peril.' He strode
forward, pushing the officials aside. But then a number of
police who had been kept in readiness, all men specially picked
for their physique and vigour, hurried up and started to push
him down the lobby stairs. Some of them took him by the
throat, others grabbed his collar, his arms, his body. But (wrote
one of the newspaper reporters who was there) 'the strong,
broad, heavy, powerful frame was hard to move, with its every
nerve and muscle strained to resist'. An almost death-like
pallor had spread over his sternly-set features. He was gasping
for breath, his body bent, his black frock-coat ripped, his collar
and shirt awry. But still there was about his mouth an expression of determination ... until at length he was overborne in
the desperate struggle and collapsed in a faint ...

This was the scene on 3 August 1881 when Charles Bradlaugh, whom the electors of Northampton had chosen to represent them in Parliament, was refused admittance and flung
down the steps. It was disgraceful, horrible, cowardly. Nothing
like it had been witnessed before in Britain's long parliamentary history and (thanks to Bradlaugh) nothing like it has been
seen since, or even attempted.

Charles Bradlaugh was born on 26 September 1833 in a
four-roomed tenement in Bacchus Walk, Hoxton, one of the
poorer quarters of north London. His father, also Charles
Bradlaugh, was a solicitor's clerk in the City; his mother had
been a nursemaid. Charles was their first-born and they moved
house several times before they settled in Warner Place South,
where they paid 7 shillings a week for six or seven rooms. The
family circumstances were never anything but narrow, since
there were seven children to be fed and clothed on a clerk's
poor salary.

At twelve his school days came to an end and he started out
in life as office boy at 5 shillings a week in the firm where his

489

father was a clerk. After a couple of years he obtained the post of wharf clerk and cashier in a coal merchant's off City Road, where his wages were 11 shillings a week.

By all accounts, he was a studious youth and he spent a lot of time hanging around the stalls of the secondhand booksellers. Of an evening he would walk to Bonner's Fields (later Victoria Park) and listen to the soap-box orators on matters of politics and religion – or anti-religion. Young Bradlaugh was shocked by what he heard from the 'infidels', as he might well be, for by this time he was a Sunday school teacher at St Peter's Church in Hackney Road. Here the clergyman was a certain Mr Packer and in 1848 he invited the 15-year-old Charles Bradlaugh to join his confirmation class. To this end the boy embarked on a course of preliminary study. He compared the Thirty-Nine Articles of the Church of England with the four Gospels and was disconcerted to find that in some points they seemed not to agree. He resolved to consult Mr Packer; and that gentleman, instead of inviting him into the vestry for a friendly talk, promptly suspended him from his Sunday school duties and wrote to Mr Bradlaugh telling him that his son had turned atheist.

As was only natural, Bradlaugh shrank from attending church, but he was so far from being an atheist that on his next visit to Bonner's Fields he tackled the 'infidel' lecturers and defended the Bible and his church with youthful vigour and confidence. Not for long, however. His juvenile arguments were shot to pieces and he was soon well on the way to becoming what Packer had accused him of being. Packer induced Mr Bradlaugh to threaten his son that unless he altered his views within three days he would write to his employers withdrawing the security he had given them, which would have cost him his job. Mr Bradlaugh may not have meant it, but his son thought he did and, at the end of the three days, packed up his few belongings and left home.

At first the youth found shelter among the little group of freethinkers to whom he had become attracted, but soon fell into debt, and when his debts amounted to £4. 15s. he happened to see at Charing Cross a poster inviting young men to join the army of the East India Company, and holding out as an inducement a bounty of £6. 10s. He enlisted on the spot and the promised bounty enabled him to settle all his indebtedness. But he found that the recruiting sergeant had tricked him and that he was not destined for India but for home service. Eventually he was enrolled in the 7th Dragoon Guards, with which regiment he served for just on three years, mainly in

Ireland, until in the autumn of 1853 he bought his discharge with £30 bequeathed by a great-aunt.

By this time his father had died and he had to help maintain his mother and sisters. Early in 1854 he obtained the post of errand-boy in a solicitor's office in Fenchurch Street at a wage of 10 shillings a week. His employer soon found that he had considerable legal knowledge and was remarkably quick in the apprehension of legal niceties. At the end of three months his wage was increased to 15 shillings and after nine months he was entrusted with the whole of the common law department. Very soon he was adding to his income by acting as the secretary of a small building society in the East End. With a hundred a year coming in he felt in a position to take a wife, and in 1855 he married Miss Susannah Lamb Hooper, daughter of a good friend of his, an ardent radical, Chartist and freethinker.

The newly married pair took a house in Bethnal Green and for some years the marriage was happy enough. So it might have remained if Mrs Bradlaugh had not developed a taste for strong drink which made her a confirmed drunkard. Bradlaugh (so his daughter Mrs Bradlaugh Bonner tells us in her 'life' of her father) was 'gentleness and forbearance itself, but his life was bitterly poisoned'. At length in 1870 the home was broken up, the two daughters taking their mother to live with them at their grandfather's in the country, while Bradlaugh lived in lodgings in London. This continued until 1877 when Mrs Bradlaugh very unexpectedly died of heart disease brought on by alcoholism.

After his marriage Bradlaugh continued in legal employment and proved so satisfactory that in 1862 he was given his articles by his then employer. After some years Bradlaugh embarked on a succession of business ventures, none of which proved very successful. In fact his heart was not in making money but in freethought propaganda; and at first under the pseudonym of 'Iconoclast' and then under his own name, he became the doughtiest opponent of the Christian churches and creeds that Britain has ever produced.

Year after year he travelled the length and breadth of the land, lecturing to audiences large and small, debating whenever some religious apologist could be persuaded to take the stand against him. Some good judges have expressed the opinion that when Bradlaugh was in his prime he was by far the most powerful orator of the day. As one wrote, 'There was something overwhelming in his force of speech when impassioned; it lifted an audience from its feet like a storm and raised their intellectual conviction to a white heat of enthusiasm.' He was a hard-hitter but he never hit below the belt. He showed no mercy to humbugs and hypocrites but he was sparing in invective and imputation and rarely, if ever, descended to the coarse ribaldry of some others of his party.

Bradlaugh was also a journalist of marked ability, writing with a plain vigour that matched his eloquence on the platform. In 1861 he was largely responsible for the launching of the *National Reformer*, a two-penny weekly, atheistic in religion and extremely radical in politics, that made a strong appeal to the rapidly growing number of educated workers. At first Bradlaugh shared the editorship but from 1866 he was in full control, and in his hands the paper became the principal organ of the freethought movement.

Another and most interesting chapter in Bradlaugh's life opened in August 1874 when Mrs Annie Besant sought and made his acquaintance. She was then twenty-seven and had recently obtained a legal separation from her husband, a Lincolnshire clergyman.

> They were mutually attracted [wrote Mrs Bradlaugh Bonner] and a friendship sprang up between them of so close a nature that had both been free it would undoubtedly have ended in marriage. In their common labours, in the risks and responsibilities jointly undertaken, their friendship grew and strengthened, and the insult and calumny heaped upon them only served to cement the bond.

Within a few days of their meeting Mrs Besant started contributing to the *National Reformer* and she eventually became co-editor and co-proprietor. For thirteen years Bradlaugh and Annie Besant were the closest of friends and associates in the causes they had at heart, until in 1886 Mrs Besant felt the lure of socialism – which Bradlaugh never did – and eventually became the high-priestess of theosophy.

Not long after their partnership had begun, Bradlaugh and Mrs Besant were the chief figures in one of the century's most sensational lawsuits.

In the winter of 1876 a man was convicted at Bristol for selling a book, *Fruits of Philosophy; or, The Private Companion of Young Married People*, written by Dr Charles Knowlton, an American physician of good repute, in which physiological details were given of the human reproductive system, together with some instruction in the douche method of birth control. The book had been on sale in England for many years and this was the first time that it had been prosecuted on the grounds of alleged obscenity. Its London publisher pleaded guilty and got off with a caution. Bradlaugh took a pretty dim view of this and decided to test the issue in the courts. In company with Mrs Besant, who had now entered into formal partnership with him under the style 'The Freethought Publishing Company', he proceeded to print a special edition of the Knowlton book, put it on sale at the company's shop in Stonecutter Street, and informed the magistrates at Guildhall and Scotland Yard what had been done.

Bradlaugh and Mrs Besant were arrested and released on bail while copies of the book were confiscated. The trial was on 18 June 1877 at the court of Queen's Bench before the Lord Chief Justice with the Solicitor General as prosecutor. Bradlaugh made a powerful speech in defence, arguing that the doctrine of family limitation was to be found in many other works in general circulation, and that physiological descriptions identical with those in Knowlton's book had appeared in medical works, many published at popular prices and some specially intended for the use of young people. The jury brought in a verdict: 'We are unanimously of the opinion that the book in question is calculated to deprave public morals, but at the same time we entirely exonerate the defendants from any corrupt motives.' The LCJ accepted this as a verdict of guilty and proceeded to sentence Bradlaugh and Mrs Besant to six months' imprisonment and a fine of £200 each. The two were released pending the result of an appeal and when the appeal was heard in February 1878 their convictions were quashed on a technical point. The trial gave an immense advertisement to the birth-control movement, and to it has been ascribed the rapid fall in the birth rate that was soon perceived.

Not long afterwards Bradlaugh was involved in another great legal battle, this time arising out of his parliamentary ambitions. He first stood for Parliament in 1868, as radical candidate at Northampton, then a two-member constituency. His candidature aroused nation-wide interest and a public subscription was opened to pay his expenses, to which tens of thousands of workers sent their threepences, sixpences and shillings. On this occasion he was beaten, as he was again twice in 1874; but his vote kept creeping up and in 1880 he won the second seat, the other being won by Henry Labouchere, the Liberal candidate.

When the new House met, Bradlaugh did *not* refuse to take the oath, as has been often stated, but asked to be allowed to affirm in lieu. When his application was rejected, he then expressed his willingness to take the oath, but this was denied him, on the ground that he had declared that it would have no binding effect on his conscience. What followed was too prolonged and complicated to lend itself to a summary description, but it should be stated that the shocking scene already described was but the worst of a long series of violent incidents, in which a band of Tory MPs, egged on by Lord Randolph Churchill (Sir Winston's father), did their brutal worst to prevent the duly elected member from taking his seat. At last following the general election of 1885, in which Bradlaugh again carried Northampton with Labouchere as his senior colleague, the new Speaker (Mr Peel) refused to allow any further interference and allowed Bradlaugh to take the oath and his seat.

In the House of Commons Bradlaugh did some useful work and in particular was successful in getting passed the Oaths Act 1888, which permits affirmation in place of the oath for all purposes where an oath is required by law.

Beyond any doubt, the long struggle to take his seat in Parliament shortened Bradlaugh's life. Early in January 1891 he was taken ill and he died on 30 January at the age of fifty-seven. As he lay on his death-bed the House of Commons passed a motion expunging from the Journals of the House the resolutions that had been passed excluding him in earlier times, but when the news came he was too ill to hear it.

He was buried in Brookwood Cemetery on 3 February. The funeral was a silent one, attended by thousands from all parts of the country. Hundreds were wearing the little tricoloured rosettes that they used to wear in the old fighting days at Northampton, and as they turned away many flung them into the grave as a final tribute.

William Cody

(1846-1917)

William Frederick Cody was born on 26 February 1846 when the American frontiersmen had barely penetrated west of the Missouri. When he died in 1917 the old West was no more. The whole territory had been explored and the Indians safely locked inside their reservations. Journeys that had taken four months by wagon in the 1840s now took only four days by train.

William Cody's parents had migrated from Ohio to the new frontier state of Iowa and it was at Scott's Farm near the small town of Le Clair that William was born. He was the fourth of eight children. In 1848 they moved again. Near Fort Leavenworth in Kansas Territory, the last outpost on the edge of barren plains and deserts, Isaac Cody built a one-roomed shack. Near it he opened a store and a tavern. The store did good business both with the soldiers from Fort Leavenworth and the stream of fortune-hunters passing on their way to California. The Indians from neighbouring reservations also used the store and young Bill Cody made many friends among them.

William was eleven years old when his father died. By then the wild frontier life had made him an expert horseman and a crack shot. Now he became the chief bread winner for a family of six. He joined the company of Russell, Majors and Waddell who, in those days, were the principal overland freighters between Missouri state and the Rocky Mountains. Their carriers were teams of twenty-five or more ox-drawn wagons. Each train was manned by about thirty men. Fifteen or twenty trains were sometimes in operation at the same time and messengers were hired to ride between them to deliver instructions from head office. Young Bill Cody applied for a job as a messenger and got it.

So Cody, still a child, embarked on his life of adventure. And thenceforward the legends around him grew and multiplied. According to his autobiography he killed his first Indian on his first trip with the freight train. He was hailed by the local press as 'the youngest Indian Slayer on the Plains'.

In between trips with the wagon trains Bill attended school

495

but, he declares, his real education came from such outposts as Ford Laramie where he listened enraptured while Kit Carson, Jim Bridger and other famous frontiersmen swapped experiences. They taught him to converse in Indian sign language and they fascinated him with their tales of frontier prowess and endurance.

Some years later Cody heard of an even more romantic and adventurous job: rider on the newly-established Pony Express. People in California had grown impatient of the length of time it took to receive mail from the east, so on 3 April 1860 Cody's old firm of Russell, Majors and Waddell started a faster method of communication by using relays of riders on fast ponies.

Cody was only fourteen but he persuaded the superintendent of the Pony Express division between Julesburg and Rocky Ridge to give him a trial. It was a job after his own heart. The letters were carried in special bags called *mochillas* which were slung over the saddle. The ponies were kept at stage stations placed about ten miles apart. At each stage a fresh and saddled pony was waiting. The rider simply flung the *mochilla* over the saddle of his new mount and was away. The usual distance covered by one rider was three stages. Sometimes a rider arrived at a stage station to find it burnt out by Indians. He was expected to carry on to the next stage regardless of hunger, exhaustion or danger.

Bill stayed with the Pony Express until, only sixteen months after its inception, the completion of the transcontinental telegraph line made it obsolete. The Civil War broke out in the spring of 1861 but there is no official record of what Cody did during the war until he enlisted in the Seventh Kansas Regiment in February 1864. He served as a scout in southern Tennessee and in the winter of 1864-5 he was sent to the military headquarters at St Louis. There he met Louisa Frederici and married her. Cody was not quite twenty-one.

After the war he worked intermittently as a teamster, scout and hunter, returning to Louisa at long intervals. He finally drifted broke and jobless into Hays City.

Hays City was one of the new end-of-track towns which had sprung up on the plains with the advance of the Kansas Pacific Railroad. The rails were laid by twelve hundred workmen and one of the main problems of the railroad company was how to feed them. The answer was the meat from the thousands of buffalo which, in those days, still roamed freely over the plains. To obtain this meat buffalo hunters were employed, Cody amongst them. He was hired not by the railway but by a firm of catering contractors. He was paid five hundred dollars a month to supply twelve buffalo a day. It was at this time that Cody earned his soubriquet 'Buffalo Bill'.

By May 1868 the railroad was finished and Bill was again out of a job. But not for long.

As the railroads pushed across the plains and the white settlers grew in number the buffalo dwindled and the Indian tribes grew increasingly hostile. They saw their land being taken from them and their principal means of existence, the buffalo, rapidly disappearing. Wagon trains and settlements were attacked. Washington ordered General Sheridan to Fort Hays to restore order. Sheridan recognized immediately how important competent scouts and guides would be to his campaign and appointed Cody chief of scouts to the Fifth Cavalry.

As chief scout Bill revelled in the opportunities to show off his daredevil courage, his stamina and endurance. So as to be easily recognized by his civilian admirers he began to dress extravagantly and allowed his hair to grow down to his shoulders. He was becoming a western 'character'.

At this stage in his career he met a man who was destined to change his life. Bill had been summoned to Fort McPherson to take part in an expedition against the Sioux. The commander of the company told Cody that a Colonel E. Z. C. Judson wished to accompany the scouts on the expedition. Judson, Major Brown explained, wrote adventure stories under the pseudonym of Ned Buntline and was looking for first-hand material. Later Buntline told Cody that he would like to make him the hero of one of his novels. Bill had no objection and recounted stories of his adventures to Buntline who wrote them with suitable enlargement and embroidery. When Cody ran out of first-hand experiences he supplied Buntline with stories he had heard around the camp fires.

Back east interest in the far west had been growing ever since 1869 when the completion of the Union Pacific Railroad enabled many easterners to see something of the west for themselves. Those too poor to afford a personal trip satisfied their lust for western adventure by reading the magazines and dime novels of the fabulous ' "Buffalo Bill", scout, Indian slayer, buffalo killer, hunter and plainsman, gallant, brave, quick on the draw, chivalrous' – a man in fact who was the embodiment of all they imagined the Wild West to be.

Trips to the west became the fashion. Rich sportsmen even travelled from Europe to see the west, and who was better qualified to lead them than Buffalo Bill. He set up a camp near Fort McPherson which he called a 'dude ranch' or 'dude wigwam' and so established a tourist industry which remains to this day. Bill, the hunting guide, dressed in a white buckskin suit fringed in white leather and a brilliant crimson shirt. His horse was snow white. His hair flowed down to his shoulders. To the dudes he was a strikingly handsome, fascinating individual.

Early in 1872 Cody's millionaire friends invited him to stay in New York. He had heard many tales of the glittering extravagant city and New York, he found, lived up to its reputation. At the Bowery Theatre one of Ned Buntline's stories, *Buffalo Bill, the King of the Border Men*, was being produced in dramatic form. Bill went to see it. When a rumour ran round the theatre that the real Buffalo Bill was in one of the boxes cheers broke out and Bill was persuaded to go on to the stage and make a speech. The audience reaction was such that the manager offered Cody five hundred dollars a week to play the part of himself in the show. Bill refused but the seed of his future career had been sown.

Cody rejoined Sheridan at Fort McPherson to continue his duties as scout but before he left for the west Ned Buntline had extracted a promise from him to appear in a stage show the following autumn. The brief interlude in New York seemed no more than a dream; reality was on the plains and in the mountains of the west. But Buntline wrote regularly to remind Cody of his promise. The name of the epic in which Cody was to appear was *The Scouts of the Plains*!

The curtain rose to a packed house who applauded rapturously at the sight of Cody. But Cody's mind was blank. He couldn't remember a word. Buntline was desperate. He tried improvising. 'Where have you been, Bill?' he asked. Cody had just returned from a hunting trip with a man named Milligan on whom he had played a practical joke. Milligan had boasted that he would enjoy an Indian fight. Cody had arranged one and Milligan fled ignominiously as a party of Pawnee scouts approached. The story had reached the press so when Bill answered: 'I'm just back from a hunt with Milligan', a roar of laughter greeted his words.

The show was so bad and yet it was a tremendous success. When it finally reached New York a critic wrote: 'Everything was so wonderfully bad it was almost good. The whole performance was so far outside of human experience, so wonderful in its daring feebleness, that no ordinary intellect is capable of comprehending it.'

When, in the following autumn, Bill returned to New York he met Major John M. Burke. As Cody's partner, friend, manager and press agent Burke had the vision to see what the legend of Buffalo Bill could be built into. He dreamed of western shows on a far greater scale than could be presented in a theatre, and it was really thanks to him that Buffalo Bill's Wild West Show was to come into being.

Before this could happen, however, Cody was recalled to the west. The government was trying to force the proud Sioux nation into the hated reservations. The Sioux preferred to fight rather than to submit. On 25 June 1876 Americans heard with shocked disbelief that General Custer and five troops of the 7th Cavalry had been wiped out at the battle of the Little Big Horn. When Cody arrived at General Merritt's HQ as chief scout to the 5th Cavalry he was still wearing his stage costume. Merritt's orders were to prevent eight hundred Cheyennes who had left the Red Cloud Agency from joining up with the Sioux.

On the morning of 17 July a party of Cheyennes were successfully intercepted, and in the action which followed Bill's famous duel with Chief Yellow Hand took place. There are many versions of the story. The most consistent one recounts that the scout and the Indian chief saw each other and fired simultaneously. Yellow Hand's pony was killed. Bill's pony stepped into a gopher hole and threw its rider. Both warrior and soldier were, therefore, dismounted and not twenty paces apart. Both men raised their guns simultaneously and fired. Cody said:

> My usual luck did not desert me on this occasion for his bullet missed me, while mine struck him on the breast. He reeled and fell but before he had fairly touched the ground, I was upon him, knife in hand and had driven the keen-edged weapon to its hilt in his heart. Jerking his war bonnet off, I scientifically scalped him in about five seconds. I swung the Indian chieftain's top-knot and bonnet in the air and shouted: 'The first scalp for Custer!'

Only six weeks after the duel Cody, lured back to the stage by tempting monetary offers, was appearing in a new play specially written for him and called *The Red Right Hand or Buffalo Bill's First Scalp for Custer*. It was wildly successful. For the next few years Bill continued to appear in similar dramas involving Indians, cowboys, scouts, lost maidens and so on. But he was becoming bored. At the back of his mind lurked something Burke had once said to him about bringing the whole panorama of the prairies to the public unrestricted by playing in a theatre.

Bill and Burke planned a show that would glorify the lives

of scouts and trappers, the exploration and settlement of the west, the stage coach, the Pony Express and the Indian wars. On 13 May 1883 Cody opened his first Wild West Show on the fair-grounds at Omaha. Next season, under the management of Nat Salsbury, the show was greatly enlarged. One hundred Indians were engaged including Sitting Bull and other chiefs who had taken part in the Custer massacre. Bears, a herd of elk and more buffalo were added to the show. Cowboys rode bucking broncos; the Deadwood mail-coach was attacked by bandits and rescued by Buffalo Bill; displays of sharp-shooting, horse racing and roping added to the noise and excitement. A girl of nineteen named Laura Moses joined the show in New Orleans and appeared under her stage name of Annie Oakley. She stayed with the show for many years.

In March 1887 the company sailed for London. The city took them to its heart. The show set everyone thinking, talking and reading about the Wild West. Bill himself was fêted and dined and wined by the most distinguished men and women of Britain. The Prince and Princess of Wales were enthralled and the Queen ordered a command performance at Windsor Castle. All that summer the show played to packed audiences at Earls Court. Then it toured Manchester and other northern cities.

Cody became a millionaire, but he could not resist a hard-luck story nor shut his ear to any appeal however hare-brained the scheme. His money went as fast as it came. Nat Salsbury, who had always attended to the financial side of the show, died in 1902 and the decline of the business was inevitable.

Bill went home to Louisa and spent the rest of his life thinking up grandiose but unsuccessful schemes for making money. His last public appearance was on 11 November 1916 at Portsmouth, Virginia. He died in Denver on 10 January 1917 and for one day made the headlines again while the nation mourned his death.

Thomas Cook

(1808–92)

The life of Thomas Cook spanned almost the whole of the nineteenth century. When he was born in 1808 Britain was still in the throes of the Napoleonic Wars and fighting for her life. The Industrial Revolution, spurred on by the demands of war to greater achievements than the eighteenth century could have dreamed of, was rapidly changing the face of the country and creating huge new urban populations in the industrial regions. When Cook died in 1892 industrial development had transformed the country from an economically depressed island of Napoleon's day to a great prosperous imperial power.

Many of the changes in social life were the direct result of the steam-engine. The development of railways and steam-engines led to a great increase in the mobility of masses of people. Cook seized upon this and, quite unintentionally at first, created an entirely new industry – the tourist industry.

Thomas Cook was born into a poor family at Melbourne in Derbyshire. His mother was the daughter of a 'hell-fire' preacher of the General Baptist Church. After the death of Cook's father (he died when Thomas was only four) she married James Smithard. The couple did their best to give Thomas some schooling but when he was ten years old he had to work and supplement the family income by hawking fruit and vegetables in the market place. In 1822 Thomas was apprenticed to an uncle who was a wood-turner and cabinet-maker. It was then that he learned to abhor the practice of excessive drinking, for every evening he saw the proceeds of a thriving business frittered away in the local pub. This hatred of strong drink was to remain with Thomas all his life.

When he was seventeen Thomas was baptized into the Baptist Church at Melbourne. The minister at that time was J. F. Winks whose life's work was 'the supplying of Baptist Sunday schools and churches with cheap and appropriate periodical literature'. Winks had a great influence on the young boy. With the help of Winks's literature Thomas became a village evangelist. He tramped the countryside distributing pamphlets and tracts. In 1828 the Melbourne Baptist Church appointed Cook 'village missionary, tract distributor and Sunday school promotor in a number of villages in Rutland and Northampton and the Lincolnshire town of Stamford'. His salary was £36 a year.

In 1833 he married Marianne Mason, a Baptist Sunday school teacher. The young couple set up home together in Market Harborough. In order to earn enough money to keep a family Cook was compelled to retire from the professional missionary business and set up in his old trade as a wood-turner. But he did not give up his evangelical work altogether.

It was at this time that another great social movement attracted his attention – the temperance movement. Cook signed the pledge on New Year's Day 1833; his wife a few months later. In 1836 Cook was appointed secretary of the Market Harborough Teetotal Society. He arranged meetings, bazaars, galas and demonstrations; attended conferences, coped with a great mass of correspondence and in general proved himself an excellent organizer. He was fully capable of handling hecklers too. He had to be, for Market Harborough was notorious for its mobs of anti-teetotal ruffians who broke up meetings and assaulted temperance workers.

Cook's temperance work was the first step in his career as a tourist agent. Gradually the links were being forged. Because of the knowledge of printing, publishing and distributing he had gained as an evangelist, he took over the organization of the South Midland Depository or Temperance Depot. There he worked not only as a distributor of tracts and pamphlets but also as the editor and publisher or two monthly temperance magazines. He was still, let it be remembered, a wood-turner by trade. All his work for the temperance movement was done in his spare time and without pay, except for a trifling commission he received on sales of the tracts.

It was at this point that the railroad entered Cook's life. On 9 June 1841 he set out from Market Harborough to attend a temperance meeting at Leicester, some fifteen miles distant. He walked. On the way he reflected on the news which he had read in the papers that the Midland Railway had recently opened a line from Derby to Rugby via Leicester and that, in consequence, an exchange of visits had taken place between the Mechanics' Institutes of Leicester and Nottingham. 'A thought flashed through my brain,' wrote Cook later, 'what a glorious thing it would be if the newly-developed powers of railways and locomotion could be made subservient to the promotion of temperance!'

In Leicester he broached his idea to the chairman of the meeting. Why not hire a special train from Leicester to Loughborough and back and allow the temperance members to attend a delegates meeting to be held in Loughborough in two or three weeks? And how about organizing a temperance gala at the same time? The conference told Cook to go ahead.

Cook went into action. First he made arrangements for a train with the Midland Counties Railway. He made the arrangements for the gala at Loughborough and for feeding the anticipated crowds. He sent out invitations to local societies in neighbouring towns. He advertised his trip: 'Mr Thos. Cook's Excn. Leicester to Loughborough and back' – eleven miles – reduced third-class fare a shilling. On 5 July 1841 570 people crowded into the nine open third-class trucks accompanied by a temperance brass band. When Leicester was reached, a procession was formed which, headed by the musicians, marched through the welcoming crowds and on to the park.

Thus, in organizing an outing in the cause of temperance, Cook laid the foundation of a vast business enterprise. For the rest of that summer of 1841 and during 1842-4 he was called upon to undertake many more of these 'amateur performances', as he called them. Cook sold his wood-turning business to become a full-time printer and publisher. In November he moved to Leicester and set up the Midland Temperance Press. Mrs Cook opened a temperance hotel nearby.

Up to now all the excursions Cook had organized had been 'amateur' – which means unpaid. By 1844 he was spending most of the summer months working on them. His name was becoming known. Obviously he could not afford to continue working at this rate for nothing, so in 1845 he decided to put the whole thing on a business basis. Calling himself an 'excursion-agent' he came to an arrangement with the directors of the Midland Railway whereby they agreed 'to place trains at his disposal while he provided the passengers'. Just how he was paid is not clear. Probably he received a percentage of the fares.

By this time annual holidays (for those who could afford them) had become an accepted part of upper- and middle-class life. The lower middle classes and working classes, however, were only just beginning to associate 'holidays' with travel. Before the advent of steam working people rarely moved away from home. The introduction of steamboats on the Thames in 1815 had provided a cheap means of transport for Londoners to Gravesend, Margate and Ramsgate. Hitherto the seaside had been accessible only to the rich and fashionable who made the journeys in coaches. The new railway companies soon introduced cheap 'excursion' trips to the seaside but these were mainly a matter of reduced fares, long delays and a pretty uncomfortable journey. What Cook organized in the summer of 1845 was quite revolutionary. He arranged a pleasure trip by special train from Leicester, Nottingham and Derby to Liverpool and back. The cost was 14s. first-class and 10s. second-class. There was no third. He also arranged for his excursionists to proceed by the steamer to Carnarvon by way of Bangor and the Menai Straits – or, if they preferred, to make an ascent up Snowdon on foot. Cook prepared everything with characteristic thoroughness. He also printed a small guide entitled 'A Handbook of the Trip to Liverpool'. It gave travellers exact times of the arrival and departure of the train at different points and included such advice as: 'Parties will have to be wide-awake at an early hour or they will be disappointed. Promptitude on the part of the Railway Company calls for the same from passengers.' The trip was such a success that a fortnight later Cook ran another identical one. It sold out. His next venture was further afield: to Scotland.

These Scottish trips proved very successful and became the backbone of Cook's excursion business for the next fourteen years. He spent two months of each summer personally conducting the tours. Although the tours catered mainly for the new richer middle classes that emerged from the Industrial Revolution, Cook did not forsake his ideal of providing cheap travel and holidays for the lower-paid classes. In the 1840s he approached several great landowners in the Midlands and asked if they would be prepared to open their grounds to 'let the people breathe'. In 1848 he persuaded the Duke of Rutland to open Belvoir Castle to the Cook excursionists, all industrial workers of the area. There was no railway so Cook transported his clients in horse-drawn coaches. Later the Duke of Devonshire was persuaded to throw open his grounds at Chatsworth to trainloads of workers.

This association with the Duke of Devonshire was to have far-reaching consequences for Cook. The Duke's agent at the time was Joseph Paxton who later designed the Crystal Palace to house the Great Exhibition of 1851. Through his friendship with Paxton Cook was introduced to John Ellis, MP and chairman of the Midland Railway. Ellis asked Cook to organize, advertise and conduct special excursion trains to carry visitors to the Great Exhibition during the season from May to October. Cook's son John was his chief assistant. Although only seventeen John was already familiar with his father's work and had spent long periods virtually living 'on the rails'.

Between them the Cooks toured the main Midland and north-ern towns helping to found 'Exhibition Clubs'. These enabled workers to pay small weekly sums towards the fares and board for their visit.

The Home Office asked Cook for advice on how to house the thousands of tourists expected to visit the exhibition. Cook, of course, saw this as a way of fostering the interests of tem-perance hotels and boarding houses.

It was during the Exhibition that Cook produced his first copy of a magazine which was to continue in publication until World War II. It was called *The Excursionist* and through its pages he advertised his trips and kept the public in touch with his plans. Incredible though it may seem, in view of the other work he got through, Cook was essentially a printer and pub-lisher. In 1854, however, Cook, as he himself said, 'found it necessary to dispose of the printing office and to devote myself more exclusively to tourist operations'.

As the century progressed Cook found competition in the tourist trade growing stronger and stronger. The railway com-panies themselves began to copy Cook's example and to organ-ize cheap excursion trips. For some time Cook had felt that he would like to expand his business overseas. He had been or-ganizing small continental tours from the time of the Paris Exhibition of 1855 and in 1864 he turned his serious attention to European travel. He toured France armed with letters of introduction to the leading French railway companies and hoteliers. With the help of his friend Paxton he was able to arrange special facilities from the London, Brighton and South Coast Railway for passenger traffic to the Continent. There-after his foreign tours continued to increase.

His first excursion to Paris was the forerunner of the modern 'package tour'. His clients were not the rich aristocrats who once toured Europe with their private couriers and their own carriages. They were the tradesmen, clerks and mechanics of the new industrial Britain who were careful with their money and who wanted to know exactly how much they would spend before they started. Being completely unused to foreign travel, they felt unbounded confidence in the calm authoritative figure of Thomas Cook or his son who organized everything for them.

From Paris, Cook's tours spread to Switzerland and Italy. Now the business began to make money and to expand. In 1865 a London office was opened at the corner of Bride Lane. The upper floors were run as a temperance boarding-house; the ground-floor office issued tickets and sold guide-books and other tourist requisites such as carpet and leather bags, hat-cases, telescopes and 'Alpine slippers'. John Cook was made a full-time partner in the firm and put in charge of the London office. By the 1870s the business had expanded so greatly that it moved to a new and luxurious building at Ludgate Circus. Cook's agents were put into uniform.

Next came expansion to the United States. Thomas Cook first crossed the Atlantic in 1865, just after the American Civil War had finished. In later years that great American, Mark Twain, was to pay tribute to the travelling Englishman.

Some of those well-to-do travellers who, before the advent of Cook, had had the monopoly of foreign travel sneered at his excursionists. Leslie Stephen in *The Playground of Europe* (1871) referred to 'Swiss valleys which have not yet bowed the knee to Baal in the shape of Mr Cook and his tourists'. *Punch* was inclined to ridicule the 'Cookites' and *The Times* was occasionally superior about them.

But it was not only the lower middle class that used Cook's. When the Archbishop of Canterbury was ordered to spend the winter of 1870–71 on the Riviera, Cook's organized the trip – in spite of all the difficulties caused by the Franco-Prussian war. In 1882 Cook's organized the visit of Prince Albert (later King George V) to the Holy Land. When Queen Victoria began to travel privately to the Riviera it was Cook's who discreetly made all the arrangements.

When the business was extended to include tours through Egypt and along the Nile, Cook's had to build their own steamers to convey the large number of passengers.

In 1872 Thomas Cook set out on his exploratory trip round the world. As a result Cook's were able to offer a world tour with five days' stay in New York, followed by stops in Niagara, Chicago, Salt Lake City and San Francisco. From there they crossed the Pacific to Yokohama, then by way of Shanghai, Singapore and Ceylon to India, returning home through Aden and Suez, Palestine, Turkey and Greece; a journey of 222 days. Thomas Cook called it his 'crowning achievement'.

But he went on to greater things. He lived to see the firm celebrate the fiftieth anniversary of its founding: that was in 1891. But by that time Cook was old and blind. The business was being carried on by his son and grandsons. Cook died at Leicester the following year. *The Times* obituary summed him up thus:

The late Mr Thomas Cook was a typical middle-class nineteenth-century Englishman. Starting from very small beginnings, he had the good luck and the insight to discover a new want and to provide for it. He saw that the great new invention of the railway might be made, by the help of a new organization, to provide large numbers of people with pleasanter, cheaper and more varied holidays than they had ever been able to enjoy before...

A sentiment expressed even more succinctly and forcefully on the plain bronze tablet set up at his birthplace in Melbourne, Derbyshire. It reads: 'He made world travel easier.'

Alfred Krupp

(1812–87)

To determine the Krupp family's share of responsibility in
Teutonic aggression is not at all easy, as the prosecution at the
Nuremberg trials discovered, and it is more rewarding to con-
centrate on their achievement, particularly on that of Alfred
Krupp, the 'Cannon King', who was the first to make the name
a world-wide symbol.

The family originated in one Arndt Krupe (or Kripe, Kripp
or Kroppens) who settled in Essen in 1587. Arndt became
prosperous selling wine, spirits and groceries and died in 1624.
It was the period of the Thirty Years War and Arndt's sons
proved equally capable in that chaotic age. The eldest sold
gun-barrels along with the soap and spices. His nephew Matthias became town clerk and bought land: some of it, outside
the city walls, would become the site two centuries later of the
great Krupp steel foundries. Within four generations the
Krupps had risen to a dominant position in the city.

In the eighteenth century it was Matthias's grandson, named
Friedrich Jodokus, who carried forward the family fortunes as
grocer, cattle-dealer and husband of a distant cousin, Helene
Amalie née Ascherfeld, first of a remarkable line of Krupp
women. Widowed at twenty-five, Helene Amalie expanded the
family business while bringing up two small children. Renam-
ing the firm 'Widow Krupp', she sold cotton goods, linens,
lottery tickers, ran a butcher's shop and started a factory for
making snuff. Everything she touched turned to gold and in
due course she bought several farms and shares in neighbouring coal-mines. Meanwhile her son married and produced an
heir, Friedrich Krupp, after whom the present firm is named,
and when the father died and Friedrich was twenty Helene
bought an iron-fulling works and took over a bankrupt iron
foundry, putting Friedrich in charge.

Friedrich was over-confident and himself went bankrupt,
but after his grandmother died in 1810, worth the modern
equivalent of about £400,000, he turned to making steel and in
1817, after initial failures, began to produce good quality
material in saleable quantities. It was a favourable moment:
the Congress of Vienna had given Prussia possession of West-
phalia with neighbouring lands on the Rhine and Ruhr in-

cluding the city of Essen, and Friedrich was able to sell dies and rolls of cast steel to Berlin for the mint as well as blocks for gun-barrels and bayonets.

But again Friedrich was over-confident, expanded too fast and within a few years was broke again, this time finally. He died in 1826 at the age of thirty-nine, leaving a widow and four children, a factory with only seven workers and debts of £10,000.

In this grim situation again a Krupp woman stepped in with energy, this time, Friedrich's widow Therese with her preco-cious 14-year-old boy Alfred. The family would have starved but for their cottage garden with vegetables and a few chickens. The safest course would have been to sell the factory and go back to grocering. Instead she and Alfred, whose only assets were a smattering of education and twelve months' experience in the workshops, got in touch at once with their best remaining customers and told them that the firm would carry on.

Years later, Alfred wrote of those early days: 'Our present works have sprung from those small beginnings, when the raw materials were purchased piecemeal and I acted as my own clerk, letter-writer, cashier, smith, smelter, coke-pounder, night-watchman, and took on many other jobs as well. A single horse could cope with our transport quite easily.' For a start he got a few orders around Essen for tools and fleshing knives. But his first big break came when an all-German customs union, or *Zollverein*, was created in 1834, abolishing dues between the still independent German states. Alfred set out at once on a grand business tour and was so successful that by the end of the year he had trebled his output and his labour force.

But the early struggle was tough and there were many obsta-cles, the most serious being that the Prussian state preferred English steel and refused to place orders with him. So Alfred took on travelling salesmen and began to seek orders abroad.

Soon Krupp steel was finding its way to France, Holland, Austria, Switzerland, even to Russia and Turkey, while the royal Dutch mint and the Sardinian mint ordered coin dies. But Alfred was not satisfied. The quality of his steel was not above suspicion and in 1838 he took a fifteen-month trip to England, where the world's best steel was produced, for what we would now call industrial espionage. Exactly what secrets, if any, he discovered is not recorded but certainly his technical knowledge was increased, and soon after he was visiting Paris, Berlin, where he sold a complete rolling mill, and Vienna, where he did the same.

But the firm was still on a shaky foundation and needed more solid outlets. As early as 1843 Alfred had made steel musket barrels, but though they were much admired nobody bought them. In 1847 he made his first steel cannon, a three-pounder and sent it to the Prussian war ministry in Berlin where it languished for two years before even being tested. Finally he was told that bronze cannons were good enough. In 1851, nothing daunted, he exhibited a six-pounder at the Crystal Place Exhibition. Victorian ladies found it 'quite be-witching', Alfred was awarded a bronze medal and became famous. But still there were no orders and not even four years later, when Alfred showed a yet bigger gun at the Great Paris Exhibition.

Finally, it was the interest and friendship of Prince William, later Kaiser William I, that in 1859 won him a first order from the Prussian government for 312 six-pounders. This was the first sign of a turning-point fateful for the world: a Krupp and a German ruler had found one another. From now on a mutual dependence grew almost inevitably.

But meanwhile the firm had been steadily expanding – from 300 employees in 1849 to over 1,200 in 1857 – owing to the demand for steel from the railways. The first line had been opened in Bavaria in 1835 and a line from Cologne to Minden, serving the Ruhr, in 1847. From this source Alfred got his first big railway contract for 500 sets of steel springs and axles. But there was a yet bigger advance to come.

It was the practice at that time to weld an outer rim or tyre on to iron railway wheels. But with the increasing speeds and loads of trains it was found that the weld cracked and this led to breakdowns. In great secrecy Alfred experimented with steel wheels and tyres not welded but rolled on while the rims were still hot. The result was a seamless product capable of with-standing much greater stress – and orders in tens of thousands.

'We now live,' declared Alfred, 'in the Age of Steel', and to a firm so technically advanced a growing flood of orders came from innumerable sources, including shipbuilding. But costs were extremely heavy and it was the weldless wheel which first gave the guarantee of prosperity, commemorated in the three interlocking rings which are still Krupp's trade symbol today.

Soon there was a world-wide demand for Krupp wheels and railway equipment; the factory was eight times as big as Alfred had found it twenty-five years before; the future was assured – but in his mind it had to be a future not merely including but dominated by Krupp steel. In 1853 he married Bertha Eichhoff, daughter of a Cologne tax inspector, but a son,

Friedrich, born in 1854 – as it turned out an only child – was marked down from birth for sacrifice on the cold grey altar and Bertha herself was soon driven to spend her life travelling, away from the thud of hammers, the smoke of Essen and her obsessive husband.

But Alfred could not stop. It was almost as though he had to go on till he exploded, like one of his cannon shells. Prince William was a friend. Now Bismarck, William's manipulator, had to be cultivated. Alfred and the man of 'blood and iron' got on well: both thirsted for power and would use any means to achieve their ends. Both were tinged with megalomania. Prussia needed the most modern weapons; Krupp could supply them and keep in the forefront of research if Prussia provided loans. It was a simple, realistic argument, one after Bismarck's own heart, and in 1866, after Krupp guns had been used on both sides in the Austro–Prussian war, Alfred got a government order for 700 guns.

Terrified by an outbreak of cholera in Essen, for the next two years Alfred roved Germany and Switzerland, while bombarding the firm with memoranda, and was only brought back from exile by news that Prussia was going to build a navy. He got the contract to equip three new ironclads.

Meanwhile Krupp steel was helping to expand the railways of Europe and North America and for many years Krupp guns had been exported to Austria, the smaller countries of Europe, Egypt, Turkey, Argentina, even to Britain. And there was a particularly fruitful trade with Russia. Only in France, where the firms of Schneider and Creusot were too powerfully entrenched, were there no sales – but even this proved an advantage.

In the Franco–Prussian war the Germans had a monopoly of Krupp breechloaders while the French only had bronze muzzle-loaders. Whether or not this factor was decisive in the war does not matter; the prestige of the victors fell on Krupp and there was an immediate and enormous demand for his weapons. As one writer had put it: 'To own a Krupp cannon was, for monarchs and megalomaniacs, the status symbol of the age.'

It was now that people began to call Alfred 'the Cannon King'. But in his sixtieth year, one of the richest men in Europe, courted by governments the world over, Alfred began to feel less, not more, secure and built himself a mansion on a hill near Essen called the Villa Hügel. Here, for the rest of his life, Alfred lived and entertained, a miserable, lonely old man.

But there was another and equal anxiety: the firm. It was too big now for Alfred to supervise personally, to see into every nook and cranny, into every workman's eyes to test his loyalty. Neither trade unionism nor political subversion could do much if labour relations were good and in this field Alfred was a pioneer. His policy was comprehensive, of the womb-to-tomb variety: Krupp settlements were built, Krupp schools, co-operative stores, hospitals, canteens, public baths, even a church and a cemetery. Pension and sick funds were started. All this did indeed foster a loyal spirit in the firm which lasts to this day, but Alfred's motive had little to do with benevolence.

After 1871, more wealth, more power came his way almost automatically. The technical race was on; the world needed guns, not once-for-all deliveries but a constant stream of the latest and best and this applied to Germany above all, with France now thirsting for revenge and paying an indemnity, imposed after the victory, of £6 million a month. So the Krupp labour force went soaring to 16,000 in 1873 and thrust Alfred on his last expansionist schemes. Iron-ore deposits were ac-quired in Spain, a fleet of ships to transport the material, over 300 mines and collieries in Germany and two big modern iron-works were bought from competitors. Alfred rode on the crest of the wave. Kaiser William was his friend; Germany was arming to the teeth; each year the world needed more and more steel to kill and to build.

All the same, Alfred could not identify himself for ever with the workshops that thundered and hissed in the valley below the Villa Hügel and it was too late to form bonds with human beings. In the echoing mansion he paced to and fro, utterly alone, snarling at the occasional guests, terrified that the ven-tilation system might fail. He could not even play a game of dominoes for fear of losing. The firm went on without him. But one hope remained: his son Friedrich, an intelligent and pliant youth whom he fondly imagined he had drilled to be-come a replica of himself. In his will Alfred directed that the firm should pass in perpetuity to a single heir, a wish that has been followed ever since.

So when he died in the arms of a footman in 1887 Alfred Krupp bequeathed an empire, though it had long since ceased to bring him any happiness. He had received many decora-tions: the Order of the Rising Sun from Japan, the Order of Vasa from Sweden and, with terrible irony, from Portugal: the Order of Christ.

W. T. Stead, crusading newspaper editor

Josephine Butler, social
reformer

Karl Marx, founder of
modern communism

James Keir Hardie, one of the
founders of the British Labour
Party

Sir John Franklin, Arctic explorer

Sir Richard Burton, traveller and writer

Sophie Schliemann wearing the jewels of 'Helen of Troy'

David Livingstone, missionary and explorer

William Whiteley

(1831-1907)

The successful men of Queen Victoria's England were noted for many qualities, but modesty would not rank high in the list. Yet even by these standards there is an almost majestic immodesty in the title claimed for himself by William Whiteley: The Universal Provider. Whiteley's claim on behalf of his department store was a large one, but he meant it. If a customer was short of guests for dinner Whiteley would supply them. If another wanted an elephant delivered to his stables that day, then Whiteley's delivered it. If someone had to look after a Zulu king during his stay in London, Whiteley's were the people. But it was not the bizarre and exotic demands that were made upon Whiteley's that made the store famous; it was the day-to-day provision of all varieties of household needs within one vast establishment. It was this that earned William Whiteley his other epithet: London's greatest shopkeeper.

William Whiteley was born in Agbrigg, a tiny Yorkshire village near Wakefield on 29 September 1831. His father was a corn-factor. At the age of fourteen he left school to work on his uncle's farm. He enjoyed the country life, was a good horseman and for a time had ambitions of becoming a jockey, but eventually settled for the more mundane life of the drapery business. In June 1848 he was apprenticed to Harnew and Glover, the largest drapers in Wakefield. After three years in the Wakefield shop, Whiteley was given his first holiday and set off, like so many of his fellow countrymen, to the Great Exhibition in London. There in the Crystal Palace in Hyde Park he saw, under the one roof, displays of all possible kinds of goods and commodities. It was here that his dream was born: to own a store where a similar range of goods could be obtained in the one place. But the dream was a long way from fulfilment. The young man still had to serve out his apprenticeship and it was not until 1855 that he was able to leave Wakefield behind and set out for the capital.

The London shops were entering a period of transition. The introduction of plate-glass had been responsible for one change. Shopkeepers were displaying their goods, which meant that the traditional pattern of shops relying on their 'connections' was being broken and an effort was being made to attract the casual buyer. Second, the wholesale and retail sides of trade were starting to separate into distinct establishments. One change in particular was vitally to affect Whiteley's plans. This was the steady movement of the shopping area westwards. In the earlier part of the century, the shopping district had been centred on the City, but now the new developments in Regent Street, Oxford Street and Bond Street were gaining prominence. This was the scene in London when William Whiteley arrived to look for work.

Whiteley chose his new job with care. He regarded this period of his life as training for the day when he would have his own shop. He opted for an old-established firm of drapers in the City, Willey and Co. of Ludgate Street. There he stayed for fifteen months until he felt he had learned all he needed to know about retail drapery and the time had come to investigate the wholesale trade. So from Willey's he went to the large, well-known Fore Street Warehouse where he remained for five years.

Whiteley was always on the look out for ways to broaden his experience, and when he was offered a job in a different branch of the retail trade – ribbons – he accepted immediately. The business was a failure and closed within the year, but Whiteley had got the experience he wanted. He now felt ready to start out on his own. He had saved carefully and had almost £700 put away.

Whiteley considered two areas for his enterprise. One was Upper Street, Islington, but this was already very fashionable and competition among the shopkeepers was becoming intense. The other was Westbourne Grove, Bayswater, which carried the discouraging nickname of Bankruptcy Avenue. Bayswater in the latter half of the century was becoming a prosperous residential area and in 1863 one of the termini of the new underground Metropolitan Railway was situated at Bishop's Road. This growing prosperity should have ensured a corresponding prosperity for local shopkeepers, but the residents were in the habit of visiting the new shops in the West End. Hence Bankruptcy Avenue. In spite of this reputation Whiteley settled for Westbourne Grove and in 1863 took out a lease on No. 31.

Whiteley hired two girl assistants and an errand-boy to work the new shop, and stocked it with fancy goods, especially ribbons. It opened its doors on 11 March 1863 and was an immediate success. Whiteley's sales technique was in marked contrast to that of his neighbours. His goods were clearly labelled with price and an accurate description, with none of the gaudy labels announcing 'Bargain' and 'Sold at Great

Sacrifice' that proliferated elsewhere. While others tried for the maximum profit mark-up on each item, he settled for a smaller profit and a larger turn-over. The customer was never harassed into buying and given very little cause for complaint. The results of the policy were soon apparent. At the end of one year the staff had been increased to fifteen assistants, a cashier and two errand-boys. New departments had been added and the original ribbons had been joined by a new range from furs to umbrellas. This pattern of expansion continued year by year until in 1867 there were seventeen departments whose sales totalled £43,000 in the year. Whiteley was ready to buy his next shop.

1867 was also the year of Whiteley's marriage to Harriet Sarah Hill, who had been one of the two girls he had first employed. The cynical were heard to comment on the advantages of having a wife who knew the business so well. And for some time the business demanded all their time and energy. Whiteley went on steadily buying shops until he owned a whole row stretching from No. 31 to No. 53 and the trade had been extended to include men's wear. Whiteley's family too was increasing, and by the time they had two sons and two daughters their original home became too small for them and they moved to nearby Kildare Terrace. Here the Whiteleys lived surrounded by their hundreds of employees who 'lived in', for Whiteley's was a keen practitioner of Victorian paternalism.

After ten years of growing success, Whiteley took the decisive step towards achieving his ambition. He began offering services to his customers which had nothing to do with his original stock-in-trade. He started with a house agency and a refreshment room, and it was then that he incorporated into his trade mark the title of Universal Provider. It was then too that he met the first check to his triumphal progress. He applied for a licence to serve wine in his refreshment room and his application was rejected. The opposing barrister, not unjustly, commented that 'Mr Whiteley had got enough irons in the fire' and added rather more oddly that the customers 'might be ladies, or females dressed to represent them, and the place might be a place of assignation'. This setback did little to deter him. Over the next few years he added new shops and new departments continuously. Soon he was selling everything from furniture to vegetables, and had added other services such as laundering. The latter remained unsuccessful for some time until he found the solution in Victorian snobbery and overcame it by wrapping servants' and masters' cleaning in different coloured wrappers. More importantly he also provided new capital for himself and a new service for customers by opening his own bank within the store.

Whiteley's expansion brought him into direct conflict with other traders in the area, who found themselves being forced out of business by the competition. The opposition found its voice through the Paddington Vestry, the local governing body, and a series of lawsuits ensued which were to drag on for years. The Vestry was backed by the local press, who were annoyed by Whiteley's refusal to advertise. In fact Whiteley foreshadowed later usage by successfully arranging to get publicity through the editorial matter of the papers. In spite of the opposition Whiteley's continued to grow, spreading out from Westbourne Grove with a warehouse in Queen's Road (now Queensway).

His next venture was to buy the Manor Farm at Finchley where he reared poultry and grew vegetables to stock his new Queen's Road shop. His shops now formed a continuous line stretching along both Queen's Road and Westbourne Grove, and he instituted one of the finest delivery services in London with two local deliveries a day, one per day in the suburbs and a rail service to country customers. A feature of Whiteley's was the hire department, which undertook to fill any order. It was this department that was responsible for supplying a vicar with an elephant.

Whiteley himself was famous among his customers for his charm and helpfulness. To his staff he presented a somewhat different aspect of strict and fierce paternalism. He was prepared to train staff well and provide decent accommodation and good wages. He also provided a whole range of social amenities from a sports ground to a library. But he was ruthless with anyone who fell short of the high standards he set. Fines were imposed for each and every minor offence, and anything more serious could lead to instant dismissal. His list of rules for employees ran to 176 items which dealt with behaviour both inside and outside the store. It was typical of the age that Whiteley felt under no obligation to apply similar high moral standards to his own private life. He and his friend George Rayner had installed two sisters, Emily and Louise Turner, in a flat in Brighton. Emily had a son who was registered as Horace George Rayner, though there was some dispute over the paternity, a fact which was to prove very significant at a later date. But for a time all went well until Mrs Whiteley discovered the arrangement. Whiteley found himself the centre of a scandal and divorce was only narrowly avoided. The Whiteleys separated and remained estranged.

In spite of these troubles in his private life the future looked unrelievedly bright for Whiteley. But on 16 November 1882 the first of a series of disasters struck. Fire broke out at 51 Westbourne Grove. Before it was brought under control six shops had been destroyed. Whiteley seemed undisturbed and rebuilding began at once. Then at Christmas there was a second fire, this time in the furniture warehouse behind Queen's Road. The warehouse, the piano workshop and the printing works were all destroyed. The trouble continued. A third fire broke out in April 1884. By then Whiteley's fires were beginning to gain such fame that special omnibuses were laid on to carry the crowds to the scene. It may have been an attraction for the crowds but it was a disaster for Whiteley. The insurance companies paid out, but Whiteley still had to find over £60,000 from his own pocket. Not surprisingly, many rumours of arson were voiced but Whiteley seemed as buoyant as ever. In 1885 he issued a catalogue for the store which ran to 1,293 pages! But in spite of this proclamation of faith, there was worse to come. Two more fires, and now Whiteley found his own share of the cost of rebuilding rising, for the insurance companies were refusing to touch anything with the name Whiteley attached. The last was the worst, and Whiteley had to borrow heavily. But still he rebuilt, and the 'Bayswater Phoenix' rose again.

Rebuilding after the 1887 fire went on quickly and soon things were back to normal – Whiteley was expanding again. In 1890 he established a flower farm and a strawberry farm and a year later a 200-acre estate in the Thames Valley which he developed as a model farm. Financially the farms were a failure, but the store went on to ever greater success. By the end of the century Whiteley had transferred from private ownership to a public company, a monument to Victorian enterprise with an annual turnover of more than a million pounds.

If Whiteley's life was one of drama, the end of it was pure melodrama. On the afternoon of 24 January 1907 Horace George Rayner walked into the store and asked to see Whiteley. A few minutes later Whiteley came out of his office and ordered an assistant to send for the police. Before anyone could intervene, the young man followed Whiteley out of the office, drew a pistol and shot him dead. Young Rayner claimed to be Whiteley's illegitimate son and to have murdered the old man because he refused to help him, but the facts have never been established. All we know for sure is that on that day the Universal Provider met a violent death under the roof of the great department store that bore his name.

Iwasaki Yataro*

(1834-83)

One of the most startling and far-reaching developments of the nineteenth century was the transformation of Japan from a closed, feudal society into a modern industrial state. The subject has fascinated historians, economists and sociologists alike. The precise nature of this transformation, its causes and the social costs as well as the gains involved, has been a matter of much controversy among both Japanese and western scholars. Among the topics most vigorously debated is the question as to who were in fact the entrepreneurs, the new capitalists of early modern Japan. What were their class origins? Some have argued persuasively that it was the *samurai* (warrior) class that laid the foundations of Japan's capitalist structure. Others have contested this.

It seems likely that the army of Japan's first modern business tycoons came from all ranks of society, with the *samurai* class providing rather more recruits than any other. Assuming this to be the case, it underlines the outstanding part played by the warrior caste, a class in Japanese society that amounted to no more than seven per cent of the entire population (of some thirty million, in the middle years of the nineteenth century).

The *samurai* class had been the ruling elite for a very long period. It was graded according to a number of sub-divisions, in the lowest of which were people whose life-style in some cases differed hardly at all from that of the ordinary peasant. There was, too, more social mobility in the seemingly rigid feudal structure than is often supposed. Merchants, for example, on occasions could acquire *samurai* rank. But in general the warrior was taught to despise the skills and the mentality of the merchant. Even the study of arithmetic, since it dealt with 'numbers', was often considered beneath the notice of the true *samurai*. The concept of profit was regarded as selfish and therefore demeaning, if not actually immoral.

It is the more remarkable, therefore, that one consequence of the shock created by Perry's brusque intrusion, in 1853 and 1854, should have been the readiness on the part of the average *samurai* so far to adapt himself to the modern world as to

* Following the Japanese custom names are given with the personal name *following* the surname.

break with some of the most deep-rooted traditions of his class. But since the clear aim of modernization was to enhance the strength of a land held to be divine, so that it should catch up with the advanced nations of the western world, a majority of the *samurai* class embraced change with a kind of ferocious zest.

One of the most successful, in the material sense, of these *samurai* entrepreneurs was Iwasaki Yataro. He was born in 1834, the son of a country warrior of minor rank in Tosa province on the island of Shikoku. The provincial lord – the *daimyo* (literally 'great name') – of Tosa ruled a singularly progressive and economically prosperous fief. Tosa, the area broadly the same as Kochi Prefecture today, was one of those fortunate regions whose climate enabled the farmer to harvest two crops of rice in a normal year. The *daimyo* of Tosa, like other great feudatories, was virtually a monarch in his own domains, subject to his continued allegiance to the *shogunate* far away in Yedo (the modern Tokyo). And perhaps more than most of his peers he encouraged the development of the local economy, including trade with other parts of Japan. Sea communications were vital for domestic commerce. Much more went by sea, from one part of Japan to another, than by land: and it was in coastal shipping that Iwasaki Yataro was to make his name and create the basis of his later fortune.

Iwasaki first became involved in this activity as a member of the Tosa *daimyo*'s treasury, in charge of the fief's financial accounts. He had won his way to this key fiscal appointment through his own merits. While still a boy his ambitious and determined character was a by-word among his neighbours; and once he had contrived to enter the direct service of the *daimyo* he pushed his way forward with unyielding persistence. The Tosa fief at this time had its own trading centre, with branches at Nagasaki and Osaka. The Nagasaki branch ran into debt. Iwasaki was commissioned to reorganize it; which he did with great success.

Meanwhile, in 1868 the Tokugawa *shogunate* was overthrown by an alliance of warriors in western Japan from the fiefs of Satsuma, Choshu, Hizen and Tosa. They established a new government under the youthful Meiji Emperor in a new capital at Yedo, renamed Tokyo, and proceeded stage by stage to dismantle the feudal structure of the country.

This process was very beneficial to Iwasaki. The fact that his own fief, Tosa, played a leading role in the overthrow of the *shogunate* gave him, like other enterprising officials of the province, opportunities for obtaining favours from the new national government. In the plan – it was indeed an armed conspiracy – to replace the *shogunate* by an imperial regime the most active participants had been lower *samurai*, men still comparatively young in years. Most of them were under forty. Thus they were Iwasaki's contemporaries. Some were his friends. Few would have seemed to him remote or senior figures. Rather, they were fellow warriors engaged on the challenging task of creating a new society. A man from his own province, Gota Shojiro, was very close to him. Goto was a figure of considerable political stature in Tokyo. His association with Iwasaki was cemented when his daughter married Iwasaki's younger brother, Yanosuke. Even more useful friendships were those which Iwasaki enjoyed with two leading members of the oligarchy in Tokyo – Okuma Shigenobu of Hizen and Okubo Toshimichi of Satsuma.

These links go far to explain the windfall that came Iwasaki's way in 1874, when the government decided to send a punitive force to Formosa against aborigines responsible for the murder of Japanese on the island. By this date Iwasaki was already a prominent figure in the shipping world. For he had secured the transfer to himself of the vessels that had once belonged to the now defunct Tosa fief and he had formed a shipping company to operate them. It had flourished and he had established its head office in Tokyo.

It was known as the 'Three Diamonds', or Mitsubishi, company. For the Formosa expedition the government chartered the company's vessels, and it also purchased abroad thirteen steamers, handing these over to Mitsubishi. Moreover, the government entrusted to Iwasaki a number of vessels that had formerly belonged to the *shogunate* and at the same time provided Mitsubishi with a generous annual subsidy.

Three years later the government again needed a quantity of shipping to transport troops and supplies, for in 1877 it was necessary to crush the serious rebellion that had broken out in Kyushu. Not only did Iwasaki provide shipping from Mitsubishi, but he also bought ten vessels from the P & O Line; and the Japanese government loaned or gave him the funds for this purpose. The loan, it may be said, was almost free of interest, repayable in fifteen years.

Such favour put Iwasaki and Mitsubishi into a position that was close to a monopoly, so far as Japanese shipping was concerned. Of seventy steamers of Japanese registry eligible for marine insurance no less than fifty-six belonged to Mitsubishi. This was the measure of Iwasaki's predominance at the end of the 1870s.

Inevitably this situation produced jealousy, not to mention

public criticism. So long as powerful friends, however, remained in the highest positions of the administration Iwasaki could rely on effective protection against possible rivals. But one of these friends was lost to him in 1878, when Okubo Toshimichi was assassinated by a gang of ultra-nationalist fanatics. Then, in 1881, Iwasaki's chief protector in the government, Okuma Shigenobu, was ousted from power.

Within a year or two of Okuma's fall Iwasaki's rivals in the business world, including members of the long-established Mitsui concern, formed a shipping company with a very large government subsidy behind it to compete with Mitsubishi. There followed a bitter struggle, a cut-throat war to secure passengers and freight, extremely costly to both companies.

Iwasaki, however, was not an easy man to defeat. He had already strengthened the resources of Mitsubishi by the acquisition of the valuable Yoshioka copper mine (the nucleus of what was to become the Mitsubishi Mining Company) and by the establishment of an exchange house (the precursor of the Mitsubishi Bank) and a warehouse business (the forerunner of the Mitsubishi Warehouse Company). Nevertheless, the two rival shipping companies incurred such losses in competing with each other that within two years both were almost bankrupt. At this juncture Iwasaki carried out a remarkable *coup*. With great secrecy he bought up over fifty per cent of the shares of the competing company.

At this moment of success his career came to an end. He had cancer of the stomach – a disease exacerbated, it was said, by many years of heavy drinking. For Iwasaki Yataro, to use a Japanese expression, 'drank like a whale'. This was consistent with the rumbustious image he presented to the world, that of a downright plain-spoken warrior turned businessman. He was no more than fifty-one when he died in 1885.

There was certainly nothing small about the personality of Iwasaki Yataro. His photograph shows us a stout but muscular figure; and the big round face with its broad moustache and humorous eyes suggests both strength and intelligence. Here, we feel, is someone whose vices and virtues must be measured by a large yardstick. It could be the face of a shrewd but magnanimous bandit or buccaneer, reminiscent of the features of Pancho Villa, if one were to place a Mexican sombrero above the kimono.

It should be remarked that Iwasaki won the friendship of the most noted intellectual figure of his day, namely Fukuzawa Yukichi, writer, teacher and 'westernizer', the founder of Keio University (just as Okuma, Iwasaki's chief patron, was the founder of Keio's famous rival, Waseda University). Iwasaki recruited many Keio graduates; and it was said that Mitsubishi was run by Iwasaki's money and Fukuzawa's men.

Iwasaki left his legacy in safe hands. His heir as president of Mitsubishi was his brother, Yanosuke – altogether a less colourful, but in no way less able, personality than Yataro. It was Iwasaki Yanosuke who derived the benefit of his brother's master stroke in securing a majority of the shares in the rival shipping company. For the government was persuaded to back the merger of the two companies, from which was born the Nippon Yusen Kaisha (Japan Shipping Company). NYK was blessed at its birth in 1885 with an undertaking from the government to guarantee an 8 per cent dividend to the share-holders for the next fifteen years. The new firm went from strength to strength, its energies devoted less to competing with other, much weaker, Japanese companies than to taking business away from foreign shipping.

In this struggle against foreign, mainly British, competition Japanese shipowners could always rely on powerful govern-ment support. Iwasaki Yataro, for example, had received government grants to enable Mitsubishi to compete success-fully with P & O for the trade between Yokohama and Shang-hai. It was not long before NYK was operating in most parts of the world. NYK, however, was only part of the huge Mitsu-bishi empire that was to blossom and reach full fruition in the twentieth century. Of the Japanese *zaibatsu* Mitsubishi was second, in size and influence, only to Mitsui.* To shipping was added shipbuilding – the Mitsubishi yard at Nagasaki is still the biggest in Japan – and banking, mining and the manufac-ture of paper, textiles, electrical equipment, manifold types of heavy and light machinery, aircraft, chemicals, glass and steel.

The career of Iwasaki Yataro and the proliferation of the Mitsubishi *zaibatsu* are admirable illustrations of one of the fundamental causes of Japan's rise to world power; namely a confident and characteristically nineteenth-century identifica-tion of personal and family profit with meritorious service to the state, so that the one necessarily implied the other. In other words, what was good for Mitsubishi was good for Japan. That, we may be sure, was how Iwasaki Yataro interpreted his own role in his country's affairs.

*The literal translation of *zaibatsu* is 'financial clique'. Mitsui was already a thriving merchant house, long established, before Iwasaki Yataro was born. Mitsui, therefore, can be said to have had a good start over its great rival.

Andrew Carnegie

(1835–1919)

Andrew Carnegie was born in Dunfermline, Scotland on 25 November 1835. He came from a family of weavers. For more than two hundred years Dunfermline had been the centre of the Scottish weaving trade. Its beautiful damask linens were in demand all over the world, including the United States. The life of the Scottish town revolved around its trade. The cottages of the weavers functioned half as shops, half as dwelling places.

William Carnegie, Andrew's father, was a shy quiet man. He had done well in his trade but had not the temperament to adjust to the factory age which threatened to imperil all that he and his cottage industry stood for. Day by day he saw new factories being built where one boy or girl could do work which had once been performed by many men. The winter of 1847–8 was a disastrous one in Dunfermline and, indeed, in the whole of Great Britain. There was widespread unemployment. Many died of starvation. Thousands of hand-loom weavers, unable to find work at home or in the factories, were forced to shut up their shops. Andrew's father was obliged to sell his looms. But for his mother the whole family might have starved. She converted the front room of her house into a small shop and sold vegetables and such delicacies as cow-heels. The family began to turn its thoughts to making a fresh start. Emigration to America was the obvious choice. Two of Mrs Carnegie's sisters and their families were already in Allegheny, Pennsylvania.

So on 19 May 1848 the Carnegies set sail from Glasgow in an old whaling schooner called the *Wiscassett*. Andrew was desolate at leaving his beloved Scotland. His father was full of doubts and fears. Only his mother had any confidence in the new country. They had no money. Every penny they received from the sale of their few assets in Scotland had gone to pay for the voyage.

Once they landed in the New World, the Carnegies headed for Allegheny. There they were welcomed by Mrs Carnegie's sisters who did all they could to help the newcomers. Times were hard. Andrew took a job in a cotton mill as a bobbin boy and earned $1.20 a week.

His first opportunity to better himself came when he was

offered a post as messenger boy in the Pittsburgh telegraph office. The job was a turning-point not only in Andrew's career but also in his cultural development. The Pittsburgh theatre of the day presented seasons of classical drama. Andrew frequently had messages to deliver to the theatre. He usually contrived to delay their delivery until the evening performance had begun and then, with the friendly consent of the manager, he would creep up into the gallery to watch the show. This was Carnegie's first introduction to Shakespeare. He acquired an astonishing knowledge of the plays.

By the time Andrew Carnegie settled in Pittsburgh, opportunities for self-improvement were not difficult to find. This was due to Colonel James Anderson, a retired businessman. One of his most treasured and pleasurable possessions was his private library. He had been moved to do something to overcome the difficulties boys had of obtaining books for study. In order to help them he opened his library to working boys on Saturday mornings and allowed them to borrow one book per week. Andrew was one of the first to take advantage of the Colonel's thoughtfulness.

In the telegraph office Carnegie was a more than industrious apprentice. The constant clocking of the telegraph key fascinated him. He itched to try his hand at sending and receiving messages. He taught himself the Morse code. Soon he was calling up associates in nearby towns. One morning when he was alone in the office an emergency call came through from Philadelphia. Could he take it? He could and he did, though somewhat fearful at his own presumption. However, the manager was delighted and raised his pay. Henceforward Andrew was sometimes asked to take over from the operator or even left in sole charge. In those days the messages were received on a thin strip of paper on which the dots and dashes were imprinted and later transcribed. Andrew, however, taught himself to take down the messages by sound. By the time he was sixteen he was promoted to the key and admiring townsfolk would drop in to watch the new telegraphist transcribe messages direct from the instrument.

On 14 March 1853 Andrew wrote to an uncle in Scotland:

... I have left my old place in the telegraph office and am now in the employ of the Pennsylvania Railroad Company, one of the three leading roads from our Atlantic cities to the Great West ... Mr Scott, the Superintendent of it, offered me 35 dollars per month to take charge of their telegraph office which the Company has in this city [Pittsburgh] for its own exclusive use, and also to assist him in writing and auditing accounts...

Once again, by a bold action, Carnegie gained promotion. Breakdowns and accidents were common on the railroad at that time and Scott was often absent from the office to look into the causes of them. One day there was a serious accident which delayed passenger trains in both directions and brought all freight trains to a halt in the sidings. Andrew was alone in the office. Most young men would have waited for the boss to return before trying to sort things out. Not Carnegie. 'I could not resist the temptation to plunge in, take the responsibility, give "train orders" and set matters going.' By the time Scott returned everything was running smoothly.

By 1859 Carnegie was the manager of the western division of the Pennsylvania Railroad. When the Civil War broke out Scott was appointed Assistant Secretary of War in charge of the transportation department. Andrew became *his* assistant. The war began badly for the North and soon Washington, the capital of the Federal Government, was in danger of being completely cut off by Confederate troops. Southern sympathizers in Maryland had destroyed all important railway and telegraph links with the North. Carnegie was given the job of repairing the damage. He collected a force of conductors, trainmen, trackmen, road supervisors and bridge-builders and rushed into action. Within three days the whole line was restored. Carnegie himself rode in the engineer's cab of the first train to enter Washington over the newly repaired track. Soon the first of the 75,000 troops so urgently needed for the defence of the capital began to arrive.

When Andrew Carnegie was twenty Scott had asked him if he had $500 with which to buy ten shares in the Adams Express. Carnegie had not even $50 but he unhesitatingly said yes. His mother mortgaged the house in Rebecca Street to raise the money. Soon Andrew was receiving a monthly dividend of $10. This event stimulated his interest in investment. Then Theodore T. Woodruff showed Carnegie a model of a sleeping-car he had invented. Carnegie immediately saw its possibilities and persuaded the Pennsylvania Railroad to build two cars. Woodruff was so grateful that he offered Carnegie a one-eighth interest in the company formed to manufacture the cars. The annual dividend from this source amounted to $5,000. Carnegie was then twenty-five years old.

In 1863 he drew up a statement of his earnings. His combined yearly income from his salary and his investments amounted to $47,860. Of this his salary amounted to only $2,400. In March 1865 he decided to become his own boss and resigned from the Pennyslvania Railroad. Now he began to devote his energies to founding great industries; to supplying the ideas, inspiration and driving power to keep them alive; to selecting with uncanny judgment men who could transform his ideas into action.

The great westward expansion in the United States after the Civil War gave rise to an enormous demand for iron. Carnegie had foreseen this, largely because of an old friend of his named Piper, a mechanic on the Pennsylvania. Piper had taken out a patent for building bridges of iron instead of wood. Only a month after leaving the railway Carnegie and Piper drew up plans for launching the Keystone Bridge Company. Soon Keystone iron bridges spanned most American rivers. In 1866 Carnegie founded the Pittsburgh Locomotive Works. By the time he was thirty-one he had at least four major enterprises under his direction.

But Carnegie was not one to believe that making money should be the main object in life; neither did he believe that a businessman should be constantly supervising his companies. Once he had organized a concern his policy was to install the best possible people to run it for him. Typically, therefore, once they were organized, he left the Union Iron Mills, the Keystone Bridge Company, the Superior Rail Mill and the Pittsburgh Locomotive Works in the hands of his subordinates and went off to Europe for a six-month holiday. Trips to Europe became a regular routine. He divided the year equally, six months in America and six months in his beloved Scotland or in Europe where he visited theatres and art galleries.

In December 1868, when he was thirty-three, Carnegie drew up a memorandum in which he set out his personal programme.

Thirty-three and an income of 50,000 dollars per annum! ... Beyond this never earn – make no effort to increase fortune, but spend the surplus each year for benevolent purposes. Cast aside business for ever, except for others. Settle in Oxford and get a thorough education, making the acquaintance of literary men ... pay especial attention to speaking in public. Settle in London and purchase a controlling interest in some newspaper or live review and give the general management of it attention, taking a part in public matters, especially those connected with education and improvement of the poorer classes. I will resign business at thirty-five but during the ensuing two years I wish to spend the afternoons in receiving instruction and in reading systematically...

Carnegie lived up to his programme. Almost every item was ultimately carried out. He did not actually settle in Oxford or London, but he did spend much time in Britain studying and promoting educational projects. He did become the proprietor of some twenty popular newspapers devoted to educating the working classes. He worked continually at educating himself, and though he did not retire at thirty-five he *did* use his surplus fortune for the benefit of others.

The main reason why Carnegie did not retire in 1870 was a chance meeting – while on a European trip – with Henry Bessemer. The Bessemer convertor, by which steel could be produced cheaply from iron, fired Carnegie's imagination. 'The day of iron has passed – steel is king!' he wrote. He built the Edgar Thomson steel rail mill, bought out the Homestead steel works and by 1888 had under his control an extensive plant served by tributary coal and iron fields, a railway 425 miles long and a line of lake steamships. In 1901 all the various Carnegie enterprises had merged into the United States Steel Corporation.

From the time he wrote the personal memorandum in 1868 Carnegie had been increasingly preoccupied with, to him, the problem of excessive wealth. In 1889 he wrote an article on the subject and sent it to the *North American Review*. This article, later referred to as his 'Gospel of Wealth', stated that 'men possessed of a peculiar talent for affairs' must inevitably make more money than they can spend judiciously upon themselves. He agreed, too, with socialists that the real creator of great fortunes was society and not the industrial 'masters'. He therefore concluded that excessive accumulations in the hands of millionaires were not, ethically considered, their own property; justice demanded that 'surplus' wealth should be returned to society which had created it. The difficulty was to reduce this theory to practical terms. This, in fact, is what Carnegie spent the rest of his life trying to do. In giving away his money he expended as much thought, energy and skill as he had spent in making it. He did not believe in men leaving great fortunes to their children.

Carnegie did not believe, either, in leaving great estates for public purposes by will. 'Men who leave vast sums in this way may fairly be thought men who would not have left it at all had they been able to take it with them.'

At the time when the article was written Carnegie's capital probably amounted to something like $30,000,000. Apart from leaving his dependants comfortable, Carnegie had publicly pledged himself to give away this vast sum. Most people were sceptical. He did not really mean it, or so they thought.

They were wrong. Remembering Colonel Anderson's library in Allegheny, Carnegie's first task was to emulate the Colonel's idea on a vast scale. By the close of 1918 he had erected 2,505 library buildings in the United States and Great Britain and other English-speaking countries. He did not, in fact, give libraries. He gave buildings to towns or boroughs which promised to support public libraries. His object was to stimulate towns into providing better educational and cultural amenities for their poorer citizens.

In 1901 he founded the Carnegie Institute of Technology at Pittsburgh and in 1902 the Carnegie Institute at Washington. The Carnegie Trust for the Universities of Scotland was founded to improve and expand the universities and to pay fees of students of Scottish birth. The Carnegie Dunfermline Trust was set up in 1903 in Carnegie's home-town. The income from the £750,000 capital may be spent on anything to improve the community. One of Carnegie's greatest satisfactions was when he bought Pittencrieff Glen and presented it to the city as a public park.

The list is endless. The Carnegie Hero Fund Commission was set up to give recognition to people who in peacetime risk their lives to save others. The Carnegie Foundation for the Advancement of Teaching (New York) provides teachers with free pensions and made possible many reforms in the educational system. The Carnegie Endowment for International Peace was founded in 1910 with a view to the 'speedy abolition of international war between the so-called civilized nations'. The Carnegie Corporation of New York – the largest of all – exists for 'the advancement and diffusion of knowledge and understanding among the people of the United States'.

Carnegie died at Lenox, Massachusetts on 11 August 1919. In all he had given away $324,657,399. Faithfully indeed had he followed the philosophy summed up in his 'Gospel of Wealth'.

Ludwig van Beethoven

(1770-1827)

At about the turn of the century it occurred to the Austrians just how many outstanding people, in varying walks of life, their country had produced over the years and how widely scattered were their final resting places. They set aside a special site in Vienna's vast Central Cemetery for a Grove of Honour, and reburied in it the remains of the great departed, exhumed from graveyards at home and abroad.

Tens of thousands go there yearly to pay homage to the famous; and one monument before which no one fails to pause bears a one-word inscription: BEETHOVEN.

No qualification is necessary, even if it were practicable to carve on a single stone all that needs to be said of him. Ludwig van Beethoven was not simply one of the two or three greatest composers of music ever to have lived. He and his work stand eternally for everything which fuses the soul and spirit of mortal man with the sublimity and awesomeness of nature, with life's joy and suffering, with the triumph and despair which attend creative endeavour and, perhaps foremost in his case, with the universal struggle against physical and spiritual oppression.

He died aged 56 on 26 March 1827 in an unkempt room in Vienna, his last illness almost unnoticed. His friends and associates were used to his frequent illnesses and had thought this last one, which was pneumonia, was just another bout. Besides, his was not the endearing nature which would have moved sympathizers to watch anxiously at his bedside. And yet, his funeral cortège, which had only some 1,000 yards to progress from the house in Schwarzspanierstrasse to the Alser church, took more than an hour and a half to cover the distance, so dense was the crowd. Almost the whole of Vienna's populace had turned out to mourn the passing of this irascible, uncouth, uncompromising genius, who, though he was not one of them by birth, they had become proud to claim as their own.

He was born in Bonn in Germany on 16 December 1770. The name Ludwig *van* Beethoven spoke of family origins in the Low Countries; his musician grandfather had come from Antwerp to become at length *Kapellmeister* to the Electoral

Archbishop of Cologne, whose seat was at Bonn. The *Kapell-meister* combined his court musical duties with dealing in wines and drinking them. Alcohol as well as art flowed liberally in his veins and in those of his wife and their sons. The son who became Ludwig's father, Johann, was a tenor in the Electoral Chapel and a constant and formidable drinker, bad-tempered and erratic. He did, however, recognize and encourage the infant boy's musical aptitudes. In those days all parents of musically talented offspring were praying for another Mozart, the phenomenon of the age.

The court organist, Christian Gottlob Neefe, who taught Ludwig the piano, confirmed the father's hopes. The boy was brought to the notice of aristocratic patrons and enabled to make his first concert tour to Vienna when he was seventeen. There the aspiring second Mozart met the original and played for him. Mozart was not unduly impressed until he asked Beethoven to extemporise. The response was so astonishingly brilliant that Mozart affirmed the youth's great promise.

What might have proved a remarkable relationship between them was prevented by Beethoven's having to hurry back to Bonn, where his mother was mortally ill. It was five years before he came to Vienna again and by then Mozart was dead.

Haydn, who had seen poor Mozart come and go, still upheld the Viennese classical tradition. Beethoven went to him for some lessons but gained little from them. His rugged individuality was already his ruler and he went his own way.

He had now adopted Vienna as his home and the discerning aristocrats who competed with one another as patrons of the arts adopted him. Mozart had refused patronage and died a pauper. Beethoven, despite his independent spirit, accepted it because he had no other means and wanted to get on. But it had to be on his own terms. He repaid their beneficence not only with brilliant piano playing but also with unpunctuality, arrogance and an utter refusal to defer to rank. He had not inherited the weakness for drink which had lost his father his post in Bonn and hastened his death, but the irritability, intolerance and personal untidiness were all there.

He was a little man with a large head made more dispropor-tionate by a mass of thick hair. His nose was stubby, his complexion dark, coarse and pock-marked, and his eyes flashed contemptuous challenge. A habitual scowl warned of the rage which would erupt if anyone showed offence at any-thing he did or disputed his opinion or, worst of all, condes-cended towards him.

Such was the tempestuous side of Ludwig van Beethoven's

personification of nature's contrasts. But after his thunder-
storm had passed his sun would peep forth as if to convey the
elements' apology for such noise and tumult, and those at
whom he had hurled his bolts would be charmed and warmed.

> Oh, ye fellow-men, who deem me hostile, who declare me
> obstinate or discourteous, how unjust you are! You do not
> know the hidden cause. My heart and my mind have, since
> childhood, yielded to the tender touch of human kindness.
> The mood was always with me to accomplish great tasks.
> But only bear in mind that for six years a disastrous affliction
> has befallen me.

He wrote those words in the autumn of 1802 when he was
just into his thirties and beginning the so-called second period
of his career. The first period had seen him achieve and consolidate fame as a virtuoso pianist, while experimenting with
composition and moving away from the influences of Mozart
and Haydn towards a unique style that astonished and offended to some extent the Viennese traditionalists. And now,
as the years of his creative greatness lay ahead of him, he knew
that he was becoming incurably deaf. He contemplated taking
his life.

It was while making a despairing visit to the thermal baths
at Heiligenstadt, on the heights above the city, that he wrote
the moving document which was found after his death and
published as *Das Heiligenstädter Testament*. Addressed to his
brothers, it was in effect a will, in which he revealed the agony
of his fruitless battle against his affliction and how he had
striven to keep others from knowing of it, even at the cost of
being thought more unmannerly and misanthropic than inherited traits had made him.

> I could not bring myself to the point of saying to people:
> 'Speak louder, shout, for I am deaf!' How could I possibly
> admit the frailty of that one sense which with me should
> have been more perfect than with others, a sense which I
> once possessed to a degree of perfection equalled by few in
> my profession, now or at any time.

It is hard to credit that the majority of Beethoven's works,
including most of the symphonies, the concerti, the opera
Fidelio, the mass *Missa Solemnis*, the sonatas and chamber
works and songs were composed by a man who could scarcely
hear, and for some years could not hear at all. The appeal of
his music is universal and enduring. People's spirits dance to
the joyousness of some of his tunes. Everyone has heard of

Beethoven, as they have of Shakespeare, and that one-word epitaph is enough; and yet he was a man alone, shut off from others by his deafness and other complaints, by depression and his forbidding personality, and by his need to work constantly, slowly and painstakingly grinding out of himself the music which he knew he had been put on earth to create.

He was alone in other respects, too. A Roman Catholic by upbringing, he abandoned the consolation and security of formal religion for a pantheism which accorded with his oneness with nature. The countryside around Vienna, especially the Vienna Woods, gave him such solace as he knew and stimulated his creativity. Strolling with his friend and biographer, Anton Schindler, he was able to recall the precise sights and sounds which had inspired the 'Scene by the Brook' second movement of the 'Pastoral' Symphony. 'The yellow-hammers, the quails, the nightingales and cuckoos all round played their parts,' he remembered; but by the time he had composed that symphony he was already unable to hear high-pitched instruments or the voices of singers. He must have been carrying those birds' songs in his mind.

It was this same ability to conceive in his mind remarkable new harmonies, from combinations of instruments which were frequently adventurous and often almost outrageous, which gave Beethoven some of his most striking effects. He justifiably termed himself a 'tone-poet', able to find the most natural sounds to correspond with each deep-felt emotion.

The piano was his principal sole instrument. He made it universally accepted and with it raised the sonata form to heights never before imagined and not since surpassed. His exploitation of the instrument's robust strength and range, compared with the small, quiet clavichord or the mechanically-limited expressiveness of the harpsichord, contributed to the positiveness of his musical thought, which in turn influenced the ideas of Schumann, Brahms and Wagner.

But his writing for strings and all the other instruments was sympathetic to their possibilities and always inventing things for them. It is a great loss to the choral repertoire that he did not live to create the many choral works he had in mind. The *Missa Solemnis* and the Ninth ('Choral') Symphony give ample evidence of what might have been. Still, more than any other composer, he contributed his share towards the permanent musical repertoire, with more than 250 major works across the whole spectrum of forms constantly being performed.

No wife was at hand to share his aspirations and ease his unrelenting task by lessening the disorder and often downright squalor amongst which he lived, ill-nourished and unhealthily irregular in his ways. He had various love affairs, some of them deep enough to add to his misery when they ended in disappointment, as all did. The woman who seems to have come closest to his heart, and may have borne him an illegitimate child, was Josephine von Brunswick, generally identified as the *Unsterbliche Geliebt* [Immortal Beloved] of some of his letters; but she was already married.

The challenge to tame him, to become the one person who could share him intimately with his art, would have been an heroic quest for any woman. She would have needed to be an exceptional person.

It has not been proven but much evidence suggests that another obstacle was between him and marriage and a family, which he lamented were denied him. He may have had incurable syphilis, contracted in his youth or inherited. It might account for some of his maladies, including his deafness – his post-mortem revealed a constitution far gone in many respects – and perhaps manifested itself in some of his rages, his despair and his virulent objection to his late brother Johann's wife for her immorality.

It was this deplored sister-in-law's son Karl through whom Beethoven tried to demonstrate himself capable of domestic affection. He fought the mother through the courts for guardianship of the child and won. It cost him money he could ill afford, for he had never managed his finances properly nor allowed anyone to do it for him. Karl proved ungrateful and undisciplined. He spent time in an institution and once tried to commit suicide. Beethoven, as a surrogate parent, had failed.

In fact he was a failed person. His life was a shambles above which his spirit soared to enrich the lives of millions of others. His age was the age of revolution against oligarchy, tyranny and oppression. Europe was shaking itself free of medieval practices and human rights were struggling for assertion. Ludwig van Beethoven, the rebel who would bend the knee to none, and whose brand of music was as individualistic and heroic as himself, was precisely the man for his time.

There was no mistaking the message of such stirring works as the 'Eroica' Symphony, the opera *Fidelio*, the overtures *Coriolanus* and *Egmont*. In our own time, the four opening notes of his Fifth Symphony heralded broadcast transmissions of news and vital messages from the BBC to the subjugated people of Europe in World War II and hearts quickened whenever they were heard. His setting of Schiller's *Ode to Joy* from his 'Choral' Symphony was chosen as the official anthem for the brotherhood of free nations, the Council of Europe.

'Oh Providence! Permit me once again to experience a day of pure happiness!'

It is unlikely that his plea in *Das Heiligenstädter Testament* was granted. He did not expect it to be and he said he advanced towards death with joy. Yet he could not kill himself because he knew how much there was still for him to do. He suffered on and wrought his magic for a further twenty-five years.

What loss mankind would have sustained had Ludwig van Beethoven given way to that despair against which his music has inspired multitudes to fight!

Franz Schubert

(1797–1828)

Vienna at the beginning of the nineteenth century was the musical centre of Europe. Yet none of the composers who had made it great, Gluck, Haydn, Mozart and Beethoven, were actually born there. Schubert became the first great Viennese composer in this golden age of musical history.

There had been many years of hardship and oppression during the Napoleonic wars and, with the Treaty of Vienna signed in 1815, the Viennese were determined to enjoy their precarious peace while it lasted. They plunged themselves with almost frenzied enthusiasm into all the diversions of life: singing, dancing, eating, drinking and entertainment of every kind.

This was the Vienna in which Schubert lived as a young man. He was born on 31 January 1797 into a humble, unsophisticated, middle-class household. His father, Franz Theodor Schubert, was a schoolmaster who had come to Vienna from the neighbouring country of Moravia where his family were peasants. His mother, Elisabeth Vietz, was of Silesian origin and had come to Vienna to find work after she and her brother and sister were orphaned. They had fourteen children, of whom the composer was the twelfth. After his first wife's death Schubert's father married again and had another five children.

The home was a musical one. Every Austrian schoolmaster of the time was expected to be a reasonably competent musician and Franz had his first lessons from his father and two elder brothers. Soon he was sent to the local organist and choirmaster, Michael Holzer, who was astonished and delighted to have such a talented pupil. But Holzer's enthusiasm made little impression on Schubert's father. He was a pious, hardworking man who had dedicated himself wholeheartedly to his chosen career and was determined that his sons should follow in his footsteps. He must have been more than satisfied when Franz, at the age of twelve, was admitted as a choirboy to the Chapel Royal, for this meant a free education at the Imperial Konvikt, the most sought-after school in Vienna.

From Franz's point of view, however, the attraction of the Konvikt was that it gave him the opportunity of taking part in music-making of all kinds. Besides singing in the Chapel Royal choir, there was the Konvikt orchestra which gave concerts each evening, usually consisting of two overtures and a symphony. Here Schubert got to know the music of Haydn, Mozart and Beethoven, besides a host of lesser composers, and at these concerts his own first orchestral pieces were played. By now he was an accomplished pianist and violinist, and chamber music – anything from piano duets upwards – was a favourite occupation. At home he played quartets with his father and brothers, his father playing the 'cello, his two brothers the violin and Franz the viola.

Towards the end of his time at the Konvikt his talents as a composer began to attract the attention of the court music director, Antonio Salieri, now hardly more than a name in textbooks but at the time a highly successful composer and one-time rival of Mozart. Schubert became his pupil and continued to take lessons from him for several years after leaving the Konvikt. He obviously admired him; many of his early works are proudly inscribed: 'Franz Schubert, pupil of Salieri'.

Schubert left the Konvikt in 1813, having completed his First Symphony which was performed at one of the evening concerts. For the time being, at least, he submitted to his father's wishes and entered a training school for teachers. Six months later he became an assistant teacher in the lowest class of his father's elementary school where he remained until 1817. However much Schubert disliked teaching, as he undoubtedly did, it gave him plenty of time for composition. The years from 1814 to 1817 were among the most productive of his whole life and it was during this period that his greatest gifts came to maturity – song-writing.

Schubert had written songs from early childhood but it was with the Goethe setting, *Gretchen at the Spinning Wheel*, composed at the age of seventeen, that his genius really showed itself. His style as a song-writer derived not only from Haydn and Mozart, his models for orchestral music, but from a flourishing school of German song-writers, now mostly forgotten, who took as their texts the new lyric verse of Goethe, Schiller, Hölty and Claudius. They represented more than any other German music the new wave of romanticism that was sweeping Europe and they had begun to explore the possibilities of the new instrument of the time, the piano, to make the accompaniment a vital part of the song instead of just a background. Their ideas made a deep impression on the young Schubert. In his lifetime he composed over six hundred songs, creating what was in effect a new genre, the *Lied*, which was used by countless composers after him – among them Schumann, Brahms, Wolf, Mahler and Richard Strauss. To gain some idea of Schubert's output during these early years, in 1815 he wrote 150 songs, six operas, two Masses, three sonatas and two symphonies.

Schubert found his life as a teacher continually more oppressive. Determined to escape in 1817 he gave up teaching, left home and moved into the lodgings of a friend, Franz von Schober. From now on he adopted a Bohemian way of living which he kept up until the end of his days. He lived at fifteen different addresses during the next eleven years, most of them the lodgings of friends. But he was no opportunist; he valued friendship as an essential part of life, almost as essential as music. The members of his circle were poets, writers and painters, most of them amateurs, whose common interest in the arts had brought them together. They instituted the famous Schubertiads, evenings of poetry, music and general merry-making, at which Schubert's songs, piano pieces and chamber music had their first hearings. Only one or two of the circle, like the dramatist Grillparzer and the painter Moritz von Schwind, ever achieved fame in their own right; but others, like Schober and Mayrhofer, were immortalized by Schubert's settings of their poetry.

Schubert wrote fourteen works for the stage (including some unfinished ones) between 1815 and 1823, none of which achieved success. His continued determination to succeed in the face of so many failures must have been partly due to financial motives. An operatic success would have meant financial security, temporarily at least, and money, or rather the lack of it, dogged Schubert through most of his life.

This was why in 1818 he took a summer post at Castle Zseliz in Hungary as music master to Count Esterhazy's children. He returned there in 1824 and it seems that on the second visit, if not the first, he fell in love with the Count's daughter Caroline. That virtually nothing is known of Schubert's romances, in spite of the highly embroidered and quite unfounded episodes which appear in some biographies, is merely an indication of the obscurity in which he spent his days.

His friends, at least, recognized his gifts and it was through them that his first songs were published by private subscription in 1821. Now for the first time his works began to be heard outside the immediate circle, at meetings of the Viennese Philharmonic Society. The Society had been in existence only a decade and was symptomatic of the changing times in providing concerts for the cultured middle classes instead of the aristocracy. The first work of Schubert's to be performed there was *The Erl King*, dating from the vintage year of 1815 and one of the few compositions which achieved fame in his lifetime.

Schubert's attempts to gain recognition in other ways were equally unsuccessful. In 1825 he sent Goethe three of his songs with a dedication but never even received a reply to his letter. Goethe preferred the music of Zelter, a minor song-writer of the time, whose settings of his poems were safe, predictable and undemanding.

A few years earlier Schubert had plucked up courage to visit his idol Beethoven with a set of variations dedicated to him. There is no reliable record of their meeting but Schubert had, for some reason, chosen an insignificant and unrepresentative work and Beethoven was unimpressed. It was only on his deathbed in 1827 that he was shown some songs of Schubert and recognized his genius. His biographer Schindler recalls how Beethoven repeated several times: 'Truly this Schubert has the divine fire,' and asked to see some of his piano pieces and operas. But it was too late. When Schubert called to see him Beethoven was only able to stare and make unintelligible signs and he died a few weeks later.

However, Schubert's friendships brought him happiness which the lonely Beethoven almost certainly never knew. With the singer Vogl he spent two idyllic summers in Upper Austria, once in 1819 and again in 1825. On the first visit he composed the 'Trout' Quintet which takes its name from the song which is used as a theme for variations in the fourth movement. The unusual distribution of instruments (it was rare to find the double bass in chamber music) was probably designed to suit the particular abilities of a group of musician friends in Steyr, Vogl's birthplace, where the two were staying at the time.

The early 1820s were a productive period, with many fine works including the Wanderer Fantasy, the song cycle *Die schöne Müllerin* [The Fair Maid of the Mill], the A minor Quartet, the Octet and the 'Unfinished' Symphony. Why Schubert only completed two movements of this symphony is still a mystery. Sketches have been found for a third movement so he obviously intended to complete it. He was habitually careless in his working methods so it may even be that he simply put it aside and forgot it with the pressure of other commitments. In any case the manuscript remained undiscovered until 1865, nearly forty years after his death.

In 1823 he became ill and it seems to have cast the first real shadow over his life. Although apparently cured by the end of the year, in 1824 we find him writing to a friend:

I feel myself to be the most unhappy wretched creature in the world. Imagine a man whose health will never be right again and who, in his despair over this, constantly makes things worse instead of better; imagine a man, I say, whose brightest hopes have come to nothing, to whom the happiness of love and friendship offer nothing but pain ...

The 'brightest hopes' probably referred to a particularly galling operatic failure in the previous year, while as far as friendship was concerned, his closest companion, Schober, had left Vienna in 1823 and Schubert felt despondent about reviving the old atmosphere of the Schubertiads without him. Nevertheless, on a more optimistic note we read that he was planning a 'grand symphony'. This was the 'Great' (C major) Symphony, completed four years later, shortly before his death.

By the end of 1824 Schubert's life had become happier again. Some of his oldest friends were back in Vienna and he took lodgings next door to one of them, Schwind. Now came the final period of composition and with it many of the greatest works. In 1826 he wrote the D minor Quartet, *Death and the Maiden*, and soon after it the song cycle *Die Winterreise*, [The Winter Journey] whose morbidity at first puzzled even as intimate a friend as Schober. It was followed by the still more pessimistic and despairing tone of many of the Rellstab and Heine settings of 1828, published posthumously under the title *Schwanengesang*. But there were confident works too, like the fine C major String Quintet, the C major Symphony mentioned earlier and two Masses.

Towards the end of the summer of 1828 his health began to deteriorate rapidly. His last occupation before being confined to his sick-bed was a study of some Handel scores which determined him to take a course of lessons in counterpoint with a well-known academic of the time, Simon Sechter. Schubert had always been conscious of the inadequacies in his technique as a composer, and the fact that he actually arranged the times of the lessons shows how unaware he was of the seriousness of his illness. He died on 19 November; the doctor diagnosed the cause of death as typhus.

Most of Schubert's music was still unknown to the Viennese public at his death. Only a fraction of it was either published or performed, except in private. And even his close friends did not know the extent of his genius, for they had only heard the songs, piano and chamber music performed at the Schubertiads. The epitaph Grillparzer wrote for Schubert's tombstone was truer than he realized: 'Music has here entombed a rich treasure, but still far fairer hopes.'

Hector Berlioz

(1803-69)

'He stands alone – a colossus with few friends and no direct
followers. His influence has been felt far and wide, but has
neither reared disciples nor formed a school.' This quotation
from an early edition of Grove's *Dictionary of Music and
Musicians* goes far towards summing up Berlioz's position in
nineteenth-century music. Indeed, to go further, perhaps his
personal tragedy was to be French at the time when Italy and
Germany were the greatest musical centres in Europe.

In Germany the works of almost-forgotten giants such as
Bach and Palestrina were being rediscovered. Music and concerts had become part of the German people. And in Italy
where the emphasis was on opera every town had its own
opera-house, its own orchestra and its own hack librettist.
Standards were often poor, as composers would be forced to
write their operas within two or three weeks, but there was a
genuine demand. France, however, had but one major musical
centre, Paris. Here Grand Opera was the rage, with its heroic
characters and fantastic rescue plots allied to a florid display
of vocal and orchestral magnificence. Its appeal was by an
immediate entertainment and excitement, which all too easily
descended to mere vulgarity.

Such was the musical scene at the time of Berlioz's birth in
1803 in La Côte-Saint-André, a small town near Lyons. His
father was a doctor and a man of considerable culture who
undertook much of his son's early education and gave him a
thorough grounding in the classics. The family were not greatly
interested in music. Berlioz's first real musical experience was
not until his first communion when, as he received the sacra-
ment, the choir began to sing the eucharistic hymn. He was
overcome and, as he explains in his *Memoires*, 'The sound
filled me with a kind of mystical passionate unrest which I was
powerless to hide from the rest of the congregation. I saw
Heaven open – a Heaven a thousand times lovelier than the
one that had so often been described to me.' From this moment
onwards he attended church regularly to hear the choir. At
home he found an old flageolet and soon learnt to pick out
popular tunes on it. Dr Berlioz knew something of the rudi-

ments of music and began to teach these to his son, who proved so apt a pupil that he was soon able to read music with ease, and to play the flute quite well. Berlioz started to teach himself harmony. He spent hours arranging folksongs and actually composed two quintets for flute and strings which were performed locally.

His father wanted him to become a doctor and taught him anatomy. Berlioz disliked the subject so intensely that he had to be bribed into continuing his medical studies by the promise of a new flute. Together with a cousin, he was sent to Paris in 1821 to attend the proper medical courses. His first experience of the dissecting room horrified him: he jumped out of the window and ran home. After that his medical studies gradually sank into the background. He went nightly to the opera and heard works by Mehul and Gluck. He discovered that the Conservatoire Library was open to the public and spent hours studying scores. Eventually he wrote to his father that he had decided to give up medicine in order to make music his career. His family gravely disapproved. His allowance was withdrawn when Dr Berlioz found out that his son was in debt. Berlioz was now alone.

At the Conservatoire Library Berlioz was given an introduction to a great teacher of that time, Leseur, who thought him promising. Under Leseur's guidance, he continued his essays in composition and in 1823 was invited to write a Mass for Holy Innocents' Day. It was a disaster because of a hopelessly inadequate performance. A wealthy friend backed a second performance, better prepared, six months later. On this occasion the work caused a great deal of enthusiasm but the concert left the poor composer owing 1,200 francs.

He was living in a garret on a diet of dry bread and fruit, earning a few francs here and there by teaching music and by working as a chorister at the Théâtre des Nouveautés. In 1827 he decided to compete for the Prix de Rome, which was then the greatest musical prize in Europe, offering three years of free study in Rome plus free board and lodging. He competed three years in succession and gained the prize at his third attempt with a piece that has never been heard since.

He was now becoming known in Paris. His overture *Les Francs Juges*, which he considered to be his first important orchestral work, and his 'Waverley' Overture were performed at a concert at the Conservatoire. Berlioz himself conducted. Soon after he suffered an emotional upheaval of catastrophic violence. An English theatre company visited Paris for a season of Shakespeare and Berlioz fell madly in love with the actress

Harriet Smithson, who played Ophelia and Juliet. He was 'struck by lightning, he raved, he was exalted'; he wrote passionate letters which were never answered. It was mainly to attract her that he conducted the Conservatoire concerts. It was with her in mind that he composed his *Symphonie Fantastique* in 1830. This most famous among his works is the first symphony to contain a detailed story. The 'Episode in the life of an Artist' is perhaps to some extent autobiographical and has – this is technically interesting – a recurrent theme, or *idée fixe*, which represents his idol. Yet Harriet Smithson refused to have anything to do with the composer.

Berlioz was not happy in Rome. He stayed for only half of the granted three years and spent much of the time exploring the country in wanderings which gave him material for a later work, *Harold en Italie*. Back in Paris, he gave a concert of his works at the Conservatoire in December 1832. Harriet Smithson was invited and attended, and now was so touched to find herself the heroine of the great *Symphonie Fantastique* which had been included in the programme that she agreed to meet Berlioz.

At the time she was in debt, she had a broken leg and she had no future engagements at all. Berlioz proposed and she accepted. They were married in October 1833. On his wedding day poor Berlioz possessed 300 francs and found himself obliged somehow to pay his wife's debts of 1,400 francs.

The marriage was altogether unhappy for Harriet, her stage career over, degenerated into a shrewish and embittered virago. To earn a living and settle their debts, Berlioz had to become a journalist. He wrote on music with an honesty that made him cordially disliked before he learnt to become a little more tactful in his critical approach to performances. It is interesting to read in his *Memoires* that he hated journalism – he could not sit at his desk for more than a few minutes without becoming bored and restive. In fact this particular chapter of his *Memoires* has the title, 'Calamity – I become a critic!' Financially and emotionally, these were sad days for Berlioz. His wife quarrelled incessantly and there were angry scenes between them frequently. The composer bore eight years of misery before a stormy separation. Then in 1841 he became friendly with a singer, Marie Recio, who was to become his second wife.

Despite his unhappiness Berlioz became a well-known figure in those years. The most important event was his meeting with the great violinist Paganini after a performance of the *Symphonie Fantastique* in 1833. Paganini had just acquired a

Stradivarius viola which he was anxious to play in public. It was on this account that he came to see Berlioz, who composed *Harold en Italie* for him, a work of four movements for viola and orchestra. As was only to be expected, Paganini was not satisfied: the solo part was not difficult enough and had too many rests! The virtuoso insisted that he wanted to play all the time.

Harold en Italie was first performed in 1834, but Paganini only heard the entire work in December 1838 when he sent Berlioz the following letter:

My dear friend, Beethoven dead, none but Berlioz could restore him to life; and I, who have tasted your divine compositions, worthy of a genius such as yours, consider it my duty to beg you to accept in token of my homage, 20,000 F ... Believe me always, your affectionate

Nicolo Paganini.

Thanks to this generous gift, Berlioz was able to concentrate entirely on composition for some time. The result was the dramatic symphony for orchestra, soloists and chorus, *Roméo et Juliette* (1839).

Soon after the Paganini incident Berlioz was commissioned by the French Ministry of the Interior to compose a Requiem Mass for the anniversary of the death of Marechal Mortier. Thus originated the *Grande Messe des Morts* which was first performed in December 1837. The *Requiem* is considered to be Berlioz's 'outstanding achievement as a rational, practical essay in the sphere of the musically gigantic'. It is scored for a colossal orchestra of 140 players, four brass choirs, four tamtams, ten pairs of cymbals, sixteen kettledrums and a choir of 210 voices. Berlioz makes full acoustic use of the four brass choirs by placing them in four different corners of the auditorium. Yet despite the huge forces involved, much of the work is eloquent by virtue of its sheer restraint. The *Requiem* is wholly original in character and romantic. It was not intended for a church service and is best described as a 'dramatic symphony for orchestra and voices which uses inspiring texts that happen to be liturgical'. Berlioz once remarked that, if faced with the destruction of all his works save one, he would plead for the survival of the *Requiem*.

In September 1838 *Benvenuto Cellini*, his first opera, was performed but only the overture was considered successful at the time. In 1840 followed the first performance of another monumental work, the *Symphonie Funèbre et Triomphale*, written to celebrate a national ceremony. From then on Berlioz spent the rest of his life travelling. In 1842, in the company of Marie Recio, he went to Brussels where he conducted several concerts of his own works. He then gave concerts all over Germany where he introduced a new composition, *Le Carnival Romain* – an overture which includes some of the best parts of his failed opera *Benvenuto Cellini*. It was on another long tour through Austria and Germany that he composed *La Damnation de Faust*, a 'dramatic legend' which is one of the most diversified and inspired of Berlioz's works.

Berlioz's travels continued, to Russia in 1847, to London in 1848, and back to France in 1849 where the election of Napoleon III inspired him to compose a *Te Deum* which, though based on a liturgical text, is hardly religious in mood. In 1850 he founded the Société Philharmonique of Paris which, under his conducting, gave one part of his oratorio *L'Enfance du Christ*. (The completed trilogy had its first performance in 1854.) However, the Société Philharmonique lasted but one year. In 1853 Berlioz returned to London which he left in despair when his production of *Benvenuto Cellini* at Covent Garden proved a terrible failure. He began to concentrate on *Les Troyens*, his two-part opera for which he wrote the libretto as well as the music, restricting himself again to the essential stages of action as related in books II and IV of Virgil's *Aeneid*. In 1862 Berlioz completed his last work – a comic opera, *Béatrice et Bénédict*, which was based on Shakespeare's *Much Ado About Nothing*. He was already a sick man. His death in 1869 was not unexpected.

Berlioz was a great romantic composer, an orchestral innovator and an incredibly ingenious experimenter with sound. It was he who established the seating arrangement of the modern symphony orchestra – part of this arrangement being that the wind players should be raised above the strings so that their respective sounds might blend better. It was Berlioz who first insisted that the conductor should face the orchestra and beat time. The acoustic experiments with the four brass choirs in the *Requiem* have already been mentioned. One may also quote the weird magnificence of the 'Tuba Mirum' where only the flutes and the trombones play. In short Berlioz treated the orchestra with the same mastery as Paganini treated the violin and Liszt the piano. The orchestra was his instrument.

Berlioz was eventually recognized as a great composer all over Europe – but not in France. He is unique in that he was subject to no influences. His intensely personal musical language evolved entirely as a result of his own strivings and experiments. It is incredible, yet true, that even as late as 1830

William Cody ('Buffalo Bill')

A poster for Thomas Cook's
first conducted excursion

Andrew Carnegie, the
philanthropic industrialist

Ludwig van Beethoven

A cartoon of Richard Wagner
from *Figaro*, 1876

A self-portrait of the
Post-Impressionist painter
Paul Cézanne

The legendary actress
Sarah Bernhardt

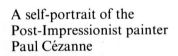

he had never heard any of Beethoven's works. His musical background was solely that of operas by Spontini and Gluck – and yet he produced early works like the *Huit Scènes de Faust*, the overture *Les Francs Juges* and the *Symphonie Fantastique* – music, that is, which is unique in form and content and unlike anything before or after. How, then, should Berlioz stand in nineteenth-century music?

He remains, as he was in his lifetime, a controversial figure, regarded by some as a genius, by others as a flawed master; yet others again treat him with a contempt amounting almost to loathing. But most will agree on one point – that his was an utterly original musical voice. The opposite poles in the controversy are perhaps best illustrated by quoting two composers. Moussorgsky remarked, 'There are two giants in music: Beethoven, the thinker, and Berlioz, who transcends thinking.' Debussy, on the other hand, contended, 'Berlioz is no musician at all ...'

Frédéric Chopin

(1810–49)

Of all the romantic composers, Chopin is the only one who has never declined in popularity. If anything, he is more popular now than in his lifetime and his works are still part of the repertoire of almost every pianist. He was unique in founding a style of piano writing which was immediately seized upon by his contemporaries but which seemed to have evolved from nowhere. It is almost impossible to trace its origins for Chopin had virtually perfected it by the age of twenty-one, on a musical diet which was limited to the narrow resources of his native Warsaw. Certain influences – the Italian operas he heard as a child, with their melodic decoration, and Polish folk music – obviously played a part but they were only facets of a whole new pianistic world.

He was an isolated figure: in an age which loved extravagance he deplored the more sensational aspects of Berlioz and Liszt; and at a time when pianistic pyrotechnics were all the rage, he refused to be drawn into empty displays of virtuosity. His favourite composers were Mozart and Bach; that he loved the latter is seen by the fact that he spent a great deal of time later in life correcting editions of the *Forty-eight Preludes and Fugues*.

He disliked Bohemianism, preferring the cultural and intellectual gatherings of the nobility, with their aura of elegance and refinement. He was fastidious over his appearance, almost to the point of foppishness, and had a manservant and a carriage. He was one of the last representatives of an age of luxury and good taste which was already beginning to crumble and which suffered a final death blow with the 1848 revolution.

But underneath all this Chopin was, above all, an ardent nationalist. Although he spent most of his adult life in France he never forgot his native country and he felt the agony of its suffering as keenly as if he had been there.

Chopin was born in the village of Zelazowa Wola near Warsaw on 1 March 1810. His father Nicholas Chopin was employed as tutor to the Skarbeks, a minor aristocratic family of the neighbourhood. He had lived in Poland only since he was sixteen; he was French by birth and came from a family of vine-growers in Lorraine. He married a Polish wife, a distant relation of the Skarbek family, in 1806. Frédéric was the second of four children, all of whom turned out to be unusually gifted. Soon after his birth the family moved to Warsaw, where Nicholas Chopin had obtained the post of professor of French at the newly founded High School. Chopin's musical talents showed themselves at an early age and, living in the centre of the town in contact with many artistic and intellectual families, it was not long before he began to attract attention. At seven his first composition was published, a little Polonaise, and at eight he gave his first public concert. This brought him to the notice of some of the most distinguished families in Warsaw and from now on he was fêted almost as Mozart was in his youth. He was constantly invited to play at aristocratic houses and acquired a taste for elegance and good living early in life.

At twelve he began composition lessons with Joseph Elsner, the head of the Warsaw Conservatory, and soon after spent three years at Warsaw High School to complete his general education – up until now he had been educated at home. During this period there were holidays in the country, where Chopin first became acquainted with Polish folk music. Mazurkas and other dances could be heard in Warsaw but here Chopin heard them as they were played and sung by the local villagers and it made a permanent impression on his musical style.

In 1826 he entered the Warsaw Conservatory as a full-time student, continuing his lessons with Elsner more intensively. Elsner was a German but had become thoroughly Polish in his outlook. His greatest hope, never fulfilled, was that Chopin would write a national opera for Poland. His chief interests were opera and orchestral music, two of the forms which least interested Chopin, but he was an open-minded teacher and allowed Chopin to develop in his own way.

By this time Chopin, well versed in everything that fashionable Warsaw life could offer, longed to travel abroad. A trip to Berlin with one of his father's friends in 1828 only confirmed this desire, and his objective became Vienna, no longer in its heyday but still a great musical centre. He made a preliminary visit the following year, during which he was given the unexpected opportunity of playing twice in public, winning widespread acclaim. This success made him all the more determined to return and he spent only another year in Warsaw, during which time he made his adult debut, playing the recently composed F minor Concerto and, later in the year, the E minor Concerto.

For his departure from Warsaw Elsner composed a farewell cantata and he was given a silver goblet filled with Polish earth as a memento. But for all these patriotic parting gestures, Chopin little knew that he would never return to Poland again.

The second visit to Vienna was doomed to failure. Hardly had he and his friend, Titus Woyciechowski, arrived and settled in than revolution broke out in Poland and Titus returned immediately to fight with the patriots. Because of his delicate health Chopin's family urged him to remain in Vienna but Chopin now found that the few concerts he gave only met with a lukewarm reception and he eventually decided to move to Paris. This he did in the summer of 1831, stopping to give concerts at Munich and Stuttgart en route. It was in Stuttgart that he heard of the fall of Warsaw and the incoherent, despairing entries in his diary speak for the agony he felt at that moment. The story that the *Revolutionary* Study, Op. 10, was written as a result seems likely, if unauthenticated.

Chopin's first impressions of Paris left him dazed and bewildered. Life was not only brilliant in its superficial aspects but the Paris *salons* were a meeting place for some of the most distinguished artists and intellectuals of the new romantic movement. Luxurious living had reached its zenith, while at the same time the country was in a state of political and artistic ferment.

Chopin had with him various letters of introduction and he was soon on good terms with most of the outstanding musicians of the time – Liszt, Berlioz, Mendelssohn, Rossini, Bellini and even Cherubini, the ageing head of the Conservatoire. He also came to know the pianist Kalkbrenner, who had a formidable reputation, and whom he admired so much that he thought of taking lessons with him. Kalkbrenner was one of the friends who helped to arrange Chopin's first Paris concert which, after being delayed by various difficulties, took place in 1832. It was a spectacular success and Chopin was immediately hailed as one of the front rank of pianists. His rare combination of virtuosity and musicianship won the approval even of dry-as-dust critics like Fétis, who wrote that he would 'make a brilliant name for himself, and deservedly' in spite of such faults as 'too much richness in the modulations' and 'some disorder in the continuity of phrasing'.

But Chopin's second concert was much less of a success. He was playing in a larger hall and the delicacy and softness of his tone, which had already aroused criticism in Warsaw and Vienna, was lost in the over-resonant surroundings. This worried Chopin enormously, for if he could not make a success as a virtuoso – and Paris was teeming with aspiring young pianists – how was he to earn his living?

But just at this time he was introduced to one of the most influential families in Paris, the Rothschilds. This was the turning-point in Chopin's career, for approval in their eyes meant approval in the eyes of the world, and Chopin suddenly found himself one of the most sought-after piano teachers in Paris, with a list of pupils consisting almost entirely of daughters of the nobility. He was invited to play everywhere and he much preferred the intimate atmosphere of the aristocratic *salons* to public appearances, which he found an ever-increasing ordeal. Besides in the homes of the aristocracy there were the émigré Polish families he had known in Warsaw, many of whom were now living in Paris. Here he was always given a warm welcome, and he cherished these remaining links with his homeland.

At the same time Chopin was beginning to find publishers interested in his music not only in France but in Germany and England as well, and by now most of the works he had written in Warsaw and Vienna, besides some more recent ones, had been published. It was his Op. 2, the variations on '*Là ci darem*' from Mozart's *Don Giovanni*, which prompted Schumann's famous remark in the Leipzig *Neue Zeitschrift für Musik*, 'Hats off, gentlemen! A genius!'

In 1835 he gave his last public appearance for several years, and that summer there was a happy reunion with his parents, who had travelled to Carlsbad to see him. On his return to Paris he stopped in Dresden to visit some Polish friends of his schooldays and promptly fell in love with their sixteen-year-old daughter, Maria Wodzinska. He proposed to her the following year but the affair came to nothing, for Maria's parents, though they liked and admired Chopin, were worried by his delicate constitution and, having heard exaggerated reports of an illness he suffered during the winter in Paris, decided that he would be an unsuitable husband.

By now Chopin had already met the woman who was to exercise the most profound influence over his life, as she had over the lives of many celebrated artists of the time, including Jules Sandeau, Alfred de Musset and Prosper Mérimée. She was George Sand, who had left her husband in 1831, come to Paris and immediately established herself as a successful not to say notorious, novelist. Her eccentric habits and her unorthodox views on conventional morality made her the personification of vice and depravity in the eyes of the respectable world. But as a person she had a maternal, compassionate nature and during the long years of Chopin's illness she became his guardian angel.

At first he was unimpressed by her, probably because he was still in love with Maria Wodzinska, but gradually their friendship grew and by the summer of 1838 they were making plans to spend the winter together in Majorca where they could avoid the malicious gossip of Paris (which could be disastrous to Chopin's career) and where, they hoped, Chopin's failing health would benefit from the mild climate.

To avoid scandal they left Paris separately and arrived in Majorca at the beginning of November. But their illusions were quickly shattered. There was nowhere to stay, the people were unfriendly and soon after their arrival the weather broke and Chopin became ill in the damp, unhealthy conditions of the house they had eventually managed to rent. Rumours went round that Chopin had consumption and when the landlord heard of it he ordered them to leave. They moved to a deserted monastery at Valdemosa in a wild, remote part of the island. Chopin wrote of it: 'Between the cliffs and the sea a huge deserted Carthusian monastery ... The cell [Chopin's room] is shaped like a tall coffin, the enormous vaulting covered with dust, the window small. In front of the window are orange-trees, palms, cypresses.' Here, in spite of continued illness, Chopin completed the Preludes, a fact that has given rise to all kinds of romantic legends, though Chopin himself always denied that any of his works had anything but purely musical significance. He disliked 'programme' music.

As soon as the weather allowed, Chopin and George Sand crossed back to Marseilles where Chopin spent several months recuperating from the disastrous winter. By now tuberculosis had set in irreversibly and the only cure the doctors could advise was rest. That summer Chopin moved to Nohant, George Sand's country home, and he stayed there until the winter season began again in Paris. This new pattern of life lasted over the next eight years, enabling Chopin, in spite of his gradually deteriorating health, to compose some of his greatest works including the two Sonatas in B minor and Bb minor, the Ballades in Ab major and F minor, the F minor Fantasia, the *Polonaise-Fantaisie*, the *Berceuse* and the *Barcarolle* – besides numerous mazurkas, nocturnes and other short pieces.

But this peaceful existence was not to last. George Sand had two children who were now almost grown up and beginning to assert their rights in the household. Her son Maurice had always resented Chopin's presence and was making his attitude increasingly apparent, while the daughter, Solange, was in disagreement with her mother over almost everything. By 1847 the situation had become so tense that Chopin felt unable to return to Nohant for the summer, and in his absence a sequence of dramatic events led to Solange marrying a young sculptor, Auguste Clésinger, entirely against her mother's wishes. In the dispute which followed Solange persuaded Chopin, who knew nothing of the intrigues behind the marriage, to take her side. Too late he realized that he had placed himself in the opposite camp to George Sand and for this she never forgave him.

This was the great tragedy of Chopin's life. He had come to depend on George Sand completely and without her he was lost. From now on his life was in decline.

In 1848 his friends persuaded him to give a concert in Paris, for he had not been heard there since 1842. It was to be his last Paris appearance; a week later revolution broke out and Chopin hastily accepted a long-standing invitation from a wealthy friend and pupil, Jane Stirling, to come to England and stay with her in Scotland. His means of income in Paris were virtually at an end, for the fall of Louis Philippe meant the decline of the aristocracy and the whole establishment which provided him with a living.

This English visit was the final blow to Chopin's health, for besides the damp climate there was the strain of the endless social round. After the London season ended, at which he had played at various aristocratic houses and appeared twice in public, Chopin went up to Scotland and stayed with Jane Stirling and some of her friends, in and around Edinburgh. She was clearly in love with Chopin and did everything she could to make his life more comfortable, but neither she nor anyone else could replace George Sand. He returned to Paris where he was intermittently bed-ridden until his death the following autumn. He felt too unwell to compose, except one or two mazurkas which he wrote down in stronger moments, and, to make things worse, for the first time in his life he was in serious financial difficulties and had to rely heavily on the generosity of his friends, including the faithful Jane Stirling who sent him a gift of 15,000 francs. The company of his sister, who had travelled to Paris to be with him, and friends like the painter Delacroix, provided his one consolation during these last agonizing months.

He died on 17 October 1849 aged thirty-nine. At the funeral Mozart's *Requiem* was sung and later, at the unveiling of a monument to his memory (designed ironically enough, by Solange's husband Clésinger), a box of Polish earth was sprinkled over his grave.

Richard Wagner

(1813–83)

Wilhelm Richard Wagner, the youngest of nine children, was born at Leipzig on 22 May 1813, the son of Johanna, wife of Karl Friedrich Wagner. However, it has long been suspected that his father was not Karl Wagner but Ludwig Geyer, a playwright, artist and actor of partly Jewish blood and a close friend of the family. The likelihood of a Jewish blood connection is particularly interesting in the light of Hitler's passion for the composer and, in recent times, Israeli government refusal to permit the playing of works by Wagner at public concerts.

Following the ravages of the Napoleonic armies came an epidemic of typhus which killed Karl Wagner, leaving the future composer fatherless at the age of five months. With seven surviving children his mother was now in desperate straits but only for a brief period, since in August 1814 she married her lover Ludwig Geyer. The family promptly moved to Dresden where in 1821 Geyer died, leaving Johanna in comfortable circumstances.

Like Schumann, Wagner's musical genius was to ripen late. And although at the age of seven he could strum the piano, he was no musical prodigy. His dying step-father hoped that 'something might be made of Richard ...'. But for a long time the direction his life would take was far from certain. From 1822 to 1827 the lad attended the Dresden Kreutzschule where, although he proved a good serious pupil, he displayed little interest in music. His music-master despaired of this young man, small in build with a disproportionately large head in which burned a pair of large and penetrating blue eyes. He was described in his report as his 'worst pupil'. His Latin teacher gave him piano lessons but predicted that musically he would come to nothing. In fact Wagner hated the piano and, like Berlioz, could never play it well. In 1828 he enrolled at the Nicholaischule, Leipzig, where his musical passion was finally awakened by hearing one of Beethoven's Symphonies. 'I fell ill of a fever,' he said at the time, speaking of this turning-point in his life, 'and when I recovered I was – a musician ...'

His fate was now sealed. Not long before this relevation of his true calling he had heard Goethe's *Egmont* with Beethoven's incidental music. He decided that he too would illustrate stories, legends and fables with incidental music. This was the point of departure into the realms of opera and operatic composition. At the outset of his new calling as a composer he wrote overtures, one of which he took to Dorn, conductor of the Royal Theatre at Dresden. Dorn was impressed and performed it. He was now beginning to compose music in earnest and with passion, learning more by doing so than by the study of books and rules.

In 1831 he entered Leipzig University where he instantly gave himself up to the excesses of student life and was soon notorious for his drinking, gambling and duelling. He worked only at his music but it was not until he read Bulwer Lytton's *Rienzi* about 1837 that he was to accomplish anything worthwhile. He was married by this time – miserably married and hopelessly in debt. He met his wife, an actress, Wilhelmena (Minna) Planer at the Wurburg Theatre where he had worked as chorus-master. She was three or four years his senior and already the mother of a six-year-old illegitimate daughter.

Wagner's company had now moved to Magdeburg where it was to become bankrupt, leaving the composer still more heavily in debt – a frequent source of embarrassment throughout his life yet one which, curiously, he bore in the most cavalier fashion. He ran deeper and deeper into debt, and his concerts at Königsberg, where his overture 'Rule Britannia' was probably first performed, made scarcely any profit. In desperation Minna left him in May 1837 and did not return until some while later when she had obtained the post of musical director at the theatre in Riga, in the Russian province of Latvia. And it was here that he wrote most of *Rienzi*, the opera that was to become his first successful work. But his debts were now so astronomical that in March 1839 he was literally hounded out of Riga by outraged creditors. With Minna he left the country, illicitly, as their passports had been confiscated.

Unable to return to Königsberg for fear of their creditors, they boarded an English ship at Pilau and arrived in London on 13 August 1839 after a prolonged, storm-tossed voyage that was to provide Wagner with his first inspirational idea for *Der fliegende Holländer*. On this terrible voyage, which lasted nearly a month, the sailors told him the extraordinary story which was to bear such rich fruit in a few years time. On 20 August the Wagners set sail for Boulogne en route for Paris.

Wagner went to Paris hoping to win fame and fortune, buoyed up by the dream of having *Rienzi* performed there. But in this ambition he was luckless. He was obliged to undertake a variety of humble and humiliating tasks in order to earn a pittance. He wrote scraps of criticism for musical journals, and was obliged to pursue such musical drudgeries as scoring arrangements for 'every imaginable kind of instrument, even the cornet ...'. His three years in Paris were a total disaster. He was twice jailed for debt and almost starved. But his enthusiasm and resolution were undiminished. He finished *Rienzi*, and wrote *Der fliegende Holländer* in five months. He now realized Paris could do nothing for him, and in the spring of 1842, he swore eternal loyalty to the fatherland.

With still more borrowed money the Wagners made their way to Dresden where *Rienzi* was performed at the Hofoper on 20 October 1842 with immediate success. He promptly rejected a Berlin offer for *Der fliegende Holländer* which was also first performed at the Hofoper, Dresden on 2 January 1843. He had now obtained a comfortable berth as conductor at the Dresden Royal Opera with an annual salary of £250, and here he was to remain (having meanwhile produced *Tannhäuser* at his theatre in 1845) until the revolution of 1848. Wagner was, as Liszt remarked, a 'born reformer'. Nothing could restrain him at this juncture. He made hot-headed republican speeches and actually fought at the barricades. He was deeply embroiled in leftist politics through his friend August Röckel, a fervent socialist. The proclamation of the Second Republic in Paris set all Germany alight. In May 1849 street fighting broke out in Dresden. Röckel was arrested and condemned to death, though later reprieved. Wagner had to flee for his life. A price was put on his head and he was obliged to seek refuge in Paris. Later with the help of his friend Liszt he escaped to Zurich.

Wagner had always been fascinated by ancient Teutonic legend and, long before the political débâcle of 1848-9 and his flight to Switzerland, the composer had begun work on *Lohengrin* and *Die Meistersinger von Nürnberg*. The former was presented by Liszt at Weimar in 1850 but Wagner was to compose nothing more until 1853, when he began *Das Rheingold*, the Prologue in four scenes to the trilogy *Der Ring des Nibelungen*.

His political interests at this time were also very much to the forefront of his mind and his activities. He almost renounced music in favour of writing provocative pamphlets on art and politics, such as *Judaism in Music* and *Art and Revolution*. The unhappy Minna, who was at heart simply a conventional German *Hausfrau*, completely failed to understand this aspect of his life. Although his public image was now a vivid combination of the powerful political rebel coupled with his ever-growing reputation as a composer, his fame and comparative material success did nothing to prevent a dramatic worsening of relations between the couple. His one constant ally and friend was Liszt who never failed to answer any of his many appeals for help. It was now, about 1850, that Wagner began work on his master project, *Der Ring des Nibelungen*, comprising *Die Walküre, Siegfried* and *Götterdämmerung*. This great cycle of operatic composition, a construction of musical architecture conceived and orchestrated on a massive scale, was to occupy him for the best part of twenty-nine years.

But what exactly *was* the nature of Wagner's contribution to the evolution of modern music, opera in particular? In his hands opera was to become an entirely new art form in which musical, poetic and scenic elements were supremely blended. Wagner was also his own librettist and in every sense his operas are sublime exercises in epoch-making stage-craft. The *Leitmotiv* system was in itself a revolutionary device. The term was invented by Hans von Wolzogen (1848-1938), the great Wagnerian authority, to distinguish the use of the constantly recurring musical motifs which play such an important part in the construction of the composer's operas. It is also a term used to describe the use of a theme associated throughout a musical composition with some particular person or idea.

The final order of the composition of his most important works is unclear but runs approximately as follows: *Rienzi* (1838-40); *Der fliegende Holländer* (1841); *Lohengrin* (1846-8); *Das Rheingold* (1853-4); *Die Walküre* (1854-6); Siegfried (1857-69); *Tristan und Isolde* (1857-9); *Die Meistersinger von Nürnberg* (1861-7); *Götterdämmerung* (1870-74); *Parsifal* (1877-82). The culmination of the master's career was reached when the gigantic trilogy *Der Ring* was performed at Bayreuth in August 1876.

As for his personal life, this was always a matter of acute ups and downs. About 1852 Wagner met Otto Wesendonck, a wealthy young businessman with an attractive wife. Herr Wesendonck at once fell under the spell of the composer's considerable persuasive charm. His first mistake was to finance a holiday for Wagner in Italy, where *The Rheingold* was conceived. In April 1857 Wesendonck bought a small, delightful house in Zurich which he let to the Wagners for a tiny rent. He and his young wife Mathilde lived in a large new villa close by. Inevitably a liaison developed between the composer and Mathilde. When it was discovered the Wesendoncks left at once for Italy. So did Minna. Wagner was left alone and proceeded to Venice. Even so, for some time he still contrived to borrow money from Wesendonck.

After more than a year's separation Wagner and Minna were together again in Paris. And at last in 1861, mainly through the intervention of Princess Metternich, Wagner was permitted to return to any part of Germany except Saxony. Meanwhile, in March *Tannhäuser* was disastrously produced in Paris. Minna left him yet again and departed for Saxony. However, in November 1862 he was finally granted permission to enter Saxony and at once proceeded to rejoin Minna at Dresden. She died there in 1866 and it is to Wagner's credit that he saw she lacked for nothing in those last years of her life.

Meanwhile he was living in Berlin until in 1864 his mounting debts forced him to move on 'pressing business' to Switzerland.

He soon made a guarded return to Germany and then came a most dramatic stroke of good fortune. Ludwig II – the 'mad King' – had just succeeded to the throne of Bavaria and at once decided to install the composer at his court in Munich. Wagner was provided with a handsome allowance and was thus enabled to finish his great work *Der Ring* in comfort. Here he met Cosima von Bülow, daughter of Liszt. They left together for Triebschen, near Lake Lucerne. In August 1870, a month after her divorce from von Bülow, she married Wagner. He was now at work on *Götterdämmerung*, the last part of *The Ring*. One of his dreams was the building of a special opera-house to be dedicated to this great work. An enormous amount of money was required to facilitate such a project. In raising this his friend the philosopher Nietzsche was of great assistance. He lent his name to the formation of Wagner societies throughout Germany for the gathering of subscriptions. In 1876 the dream was realized when the theatre was completed at Bayreuth.

On 13 August in that year, and during the following four days, the entire *Ring* was given its first performance at Bayreuth. It was a staggering success. This resounding triumph was followed by a Wagner Festival in London. It was presented at the Royal Albert Hall with Wagner himself conducting.

When *Parsifal* was produced at Bayreuth on 26 July 1882 the composer's heart was already weak and the stress of a lifetime of failures and successes was beginning to take its toll of him. It is said that he wanted to include a certain lady in the cast of *Parsifal* and that this made Cosima angry and jealous. In a fit of temper Wagner retired to his room. The date was 13 February 1883. At lunch-time his bell rang violently. Cosima rushed to his room, only to find him dead. He lies where his faithful dog Russ had been buried, in the garden of his house, Wahnfried, at Bayreuth.

Jenny Lind

(1820-87)

In her best years she was probably the finest soprano singer of all time. Her purity of tone and brilliant technique brought her the nickname 'the Swedish Nightingale'. She could act better than all the greatest actresses, raising operatic performances to unimagined artistic heights. But the additional quality which made her a phenomenon was the goodness of her soul. It transformed her physical plainness into beauty every time she began to sing, and shone through the performance to move the most critical audiences to tears and unsurpassed enthusiasm.

Jenny Lind was the illegitimate child of a shrewish mother who, although deeply pious, chose to live with a man five years her junior until the death of her divorced husband, when she married him. Jenny, as Johanna Maria was always called, was an unwanted child. Her father was a weakling and a sponger. Her mother kept ends together by running a school, in which Jenny was enrolled.

Jenny was still only four when she astonished her kindly grandmother by going to the piano and playing, almost correctly, a tune she had heard a marching band play. At the Home for Widows, where she was sent to live with the old lady for some time, she amazed another hearer even more. She was nine at the time. Sitting in a window overlooking the street, she sang to her cat and was heard by a passing servant, who went home and told her mistress, a dancer at the Royal Theatre, that she had never heard any sound so sweet. Mademoiselle Lundberg summoned Jenny and her mother to her. When she had heard the child sing she declared her a genius and offered to introduce her to the theatre directors. Jenny's mother refused indignantly; partly perhaps because some formality might compel her to admit that she was an unmarried mother, partly because her rigid religious scruples would not tolerate the thought of her daughter entering the loose-living theatre world.

Mlle Lundberg persisted, though, and Jenny's mother at last consented to take her to sing for Craelius, the principal teacher of the opera company. The performance of an obscure operatic air by the shy, almost ugly child of nine moved the professor to tears. He hurried to his chief, Count Puke, and asked him to

557

come and listen. Puke replied sarcastically; but he came – and stayed to weep. Jenny was offered an immediate place in the opera school, although she was nearly five years below the customary entrance age.

At the opera school she studied singing, dancing, acting and deportment. She worked hard and was soon displaying uncommon gifts all round. Her first appearance in grand opera was in 1836. The opera, by Adolf Fredrik Lindblad, who would become a lifelong friend, was a failure, but the fifteen-year-old soprano's singing and acting were given contrasting praise. She was offered full actress status with the company the following year. There were plenty besides her mother to warn her that this was a certain step towards moral ruin, since most actresses were loose-living and newcomers were expected to follow their example. Jenny Lind had no fears. Her art had not, and never would have, anything of vanity in it. It came from God. She was as uncompromisingly opposed to immorality as any Puritan.

It was as well for her that she could be so disciplined, for she was soon being lionized by society to a degree which must have spoiled anyone more susceptible. She was the unquestionable star of the Swedish opera, commanding full houses, invited everywhere. Still, she went about in almost drab dresses and used no make-up to try to improve her broad, sallow face with the flat, heavy nose. When she walked on to the stage she was plain to the point of ugliness. From the first note she sang she was transformed into a radiant beauty.

At nineteen she had yet another in a succession of hateful quarrels with her mother and left home with her sister Louise. She would never live with her parents again, though as long as they lived they pestered her for money, which they demanded as a right, and she, guilt-stricken that her affection for them could not be perfect, went on paying.

Now she went to live in the home of the composer of her first opera, Lindblad, and his wife. Though not a great composer, Lindblad was well known and respected for his simple songs, full of Swedish character. Jenny Lind made them her own, singing them as no one else ever would.

Feeling in need of advanced tuition, she went to Paris and presented herself to the Spanish maestro, Manuel Garcia. He asked her to sing. She chose an aria from *Lucia di Lammermoor*, an opera she had sung with never-failing success in Stockholm. When she had finished, Garcia said, 'It would be a waste of time teaching you, Mademoiselle. You haven't enough voice.'

She knew that it was true, for she had broken down during the aria. For her age her voice had been over-used and not used properly. Her breathing was quite wrong. Another few months – although she had not realized crisis to be so near – and she would have strained her voice beyond repair. She begged Garcia to reconsider. Reluctantly, he agreed that if she would rest completely for six weeks, not even speaking more than she had to, he would hear her again. He did and consented to teach her. When she left him, less than a year later, she was a new singer; and her breathing-control had become her greatest asset, enabling her to produce incredibly sustained notes, dazzlingly swift shakes and other ornamentations, and yet the most perfect pianissimo, scarcely a sound at all but audible all over a packed theatre.

She returned home in August 1842 to face the ordeal of a new debut in the title role of Bellini's *Norma*. It was a triumphant homecoming. Praise was ecstatic and marked the outbreak of the so-called 'Jenny Lind fever' that would rage through several countries. Whether she sang Norma, or Agatha in *Der Freischütz*, Alice in *Robert de Normandie*, or Amina in *La Sonnambula*, she scored equal success with the quality of her sound and the intelligence of her interpretation.

The Berlin Opera House management offered her a debut in a work of her choice. She asked for *Norma*. For the first time ever the critical, disciplined Berlin audience was unable to resist applauding wildly after an aria and calling for an encore. Jenny Lind had conquered again. Triumph followed triumph in Germany, but exhaustion always threatened her happiness. She would suffer throughout her career from overwork and nervous strain, bringing migraine headaches.

She was worried, too, by having signed too hastily a contract to appear for twenty performances at the Italian Opera House, Drury Lane in London. She had agreed to too little fee, had not time to learn English, in which she was to sing, and shrank from having to submit herself so soon to yet another public. Alfred Bunn, the licensee, refusing to release her, wrote threatening, wounding letters. 'I shall never in my life go to London!' she cried. Yet she did, in the spring of 1847, persuaded by Bunn's rival, Lumley, of Her Majesty's Theatre, and convinced by Felix Mendelssohn, who had become a warm friend, that she would meet with a reception that would outmatch anything she had experienced.

She appeared in *Robert de Normandie* on 4 May 1847. It was to be an historic occasion. Every seat was sold at exceptional prices. Immense crowds of people and carriages jammed

Haymarket. The Queen and Prince Consort, who had had the advantage of hearing Jenny sing in Bonn and had paid her many compliments, were in their box with other royal persons. Excitement was feverish amongst the audience, many of whom sat in ripped clothes and aching from the fight to get to their seats.

Some of the bursts of applause which punctuated the entire performance lasted up to twenty minutes. One aria was encored verse by verse. Such cheering as burst out at the end had never been heard. The Queen broke all precedent by throwing her own bouquet at the curtseying Jenny's feet. It was perhaps the greatest and most significant of all Jenny Lind's triumphs, for it showed her she was completely accepted by a people whose country and manners her brief sojourn had already shown her were exactly suited to her personality. She took the first of her many English homes, a house in Old Brompton where she could rest quietly and study the language before driving every night to Her Majesty's Theatre to receive an acclaim that would equal that of her debut.

She returned to Berlin for her final season there. She was only just turned twenty-seven but talk of retirement had been constantly on her lips. It was the stage, chiefly, of which she was heartily weary. It involved too many strains, too much trivial business. Yet she was ready to give up singing itself, and followed her German visit with a farewell return to Sweden.

She had been much affected by the sudden death of Mendelssohn who had helped her in so many ways and whose songs she had come to interpret supremely; and there had been the strain and bitterness of the protracted quarrel with Bunn, ending in a lawsuit which he won, thus tarnishing her image in uprightness. She was exhausted, nervous, ill. A doctor found that her heart was tired and ordered her to rest.

After six months she was ready to sing again and did so in Hamburg in recitals with a young Jewish-born pianist, several years her junior, named Otto Goldschmidt. He introduced her to the glories of the art songs of Schubert, Schumann and others of the German school which henceforward bulked large in her repertoire and received superb interpretation from her. Another recent discovery had been oratorio, the music-form in which Jenny Lind scaled her greatest artistic heights. Mendelssohn had written the soprano part in *Elijah* especially for her, but had died before she could sing it. When at length she performed it in London in order to raise money for the Mendelssohn Scholarship for composers she created a sensation of a different order from her operatic ones. It was through oratorio – *Elijah*, *The Creation* and especially *Messiah* – that she penetrated most deeply into English hearts. Her unflamboyant manner and the moving conviction with which she sang the religious works were exactly in tune with Victorian English notions of morality and art.

Before she could consolidate this new reputation she fulfilled an agreement with that astutest of showmen, P.T. Barnum, to visit the United States. Her work was little known there but by the time she arrived in September 1850 Barnum's pre-publicity had whipped that nation into frenzied anticipation. Her first performance in New York justified every superlative that Barnum had caused to be used about her. The audience went wild and, characteristically, Jenny gave the whole of her large fee to American charities.

She stayed in America for two years and if their last months were anti-climactic for her public there, she had had a triumph that would become legendary. She lingered a little too long and became too familiar; but the chief cause of decline in her popularity was her break from Barnum's management and her marriage to Otto Goldschmidt, whom she insisted thereafter should be given the deference her audiences reserved for her alone. Tasting the domestic bliss she had longed for, she did not care and happily returned to Europe and retirement. After some four years in Germany and the birth of two sons and a daughter she reappeared in England in 1856 to give many notable performances in oratorio. Her voice was no longer dazzling, but it remained pure enough and her sincerity great enough to enable her to earn nearly twice as much money as any other artist in a single English season.

The warmth of friendship which the Goldschmidts enjoyed from all sides determined them to settle in England for good. They identified themselves completely with English musical life. In 1883 the Prince of Wales invited Jenny to become First Professor of Singing at the Royal College of Music. Otto had already been Vice-Principal of the Royal Academy of Music and was still one of its governors and examiners.

In January 1887, while taking her customary winter holiday at Cannes, Jenny learned that she had cancer. She fought it and thought she was getting better; but in September a stroke paralysed her. She died on 2 November. The day of her funeral at Great Malvern was one of widespread mourning. Seven years later a plaque was put up to her memory in Poets' Corner, Westminster Abbey. England has produced many great women but 'the Swedish Nightingale' is the only one to have been thus honoured.

Sir John Everett Millais

(1829-96)

'No good man is ever unsuccessful in life.' The statement is almost a parody of Victorian complacency. An elderly self-satisfied, self-made capitalist, surrounded by his large family and every adjunct of material prosperity, might have declared his creed in just such words. Yet they were spoken by a man aged just twenty-six, poor and struggling, leading a Bohemian life at the heart of the most revolutionary movement in the history of art: the Pre-Raphaelite Brotherhood. The calm positiveness of the credo was characteristic of John Everett Millais, his sanguine temperament, his self-confidence and the astounding luck which accompanied him through life. 'He was the kind of man who always got other people to carry his parcels for him,' said Holman Hunt, his best friend; and he did not mean it unkindly.

Like so many artists, Millais had Gallic blood. His lively, charming mother and his musician father came from Jersey. 'Johnny', or Jack as they called him, was born in Southampton in 1829 and brought up in London, but the atmosphere of the Millais home was full of Latin gaiety. 'Old daddy's' guitar twanged when he was not sitting as model to his precocious son; 'He's really capital,' boasted Johnny, 'and *she*'s very clever,' rubbing his curly head against his mother's brow and patting his father on the back. There was a sister Emily and a devoted brother William. 'Dear creatures!' said Johnny of them all.

From infancy it was obvious that the slender, delicate child with the angel's face, cupid's-bow mouth and 'cockatoo crop' of thick fair curls was going to be a genius. His early talent was the cause of the family move to London, where Johnny's mother was told by Sir Martin Archer Shee, RA, 'Madam, it is your duty to bring the boy up to Art.'

He had every advantage in training – at eleven he entered the Royal Academy Schools, the youngest pupil they had ever admitted – but his real school was the world of life, letters and intellect to which his parents gave him the key.

His best education, said the old Millais, looking back, had been gained by association with great men. At breakfast with

Samuel Rogers, when he was only fourteen, he heard Hazlitt and Macaulay 'favouring the company with their ideas'. A few months later he sat at table with Wordsworth. Young as he was, he formulated a rule for life: 'He who would do great things must familiarize himself with the spirit of the great, with their pictures, their busts, their poems and, above all, by their living presence and conduct.'

In 1843 art in England was in a poor way. The great painters of the late eighteenth and early nineteenth centuries were gone, only the ageing Turner remaining. Conventional subjects monopolized the field: fancy pictures of eighteenth-century scenes from literature; sentimental portraits; still-lifes; portrayals of the young Royal Family, stolid in court dress or contemplating the bleeding corpses of game; stags and gods galore from the prolific brush of Landseer. Nevertheless sixteen-year-old William Holman Hunt, brought up in a gloomy Puritan home, longed to be an artist and had already acquired a card to attend lectures and such functions as prize-giving days. At the 1843 prize-giving he first saw 'the wonderful young draughtsman' of whom he had already heard. The slender boy Millais, white-collared and aureoled with his own fair curls, appeared to receive the first prize and was greeted with cheers, smiles and loud applause. He was 'exactly what I had pictured him', said Hunt. The youths met, liked each other: the foundations of their 'sacred friendship' were laid.

They were temperamental opposites who complemented each other perfectly. Together they talked, studied, painted. The serious, didactic Hunt impressed on the carefree Millais the sad plight of Art. In a new book by one John Ruskin, a young Oxford man, he found his text, for *Modern Painters* was a spirited defence of the much-criticized giant Turner – and something more. 'Go to nature in all singleness of heart, selecting nothing, rejecting nothing,' advised Ruskin. Hunt obeyed him and Millais took fire and followed. They began to paint in their own way, and it was not the way of the Royal Academy.

Even their materials were revolutionary. Instead of the dangerous asphaltum, the 'pernicious Dead Sea pitch' whose bitumen had threatened the permanence of earlier paintings, they were lucky enough to have the use of chemist George Field's 'precious pigments' – clear, delicate colours, brilliant chromes, glowing vermilions, vivid greens and blues. A quality as of good stained glass permeated their work: significantly medieval in feeling, for their intention was to go back to the (supposed) standards of art before the age of Raphael (1483–1520). If their vision of a re-created Middle Ages was but a dream, it was a vivid one and a natural result of the artificiality of the eighteenth century and the growing materialism of the nineteenth, with its aesthetic horrors proceeding from the Industrial Revolution and its enthronement of the Gods of Wealth and Commerce.

They were joined in 1847 by an amazing young man, Dante Gabriel Rossetti. Half-Italian, poet, mystic, at once genius and dilettante, 'a bard-like spirit, beautiful and free' in his youth, he excited the two friends and opened up new vistas of development for their little Brotherhood. Soon they were seven: other friends had joined them. Their ideals clarified. They were to be leaders of a new romantic movement, strongly grounded in the great poetic Romantics who had gone before. Hunt had introduced Millais to the poems of Keats, for whom he developed a passionate affection. His first great picture *Lorenzo and Isabella* was inspired by Keats's poem and featured his father and Rossetti as models. It was accepted by the Royal Academy. In 1850 followed *Christ in the House of His Parents*, a complete breakaway in its portrayal of Christ's earthly family as ordinary working-class people. It was fine, brave work, by today's standards beautiful and moving. From contemporaries it aroused a storm of indignation, used as they were to lady-faced milksop Christs and raptly respectable Madonnas. Dickens, in *Household Words*, raved against the showing of the child Christ as 'a hideous, blubbering, red-haired boy in a night-gown' and the other humble figures of the carpenter's household.

'All my early pictures were damned by the critics, and my parents were so discouraged that my father said over and over again, "Give up painting, Jack, and take to something else."' But Millais did not give up painting. Canvas followed canvas, the idyllic *Woodman's Daughter* with its atrocious figure-drawing, the tragic parting lovers of *The Huguenot*, the immortal *Ophelia* – Rossetti's love and model Lizzie Siddal floating in a bath of rapidly cooling water. It was a picture that would have rejoiced Shakespeare, whose spirit (as well as his own) Millais had captured in it. In the next year 1853 came the most significant picture he was ever to paint, *The Order of Release*. It shows a scene of 1746, after the failure of Prince Charlie's campaign. The model, 'absurdly like', but that the hair was painted dark instead of auburn, was Effie Ruskin, wife of the author of *Modern Painters*, *The Seven Lamps of Architecture* and *The Stones of Venice*.

John Ruskin had never really meant to marry Effie Gray, the lovely, lively Scots girl as unlike him as chalk from cheese. Remote, ascetic, namby-pambied by his parents, he had been cajoled by them into taking a wife. Dear John ought to marry and this distant cousin, so malleable and gay, was as innocuous a match as any. The Ruskins felt they could mould her to their image.

They were wrong. Effie had a strong will and personality of her own. She disliked being treated like a child or a fool by the elder Ruskins and like a not very favourite sister by her husband; for the marriage had never been consummated. Recent research and discoveries indicate that Ruskin's ideal of womanhood was best expressed in stone or marble, and preferably draped. Female flesh, as revealed in the seclusion of the marital bedroom on the wedding night, horrified and repelled him as brides were traditionally horrified and repelled. Effie was hurt and insulted. For some four years she bore the situation without protest, except in veiled terms to her intimates. In 1851 she and Millais had met, but she had taken little notice of the tall, gangling, picturesque young man, charmed though he had been by her beauty. When in 1853 she sat for the figure in *The Order of Release*, they were mutually attracted, both young, vital and (for all Millais's genius) normal people. The picture had a tremendous *succès d'estime* and was particularly admired by Ruskin, who began to cultivate Millais's friendship. In June 1853 Ruskin, Effie and Millais, accompanied by William Millais and a friend went on holiday to the Scottish Highlands.

Though conventional feeling and good taste prevented anything being said, the wildly beautiful surroundings, the pastoral pleasures, the cosy conversations when the rain kept the party indoors, all fed the flame of attraction between Millais and Effie.

Millais and Effie returned to London after a fifteen-week holiday deeply in love. Millais was tormented, 'dreadfully unwell', beset with nervous headaches and melancholy. He had begun to hate Ruskin. He knew Effie's marital situation and pitied as well as loved her. Effie, more practical, was goaded into action. In April 1854, as the climax of a neat conspiracy, she left home on an ostensible visit to her parents and never returned. A suit for nullity was successful, though a great ordeal for Effie. By July 1854 she was a free woman; just one year later she and Millais were married.

It was a happy union, though Effie's nerves never completely recovered from her existence with Ruskin, and she and Millais found things to criticize in each other – he disliked her passion for sightseeing, she was bored with his new obsession with blood-sports. For a great change had come over the youthful idealist. With a wife and family to support (nine children arrived in thirteen years) he could not afford to dream in paint. In the year of Effie's enfranchisement the Pre-Raphaelite Brotherhood died a natural death. Millais, one of his biographers has said, was like a man waking from a dream. Hunt might wrap himself in religion, Rossetti drift into decadence: Millais was elected to the Royal Academy.

Romanticism died hard in Millais. In 1856 came the lovely *Autumn Leaves*, in 1857 *Sir Isumbras at the Ford*, the melancholy *Vale of Rest*, a late, enchanting *Eve of St Agnes*. Then the pot-boilers began, soon to hang in reproduction on thousands of Victorian parlour walls: *The Boyhood of Raleigh*, *The North-West Passage*, *A Yeoman of the Guard*, portraits of statesmen, the 'sweetly pretty' child pictures which drew oohs and aahs from countless admirers – *My First Sermon* and *My Second Sermon*, *Cherry Ripe* and *Bubbles*, which to Millais's fury was snapped up as a soap advertisement.

By 1867 he was making £100 a day from water-colour copies, with a potential income of between £30,000 and £40,000 a year. Her Majesty was pleased to approve his portrait of her favourite Disraeli, though she refused to receive Effie because of the odium of divorce. The Millais family mixed with the most brilliant society; with nobility, intellectuals, the great in all spheres. When not shooting and hunting, Millais lived in a mansion at Palace Gate, Kensington, built for him in Renaissance style.

By 1885 he was no longer Mr Millais: Gladstone's government had bestowed on him a baronetcy. A typical John Bull, handsome, florid, jolly, earthy, he thoroughly enjoyed the honours and riches heaped upon him. He had forgotten Ruskin, forgotten the ardours of the Pre-Raphaelites. When throat cancer crept upon him in 1896 he was 'ready and not afraid'. 'I've had a good time, my boy, a very good time,' he whispered hoarsely to his friend Philip Calderon.

One of his last thoughts, typically, was for his beloved Effie, who was constantly at his bedside. He begged the Queen to receive her at last and Victoria, astonishingly, consented. On 13 August 1896 he died and was buried in St Paul's as befitted his status.

'No good man is ever unsuccessful in life.' He had been good and he had succeeded, though not as his early comrades would have wished. Yet the legends in paint endure: Ophelia still floats among the blossoms; smoke rises still from the bonfire of autumn leaves; the small humble Christ-child, outlasting criticism, receives eternally His Mother's kiss.

Sir Henry Irving

(1838-1905)

The baby, christened John Henry Brodribb, had dark hair, long legs and was very vocal. These were unremarkable facts; so was the coincidence that the child had been born in 1838 in his father's thirty-eighth year. But father Samuel, an easy-going, somewhat improvident travelling salesman for the village store in Keinton Manderville, Somerset, thought them extraordinary and duly noted them in one of his scrapbooks. Samuel was intrigued by externals; his wife Mary, on the other hand, who came from a devoutly Methodist Cornish family, went straight for the soul and, feeling an imperious need to save her offspring from the devil, began to read to him from the Bible as soon as he stopped yelling.

The child grew and prospered until his father decided to seek better-paid employment in Bristol and his mother, fearing the effect of town life on him, sent him to live with her sister, married to a rumbustious overseer of tin mines, at Halsetown, a modern village overlooking bleak moors behind St Ives.

Here Johnnie lived happily till he was ten and here by a mysterious process it came to him that he was born to be an actor. Certainly he found drama in the Bible and in his aunt's other book, *Don Quixote*. Of course he watched the itinerant players who set up their tent in the villages and performed melodramas for the tin-miners. The grim Atlantic crashing on desolate shores, the dark granite cliffs, the lonely cry of the curlew, supernatural tales whispered on wind-filled winter nights by half-Christian, half-pagan Cornishmen: all of this excited him as it did other children. But only in him did these ingredients merge with the conviction that he must mime the drama of life.

On hearing of this, his father noted it as another curious item for his scrapbook, but his mother was horrified. In those days actors were looked upon as the dregs of society; the church fulminated against them and the theatres which offered only trash, a tinselly coat trailed only too obviously by the Evil One. Mary and her sister combined to propel him towards the ministry, but Johnnie had his ballast to offset them: a spiritual experience amounting to ecstasy which overpowered him when he was ten in Halsetown church and did not weaken but strengthened his resolve.

Soon after this, Johnnie went to London to join his parents where they had established themselves in Old Broad Street. Education at the City Commercial School, where a kindly headmaster helped to cure a slight stammer, was followed by a junior clerkship in a law firm off Cheapside. As he walked to the office astonished bystanders heard him spouting Shakespeare to himself; in the intervals of pen-pushing and inkpot-filling he recited verses to the staff and in the evenings, as often as he could, he went to Sadlers Wells theatre.

Samuel was earning little money, apparently as a caretaker, and before he was sixteen Johnnie, who had an affectionate nature, was quite happy to fall in with his parents' wish that he should get a better-paid job with an East India merchant in Newgate Street. What did it matter? His spare time was his own and in the evenings he attended elocution classes, took fencing lessons and did some amateur acting. Two years later, after early-morning coaching from a friendly actor, he was being interviewed by the great Samuel Phelps himself. Phelps heard him recite, then bluntly but kindly told him: 'Sir, do not go upon the stage. It is an ill-requited profession.' Whereupon the young Brodribb said that he did mean to go on the stage. 'In that case, sir,' said Phelps, 'you'd better come here [Sadlers Wells] and I'll give you two pounds a week to begin with.'

The offer could well have turned a weaker head but the aspiring actor cautiously declined. Soon after, he was given an introduction to the manager of the New Royal Lyceum Theatre in Sunderland.

So the eighteen-year-old youth set off, having promised his mother he would never tarnish the name of Brodribb but would act under the pseudonym of Irving. Physically he was not well-equipped: an interesting but by no means handsome appearance, long spindly legs, an ungainly gait, a voice that he never learnt fully to control – and a strong West Country accent. All this made him a doubtful starter, even for a provincial theatre where tough audiences insatiable for entertainment swallowed farce, melodrama and burlesque in huge, undiscriminating mouthfuls.

But with the stock company that Irving joined he at least established himself and acquired massive experience. The evening programme often consisted of two or three pieces and was changed several times a week. He had to learn fast and adapt himself to an extraordinary variety of parts, playing for his first appearance the Duke of Orleans in Bulwer

Lytton's *Richelieu*, followed by the role of a cook in an 'oriental pantomime', next evening a French officer in *The Lady of Lyons* and, the same week, Cleomenes in *The Winter's Tale*.

Sunderland led to an engagement at the Theatre Royal, Edinburgh (the juvenile lead) and from there he moved to Glasgow and Manchester, playing in three years of hard work and poor pay no less than five hundred parts ranging from 'Scruncher the Wolf' in pantomime to the king, the ghost, Laertes and Horatio in *Hamlet*. But fifteen years in all were to pass before his strange power was fully recognized. He became well known in many provincial centres and did a triumphant season in Dublin. But dramas in those days were written and performed in a verbose, declamatory style. Actors seldom got inside their parts (if there was an 'inside' to them at all), but made their 'points', stumping and roaring about the stage in a form of animated recitation. His flair for eccentric comedy was soon recognized; in melodrama his actions and appearances were often hailed as masterpieces of impersonation, but the characters themselves could not come alive, partly because the material was lacking, partly because Irving could not free himself from the traditional style of acting.

So the true fires of his genius simmered till 1871 when, after performing in London for some time, he was in partnership as leading actor and stage-manager at the Lyceum with the American impressario H.L. Bateman. The play was *The Bells*, an adaptation from the French, a psychological drama about an Alsatian innkeeper who in early life murdered a travelling stranger for his gold and fancies he hears, on the anniversary of his death, the bells of his sleigh coming down the road, and in the space of twelve hours is literally killed by his guilty conscience. This play, though not on the highest level of writing, became the corner-stone of Irving's fame and he performed in it hundreds of times. At the premiere, in 1871 for the first time in anyone's memory of the theatre, all cheap stage effect was laid aside, the last wisp was dispersed of the insincerity that had befogged it for generations and Irving was that innkeeper, to the last tremor of hands and voice, as it seemed to the audience, to the last hair on his head. It was a terrifying portrayal of remorse, something of universal significance, as though the guilt of Cain, dormant in humanity through millenia, were surging to the surface, as though all the little murders that people perpetrate every day were comprised in that huge dark stain that overwhelmed the character. And though Irving used all his lung-power, every sound and move in the performance was carefully calculated. It was art, as one critic said, 'beating with the pulse of nature'.

For Irving the triumph was complete. But that same night, after his last curtain-call to a shouting and cheering audience, a wound was opened in his private life which never healed completely. For two years he had been married to a young lady, daughter of Surgeon General O'Callaghan of the Indian Army. The marriage had come about through an infatuation which had little to do with the real personalities of husband or wife. Irving's real love, a charming young actress named Nellie Moore, had tragically died of scarlet fever. Lonely and sick at heart, he had fallen into the arms of the determined and apparently admiring Florence O'Callaghan.

Florence professed a love of the theatre, but she soon proved suspicious and quarrelsome. Now, after the first night of *The Bells*, they attended a supper party in his honour. At one end of the table sat the actor, relaxed and basking in the praise of his friends. At the other, Florence held aloof, tight-lipped and austere, exuding an almost palpable chill, complaining that Irving was boring the company.

If he noticed this vicious behaviour he said nothing, but later on the way home laid a hand on her arm and said: 'Well, my dear, we too shall soon have our own carriage and pair.' There was silence, then her furious jealously broke forth: 'Are you going on making a fool of yourself like this all your life?'

Irving did the only thing possible. He stopped the conveyance, got out, told the coachman to drive on and for the rest of his life never spoke to his wife or visited their home again. At this time they had one son and another on the way.

From now on he rose to be the greatest actor on the English-speaking stage, from 1878 as sole manager of the Lyceum where annual seasons alternated with provincial tours and highly successful visits to America. Everything at the Lyceum was larger than life: gorgeous spectacle, tremendous scenic effects, Irving himself on a grand scale, staging lavish productions, accurate to the last realistic detail of a Grecian cornice or a medieval crozier. Some people thought his realism went too far, sometimes dwarfing the weaker plays, but the combination of light, sound and pictorial effect which he blended with scrupulous care, the unified impression which his productions usually conveyed, was something completely new in those days and audiences loved it.

He knew his public, gave them romantic comedy and stirring drama – stuff which the young Bernard Shaw stigmatized as 'schoolgirl charade and obsolete tomfoolery' – as well as new and intelligent interpretations of Shakespeare, far from the welkin-splitting tradition; and his Shylock, Hamlet, Richard III and Wolsey were very successful psychological studies, the direct forerunners of the modern approach. Aspects of his complex personality found expression in a gruesome portrait of the senile autocrat Louis XI, in an old soldier of ripe eccentricity re-enacting his experiences at Waterloo (adapted from Conan Doyle), in Richelieu, Dante and the warrior priest of Tennyson's *Becket*. 'It would be almost impossible,' wrote a critic, 'for Mr Irving to fail in an ascetic character. Nature designed him for a prince of the church.'

A contemporary wrote of 'that Lyceum-land where, as in the isle of the lotos-eaters, it is always afternoon'. Here, alternately enchanted, terrified and amazed, a devoted public, from the Prince of Wales and Gladstone to London cabbies, flocked for twenty-five years to see the phenomenon of Irving, supported for much of that time by Ellen Terry, dance out his parts, not merely walk them, sing, not merely speak, in an extraordinary combination of the natural and the artificial which raised serious drama to the status of a semi-religious ritual.

It is hard to get at the core of an actor whom one has never seen. Irving seems to have had a sense of almost priestly vocation, to have been preoccupied all his life with the eternal conflict between the light and the dark, good and evil, sin and salvation. As it is indeed between these poles that the whole human drama oscillates, he could not but seek, and with success, to gain reputation for the theatre's educative value and the blessing of the church on it. As for his place as an actor, Ellen Terry's son Gordon Craig, writing in the 1930s, claimed that he had never known or seen or heard a greater.

Towards the end of his life, around the turn of the century, naturalism was beginning to clash with the romantic drama he personified, But it was production costs, not any loss of public, which eventually nearly ruined him and forced the Lyceum to close. After that, though a sick man, he went on tour and it was at a hotel in Bradford in October 1905, after an evening performance of *Becket*, that he died.

He had raised the theatre from its disreputable and degenerate state of the early nineteenth century to the standing of a national institution and made it again a mirror of the human condition. He had installed Shakespeare in the national consciousness after long years of neglect. He had formed a link between the theatres of Britain and America. And he was the first actor ever to be knighted.

Paul Cézanne

(1839–1906)

Paul Cézanne was born at Aix-en-Provence on 19 January 1839. His father Louis-Auguste was a prosperous hat-maker who was to become an even more prosperous banker. His mother was the daughter of an Aixois cabinet-maker. By 1859 Cézanne *père* owned a town house in Aix and an extensive country property called Le Jas de Bouffan set in some thirty-seven acres outside the town. It was approached by an avenue of chestnut trees and had a vineyard and a farm. It figures in many of Cézanne's paintings.

In 1849 the lad was sent as a day-boarder to the Pensionnat St Joseph, an Aixois school where Emile Zola was also a pupil. They were to become close friends. In the school band on *jours de fête* Cézanne played the cornet and Zola the clarinet. He was by all accounts an industrious scholar, winning prizes for Greek, Latin, history and mathematics. It was while at school that he discovered his passion for drawing, and when he was nineteen he began attending evening classes at an art school attached to the Aix Museum. He took his *lycée* degree in Letters in 1859 and wished to go to Paris to study art. It was at this point that he first came into direct conflict with his father, a man of powerful and overbearing personality, who strongly opposed the young man's wishes and insisted that he study law. This he did from 1859 to 1860, devoting all his spare time to drawing and painting.

Meanwhile Zola, who was now settled in Paris, wrote long stimulating letters to Paul who became even more dissatisfied with his lot and longed to join his friend. In 1861 Cézanne's father reluctantly agreed that he should spend a trial period in the capital on a small allowance. He remained in Paris for six months, taking rooms near Zola on the Left Bank in the vicinity of the Pantheon. In the mornings he attended the Académie Suisse, in the afternoons he studied and copied in the Louvre or painted in the studio of a friend. He was passionately fond of landscape, still-life and portraiture, and began a portrait of Zola as soon as he had settled down. But the writer found him difficult, moody and obstinate. 'To convince him of anything,' Zola wrote to a friend, 'is like trying to persuade the towers of Notre-Dame to dance a quadrille ...'

At the end of his trial period, and greatly discouraged by his lack of success as an art student, Cézanne returned to Aix to work in his father's bank. But in the autumn of the following year, 1862, he could no longer endure the family business and decided that he would only be happy as a painter. He returned to Paris with an increased though still meagre allowance, and in November of that year he rejoined the Académie Suisse. From there he applied for admission to the École des Beaux Arts but was not accepted. However, he was now beginning to make friends among the other young painters working in Paris at that time, many of whom were themselves destined for fame. Camille Pissarro was the one who was to exert the greatest influence upon him, but he also became friendly with Bazille, Monet, Renoir and Sisley.

He spent the whole of 1863 in Paris where he visited the now celebrated *Salon de Refusés;* literally, salon of the refused ones. This was set up on the instructions of Napoleon III in 1863 as a result of the scandal that followed the refusal by the official salon to accept works by such already distinguished artists as Edouard Manet. However, his chief exhibit at this exhibition, *Déjeuner sur l'herbe* [Luncheon on the Grass], outraged both the Emperor and the Empress and gave rise to further scandal. But the exhibition proved to be a lodestar of the rising *avant-garde* and rallied young artists – among them Cézanne – to Manet's side. At this time Cézanne was primarily interested in the paintings of Delacroix and Courbet, and his own version of the romantic manner was expressed in dark tones. This style persisted until 1872. He returned to Aix in 1864 and until 1870 divided his time between there and Paris. In these years he painted a series of murals around the walls of the drawing-room at Le Jas de Bouffan, a number of landscapes around Aix and l'Estaque and a series of portraits. He also painted many still-life pictures. During this period he also regularly submitted paintings to the Salon and was as regularly rejected.

So far as his private life was concerned, sometime before 1860 Cézanne became involved with a young model, Hortense Fiquet. She was to become the mother of his son. As always the young artist greatly feared his father and the wrath that would surely follow should Cézanne *père* discover that he was not only pursuing a career of which he had never approved, but that he was also keeping a mistress on his father's allowance. But the secret was well kept – at the outset.

On 19 July 1870 France declared war on Germany. When war broke out Cézanne moved to l'Estaque where he lived and worked peacefully until some time in 1871 when he returned to Paris. Hortense, whom he subsequently married, was now living with him and his son Paul was born in Paris on 4 January 1872. Shortly afterwards he established himself at Auvers near Pontoise, where he worked with Pissarro and made the acquaintance of Dr Gachet, who was later to become physician to Van Gogh. He was to remain in that region until 1873, painting many landscapes and the *Maison du Dr Gachet*. In the spring of 1874 he once again returned to Paris and sent three pictures to the first Impressionist Exhibition, one of which – *La Maison du Pendu* – he sold to Count Doria. At this point he spoke to his mother for the first time about his liaison with Hortense but still kept the secret from his father.

Cézanne's participation in the Impressionist Exhibition was widely criticized and denounced. In view of this he refused to take part in the second Impressionist Exhibition but sent no fewer than sixteen pictures to the third Exhibition of 1877. By 1878 he had broken with the Impressionist system to concentrate on that area of visual exploration and analysis which places him squarely in the twentieth century. This study involved the analysis of form, a concept of visual aesthetics which, within a few years of his death in 1906, would lead Picasso and Braque to the discovery of Cubism. He was therefore, notwithstanding his early association with the Impressionist movement, essentially a Post-Impressionist painter – as were Van Gogh and Gauguin. Although Cézanne was in time a man of the nineteenth century, in aesthetic spirit he was of the twentieth century – a bridge. In his later work he foreshadowed the immense changes in the whole structure of modern aesthetics that were to take place within a few years of his death: changes in which his own philosophy of the nature and function of art was to play a key rôle. He was the supreme catalyst, the break-point between the old and the new. This is best illustrated by comparing the objectives of Impressionism with those of Cubism. For although Cézanne himself was not a Cubist – the term was not invented until after his death – his concern with the analysis of form was entirely commensurate with the birth of a new aesthetic: one that was to alter the whole course of twentieth-century art not only in terms of painting and sculpture, but also in every area of the applied arts from architecture to furniture design.

The basis of Impressionism was the analysis of light. The leading figures of the Impressionist movement were Pissarro and Monet. Together with Renoir, Sisley and, to a much lesser degree, Cézanne, their basic argument was that since we see only by the light of the sun – and they were principally land-scape painters – the painter should, literally, paint with sun-light. If he was to have any chance of capturing the effect of sunlight on landscape – of pure light – then, it was argued, he should paint only with colours that make sunlight. Unlike his predecessors (Turner excepted: he was perhaps the first Impres-sionist) the Impressionist painter would henceforth omit black and brown from his palette – two agents hitherto used even by the greatest landscape painters. If, as the chemist Michel-Eugène Chevreul had noted, a ray of sunshine passed through a prism is fractured into the seven colours of the rainbow – red, orange, yellow, green, blue, indigo and violet, then the landscape painter should use only the colours of the spectrum, totally omitting black and brown. And indeed, by limiting themselves to the 'spectrum palette' the Impressionist painters were able to capture for the first time the sense and feeling – and the appearance – of sunshine. Their summer landscapes shimmered with heat. Shadows, hitherto black and muddy, glowed with deep purples and blues. But the results were also amorphous – formless. Light destroyed the perception of the basic shapes and forms of which nature is comprised. It is at this point and for this reason that Cézanne broke with the Impressionist system and philosophy. Whereas they were con-cerned with the analysis of light, Cézanne was primarily inter-ested in the analysis of form. Late on in life he was to outline this philosophy in a letter to the painter Emile Bernard (Aix-en-Provence, March 1904): 'May I repeat what I told you here: treat nature by the cylinder, the sphere, the cone, everything in proper perspective so that each side of an object or a plane is directed towards a central point...'

This is of course a pre-figuration of the basic principles of Cubism. You have simply to add the elements of the square, the rectangle and the sharply cut geometric facets that Picasso derived from his study of African sculpture and you have Cubism. These sharply cut facets can be seen in many of Cézanne's later studies of La Montagne Sainte-Victoire. Had he lived beyond 1906 – and he was only sixty-seven when he died – he would certainly have escalated his vision into the new way of looking. Returning to the life of the artist, he continued to shuttle between Paris and the South of France, Aix and l'Estaque, where Renoir visited him in 1882. Cézanne was now forty-four and completely independent since the securities from which he drew his regular allowance were registered in his name. However, compared with the reputation enjoyed by such contemporaries as Pissarro, Degas, Monet, Renoir and

Sisley, he was still relatively unknown. The struggle for recognition was always a great burden to him.

From 1884 to 1888, while Cézanne was staying chiefly at Gardanne, a small hill-side town near Aix, the formal, architectonic element in his painting became increasingly clear. He was examining the structural basis of nature with an ever-sharpening sense of its inherent geometry. The culmination of this search can be seen a few years later in the three groups of paintings he produced in 1892: *The Card Players*, the *Baigneuses* series (of which there is a superb version in the National Gallery, London) and the various studies and depictions of *La Montagne Sainte-Victoire*. In 1885 he went north to Vernon where he was close to Zola at Medan and Renoir at La Roche-Guyon. He stayed with Renoir and visited Zola. At this time he was also involved in a love affair of which, to date, no details are known. Letters passed between the lovers through the offices of Zola, but the affair lasted little more than a month. 1886 was to be a momentous year for Cézanne. In April he married Hortense Fiquet and in October his father died, leaving him Le Jas de Bouffan, various other properties and 1,200,000 francs. He no longer had to worry about money. In this year he also quarrelled mortally with Zola who, in his book *L'Oeuvre*, based one of the characters, an unsuccessful painter, only too obviously upon the life and fortunes of Cézanne.

Cézanne was slowly beginning to achieve recognition. But unhappily his health began to fail. In 1891 he had his first attack of diabetes and in the summer of that year, possibly on doctor's orders, he went to Switzerland. This was the only known journey he ever made outside France. He was an orthodox Catholic and it is recorded that while at Fribourg on his Swiss visit he was so distressed by an anti-Catholic demonstration that he left the town immediately. The gesture provides a clue to the acute sensitivity of his nature. He was still relatively unknown when, in 1895, he met the great pioneer art dealer Ambrose Vollard in Paris. In that year Vollard gave him his first one-man exhibition. Ignored by the public, it was widely acclaimed by artists and connoisseurs. It was the beginning of the artist's later reputation. The young men admired his art; the wealthy dilettanti bought it. The eccentric nature of the man, his cantankerous oddity, is well demonstrated by the fact that when this vital exhibition opened at Vollard's Gallery in December 1895 the artist chose to remain in Aix. His interest was minimal. He simply instructed his son Paul to dispatch the paintings to Vollard, and these are reputed to to have arrived in Paris unframed, not on stretchers, but just rolled up.

Exhibitions followed at Brussels in 1887 and 1901 and, more notably, at the big Central Exhibition in Paris in 1900. But the greatest personal triumph of his life was at the Salon D'Automne in 1904. Here, in the heart of Paris, Cézanne was given an entire room in which to display his work. In the autumn of 1897 his mother died. She had been a good and close friend of his, and her death distressed him greatly. He could no longer bear to live at Le Jas de Bouffan and he sold the property for 80,000 francs. In 1899 he rented a house close to Aix – the Château Noir – and lived there until 1902 when he finally settled in a new house and studio he had built on the Chemin de Lauves – a hill overlooking Aix. He continued to visit Paris from time to time, meanwhile living very simply. On Sundays he would dress in conventional, bourgeois clothes and drink coffee with his friends at the local cafés. On weekdays and for painting he wore the clothes of a country farmer.

By the beginning of 1906 his diabetes became much worse and he began to suffer from severe and frequent headaches. But he carried on with his painting, going out almost daily to *le motif*, as he liked to call the site of his landscapes. He wrote to Emile Bernard: 'I am old and ill but I have sworn to die painting ...' It was a prophetic remark. Shortly afterwards, while trudging painfully to *le motif* carrying all his equipment, he was caught in a violent storm and collapsed by the roadside where he was eventually picked up by a passing laundry cart. He developed rheumatic fever and died a week later. Officially he died of congestion of the liver. He is buried in the cemetery at Aix-en-Provence.

Claude Monet

(1840–1926)

Claude Oscar Monet was born at rue Lafitte, Paris on 14 November 1840, the elder son of a grocer. Because of financial difficulties the family were obliged to move to Le Havre about 1845, where the artist's father went into partnership with his prosperous brother-in-law, a ship-chandler and grocer. The young Monet was a precocious youngster, for while he was still at school he was already making a reputation as a political caricaturist.

In 1856 the seacape painter Eugène Boudin – later to become Monet's friend and tutor – was astonished to discover in Le Havre a group of brilliant caricatures by the artist who was then a mere sixteen years of age. These he was selling at prices between 10 and 20 francs in a local stationer's and frame-maker's shop which only a little earlier had been owned by Boudin himself. Boudin (sixteen years Monet's senior) and the young artist soon became close friends, and although at the outset of their association Monet did not care for Boudin's work or for landscape painting, he was persuaded, very much against his will at first, to take up the practice of painting out of doors.

The two artists began to work together – *en plein air* – an experience which was to lead Monet to an entirely fresh awareness of the meaning and function of painting. Hitherto and traditionally landscape painting had usually been carried out in the studio from sketches made on the spot. The idea of painting in the open was a revelation to the young artist: 'as if,' he said, 'a veil had been torn from my eyes. I understood. I grasped what painting was capable of being. My destiny as a painter opened up before me ...' Here too was the flashpoint for Monet's contribution to the evolution of Impressionism. Painting in light – and with light. What Cézanne was to the analysis of form, Monet was to the analysis of light.

Between 1856 and 1858 Monet was Boudin's pupil. Around this time too his picture *View of Rouelles* was accepted for exhibition at Rouen, a city he was later to immortalize in a series of views of the cathedral. At the age of sixteen he had competed for a municipal art scholarship to take him to Paris:

578

he failed. In May 1859 he persuaded his parents to permit him to pay a short visit to Paris where, encouraged by the landscape painter Constant Troyen (1810–65) and much against his parents' wishes, he established himself permanently in the capital, first at 35 rue Rodier and then at 28 rue Pigalle. He further infuriated his family by refusing to study at the École des Beaux Arts, preferring to work instead under the painter Charles Jacque and at the 'free' Académie Suisse where he first met Camille Pissarro, himself destined for fame along with Monet as one of the key figures of the Impressionist movement. So outraged were his parents that his allowance was drastically cut. Monet was to be more or less chronically hard up until well into middle age.

The evolution of Monet's art was conditioned by three main factors: Boudin's influence in getting him out of doors and teaching him to use brushes and palette; his military service in North Africa; and the painting he did in London during the years 1870–71, when he and Pissarro left France at the outbreak of the Franco–Prussian war.

In the autumn of 1860 Monet was called up for military service and sent to Algeria where he served with the Chasseurs d'Afrique. The light and colour of North Africa were a revelation to him and, as he later admitted, had important consequences for the future of his painting. However, in 1862 he began to suffer from anaemia and was sent home to convalesce for six months, at the end of which the doctors warned that a return to Algeria might have fatal results. His family were obliged to buy a substitute for the remaining four years of his military service.

Once again he persuaded his reluctant parents to allow him to return to Paris, on condition that he studied under a 'serious' teacher. He enrolled at the Académie Gleyre where he met the painters Jean Bazille, Alfred Sisley and Auguste Renoir, all destined to become members of the Impressionist movement. In 1863, because of financial difficulties and his failing eyesight, Gleyre was obliged to close his studio. But by this time Monet felt in no further need of instruction and had become actively associated with the radical Café Geurbois group, of which Manet was a prominent figure.

By 1867 he had a mistress, Camille Doncieux. In June of that year she became pregnant and he was compelled to throw himself yet again on the mercy of his parents. They agreed to help him but only on the understanding that he left Camille and went to live with his aunt, Madame Lacadre at Sainte-Adresse. In July he temporarily lost his sight and Camille gave birth to his son, Jean Monet. He moved to Honfleur and in the autumn of 1867 returned to Paris to stay in Bazille's studio. In 1869, a particularly bad year, he moved to Saint-Michel near Bougival where Renoir was also living with his parents. He was often without money, either for food or materials. Bazille continued to support him with small sums of cash, and Renoir supplied him with bread stolen from his mother's table.

In the autumn Camille rejoined him at Saint-Michel, and his family immediately stopped the small amount of help they had been giving him. A year later, in 1870, he was rejected by the Salon and on 26 June that year he married Camille. He promptly moved to Trouville where Boudin was working, and installed himself and his family at the Hôtel Tivoli. Unable to pay his bill, he left Camille and his young son in the care of Boudin and set sail for England. With the outbreak of fighting between France and Germany he felt no obligation, as a socialist, to fight for the Empire. He made directly for London, taking accommodation first at 11 Arundel Street, Piccadilly and then at 1 Bath Place, Kensington. His family soon joined him in London, where Pissarro was also living, having himself fled from France at the outbreak of war. And it was in London – not in France – that Impressionism was born.

The two artists were excited by the work of Constable and Turner (both in their way 'Impressionists'). Together they painted pictures of the Thames and the London parks, using the diffuse, amorphous style which is the essence of the impressionist vision. They created general impressions of scenes like the Houses of Parliament seen through the veils of hazy river mist. Nothing was detailed. The style was revolutionary, as were the colours they used, both artists restricting their palettes to the seven colours of the spectrum: no black or brown.

While in London Monet was introduced to the influential French dealer Durand-Ruel, who himself had taken refuge in the capital and opened a gallery at 158 Bond Street. He began to buy Monet's paintings.

In the winter of 1871 Monet returned to France and in 1873 persuaded his fellow Impressionists to found an exhibiting society, Société Anonyme Co-opérative d'Artistes-Peintres, Graveurs et Lithographes, with premises in the former studio of the photographer Nadar. And it was here that the Impressionists held their first exhibition in 1874. The exhibition was received with ridicule and scorn by public and critics alike. The name of the movement – although appropriate – was accidentally and maliciously derived from the title of one of Monet's paintings: *Sunrise: an Impression*. The picture earned the group what was intended at the time to be a derogatory title – Impressionists.

Monet's struggles continued, although he was now selling many of his paintings. In 1879 Camille fell desperately ill and Monet was obliged to pawn his possessions in order to pay the medical bills. But in September of that year she died. In 1880 one of his paintings was accepted by the Salon, but he was roundly accused by Degas of treachery, for attempting to compromise with officialdom, and he never exhibited at the Salon again. The year 1883 was the next crucial landmark in Monet's career, for it was in April that he moved to a house at Giverny which he at first rented and then bought in 1890. Here he built a boat-house and started to plan and landscape the water-garden where, over a period of some twenty years, he was to work on the greatest of his achievements, the 'Water-lily' series. In these pictures, of which there are a great many, Monet explored the infinite range of the reflections cast by the leaves and flowers of the water-lilies in the sheet of water which held them. The reflections from the sky, the effect of beams of sunlight, the disturbance of a passing ripple, all added to this rhapsodic ever-changing kaleidoscope. In 1891, after severe attacks of rheumatism, the result of working out of doors in all weathers, he continued to work on his 'Haystack' series and in May Durand-Ruel exhibited twenty-two of his paintings, including fifteen of the 'Haystack' series. Every picture was sold in the first three days for prices between 3,000 and 4,000 francs.

At Giverny he built a Japanese bridge over the lily-pond formed by damming a tributary of the river Epte. This bridge he often painted. In 1892, now finally established at Giverny, he moved for a while to Rouen where he began his other great series of paintings: views of the cathedral at Rouen. And in the summer of that year he married his second wife, Madame Ernest Hoschede, who had been his constant companion for the past ten years or so. He continued to work on the cathedral series into 1893, then returned to Giverny.

He was now quoting very high prices for his paintings and even Durand-Ruel baulked at the asking price of 15,000 francs for one of his Rouen Cathedral pictures. Yet a collector bought no fewer than four at this price. By 1895 his reputation was higher than that of any other Impressionist, particularly in America. He consistently executed atmospheric studies of landscape, and Degas recalled an amusing and revealing story. One day he saw Monet arriving in a little carriage at Varengeville. The painter got out, looked up at the sky and said: 'I am half an hour late! I'll come back tomorrow ...' One of the painter's systematic methods was to work on a series of canvases each linked to a particular time of day when the light was more or less the same. He would often call out to his family at Giverny: 'Bring out the eleven o'clock canvas!' or: 'Let me have the nine-thirty canvas!'

In 1900 he made another visit to London, staying this time at the Savoy Hotel, and resumed work on his Thames series, painting the Houses of Parliament from a room in St Thomas's Hospital. But the London light irritated him. 'It changes too much and too often,' he said on his return to his beloved Giverny. Nevertheless he was fascinated by the Thames and in 1901 returned yet again to the Savoy Hotel and his painting of the river.

After the death of Cézanne in 1906 Monet grew increasingly neurotic about his work and had great difficulty in coming to terms with his dealer, Durand-Ruel. He was also beginning to have bouts of illness and trouble with his sight. In 1908 he visited Venice with his wife and was sufficiently restored to health to begin a series of Venetian studies. In 1909 Durand-Ruel exhibited forty-eight of his *Nymphéas* [Water-lily] paintings. They were widely acclaimed. Thereafter the artist, once so poor and unsuccessful, was plagued by admirers, entrepreneurs and importunate dealers.

1911 was a year of tragedy. Madame Monet died in May and this loss, coupled with the progressive deterioration of his sight, turned the artist, who was already something of a recluse, into a misanthrope convinced that in the final outcome he was a failure. From now on Monet seldom left Giverny. In 1914 his son Jean died after a long illness. 1921 saw a great retrospective exhibition of his work at Durand-Ruel's, and he made over a series of *Nymphéas* decorations to the French state. They are now in the Musée de l'Orangerie, Paris.

By 1922 Monet was unable to work because of a double cataract. An operation partially restored the sight of one eye. But although he struggled to paint, it was fast becoming impossible. It was Clemenceau - whose portrait he had painted - who finally persuaded him to stop. On 6 December 1926, after a few days of total blindness, the artist died at Giverny in his eighty-seventh year.

Sarah Bernhardt

(1844-1923)

There are some vessels which, until filled with the right wine, are mere containers; attractive enough but unfulfilled. You pour from the appropriate bottle and immediately they sparkle or glow with life and promise. This is how it is with many actors and actresses. When not actually at work they are waiting for that infusion of a part to play which will justify their being.

It was not so with Bernhardt. She acted on the stage and off. She never stopped. Wherever she was, whatever her age or fortune, she remained the *prima donna assoluta* of life, a being of constant energy, enthusiasm, extravagance and elegance. She was the sort of *grande dame* actress often portrayed in plays and films, though increasingly seldom met in real life. Yet she might have been a nun.

She was born on 23 October 1844, the illegitimate child of a Dutch-Jewish cocotte, Judith Van Hard, and one of her lovers, a well-to-do former lawyer named Edouard Bernhardt. After an unsatisfactory infancy in the care of nurses and relatives, she was placed in a convent at Versailles while her mother flitted about the world from lover to lover. Religion brought her the security she needed. She became studious and mystical, and felt she never wanted to leave the convent walls.

Sarah was almost fifteen when a 'family' council discussed her future. It was no relative but her mother's current lover, the Duc de Morny, half-brother to the Emperor Napoleon III, who made the decisive suggestion that she be sent to the Conservatoire to study acting. With his influence there was no doubt that she would be accepted but the formality of an audition had to be undergone. Although she still wanted above all to be a nun, she dutifully studied the works of Racine and Corneille which she was given and then submitted herself to the board of examiners. To the professors' surprise the pale, thin child chose to recite the fable *Les Deux Pigeons* by La Fontaine. The fresh quality with which she invested the too-familiar seventeenth-century story astonished them; but what impressed them more was the golden quality of her voice. She was welcomed to the Conservatoire and took the second prize for tragedy at her first examination. When the time was ripe, the Duc de Morny made sure that she was enrolled with equal ease into the company of the Comédie Française.

She was not quite eighteen when she made her debut in *Iphigénie*. She was almost overcome with nervousness but got an approving notice from a leading critic. Her future was distinctly promising; yet within a few weeks she was no longer a member of the company. At the annual celebration of the birthday of the playwright Molière, the actors were assembling when Sarah's youngest sister, whom she had taken along, trod on an older actress's train. The woman knocked her down: Sarah unhesitatingly slapped her. Called to make a formal apology next day, she resigned instead.

She had acted angrily and sincerely and without thinking that, with her influential backers, she would have no trouble finding another appointment. But it was true. She was soon signing a contract with another theatre, the Gymnase, with the promise of important roles. All went well until she was given a part which she felt was beneath her, a dissatisfaction which coincided with a more tangible event: she had become pregnant by one of the first of the many lovers she would have in her lifetime. Not to be outdone by her mother in the matter of nobility, she had become the mistress of the Belgian, Henri, Prince de Ligne. Less than three weeks later her son – the only child she would have – was born. She had him christened Maurice.

Sarah had received an inheritance from her father, now dead, and was in no need of money. When the juvenile lead in a play at the Porte-Saint-Martin theatre fell ill and she was begged to replace her she wanted to refuse. It was a light entertainment piece which she had enjoyed several times from the audience; but she was an actress trained for the Comédie's classical tradition. Persuasion won. She took the role and was offered a three-year contract when the curtain fell. But it was with the Odéon, the best of the popular theatres, that she signed. It was there that she would be most happy in her career and there leapt to fame in 1869 as Poetry in a dreamy love-idyll, *Le Passant*, by a young civil servant named Coppée.

She was suddenly the idol of Paris – an attractive idol, too. She was slim, almost to the point of a model's thinness. Her hands were delicate, her face pale, with fine hair like a halo over it, her eyes damson and long-lashed, with a soulful, poetic gaze. For all the hurly-burly of her boudoir and her frank appreciation of the physical pleasures, her looks were more of an idealization of woman as lover, a sort of dream-figure.

When the Franco-Prussian War broke out in July 1870 the intensely patriotic Sarah set up a hospital in the Odéon Theatre. She used her great vitality and irresistible persuasive powers to obtain all she needed in the way of medical supplies, clothing, food and wine, even demanding all her friends' overcoats and cajoling from the chief of police, who had been her first lover when she was not long past her childhood, the empress's own stores from the Tuileries. (Ironically enough, she had probably been more than just 'good friends' with the Emperor, too.)

Her hospital work earned her a gold medal and when, later in life, she was made a Chevalier de la Legion d'honneur, her war work took precedence in the citation over her services to the stage. It also did something for her character, deepening her understanding of others, which in turn gave a new dimension to her playing when the Odéon became a theatre again. She reaffirmed her qualities as the Queen in a revival of Hugo's *Ruy Blas* in 1872 and may have had an affair with the seventy-year-old playwright into the bargain. The role strengthened her reputation with the critics and brought an invitation from the Comédie Française to rejoin that most august of companies. Ignoring the fact that she still had a year's contract to run with the Odéon, she signed.

At the Comédie Française she acted with a new intensity which shattered the composure of some sensitive members of her audiences. Her private life quickly became the talk of Paris and acquired the inevitable colouring of rumour. She had a hotel built for herself in a fashionable quarter, helped to supervise the work and summoned a host of friends to help with it. When installed, she placed near the bed in her apartment a coffin, ready-made to measure and lined with rose-pink quilting. Occasionally she slept in it.

Sarah Bernhardt was first seen in England in 1879. Her reputation was such already that a huge crowd was at Folkestone to see her disembark, with Oscar Wilde and Johnston Forbes-Robertson bearing flowers for her. She made her debut in one of her greatest roles, Phèdre, at the Gaiety Theatre on 2 June, half-dead with nerves and almost having to be carried on and off stage, so near was she to sheer collapse. Her performance was a tremendous success, and a wave of Sarah Bernhardt mania swept London. Many who had sat entranced by her acting were ready to declare her the greatest of all time.

She went to America and instant acclaim in the spring of 1880, having severed her connection with the Comédie Française once and for all at the cost of an enormous financial penalty in lieu of the fifteen years her contract still had to run.

She was on her own from now on, heading her own companies, cashing in on her own fame and the publicity value of her flamboyant private life. The name 'Sarah Barnum' bestowed on her in a libellous book by a jealous colleague, whom Sarah paid back with a horsewhip, was not entirely unearned.

Sarah was by now so identified with self-publicity that the announcement in 1882 that she was about to marry was greeted by many newspapers as yet another advertising stunt. That spring in London she did marry a Greek named Damala, ten years her junior. It was a short-lived union. Damala was an actor and a bad one. After the public's initial politeness towards newly-weds had worn off he was soon being harshly criticized. Sarah defended him but early the following year he had left her and she had taken yet another lover. Her public showed its wholehearted approval.

In 1891 Sarah set forth on her longest tour. It would last over two years and take in North and South America, Australia, Russia and many European capitals. She loved the constant travelling, which would have worn out many much younger than she, and revelled in the adulation. She played in *Phèdre*, *La Tosca*, and the new play written for her by Sardou, *Cléopâtre*, which included that scene of utter frenzy from the Queen of Egypt which moved a woman in one of her London audiences to make the celebrated remark, 'How very different from the home life of our own dear Queen!' The role also inspired Ellen Terry, a fervent admirer of hers, to urge her to play Shakespeare, Juliet in particular. She never did play Juliet; but in a *tour de force* as astonishing for its boldness as for its effects, she played Hamlet.

Sarah was now fifty-four and no longer receiving the blind adoration of her prime. Undeterred, she went back to Paris to run her own theatre, the Théâtre Sarah-Bernhardt, which she conducted like an empress, holding court to the famous in her enormous, empire-furnished suite of rooms there. One of her first enterprises, as audacious in its way as her Hamlet, was her impersonation of another male, the young Duc de Reichstadt, son of Napoleon, in Rostand's new play *L'Aiglon*. She rehearsed for months, perfecting every detail and wearing men's clothing for weeks in order to accustom herself intimately to her role. The impact of her play, with its patriotic theme and sentimental evocation of past glories, was colossal.

However much she might exclaim that she was exhausted, Sarah Bernhardt did not know the meaning of repose and did not want to. She dashed about Europe and to America, performing, organizing, arranging for new productions and hugely enjoying herself. But in 1905 a mishap occurred which was to affect her permanently. Playing *La Tosca* in Rio de Janeiro, she flung herself as usual from the parapet of the Castel Saint Angelo just before the final curtain, but instead of falling on to the usual pile of soft mattresses she hit the bare stage. Someone had forgotten to put the mattresses there. The main impact was on her right knee. She fainted. They took her to her hotel on a stretcher and called a doctor; but when she came round and saw his dirty hands she absolutely refused to let him touch her. Against all advice she waited until her arrival in New York three weeks later before she would see a doctor. It was too late. Year by year the injury affected more of the limb, making her resort to pain-killing injections before she acted. In 1914, after nine years of increasing suffering but never decreasing activity and spirits, she agreed to the amputation that alone could save her life. She telegraphed to Mrs Patrick Campbell, 'Doctor will cut off my leg next Monday. Am very happy. Kisses. All my heart.' She was seventy.

'I shall not die until I am ready,' she had declared. The operation was a success. After only a few weeks convalescence she was back in Paris, appearing in matinées for wartime charities, playing in a film. She did not have a false leg: she was carried on a litter to where she would sit, contriving to do with her wonderful voice alone what she could no longer do with movement. She had herself taken to the Western Front to perform for the troops and even toured parts of Europe and America; but the applause now was more inspired by affection and some pity than by her art. She could no longer play her great parts. Meretricious fragments were all that were left to her from which to build her programmes.

In 1921 aged seventy-six she made her last visit to England and performed wonderfully at the Princes Theatre as a dying old man in *Daniel*, a play specially written for her by Louis Verneuil. After the final curtain Ellen Terry and leading English actors and actresses came up to pay homage to her and present her with a gold-bound book of signatures.

The following year she became the victim of chronic kidney disease. Refusing to rest, she went on rehearsing a new play and filming, but inevitably collapsed. She died on 26 March 1923 and the pink-quilted coffin that had been the subject of so much publicity years before was at last put to its intended use.

Index

Albert, Prince, 111–16; character and achievement, 111; early years, 111–12; marriage to Queen Victoria, 112; English opinion of, 113; reforms royal estates, 113; supports arts and sciences, 114; President, Royal Society of Arts, 114; masterminds Great Exhibition, 114–15; created Prince Consort, 116; treatment of Edward VII, 116; death, 116

Applegarth, Robert, 434–9; marriage, 434; joins Carpenters' Union, 434; growth of trade unions, 434–6; General Secretary, Amalgamated Society of Carpenters and Joiners, 436–7; political aims, 436–8; member London Trades Council, 437; campaigns for Reform Act, 438; social work, 438; pioneers legalization of trade unions, 439; achievement, 439

Arnold, Thomas, 379–84; influence and character, 379–80; education, 380; religious and moral principles, 380–1; marriage, 381; at Laleham, 381; headmaster of Rugby and reforms implemented, 382–3; Regius Professor of Modern History at Oxford, 383; death, 383; later criticism of his ideals, 384

Balzac, Honoré de, 234–9; *Cromwell*, 234; and Mme de Berny, 234; as debtor, 234–5; enters Paris society, 235; writing habits, 235–6; *La Comédie Humaine*: begins, 235; as portrait of French society, 236–7; characterization in, 237–8; marriage, 238–9; death, 239

Bates, Henry Walter, 477–82; the Victorian naturalists, 477; influence of Humboldt, 477; Amazon travels and *The Naturalist on the River Amazon*, 477–82; contracts yellow fever, 479; explores environs of Santarem, 479–81; excursions from Ega, 482; tribal encounters, 481–2; return to England, 482; assistant secretary to Royal Geographical Society, 482; his collections and work on mimicry, 482; death, 482

Beethoven, Ludwig van, 529–34; achievement, 529; death and funeral, 529; first concert tour and meeting with Mozart, 530; appearance and character, 530–1; as virtuoso pianist, 531; deafness and *Heiligenstädter Testament*, 531–2; pantheism, 532; as 'tone poet', 532; use of piano and strings, 532; love affairs, 532–3; as guardian, 533; as man of his time, 533–4

Bell, Alexander Graham, 194–9; grandfather as teacher, 194–5; father's invention of Visible Speech, 195–6; teaches vocal physiology, 196; works on multiple telegraph, 196–7; invents telephone, 197–9; designs telephone system for Post Office, 199; designs first gramophone and aeroplanes, 199; researches transmission of sound along light beam, 199; death, 199

Berlioz, Hector, 540–5; French musical scene, 540; first musical 'experience', 540; gives up medicine, 541; mass for Holy Innocents'

589

Berlioz (*cont.*)
Day, 541; wins *Prix de Rome*, 541; marriages, 542; *Symphonie Fantastique*, 542; *Harold en Italie*, 542, 543; as journalist, 542; meets Paganini, 542-3; *Roméo et Juliette*, 543; Requiem, 543; operas, 543-4; *La Damnation de Faust*, 544; travels, 544; *Te Deum*, 544; *L'Enfance du Christ*, 544; orchestral innovations, 544; uniqueness and achievement, 544-5

Bernadette, St (Bernadette Soubirous), 361-6; childhood, 361; visions, 361-5; examined by authorities and Church, 364, 365; discovers healing spring and first miracle at Lourdes, 364; vision identified as Immaculate Conception, 365; fame of Lourdes, 366; becomes a nun, 366; declared a saint, 366

Bernhardt, Sarah, 583-97; convent upbringing, 583; studies acting, 583-4; with Comédie Français, 584, 585; debut, 584; with Gymnase, 584; with Odéon, 584, 585; appearance, 584; son born, 584; hospital work, 585; marriage, 586; foreign tours, 585, 586, 587; runs Théâtre Sarah-Bernhardt, 586; injury, 587; entertains troops, 587; death, 587

Bismarck, Otto Edward Leopold von (Prince Bismarck), 105-10; education and marriage, 105; Prussian ambassador, 106; Prime Minister and Foreign Minister of Prussia, 107; wars against Denmark and Austria, 107; Franco-Prussian war, 108; becomes prince, 108; growth of German empire, 105, 108; Chancellor, 108; *Kulturkampf*, 109; opposes socialism, 109; welfare measures, 109; resignation, 110; character and political achievements, 110

Blackwell, Elizabeth, 416-21; emigrates to USA, 416; as teacher, 416-17; decides to study medicine, 417-18; at Geneva University, 418-19; becomes first woman doctor, 419-20; studies in Paris, 420-1; eye injury, 421; works at St Bartholomew's, 421; opens women's hospital in New York, 421; professor of gynaecology, 421; death, 421

Booth, William, 350-5; parentage, 350; pawnbroker's apprentice, 351; supports Chartists, 351; 'conversion', 352; moves to London, 352; begins preaching, 352-3; marriage, 353; as Methodist lay preacher, 353-4; founds Salvation Army, 354; character, 354-5; *In Darkest England and the Way Out*, 355; social work, 355; death, 355

Bourne, Hugh, 320-4; history of Methodism, 320-1; founds Primitive Methodism, 321; conversion, 321; preaches and forms new Methodist connection, 321-2; characteristics of Primitive Methodism, 322-3; influence on trades-union movement, 322-3; influence in Australia and America, 323-4; achievement, 324

Bradlaugh, Charles, 489-94; refused admission to Parliament, 489; childhood, 489; becomes freethinker, 490; as soldier, 490-1; legal employment, 491; break-up of marriage, 491; lectures against Church, 491-2; editor of *National Reformer*, 492; friendship with Annie Besant and trial, 493; political career, 493-4; pioneers Oaths Act, 494; death, 494

Bright, John, 391-6; Quaker background, 391; political work in Rochdale, 391-2; joins Anti-Corn Law League, 392-3; and Cobden, 392, 394; MP for Manchester, 393; attacks Crimean War, 393; Liberal MP for Birmingham, 394; public image and character, 394-

5; campaigns for extension of suffrage, 394, 395; under Gladstone, 395-6; death, 396; political ideals, 396

Brontë sisters, the, 274-80; death of Mrs Brontë, 274; Rev. Brontë, 274, 275; at Cowan Bridge, 274-5; deaths of Maria and Elizabeth, 275; childhood of, 275; publish poetry, 276-7; assume pseudonyms, 277
  Anne: *Agnes Grey*, 277; *Tenant of Wildfell Hall*, 279; death, 279
  Branwell: 276; death, 278
  Charlotte: in Brussels and M. Heger, 276; *Jane Eyre*, 277; visits to London, 277-8, 279; character, 279; *Shirley*, 279; marriage, 279; death, 279
  Emily: poetry of, 276-7; *Wuthering Heights*, 277; death, 278-9

Brown, John, 483-88; frontier and Nonconformist background, 483; becomes abolitionist, 483; marriages, 484; devotes life to slave emancipation, 484; directs 'Pottawatomie executions', 485-6; attack on Harper's Ferry, 486-7; imprisonment, 497; hanged, 498; becomes abolitionist martyr, 498

Brunel, Isambard Kingdom, 153-8; achievements, 153; family background, 153-4; directs work on Rotherhithe Tunnel, 154-5; Clifton suspension bridge, 155; chief engineer, Great Western Railway, 155-7; supervises construction, Royal Albert Bridge, 157; builds steamships, 157-8; death, 158

Burton, Sir Richard, 465-70; travels to Mecca, 465; education and character, 466; as soldier, 466; as interpreter, 466-7; explores Somaliland, 467-8; discovers Lake Tanganyika, 468-9; fails to discover source of Nile, 469; visits Salt Lake City, 469; marriage, 469; as consul, 469-70; made KCMG, 470; translates *The Arabian Nights*, 470; death, 470

Butler, Josephine, 422-7; unpopularity, 422; background and marriage, 422; at Oxford, 423-4; views on women, 423-4; at Cheltenham, 424; death of daughter, 424; social work in Liverpool, 424-5; campaigns for repeal of CD Acts, 425-7; campaigns for female equality, 427; death, 427

Canning, George, 43-8; birth and parentage, 43; education, 44; break with Whigs, 45; elected MP, 45; friendship with Pitt, 45, 46; marriage, 45; Foreign Secretary under Portland, 46; duel with Castlereagh, 46; Foreign Secretary (1822) and policies, 47; fight for premiership and success, 47-9; death, 49

Carlyle, Thomas, 216-21; philosophy and influence, 216, 220; education, 216-17; and Edward Irving, 217; religious stance, 217; translates *Wilhelm Meister*, 217; marriage, 218; *Sartor Resartus*, 218-19; moves to Chelsea, 219; and John Stuart Mill, 219, 220; *The French Revolution*, 219-20; *Life and Letters of Oliver Cromwell*, 220; unhappy home life, 220; *History of Frederick the Great*, 221; Rector, Edinburgh University, 221; *Reminiscences*, 221; death, 221

Carnegie, Andrew, 523-8; family emigrates to USA, 523; as bobbin boy, 523; works in telegraph office, 524-5; cultural development, 525; works for Pennsylvania Railroad, 526-7; early investments, 526-7; establishes companies and travels, 527; personal programme, 527-8; buys

Carnegie (*cont.*)
newspapers and promotes education, 528; merges enterprises into US Steel Corporation, 528; gospel of wealth, 528–9; death, 529

Cézanne, Paul, 572–77; and Zola, 572, 576; at Académie Suisse, 572, 573; exhibits at Salon de Refusés, 573; early romantic style, 573; affair and marriage to Hortense Fiquet, 573, 574, 576; Impressionist exhibitions, 574; as Post-Impressionist and forerunner of Cubism, 574–6; recognition, 576; exhibitions, 576–7; death, 587

Chadwick, Edwin, 385–90; works for Bentham, 385; secretary, Poor Law Board, 385–6; public health campaigns, 386–89; Public Health Act, 388; member, Central Board of Health, 388–9; character, 389; housing, burial and social reforms, 389–90; knighted, 390; death, 390

Chamberlain, Joseph, 123–8; Nonconformist education, 123; in business in Birmingham, 123–4; mayor of Birmingham, 124–5; MP under Gladstone, 125; resignation, 125; becomes Liberal Unionist, 125; Colonial Secretary in Boer War, 126; founds Tariff Reform League, 127; stroke and death, 128; marriages, 128

Chopin, Frédéric, 546–51; character and musical influences, 546; early musical talent, 546–7; at Warsaw Conservatory, 547; concert debut, 547; in Vienna, 547, 548; moves to Paris, 548; early concerts, 548; patronage of Rothschilds and piano teaching, 549; work published, 549; and George Sand, 549–51; some of greatest works, 550; visits England, 551; death, 551

Cody, William, 495–500; frontier background, 495; wagon-train messenger, 495; on Pony Express, 496; marriage, 496; as buffalo hunter and earns name 'Buffalo Bill', 496–7; chief scout to Fifth Cavalry, 497; hero of Wild West novels, 497; promotes tourism in Wild West, 497–8; works in theatre, 498, 499; duel with Chief Yellow Hand, 499; Wild West shows, 500; death, 500

Cook, Thomas, 501–7; apprenticed to cabinet-maker, 501; Baptist evangelist, 501–2; marriage, 502; temperance work, 502; first railway excursion for temperance meeting, 502–3; becomes printer and publisher, 503; organizes first pleasure trips, 504; runs excursions to Great Exhibition, 504–5; *The Excursionist*, 505; pioneers 'package tour' abroad, 505–6; offers world tours, 506; achievement, 506–7

Darwin, Charles, 159–64; studies medicine and theology, 159; voyage on HMS *Beagle*, 160–2; formulates theory of evolution, 161–2; marriage, 162; Fellow of Royal Society, 162; *The Origin of Species* and its reception, 163; *The Descent of Man*, 163; family life, 164; death, 164

Dickens, Charles, 263–7; childhood, 263; works in blacking factory, 263–4; as parliamentary reporter, 264; and Maria Beadnell, 264; *Sketches by Boz*, *The Pickwick Papers*, 264; marriage, 264–5; *Oliver Twist*, *Nicholas Nickleby*, *Barnaby Rudge*, *The Old Curiosity Shop*, 265; visits America, 265; *American Notes*, *Martin Chuzzlewit*, 265; portrayal of children in *Dombey and Son*, *A Christmas Carol* and *David Copperfield*, 266; founds *Household Words*, 266; public readings, 266; produces *The Frozen Deep*, 266; and Ellan Ternan, 266; the later novels, 266–

7; travels and railway accident, 267, *Edwin Drood*, 267; death, 267
Disraeli, Benjamin (Earl of Beaconsfield), 73-8; background and education, 73-4; *Vivian Grey*, 74; enters politics, 74; elected MP, 75; *Sybil*, 75, 76; marriage, 75-6; MP for Shrewsbury, 76; *Coningsby* and *Tancred*, 76; Chancellor of Exchequer and Leader of House of Commons, 76; rivalry with Gladstone, 76-7; Prime Minister, 77; and Queen Victoria, 77; foreign policy, 77-8; Congress of Berlin, 77-8; defeat, 78; *Endymion*, 78; character and death, 78

Faraday, Michael, 147-52; Faraday Lectures, 147; as bookbinder's apprentice, 147; laboratory assistant to Sir Humphrey Davy, 148-9; marriage, 149; makes first electromagnet, 150; Director of Laboratory at Royal Institution, 150; makes first dynamo, 151; discovers lines of force in electromagnetism, 151; develops basic laws of electrolysis, 151; as forerunner of Einstein, 151; invalidism and death, 151-2; religious faith, 152
Franklin, Sir John, 452-8; midshipman and under command of Flinders, 452; first expedition seeking North-west Passage, 453; expedition to Arctic, 453-4; Fellow of Royal Society, 454; maps north coast of America, 454; knighted, 455; lieutenant-governor of Tasmania, 455; second expedition seeking North-west Passage, 455-6; polar exploration by others, 456; fate of expedition and its achievement, 456-8

Gladstone, William Ewart, 98-104; background and education, 98; elected MP, 98; marriage, 99; vice-president, Board of Trade, 99; criticises government of Two Sicilies, 100; opposes Disraeli, 101; Chancellor of the Exchequer, 101-2; Prime Minister and leader of Liberal Party (first term), 102; second and third terms, 103; supports Home Rule, 103; Leader of the Opposition, 103; resignation, 103; death, 104

Hardie, James Keir, 141-6; background and early years, 141; as coal miner, 141-2; marriage, 142; campaigns for mining reforms, 142; conceives idea of labour party, 142-3; political principles, 143; first Independent Labour MP, 144; editor of *The Labour Leader*, 144; sets up Labour Representation Committee, 145; MP for Merthyr Tydfil, 145-6; leader of PLP, 145; campaigns against World War I, 146; death, 146
Hegel, Georg Wilhelm Friedrich, 200-4; main events of life, 200; major books, 200; impact of revolution and Enlightenment on, 201; belief in reason, 201; concept of history and change, 201-2, 203; *The German Constitution*, 202; *The Philosophy of Right*, 202; idealization of the state, 202-3; concept of freedom, 203; influence on conservatism and communism, 204
Heine, Heinrich, 228-33; *Buch der Lieder*, 228; *Die Lorelei*, 228; quality of verse and influence in Germany, 228; childhood and education, 229; apprenticed to banker, 229-30; first love, 230; love in his poetry, 230; studies law, 230; early reputation, 230-1; *Die Harzreise*, *Die Nordsee*, *Reisebilder*, 231; European travels and settles in Paris, 231-2; marriage, 232; later poetry and death, 232-3; fear of nationalism, 233
Hill, Octavia, 440-5; childhood and grandfather's influence, 440; early

Hill (*cont.*)
    employment and teaching, 441;
    establishes and manages model
    lodging-houses, 442-4; aims and
    philosophy, 443-4; pioneers social
    work as career for women, 444;
    influence abroad, 444; pioneers
    provision of open spaces, 445;
    helps found National Trust, 445;
    death, 445
Huxley, Thomas Henry, 177-82;
    character and background, 177;
    studies medicine, 177-8; ship's
    surgeon, zoological and scientific
    papers of, 178-9; Fellow of Royal
    Society, 179; marriage, 180; pro-
    fessor of natural history at School
    of Mines, 180; supports Darwin,
    180-1; *Man's Place in Nature*, 181;
    books popularizing science, 181;
    agnosticism, 182; work on royal
    commissions, 182; death, 182

Ibsen, Henrik, 302-7; childhood,
    302; apothecary's apprentice, 302;
    early plays, 303, 304; works for
    National Theatre, Oslo, 303; mar-
    riage, 303; *Brand*, public acclaim,
    304-5; *Peer Gynt*, 305; plays of
    middle period, 305; *A Doll's
    House*, 305-6; *Ghosts, An Enemy
    of the People, The Wild Duck,
    Rosmersholm, Hedda Gabler,
    When We Dead Awaken*, 306;
    death, 306; influence and origin-
    ality 307
Irving, Sir Henry, 567-71; child-
    hood, 567; decision to be an actor,
    567-8; early employment, 568;
    joins New Royal Lyceum Theatre,
    568-9; adopts pseudonym, 568-9;
    works in provinces, 569; flair for
    comedy, 569; *The Bells*, 569-70;
    leaves wife, 570; fame and works
    as manager of Lyceum, 570; tours,
    570; acting talent, 570-1; closure
    of Lyceum, 571; death, 571;
    achievement, 571

Jackson, Andrew, 30-6; birth and
    character, 30; marriage, 31; mili-
    tary career, 31; 1824 election cam-
    paign, 32-3; 1828 election cam-
    paign and Presidency, 33-4; feud
    with John Calhoun, 34-5, 36; pol-
    icies and states' rights, 35-6; trea-
    ties with Indians, 36; death, 36
James, William, 308-13; theory of
    pragmatism, 308-9; childhood,
    309; studies medicine, 310; rejects
    determinism, 310; lectures in
    psychology at Harvard, 311; mar-
    riage, 311; *The Principles of
    Psychology*, 311-12; religious
    philosophy, 312; later books, 312;
    death, 313
Jefferson, Thomas, 11-16; back-
    ground, 11; studies law and enters
    politics, 11; marriage, 12; architec-
    tural work, 12, 16; contributes to
    Declaration of Independence, 12;
    Act for Establishing Religious
    Freedom, 12; governor of Virgi-
    nia, 12-13; books, 13; travels to
    France, 13-14; elected President,
    14; Louisiana Purchase, 14-15;
    second term, 15; founds Univer-
    sity of Virginia, 15-16; death,
    16
Jowett, Benjamin, 397-403; funeral,
    397; childhood and education,
    397-8; early Balliol career, 398-9;
    Master of Balliol and Vice-Chan-
    cellor of Oxford, 399; campaigns
    for university extension and re-
    form, 399-400; academic ability,
    400-1; translates Plato, 400; intro-
    duces Hegelian philosophy, 401;
    extends 'Greats' course, 401; in re-
    ligious controversy, 401-2; per-
    sonal life, 402-3; epitaph, 403

Keats, John, 222-7; death, 222; epi-
    taph, 222, 227; family life, 222-3;
    studies medicine, 223; early poetry
    and *Endymion*, 223-4; *Isabella*,
    224; *Hyperion*, 224, 225; *The Eve
    of St Agnes*, 224, 225; *Lamia*, 224-

5; and Fanny Brawne, 225; the *Odes*, 225-6; *Otho the Great*, 225; the letters, 226; views on poetry, 226

Kierkegaard, Soren, 344-9; parentage, 344; education, 344; appearance, 345; at university, 345; social life, 345; first book, 346; and Regina Olsen, 346-7; *Either/Or: A Fragment of Life*, 347; *The Repetition*, 347; religious beliefs and teaching, 348; as founder of existentialist philosophy, 348; his writings, 349-50; death, 349

Koch, Robert, 189-93; achievement, 189-90; as doctor, 190; researches into cause of anthrax, 190-1; formulates basic bacteriology techniques, 191; develops culture-growth, 191; discovers tuberculosis bacillus, 191-2; discovers tuberculin, 192; works on cholera bacillus, 192-3; Director, Berlin Institute of Infectious Diseases, 191-3; works on immunity and development of vaccines, 193; awarded Nobel Prize, 193; death, 193

Krupp, Alfred, 508-12; ancestry and growth of family steel business, 508-9; trebles output and labour force, 509; makes first steel cannon, 510; develops weldless wheel, 510-11; and Bismarck, 511; supplies weapons world-wide, 511-12; treatment of workers, 511-12; loneliness, 512; death and honours awarded him, 512

Lee, Robert E., 79-85; background, 79; marriage, 79; Mexican War, 79; Civil War begins, 80; commander of Virginian forces, adviser to President, 80-1; defends Richmond, 81; invades Maryland, 82; defeat at Antietam, 82; victories at Fredericksburg and Chancellorsville, 83; defeat at Gettysburg, 83-4; battles against General Grant, 84-5; treaty at Appomattox, 85; military skills, 85

Lincoln, Abraham, 92-7; character and achievement, 92; frontier background, 92-3; marriage, 93; elected to House of Representatives and practises law, 93; views on slavery, 93-4; campaigns as Republican, 94; elected President, 95; Civil War, 95-6; second term, 96; assassination, 96-7

Lind, Jenny (Johanna Maria), 557-61; early talent, 557; first stage appearance, 558; as actress, 558; trains in Paris, 559; 'Jenny Lind fever' and acclaim in Europe, 559; first English appearance, 559-60; final Berlin season, 560; sings oratorio, 560-1; works for Barnum in America, 561; marriage, 561; professor of singing at Royal College of Music, 561; death, 561

Livingstone, David, 459-64; studies medicine and theology, 459; sent by London Missionary Society to Kuruman, 459; marriage, 460; establishes mission, 459-60; discovers Lake Ngami, 460; discovers Zambezi River and Victoria Falls, 460; discovers Lake Nyassa, 461-2; disappearance, 462; found by Stanley, 463; death, 464; achievement, 464

Macaulay, Lord (Thomas Babington), 240-5; childhood and early writings, 240; at Trinity College, 240; as conversationist, 241; writes for *Edinburgh Review*, 241-2; political career, 242, 243; administrator in India, 242-3; *Lays of Ancient Rome*, 243; *History of England*, 243-5; becomes peer, 245; death, 245

Marx, Karl, 281-6; political background in Germany, 281; university studies, 281; marriage, 281; moves to Paris, 281; friendship with Engels and co-authors *The*

Marx (*cont.*)
   Communist Manifesto, 282, 283, 284; editor of *Rheinische Zeitung* in Germany, 282; moves to London, 282; first volume *Das Kapital* published, 282; death, 283; character, 283; concept of change, 283; insistence on class struggle, 283-4; theory of surplus value, 284; views on capitalism, 284; philosophy, 284-6; influence, 286

Maxwell, James Clerk, 183-8; early interest in science, 183-4; academic posts, 184, 185; researches perception of colour and Saturn's rings, 184-5; marriage, 185; supervises founding Cavendish Laboratory, 185-6; research into colour-blindness, 186; *Treatise on Electricity and Magnetism*, 186, 187; death, 186; founds statistical mechanics and studies kinetic theory of gases, 186-7; Maxwell Equations and electromagnetic theory of light, 187-8

Melbourne, Viscount (William Lamb), 55-60; birth and parentage, 55; marriage, 55-6; elected MP, 56; Lord Lieutenant of Ireland, 56; Home Secretary, 57; supports Reform Bill, 57; elected Prime Minister, 57-8; and Queen Victoria, 58-9; resignation and reappointment, 59; fall of his government, 60; death, 60

Mendel, Johann Gregor, 171-6; education, 171; becomes monk, 171; at Vienna University, 172; as supply teacher, 172; contemporary knowledge of plant genetics, 172-3; theory of mechanism of heredity, 173-4; lack of public interest in his work, 174-5; becomes abbot, 175; death, 175; work recognised as pioneering science of genetics, 176

Metternich (Prince Clement Wenzel Lothar von Metternich-Winneburg-Beilstein), 49-54;

marriage, 49; political aims, 49-50; Congress of Vienna, 50; character, 51; congress system and quadruple alliance, 51, 52; European revolutions, 53; dismissal as Chancellor, 53; exile in England, 54; return to Vienna and death, 54

Mill, John Stuart, 246-51; father's influence, 246-7; joins East Indian Company, 247; writes for *Westminster Review*, 247; and Harriet Taylor, 248-9, 250; *System of Logic*, 249; *Principles of Political Economy*, 249-50; marriage, 250; *On Liberty*, 250-1; wife's death, 250-1; later writings and campaigns for female emancipation, 251; parliamentary defeat, 251; *Autobiography*, 247, 248, 250; death, 251

Millais, Sir John Everett, 562-6; background, 562; at Royal Academy Schools, 562; member of Pre-Raphaelite Brotherhood, 563-4, 566; *The Order of Release*, 564-5; love affair with Effie Ruskin and marriage, 564-5; elected to Royal Academy, 566; romantic paintings, 564, 566; 'pot-boiler' paintings, 566; lifestyle, 566; made baronet, 566; death, 566

Monet, Claude, 578-82; as political caricaturist, 578; pupil of Boudin, 578; influences, 578, 579; in Paris, 579; military service, 579; marriage, 579-80; in London, 580, 582; contribution to Impressionism, 578, 580-1; move to Giverny and Water-Lily series, 581, 582; second marriage, 581; reputation, 581; in Venice, 582; becomes recluse, 582; retrospective exhibition, 582; blindness and death, 582

Monroe, James, 23-9; early career, 23-4; Governor of Virginia and foreign missions, 24; War of 1812 and Secretary of State, 24-5; elected President, 25; Panic of

1819, 25–6; Missouri Compromise, 26–7; foreign policy and Monroe Doctrine, 28–9; character, 29; death, 29

Napoleon Bonaparte (Napoleon I), 37–42; birth and education, 37; early army career, 37–8; marriage to Josephine, 38; Italian campaign, 38; Egyptian campaign, 38; First Consul, 39; marriage to Marie Louise, 40; legal policies, 40; educational policies, 40–1; religious policies and Concordat, 40–1; becomes Emperor, 41; Austerlitz and Jena, 41; Treaty of Tilsit, 41; Continental System, 41; war with England, 41; march on Moscow, 41; downfall of Empire, 41–2; character, 42; Waterloo, 42

Napoleon III (Charles Louis Napoleon Bonaparte), 86–91; political background and rise to power, 86–7; elected Napoleon III, 87; political ideology of Second Empire, 88–9; marriage, 88; economic policy, 88, 90; foreign policy, 89–90; growth of opposition, 90–1; grants new constitution, 91; French defeat in Franco-Prussian war and proclamation of republic, 91; exile and death, 91; character, 91

Newman, Cardinal John Henry, 331–7; childhood and education, 331; elected Fellow of Oriel, 332; ordained, 332; contracts typhoid, 332; questions Anglicanism, 332–3; *Tracts for the Times*, 333; joins Oxford Movement, 333; joins Roman Catholic Church and ordained, 334; joins Oratorians, 334–5; founds Catholic university in Dublin, 335; founds the Oratory School, 335; editor of *The Rambler*, 335–6; *Apologia pro Vita Sua*, 336; created Cardinal, 336; death, 336

Nightingale, Florence, 410–15; state of nursing in England, 410; trains as deaconess, 411; superintendent at Home for Gentlewomen, 411; Crimean War and poor medical treatment, 411; reforms and directs nursing in Crimea, 412–14; returns to England, 415; *Notes for Nursing*, 415; hospital and nursing reforms, 415; invalidism, 415; appointed to Order of Merit, 415; death, 415

Owen, Robert, 373–8; achievement, 373; draper's assistant, 373; manager of cotton-spinning factory, 374; marriage 375; buys cotton mills at New Lanark, 375; reforms at New Lanark and infant schools, 375–6; *A New View of Society*, 376; campaigns for Factory Bill, 376; 'villages of cooperation', 377; leader of Grand National Consolidated Trade Union, 377; death, 378; as pioneer of cooperative movement, 378

Palmerston, Viscount (John Henry Temple), 61–6; parentage and education, 61; elected MP, 62; character, 62; Secondary at War, 62–3; joins Whigs and Foreign Secretary, 63–4; marriage, 64; 'Don Pacifico Case', 64; at Home Office, 65; first ministry, 65–6; second ministry, 66; death, 66

Parnell, Charles Stewart, 129–34; influence of English in Ireland, 129; family background, 129–30; character, 130; MP for Meath, 130; MP for Cork, 131; leader of Irish Party, 131; affair with Mrs O'Shea, 131, 132, 133; jailed for Land League activities, 131–2; Phoenix Park murders, 132–3; supports Home Rule Bill, 133; loses leadership Irish Party, 134; marriage, 134; death, 134

Pasteur, Louis, 165-70; achievement, 165; education, 165-6; pioneers stereochemistry, 166-7; academic posts, 167, 168, 169; marriage, 167; work on microbes, 168; elected to Academy of Sciences, 168; originates pasteurization, 168; work on silkworms, 168-9; work on vaccination and immunology, 169-70; Pasteur Institute founded, 170; death, 170

Peel, Sir Robert, 67-72; enters parliament, 68; Secretary for Ireland, 68; marriage, 68; Home Secretary, 68-9; criminal law reform and founds Metropolitan Police, 68-9; supports Roman Catholic Emancipation Bill, 69; Reform Bill, 69-70; Prime Minister, 70; free-trade policies, 70-1; resignation, 71; death, 71-2

Pius IX, Pope, 325-30; Archbishop of Spoleto, 325; and the revolutionaries, 325-6; becomes Pope, 326; liberal measures and foreign policy, 326; flight and re-establishment, 326; character, 327; restores hierarchy in England and Holland, 327; doctrine of Immaculate Conception, 327; First Vatican Council and papal infallibility, 328; political role, 328-9; 'prisoner of Vatican', 329; Law of Guarantees, 330; as spiritual leader, 330; death, 330

Place, Francis, 367-72; parentage, 367; as breeches-maker, 368; marriage, 368; sacking, 368; secretary Breeches-makers' Society, 369; chairman, London Corresponding Society, 369; opens tailor's shop, 370; political activity and radicalism, 371; helps obtain repeal Combination Acts, 371; drafts People's Charter, 371; second marriage, 371; death, 372

Reuter, Baron Paul Julius de, 404-9; baptism, 404; marriage, 404; as publisher, 404; Paris news agency, 405; Berlin news service, 405-6; London news agency, 406; becomes British subject, 406; Reuters founded and first scoop, 407; employs overseas agents, 407-8; private telegram service, 408; world-wide offices, 408-9; made baron, 409; death, 409

Roberts of Kandahar, Lord, 117-22; early army career, 117-19; Indian Mutiny, 118; awarded VC, 118; administration and military service in India, 118-19; command in Afghanistan, 119; march from Kabul, 120; defends Kandahar, 120; made baronet and GCB, 121; Commander-in-Chief, India, Ireland and in Boer War, 121-2; military reforms at home, 122; death, 122

Schliemann, Heinrich, 471-6; his 'Trojan' palace, 471; early years, 471-2; linguistic skills, 472; business acumen, 472; 'discovers' Troy, 473, 474; marriages, 473-4; excavations at Mycenae, 474-5; discovers Homeric pottery, 475; intellectual bankruptcy of, 475-6; work by others, 476; death, 476

Schubert, Franz, 535-39; childhood, 535; at Imperial Konvikt, 535; pupil of Salieri, 536; First Symphony, 536; as teacher, 536; creates Lied genre, 536-7; Schubertiads, 537; Erl King, 537; meets Beethoven, 538; Trout Quintet, 538; early works of 1820s, 538; illness, 538-9; 'Great' Symphony and final works, 539; death, 539; lack of fame in lifetime, 539

Shaw, Richard Norman, 428-33; early life, 428; works for William Burn, 428; wins Royal Academy medals, 428; travels, 428; partnership with Nesfield, 429; marriage,

429; designs houses for aristocracy, 429-30, 433; architectural styles and influence, 430-2, 433; new materials and methods of, 432; declines honours, 432; character, 433

Shelley, Percy Bysshe, 210-15; at school, 210; breaks engagement, 210-11; and William Godwin, 210, 212, 214; *St Irvyne*, 213; sent down from Oxford, 211; first marriage, 211-12; *Queen Mab*, 212; elopes with Mary Godwin, 212; *Alastor*, 213; and Byron, 213, 214, 215; *Frankenstein*, 214; marriage to Mary Godwin, 214; *Laon and Cythna, The Cenci, Prometheus Unbound, Epipsychidion*, 214; *Adonais*, 214-5; drowns, 215

Smiles, Samuel, 268-73; *Self-Help*, 268, 270, 272; views in context of time, 268, 271-2; as doctor, 269; tours Europe, 269; *Physical Nurture and Education of Children*, 269; editor, *Leeds Times*, 269; political career, 269-70; as railway administrator, 270; *Lives of the Engineers*, 270, 272; *Character, Thrift, Duty*, 270-1; influence of his writing, 272-3; marriage, 273; *Autobiography*, 273; death, 273

Smith, Joseph, 338-43; childhood, 338; vision and *Book of Mormon*, 338-41; growth of Mormons, 341-2; Nauvoo built, 342; campaigns for presidency, 342; polygamy of, 342; imprisonment, 342-3; assassination, 343

Spurgeon, Charles Haddon, 356-60; Calvinist upbringing, 356; becomes Baptist, 357; pastor, New Park Street, 357; marriage, 357; popularity, 357-8; Metropolitan Tabernacle, 358-9; writings, 359; Pastor's College, 359; social reforms and political views, 359; impact on working classes, 359; leaves Baptist Union, 360; his

preaching and achievement, 360; death, 360

Stead, William Thomas, 446-51; drowns on *Titanic*, 446, 451; childhood, 446; clears local slum, 446; marriage, 446; writes for *Northern Echo*, 446-7; editor of *Pall Mall Gazette*, 447; social reforms through journalism, 447-50; and General Gordon, 448; campaigns against juvenile prostitution, 448-50; imprisonment, 450; founds *Review of Reviews*, 450-1; becomes Spiritualist, 451; as pacifist, 451

Stendhal (Henri-Marie Beyle), 205-9; as soldier, 205; love of Italy, 205, 206; love affairs, 206-7; *De L'Amour*, 207; *Le Rouge et le Noir*, 207, 208; *La Chartreuse de Parme*, 207, 208, 209; consul in Italy, 207; writing style, 208; moral standpoint, 208-9; attitude to writing, 209

Talleyrand (Charles Maurice de Talleyrand-Périgord), 17-22; and Napoleon, 17; and the Church, 17-18; President of National Assembly, 18; flees to England, 19; in America, 19-20; French Foreign Minister, 20; negotiates treaties of Luneville and Amiens, 20; plots with Russia, 20-1; downfall of Napoleon, 21; Foreign Minister under Louis XVIII, 21; Congress of Vienna, 21-2; ambassador to Britain, 22; death, 22

Tennyson, Alfred, Lord, 252-7; death, 252; childhood, 253; at Trinity College, 254; and Arthur Hallam, 254; poet laureate, 254; *In Memoriam*, 254; character, 255, 256; marriage, 255; *The Idylls of the King*, 255; other poems, 255; contemporary influence, 256; made baron, 256

Thackeray, William Makepeace, 258-62; Indian childhood, 258;

Thackeray (*cont.*)
education, 258; early travels, 259; character, 259, 262; marriage, 259; as satirist and *Yellowplush Papers*, 259; wife's insanity, 260; writes for *Punch*, 260; *The Luck of Barry Lyndon*, 260; and Jane Elton, 260–1; *Vanity Fair*, 261; later novels, 261–2; editor, *The Cornhill*, 261; death, 262

Tolstoy, Count Leo Nikolayevich, 292–6; death, 292; childhood, 292–3; at Kazan University, 293; returns home, 293; travels to Moscow and St Petersburg, 293; fights in the Caucasus, 294; *Childhood, Boyhood and Youth*, 294; travels abroad, 294–5; establishes schools, 295; marriage, 295; *War and Peace, Anna Karenina*, 295; desire for simple life, 296; character, 296; later work, 296

Turgenev, Ivan Sergeyevich, 287–91; as nihilist, 287, 291; background and mother's influence, 287–8, 289; concern for Russian people and as revolutionary, 288, 289, 290, 291; inherits from father, 288; at St Petersburg University, 289; novels of, 289–90; leaves Russia, 290; depression of, 291; death, 291

Verne, Jules, 297–301; studies law, 297; and Dumas, 297–8; first play, 297; secretary of Théâtre Lyrique, 298; *Martin Paz*, 298; as stockbroker, 298; marriage, 298; *Five Weeks in a Balloon*, 299; signs book contract, 299; *Twenty Thousand Leagues under the Sea*, 300; awarded Légion d'Honneur, 300; conscripted, 300; *Around the World in Eighty Days*, 300–1; travels and later novels, 301; in politics, 301; death, 301

Wagner, (Wilhelm) Richard, 552–6; parentage, 552; discovers musical talent, 552; composes overtures, 553; at Leipzig University, 553; marriage, 553; in debt, 553; *Rienzi*, 553, 554, 555; *Der Fliegende Holländer*, 553, 554, 555; in Paris, 553–4; conductor, Dresden Royal Opera, 554; *Tannhäuser*, 554, 555, 556; political activity, 554; *Lohengrin*, 554, 555; *Die Meistersinger*, 554, 555; the Ring cycle, 554–5, 556; contribution to opera, 555; private life, 555–6; marries Cosima von Bülow, 556; Bayreuth completed, 556; *Parsifal*, 556; death, 556

Whiteley, William, 513–17; the 'Universal Provider', 513, 515; draper's apprentice, 513; in London and learns wholesale trade, 514; opens first shop, 514; marriage, 515; expands business, 515–16; treatment of staff, 516; estrangement from wife, 516; fires at shops, 517; Whiteley's becomes public company, 517; murder of, 517

Wilde, Oscar, 314–19; parentage and education, 314; university honours of, 314–15; at Oxford, 315; as exponent of Aestheticism, 315; enters high society, 315–16; as conversationist, 316; visits America, 317; marriage and homosexuality, 317; early writing, 317–18; plays of, 318; trial and imprisonment, 318–19; exile in Paris, 319; death, 319

Witte, Sergei Yulieyevich, 135–40; background, 135; works for Imperial State Railways, 135; general manager, south-western railway in Russo/Turkish war, 136; pioneers trans-Siberian railway, 136–8; Finance Minister, 138; Prime Minister, 139; dismissal, 139; war with Japan, 140; supports Duma, 140; dismissed from Council of Ministers, 140; urges neutrality in World War I, 140

Yataro, Iwasaki, 518-22; growth of *samurai* entrepreneur, 518-19; reorganises finances of Tosa fief, 519; and new Tokyo government, 519-20; forms Mitsubishi, 520; ex-, pansion and competition with Mitsui, 521; death, 521; character, 521; future expansion and founding of NYK, 522; reasons for success, 522